THE DIE BROKE

Complete Book
of Money

Also by Stephen M. Pollan and Mark Levine

Die Broke

Live Rich

The Die Broke Financial Problem Solver

THE DIE BROKE

Complete Book
of Money

Unconventional Wisdom about Everything
from Annuities to Zero-Coupon Bonds

Stephen M. Pollan *and* **Mark Levine**

HarperBusiness
An Imprint of HarperCollinsPublishers

Disclaimer

This book is designed to provide readers with a general overview of personal financial strategies. It is not designed to be a definitive guide or to take the place of advice from a qualified financial planner or other professionals. Given the risk involved in investing of almost any kind, there is no guarantee that the investment methods suggested in this book will be profitable. Thus, neither the publisher nor the author assume liability of any kind for any losses that may be sustained as a result of applying the methods suggested in this book, and any such liability is hereby expressly disclaimed.

FIRST EDITION

Designed by Leah Carlson-Stanisic

Library of Congress Cataloging-in-Publication Data

Pollan, Stephen M.
    The die broke complete book of money : unconventional wisdom about everything from annuities to zero-coupon bonds / by Stephen M. Pollan and Mark Levine.
        p. cm.
    ISBN: 0-06-661993-9
    1. Money. 2. Finance, Personal. I. Title: Complete book of money. II. Levine, Mark, 1958-   III. Title

HG221.P757 2001
332.024—dc21
                                                            00-046084

        00   RRD   10   9   8   7   6   5   4   3   2   1

TO HARRIET POLLAN

CONTENTS

ACKNOWLEDGMENTS

This book represents the sum total of more than thirty years of consulting and writing. It draws on all the advice and guidance we have received in that time. For that reason we need to thank all those whom we've interviewed in the course of researching our 15 books and nearly 100 articles. Of course, we also need to thank all the clients of Stephen M. Pollan PC, without whom none of this would have been possible.

Over the course of our collaboration, we have tried hard not to repeat ourselves, and we've continued that effort in this work. However, in a book of this scope it was necessary at times to draw on our earlier works. Some of the concepts and ideas contained in this book, and, admittedly, even some of the language, have appeared previously in other of our books and articles or been the subject of appearances on television or radio.

Such duplications arise simply because we have not been able to come up with a better way of saying something, and that's a credit to all those editors, producers, and publishers who have worked with us during the past two decades. We'd like to thank them all for contributing to our growth as a writing team, but we'd particularly like to thank Debbie Harkens, who gave us our start; Diane Harris, who helped us develop a broader audience; John Koten, who worked with us to refine our voice; and, most of all, Adrian Zackheim of HarperCollins, who gave us the vision and guidance we needed to put it all together.

We've never hesitated to draw on the expertise of others. In the preparation of this book we tapped into the wisdom of an exceptional group of knowledgeable individuals. Special thanks go to five experts who graciously put up with our obsessiveness: Gary Ambrose, director/senior financial consultant, Personal Capital Management, Inc.; Richard Koenigsberg, CPA, Spielman, Koenigsberg & Parker; Wendy Parmet, Esq., partner, Parmet & Zeif, PC; David Paul Pollan, Esq., Atlanta, Georgia, member of the National Academy of Elder Law Attorneys; and Allen N. Ross, Esq., partner, Warshaw Burstein Cohen Schlesinger & Kuh, LLP.

We also must thank the following individuals who unselfishly let us take advantage of their unique expertise: Mimi Barker, journalist; Edgar H. Booth, Esq., partner, Warshaw Burstein Cohen Schlesinger & Kuh, LLP; Roger L. Cohen, Esq., partner, Warshaw Burstein Cohen Schlesinger & Kuh, LLP; Michael Costa, CPA; Warren P. Graham, Esq., partner, Warshaw Burstein Cohen Schlesinger & Kuh, LLP; Connie LaMotta, president and CEO, LaMotta Strategic Communications; Robert A. Mogil, president, The Mogil Organization; David Rosenfeld, president and CEO, Eagle Growth Investors; Gabriella Rowe, president, Grow Associates Management Consultants; Leslie Smolan, partner, Carbone-Smolan Agency; and Robert P. Wittes, Esq., partner, Warshaw Burstein Cohen Schlesinger & Kuh, LLP.

Mike Powers, an exceptional author in his own right, did a magnificent job compiling and organizing the research necessary to write this book. We could not have written this book without him.

Stuart Krichevsky, while formally our agent, has actually served a far more important role in our careers. Without his advice, encouragement, guidance, and friendship we never would have come this far.

Most importantly, we need to thank Corky Pollan and Deirdre Martin Levine for showing us that there's more to life than money.

UNCONVENTIONAL WISDOM:
LIVE RICH AND DIE BROKE

Unconventional wisdom. That's what I've been offering my clients and readers like you for more than three decades now. Some have even called my ideas heretical. So be it. I come by my heresy honestly.

Unlike most of the authors of personal finance, small business, and career books, I'm a hands-on practitioner. I practice what I preach. I have a coterie of dedicated clients, individuals just like you, who pay me to help them with their legal, financial, career, business, and consumer problems.

After careers as a real estate developer, venture capitalist, banker, and college professor, I launched a private legal and financial consulting practice on New York City's Upper East Side. Most of my clients are baby boomers from what used to be called the upper middle class. While only a few of them can be counted among the new breed of e-millionaires, most aspire to that level of financial success. They have combined incomes of well over $150,000, live in apartment buildings with doormen or rural homes on more than an acre of land. They take vacations to Europe or St. Bart's, go out to restaurants at least once a week, buy wine by the case, and drink single-malt scotch. They belong to gyms and spend most of their few free moments doting on, and catering to, their spouses and children.

Unconventional Because It's Practical

While there are some uniquely New York elements to my clients' personas and while they may be more affluent than the average, in the most important ways they're just like most successful Americans, including you. They've acquired more possessions and experiences than their parents had at their age. They hold down decision-making and policy-setting positions in corporations, they are running their own successful small companies, or they have made a name for themselves in a competitive creative field. And they lead complicated lives filled with a variety of financial obstacles, from the monumental to the mundane. They've taught me, and continue to teach me, the real money problems that people face. I know how vexing seemingly ordinary tasks—like deciding on a child's allowance, dealing with office politics, selecting an answering machine system, and shopping for a checking account—can be.

Unconventional Because It's Effective

Not only do my clients regularly teach me what matters most to real people like you, but they also hold me to a high standard: my advice must work; otherwise they won't continue as clients.

That means I can't be doctrinaire about money issues. My clients' money problems aren't hypothetical exercises; they're real-life dilemmas. So my approach to issues can't be theoretical and abstract; it must be pragmatic and practical. That holds true for my books as well as my consultations. I know the advice I'm offering you in this book works because it has worked for hundreds of my clients. It has helped people win employment contracts, negotiate business loans, finance postretirement careers, and purchase weekend homes.

Unconventional Because It's Direct

Because I work with clients my advice also needs to be unambiguous. I've found that when people are paying for advice, they want to be told what they should do. They come to me to get an answer, or at least my opinion, not to engage in a Socratic dialogue. In both my consultations and my writing, I'm direct about issues. You won't have to read far into an entry in this book to learn my opinion on a topic. You may not always agree with me or like what I have to say, but it's my best advice. Giving my clients—or you—any less would be unconscionable. I say you should always be looking for another job, you should lease rather than buy a car, you should never buy whole life insurance, and you should terminate any employees you possibly can.

I don't abandon clients who don't agree with me; if they wish, I continue to help them pursue their goals in the manner they've chosen. Similarly, in this book I'll provide you with enough information and guidance that you can follow paths other than those I recommend. If things work out, bully for you. If they don't, you can start over. I promise I won't say I told you so.

Unconventional Because It's Holistic

Dealing with real people day in and day out, I've learned that money issues can't be neatly divided and filed into separate categories like investing, career, real estate, business, shopping, and personal life. Most authors limit their scope to one of these topics because their experience is more conventional than mine. This is understandable: having been trained as specialists, they focus on their area of expertise. I'm not a specialist. My clients have trained me to be a generalist. Through them I've learned that all the areas of our money lives must be viewed as a unified whole. When clients come to me for help in buying a home, I need to learn about their career status, investment portfolio, marriage and parenting plans, and even their health, before I can give them sound advice.

I've counseled clients to have physicals before undertaking a job search and to have children before buying a summer home. I've taught clients how to be savvier when shopping at supermarkets and when buying mutual funds. I've helped clients pick out engagement rings as well as real estate. In my practice I deal with any and every area of a client's life that is touched by money because I've learned that all these areas interact. That's why you'll find the first truly comprehensive approach to money in this book, with entries on legal, financial, career, business, consumer, and even some personal topics. You'll find entries on things you never think of in financial terms: topics like listening, reading, garb, and pets.

Unconventional Because It's Cutting Edge

Finally, working with clients has led me to appreciate just how much the money world has changed. It's one thing to read survey results or view stock market tables. It's quite another to have a real-life embodiment of the information age sitting across the table from you, asking for your help.

During the past ten years many personal finance authors and pundits have been discussing Roth IRAs as if they were still state-of-the-art in financial planning, talking about refinancing your mortgage as if it was daring, and offering tips for landing a grand title and a corner office. They've been bending and tweaking and jury-rigging the conventional financial wisdom of the industrial age (in some cases, even the agrarian age) and trying to make it work in the information age. Another set of authors have been focusing on the lifestyles of the superwealthy, either self-made or accidental, suggesting that these silicon sagas are today's Horatio Alger tales.

During that same time I've been talking with my clients about viaticals, d4C trusts, prepaid tuition plans, and headhunters. I've been offering practical twenty-first-century money advice.

The Old Rules No Longer Work

You see, I've learned that the traditional rules and ideas of the industrial age no longer work in the new information age.

In the old world, if you did your work you kept your job; if you did your work well you were promoted; if you kept your job you got regular pay raises; if you got promoted you got a sizable pay raise; if you were loyal to the company, the company would be loyal to you; an entrepreneur's success was directly tied to his or her company's success; and in order to be happy our work had to be meaningful.

In the new world, there's no justice in the workplace; you can't count on paternalistic employers; the days of automatic pay raises are gone; there's no such thing as corporate loyalty; the interests of a business and its owner are not identical; and, while deriving self-actualization from work is still wonderful, it is less likely than ever before and pursuing it at the expense of more basic needs is dangerous.

In the old world, credit cards were tools that let you painlessly live out your dreams; retirement was an idyllic reward for years of toil; and money was made to be saved and passed on to the next generation.

In the new world, buying on credit can lead to financial ruin; retirement at any age may be foolish; and trying to build up and maintain an estate can be downright dangerous.

We're living in a scary time—the passage from one world to another, from one age to another, is always frightening. But you can't keep playing by the rules of the old world. You must adopt new financial rules, or at least a new approach to money, to survive and flourish. I've developed just such an approach.

Believe me, I don't claim any special magical insight. What I have is a window on the future: my clients. They're the ones who forced me to set aside outdated ideas about finances and abandon preconceived notions. And they're the ones who led me to a holistic twenty-first-century approach to money that I call Live Rich and Die Broke.*

The Goal: Live Rich

Live rich. When you come down to it, isn't that what we all want? To live the life of our dreams?

For some, living rich means owning a well-appointed villa in Tuscany. For others, it's being able to buy a Mercedes without worrying about the price tag. Still others think it means traveling the globe and staying in four-star hotels. Creative individuals may dream of being able to paint without worrying about paying their rent. The spiritually motivated may want to spend their time with the Dalai Lama. We each have our own personal vision of what goes into a rich life.

The one common element, however, is *freedom*. Look at all the different dreams of a rich life and you'll see each is based on having the freedom to do whatever you want to do. Living rich is having the freedom to live where you want, buy whatever you want, travel the world, create art for art's sake, or spend your life in meditation and prayer. Living rich is also having the freedom to set aside your fears and seize the reins of your life. To live rich is to be free, and to be free is to live rich.

Living rich isn't the same as being rich. No one sane truly equates a rich life with being wealthy. It isn't money that we want. It's what money can buy.

Obviously it takes money to buy a magnificent home, beautiful things, and first-class travel. But it also takes money to do nonmaterial things, like create art or lead a life of prayer. All of us, even artists and contemplatives, live in a capitalist world. It takes money to obtain the necessities of life—food, clothing, and shelter. That money comes from our own work or from the work of others.

Someone, somewhere—perhaps a spouse or a parent—is earning money so the idealistic artist can spend her time painting. And someone, somewhere—perhaps some wealthy materialist paying $10 for a jar of preserves—is earning money so the devoted Trappist monk can spend many of his waking hours at prayer.

While money plays a big part in whether or not you're able to live rich, to be free, the key is to learn to truly work for ourselves. That sounds simpler than it is.

Truly Work for Yourself

Just because you're self-employed doesn't mean you're working for yourself. Far from it. Few entrepreneurs really work for themselves. Deep down, most of us work for someone or something else, whether it's our company, our employees, our parents, or our spouse and children. By the same token, you can get a paycheck and still truly work for yourself. Working for yourself has nothing to do with who signs your paycheck. It means working to satisfy your own real needs, not just your perceived needs, and not the needs of someone or something else.

---

*This approach is a synthesis of the spending and earning approaches I outlined in my two earlier books: *Die Broke* and *Live Rich*. For a fuller explanation of my ideas I suggest you take a look at those two works.

You're not working for yourself if you're pursuing a profession in order to please your parents or boss or teacher. You're not working for yourself if you're always putting the needs of your boss and coworkers before your own. You're not working for yourself if you're in a particular job because you think it pleases your spouse. You're not working for yourself if you're satisfying needs you "think" you should have—whether it's owning a four-bedroom split-level or holding a job feeding the hungry. You're not working for yourself if your goal is satisfying your company's needs. You're only truly working for yourself when you're satisfying your own real needs.

You can develop an understanding of your own true needs through soul searching, self-analysis, prayer, meditation—whatever method you like. No one road to the truth is any better or quicker than another. Just as we each have our own needs, we also have our own best path toward discovering those needs. I wish I could help you uncover those truths, but I'm not a psychotherapist or a seer.

Ironically, while I can't help you uncover your true needs, I can help you achieve them. There are new maxims that can help you live rich. So replace those outdated assumptions and expectations, and apply these new maxims to your money life.

Make Money

Sounds simple. We all want to make money. Then how come so few of us feel like we have enough? I think it's because, for a variety of psychological and cultural reasons, we subconsciously feel there's something wrong with making money. We believe that money is somehow crass, venal, and dirty. That's ludicrous. I don't think there's anything wrong with money; in fact there's a lot right with it. In order to survive and thrive in the twenty-first century you need to make the acquisition of money a high priority.

That doesn't mean money must be your exclusive goal—although there's nothing wrong with that. It means that in our capitalist society money is a necessary tool to achieve happiness and to satisfy work-related needs, whatever they are.

Money in and of itself can do nothing. When the paper dollar stopped being backed by silver, and when coins were no longer worth their weight in precious metal, money lost its intrinsic value. But it's invaluable extrinsically. Taken as a tool, money can do almost anything. It may not be able to buy you happiness, but it can buy most of the things that bring happiness, including health to some degree. Certainly, the lack of money can make you miserable.

The search for work that's emotionally fulfilling is noble but quixotic, especially today. I'm not saying it's impossible, just improbable. And pursuing such a utopian mission can lead to frustration.

If you've been lucky enough to find gratifying work, that's wonderful. But I don't think it's enough. You can't let your emotional satisfaction get in the way of a vital truth: work is the only area of your life that has the power to generate money for you. Gratification, on the other hand, can come from every other area of your life: hobbies, church, family, exercise—you name it. But none of those can give you the money that work can. Your goal for work should be to make money. If you can make sufficient money doing something you find emotionally gratifying, offer a prayer of thanks: You're one of the few. But if you're not generating sufficient income, please don't let your love of what you're doing blind you to your need to find another way to make money.

Remember: Work is the area in your life that gives you the best chance to earn money. And it's the other areas of your life that give you the best chance at self-actualization. You can help the world by volunteering. You can be creative through a hobby. You can get a sense of purpose and a feeling of joy by caring for your family. You can be spiritually uplifted at a house of worship. My advice is to render unto work that which is work's—the ability to make money—and render unto God, and family, and community, that which is God's, the family's, and the community's—the ability to provide psychological, emotional, and spiritual fulfillment.

Don't Grow: Change

It's obvious that the implied contract that once bound workers and their employers has been torn to shreds. There's no longer any guarantee that if you do your job you'll keep it, or that if you do your job well you'll get a raise or promotion. There's also no longer any reward for length of service or sacrifices for the company. The skilled bookkeeper who has been with the company for 20 years is as likely, perhaps more likely, to be laid off than the neophyte clerk who started yesterday. The sales executive who moves his family across the country when the company suggested a transfer can be out of work before he finishes unpacking his golf clubs. In the twenty-first century there's no career or job ladder to climb, there's no loyalty, and there's no justice. All the signs and markers on the path to career success have been removed. You're on your own with your new attitude, new rules, and innate sense of direction to guide you.

Similarly, there's no longer a set pattern of business. Small companies used to get a foothold by carving out a niche in existing market and then climb by increasing their market share. In the process they grew in size and scope. Some brought more of the functions they relied on in-house. Others opened new outlets in new geographic areas. In both cases, staff and plant grew. In this way, a one- or two-person operation could become a $1 million corporation with a staff of hundreds, if not thousands.

Yet for the past decade large, established companies have been doing the exact opposite. In reaction (some would say overreaction) to the new economic environment, corporations are downsizing and focusing on their core functions. Meanwhile, most small businesspeople are still thinking of growth or expansion.

Rather than focusing on climbing a ladder or developing a company, you must invest financially and emotionally in yourself alone. As an employee or entrepreneur, my suggestion is to increase your own skills and do things that increase your income, your marketability, and most of all, your profitability. Don't let yourself be detoured by psychic benefits like corner offices, impressive titles, larger facilities, or bigger staffs. What counts is that your company or job is making you money.

Try to stop doing things that interfere with those goals. Don't put down roots in either a company or a business if you can help it. You'll be better off both physically and emotionally if you're able to pull up stakes and move quickly. If you're an employee, that may mean living, to the greatest extent possible, out of your briefcase, keeping your résumé in circulation, and becoming a regular at networking functions and organizations, not just in your industry but in other industries and your community. If you're an entrepreneur, that could mean not renting space but working from home if you possibly can, or selling your products via the Internet or a catalog. It might even mean not hiring *any* employees, and using temps and freelancers instead. For everyone, it means focusing on your own personal bottom line, whether you're an employee or an entrepreneur. Your bank balance is what counts, not the company's coffers or your business's books.

In the twenty-first century, if we're going to flourish we all have to get used to being ready to move in any direction. It's going to be very difficult to earn money by doggedly following a prescribed pattern, whether it's climbing the next rung on an organizational chart or increasing your market share by 10 percent. I think employees should now look for opportunities rather than promotions. I tell my entrepreneur clients to look for new markets rather than increasing market shares. If you're an employee you should be looking for another project—inside or outside your present company—or an opportunity to become an entrepreneur. If you're already an entrepreneur you should be looking for the next business to start, the next product or service to offer—or perhaps even an opportunity to work on a project inside a company.

Take Charge

In the twenty-first century you can no longer be reactive. You need to take charge of your own life in order to live rich. You may think you're already taking charge, but I'll wager you're still reacting to others, whether they're your superiors, customers, clients, or suppliers. Are you waiting for a raise or promotion or a new project? Are you waiting for payment or for customers to come to you or for suppliers to let you know about new products? That's not going to cut it in the twenty-first century. Instead, you must become positively proactive and start taking measured risks.

If you're like most of my clients you do things to yourself you'd never let others get away with today. You let self-centered fears keep you from taking the actions necessary to thrive. You need to get out of your own head, stop blaming others, stop judging your success or comparing yourself to others, and start taking forward steps. The worst possible result of an action is seldom as bad as you imagine it in your head.

Blame and fear freezes you in place, and the status quo spells doom in the twenty-first century. You have to be courageous, raise your sails, take risks, set goals and priorities, stop measuring yourself.

You need to wake up to life and cherish each and every day. You need to develop the courage to take responsibility for yourself, realize that taking risks isn't the same as gambling, and accept that life isn't ad hoc. You have to set goals and priorities. Most of all, you have to stop living in the past and worrying about the future and, instead, live rich in the present.

Create Yourself, Inc. or Become a Mercenary*

If you're an entrepreneur, you are not your business. Your business is nothing more than an avenue for profit. It should not be an entity in and of itself. Treat your business as a separate entity and you start doing things for it, rather than for you. You start worrying about how *it's* doing, rather than how *you're* doing. You start focusing on its growth, rather than your wallet. You start thinking of its image, rather than your lifestyle. You start worrying about its future, rather than your present. Your business exists solely to satisfy your own real needs. It should have no needs of its own—at least none you should care about.

Instead, I suggest you create your own personal company, which I call Yourself, Inc. Yourself, Inc. isn't the particular business you're in at the moment; it's the work or commercial aspect of your life. Yourself, Inc. is the vehicle through which you can start or buy new profitable businesses, kill off or sell old ones, or perhaps even form a joint venture with another organization or an employer for a time. What's key is that Yourself, Inc. never has any agenda other than meeting your personal needs and wants. Just as Warren Buffet has Berkshire Hathaway to represent his (and his shareholder partner's) financial interests, so you should have your own Yourself, Inc. It's the infrastructure for all your commercial efforts, the common thread that ties together all your efforts to make money.

If you're an employee, you've spent the past decade listening to workplace pundits offering hundreds of suggestions—some savvy, some silly—about how employees can deal with the changing economy and come out on top. I think all employees need to reach back in time and emulate the *condottiere* of the Renaissance.

The *condottiere* were soldiers for hire who had a personal code of conduct, who were loyal (as long as they were paid), and who readily joined units with other professional soldiers. Perhaps you know them better by the name they were given in England: free lances. The *condottiere* were ultimately answerable only to themselves, responsible for their own security and safety, their own growth of skills, their own savings, their own futures. They were always looking for the next battle to fight.

Pay Cash

Since the end of World War II we've become a nation of debtors. Americans in the eighteenth century had Ben Franklin's Poor Richard as their role model. We're entering the twenty-first century emulating conspicuous borrowers and spenders and refinanciers like Donald Trump. Powerful advertising promotes the joy of consumption. Increasingly available consumer credit and a mass psychology of self-indulgence and immediate gratification are turning us into a country that, collectively and individually, lives beyond its means.

Years ago it all seemed to make a lot of sense. Inflation was high, so credit-card buying

---

*In my book *Live Rich* I used the term "Yourself.com" rather than "Yourself, Inc." I've since realized that the Internet implications of that phrase led some to think it only applied to e-businesses. In an effort to make the concept's universality more obvious I've changed the name.

looked like a brilliant idea. We all bought into this consumerism. If you've been brought up using a dishwasher rather than a Brillo pad and the only time you're inside a coin-operated laundry is to use the pay phone, it seems only right to buy appliances right away—even if you have to charge them. And when new, more sophisticated or stylish appliances (or cars, or furniture, or clothes, or anything) come along, you can buy them on credit, even if you haven't finished paying for the one you just replaced.

But in this new world where incomes can shrink or disappear overnight, excessive borrowing is the seed of financial ruin. The maxim for such a world is to pay cash whenever you can. Don't reach beyond your grasp. Save and wait, and then buy something—whether a home or a car or a dishwasher—that will last long enough to justify either the cost of borrowing or the time spent saving. Wait, study, and research, and then use cash to buy something that will last you for a long time, rather than jumping to buy today's hot item on credit.

Don't Retire

It's remarkable how pervasive the relatively recent notion of retirement has become. Retirement as we now know it didn't exist prior to the 1930s. Social Security was developed and promoted by FDR and his New Dealers as a way to convince older workers to retire in order to open up jobs for young people during the Great Depression. Since then, Social Security benefits have expanded dramatically. From the 1930s to the 1980s private pension plans also boomed. The financial services industry saw money to be made and began relentlessly promoting retirement. In less than half a century it had evolved from a social experiment to a presumed entitlement.

Retirement made a lot of sense at a time when you weren't going to live much longer than age 65, when your job was back-breaking, when you got less productive as you got older, and when society had to make room in the job market for lots of young people. And an idyllic retirement was actually possible for your parents, who could take those expanding benefits and pensions and add to them a windfall profit from the sale of their real estate.

But in this new age retirement is not only not worth striving for, it's impossible for most—and something you would do best to avoid. The premises that underlie it are simply no longer true.

When age 65 was chosen as the retirement age, most people died at 63. Today, not only are you likely to live into your eighties or nineties, but your older years are going to be active and productive ones. Retiring at age 65 would mean spending two decades doing needlework and gardening.

When retirement was first developed, everyone thought leisure was automatically more fulfilling than work. You know better. You take pride in a job well done, enjoy being part of a team, and know that work—of one form or another—is as integral a part of your life as play.

When retirement took hold in the American mind, most work was physical in nature. It was obvious then that older workers were less productive than younger workers: they simply couldn't lift as many bales of cotton or carry as many bricks. Today, probably the most physically demanding part of your job is pushing the buttons on your cell phone or dragging a stylus across your Palm Pilot. There's absolutely nothing that indicates older workers are less productive. In fact, most evidence indicates they're *more* productive.

When retirement was first being promoted, the United States had a large generation of young people that it had to absorb into the workforce. It made some sense, therefore, to open up spots. Today, however, the twenty-somethings waiting in the wings are a small generation. They don't need to have lots of spots opened for them. In fact, there aren't enough of them to fill all the jobs the preceding generation is doing.

Finally, the financial trends that made it possible for your folks to retire have been reversed: Social Security is questionable, private pensions are vanishing, and real estate values have, in most of the country, stopped soaring.

Forget about retirement. Take it from someone who, at the age of 70, launched yet another career (my sixth or seventh—I've lost count), joining a law firm as a partner. Giving up the living death of retirement is actually an empowering act that opens up undreamed-of opportunities for your personal, professional, and financial growth. Emulate the ancient Greek hero Ulysses, rather than model yourself after a lemming. Look at your working life as a lifelong journey up and down hills, rather than a single climb up a steep cliff that ends with a fatal step off the edge (and into the abyss) at the arbitrary age of 65.

Die Broke

Die broke. I know, at first the phrase sounds insane. It's something to avoid, not something to pursue. It generates images of Dickensian poverty and Depression-era mortgage foreclosures. But fight past those reflexive responses and think about it for a minute. What's wrong with dying broke? What good will money do you when you're dead? Isn't it ironic to hoard money for a time when you can't spend it? But what about your family? you wonder. Why not take care of them when you're alive? Why should they wait for your death to be taken care of?

Inheritance made sense when it consisted of fixed assets—like a family farm, a business, or a set of tools—and was part of an implicit contract between generations—oldest son Jeb gets the farm when Dad dies in exchange for supporting Mom. But when it consists primarily of mutual funds, Treasury bills, and a condo in Del Boca Vista, and carries with it no obligations, it's nonsensical.

Creating and maintaining an estate does nothing but damage the person doing the hoarding. It will force you to put the quality of your death before the quality of your life. You'll be forced to choose not to spend on something for yourself so your kids can use the money.

Inheritance also hurts society. Funds maintained in an estate are generally kept in frozen investments, which contribute very little to the productivity of the economy.

Estates and potential inheritance can also hurt families. By inserting economic self-interest into emotional decisions, they can damage family dynamics and relationships. Suddenly, your son views your purchase of a new sailboat not as your lifelong dream being fulfilled but as money coming out of his own pocket. You begin to suspect the motivations behind your daughter's trip to visit you for the holidays. "Does she really want to see me, or is she just worried about maintaining her share?"

There's even evidence that inheritance hurts the recipient. Studies show that the expectation of an inheritance erodes the drive and motivation to work. And what do you think it would do to your soul to have a reason to look forward to the death of a loved one?

Finally, inheritance is an incredibly inefficient means of passing along wealth since it's subject to a significantly greater tax bite than any other type of income.*

Rather than looking to acquire assets in some futile quest for immortality, in the new world you should focus instead on getting the maximum use out of your assets and income. There are financial tools available—such as annuities and reverse mortgages—that can insure you won't outlive your money while guaranteeing you'll leave nothing behind. Free from the burden of building an estate, you can use your money to help your family and improve your own life.

You can help your children when they're young and need it most. Rather than leaving them money when you die, you can send them to Europe for the summer, help them buy a car, supply the down payment for their first home, or provide start-up capital for their own business. Given wisely, such gifts can have a far greater long-term impact on their lives. When your child is 25, $10,000 from you could spell the difference between renting an apartment and buying a home. When your child is 50, that $10,000 will end up funding a one-week European vacation. Besides, if you give the money while you're alive, you'll be around to see their joy and receive their thanks.

By giving up the goal of maintaining an estate, you can also lead a far richer life of your own. You can take that month-long trip to England, study Renaissance art in Italy, buy a summer home in the Adirondacks, renovate your kitchen, or simply go out to dinner and the theater more often. I tell my clients that the last check they write should be to the undertaker—and that it should bounce.† Ironically, by striving to die broke you guarantee you live rich.

The Ultimate Reward: Freedom

Make money; don't grow: change; take charge; create Yourself, Inc.; become a mercenary; pay cash; don't retire; and die broke. Following these eight maxims can unlock an incredibly rich future for you, one far better than was possible under the old rules. That's because there's a fundamental philosophical difference between the new maxims and the old rules that makes all the difference in the world.

The old rules were based on a whole litany of values; some of them good, some of them not so good. The new maxims are based on just one underlying principle: Set your own goals and do the best you can to achieve them.

You can find freedom in the new economic world. Free from living the kind of life you've been told to lead, you can start to lead your own. By giving up the outmoded rules of the past

---

*As this book is being written legislation has been proposed to eliminate or scale back estate taxes. Whatever the eventual outcome of that effort, I still believe the remaining arguments against leaving an inheritance are overwhelming.

†Funeral directors aren't my favorite people. For the reasons why, read the entry on funerals.

and by establishing your own goals and paths, you can stake a claim to your own hopes and dreams. You can have a chance to follow your bliss and uncover paths that truly bring you joy, satisfaction, and even prosperity.

When you truly live for yourself, you're living rich. By figuring out what your own real needs are, and by working to achieve them, you'll finally start to feel good about yourself. You'll feel a new and unique sense of freedom and personal empowerment. Remember: To be free is to live rich, and to live rich is to be free.

When you're not following your own dreams, you're a slave. Granted, you may be wearing chains of your own creation, consciously or unconsciously, but those are in fact the strongest restraints.

A man can be kept in physical slavery by others, with shackles binding him, but if his will is unbroken he remains free in spirit. On the other hand, a man who restrains his dreams feels no such sense of personal freedom. He may be physically free, but his spirit is in chains. He lives a poor life, regardless how much money he is earning through his servitude. But if he breaks those psychological chains, he is free to soar as high as his dreams will take him.

USING THIS BOOK

The entries in this book are in alphabetical order. Since not everyone will read this book in chronological order, there are some intentional redundancies in related chapters. However, these have been kept to a minimum so as not to bore those who do read the work from cover to cover. Cross-references to other entries that may be useful and provide more information are listed at the end of each section.

Rather than crowding the prose with gender-neutral phrasing—"he or she"—or simply alternating genders chapter by chapter, we've tried to give the text its own internal consistency. For instance, every accountant is male, while every lawyer is female; every contractor is male and every real estate broker is female; every parent is female and every child is male. Genders were assigned for convenience purposes only and do not reflect anything other than the authors' whims.

As ever, comments and questions are not only welcome but encouraged. The best way to contact the authors is either by post, care of HarperCollins, or by email at smppc@aol.com or mark4smp@aol.com.

ACCESSORY APARTMENTS

Let's be honest. Your family probably isn't the Waltons. Neither the homes nor the lifestyles of today's average American family easily lend themselves to multigenerational households. That doesn't keep many seniors from expressing the desire to move in with their children in their later years.

One possible solution to this dilemma is the accessory apartment: a small living unit that's usually attached to the home of a son or daughter. It has a private entrance and its own kitchen and bathroom. It may or may not have an interior entrance into the rest of the house.

Accessory apartments can provide seniors and their families with the best of two worlds. They help seniors retain their independence; technically, they're still living alone. Accessory apartments also allow seniors to remain with their families, which provides important emotional benefits and adds to their sense of security. For the family, it's a much better arrangement than having the parent share living space with the rest of the clan. Everyone has more privacy, and family members can choose to spend time together or not as fits their needs and their moods. Just having a wall between everyone significantly reduces the friction that can occur when everyone is in the same home.

You may find your home is already set up to house an accessory apartment. Or you may need to hire a contractor to do some home renovation. If financing is an issue, I have two suggestions. The first is to use some of the money from the sale of your parent's home to finance any necessary renovation or construction. The second is to obtain a home equity loan and cover your payments with part of your parent's income. If you wish, once your parent is no longer living in the apartment, you can continue to rent it to provide an income stream, or you can reincorporate it into your own living space.

A variation of the accessory apartment concept is what's known as the "granny flat." The idea began in Australia: Under a government program, a prefabricated housing unit is installed on the property of an adult child. When the unit is no longer needed, it is removed.

In the United States, granny flats are known as ECHO homes (Elder Cottage Housing Opportunity). Here, the financing and installation costs are the responsibility of the family. Some home manufacturers are tapping into this market by offering ECHO units in the $15,000 to $20,000 range. When they're no longer needed, the units can be converted to another use or removed and resold.

The downside of both accessory apartments and ECHO units is that they may raise your property taxes. They can also generate problems with neighbors. ECHO units, in particular, tend to become a point of dispute. You may also run into zoning problems. I think the increased need for senior housing will eventually force the removal of these regulatory problems, as more and more communities amend zoning laws to accommodate ECHO units. In the meantime, you may need to petition your local government to change its zoning ordinances. Recruiting local seniors organizations or religious groups to help will further your cause.

There are legal, tax, and insurance ramifications attached to these housing arrangements. Check with your lawyer and accountant before you decide to build an accessory apartment or install an ECHO unit. Speak to your insurance agent as well to make sure you have coverage for the new addition to your property.

Sure, it may be a bit of a pain to set up an accessory apartment or ECHO unit for a parent. But in my experience, it is less problematic than taking a parent into your own home.

(See also home equity loans, home improvements, property taxes.)

ACCOUNTANTS

NEVER TRUST a rakish accountant. Okay, I'm overstating things, but just a bit. There's a very fine line between charisma and sleaze. You want an accountant who projects stability, dependability, and integrity—someone who makes Steve Forbes look like a libertine.

But just because you want a conservative-looking and acting accountant doesn't mean his role in your financial life is colorless and unimportant. Sure, his job description—an individual trained to prepare, maintain, and analyze personal and business financial records and statements—leads most people to think of him, if ever they *do* think of him, as a bit player in your life. That's a big mistake.

A good accountant can help you as much as, maybe even more than, the flashiest stockbroker or financial planner. Your accountant can save you or your business a fortune by minimizing your tax bills and preparing financial statements. Accountants aren't all the same. For instance, income taxes are far more subjective than you might imagine. Every year *Money* has a panel of tax preparers, enrolled agents, and accountants prepare a tax return for the same hypothetical couple. Rarely do any two of the returns end in the same result or agree with what the IRS believes is the right answer.

An accountant can also take advantage of this subjectivity of numbers by helping package your financial information in a way that enhances your personal credit and your business's bankability and attractiveness to investors.

In order to get those kind of benefits from an accountant, you need to treat his hiring as a serious matter. Forget about dropping into the temporary storefront set up in the mall by a tax preparation service. Steer clear of your nephew, who just got out of college but is a real financial whiz—according to his parents. No one, repeat, no one, should use anyone other than a certified public accountant (CPA) or enrolled agent as a tax preparer.*

Hire a CPA

CPAs have earned those initials by passing rigorous exams. The general public might think of them as boring and unimportant, but they're highly respected by the business world. That's because, first, they're required to constantly upgrade their knowledge, and second, their training has as much to do with ethics as it does with accounting.

CPAs can lose their credentials if they don't maintain their professional standards and practices. In a world of sharp talkers, CPAs are almost always straight shooters. (Note the word "almost" and read the sidebar at the end of this item.) I've been with bankers who have questioned entries on a client's loan application. When I've offered them letters from a CPA validating the information, they've treated the notes as an imprimatur. Of all professionals, the CPA has traditionally ranked at the top of the list for the most trusted adviser.

Another obvious advantage to CPAs is that they are year-round financial professionals. That's obviously a necessity for business owners who pay taxes and borrow money throughout the year and need constantly updated financial information to make savvy decisions. But it's also important for those who use an accountant solely for their personal tax returns.

Tax preparers hang out a shingle from January 1 through April 15 and then take off their accounting hats until the following year, returning to their full-time jobs as teachers, travel agents, and plumbers. A CPA, on the other hand, is available during the entire year to advise you on tax issues or other financial questions. And he will be right by your side if you're audited. Try finding that fly-by-night tax preparer when you need help responding to a spaghetti letter from the IRS.†

---

*It's distressing how many lower- and middle-income people don't get their fair share of tax credits and refunds because they don't know to hire an accountant. To their credit, many social service agencies arrange for civic-minded accountants or enrolled agents to provide free advice to clients.

†A spaghetti letter is the nickname of the most common type of IRS inquiry: a letter asking for clarification of something the IRS thinks might, perhaps, potentially indicate that you owe more money. It's called a spaghetti letter because it's just the IRS throwing something against the wall to see if it sticks. A good CPA knows how to respond so that it doesn't stick.

Although I have great respect for accountants and their skills, I don't feel most are qualified to act as business consultants or financial planners. Hire them to prepare your taxes, your business's financial statements, and maybe your money tactics. Use them to help trim your tax bill and improve your chances of obtaining loans or enticing investors. But don't rely on a run-of-the-mill CPA for strategic advice on what mutual fund to invest in or on how to develop your business. That's a job for a specialized financial planner or an MBA-trained business consultant.

Look for the Young and Hungry

I think the best way to find a good CPA is through word of mouth. Ask your other professionals, particularly those whose businesses rely heavily on accounting services—physicians, bankers, lawyers, financial planners—for recommendations. If you're looking for an accountant to represent you or your sole proprietorship, keep an eye out for a young individual or a small firm eager to build a client base. Although he may not offer the services or clout of an older, established CPA, he'll likely charge far less, be more willing to work hard and go out of his way to meet your needs, and he's more apt to be on top of the latest developments in his field.

I always look for young accountants who have worked for medium-sized firms but have just recently gone out on their own or started their own firm. Young accountants like that generally have a broad background and are often willing to grow with a client, learning about your specific industry or unique personal financial situation, yet they are still able to help you save money, keep records, and generate statements.

There are just two caveats about hiring a young and hungry individual or firm. If your business is in a highly regulated industry, it probably makes sense to hire a seasoned CPA with specific experience in your business or a midsized firm. And in your search for youth, make sure to check for baby fat. Youthful energy and enthusiasm are invaluable, but they must be balanced by common sense and candor. I don't mind if an accountant doesn't know the answer to a question and says he'll find out. That's better than winging it and covering up a deficiency in order to impress.

Look for Midsized Firms

If you're looking for an accountant for your business and you're either a partnership, a limited liability company, or incorporated, I'd suggest a medium-sized accounting firm. It's great if you're a business owner and your accountant has contacts with financial institutions, has a tax department on hand, and has estate expertise as well. You're more apt to find that in midsize firms. Having an accountant with a good personal Rolodex, or whose firm has many contacts, is also a plus since he may be able to turn other clients into investors. After all, who has a better handle on how a company is doing than its accountant. And if that accountant or his firm also represents the investors' interests, it can be an excellent match.

It's also good if a business owner's accountant has some teaching skills. He can help you become conversant with financial ratios, projections, and statements, making you that much more of an attractive investment or borrower.

Interview Each Candidate Thoroughly

Once you have a list of candidates, make appointments with each to discuss your needs. Bring tax returns and financial statements from previous years and be prepared to have a frank discussion of your financial situation. If any candidate refuses to meet with you or wants to charge for this initial conversation, scratch his name off your list.

Look around the accountant's office when you arrive. Does the office look well-organized? Does the staff seem well-trained? Sure, these are superficial judgments. But if a candidate's own office is a mess, he probably isn't going to be very good at organizing your financial records. And if a candidate's own staff appears incompetent, he's probably not going to be very good at teaching you or your staff.

Look for someone who, while technically proficient, is also capable of speaking and writing in language you understand. If you don't understand the advice you're being given, it won't do you any good.

Ask each candidate if he has other clients whose financial situation or business is similar to yours. Knowing your industry and the players in it can be a real plus. Find out if he will be handling your business personally or whether it will be assigned to a staff accountant. And ask the candidate about his education, both past and current. Any CPA worth his fee will regularly attend seminars and classes to keep up with the changes.

Speaking of fees, don't forget to discuss them. Charges for accounting services vary according to location, experience, and the size of the firm, so it's tough to generalize. But be prepared to pay between $200 and $1,500 for the preparation of a personal tax return, depending on its complexity. Your business should expect an annual bill of between $2,000 and $6,000 for tax preparation, and the occasional special statements for loans and other purposes. Make sure the fee and the ownership of documents is agreed on and spelled out in writing in an engagement letter. This will prevent any misunderstandings or problems down the road.

Granted, these fees may seem expensive, particularly if you're accustomed to using a tax preparation service or preparing your returns yourself. But keep in mind that unless your financial situation is especially convoluted, you'll only need a few hours of a CPA's time

---

You Know an Accountant Is a Crook if He . . .

• Has you sign a blank tax return or a return filled out in pencil

• Asks you to have your refund sent directly to him*

• Tells you he knows how to "get away with" not paying any taxes

• Promises you a refund without having looked at your numbers

• Takes a percentage of what he "saved you" as his fee

---

*A caveat: If you've hired an accountant to serve as your personal money manager, in charge of your banking and bill paying, it's okay for him or her to receive any refund directly.

every year, so you're really only talking about a few hundred dollars. Believe me, it's worth it just to know there's a professional standing behind you. Consider it an investment in peace of mind.

If you're a business owner, you should feel no compunction about trying to negotiate the accountant's fees downwards.

Negotiate Your Accountant's Fees

The secret to successfully negotiating your accountant's fees downward is to never imply he isn't worth the stated amount. Instead, cite your own budget as the reason for negotiating, and discuss everything other than the value of the services.

Subtly suggest that you can compensate for paying a lower fee by bringing other clients to the accountant. For instance, your membership in a local business association or service organization can be an enticement for a young accountant looking to expand his client base.

An older, established accountant, or a midsized firm may not find that as valuable, however. In this case, the best way to save money is to ask for a reduction or the elimination of any advances or retainers. The very fact that the accountant is established or is part of a firm means there's less of an need for such up-front money.

How to Ask the Uncomfortable Question

All CPAs believe that while tax evasion is illegal, tax avoidance is every citizen's patriotic duty. Loopholes are written into the tax code intentionally. And most parts of the code are open to interpretation, at least until the IRS issues a ruling. That being said, a CPA must abide by a strict set of ethical rules and standards. He does not want to be asked for help in "evading" or advice on "how much to cheat." On the other hand, if you're like most taxpayers, you're concerned that you may not have taken full advantage of all your possible deductions or be deducting as much as others in a similar financial situation. How do you get around asking what might be an uncomfortable question?

The key is to choose your words carefully. Explain to the accountant that while you've done a careful job of adding up your receipts, you're only human and may have missed a few expenses. Note that you want to take an aggressive approach to your return without triggering any audit flags. Then ask if there are any areas where you appear to be claiming less than the average return of someone in a similar financial situation.* Conclude by explaining that if there are any such areas, you'll go back and double-check your numbers now and make sure you're more thorough on next year's return.

---

*The average deductions taken the previous year by taxpayers in the different income brackets is public information and your accountant should have the numbers handy.

Another option is to ask the accountant to provide fewer services in exchange for a lower fee. Perhaps you don't need quarterly statements or you could outsource your payroll returns.

(See also audits, banking and bankers, financial planners, financial ratios, lawyers, location, negotiating, sole proprietorships, tax preparers, word of mouth.)

ADOPTION

I THINK ONE of our society's greatest advancements has been the shift in criteria for adoption. No longer are adoption rights granted only to people who satisfy some arbitrary notion of "normalcy." Today, the criterion for adoption, quite rightly I believe, is what's best for the child.

Most adoptions are regulated by the states. They either administer their own agencies or oversee agencies that they license and monitor. The agencies play the role of broker in bringing together children, adoptive parents, and birth mothers. Some adoptions are of infants. Others are of older children, sometimes in their teens, who have spent some part of their lives in foster care. If the process begins before the child is born, it's quite common for adoptive parents to pay the birth mother's medical costs and legal expenses associated with the adoption.

You may also have the option of a private adoption. Rather than being overseen by an agency, private adoptions occur when a couple seeking to adopt a child and a woman who wants to surrender a child are brought together by an intermediary. (In some states, however, intermediaries are not permitted.) Often this role is played by a lawyer, physician, or friend. Private adoptions have become more common in the United States in recent years. It's not unusual to see classified ads placed by prospective adoptive parents seeking women who are looking for a home for a child.

As these adoptions have become more common, the issue of payment has come to the fore. It's illegal to "buy" a child. Any money that changes hands is supposed to cover the legal expenses of the adoption and the medical expenses of the birth mother. If the intermediary receives any kind of fee, she risks prosecution—and so do you. However, the nature of private adoptions makes it very difficult to monitor such transactions.

International Adoptions

Many parents today are choosing to adopt children from other countries. Because of the complexity, most choose to go through agencies that specialize in international adoptions. There's an incredible amount of paperwork to be filled out and a great deal of interaction with the Immigration and Naturalization Service. You'll also need to be prepared to spend a lot of money. Some international adoptions can cost $20,000 or more.

You may be able to simplify the process by looking for people who have already adopted internationally and getting the names of private agencies and lawyers who assisted them. There are also support organizations that may be able to answer your questions and provide you with guidance.

Open Adoptions

In some cases, the relationship between the birth mother and the adoptive couple can become problematic. Most states have a waiting period during which the birth mother can change her mind and take the child back. Sometimes the birth mother will petition for the return of her child years later, claiming she was coerced or otherwise manipulated into giving up her child.

The growing trend toward open adoption has reduced such conflicts. In an open adoption, the birth mother relinquishes all legal rights and responsibilities, but rather than disappearing, stays in contact with the adoptive parents and her child. Visiting arrangements are sometimes worked out and she plays an active role in her child's life.

The birth father must also be considered. Most states require that the birth father be notified of an impending adoption. If he wishes, he can agree to an open adoption. He can also choose to raise the child himself, assuming no questions are raised about his fitness as a parent. If he doesn't choose to raise the child, however, he cannot prevent the adoption. The state will terminate his parental rights and free the child for adoption.

Adoption Records

In most states adoption records are automatically sealed to protect the privacy of everyone involved. In recent years, however, there has been increasing pressure to make the records accessible. There are provisions in some states to make adoption records available to children once they reach age 18 so they can learn the identities of their birth parents if they wish. Some states only allow this information to be revealed when the birth parents give permission. In some cases, if the adopted child learns that he has a serious health condition, the state will allow the records to be opened so any useful genetic information can be obtained.

Much of this controversy will become moot as states adopt Measure 58, a federal law giving adoptees the right to examine their records.* The law was passed in 1998 but was put on hold while the courts reviewed a lawsuit brought by several anonymous birth mothers. The Supreme Court released the hold in May 2000, and the first states to adopt it were swamped with requests.

(See also lawyers.)

ADVERTISING

THERE'S AN OLD TRUISM in the world of business: Half of all advertising is wasted, but the problem is, nobody knows which half it is. Here's my updated version of that apho-

---

*Note, also, that an adopted child has the exact same legal rights in regard to his parents' estate as does a birth child.

rism: Almost all small business advertising is wasted, but the problem is, nobody wants to admit it.

Advertising is the most common form of marketing because, in theory, it offers the best chance to reach a great many people in a short period of time. In practice, I think advertising is the most popular type of marketing because it provides the biggest ego boost to the business owner. But this doesn't mean that a small business shouldn't advertise as part of its marketing plan—only that every business needs to weigh the pluses and minuses.

Traditional advertising is far and away the most difficult and expensive type of marketing. In my experience, most small businesses can more effectively spend their marketing time and money on publicity and promotion, or on nontraditional forms of advertising, such as the Internet. If, on the other hand, you're a retailer or own another business that needs to advertise, roll up your sleeves and start doing some further analysis.

There are five major advertising mistakes: not spending enough; spending too much; not being ready for sales; poor positioning; and not knowing the customer. To avoid these mistakes, and to come up with a program that fits your business's unique advertising needs, it is essential that you make a careful study of your market, dollar projections, and available advertising avenues.

Who, Why, How Much, When, What . . .

First, analyze your existing and potential customers. Who are they? Which of their needs are you meeting? What advantages does your product or service have over the competition?

Second, decide why you're advertising. Is it to generate awareness of your business and its products? Is it to unveil a new product? Is it to sway customers from a competitor's offerings to your own? Whatever the reason, your goal must be clear, because that's what will determine the type and content of your advertising.

Third, come up with a budget. The best method is to think of advertising as just another cost of doing business. Consider your advertising, whatever its frequency or price, as an annualized cost. Advertising should never be undercapitalized. That will only lead to its failure. Research whether there are cooperative advertising funds available in your industry. Many manufacturers, for example, will provide funds for retailers to place their own ads touting the vendor's products. There are also some advertising combines made up of businesses that have some aspect in common—location, for example.

Fourth, decide when to advertise. Here again, consult your market research. Does your business have seasonal ups and downs? Are the products or services bought habitually, or does the purchase need to be encouraged? How often can the customer be expected to make a purchase? Package goods companies generally advertise right away to launch a new product. But it can be self-destructive for a business to advertise too soon. One of the worst things you can do is advertise and not be able to handle the demand you've created. Customers you turn away empty-handed will never return.

The three most common advertising patterns are during peak seasons, during off seasons, and constant advertising. For example, if your customers act habitually, it's important to advertise heavily before peak periods but also to keep a steady advertising presence all year. A ski equipment company, for example, will advertise most heavily in the fall and winter, but by spring their ads will have disappeared. A golf equipment business, on the other hand, will be more likely to advertise year-round, since golf is a year-round sport.

Fifth, give thought to the message you'd like to convey to your customers. To be effective, every advertising message must get the target's attention, hold it, address a need, and foster an action, in that order. Failing in just one part of this sequence will result in an ineffective ad. Examine the competition's advertising message and try to find an opening for your own, different message. Advertising agencies can be a real help in this area, but depending on the budget you've allocated, such assistance may be too costly.

. . . And Most Importantly, Where

Sixth, and perhaps most importantly, you need to select one or more advertising media. Weigh each by reach, frequency, demographics, and cost. Reach is the number of people who see the message and frequency is the number of times they see it. If you are looking to create awareness, you go for a broad reach; frequency, on the other hand, creates sales.

Because of the number of people reached per dollar spent, newspaper advertising is, in my opinion, the best deal available. For a relatively modest cost, you can reach tens of thousands or even hundreds of thousands of readers. The problem is, newspaper ads can become lost in the visual jumble of the pages. Small ads are easily missed.

Magazine advertising is more focused. Most magazines have a fairly specific audience, and this makes it easier for advertisers to reach their own target audiences. But magazine advertising can be expensive and, as with newspapers, an ad can disappear among the clutter.*

Telephone directories are effective because they reach people who have already made a decision to spend their money. How many times have you decided to buy something and reached for the telephone book? But what happened when you got to the listings of the product or service you were interested in? There were probably a confusing number of entries. Once again, an ad can easily be overlooked.

Direct mail, on the other hand, is impossible to overlook. This makes it one of the most effective methods of reaching customers. It's selective, it reaches a broad audience, and when it works, it generates quick action on the part of customers. But it's also expensive, and although it's hard to overlook, it's easy to discard. A lot of it ends up unopened in the recycling bin with the rest of the junk mail. The big advantage of direct mail is that years of study and analysis have turned it into a science. Experts can often predict response rates to within 1 or 2 percentage points. That means the direct mail decision usually comes down to whether or not you can afford to spend enough on the advertising for it to be profitable.

---

*One way of cutting the costs of advertising in expensive media is to enlist the services of a media buyer. These individuals or agencies function as a sort of advertising space consolidator, buying up unsold space and time from media in bulk and offering it to clients at a discount.

Private sale advertising can be extremely effective in creating and maintaining a stable of loyal repeat customers. A mailing or series of telephone calls to a solid customer list, offering a special "regular customer only" price, is an excellent way to firm up your business's foundation of support.

Trade shows and conventions are popular with manufacturers and wholesalers interested in attracting distributors and retailers. They are effective methods of directly reaching a target market. The downside is the expense of travel, lodging, and having an exhibit designed and shipped to the site.

Billboards and transit advertising are effective in that they reach thousands of people. The problem is that each of those viewers only gets a passing glance at your message. A fair amount of market saturation is needed to make this form of advertising pay off.

Television reaches enormous numbers of people. And because it has the added advantage of mixing audio with visual images, it's very effective at grabbing people's attention. But expense is a serious issue, as is effectiveness. Even seasoned advertising pros concede it's almost impossible to know if a television ad is reaching its intended audience.

Radio is much more affordable than television. It has the ability to reach large numbers of people and allows you to target a specific audience. Since the advent of television, radio has been forced to do an excellent job of closely tracking audience demographics and, as a result, offering a great deal of bang for the buck. But radio is also notoriously difficult to do well. Most people require the assistance of an ad agency or the station itself in creating a truly effective ad.*

The Internet, particularly the World Wide Web, is the newest and the arguably the most trendy advertising medium. Although the effectiveness of advertising on the Internet has been hard to measure so far, there's no question it's a viable place to put your message. The growth of the Internet has been exponential and it's rapidly becoming a major marketplace. The problem is the nature of the medium itself. It allows consumers to control where they go and what they see. If they choose to ignore advertising, it's easy for them to do. On the other hand, if they do become interested in an ad, the interactive nature of the Web allows advertisers to give customers more information than any other advertising venue. If you have an online business, your Web ad can even bring them right to your digital doorstep.

Track Your Results

After selecting which advertising media you'll use, your final task is to devise some way of tracking the effectiveness of your advertising. You want to be able to compare your stated goal with the actual results. Among the best techniques are coupons, ad-mention discounts or rewards, and inquiries. Why is tracking so important? Unless you track your results, you won't be able to determine whether the money you're spending on advertising is worthwhile.

---

*In general, if you can afford the services of an established advertising agency, it always makes sense to hire one. They are experts at creating and placing ads that work. If their ads didn't work, they wouldn't be in business very long.

The Advertising Medium of the Future

I believe that by the end of the decade the Internet will be the primary advertising medium for small specialty businesses, whether they're retailers, service providers, or manufacturers. Why?

- It's interactive. No other medium allows a true back-and-forth dialogue with customers.

- It's cheap. Spend $20 a month on an Internet connection and download some free software and you have the tools and ability to reach millions of customers.

- It's self-defined. Internet users already gather in "places" with other people with similar traits or interests. Pardon the expression, but it's like shooting fish in a barrel.

- It's flexible. No other advertising medium lets you change your message so quickly and so cheaply to fit any variation from gender to geography—and then change it back the next day.

- It's addictive. People are hooked on the Internet the way they were hooked when radio and television first appeared. And every day more people get online.

- It's fast. No other medium lets you create a marketing package in hours, compile a list of customers in minutes, and send it to all of them in seconds.

- It has great demographics. Internet users are young, educated, and affluent consumers, and in just about every business in the world.

- It's global. Your reach is limited only by your imagination. Your e-mail gets to Zaire as quickly as to Toledo, and your Web page can be seen just as clearly in Cologne as in Hoboken.

Ad Bartering and Discounts

Businesses that are low on cash but still need to get the word out to the public to build or maintain a customer base have alternatives to spending heavily for advertising. In some instances, they can turn to barter arrangements for everything from ad agency assistance in creating and laying out a campaign to swapping air time on radio and television in exchange for goods or services.

Barter time for radio and television advertising once flourished in the 1960s and 1970s. A "swap" was arranged: services or merchandise for programming. Today such arrangements are uncommon, but some radio stations may still enter into barter agreements, and it may be worth a few hours of telephoning to see if media time can be swapped for your company's merchandise.

The Internet has expanded the world of bartering. According to industry reports, barter amounts to an estimated $16 billion a year, and some 1.2 million businesses are forecast to barter in North America alone within the next decade. Consolidation is underway in the industry, with three or four major players dominating the field. Online B2B (business-to-business) exchanges, including local ones, can list ad agencies and design firms that are willing to barter their services, along with printers and other suppliers you may be able to swap services with. Investigating these resources can prove a worthwhile investment.

In print media, magazine "remnants" of unsold space and newspaper "standbys" for ads that run when major advertisers cancel can provide important savings. Remnants in weekend newspaper supplements and television program guides can provide as much as a 40 percent discount while providing effective reach. The rules of the game are strict: the advertiser has hours, not days, to decide whether to take the space, and the ad must be ready to be placed immediately.

AGE DISCRIMINATION

EXPERIENCED, SAVVY, SKILLED PEOPLE in their forties, fifties, and sixties are regularly being canned and replaced with inexperienced, naive newcomers. Sometimes it's because the younger person will accept far less in salary and benefits. Other times it's simply because youth is "in" right now. Superficial corporate executives think they can boost their company's share price by hiring some kids with nose rings and tattoos and setting up a Web site.

Unfortunately, this will remain a pattern until about 2008. Then, when most baby boomers will have hit the age of 60, the gray hairs will rule the roost. Until then, if you're over 40 you'd better join me in keeping one eye open.

Think it can't happen to you? It can. People from all walks of life and in all careers are discriminated against because of their age. Corporate vice presidents are just as vulnerable as folks who work in the shipping department. Some are quietly fired from jobs they've held for 20 years or more to make room for younger employees who are judged to have more energy and who definitely command lower salaries. Others are "shelved," moved into positions of less responsibility and with no chance of further advancement. Then there are those who are discriminated against in the hiring process by employers who feel they'll be less productive, reluctant to learn new skills, and more likely to miss work because of illness.

Age discrimination can be particularly hard on women, and not just those over 40. Women in the 25 to 35 age range are often overlooked for promotions or new jobs because employers think they'll soon leave to have children. Women are also under more pressure than men to have a "youthful" appearance. By the time they're in their fifties, many women find it difficult to even get a job interview.

I take this issue personally since I celebrated my seventy-first birthday during the writing of this book. I'm living proof that age isn't a handicap in the workplace. In fact, I started down a new career path as I entered my eighth decade of life by closing my private office and joining an established law firm as a partner. My age wasn't an issue with any of the seven different law firms who pursued me. What they cared about was my ability to attract and serve clients. That's all that should matter. And according to the federal government, that's all that legally can matter.

Your Legal Protections

The Age Discrimination in Employment Act of 1967 protects individuals who are 40 years old or older from employment discrimination based on age. The ADEA's protections apply to both employees and job applicants. Under the ADEA, it is illegal to discriminate against a person because of his or her age with respect to any term, condition, or privilege of employment. This includes hiring, firing, promotion, layoff, compensation, benefits, job assignments, and training. The ADEA applies to employers with 20 or more employees, including state and local governments and the federal government. It also applies to employment agencies and labor organizations.*

In 1990, the ADEA was amended by the Older Workers Benefits Protection Act. This legislation specifically prohibits employers from denying benefits to older employees. It states that an employer can reduce benefits based on age only if the cost of providing the reduced benefits to older workers is the same as the cost of providing benefits to younger workers. In other words, every worker must receive benefits costing the same amount.

We're all also protected by the Age Discrimination Act of 1975, which applies to people seeking financial assistance from the federal government. The ADA forbids discrimination at all age levels, ensuring that students seeking federal assistance for their education are protected.

Despite these laws, age discrimination charges are brought against employers every day. The Equal Employment Opportunity Commission receives more than 16,000 complaints every year. Many end up in court, where verdicts are shifting in favor of the plaintiffs. A landmark 1996 Supreme Court ruling found a company guilty of age discrimination for replacing a 56-year-old employee with an employee who was over 40. Prior to that case, most rulings held that age discrimination had not occurred unless the new employee was under 40.

---

*Just because you work for a firm or organization with fewer than 20 employees doesn't mean you aren't protected. Each state has its own age discrimination statutes that may apply to companies not targeted by the federal legislation.

Preempting Age Discrimination

Of course, everyone wants to avoid a legal battle, in which the big winners are always the lawyers. That means you need to preempt the discrimination by insuring you aren't outdated or perceived as obsolete.

Take a realistic look at your skills and abilities and how they fit into your industry's rapidly changing environment. Are you adept at all the new technologies and ideas in your business? If you're not currently as comfortable with new processes and procedures as your younger peers, get on the ball. Immediately seek the training and education you need to be as up to date as anyone else in your business.

Don't stop subscribing to the long-established industry bibles, but add the new hot publications to your reading list as well. For instance, read *The Red Herring* and *The Industry Standard* as well as *The Wall Street Journal*—and let everyone see your reading list has expanded.

Make a conscious and visible effort to network with younger people, not just your old cronies. And don't bore them with your old war stories. Listen to what your juniors are saying and thinking. Wisdom comes from experience, not age.

Work on your image as well as your substance. That doesn't mean trading in your Brooks Brothers suit for a Hugo Boss outfit. There's nothing more pathetic than a 60-year-old trying to look like a 30-year-old. Instead, focus on your attitude and mannerisms. Smile. Be enthusiastic and optimistic. Exude energy and vitality. Walk with your head held high and a bounce in your step.

Don't immediately shoot down new ideas in meetings by relating them to past failures. Use your knowledge and experience to help make those new ideas work by avoiding the pitfalls of the past. Most of all, show flexibility; demonstrate that you're ready, willing, and able to change with the times.

If You're Fired Because of Your Age

If you're too late in demonstrating your youthful attitudes and flexibility and you suspect you're about to be fired because of your age, you need to raise the issue calmly but forcefully and immediately.

As soon as you realize you're being terminated, politely interrupt the designated executioner and ask for a pencil and paper to take notes. Say as little as possible, just asking for information to be repeated so you can "make sure you take everything down correctly."

Don't nod reflexively, as most people do, whenever the other parties speak. Your acceptance is a valuable commodity, especially now. This will very subtly demonstrate your pique and determination.

When you're asked to sign a release, refuse. Say that this has come as a shock to you and you're in no condition psychologically or emotionally to sign anything. Explain that before you can respond to what has just transpired, you need to speak with a lawyer about the "special circumstances" surrounding your termination—unless of course they'd like to reconsider their action.* If you're pressed to sign or they threaten to withdraw their "generous" severance package, say you're making note of their threats, stand up, say they will be hearing from either you or your lawyer in the next couple of days, and leave. As soon as you can, contact your lawyer and get the name of a lawyer who specializes in employment law.

Signs of Current or Pending Age Discrimination

How can you tell you're about to get canned because you remember the Kennedy administration? Here are a few signs:

- You're rejected for one job after another even though you're clearly qualified for the positions.
- You're transferred from a position of responsibility within your firm to one with little responsibility.
- You're moved from a position where you supervise many people to one where you supervise a few.
- After years of being trusted, your decisions are constantly questioned by your superiors.
- There are suddenly inconsistencies in how your job performance is evaluated by your superiors.
- Your company begins to hire large numbers of young people.

(See also benefits, employees, employment agencies, job interview, lawyers, layoffs, networking, promotions, reading, termination, Web site.)

ALIMONY

ALIMONY ISN'T AWARDED as often as most people think. Judges consider a variety of factors when making this decision. Among them are each person's age and health, the length of their marriage, and their ability to earn money, both now and in the future. In some states, they also consider the amount of property that's involved and the conduct of the two parties. In

---

*If they actually do reconsider, don't think the story is over. Once you have been targeted for termination, and have avoided it only through subtle threats, you have no future in this company. Use any reprieve as a chance to find another position as soon as possible.

most states, judges won't award alimony unless one spouse has been completely dependent economically on the other for most of the marriage.* While that characterizes many marriages among the World War II generation, it's less common among their baby boomer children.

The size of an alimony award isn't the only concern; tax deductibility can be an issue as well. Even if alimony isn't awarded by a judge, it often makes sense economically to agree to pay alimony rather than child support. This is because the IRS taxes alimony and child support differently. Child support payments are not taxed as income for the recipient, nor are they tax-deductible for the contributor. Alimony, on the other hand, is both taxable and tax-deductible.

Alimony in lieu of child support makes sense when one party makes a great deal more money than the other. For example, let's say a couple—we'll call them Bob and Mary—agrees to divorce. Bob makes $200,000 a year and Mary makes about $25,000. She keeps custody of the kids and he agrees to contribute to their support.

If Bob and Mary can communicate effectively enough in the midst of all the emotional upheaval they're experiencing and crunch the numbers, they'll discover that it's to both their advantages for all the support to come in the form of alimony. First of all, Bob is in a higher tax bracket than Mary. The tax deduction that he'll receive from his alimony payments will allow him to more than make up for the extra taxes Mary will have to pay. She agrees to not ask for child support and he agrees to pay more in alimony. Under this arrangement they both end up with more after-tax income.

There's just one problem. Uncle Sam doesn't operate with blinders on. The IRS is fully aware of the advantages of paying alimony rather than child support and will examine your situation very carefully if it becomes apparent that you're pursuing this strategy.

The IRS has strict rules about what constitutes deductible alimony and how it must be paid. First of all, the payment of alimony must be described in a court decree or in a written agreement between the two parties. Any money paid informally before an agreement is signed is not considered alimony.

Second, alimony must be paid in cash or by check. It can't be provided by services in lieu of payment or by the transfer of property. The payments can't be deducted during any year for which the couple files a joint tax return.

There are also rules regarding the relationship between the two parties. If you're both living under the same roof, any payments won't be considered alimony. It doesn't matter if you're in separate wings of the house and go weeks without laying eyes on one another, you still won't qualify. You must live in separate residences.

The best approach is to find the combination of child support and alimony that provides the best economic advantage without triggering an audit. My advice is to try to negotiate an alimony agreement you both can live with. If you can't communicate effectively enough to reach an agreement yourselves, have someone who does divorce mediation get involved. You may find this

---

*In most states courts attempt to preserve the preseparation standard of living—especially in long-term marriages.

strategy provides you both with the best solution. And once you reach an agreement, honor it.

An alimony agreement can be changed or stopped at any time with the consent of both partners. For example, the spouse receiving alimony may find a job with a significant increase in salary and agree to receive less each month. Or the opposite can happen: The providing spouse might agree to funnel some additional income to the recipient spouse. If the recipient spouse remarries, alimony is terminated unless both parties agree otherwise. Of course, alimony also stops when one of the parties dies.

(See also audits, child support, divorce.)

ALLIANCES

A LLIANCES ARE NECESSARY EVILS. They are solely a means to an end you could not otherwise accomplish on your own, whether it's evicting Saddam Hussein's forces from Kuwait or landing the Microsoft account. I think the most realistic approach to alliances was that of Lord Palmerston, a nineteenth-century prime minister of England. He said, "We have no eternal allies and we have no perpetual enemies. Our interests are eternal and perpetual, and these interests it is our duty to follow."

What was true for the politics of the British Empire is also true for your business. Forming a business alliance isn't the same thing as forming a partnership. You aren't looking toward a long-term relationship. Instead you're looking to develop a short-term relationship between your business and another business that facilitates the accomplishment of common goals that serve your interests.

The Basics

Business alliances can be defined by legal contracts that describe the responsibilities of all the parties involved, or they can be as simple as a handshake. They can be between two businesses or they can involve hundreds. Whatever their numbers, the members will be linked by a common need that can better be met by operating as a group than by remaining independent.

While there have always been alliances in business, they've become more common as the number of small service and technology-based companies has grown. Today's information technology makes it possible for a single person in a week to do what it used to take 10 people to do in a month. But what if that one person is confronted by a project that requires more time and effort than he or she can do alone, even with the latest technology? What if that one person wants or needs to give the appearance of a larger organization in order to solicit work or clients that are beyond her individual capabilities? The answer is to form alliances with other small businesses. The alliances you create will be determined by your expertise, skills, and abilities and by the needs of your clients. If you don't have all the expertise, skills, and abilities to fill those needs, you will have to find others who do.

Let's say you're an independent public relations expert. You think you'll be able to sell a publicity campaign to a large retailer you've been pursing. However because of the size of the project, you won't be able to do more than the planning and coordination role. Rather than avoiding the project because it's too big for you, you look to form alliances with a handful of other businesses. You speak with a public relations writer you've known in the past who's now out on her own. You contact a graphic artist who was once a coworker of yours and who now works from his home. You telephone a direct mail consultant you met at the local chamber of commerce. The writer puts you in touch with a freelance commercial producer and the artist introduces you to a good local photographer. Suddenly you're not a one-person operation but a six-person agency.

That six-person alliance—or any alliance, for that matter—allows a small business to take on larger or more projects, offer greater and wider expertise to clients, do things faster and for less money, trim expenses and increase revenues. In effect, alliances let you retain all the advantages of your small operation while adding many of the benefits of a larger organization; you get the best of both worlds. In addition, your allies can eventually become marketing arms for your business, bringing in clients and opportunities you might never have gained on your own.

Structuring and Formalizing Your Alliances

These alliances can be structured in any number of ways. You could be a general contractor and the rest of the team could be subcontractors to whom you simply farm out work. You and one or more of your allies could form a limited partnership. Forming a virtual corporation isn't out of the question, if the project is large enough. What matters isn't so much the exact form of the alliance, but that the relationship is formalized and documented by a binding agreement. Again, this could be a simple letter pact or it could be a comprehensive contract, depending on the situation. Whatever the form of your agreement, it's prudent to get your lawyer involved in the drafting of the document.

However simple your agreement, it should contain all of the following:

- The names of the individuals involved and their businesses
- The date of the agreement and the term of the relationship
- A general description of the project or goal of the alliance
- A specific description of the responsibilities of all the allies, including deadlines
- A specific description of the financial and nonfinancial contributions of all the allies
- A specific description of how and when money will be spent, collected, and divided
- Criteria for judging the quality of work
- Criteria for resolving disputes and dissolving the alliance

Finding Allies

It's fairly easy to find allies within your own industry or profession since you can draw on your networks of former coworkers and peers. But no one's network is ever big enough. Be on the lookout for future allies at professional seminars, trade shows, or other industry functions.

If you need to find allies in other professions or industries, see if you can form a bridge using your existing network. Let's say you need to find a Web site designer, but all your contacts are in the magazine industry. Ask your magazine contacts about any experiences or information they have with Web site design. Perhaps one of your art director friends could come up with a name for you, or at least a lead. Use that lead to start developing a Web site design network of your own.

You can also draw on your personal network if your professional contacts don't provide enough leads. Ask friends, relatives, and people you know through social and community activities. Speak with your accountant, lawyer, and banker. Call up your dentist. Leave no stone unturned. Sometimes you find the best people in the most unlikely ways.

In selecting allies from among a group of candidates, pay as much attention to character as ability. If the people with whom you associate are professional and ethical, you will enhance your image. If they're amateurish and corrupt, you'll do more than lose this one project; you'll tarnish your reputation.

(See also banker, corporations, laywers, networking, partnerships, Web sites.)

ALLOWANCES

Your child's financial future is in your hands. You can help turn him into a dollar dunce or a monetary master. This power doesn't come from the money you save or invest for your offspring's future. It comes from the pocket change you give him at the beginning of every week.

An allowance gives a child his first hint of the independence to come later in life and teaches him the basic financial discipline so many of the rest of the world is lacking. Since a child doesn't have access to credit, he'll quickly learn that the only way to get what he wants is to save for it.

To be effective, an allowance must be provided on a regular basis. I recommend a weekly allowance. Your child must understand that it's up to him to make decisions about how much he can afford to spend and what purchases carry the most priority. If you simply give him money when he needs it or wants it, you, not he, become the decision maker.

Don't tie allowances to an accomplishment like good grades. That brings an entirely different value system into play and distorts the real purpose of the allowance. Money for good grades is really just a form of bribery. What your child should be learning is that the real reward of hard work is the accomplishment itself.

Since planning is an integral part of money management, allowances should be given on the same day of the week. This gives a child a basis on which to make some rudimentary budgeting decisions. You should start an allowance at age 5 or 6. Prior to that, it's a good idea to let your child pay for small purchases by giving him the money and letting him take care of the transaction. While this won't teach him about budgeting, it will provide him with a basic understanding of the money-exchange process.

It's important to step back and let your child make his own mistakes. If he doesn't have the money for something he really wants because he squandered it on silly impulse purchases, that's an important lesson learned. It teaches him the value of putting money aside for things that are really important. It may take a while, though. Most children are 8 or 9 before the concept of saving for a rainy day finally sticks. One way to give your child an early start is to have him target a particular toy he wants and then save the money needed to purchase it.

The amount of allowance you give your child will depend on your income, the socioeconomic level of your community, the age and maturity level of the child, and the type of purchases it's intended to cover. Allowing a child to have a voice in the decision can be useful, but don't let things get carried away. I'll guarantee you that his idea of what's necessary and your idea of what's necessary won't be anywhere close.

By the time your child is 12 or 13, you should be giving him enough of an allowance to cover his clothing and entertainment. You also can move the allowances to every other week or even monthly. By gradually making your child responsible for more of his own needs and forcing him to budget over longer periods, by the time he gets to college he'll be able to handle lump sums of money meant to last an entire semester.

Your child can also learn from participating in your financial activities. Although I don't suggest you go so far as to divulge your income to him—at least until he's old enough to put it in perspective, anyway—showing him how you manage your household budget can be very instructive. If you're saving for a new couch, explain how you elected to not go out to dinner and a movie one night and instead chose to put the money toward the couch fund. When the bills come for credit card purchases he saw you make, explain how you now have to write a check to the bank that paid the merchant for your purchases. You can also explain that if you don't pay the entire amount by a certain date, the bank will assess an interest charge.

Keep one thing in mind as you teach your child about money. Although he'll learn a lot from managing his own allowance, he'll learn as much by watching you. Explain to him why you make or don't make certain purchases, how you're saving for his education, and why price is not necessarily an indication of value. If you're wise with your money, he'll learn to be wise with his.

(See also budgeting, clothing, credit cards, entertainment.)

ANNUAL REPORTS

ANNUAL REPORTS are just about worthless as sources for investment information. Fledgling investors, prowling the financial horizon for promising places to put their money, think that annual reports are good places to start scouting. After all, publicly held companies must issue an annual report at the end of every fiscal year. The report typically includes information on the company's philosophy and mission, detailed descriptions of its operations, a review of the year just past, and its future directions and opportunities. Sure, they provide a broad introduction to the company, its goals, and its products or services. There's just one problem—annual reports are prepared by the companies themselves, which make every effort to appear as appealing as possible.

I know all about this packaging. When I was president of an American Stock Exchange–listed small business investment company, I spent as much time, or more, preparing our annual report and choreographing our annual meeting as I did running the company.

The One Kernel of Truth

Note that I said annual reports are "just about" worthless. I equivocated that little bit because there's one section in every annual report where the naked truth is actually revealed. Usually in the back—after the cheery message from the company president and page after page of color photographs picturing happy employees and customers and endless paragraphs boasting of the company's stunning accomplishments and bright future—are the numbers that paint the real picture of a company's financial health.

That's why I always tell my clients to start at the back when they're reading an annual report, find the numbers, tear those pages out, and throw away the rest.

What to Look For

Here are some of the questions those numbers will answer, beginning with two of the most important.

What was the company's profit (or loss)? The annual report will include a statement of earnings and expenses that answers a most basic question: Is the company making money? Most annual reports will compare the current year with the two or three previous years to give you some perspective.

What are the company's assets and liabilities? The annual report's balance sheet will compare the company's assets and liabilities. Among other things, it will tell you how much money the company has in cash and short-term investments, how much long-term debt the company is carrying, how many shares of stock are outstanding, and the value of the stock.

What are the earnings per share? This is easily calculated by dividing a company's profit by the number of shares in the company. A company that's growing will show a steady increase in earnings per share. This figure is often included in the consolidated statement of earnings.

What's the payout ratio? What percentage of its net earnings is the company paying its investors in dividends? Traditionally, payout ratios are between 25 and 50 percent. If they're higher, it may mean the company isn't earning enough to meet its obligations and still have a healthy profit left over. Be aware, however, that today, dividends aren't viewed with the same importance as in years past. Most of the high-flying high-tech firms avoid paying dividends.

What are the company's key policies and objectives? This is becoming increasingly important to some investors, who have certain political or environmental expectations in addition to the more traditional concerns about product, marketing practices, and return on investment.

Don't Ignore the Fine Print

Since annual reports have more to do with marketing than they do with providing information, any potentially bad news is often hard to find. You can usually assume that the smaller the print, the less desirable the information.

Often the fine print is found in footnotes reserved for information about liabilities, debts that may be coming due, or lawsuits that are pending. Other times the footnotes will contain clarifications to statements made in the report's text. It can be a chore to read it all, and that's what the company is counting on. That's all the more reason to read it carefully.

Do Additional Research

Obviously, on its own, the information in an annual report is insufficient for making an investment decision. You should scour the financial press for articles on the company and obtain additional company-prepared material, such as prospectuses and quarterly reports. The company's investor relations department will be able to provide you with these documents.

You'll also want to contact the Securities and Exchange Commission for copies of the company's 10K or 10Q forms. These are required by the SEC and contain detailed financial information presented in a completely objective light. You'll need to consult with independent rating services and get their take on the investment. Ultimately, this is the kind of information that

Every annual report should include a statement from auditors with an outside accounting firm that states they have examined the report's financial statements and find them accurate. If the company claims accounts receivable of $10 million, the accounting firm will have called its customers to make sure the number is correct. If the report states that the company has 1 million widgets in its warehouse, the auditors will have visited the warehouse and conducted a physical inventory to make sure the widgets are really there and that they're not obsolete.

The Critical Three Points

If you are going to review the entire annual report, these three items should be your primary focus:

1. *Listen to the message.* Although written in a strictly positive light, there will be underlying subtle messages interwoven throughout the narratives. Has there been senior management turnover? Is the industry facing regulatory changes? Are there profitability concerns? Even painted over, such issues will need to be touched on and addressed.

2. *The business isn't static.* Don't make the mistake of just looking at this year's report. Go back two or three years. How has the message changed? How have the numbers changed? Is the company growing? Is profitability improving? Are costs getting out of control? Trends are far more telling than static numbers.

3. *Cash is king.* Income statements tend to blur operational results with noncash entries such as depreciation. Focus in on the statement of cash flow. How has cash changed as a result of operations? This is a critical determinant as to how the business is really doing.

should help you decide whether a company is a good investment or if you and your money should look elsewhere.

(See also employees, inventory, lawsuits, receivables.)

ANNUITIES

IN MY MIND, the single-premium immediate fixed annuity is the magic bullet of personal finance, solving the biggest problem facing most of my clients. Yet annuities remain the most maligned financial instruments around. While they are unique among investments in that they can provide you with a guaranteed income for as long as you live, for most of the twentieth century they were misunderstood. One type of annuity—the fixed annuity—was seen as a prudish kind of retirement plan favored by rich old maiden aunts. Another type—the variable annuity—was viewed as an aggressive tax-avoidance technique for mercurial investors. Before I get into its magical curative properties, let me back up and provide some background information.

All about Annuities

An annuity is simply a contract that guarantees a lifetime income. Generally it's an agreement between an individual and an insurance company, although other institutions, including charities and corporations, enter into annuity agreements.

Annuities can be categorized by the nature of their income, premium, and payouts. If the amount of the income is established at the time the contract is signed, it's called a fixed annuity. If the amount of the income is determined by the performance of an underlying investment portfolio, it's called a variable annuity. In a single-premium annuity an individual makes just one lump-sum payment to the insurer. In a periodic-payment annuity an individual makes a series of smaller payments for a predetermined length of time and at set intervals, say, monthly for 30 years. Immediate annuities start paying an income immediately (actually, 30 days) after the total premium is paid. Deferred annuities don't start paying out until some predetermined point is reached, say, age 65.

String these definitions together and you get a nearly total understanding of the product. For instance, a single-premium immediate fixed annuity is one in which you make one payment to the insurer who promises to immediately start paying you a fixed amount. On the other hand, a periodic-payment deferred variable annuity would require you to make a series of payments to an insurer who promises to pay you an income, of an amount to be determined, at a date some time in the future.

There are also options on how long the income from an annuity is actually paid. A single-life annuity pays an income only as long as the person who bought it lives. A life-with-period-certain annuity pays an income either for as long as the person who bought it lives or for a set number of years, whichever is longer. If the person dies before the period certain expires, her heirs get the income for the remaining years. A joint-and-survivor annuity pays an income for as long as both the person who bought it and her named beneficiary (or beneficiaries) live. You get the highest return on a single-life annuity, since it will pay out the shortest length of time, and the lowest return for a joint-and-survivor annuity, since it will pay out for the longest length of time.

The Advantages of Annuities

Annuities have three distinct advantages.

They provide a *lifetime income.* It's possible to outlive the income from every other investment, regardless of how conservative or risky it may be. Buy an annuity and you can rest assured you will never outlive your money—they truly are longevity insurance.

They provide a *guaranteed income.* The stock market can turn bullish or bearish, interest rates can climb or plummet, but the income from a fixed annuity will never change. If you buy an annuity that promises to pay an 8 percent return, it will continue to do so even if interest rates fall dramatically.

They provide *partly tax-free income.* A portion of the income you receive from an annuity will be tax-free. That's because a part of each payment is considered repayment of the money you put in, not income. The older you are when you buy the annuity, the larger the payment you'll receive and the larger the portion of the payment that will be tax-free.

The Disadvantages of Annuities

Of course, not even penicillin is without side effects, and my financial magic bullet has its downsides too. I call them the "three i's."

Annuities are *irrevocable.* Once you hand over your money and buy an annuity, you can't get it back for any reason. There are some exceptions to the rule in some new products that will let individuals get back a percentage of their money for a period of time in order to pay for medical emergencies. That "out" comes with a price, however: lower rates.

Annuities are subject to *inflation.* What was a nice monthly income in 2000 may not stretch as far in 2010 if those were 10 years of high inflation. Fixed incomes are always mixed blessings.

Annuities are subject to *insolvency.* An annuity isn't backed by the government. Your money is only as certain as the financial solvency of the insurer or charity that issued it. When you buy an annuity, you're depending on the issuer being around to pay that promised income as long as you're around to collect it.

One oft-cited downside of annuities is the risk that you could die soon after buying one, not collect that much in income, and have the bulk of the money end up in the insurer's hands rather than in your heir's. However, if you're like me and other Die Brokers, and you plan on spending everything, that's not an issue. And even if you're not a Die Broker, this risk is the same one you assume when you buy almost any insurance product. You could end up paying tens of thousands of dollars in auto, disability, home, and health insurance premiums and never collect as much as you've paid. You could pay term life insurance premiums for decades and end up dropping the policy when it's no longer needed.

Mitigating the Downsides

One of the reasons I'm so enamored of annuities is that there are easy ways to mitigate all the potential downsides.

Simply by making sure you have adequate home, auto, liability, and health insurance and, when it makes sense, long-term care insurance, you're providing all the protection from financial disaster you need. If you have a sound insurance package you'll never need the money for an emergency, so the irrevocable nature of annuities won't be a problem.

The inflation risk attached to annuities can be lessened by following a savvy purchase strategy. It can be summed up as follows: Buy only as much income as you need, as late as you possibly can.

Finally, the risk of insurer insolvency can be mitigated by researching the financial health of insurers and only buying annuities from those that are judged highly. Don't limit your purchases to one company. As your portfolio of annuities grows, diversify the risk by purchasing from two or more companies that each satisfy your financial criteria.

Buy Only Single-premium Immediate Fixed Annuities

These are the annuity equivalent of straight term life insurance: plain vanilla products. They offer all the features you need with none of the frills and complications that could make comparison shopping difficult. If you just focus on single-premium immediate fixed annuities, you'll find it very simple to compare rates.

Buy As Late As You Possibly Can

As I noted earlier, the older you are when you buy an annuity, the higher the rate of return it will offer and the larger the portion of the income that will be tax-free.* I think the best time to start thinking about buying an annuity is when you can see that simple earned income may no longer be enough to maintain your lifestyle.

If you're not going to retire completely, your earned income will continue past age 65. But even though it's not stopping entirely, it may drop below the peak levels you experienced in your fifties and early sixties, either intentionally or unintentionally. While the exact timing of when you buy your first annuity will depend on your own unique circumstances, as a general rule most of my clients enter the annuity market when they're about 70. By then most have a good idea of what their income and expenses will be in the latter portion of their lives.

Buy Only As Much As You Need at the Time

Just because you see your earned income beginning to drop at age 70 doesn't mean you should turn your entire investment portfolio into an immediate annuity right away. Since the rate of return on an annuity is locked in when you buy it, you could be dooming yourself to a lifetime of below-market interest. As long as you don't need the income, you can do better investing it in equities.

A more sensible approach is to start by taking only a portion of your nonqualified savings—those savings not in IRAs, SEPs, or 401(k) plans—and buy just enough of an income to compensate for the drop in your earned income. Then, when you once again see your income dropping below the level you'd like, buy yet another annuity, locking it in at the then-current rate. In this way, you keep from locking all your money in at what might turn out to be a low rate. Because you waited and got a few years older, you'll automatically get a better deal and

---

*An oft-cited rule of thumb is that the yield on an annuity will increase about 0.02 percent for every year you delay buying it.

Rating Insurance Companies

A. M. Best is the rating service that rates more insurers than any of the other firms, so start with it. Write down the list of insurers from whom you're thinking of buying an annuity, and telephone the A. M. Best customer service center. You can get the telephone number either online or from your local library. You'll receive a Best ID number for each of the insurers you're interested in. Then call Best's automated-ranking telephone line. You'll be prompted to enter the ID numbers to receive the latest Best rating of the insurers. It will cost you a small per-minute fee to use this automated service.

I wouldn't stop there, however. Every rating firm has its own criteria. Play it safe and make sure more than one of the rating services gives your insurer high marks. The second call I'd place would be to Weiss Research. For a fee of $15 it will provide you with an oral report on a company. Obviously, only ask for reports on insurers that you've already learned Best rates highly.

Now you'll have a list of insurers rated highly by two services. As a final check, call the three other firms that rate insurers: Moody's, Standard & Poor's, and Duff & Phelp. They all provide one free quote over the telephone. Ask each for a rating of one of the insurers you've found were highly rated by both Best and Weiss. That will give you three independent judgments on three of your candidates.

If you have more than three candidates or aren't satisfied with just three judgments, check all the candidates by using Standard & Poor's ratings on the Insurance News Network Web site. If you don't have Internet access, you can find books listing Moody's and Standard & Poor's ratings in the reference section of a good library.

Don't let half of a percentage point sway you into buying an annuity or policy from an insurer that isn't given top marks. That additional return will be worthless if the insurer goes belly up. Stick with companies rated A or better.

The Charitable Option

Insurance companies aren't the only institutions offering annuities. The most interesting alternative is to purchase a charitable-gift annuity. Rather than giving the lump sum (or series of payments) to an insurer, you give it to a charity, which in exchange promises to pay you (or you and your survivor) a lifetime income, starting either immediately or when you turn 65.

The most obvious advantage of charitable-gift annuities is that they offer a tax deduction as well as income. That can have a substantial increase on the buying power of whatever income you receive. That could also compensate for having to fund an annuity with qualified dollars that, having been withdrawn, are now subject to high taxes. Of course, you also get the joy of giving to a service organization rather than an insurance company. And since you're making the gift while you're alive, you'll get to be there when they name the building after you.

The most significant disadvantage to charitable-gift annuities is that you're relying on the continued financial solvency of a charity rather than on an insurance company. There's no A. M. Best or Weiss rating for charities, so there's no way you can make that kind of judgment. Instead, you need to rely on the regulations of the insurance fund in the state in which the charity is based. New York State, for example, has very strict guidelines on how much a charity that offers annuities must keep in reserve and how it invests that reserve money. Other states are less stringent. Some offer no protection. Therefore, when you shop for a charitable-gift annuity, you have to shop not only on the basis of the financial return and how you feel about the charity's mission but also on the policies of the charity's home state. Don't rely on the word of a fund-raiser; pick up the telephone and call the state's insurance department and get the information directly from the source.

you'll have helped offset the impact of inflation on your income. As your earned income continues to decline naturally, just keep annuitizing your savings and investments (both nonqualified and qualified) until you're invested entirely in fixed annuities.

There's nothing to fear about eventually being entirely invested in annuities—in effect, giving away all your principal. The reasons traditional financial advisers tell people to shy away from tapping into their principal is to preserve their estate and ensure that they don't outlive their money. But if you're not planning on leaving an estate, that's not an issue. Besides, since you've bought annuities, you can't possibly outlive your money.

Buy Only from High-rated Insurers or Solvent Charities

When you buy an annuity, you're counting on the issuer being solvent longer than you live. While state insurance funds may step in to make good on claims against failed insurers, that's not something you want to rely on. Instead, make it your business to personally check the health of every insurer you're shopping. (See "Rating Insurance Companies," page 28.)

Shop Around Before You Buy

Do not, I repeat, do not, take the easy way out when shopping for an annuity. While single-premium immediate fixed annuities are plain vanilla products, there are price differences. Every insurer has its own actuarial table, investment projection table, and desired profitability. That means individual annuity products will very likely offer different incomes to the same person.

Couples Should Opt for Joint-and-Survivor Annuities

If you have a life partner I urge you to buy a joint-and-survivor annuity, which will continue to pay an income as long as one of you is alive. (Federal law requires that this option be offered to everyone purchasing an annuity, and that spouses sign a waiver if it is not selected.)

Granted, this will result in a lower income than if you took out a single-life or life-with-period-certain annuity. However, you can lessen the effect somewhat by electing for the survivor to get either ⅔ or ½ of the benefit rather than the exact same income. Just make sure you figure out the actual drop in expenses after the death of one spouse before you select one of these options.

————————

(See also charities, health insurance, inflation, IRAs, life insurance, long-term care insurance, Web sites.)

ANSWERING MACHINES AND SERVICES

As a lifelong supporter of organized labor I hate to admit it, but my new rule is, Replace humans with machines whenever possible. My opinion isn't universal. I know some older businesspeople who hate answering machines and will only use answering services when they're away from their offices. They argue that answering machines are impersonal, that people prefer to speak to another person rather than a machine, that many people will hang up rather than speak to a machine, and that in an emergency, an answering machine is of little use.

Machines Are Fine for Everyone Other than Doctors and Vets

The only argument that holds water is the last one. And even that's questionable. With all of today's telecommunications options it's relatively simple either to have a client's call forwarded in an emergency or to have that client contact you via a beeper or cellular telephone. I believe the only people who truly need answering services are doctors and veterinarians, who must be prepared to deal with life-and-death situations at any moment and whose clients will need almost immediate attention. People like plumbers, who are certainly desperately needed when pipes burst at 3 A.M. on a cold night, can always be reached via beeper.

For all other businesspeople, answering machines and voice mail systems work just fine. I'm a lawyer and financial adviser. If I have a client who decides to buy a million-dollar beach house in the middle of the night, I can wait until I get to the office in the morning to learn about it. If she just can't contain her excitement, she can call her friends and wake them up. In all seriousness, most of the true emergencies I deal with are work- and finance-related, and therefore develop during business hours.

There certainly was a time when people felt uncomfortable with answering machines, and perhaps there are still a few people who get flustered by them. But these days I truly believe most people find an answering service more intimidating than a machine. This is particularly true after business hours: people now expect to get a machine, and getting a real live person can be unsettling.

Then we must consider the competence of the person taking the message. Let's face it, these are not the best-paying jobs in the world and the hours are terrible, so they don't attract the best and the brightest. Frankly, I wouldn't be very comfortable having some of these people deciding what's important in my life and what isn't.

You can also check with your local telephone company to see what kind of answering services it offers. You'll probably find that the sound quality of the telephone company's voice mail system is better than that of any of the machines you test. The downside is that you have to call in to change your message. You'll also find that most companies offer few, if any, options and that, over time, the cost is much higher than buying your own machine.

Selecting a Machine

Most businesspeople can get by with a basic answering machine for their personal use. They have fewer options than an answering service but they're also a lot less expensive. Just make sure the model you buy has the features you need. Test the sound quality of incoming and outgoing messages and check to see if it's voice-activated, so clients won't be cut off in the middle of their messages. It should also have automatic interrupt so you won't have to shout over your own voice if your message comes on before you can get to the telephone. I also think it should provide for multiple answering machine messages and announcements.

One feature I prize is the ability to record conversations. I frequently interview people for magazine articles and books and, with their permission, use my answering machine to tape the interviews. It's much easier than using a cassette recorder. Machines with remote control of all their functions are also quite useful.

For people whose communication needs are more complex, a voice mail system provides many options. These systems are really like an electronic receptionist. They can direct calls to other telephones, a fax, a modem, or pagers. They can also field calls and take messages for a number of different people. They're perfect for small businesses that have a number of people who are in and out of the office all day.

If you disagree with me and decide you can't live with an answering machine or voice mail system and must have that human touch, then look into answering services. But choose carefully. As with any other "agents" you associate with, an answering service becomes an extension of your own business. If the people fielding your calls are rude or inept, your callers will likely ascribe those same qualities to you. That's something no businessperson needs.

(See also answering machine messages, doctors, cellular telephones, lawyers, pagers.)

ANSWERING MACHINE MESSAGES

JUST BECAUSE YOUR WIFE THINKS you do a great Jerry Seinfeld imitation doesn't mean you should subject the rest of the world to it.

I'm appalled by some of the answering machine messages I've heard used by businesses. Some are feeble attempts at humor. Others are silly. A few are simply rude. These kinds of messages would be inappropriate for private telephone numbers. For business lines, they're unforgivable.

First impressions are lasting impressions. Your answering machine message is often the first contact you'll have with a new client or customer, so you need to present your business in a professional manner. Never let a child record a message for your home-based business. Try to be cute or clever with your message, and you could leave people with the impression you're an imbecile.

Answering machines can be tools for business, so their messages should be as businesslike as possible. Identify yourself in a clear voice and politely explain that no one is available to take the call. Ask callers to leave a message and perhaps an explanation of why they're calling. Then, tell them you'll call them back as soon as possible. When you receive their message, live up to your word and return it as soon as possible.

If you have a voice mail system that has multiple message boxes, you can offer callers a choice. They can press 1 to leave a message for you, 2 to leave a message for your assistant, 3 to get your mailing address, 4 to get your e-mail address, 5 to get your fax number, and 6 to reach your beeper or cellular telephone (in an emergency). However, be careful that your voice mail menu isn't too complex and always offers callers an easy escape.

When recording a message for your personal extension in a large office voice mail system, consider adding the word "confidential" (as in, "you can leave a confidential message after the beep"). That could help dispel fears about a perceived lack of privacy.

Work from a prepared script when recording your message. Write down what you want to say, practice it a few times, and then record it. Play it back to hear how you sound. Pay careful attention to your diction and inflection. If you don't like the way you sound, keep rerecording until you do.

If you don't ordinarily answer your own telephone, have your message recorded by the person who does. My office's voice mail has a message in my assistant Bridget Bradley's voice since she not only answers most of the calls, but she also has a very pleasant voice. Regular customers

Personally, Say As Little As Possible

While the messages on your business answering machine should be somewhat forthcoming, it's sensible to provide as little information as possible on your personal answering machine. Security experts advise not declaring that you're away from home. Some even suggest you don't use your name. What should you say? Short and sweet is best.

> You've reached 555-1234. Leave a message after the tone.

Three Wise Messages

I suggest you use three different messages on your business answering machine. The first should be used whenever you're away from the telephone during business hours. It should state your name, that you're only temporarily unavailable, and that you'll return the call as soon as possible. Here's an example:

> You've reached John Smith. I'm away from my desk or on another call. Leave a message and I'll return your call as soon as possible.

The second message should be used whenever your office is closed during the week. It should also state your name, your normal office hours, and note that you'll return the call the next day. If you need to provide 24-hour service to your clients, you could also provide them with another telephone number or a beeper number.

> You've reached John Smith. I'm normally in the office from 8 A.M. to 4 P.M., Mondays through Friday. Leave a message and I'll return your call first thing tomorrow morning. If this is an emergency you can have me paged by calling 555-2345.

Your third message is for when your office is closed, either for the weekend, a holiday, or any other extended period of time. In addition to stating your name and explaining your absence, you can either solicit a message or set the machine to announce-mode only and ask the person to call back when you return. In the case of weekend or holiday closings I think an announcement alone is sufficient. However, if you're away on a business trip you should solicit messages and return them from your remote location. Once again, if necessary, provide an emergency access number. Here's a simple announcement-only weekend message:

> You've reached John Smith. My office is closed for the weekend. Please call back after 8 A.M. Monday morning.

A holiday message might be as follows:

> You've reach John Smith. My office will be closed from Wednesday, November 24, through Sunday, November 28, for Thanksgiving. I'll return to the office on Monday, November 29. Please call back then.

And finally, here's an appropriate message if you're going to be out of the office on business:

> You've reached John Smith. I'll be working outside the office from Monday, December 10, through Thursday, December 13. However, I'll be in constant contact with this machine. Leave a message and I'll return your call as soon as possible.

or clients will derive a sense of assurance from hearing the same voice every time they communicate with a business. But don't try to fake it: If you're flying solo in a tiny office, having someone else's voice on your answering machine isn't going to impress anyone. The ploy will become obvious as soon as you get back in touch with the caller. I know one accountant whose answering message was recorded by a young woman with a British accent, even though his regular receptionist comes from the Bronx. At that point a fake receptionist makes you look sleazy rather than impressive.

Don't forget to change your message when you're going to be away for any length of time, even if it's just a day. Let people know how long you'll be away. If appropriate, leave another number where they can be assisted or where you can be reached in an emergency. If nothing else, note that you'll be in regular touch with the machine and will return urgent calls as soon as possible. Assure all callers that you'll get right back to them when you return.

Your answering machine message says more about you than you think. Play it straight and keep your message to the point. If you want to entertain people with your Jerry Seinfeld impression, wait until you get to know them a little better.

(See also answering machines and services, cellular telephones, e-mail, home-based business, location, voice mail.)

ANTIQUES AND COLLECTIBLES

Buy antiques and other collectibles for their beauty and craftsmanship, not as investments.

Trying to make money on antiques and collectibles is very difficult. Sure, you might buy an old armoire that appreciates nicely while you own it. Or you may buy a painting at an old barn sale, go to the Antiques Roadshow and learn it's by a famous artist, and be able to turn around and sell it for hundreds of times what you paid for it. These things do happen. But almost always they're happy accidents, not planned investments. Buy something you think is a steal and you're apt to be the one that's taken.

Instead, enjoy what you have and don't worry about the asset end of things. Down the road, if something you bought should turn out to be worth a lot more than you paid for it, just consider it good luck.

Buying Antiques

Having said that, I will admit that genuine antiques can almost always be counted on to at least hold their value. They're also comparable in price to new furniture. Bought at auction, average-quality antiques are a much better buy than their contemporary showroom counterparts. They're usually better made, they don't go out of style, and they maintain their value or even appreciate a bit.

The trick is to buy functional antiques—beds, bureaus, tables, and chairs. It is their usefulness that will make them desirable to future buyers. An antique chamber pot, on the other hand, will have a limited appeal and will therefore be harder to sell.

Buying antiques requires that you educate yourself. Learn about different furniture periods and become familiar with different construction techniques. Reading trade magazines and price guides will help. So will reading books on antiques. Your best bet, however, will be to take classes. If you have a university or museum nearby, find out what sorts of classes are offered.

You can also learn a great deal by going to auctions. Go early so you can inspect the items that are being auctioned and talk to the auctioneer and dealers who are in attendance. Make note of what items attract heavy bidding and what kinds of prices they bring. Pay attention, too, to those items that don't attract a lot of attention. Over time, you'll begin to get a sense of market value and the factors that make one piece more desirable than another.

At that point you'll be ready to buy. Know what you're after and take the time to find it. When you discover a piece you're interested in, be ready to negotiate the price and give reasons why you think your offer is fair. For example, you will have learned that a piece that has been extensively restored is less valuable than one that's in original, albeit poor, condition. This kind of knowledge will enable you to offer an informed price and prevent you from paying more than you should.

When you buy a piece, you should always get a receipt that describes it in detail. The receipt should include the date the piece was made and its condition. You should also be given a money-back guarantee. If the dealer refuses to do either of these things, walk away from the deal.

Buying Collectibles

The long-term value of collectibles is even more difficult to predict than that of antiques. Not surprisingly, the demand for collectibles is usually driven by nostalgia, as people search for a piece of their youth. Many collectibles enjoy a brief period of great demand and interest, which in turn drives up prices. But the excitement can stop just as quickly as it started, resulting in prices dropping like a stone.

This is yet another reason to collect things because you're in love with them and not with the intention of making money. Some people buy contemporary collectibles, items that are manufactured today but designed to be one-of-a-kind. Commemorative plates are an example of this, as are holiday items like Christmas ornaments. Others scour flea markets and garage sales for old items like record albums or glassware from certain periods. I know a man in upstate New York who collects old milk bottles. His collection is a fascinating history of dairies throughout the northeastern United States dating back to the late nineteenth century.

Like antiques, the key to collectibles is to have as much knowledge about what you collect as possible. Since most collections are the result of personal obsessions, the learning usually takes care of itself. But if you've decided to collect something for other reasons—perhaps you really do think you can make money at this—then do your research before you start.

Spotting Fake Antique Furniture

Here are some signs of fake antique furniture.

- Light and new-looking wood is showing through worn areas.

- Paint comes off in strips.

- There are different underlayers of paint on different parts of the piece.

- It has a pristine finish.

- It is completely painted.

- It is taller than normal due to the addition of casters.

- The feet have uneven bottoms.

- Rollers are smooth or even.

- The seat is more than 18 inches above the floor.

- The legs are perfectly round.

- The wear on the legs and back is even.
- The seat consists of two or more pieces glued together.
- The bed frame matches a modern-sized mattress.
- There's no wear on the rope holes of a bed frame.
- A bed frame has no extra screw holes from previous mattress supports.
- All the wooden boards are perfectly flat and level.
- It's a dining and drop-leaf table that's 30 inches high.
- The table top has sharp edges.
- There's no wear on the base or stretchers of a table.
- The table top is secured with L brackets or screwed from the top.
- The table top is made of many narrow boards.
- The back or bottom is painted or stained.
- The back is made of one piece.
- Plywood or fiberboard is present.
- There are empty nail holes.
- There are light-colored areas on the bottom, indicating that feet have been moved.
- There's a lack of wear on the bottom indicating it may have been the top of a two-piece unit.
- The boards on the back match and are of good quality.
- Butt joints are used to construct the doors or drawers.
- The doors are worn in the wrong areas.
- The insides of drawers are finished.
- The drawers are joined with precise, even dovetails.
- The drawer interiors don't match.

(See also auctions, furniture, reading.)

APARTMENT LEASES

APARTMENT LEASES ARE the world's most one-sided legal documents. They're prepared by the landlord's lawyer or an agent representing the landlord, so every term and condition governing occupancy—including the rent—is structured for the landlord's benefit. The tenant is almost completely stripped of rights and power.

Making the situation worse is that few tenants actually read their leases. There are often significant differences between what the landlord or his agent promises orally and what actually appears in the lease document.

This is why it's essential to carefully read every page of a lease agreement, bearing in mind that everything is potentially negotiable. Don't back off if you're told you're being asked to sign the "standard contract." Your goal should be to craft a unique document that's tailored to your needs as well as the landlord's.

Begin with the term of the lease. The longer the lease the more protected you are from rent increases, but the more danger you'll be stuck being responsible for rent you don't want to pay. The best compromise is a long lease that gives you the right to sublet, or better yet, cancel, under certain reasonable circumstances.*

If you're only going to need an apartment for six months, don't sign an agreement for a year assuming you'll be able to sublet the apartment for the last six months. Instead, ask for a six-month lease. If the landlord refuses, ask for a month-to-month lease with a mutually agreeable timetable on how much notice you need to give when you decide to move out. If you're certain your residence will be a short one, and you know roughly when you'll be leaving, offer three months notice.

See if there are any restrictions on who or how many people can live in the apartment. Some leases bar children. Others may make it impossible for you to bring in a roommate if you want one, regardless of the person's gender. And of course, make sure it allows you to have a pet if you own one. Some landlords may require extra security if you have a pet to cover the costs of any damage. That's a reasonable request. Just make sure any existing damage to the apartment is noted by the landlord when you move in. Otherwise he could try to claim it was caused by your pet and keep part or all of your security when you move out.

Examine the language governing alterations to the apartment. It should specify that you can make alterations with the landlord's permission, which won't be unreasonably withheld, and that any improvements you make are yours and not the landlord's. That gives you the right to take them with you when you leave. In return, you can agree to restore the apartment to the condition it was in before the alteration.

You'll want to look carefully at the terms for renewal. Check to see if there are any fees or

---

*Reasonable circumstances might include a job transfer or an increase in the size of your family.

built-in rent hikes if you choose to renew. If there are no terms for renewal, make your own and have them added to the document. For example, you might agree to give the landlord a minimum of 60 days notice if you intend to renew the lease.

Find out who is responsible for repairs and maintenance. Many renters foolishly sign leases making them responsible for all repairs and maintenance. They end up having to buy new refrigerators or pay hefty plumbing bills. Major maintenance and repair costs of a permanent, structural, or mechanical nature should be borne by the landlord. Minor cosmetic repairs should be the tenant's responsibility, as should any repairs needed due to problems caused by the tenant.

If you work from home, make sure you can operate your business from the apartment. Granted, the landlord is within his rights to limit the kind of activities you can engage in. But if you're in a profession that doesn't create a lot of visitor traffic to the apartment or otherwise detract from the quality of life of others in your building and neighborhood, there's no reason you shouldn't be allowed to work at home.

Can you live with the terms governing termination of the lease and subletting? You want to keep your options open, so your goal should be the ability to terminate the lease with sufficient notice to the landlord. Likewise, you should also be able to sublet the apartment if you choose. The more control you can retain over the apartment, the more valuable the lease will be to you. Of course, these are two areas where most landlords are loathe to compromise.

Finally, don't ignore the fine print. This is where truly dangerous terms can be hidden. It might state that the landlord can show your apartment at any time without your permission; that the lease is voided if the property is sold; that there will be a fee for every day you stay in the apartment after the lease is up; or that certain charges, like increased taxes, can be passed on to you. You need to realize that everything in the fine print is going to be for the benefit of the landlord. Read it carefully. If you need to, have a lawyer look at it.

Keep in mind that rental markets are driven by the same supply and demand that drive other markets. The weaker the rental market in your town or city, the more leverage you'll have in negotiating the terms of your lease. But if demand is high, the landlord will have more power.

(See also lawyers, negotiating.)

APPLIANCES

APPLIANCES SHOULDN'T BE either status symbols or fashion statements, but for many of my clients, they are both. I'm afraid we're following the same path with appliances that we did with automobiles, moving from utilitarian product to expression of personality. I urge you to wage the good fight against this absurd trend and focus on buying appliances for their reliability and efficiency rather than their sexiness. Here are some strategies for finding affordable appliances that won't break down the day after the warranty expires.

Buy the Most Reliable

The best way to avoid appliance problems is to purchase the most reliable brands on the market. The best source of information on reliability is *Consumer Reports*. The magazine's staff have been testing everything under the sun for decades. If Frigidaire comes out with a new refrigerator, it's immediately dragged into the magazine's laboratories to be poked and prodded to see how well it performs. That information is then published in the magazine's next issue on kitchen appliances for all the world to see. Thousands of other products are given the same scrutiny every year.

Here's another hint. Rather than buying a name-brand appliance, check out the appliances offered by national retailers like Sears, J. C. Penney, and Montgomery Ward. Although they have the company name on them (Sears markets its appliances under the Kenmore label), they're actually produced under contract by major appliance manufacturers, who simply remove some bells and whistles. It's usually easy to find out which company built a product. The department manager or store manager should be able to supply you with that information. If it's a company you're familiar with, you can usually be assured you're getting a quality product at a cheaper price.

Check Operating Costs

Most appliances these days run on electricity. That's an expensive source of energy, so you'll want to make sure any appliance you're considering buying uses as little electricity as possible.

For the past 20 years, the government has required that all major appliances carry a label stating how much energy the appliance will use in a year and its approximate cost. Just make sure the price per kilowatt-hour on the label is the same as what you're charged by your local utility.* If it's not, you'll need to do your own calculations to come up with a useful figure.

Appliances that produce heat are the most expensive to operate. The worst energy guzzlers by far are electric dryers and electric ranges. Hair dryers, toaster ovens, and space heaters are next, although they only consume a third of the energy of dryers and ranges. Air conditioners also consume a great deal of energy and are comparable to toaster ovens and space heaters.

Most other appliances are much more reasonable to operate. Since they're operational 24 hours a day and cost more than any other appliance, most of us are concerned about our refrigerators. You'll be pleased to know they're quite efficient these days and use less electricity than a television, stereo, vacuum cleaner, or washing machine.

Warranties and Extended Service Contracts

All appliances come with a warranty—a guarantee by the manufacturer that they will repair or replace the appliance free of charge for a certain period of time after the product is purchased.

---

*Your utility bill should contain your cost per kilowatt-hour.

A "full warranty" means everything is covered. A "limited warranty" means there will be a lot of fine print involved. For example, the manufacturer may not guarantee the product against damage from what it considers misuse by the consumer. This means if your kids use the blender to try to chew up a bunch of rocks, the manufacturer won't feel obligated to fix the damage.

Make sure you read the warranty information thoroughly with any appliance you're considering purchasing. And when you do buy it, remember to fill out the warranty card and send it in. The warranty might not be honored if you forget.

When you purchase an appliance, the salesperson will usually try to sell you an extended service contract that will become effective when the warranty expires. These generally aren't worth the money. If you had a service contract on every appliance you own you'd probably be shelling out a couple of hundred dollars a year. Most appliances are deceptively simple and there's not much that can go wrong. Granted, an extended service contract is insurance if you do have a major problem, but it's cheaper over the long haul to take your chances and pay for problems as they appear.

Savvy Shopping

Appliances are so costly these days that it's essential to become a savvy shopper. Here are some pointers:

Do not become an early adapter of new technologies. While there may be some social status attached to being the first on the block with a new product, that prestige comes at a high cost. Early generations of new products are invariably the most expensive, the most basic, and the least reliable. Wait and you'll pay less and get more features and dependability for your money.

Time your purchases. Appliances are seasonal. The worst time to buy an air conditioner is the summer. Want to spend top dollar for a snow blower? Shop for one in January. You can save a great deal of money buying before the season begins, when retailers are looking to make space for new models, or after the season ends, when retailers are looking to clear out their overstocks. There are also traditional clearance cycles that take place after Easter, around Independence Day, and just after Christmas.

Don't fall for marketing gimmicks. The latest schtick seems to be offering a "commercial" line of appliances to the consumer. Make no mistake about it: most of these commercial appliances are simply consumer products dressed up to look professional. Few truly commercial appliances could fit in a residential kitchen.

ARBITRATION

I'M A LAWYER, and even I think arbitration is the best way to resolve serious financial disputes.

Whenever two parties in a dispute reach an impasse, they generally have two options. One is to take the issue to court and present their arguments before a judge. The other option is arbitration.

The arbitration process allows a neutral third party to conduct an evidentiary hearing and a review of written submissions from the two parties. By agreeing to arbitration, the disputing parties agree that the arbitrator will have the final say in how the dispute is settled. Her decision will be legally binding, although it can be appealed under certain circumstances.*

When Is Arbitration Necessary?

Arbitration becomes necessary when both sides in a dispute feel they are no longer capable of reaching an agreement without outside intervention. Until that point, they have the option of using a mediator rather than an arbitrator. Rather than rendering a decision himself, a mediator works with both parties to help them negotiate a mutually acceptable agreement on their own.

Once an arbitration process begins, both parties will agree to adhere to the arbitrator's decision. An arbitrator will typically have a prehearing session or sessions to allow both sides to present disputes or questions. After she rules on those issues, the arbitration session itself will occur. After she's heard all the evidence, the arbitrator will issue her decision.

Arbitration hearings are closed to the public. The cast of characters can vary, but it usually includes the two parties involved, their lawyers, any witnesses who will be testifying, and the arbitrator. The atmosphere is more informal than a courtroom proceeding. Hearings are often held in conference rooms.

An arbitration hearing follows a process similar to a legal hearing. Each party makes an opening statement, presents evidence, questions and cross-examines witnesses, and makes a closing state-

---

*If they choose, the parties can select nonbinding arbitration. In that case, the arbitrator will give an advisory opinion. The decision to follow her advice is completely up to the two parties.

Mitigating Damages through High-Low Arbitration

One of the best examples of how flexible and efficient arbitration can be is the use of high-low arbitration. Both parties in an arbitration hearing can agree beforehand on maximum and minimum limits on the amount of money that can be awarded. By using this technique both parties can mitigate the potential damage of a defeat without having to give up their chances at victory, as they would if they settled a legal case. Generally this is done without the arbitrator's knowledge so as not to influence the decision. If they've established a ceiling of $75,000, for example, and the arbitrator awards $100,000, they'll settle privately, with only $75,000 changing hands. Likewise, if they set a low limit of $50,000 and the arbitrator awards $25,000, the higher amount will be paid.

ment. In some cases, the hearing can be conducted with written submissions rather than in-person testimony. When a decision is reached, it's usually not a matter of public record.

The Advantages of Arbitration

The arbitration process has several advantages over a courtroom proceeding. One is *speed*. The process is fairly simple to set up, so most disputes can be settled in two or three months.

Arbitration also provides a great deal of *flexibility*. Because it's a private activity, the two sides can tailor the proceeding to their own tastes. For example, they may agree to limit the number of witnesses that can be called or the kind of evidence that can be presented. They may even agree to put a cap on the amount of damages that can be awarded.

Another advantage is *cost*. The arbitration process eliminates many of the time-consuming activities associated with a court hearing. That translates into lower legal fees and less time missed from work.

Arbitration also allows the disputing parties to bring in an arbitrator who has expertise in the area of the dispute. There are arbitration specialists in almost every industry, including securities and investments. If you think your broker has been reaping excessive commissions by churning your account, for example, the two of you will likely end up in binding arbitration.

Arbitration Clauses

My advice is to insert an arbitration clause into any contract you're about to sign that doesn't already include one. Here's a clause that provides for arbitration before the American Arbitration Association, one of a number of reputable organizations that facilitate this process:

> **Any controversy or claim arising out of, or relating to, this agreement, or to its making, performance or interpretation, shall be settled by arbitration under the [commercial] arbitration rules of the American Arbitration Association then existing. Judgment on the arbitration award may be entered in any court having jurisdiction over either of the parties.**

An alternative is for the parties to agree to private arbitration. An appropriate clause for that would be:

> **The parties agree to settle their dispute concerning this agreement by binding arbitration before _____ [or alternatively, three arbitrators, one of whom shall be selected by each party and the third by the two designated arbitrators]. Judgment on the arbitration award may be entered in any court having jurisdiction over either of the parties.**

You probably signed an agreement to that effect when you opened your account—although you may not remember it. In fact, arbitration is often mandated in many agreements today. (See "Arbitration Clauses," page 43.)

As an alternative to arbitration, nonbinding mediation before a mutually acceptable and respected third party can often resolve controversies. Essentially, the parties are calling upon a third party who is not personally interested in their dispute to bring her experience and wisdom to bear on the problem in an effort to find a peaceful solution. Obviously, if mediation can work, it saves time and money. I've included a sample mediation agreement in the entry on divorce.

––––––––––––––––––––––

(See also divorce, lawyers.)

ASSET ALLOCATION

NEVER TRUST any financial professional who advocates off-the-shelf asset allocation formulas. No two people are identical in their circumstances, needs, or personalities, so no two asset allocation formulas should be identical; it should always be a custom job.*

The concept of asset allocation is based on the three most important factors of investing: risk, growth, and time. It's a strategy for the long haul that recognizes that at any point in time different kinds of investments move in different directions. By allocating your money toward a variety of investments, you minimize risk and avoid loss in your overall portfolio.

It's based on the same diversity theory underlying mutual funds. By diversifying, you're increasing the likelihood of profit. The fact that you have your money spread out among many different investments means that the upward movement of the bulk of your investments will negate the losses experienced by a few.

How you choose to allocate your money—and it should be you, not your financial professional, making the final choices—depends on your individual needs, goals, circumstances, and appetite for risk. If you're young and can absorb some risk, you'll likely be a bit more swashbuckling than if you're nearing retirement and are concerned with solid, predictable returns.

Fixed or Flexible?

There are two prevailing schools of thought in developing asset allocation formulas. The first assumes that you should pick the best combination of investments to help you reach your goal

––––––––––––––––––––––

*The standard asset allocation formulas, such as those that appear in the box on page 47, should be used like boilerplate legal documents: they're good starting points from which to craft customized products.

and then stick with that combination by creating a fixed portfolio. Let's say you've decided to keep half the value of your portfolio in growth stocks and to split the other half equally between mutual funds and Treasury bills. The fixed-portfolio theory says that although you may change your holdings within each of the three categories of investment, your overall allocation between the three should remain the same year after year.

To maintain the balance in your portfolio, you'll need to periodically adjust your holdings. For example, if your stocks have been increasing in value faster than your mutual funds and T-bills, it won't be long before they represent a lot more than 50 percent of the value of your portfolio. At that point, you'll need to sell enough of your stocks to get the percentage back to the 50 percent you started with. The theory holds that you should do this any time your investment percentages get 5 to 10 percent out of line.

Why should you unload stocks when they're performing so well? Let's suppose the market suddenly takes a nosedive. Since you'd have more than your planned 50 percent of your assets in stocks, the value of your portfolio would decrease more than it should. You need to remember that maintaining a steady level of risk is the main goal of the fixed-portfolio approach to asset allocation.

If you just can't imagine selling something that's appreciating so quickly, you'll likely be more comfortable following the flexible-portfolio theory. This approach assumes that you'll change the makeup of your holdings in reaction to market conditions. Rather than keeping a firm 50 percent of your portfolio in stocks, you might decide to keep between 25 and 75 percent, adjusting your holdings in reaction to market conditions. If stocks are going through the roof, you'll dump your T-bills and buy more stocks. If the market begins to sag, you'll sell stocks and reinvest in T-bills.

The obvious downside to the flexible-portfolio approach is that it increases risk. It requires you to pay careful attention to the markets in each of the investments in your portfolio and try to predict their movements ahead of time. Remember, there are professionals who lose money trying to do this. If they have a tough time with it, imagine how you'll do. That's why I suggest my clients follow the fixed-portfolio approach.

Risky or Conservative?

Regardless of which approach you take, fixed or flexible, you can adjust your risk even further by the kinds of investments you choose to keep in your portfolio. This requires a basic understanding of how different investments behave. Blue-chip stocks are less risky than growth stocks. Stock mutual funds are less risky than individual stocks. Government bonds are less risky than corporate bonds. T-bills, certificates of deposit, and money market funds are less risky than any other investments.

By understanding the risks inherent in any given investment, you can create an overall level of risk simply by the investments you choose for your portfolio. An aggressive portfolio comprised largely of individual stocks and stock mutual funds, for example, will be more risky than one comprised of government bonds and CDs. Once you've created a portfolio with a desired level of risk, you can take the fixed-portfolio approach and keep that level of risk fairly constant. If you apply the flexible approach, your risk will increase or decrease depending on market conditions.

Different Strategies for Different Age Groups

This is where time and investment goals become factors. All other things being equal, the younger you are, the more time you'll have to weather market ups and downs while locking in overall long-term growth. This means you can create an asset allocation that assumes more risk but offers higher potential returns. If you're older and your time horizon is shorter, you'll be more interested in guaranteed short-term growth. Risk will be much less palatable.

No matter your age, you'll need some liquid cash reserves—money kept in a bank or money market fund. When you're younger, growth stocks, stock funds, and zero-coupon bonds could allow you to save for your children's college educations and start your own retirement funds. As you age, owning a house might provide a hedge against inflation while you continue to invest in stocks and stock funds and expand into Treasury bonds. As you get older, you might want to reduce risk by unloading many of your stocks and move the money into more predictable stock index funds, bonds, and bond funds.

Know Where You're Headed

The concept of asset allocation is designed to help people reach their goals, regardless of whether they're 40 years off or just around the corner. Be realistic in your expectations. Set aside as much money as you can each month. Become a student of investing and learn to do your own research. Acknowledge your own comfort level. Choose a mix of investments that won't keep you awake at night with worry. And above all, be patient. Successful investing is as much a factor of time as anything else. By setting up a customized allocation of assets in your portfolio and allowing time to work its magic, you'll get where you want to go.

Portfolio Models

There are no off-the-shelf asset allocation formulas. Clearly, your portfolio has to generate required current income while growing to meet future goals. What follows is a model based upon age and life cycle. use this as a starting point in customizing your portfolio.

Asset Allocation Formula (% of Investment Income)

	Age 20 Single	Age 40 Married with children	Age 60 Pre-retiree	Age 80 Retired
Cash*	5	10	10	10
CDs/short-term bonds	5	10	10	20
Long-term bonds (laddered)	0	0	20	30
Large-cap domestic equities	45	25	20	10
Small-cap domestic equities	30	20	10	5
International equities	15	15	10	0
Real estate†	0	20	20	25

* For emergency purposes and investment opportunities.

† Inclusive of home.

(See also bonds, certificates of deposit, mutual funds, stocks, Treasury bills.)

ATMS AND CASH CARDS

SOMETIMES A LITTLE INCONVENIENCE is a good thing. I'll bet some of you haven't physically cashed a check in more than a decade. The steady proliferation of automated teller machines (ATMs) has made access to cash easier than ever. They're in every bank as well as in grocery stores, hotel lobbies, malls, gas stations, convenience stores, and even highway rest stops. The ATM and its partner, the cash card, have made getting cash simpler, quicker, and easier.

But ATMs and cash cards have also resulted in increased problems with uncontrolled spending. I've become aware of this over the years by talking to some of my clients about their financial problems. When I ask them to track the movement of their cash each month, most of them can't account for 30 percent of it. One moment it's in their wallet and the next moment it's gone.

The funny thing is, at my urging, many of these folks have already sworn off credit cards because of previous problems with plastic and have switched to the "cash only" approach to spending. But in their attempt to restore their financial life to health, they've staunched one wound just to open another.

There's no question that ATMs have changed people's attitudes about cash. Before ATMs, people would head to the bank every Friday on their lunch hour and cash a check for a certain amount of money that was intended to last for a week. They'd stand in line with everyone else, visit with the teller while she cashed the check, and then head back to the office.

Because that money was to last a week, people were extremely conscious of how much they were spending and what they had left in their wallet. Part of the reason for this vigilance was frugality. But an equal part was dread over having to use up another lunch hour to get more cash.

In retrospect, that Friday trip now seems like such a waste of time that many of my clients can't believe they did it. Now they just run out the front door of their building to get cash just a few brisk paces away. They probably use the ATM three times a week on average; I have some clients who use it five or six times a week.

Therein lies the problem. Since it's so easy to get cash, you're never out of cash. The spending wheels are permanently greased. If you decide on the spur of the moment to go out to dinner but don't have the cash, you can run to the machine. A day later, having spent all but a few dollars of that withdrawal on dinner, you realize you're low on cash and stop at another ATM. Unlike the old mind-set, which was to make sure the cash in your pocket lasted you a week, the new attitude is to make sure the cash in your pocket never falls below a certain level. You've taken the minimum account balance model and adapted it to your wallet. It's no wonder so many people have problems with ATMs.

If, like so many of my clients, you have a problem managing your cash withdrawals, I have a very simple suggestion for you. Put

Cash Card Security

There's another good reason to keep that cash card tucked away in a safe place: security. Most cash cards today double as debit cards, allowing their use without access to your personal identification number (PIN). If you lose your credit card and report the loss immediately, your liability is limited to $50. Lose your cash card and your liability can be up to the entire the balance in the accounts linked to that card. Sure, cashiers are supposed to check signatures against those on the back of the card. But how often do you see that done anymore?

the card away in a drawer and leave it there. Switch to the old method of getting cash. Once a week, take a few minutes to think about your plans for the week and what money those plans will require. Then go to the bank and cash a check for that amount. If that's too much trouble, take the card out of its hiding place, walk or drive to the ATM, take out exactly as much money as you'll need to get through the next seven days, and return the card to its hiding place.

Then let your activities be determined by how much cash you have in your wallet, not by your proximity to an ATM. If that spur-of-the-moment dinner crops up again, a quick look in your wallet will tell you just can't afford it right now. To control your cash flow you need to learn to "just say no."

(See also cash flow, credit cards, debit cards.)

AUCTIONS

MORE PEOPLE GET TAKEN at auctions than come away with bargains. But just as you never hear about people losing money by day-trading stocks, you rarely hear about auction scams. They're often just too embarrassing. This reticence to reveal ripoffs has maintained the popularity of auctions.

In fact, you could say that the past couple of years have been the golden age of auctions. Today you can buy almost anything at auction. In addition to the old standbys—antiques, art, and other collectibles—you can buy items ranging from cars to real estate. Even the federal government has gotten into the act, offering confiscated and surplus items at auction. And most dramatically, a new venue has entered the picture: the online auction. Web sites such as eBay and Amazon.com allow buyers and sellers to come together and wrangle over everything from stuffed aardvarks to old zoology textbooks. These sites have proven to be among the most popular on the Web, despite the fact that people are bidding on objects they've never seen in person.

This is probably because the auction is—on the surface, anyway—such a pure form of capitalism. It's supply and demand at its most basic. A group of people gathers together, examines the items available for purchase, and begins the bidding process. The person willing to pay the most wins. It couldn't be simpler.

Admittedly, auctions can also be a lot of fun. The act of bidding against one or more competitors is surprisingly exhilarating—so much so that sometimes all rationality flies out the door as bidders get caught up by the desire to win, regardless of the value of the item up for sale. That's why it's essential to establish a budget before you bid at an auction, and then stick to it. Otherwise it's easy to spend more than you should. (See "Tips for Buying at Auction," page 50.)

Buyer Beware

Despite it's superficial image as pure capitalism, there's often more going on at an auction than meets the eye, and a lot of it is designed to work against you and other bidders. This is because

Tips for Buying at Auction

You need to be as careful with your money at an auction as you would anywhere else. Here are some basic rules for buying at auction.

- Learn the rules of the game. Visit several auctions before participating. Carefully examine an item before bidding on it. Auction items are usually sold "as is." If you discover a problem after you've purchased something, you'll have little chance of getting your money back.

- Don't assume an antique, art work, or other collectible is of exceptional value unless you've had your own independent expert authenticate it as such.

- Often most of the people attending an auction are dealers. If there's no bidding on an object, there's probably something wrong with it. Conversely, don't assume that lively bidding on an object means it has unusual value.

- Arrive at an auction with a budget and stick to it. Also, decide beforehand on the maximum price you'll pay for an item and stay within that amount. Otherwise, you're likely to get caught up in the excitement of bidding and pay more than you should.

- Just because an auction is being held in a barn in the middle of nowhere and not at Sotheby's doesn't mean you're more likely to find bargains. The best place to get good buys is at an estate auction. The objects being auctioned won't have entered the antiques or collectibles market, so you may be able to find some bargains.

- Be particularly cautious when bidding online. Paying money for an object you can't examine beforehand is extremely risky.

people don't have to attend an auction to participate in it. While you're sitting in the audience with your numbered paddle or card, there may be people sending in bids over the telephone to auction representatives. Often the telephone bidder is an agent—sometimes a hired expert—representing the person who is actually interested in buying the object.

This opens the door to all sorts of scams. One is the "phantom bidder." Some unscrupulous auctioneers will announce bids they claim have been delivered over the telephone just to drive up the price of an object. Others will plant shills in the audience to artificially drive up the bidding.

Bids can be entered any number of ways. One is the "order bid." People who can't attend an auction may fill out a form with the auction house that states the maximum they're willing to pay for an object. Then a representative of the auction house will bid for them. If the auction house is honest, the bidder will try to get the object as cheaply as possible. A dishonest auction house, knowing that it has a certain bid in hand, may use shills to make sure the bidding reaches the prearranged price offered by the absentee bidder.

Sometimes the seller of an object and the auction house will agree ahead of time on a minimum price they'll accept for an object. This is called the "reserved price." If the bidding doesn't reach that level, the auctioneer will announce the item was "bought in," meaning it remains the property of the seller.

You may also find yourself up against a group of dealers who are working together to keep prices down. They'll get together before the auction to decide which items they want to buy. Then only one dealer will participate in the bidding on each object. Later they'll get together and conduct their own auction to determine who gets what.

Auction houses have other tricks they use to pad the bottom line. For example, both buyer and seller may be hit with charges over and above the selling price for commissions, insurance, shipping, and other services. Although many of these are legitimate, some auction houses are not above padding them a bit. Some charges can be as high as 15 percent of the selling price.

Finally, take any catalog information or online description about the items up for bid with a grain of salt. Remember, the auction house doesn't make any money unless items sell, so the text will be written to make them appear as desirable as possible. Make sure you read the fine print, too. That's where the bad news will often be found. You don't want to wait until you arrive home with your antique grandfather clock to find out it doesn't work.

(See also antiques and collectibles, stocks, Web sites.)

AUDITS

FOR MANY YEARS, finding a letter with an Internal Revenue Service return address in your mailbox could turn the knees of even the most self-assured individual (including me) to jelly. The IRS loved that it struck such fear in the hearts of taxpayers, since the fear of audit was its greatest preventive weapon, keeping taxpayers on the straight and narrow. I'm going to let you in on a little secret, however. The IRS isn't the demon it used to be.

Sure, being audited is still no picnic. But the chances of your being audited these days are less than they were a few years ago. Back then agents apparently operated under a quota system and were expected to uncover a certain number of miscreants every year. But in response to taxpayer complaints and public embarrassment over a number of cases in which people were subjected to horrendous treatment, Congress passed the Restructuring and Reform Act of 1998.

The result is a more user-friendly IRS, one in which agents can be fired for things like assault or battery on a taxpayer or threatening an audit for personal gain. As a result, audits are down and complaints have also been reduced. Fewer than 2 percent of returns have been audited each year for the past several years. In 1998, less than 1 percent were audited, largely because of a 19 percent reduction in the number of IRS auditors.

What Triggers an Audit?

Okay, the odds have improved, but don't kid yourself: the IRS still examines returns very carefully to spot cheaters. Information on IRS audit strategies are as closely guarded as nuclear secrets. Actually, based on recent spying allegations in the Department of Energy, they're apparently *more* closely guarded than nuclear secrets.

Still, it's believed that the primary strategy the IRS follows is to look for returns with high "discriminant functions." These are scores assigned to your return and are based on a norm for your occupation and income. Let's say, for example, you're a school teacher and you claim a number of airline tickets as a business expense. Since a school teacher is unlikely to travel much, if at all, for work, the IRS computers will assign your return a high score and it will be kicked out for possible audit. At that point the return lands on the desk of an examiner, who will attempt to determine whether the discrepancy noticed by the computer can be explained. If it can't, she'll send out an audit notice.

Even if you don't score a high discriminant function, there's still a chance you'll be audited. Sometimes the IRS will select a certain number of returns at random for a line-by-line audit to get a sense of what percentage of people are making mistakes on their returns. If you get snagged with a faulty return, you can count on paying the overdue tax, interest, and possibly a penalty. If you're a big-time tax cheat, you can be prosecuted. (See "Big Penalties for Cheating," below.)

Here are some other situations that may trigger an audit:

You own your own business, deal in large amounts of cash, and file Schedule C. In 1998, 3.25 percent of taxpayers filing Schedule C and reporting more than $100,000 in primarily cash income were audited.

Big Penalties for Cheating

Cheating on your taxes is foolish. If you're caught, whether through an audit or some other means, it will definitely cost you lots of money, and it could even result in some time in the slammer. Here are three situations in which you can be charged with a crime:

1. If your unpaid tax is more than $500, you can be charged with a misdemeanor for delivery or disclosure of false returns.

2. If you're caught in a tax evasion scheme that results in $10,000 or more in unpaid taxes, with at least $3,000 from any single year, you can be charged with a felony.

3. If it's determined you willfully failed to file returns or filed false returns resulting in at least $2,500 in unpaid taxes a year over a three-year period, you can be charged with a felony.

Audit Tactics

There are definite tactics involved in dealing with IRS examiners. Most professionals who represent clients before the IRS follow similar tactics. Most tend to immediately accept the date and time of the meeting proposed by the IRS to signal they're prepared and organized. Then they actually do prepare exhaustively. Generally, they use the first few minutes of the audit to tout the client and establish their own credibility. Polite small talk helps build personnel rapport and takes some of the examiner's limited time away from the audit itself. Discussion is first steered to the issues on which the documentation is strongest, hopefully compensating for later areas that lack strong documentation. Some professionals prepare the schedules they know the examiner will need on their own. Not only does it make the examiner's job easier, but sometimes the numbers will be accepted with little or no checking.

Tricks That Don't Work

Some of the tricks that won't help you during you an audit include:

- Having garlic or otherwise offensive breath or body odor
- Inviting the auditor out to lunch
- Bringing a crying baby with a dirty diaper to the audit
- Setting up an appointment for late on a Friday afternoon

You take a home office deduction. This is an area full of ambiguities and confusion. If your home office is your only office, your odds of being audited drop.

You write off large amounts of travel and entertainment expenses. One legendary IRS story concerns a businessman who tried to write off the cost of his daughter's wedding as a business expense on the grounds that all the guests were his customers. It didn't work.

You claim large business losses year after year. The IRS understandably starts to wonder whether you're really in business to make a profit. If your business is one in which there are traditionally lots of lean years compared to a handful of good years, for example, writing, recurring losses aren't as problematic.

You do business with someone else who has been audited because of irregularities in his or her return.

Your accountant or tax preparer is under scrutiny by the IRS.

You take a large casualty-loss deduction. Since so few people qualify for these deductions, they're almost always checked. That's why it's important to provide documentation along with your return.

Your stated income doesn't match up with the sum of your W-2s, 1099s, and other reports of income the IRS has received.

You file an estate tax return. Because of the amount of money involved, these draw unusually heavy scrutiny. In 1998, the IRS audited approximately 13 percent of all estate tax returns. When the value of the estate was $5 million or more, nearly half were audited. Here is yet another reason to die broke.

Your Rights in an Audit

If you are informed your return will be audited, don't panic: you have protection. The taxpayer's bill of rights states that audits must be held at a convenient time and place; you can have someone represent you; and you can adjourn a meeting and call in expert assistance. If a ruling is made against you, you have the right to appeal, and you can sue if you feel you've been abused or the agency has recklessly disregarded your rights.

In many cases the IRS is more concerned with documentation of a number than it is with documentation of the context of that number. Let me explain. While the IRS may question the total of your business entertainment deductions, they may be satisfied if you provide sufficient receipts rather than more subjective proof that each meal was in fact a business meeting.

My Advice: Find a Hired Gun and Play It Straight

I think the most important secret to surviving an audit is to stay home and hire someone else to endure the interrogation. The taxpayer's bill of rights lets you have a CPA, a lawyer, or an enrolled agent (someone who has taken and passed the IRS examination for tax preparation) who has been given power of attorney to represent you at the proceedings. Bookkeepers and tax preparers may appear with you but they can't take your place. CPAs will charge you from $100 to $200 per hour for audit representation; tax lawyers will charge from $150 to $350 per hour; and enrolled agents will charge from $75 to $125 per hour.

If you prepared your own return and the audit appears to involve just tax or financial issues, hiring an enrolled agent should suffice. If a CPA prepared your return, either he or someone else from his firm who specializes in audit representation should be your surrogate. If it appears the IRS suspects fraud, or the audit involves trust, estate, charitable foundation, or partnership issues, you should spring for the extra money and hire a tax lawyer to sit in your chair.

Besides saving you some emotional turmoil, not being at the hearing may actually improve your chances. IRS examiners are taught a very subtle interrogation technique than encourages taxpayers to divulge more information than may be needed to resolve the initial limited inquiry.

Most people are nervous at an audit. Thinking that the more information they provide, the better off they'll be, they babble on and often provide grounds for further investigation. Professionals know how to respond as concisely and narrowly as possible and are confident enough to say very little. Because the chances for "winning" are lower, tax examiners are more willing to compromise when faced with another professional. The audit takes on the atmosphere of a negotiation rather than a confrontation.

And make no mistake: it *is* a negotiation. If your return has been selected, odds are the IRS can come up with some reason to increase your tax bill. The secret is to restrict the scope of the examination and minimize the increased bill. Professionals will usually gain leverage with the examiner by showing a willingness to delay as long as possible and pursue all the available appeals options. Examiners are under pressure to close cases and know that the higher up the ladder the case goes, the lower the final adjustment is likely to be. They'll compromise in exchange for closure.

Here's a final word of advice. If you don't cheat on your taxes, you won't have anything to worry about. Tax evasion is illegal. Tax avoidance is downright patriotic. Take advantage of every legal loophole and every legitimate tax-planning strategy and tactic you can. Pay no more—or less—than your fair taxes and you won't have a problem. In fact, the IRS will consider you a great customer. So play it straight and you'll sleep well at night.

(See also entertainment, home offices, lawyers, partnerships, tax preparer.)

AUTOMOBILES

I HATE AUTOMOBILES. Having been born and raised in New York City, I didn't grow up viewing the car as an essential part of daily life. By the time I moved to an auto-centric suburb with my young family, my internal combustion values had been set. To me, cars were a poor replacement for public transportation, nothing more. And driving was a chore, not a joy. When my family moved back to the city after a decade in suburbia, I was happy to use a car rarely. We survived with an efficient little Honda Civic for quite a few years.

Once my wife and I bought a weekend home in Connecticut, we did start to use our car more. Since we're often carting around groceries and grandchildren, we've graduated to a Volvo stationwagon, selected for its spaciousness (groceries) and safety (grandchildren). During the week our car sits in its rented underground parking space (arguably some of the most expensive real estate per square foot in the world) waiting to make its two-hour trip to the country on Friday evening and its return trip Sunday afternoon.

Because I've no emotional attachment to automobiles and, admittedly, because my lifestyle allows me to do without one most of the time, I'm uniquely able to view them objectively. While, in theory, they're assets, they're rather poor performers, since almost all depreciate immediately and dramatically. Therefore, in practice, most cars should be viewed as expenses. They are tools rather than extensions of your personality. They are tools that are expensive to maintain and repair. And many are tools that generally don't last very long. Unless you can afford to buy one of the handful of models that have historically maintained their value and lasted for decades, you shouldn't spend any more money on a car than you need to.

Function, Not Fashion

That's why I advise getting something reliable and functional, not something fashionable. Every day I walk down the streets of New York and see people driving around in expensive four-wheel-drive Lincoln Navigators and Land Rovers. From a practical point of view, it's absurd. These people live and work in the most paved piece of real estate on the planet, with the most extensive mass transit system on Earth, yet they're driving cars designed for those who need to negotiate the Grand Canyon to get home every night.

You certainly don't need to spend a fortune to have an efficient car. The automobile industry has never been as competitive as right now, and the quality of its products is proof. There are plenty of efficient cars on the market than can be leased or purchased for a reasonable price. Approach selecting a car as you would getting a computer system for your business, not as you would choosing a work of art for your dining room. How much car do you need? What will you be doing with the car? What's the car's reliability record? What kind of gas mileage does it get? Is it comfortable? How has it performed in safety tests? How much can you afford to spend, either in total, if you'll be paying cash, or monthly, if you'll be borrowing or leasing?

And don't worry that your clients or neighbors will think less of you because you're not driving around in a Mercedes or a BMW. Savvy clients will be impressed by your practicality. They won't think your fees are too high just so you can afford to drive around in a Jaguar. What your neighbors think doesn't matter.

The Case for and against Leasing

Today, almost one-third of all new cars and trucks are leased rather than purchased. Automobile leasing came into its own as a viable alternative just about the same time the phrase "sticker shock" entered the language. Once auto prices climbed above a certain level and sales of new cars started falling, auto makers and dealers began promoting the lease alternative.

I believe leasing makes sense in most instances. The basic concept of an auto lease is that you are paying for use of the car for a set period—the lease term. At the end of that term the car goes back to its owner—the leaseholder—who can then sell it to you or someone else. Down payments and monthly lease payments are invariably lower than loan payments because you are buying temporary use of the car, not permanent ownership, but at the end of the lease term you own nothing. It's comparable to renting a home rather than buying one. Of course in this case the asset is depreciating rather than appreciating.

Leasing clearly makes the most sense if:

You need a certain type of car that you couldn't otherwise afford to buy. Let's say you need to buy a new, somewhat luxurious four-wheel drive vehicle because you drive clients around and live in the snowbelt. It will cost you far less each month to lease rather than buy that Ford Explorer.

You know you'll remain within the mileage allowance, typically 12,000 miles annually. Turn in the car with more than the allowable miles and you'll end up paying 10 to 25 cents per mile. If you know you're apt to exceed the allowance, negotiate a larger total, say 15,000 miles per year, when you first sign the lease.

You'll be keeping the car until the end of the lease. Turn a leased car in early and you'll be forced to pay thousands of dollars in penalties.

You'll be maintaining the car well. Charges for "excessive wear and tear" can be expensive, especially if you're not simply rolling the car over for another leased vehicle from the same dealership.

You'd be trading the car in at the end of three years anyway. If you're only planning on owning it for three years you might as well lease it and pay less out of pocket.

You own your own business and will be using the car for business. A business owner can deduct all the costs of a leased vehicle used solely for business, including the monthly payments, insurance, maintenance, fuel, and repairs.* A relatively small "lease add-back" amount, based on the value of the car, must be added to your income to represent it being part of your compensation.

On the other hand, some experts believe buying makes sense if the following apply:

You don't need to buy a particular type of car and can select a model based on your budget instead.

You'll be putting more than 15,000 miles a year on the car.

You're not sure if you'll be keeping the car for three years.

---

*Just remember that the tax form on which you claim business use of a motor vehicle asks if you have another car available for personal use. If you claim you are using a vehicle 100 percent for business, you had better have another car available for personal use if you don't want the IRS to drop you a line.

You and your environment are very hard on your vehicles.

You were planning on using the car for more than three years.

You don't own your own business.

Buying and Leasing Dos and Don'ts

Everyone knows that to get the best deal when buying or leasing a car you don't negotiate down from the sticker price, but up from the dealer's invoice price. Dealers' invoice prices can be obtained from *Consumer Reports* mail, telephone, and online services, as well as from a number of other Web sites. A good first offer is about 1 percent above the dealer's invoice, and a smart bottom line is 3 percent over invoice.

Here are some other buying and leasing dos and don'ts:

- Do all your research about various models' performance, repair, and safety records before you go to a dealer.

- Don't select a car without first checking with your insurance broker about how much coverage on that particular model will cost.

- Don't buy or lease from a particular dealer until you contact your local office of the Better Business Bureau and ask about any complaints on file.

Let Your Fingers Do the Shopping

Shopping for cars is easier than ever before. (See the entry on automobile shopping for a less idiosyncratic approach.) Today, I don't even bother going to a dealership unless it's to pick up the car. Once I know exactly what car I want and what features I need, I telephone dealerships within an hour's drive of my home, tell them what car I want, that I'm ready to buy or lease that day, that I'll be calling the 10 or so dealerships in the immediate area, and then ask for their best price. If I'm leasing, I ask them all for a monthly payment figure, based on the same deposit and mileage allowance. If I'm buying, I ask them all for a bottom-line, all-inclusive price.

Once I have all my price quotes, I call back the dealer with the second lowest price and give him or her a chance to beat the lowest price. If they do, I agree to the deal right then. If they don't, I call back the lowest-price dealer and seal the agreement. I always insist that the salesperson double-check and then triple-check the deal before I get off the telephone, explaining that if the deal changes when I arrive in person, I will walk right out the door. That's only happened to me once. The moment I stepped out the door, they were miraculously able to make the deal after all.

- Don't let the dealer see your current car—that will keep him from making judgments on what you can afford.

- Do try to sell your old car on your own rather than trade it in. You'll get more money and the buy/lease deal will be less complicated. If you can't be bothered selling it on your own, ask for a trade-in equal to 90 percent of its value in the *Kelley Blue Book*—and don't settle for less than 75 percent. If you're leasing, your trade-in's value should be deducted from the car's capitalized cost.

- Do look for a "subvented lease," which will be subsidized by the manufacturer.

- Don't pay preparation charges, dealer exchange fees, ADM (additional dealer markup) charges, or for Scotchgard treatments or rustproofing you haven't ordered on your own. Advertising and destination fees, on the other hand, are legitimate charges.

- Do make sure the definition of "excessive wear and tear" is spelled out in the lease document.

- Don't sign the dealer's loan offer right away. While you'll usually get a better loan interest rate from a dealer than a bank, double-check to see if your bank will beat the dealer's best offer.

- Don't drive away with the car until you're completely satisfied with the car's condition. Drive the car off the lot and it's now your problem.

(See also advertising, automobile leasing, automobile shopping, down payments, Web sites.)

AUTOMOBILE INSURANCE

THE BEST WAY to cut your auto insurance bill is to move to North Dakota. Nothing affects auto insurance rates more than location. The lower the population density of an area, the lower the auto insurance rates. If I moved out of the New York City metropolitan area to another part of New York State, I could save $1500 a year on my auto insurance. New Jersey has the highest auto insurance rates in the nation partly because it's so densely populated. Since no one in his right mind relocates just to cut his auto insurance bill, you'll have to settle for some other less dramatic ways to trim your premiums.

Why Is Automobile Insurance So Expensive?

And make no mistake, trimming your bill is essential. Auto insurance rates are exorbitant. Why? It's simple, really. Insurance premiums are based on statistical probability. The greater the likelihood that a company will need to pay a claim on a policy, the higher the premiums for that policy.

This is one reason why homeowner's policies are generally so reasonable. The likelihood of your house burning down or being damaged by severe weather is really quite small. Therefore, the chances of you filing a claim are equally small.

But people are always having car accidents. There are thousands every day. That's why the premiums for automobile insurance are so high.

Many factors are calculated in determining premiums. As I mentioned, if you live in a city you'll pay more than people living in rural areas. Different states also have different insurance regulations, and these affect premiums. Age and sex are big factors. Teenagers have a very high accident rate. And men tend to be involved in more accidents than women.

Driving record will also affect premiums. If you have a history of speeding tickets, accidents, or drunk driving, you'll pay more than someone with a clean record. If your record becomes bad enough, you may even become uninsurable.

The kind of car you drive will affect what you pay. Makes that are expensive to repair, prone to accidents, or stolen more often will cost top dollar to insure. All else being equal, the owner of a Porsche will pay a much higher premium than the owner of a Plymouth Breeze.

Fault and No-Fault

You live in either a "fault" state or a "no-fault" state. In a fault state, the person responsible for an accident (and the insurance company) is also responsible for paying for damages and injuries to the other party or parties. In a no-fault state, neither party is considered at fault and each party (and each insurer) is responsible for paying for his or her own damages and injuries.

Trimming the Coverage

Auto insurance policies are actually packages of various types of coverage. You can trim your costs by eliminating coverage you don't need and trimming coverage wherever possible.

1. *Bodily injury and property liability insurance.* In many states, liability insurance is required for all car owners, regardless of the age or value of their cars. It covers injury you cause to pedestrians, other cars, and the passengers in other cars. Conversely, if someone should run into you, his or her policy will cover injury or damage to you and your vehicle. The amount of coverage you need is tied to your vulnerability to a lawsuit if you cause an accident. The more assets you have, the more liability insurance you should purchase. Basic coverage should include $100,000 worth of coverage for each injured person, with a maximum of $300,000 per accident. If you have a lot of assets that could be pursued by a plaintiff's lawyer, you may want to purchase even more. However, it's invariably cheaper to buy an umbrella liability policy that supplements both your auto and homeowner's packages than it is to increase this part of your auto package. One caveat: you should never be insured for more than your net worth.

2. *Collision insurance.* This covers damage to your vehicle. Your premium will depend on the age and value of your car and the deductible you choose. If you have a new car, you can

lower your premiums by selecting a higher deductible. Cars depreciate in value quite rapidly, and the need for collision insurance decreases right along with it. If you have an old car, collision insurance makes no sense at all. This is because when you have an accident, your insurer will pay you either the cost of the repair to the car or the book value of the car, whichever is less.

3. *Medical payments insurance.* This covers the medical costs (or, God forbid, funeral bills) of the policyholder, other family members, and any passengers who are injured in an accident involving the policyholder's car, regardless of who caused the accident. Since an injured person's health insurance will pay for medical bills, your auto policy's medical payments coverage need only cover the deductibles. If the parties have no health insurance and sue you, your liability coverage will protect you.

4. *Uninsured motorist coverage.* Despite the fact that liability insurance is often required by law, there are a lot of people who don't have it. Of course, they're usually the worst drivers on the road. Many have had their coverage canceled because of their poor driving histories. If one of these people should hit you, whether you're in your vehicle or just walking down the road, collecting for damages will be a nightmare. Uninsured motorist coverage protects you against such situations.

5. *Comprehensive coverage.* Comprehensive coverage protects you and your automobile against anything the other elements of the package don't cover—theft, vandalism, collisions with animals, and many other risks. Whether you need comprehensive coverage is really tied to the value of your car. Like collision coverage, damage is limited to the value of the car. And you may be covered against theft by your homeowner's coverage.

6. *Rental car reimbursement.* Some policies will pay a small daily stipend to allow you to rent a car while your car is being repaired. It's useful if you use your car to make a living. But if you can live without your car for a few days, I don't think the coverage is worth the money.

7. *Towing reimbursement.* This will pay for the cost of being towed if your car breaks down or you're in an accident. You can get the same benefit, and much more, by joining the AAA or another auto club.

Other Ways to Save
Besides trimming the various parts of your auto insurance package you can also save premium dollars in some other ways.

- Insuring more than one vehicle with the same insurer

- Buying your auto, homeowner's, and umbrella liability insurance from the same insurer

- Letting your insurer know your car is garaged or otherwise parked off the street and isn't used for commuting

- Not letting your teenagers have their own car or use your car more than 50 percent of the time

- Sending your teen to college more than 100 miles from your home

- Taking advantage of discounts for defensive driving courses and student drivers who get good grades

- Buying cars with passive safety devices like air bags, antilock brakes, and automatic seat belts

- Buying cars with antitheft devices

- Paying the premium bill in full rather than incurring interest charges

- Shopping around for better rates from known low-cost insurers such as GEICO and USAA.

(See also funerals, health insurance, liability insurance, location, networking.)

AUTOMOBILE LEASING

IF YOU CAN'T PAY CASH for the car you need, lease it rather than taking out a loan to buy it. Why am I so enamored of leasing? First, there's the cost. When you buy a car, you need a fairly sizable down payment, maybe 10 to 20 percent, since few lenders offer 100 percent financing. You also need to pay sales tax. If you take out a loan for three years (the average lease term) you'll pay hundreds of dollars more each month, cutting a sizable chunk out of your stream of income. Granted, at the end of that loan term you will own the vehicle. But it will have depreciated enormously. While you can reduce your monthly payments by taking a loan for 48 or 60 months, that will increase the total amount out of pocket you pay for the car, and leave you with an asset that has depreciated even further.

Now look at leasing. You go to the dealer, make a modest down payment or none at all, pay taxes up front or have them rolled into the lease payments, sign a few papers, and drive away with a brand new car. Your lease payments will be about half of what they'd be if you were buying the car. When the lease expires, you return to the dealer and turn the car in, sign a new lease agreement, and drive away in another brand new car.

The other major downside of car ownership is the cost of repairs. During the first three years repairs are rarely an issue, regardless of whether you lease or buy. That's because manufacturers' warranties these days provide near complete coverage against problems for at least three years or 30,000 miles. This means you only have to worry about routine maintenance, such as changing the oil.

When you lease, you have constant warranty protection. Not only will your chances of having a mechanical problem be reduced, since you'll always be driving a relatively new vehicle; if you do have a problem it is unlikely to cost you a penny. When you own a car, you're responsible for repairs once the warranty expires. And once a car becomes four or five years old, you never know what might happen.

If you're self-employed and use your car entirely for business, leasing provides you with an opportunity to deduct all the expenses related to that car, including the lease payments themselves. Granted, you will need to add an amount (determined by the model and age of the vehicle) to your income to represent the value of having a "company" car. Still, the amount is usually quite low. In addition, if you are using the car 100 percent for business you'll need to be certain to note on the relevant tax form that you do indeed have another vehicle available for personal use.

Basically, leasing allows you to always drive a late-model vehicle for almost nothing down, relatively low monthly payments, and little or no repair costs. If you're an entrepreneur who leases, all your business auto expenses may be deductible. Buying, on the other hand, requires more money up front, can as much as double your monthly payments, and leaves you with an asset that has depreciated in value and may be facing considerable repair costs.

Bargain Leases

Just as there are bargain buys out there among auto dealerships, there are also bargain lease deals. Manufacturers tailor their lease programs to their inventories. If a certain model isn't selling well and inventories are backing up, the manufacturer starts a lease program with very attractive terms in order to reduce inventories. If you're flexible about what kind of car you drive, you can usually find great deals.

If you really want to minimize your driving costs, you might consider leasing a vehicle that's a few years old. There are a glut of automobiles in the United States these days, and many dealers will lease an older car just to keep their inventories moving. In the metropolitan New York area, you can lease a four- or five-year-old car for little more than $100 a month.

When Buying Does Make Sense

Having made the case so strongly for leasing, let me offer a couple of caveats. There are two situations in which I think buying a car makes sense. One is if you need a second car for puttering around town—to get you to the train station in the morning, for example, or to allow your child to drive to school. Most families reach the point where such a vehicle becomes a necessity. In this case, save up the money and pay cash. You'll probably only need a couple of thousand dollars at most. The only other time I think buying a car makes sense is when you can afford to pay cash for it. I don't believe in taking out loans unless you need to, so if you have the money to buy the car you want, by all means do it. If you don't have the cash, lease the car.

You have to be careful, though. The warranties on these vehicles are limited. Some are only for 90 days. After that, you're responsible for any repairs. But there are manufacturers out there whose vehicles are known for providing years of trouble-free driving. By selecting one of their cars, you can reduce your chances of facing expensive repair costs.

(See also down payment.)

AUTOMOBILE LOANS

SINCE YOU'RE READING THIS CHAPTER, you probably don't agree with me that leasing an automobile is smarter than buying. That's okay. Let me just tell you a few quick things about auto loans.

I'm always amazed at the number of people who spend weeks driving from dealer to dealer just to shave a few dollars off the purchase price of a car and then make a single call to their bank to arrange the financing. Or, even worse, they simply accept the dealer's offer to arrange financing. It never occurs to them to spend the same kind of energy they spent haggling over prices in looking for a good loan rate. It's silly. A difference of just one interest point can result in hundreds of dollars in out-of-pocket expenses over the term of a loan.

Consider this example. Let's say you want to borrow $20,000 over 48 months. If you take out a loan at 9 percent, your monthly payments will be $497.70 and your total cash outlay over the 48 months will be $23,889.60.

But if you find a source of financing at 8 percent, your monthly payments drop to $488.26 and your total outlay is 23,436.48, a decrease of $453.12. And keep in mind that it's not unusual to find a range of three to four points among all potential auto lenders. If you don't take the time to shop around for the best deal, you can cost yourself a lot of money.

Nondealer Financing

I'd advise you to start your shopping with a nondealer source: a local credit union. These institutions are nonprofit and member-owned and are geared to just this kind of small-scale lending, so they often offer the best terms. Credit unions might even offer 100 percent financing. You may need to join the credit union by opening a checking or savings account, but that shouldn't be a problem. The terms of those services are often equally attractive.

Commercial banks and savings and loan associations are other sources of auto loans. Their rates will vary dramatically, so take the time to comparison-shop. Be careful to factor any up-front fees and one-time charges into the mix. Some lenders will entice you with lower rates but also add on charges. When you do the math, you often find your total out-of-pocket costs are higher than they would be if you obtained a no-fee loan at a higher rate. You should also steer clear of variable-rate loans. Although they'll start out at a lower rate than fixed-rate loans, there's

Taking Out a Loan versus Paying Cash

If you've sworn off leasing and are trying to decide between paying cash or taking out a loan to buy a car, you can do some simple calculations.

Since almost all vehicles depreciate in value rather than appreciate or maintain value, you shouldn't treat this as an investment. Instead, compare the cost of borrowing—the interest rate on the loan—to the cost of spending rather than saving the money.

Let's say you're earning 7 percent interest on the cash and an auto loan will cost you 5 percent interest. In that instance it makes sense to obtain the loan and earn 2 percent more than you'll be spending. On the other hand, if you're earning 4 percent interest on the money and the loan will cost you 5 percent, it makes sense to pay cash. If the rates are roughly equal, you'll need to factor in your need for liquidity.

often no cap on how high they can rise. If you do a great deal of business with a particular bank and are a "preferred depositor," you might find that it will offer a very attractive auto loan rate simply as a service to keep your business.

Dealer Financing

The sources of dealer financing vary. Sometimes the dealer will go through a commercial bank. Other times the financing will be offered by the company that manufactures the car you're purchasing.

The terms offered by a dealer will be in direct correlation to sales. When times are good and sales are booming, the rates will be high. If sales are in a slump, however, the rates can be quite attractive. If you pay attention to ads in the media, you'll frequently see offers from automobile manufacturers for financing at very low rates, say 2.9 percent or 3.9 percent. These rates are hard to beat. But they're usually for very short terms, maybe just a year or two, so you need to make sure you can afford the exceptionally high monthly payments. They're also usually tied to a specific model that hasn't been selling well, so you need to be flexible in the kind of car you want.

Dealer financing is often the best option for those with credit problems. Dealers and auto manufacturers are in the business of moving vehicles, not making loans, and therefore are liberal in their lending. Many dealers even advertise their willingness to deal with buyers who have bad credit histories.

Borrowing from Yourself

Another potential source of financing is to borrow from your own assets via a home equity loan. The rate can be quite attractive and the interest, within some restrictions, will be tax-deductible.

Despite these obvious advantages, I feel you should avoid tapping into that particular area of credit to finance a car. The equity in your home is a very valuable asset, and when you borrow against it you're risking losing your home if you're unable to pay back the money. I think home equity loans should be reserved for investing in your future—such as home renovations, purchasing securities, or educating your children—rather than making a purchase.

Make It Quick

One final point: Borrowing money is expensive. Your job is to find the cheapest loan and pay if off as quickly as possible. Decide how much you can afford each month and then find terms that fit. And if you find yourself with a chunk of cash and can pay off the loan ahead of time, by all means do it. Then the next month you can put the money you'd have put toward your car loan in a mutual fund instead.

(See also home equity loans, savings accounts.)

AUTOMOBILE OWNERSHIP

CARS ARE MONEY PITS. I guess my problem is, I only see them from a financial perspective and I recognize them for what they are—an expense. They're costly to own and operate. Plus they depreciate like crazy. But, like most people, I need one, so I own one.

Calculating Ownership Costs

Next to the purchase of a home, buying a car is the second most expensive transaction most of us will make. Yet because our culture attaches so many odd values to cars, people base their purchase decisions on all the wrong things. They fall victim to advertising and see cars as an extension of their personalities rather than what they really are, a tool. As a result, they act impulsively and emotionally and end up spending more money than they need to, or buying a car that's not appropriate for their needs. Many people do both.

I believe you should approach the purchase of a car, new or used, by evaluating the costs of ownership. Here are some of the factors you need to analyze. I suggest you consult www. edmunds.com to get much of this information on particular cars. Maintained by the same company that publishes automotive magazines, this Web site provides a wealth of information on both new and used cars.

Depreciation

A new car begins to depreciate (decrease in value) the instant you drive it off the lot. It will depreciate most quickly during the first three or four years that you own it. A four-year-old used car will depreciate more slowly than a new car. The more your car has depreciated, the lower its resale value and its value as a trade-in.

There are significant differences in the depreciation rates of various makes and models. Four-wheel-drive vehicles tend to hold their value better than two-wheel-drive vehicles since, at least until recently, they were seen as utilitarian. A bit of rust and some dings didn't matter as much. They could still do the jobs they were built for, and that's what counted. Some manufacturers are known for building reliable cars that will last 10 or 15 years with the proper care and maintenance. Not surprisingly, their vehicles hold their value much better than those of other manufacturers. A couple of well-known examples are Mercedes and Volvo. Purchasing a vehicle from one of these manufacturers may be the most cost-effective over the long term. Of course, their initial costs are relatively high.

Insurance

Auto insurance can be an enormous expense. Insurance rates are tied to the age and value of a car, the age and sex of its driver or drivers, the location where the car will be driven and parked, and the likelihood of the car being stolen.

Call your insurance agent and get quotes for any vehicle you're considering buying. Depending on the car's age, you may want to forget about comprehensive coverage and just insure it for liability.

Finance Charges

If you're going to be taking out a loan to finance a car, you'll also need to consider how much you'll be paying in finance charges (interest). The total amount of your finance charges will depend on how much money you borrow, the interest rate, and the duration of the loan. My advice is to make the duration of the loan as short as possible while making sure you can still afford the monthly payments. Even better, pay cash.

Taxes and Registration Fees

Registration fees vary widely. In some states, the cost of registering your car is tied to its age. The older it is, the cheaper it is to register. In other states, everyone pays a flat rate, regardless of the age of the vehicle. Taxes on vehicle sales are most often tied to state sales tax rates. Your insurance representative or your local motor vehicle office can provide you with tax and registration information. If you're buying the car from a dealer, your salesperson will also be able to tell you.

Maintenance

Basic maintenance will include work like brake jobs, tire rotation, engine tune-ups, oil changes, and replacement of various fluids and filters. You can get a rough idea of what your annual maintenance costs will be by reviewing the maintenance schedule in the owner's manual. If you're buying the car from a dealer, talk to the manager of the service department. If not, you might want to consult with a mechanic.

Repairs

Repairs are the big crap shoot of car ownership. One of the advantages of driving a new car is that most everything will be covered by warranty for the first three years or for a certain number of miles, usually 30,000. Of course, this benefit will be somewhat diluted by the fact that you'll be paying more in finance charges, taxes, and insurance. Similarly, if you lease the car for three years, you'll also be covered for the duration of the lease.

A used car, on the other hand, will cost less in taxes, insurance, and finance charges. But it's also going to be a potential source of endless repair costs. Once a car reaches four or five years of age, anything and everything can go wrong. The Edmunds Web site rates the reliability of vehicles. These ratings can serve as a guide to how likely it is you'll face major repair bills.

Fuel

Despite the vagaries of OPEC, this is really your most predictable cost. The gasoline use of all vehicles is well-documented. If you have a rough idea of how many miles you'll be driving the car each year, it's quite simple to calculate your annual fuel costs.

Using Your Information

Once you have a list of candidate vehicles, you can calculate costs in all the above categories and add them up to see what your annual costs of ownership will be for each vehicle. After that, it's your decision. You already know what my advice would be: go with the one that costs the least. However, I learned long ago that when it comes to cars, rational behavior and common sense usually fly out the window, particularly where middle-aged men are concerned.

(See also advertising, Web sites.)

AUTOMOBILE RENTALS

RENTING A CAR is one of the least consumer-friendly transactions you'll ever face. Prices fluctuate from company to company, from day to day, and from airport to airport. Companies themselves offer various special packages and options. The rental contracts are lengthy and full of fine print. Hidden charges can often fatten the final bill. Getting the best deal on a rental car requires some research and a careful analysis of your needs and the options offered by the rental company.

Will You Even Be Able to Rent a Car?

Don't assume so. You might not be eligible. When you rent a car, the rental company will feed your name and driver's license number into a computer that's connected to a network of databases containing motor vehicle department information from around the country. If the search reveals you have a poor driving record, the company may decide you're too risky and turn you down.

The criteria for refusal vary, but they're all pretty tough. If your driver's license has been revoked or suspended, or you've been convicted of driving under the influence of alcohol or drugs during the previous four to six years, you'll be turned down. You'll also likely be turned down if you've been involved in a fatal accident in the last four to six years. Some people have been turned down because of accidents that weren't their fault.

If you are turned down, you may or may not be given a reason. Some companies will merely give you the list of offenses than can result in rejection and let you interpret it accordingly. Regardless, you don't want to find out at the last second that you won't be able to get a car. You should reserve rental cars ahead of time as often as possible. When you make a reservation, give the clerk your driver's license number and ask that it be checked while you wait.

Young people also have problems renting cars. Many companies won't rent to people under a certain age—anywhere from 21 to 25—under the assumption they're more likely to have an accident. Although this is clearly discriminatory and may, in fact, be illegal, the practice is widespread.

Finally, if you don't have a credit card you can't rent a car. Rental companies demand the security of having your credit card account number before they'll hand you the keys to one of their cars.

Insurance Coverage

If you're driving around in a $25,000 car that belongs to someone else, you'll want to make sure you're completely covered if you have an accident or the car is stolen or damaged. Start by checking your own auto insurance policy. Most include coverage for rental vehicles as well as your own. Some states, such as New York, mandate that rental vehicle coverage be included as part of your policy.

If you're not covered, you'll have the option of purchasing a collision damage waiver that absolves you of any damage to the vehicle, regardless of the cause. These are real money-earners for rental companies, and they promote them endlessly, even when they know you don't need them. They may even try to tell you that the waiver is mandatory.

Pay particular attention to your liability coverage. Your own auto policy likely offers it, and your credit card company may even provide it, but don't take any chances: check. You're just an accident away from a million-dollar lawsuit. If you don't have liability coverage through your personal policy or your credit card company, you can purchase it from the rental company. Some companies may provide you with liability coverage free of charge, but it's usually not a lot. If you have significant assets, you'll probably want to purchase the supplemental coverage.

Protecting Your Wallet

Car rental companies have many tricks up their sleeves to generate revenues. Selling unneeded insurance is just one of them. Here are some others:

Rent your vehicle on the weekends if you can. Many of the cars that serve business travelers, the primary customers of car rental companies, sit idle on weekends, so rental companies will lower their rates to keep them on the road. Just make sure you have the car back on time. If you don't, you can be hit with painful extra charges.

Additional driver fees. Some companies will charge a fee if anyone but you will be driving the car. Fees can range from $10 to $25.

Mileage deals. Among the many options you may be offered is "free" mileage. And it is free, as long as you don't go over the limit. If you do, count on being charged 30 cents a mile or more on the overage. Make sure you ask what the limit is. It might not be that evident in the rental agreement, and you can't count on the agent to tell you.

Cancellation fees. They're not charged for every type of car, usually just for luxury cars, minivans, and other "special-order" vehicles. The charges can be ridiculous, $100 or more. Be sure to ask if there's a cancellation fee and how much notice must be given, regardless of what kind of car you're renting.

Fuel charges. Rental companies want you to return their car with the same amount of gas as it had when you drove it off the lot. If you don't, they'll charge an exorbitant fee. They may offer you the option of paying more up front and not having to return the car with a full tank, but even with fuel prices sky-high the option is rarely worth the cost.

(See also credit cards.)

AUTOMOBILE REPAIRS

WHEN I OPEN THE HOOD of a car, I might as well be looking at the innards of the space shuttle. It's totally meaningless to me. So when I need repairs done on my car, I'm ripe for the picking: a mechanic could tell me just about anything and I'd have no choice but to believe him.

The only thing that makes me feel better is, I'm not alone. It has been estimated that of the more than $100 billion Americans spend on car repairs each year, as much as 40 percent may be for work that either doesn't need to be done or isn't done. Is it any wonder car repairs are consistently at the top of consumer complaints to the Better Business Bureau and other consumer advocacy groups?

Finding a Repair Shop You Can Trust

When it comes to car repairs, you can take your car to a dealer's shop or to an independent shop. I think if you have an older car, your best option is an independent shop, particularly if it's someone who comes highly recommended and with whom you can build an ongoing relationship. Look for shops endorsed by the American Automobile Association and certified by the National Institute for Automotive Service Excellence.

This is not to say dealers are dishonest. The problem is, dealers depend on their repair shops to generate the bulk of their revenues—as much as 90 percent in some cases. Their labor charges are usually higher than those of independent shops. Parts are also expensive. On the other hand, their mechanics are expertly trained in servicing your make and model of vehicle. The best dealers also place a premium on quality service and back up their work unconditionally. If you have a fairly new vehicle, which is less likely to need major mechanical repairs, it probably makes sense to use a dealer's repair shop.

What to Watch Out For

There are any number of ways you can be taken by a crooked car repair shop. Here are some of the most common complaints:

Poor-quality work. As many as one in three vehicles that are repaired must be returned to the shop for further work.

Unnecessary repairs. Most car owners are, like me, totally clueless. If they're told their whatzimajiggit needs to be replaced, they pay to have it replaced.

Charges for work not done. There was a story in the news a few years ago about a minister who took his car in for work. Rather than leaving, he brought some paperwork with him and stayed in the customer lounge—in a seat from which he could see his car. A couple of hours later the service manager came in and told him his car was ready. It hadn't been touched.

Pricing. Repair shops lure customers by advertising a certain price for a certain service. Once the car is on the lift, however, the mechanic finds many additional problems.

Warranty disputes. Many dealers will claim your warranty will no longer be valid if work is performed on your car by anyone other than the dealer. In fact, you can have basic maintenance performed by anyone and the dealer must still honor the warranty.

How to Protect Yourself

Here are a few precautions to take when you need car repairs. They could save you hundreds of dollars.

1. *Require authorization.* Don't sign a repair authorization unless the specific problem has been written on the repair order. If the mechanic is unsure of the problem, ask him to call you later with a description of the problem and an estimate. He can then proceed only with your permission.

2. *Get a second opinion.* This is particularly important with expensive repairs or if you're in a situation where you've had no previous experience with the repair shop.

3. *Patronize specialty shops.* Routine maintenance such as oil changes can be handled inexpensively by franchised chains that specialize in that particular service.

4. *Don't pay for work you didn't ask for.* If there are charges on your bill for work you didn't authorize, don't pay for it.

5. *Talk to the mechanic.* Speak directly to the person who will be performing the work on your car. If you communicate through a service manager, it can lead to unnecessary confusion.

6. *Use rebuilt parts.* They're much cheaper than original parts. The only downside is the guarantee on the parts will be for a shorter period of time.

7. *Check your warranty.* Always check your warranty to see if the repair is the responsibility of the dealer.

Last Resorts

If you have a problem with a car repair shop that you can't resolve on your own, contact your local better business bureau or other consumer affairs agency. If problems persist, contact the attorney general's office in your state.

AUTOMOBILE SHOPPING

FEW PEOPLE ACTUALLY BUY CARS—cars are sold to them instead. It's rare for anyone to view auto shopping as a proactive, pragmatic process. Instead it's usually a quick, reactive purchase. Selecting a car, whether you're buying or leasing, is a major decision. As has often been noted, cars are the second most expensive items most people will ever buy, next to their houses. And auto leases are likely to be the second highest monthly expense most people will carry, next to their rent or mortgage payment. The wisest approach to this transaction is to spend more time researching and investigating, and less time at the dealership.

Decide What You Need

As I've mentioned in many of the other automobile entries, I take a very utilitarian approach to cars. To me, they're simply tools for transportation. I approach the search for a new car using the same criteria I would use if I were looking for a new telephone answering machine. It has a defined function and as long as it carries out that function reliably, safely, and comfortably, I'm quite satisfied. In other words, I don't need a Mercedes to be happy.

Before you start shopping, you need to decide what kind of a car you need. First, what kind of driving do you do? Are you a city dweller who rarely leaves town or do you live in a rural area and spend a lot of time on the road? Will there typically be many people in the car or just one or two? If you're a soccer mom, your needs may be much different from your own mother's needs. Do you live in an area where there is severe weather or in a more moderate climate? People who live in snowbelt states generally find four-wheel-drive vehicles to be quite useful.

People who live in areas with little snow, who don't go "off-roading," do not need four-wheel drive. Of course, you wouldn't know that by looking at the streets and highways in our temperate-zone big cities. That's because most drivers are being sold an image and rather than buying based on their needs, they are buying based on their wants.

Decide What You Can Afford

Unless you plan to pay cash for the vehicle, forget about the total price of the vehicle. Instead, focus on the monthly payment. You need to decide how much money you're comfortable parting with every month. Add to that the cost of fuel, insurance, maintenance, and repairs to come up with a total monthly cost.

Do Your Research

Once you've decided what you need in a car and what you can afford, you need to start evaluating different models. Since automobiles are such a big business, information about automobiles is an equally big business. There are hundreds of publications and Web sites devoted to every facet of automobile ownership.

I personally find the Internet to be the best source of information. One of the best automobile Web sites, in my opinion, is www.edmunds.com, which is operated by the publishing company of the same name. This site contains information on just about every make and model, both new and used, including price, features, and performance. Each car is given a rating from 1 to 10 in categories such as reliability, safety, and comfort. You can even calculate your monthly payments by plugging in the amount you want to borrow, the interest rate, and the length of the loan. Equally important, you can find out what dealers pay for the car. This will be critical once you begin the negotiating process.

Dealing with Dealers

At this point, you'll be more than ready to start visiting dealers. Begin with telephone calls. (For my personal telephone shopping strategy, see "Online Auto Shopping" above.) Call the dealers who carry the models you're interested in and ask to speak to a salesperson. Tell her what you're interested in and make it clear that you've done your research—including the fact that you know what the dealer paid for the car. Let her know you're comparison-shopping and you're only interested in discussing price based on her cost, not on the sticker price.

Now, car salespeople have not earned their reputations by accident. There are all sorts of ploys they'll try to get as much money as possible out of you. Here are a just a few of them and some advice on how you should respond:

She'll tell you to visit other dealers and come back with the best price you're offered. *Your response:* "I would like a firm price from you now or I won't be coming back."

She'll offer you a price but insist you must buy the car that day for the offer to stand. *Your response:* "I don't intend to be pressured. Any price you offer me today should be good tomorrow."

She'll argue with you about what she has paid for the vehicle, insisting your numbers are wrong. *Your response:* "Okay, show me your invoice. If I'm wrong, we'll use your numbers. But if I'm right, that means you've lied to me and I'll take my business elsewhere."

She'll give you what you know is an unrealistically low price with the intention of making up the difference by adding additional charges into the sales contract. *Your response:* "This is an attractive offer. I'd like to speak with the sales manager to confirm that she has authorized this price and there will be no other charges attached to the transaction."

She'll try to steer you to vehicles with expensive extra features. *Your response:* "No, thank you. I'm familiar with the options available for this vehicle and I'm quite satisfied with those I've already selected."

Keep the conversations about price separate from any discussions of financing or leasing. Once you've agreed on a price you can then move on to the financing or leasing details. Also, don't agree to purchase extended warranties or other kinds of service contracts. These are huge money-makers for dealers and rarely worth the money.

(See also automobile ownership, e-mail, negotiating, Web sites.)

BANKING AND BANKERS

Only a fool feels loyalty to a bank. Sure, banks can be wonderful institutions—until you need to borrow money. Then they get a bit standoffish. They may wrap themselves in the garb of community service, but when push comes to shove they're as fixated on the bottom line as any other business. Still, they are necessary, so let's ignore their flaws for the moment and look at their virtues.

Banking is an extremely competitive industry, so banks go out of their way to lure new customers. They offer a variety of deals on different checking and saving accounts. They offer credit cards and debit cards. They can offer personal and business loans for a variety of needs, ranging from home mortgage loans to business lines of credit. They may provide financial services, offering to take care of our mortgage payments, car payments, and other bills with automatic debits from designated accounts. They have ATMs so we can do our banking from different locations, 24 hours a day. They manage trusts and provide services for small businesses. They've even moved into investment services in the last decade, through separate sister companies due to the archaic banking regulations.

Choosing a Bank

In this sense most banks are about the same. This is why it's often difficult to decide which one you want to do business with. My advice is to ignore interest rates and fees. By the time you read through all the small print, they're virtually identical from one bank to another. I think the best way to select a bank is to pay attention to advertising and determine who it is each bank is trying to attract. For example, a bank that's interested in attracting the business of younger people will promote its mortgage, consumer loan, and credit card services and have plenty of 24-hour ATM locations. Some banks are interested in working with small businesses and offer special account services and electronic credit card transaction services. Trust companies specialize in helping people manage inheritances and other large sums of money. Pay attention to the services banks are touting and decide which ones best meet your needs.

When you're shopping around, don't be impressed by a bank's size. You'll often find that a small, locally owned bank with a few offices around town will provide you with better—and cheaper—service than a huge conglomerate that boasts offices in every major city in the country. When I recently started shopping around for a new bank, I discovered that some of the smaller banks, which didn't have branches near me, were even prepared to make regularly scheduled stops, mornings and afternoons, at my office to compensate. As a banking customer, it's better to be a big fish in a small pond. Just make sure the bank is insured by the Federal Deposit Insurance Corporation (FDIC). And don't keep more than $100,000 in any one bank. That's the limit on FDIC insurance.

Choosing a Banker

There's one other criterion you need to be aware of in your search. You're not just looking for a bank, you're also looking for a banker, a specific individual to address your needs. You want someone to expedite transactions, deal with problems, and gently shepherd you through the maze of red tape and bureaucracy. For a business, a personal banker can sometimes provide access to lines of credit or take advantage of cash management programs that allow you to squeeze every last drop of interest out of the cash in your accounts. For an individual, a personal banker can serve as your advocate in front of the loan committee or simply help you manage your accounts, ensuring that you receive the maximum return possible.

Most banks are more than happy to provide you with a personal banker. If you have a large business with a lot of cash flow, sizable accounts, and a variety of financial needs, or if you have sizable personal funds on deposit, they can get positively giddy. They even have names for this kind of personal service: "core banking," implying you're on the inside, or "select service," implying you're a VIP deserving of special treatment.

When interviewing potential personal bankers, ask about the candidates' educational backgrounds. An MBA in finance is a good credential for any banker and a particularly fine one for someone who'll be providing your business with advice and guidance. Find out the extent of each candidate's authority. Will the banker need to go to a loan committee for everything, or does he have the power to make some loans on his own? Ask how long each candidate has been in banking, and with their current bank. The longer they've been a banker, the more wisdom you can expect. The longer they've been with their current bank, the more power they'll probably have.

Once you've chosen a personal banker, that person will join your lawyer, accountant, financial planner, and other professionals as part of the team that gets you through your personal and business life. Cultivate a relationship that extends beyond business. Invite him for dinner or take

The Credit Union Alternative

Credit unions are nonprofit private institutions that provide banking services to their members. Most are federally insured. While credit unions usually limit their services to either employees of a particular company or members of a certain profession, others operate in a specific location, offering membership to everyone in that area. Because they are nonprofit and oriented toward serving their members, credit unions charge lower fees and usually have more liberal lending policies. The downside is that they may not offer all the financial products or services you need. If you qualify for membership and can work around their limitations, credit unions are an excellent alternative to commercial banks. For the names of credit unions near you consult your local telephone directory or log onto the Credit Union National Association's Web site.

him to a sporting event or the theater. Let him know you value his advice and keep him apprised of developments in your life and business. And if he moves to a job with a different bank, move your business with him as well. That's what I did recently when my longtime personal banker shifted jobs. Instead of being loyal to a bank, be loyal to a banker.

The one thing your personal banker might not be able to help you with is getting a small business loan. As I mentioned earlier, this is where the Jekyll-and-Hyde personality of most banks kicks in. They love to have your money, or to make secured loans, but they're extremely conservative when it comes to providing seed money, or perhaps even operating capital, to fledgling businesses. Their attitude improves once a business has "become bankable," meaning it has managed one or two downturns or established a firm financial footing. Of course, that's when you'll have less need for their services. That's just part of the irony of banking: When you need a loan, they won't give you the time of day; but when you don't need the money, they'll be banging down your door offering loan deals.

It's easy to hold this reticence to lend seed money against banks. But I was once a banker and a venture capitalist, so I understand. Banks are businesses. They don't make money by providing financial backing to questionable business endeavors. What they will do is lend money to you rather than your fledgling business through a secured personal loan. That way, if you default on the loan, they can come after your home, your car, and your other assets to get their money back. When you look at the situation objectively, you really can't blame them.

(See also accountants, advertising, automated teller machines and cash cards, cash flow, checking accounts, credit cards, debit cards, financial planners, lawyers, location, mortgage loans, savings accounts, seed money, Web sites.)

BANKRUPTCY

I DON'T CARE how easy it sounds or how liberating it might seem, declaring bankruptcy is still the financial mark of Cain. So unless you want to spend the rest of your life with the word "deadbeat" stamped on the front of your financial profile, dig yourself out of the hole instead.

It's not that I'm unsympathetic. I began my personal consulting career offering advice on credit, and the first book I wrote almost two decades ago was on credit. As a result, I've probably seen and heard more tales of credit woes than anyone outside a collection agency. I myself fell into a deep financial pit in the 1970s when I came down with tuberculosis, lost my job, and had to survive on my disability insurance payments. But despite all I've heard and seen and been through, I'm still against personal bankruptcy.

In the short term, declaring bankruptcy may indeed be less painful than facing up to your problems, changing your lifestyle, and making personal deals with each of your creditors. The long-term pain and impact, however, will be far worse. Besides, this is one of those cases where some pain could be a good thing, since it delivers a worthwhile lesson.

Rather than bankruptcy, I encourage my clients to to seize control of their financial lives by proactively contacting their creditors as soon as they sense they're in trouble. I tell them to "push the up button" in their telephone conversations until they get to supervisors or managers with the power to make repayment plans. Throughout the process I advise stressing the desire to pay back the entire debt and the willingness to stick to repayment plans—as long as they're feasible. In most cases, creditors are willing to take a chance with you in order to get something, since the alternative, as you'll indicate on the telephone, is a declaration of bankruptcy, which is apt to result in their getting nothing.

Bankruptcy Basics

When you declare bankruptcy, you're petitioning the court for legal protection from your creditors. You're asking for a time-out of sorts to restructure your finances and come up with a plan to get out of debt. Bankruptcy will free you from most of your obligations—but not all of them, and not without serious consequences.

There are two primary types of personal bankruptcy: Chapter 7 and Chapter 13. A third, Chapter 11, is almost always used by businesses, although it sometimes is the best route for individuals with significant assets and the money to pay their legal bills.

Before you decide to file for bankruptcy, you should consult with a financial planner or credit counselor and your own lawyer. Try to get a recommendation for a reputable, experienced bankruptcy lawyer. Many bankruptcy lawyers are ready and waiting to take you by the hand and lead you through the bankruptcy process, whether it's the right path for you or not. It's not that they're unethical; they're simply fixated on their specialty. Just as a surgeon will almost always suggest surgery, a bankruptcy lawyer will almost always suggest bankruptcy. Instead, consult a skilled generalist lawyer who can help you look at your circumstances more objectively and, if need be, use a bankruptcy lawyer she recommends. One other warning: Don't use a lawyer who offers help in return for a percentage of your debt. You're already going to be in enough trouble. You don't need any more.

Going into bankruptcy involves more than filling out a set of forms. Be careful: Mistakes can haunt you for a long time, so avoid the bankruptcy mills that specialize in preparing forms cheaply and will not provide effective representation in court.

Chapter 7 Bankruptcy

Chapter 7 bankruptcy, or "straight bankruptcy," carries the most severe consequences. It provides the least amount of protection for your personal property, so you'll be expected to sell most of your nonexempt belongings to pay off your debts.

You can file for Chapter 7 protection of your own accord. You can also be forced into it by creditors. Once you've filed the proper papers an automatic stay protecting you against further harassment from creditors goes into effect. A trustee will be assigned to oversee the liquidation of your assets. Because your debts so far outweigh your assets, your creditors will often receive nothing, or at best only a portion of what they're owed. If no objection is made, the court will grant you a discharge of your debts that voids most judgments previously made against you. It is assumed that you've learned your lesson because you cannot file for bankruptcy again and get a discharge for six years. If you get into financial trouble again during that time, the consequences will be even more serious.

Chapter 7 will have an enormous impact on your life, but it won't leave you completely destitute. Exemptions vary from state to state. For instance, in Florida there is no limit on the value of the personal residence that is exempt, while in New York the limit is $10,000 in equity. There are also various exemptions for one motor vehicle, personal property such as clothing and appliances, jewelry, professional items such as tools or books, cash-value life insurance, and income from benefits like Social Security, veterans benefits, disability payments, unemployment, alimony, welfare, and pensions.* If you're married and filing jointly for bankruptcy, the exemption amounts may double. Your lawyer needs to check state laws because the specific amounts can vary dramatically.

What Chapter 7 won't do is let you off the hook for certain debts. These include a variety of taxes, including certain income taxes; unpaid withholding and Social Security taxes; financial liabilities incurred because of willful or reckless acts against another person or property; loans not listed in your bankruptcy petition; and student loans less than five years old. Bankruptcy will not free you from spousal maintenance or child support payments, nor will it provide pro-

---

*As of the writing of this book the U.S. Congress is considering major amendments to the bankruptcy law that could affect some of the facts I've written here. The legislation is being pushed by the credit card and banking industries, so not surprisingly, the changes appear to be focused on making it impossible to discharge credit card debt. There is still some uncertainty as to when, or even whether, this legislation will become the law.

tection for cosigners on your accounts. Your creditors can immediately demand that your cosigners repay any outstanding loans they agreed to guarantee.

Chapter 7 will also hold you responsible for debts you incur for luxury items purchased within a certain number of days of the filing date. This is to keep people from going on spending sprees with the knowledge that they're shortly going to be declaring bankruptcy. So if you think you can finance a trip to Europe with cash advances and then come home and file for Chapter 7 protection, forget it.

Chapter 13 Bankruptcy

Chapter 13 bankruptcy leaves your assets intact. It assumes that, given a little time, you can come up with a plan to restructure your finances and pay off a portion of your debts. In fact, the full legal term for Chapter 13 is "Adjustments of Debts of an Individual with Regular Income."

As with Chapter 7, Chapter 13 provides you with protection from creditors. It also protects cosigners of your loans, at least for a period of time. Your creditors can only go after them after the court-approved plan makes it clear that you won't be able to repay your creditors in full. Your cosigners will then be responsible for any amounts you were not able to pay.

Chapter 13 protection requires that you present the court with a monthly budget showing how much money you'll have left over after your minimal living expenses are covered. The court then approves or modifies your plan. Then you can begin to whittle away at your debts by payments to the trustee over three years, or in some cases not more than five years, repaying anywhere from some small percentage of the entire amount to almost the total debt. At the end of that period, the court will discharge you from all further indebtedness.

Life after Bankruptcy

Bankruptcy is a source of incredible emotional stress for individuals and families. Not only does it put severe limitations on your lifestyle, it destroys your credit rating. It will be years before you are free and clear of the black mark on your financial history. In some cases, you may never be free of it.

The best way to get back on track after a bankruptcy is to build a healthy credit history all over again. The first step is usually to obtain a secured credit card from a bank. Use it for small purchases and pay the bills in full as soon as they arrive. Over time, as you accumulate some savings, you can use them as collateral to take out a secured loan. Stick to the repayment schedule and pay off the loan on time.

Only by operating in this manner can you restore your credit rating. And it won't happen quickly. Most people take four or five years to restore themselves to full creditworthiness. And a bankruptcy won't disappear from your credit report for 10 years. (Check to make sure it does. It isn't always expunged automatically.)

If you can demonstrate that your personal bankruptcy was caused by the failure of your business, rather than your own financial irresponsibility, you'll find that the road back from

Ten Signs You're in Credit Trouble

Credit trouble doesn't occur overnight. It's usually the result of years of financial mismanagement. Here are some of the signs you may be headed for trouble:

1. You start to fall behind on your mortgage, rent, utility bills, and other regular monthly expenses.

2. You can only pay the minimum on your credit card bills.

3. You take cash advances from one credit card to pay off another card.

4. You take cash advances to pay for basic living expenses like groceries and rent.

5. You begin to play payment games: You send the telephone payment to the bank and the VISA payment to the telephone company to buy time. Or you "forget" to sign your checks.

6. You take out a debt consolidation loan and then begin to run up your credit card balances all over again.

7. This month's bills are already arriving before you've paid last month's bills.

8. You begin to take money out of savings accounts to meet your monthly payments.

9. You get turned down for credit.

10. You're being dunned.

bankruptcy is far smoother. Otherwise, it will be a long, painful process. But there is a silver lining: At least there are no more debtors' prisons.

(See also alimony, appliances, banking and bankers, child support, clothing, credit cards, credit report, debt consolidation loans, disability insurance, financial planners, jewelry, lawyers, mortgage loans, savings accounts, Social Security, withholding.)

BENEFITS

BENEFITS ARE NEVER AS GOOD as cash. Most employers offer benefits, not because they're benevolent souls but because, in the final analysis, it costs them less than the cash equivalent if they want to attract and retain quality workers. For example, despite all the justifiable gripes about the high cost of providing health insurance for employees, it still costs a company less to buy group health coverage than it would to provide every employee with enough in salary to buy their own individual coverage, thanks to economies of scale.

As a result, today employee benefit plans are the primary source of medical, dental, and disability insurance. They may also provide assistance for family problems and opportunities to save on taxes and invest for retirement. For the average working family, benefit plans have become a critical source of financial security. Without benefits many families simply couldn't afford to keep their heads above water.

The most common employee benefits are paid vacations and holidays, life insurance, medical insurance, paid sick leave, and dental insurance. Less common are employer contributions to retirement plans, disability insurance, and paid personal leave. Flex time and flex place options are rarer still. Upper-level personnel may have perquisites added to their benefits package, such as company cars, health club memberships, clothing allowances, expense accounts, or even deferred compensation packages. Paid maternity and paternity leave are still almost unheard of whatever your rank in the company.

Most savvy employers, knowing they need to offer benefits to attract and keep good people, but faced with increasing costs, are trying to scale back benefits rather than eliminate them. For instance, they're shifting from a traditional fee-for-service health plan to an HMO, increasing deductibles and copayments, or offering a menu rather than a set package—letting employees choose either medical, life, disability, or long-term care insurance coverage, for example. This has resulted in a confusing situation requiring employees to very carefully select benefits that best meet their needs, which will vary with their ages and the characteristics of their families.

Important Insurance Benefits

With the cost of health care at an all-time high, medical insurance is unquestionably the most critical employer-provided benefit to working Americans and their families. More than 80 percent of the people working for companies with more than 100 employees sign up for medical insurance. Most companies include employee assistance programs (EAPs) as part of their health coverage to provide treatment for substance abuse and personal problems. The availability of medical coverage is often the number one criteria for people who are looking for a job.

Life insurance can also be a valuable benefit. Most plans provide a minimal amount of coverage tied to an employee's annual salary. Employees then have the option of purchasing additional insurance themselves and having the premiums withheld from their paychecks. Because employees are taking advantage of group coverage, it's often an inexpensive way to obtain life insurance. It may also provide individuals who would have trouble buying a policy on their own a chance to get coverage, since the risk is now spread among the group.

Dental insurance is another valuable benefit to some families. Not all employers offer it, and those that do are usually larger companies. The coverage can include regular checkups and a portion of the cost of procedures such as fillings, root canals, and periodontal work. Some plans provide partial or full coverage for orthodontia, an important consideration for families with adolescents.

Disability insurance provides an income when you are unable to work due to illness or injury. Some companies will "self-insure" for disability, paying your salary for the first few months when you become disabled, after which your salary will be picked up by supplementary long-term disability coverage. Long-term in this case is a misnomer since it often extends for only three years, requiring you to take out supplemental coverage of your own. It's not unusual for an employer to pass some of the cost of disability insurance premiums on to their employees. But the cost is more affordable than buying it on your own.

Retirement Benefits

Employer-provided benefit plans can do more than protect you from illness and injury. An equally important function is to help you prepare for retirement. Fewer and fewer companies these days offer traditional defined-benefit pension plans, which provide employees with a fixed monthly check after retirement. Instead, they offer retirement savings plans that put more responsibility on the employee to put money aside and select investment options.

Some of the most popular retirement investment plans are 401(k)s—for employees of businesses—and 403(b)s—for employees of colleges, hospitals, school districts, and nonprofit groups. These plans are often called "defined-contribution plans" because the employee will contribute a certain amount to the plan each year. The great thing about these plans is that contributions are deducted directly from employees' paychecks and are not subject to taxes. Uncle Sam doesn't take his chunk until an employee begins to withdraw money upon retirement or at age 70½, whichever comes first. By then not only will the employee have the initial investment to draw upon but the gains that money has earned over time. And this income will now be taxed at what presumably will be a lower rate, assuming a lower income upon retirement.

Some lucky workers enjoy the benefits of employer contributions to their retirement accounts. Most are in the form of profit-sharing plans, which can be as much as 15 percent of an employee's annual salary (but no more than $30,000). Most plans allow the employee to make contributions as well. As with 401(k)s and 403(b)s, the money is not taxed until it's taken out after retirement. Employee stock ownership plans (ESOPs) are another way companies contribute to their employees' retirement packages.

Highly compensated executives, whose qualified (tax-free) retirement plan contributions have been severely limited by recent legislation, may be offered supplemental employee retirement plans (SERPs), which provide avenues for nonqualified retirement savings, usually through some form of deferred compensation.

If you have small children or care for elderly parents, you might find flexible spending account benefits useful. Money is withheld from your paycheck and then doled out to you as reimbursement for child-care or elder-care costs. Most plans also allow you to be reimbursed for health care costs that aren't covered by your medical insurance. As with 401(k) plans, the money withheld from your pay is not taxed, so these plans also reduce your tax burden. The few companies that offer these plans have limits on how much you can contribute to the accounts.

(See also clothing, disability insurance, employee stock ownership plans, employees, flex time and telecommunting, health club, health insurance, life insurance, long-term care insurance, negotiating, pension plans.)

BILL COLLECTORS

B ILL COLLECTION AGENCIES have earned their reputations. The abusive tactics—threats of arrest, profane language, public embarrassment, telephone calls at all hours of the day and night—used by many of the less sophisticated members of the industry have led to the business being almost universally reviled. These folks have had even greater opportunities to ply their craft in the last decade as credit card and other consumer debt have reached new heights. More people than ever are finding collection agencies knocking on their doors or calling them on the telephone.

You Do Have Protection

While I'm not suggesting you don't have a responsibility to pay your debts or that collection agencies don't serve a useful purpose—I use them myself to obtain payment on long-outstanding bills—I don't think anyone should have to put up with abuse and scare tactics. Congress feels the same way. The Fair Debt Collection Act of 1977 was passed to protect consumers from such behavior.

The act applies specifically to those businesses that are contracted to pursue collections on behalf of another party. It doesn't apply to department stores, banks, gasoline companies, or other creditors who may contact you directly. If, however, they contact you under the guise of another entity, they fall under the provisions of the act.

The act is designed to protect your privacy and save you from embarrassment. It limits the number of people a bill collector can contact about your debt, excluding friends, relatives, and your employer. It does allow them to contact your lawyer, its own lawyer, and consumer-reporting agencies. It can also contact other people if so authorized by the court or if it has the authority to enact a

What's the difference between a perquisite and a benefit? A perquisite has psychological or lifestyle impact but adds nothing tangible to your bottom line. A benefit has a definite financial impact but may do nothing for your ego. For instance, a corner office may be nice, but it doesn't add a penny to your pocket. A disability policy paid for by your employer may not be as impressive, but it has a far greater impact on your life. Trust me, whenever you're looking at a compensation package it's important to separate the perquisites from the benefits, negotiating for more of the latter, even if it comes at the expense of the former.

Tips for Dealing with Bill Collectors

Here are a few suggestions for dealing with bill collectors.

- Don't ignore them. If you're contacted, respond, even if it's to tell him to get lost. Otherwise, he'll think the debt is legitimate and keep hounding you.

- Keep records of all correspondence and conversations with the bill collector. Remember that the Fair Debt Collection Act only protects you if you put all your communications with a bill collector in writing. Be calm but firm. State your position and, if there's an error, make it clear you will not pay the debt. If the collector tries to harass you, point out that he's in violation of the Fair Debt Collection Act and that if he continues to bother you you'll contact authorities.

- Pay attention to your mail. If you manage to scare off the bill collector, you still may be sued. Make sure you answer the summons. Otherwise you may have a default judgment made against you and end up paying the same debt you previously fought.

- If you do settle, make sure your credit file appears positive. You don't want potentially negative terms liked "settled," or "written off," to appear in your report.

- The older the debt the less the creditor or bill collector will settle for. Accounts receivable can't be left on balance sheets forever. At some point they are "written off," which means they are claimed as a deduction on a tax return. Once that occurs, any subsequent repayment must be recorded as income. At that point creditors will usually settle for 30 to 50 percent.

judgment like a wage garnishment. Obviously, in the latter situation your employer would need to be contacted.

In contacting you, collectors can use the telephone, letters, or telegrams. They cannot use postcards, nor can there be anything on the letters or telegrams that indicates that the correspondence is in regard to a debt. For example, if the business name is A to Z Collection Agency, it cannot be printed on the envelope.

Bill collectors can also visit you personally, but only during convenient hours, usually considered to be 8 A.M. to 9 P.M. If they know you have a lawyer, they're required to contact her first. If the lawyer doesn't respond within 30 days, the bill collector can contact you directly.

When bill collectors contact you, they must identify themselves immediately and state the purpose of the call. If they threaten or imply any abusive action, such as having you arrested by the sheriff or going to your employer about your debt, they're breaking the law. The act prohibits coercion, threats of violence, or other criminal acts, and embarrassing you by contacting your friends and relatives or publishing your name in a list of debtors.

If You Dispute the Debt

If you dispute a debt, the Fair Debt Collection Act requires that you notify the bill collector in writing within 30 days. He then must verify the debt and the identity of the creditor. The act doesn't specify what constitutes verification. It could be a copy of any judgments that have been made against you. It could also be a copy of a contract or an invoice you've signed. If you are presented with documentation, you need to decide whether to continue to dispute it. It could be that the debt was already paid and the creditor is in error. It could be for merchandise you returned or a service that you felt was unsatisfactory and therefore refused to pay for. Or it could be a legitimate debt.

If it's legitimate, pay it. If you need time, propose a payment schedule. If it's not legitimate, respond again in writing to the bill collector, telling him why you dispute the debt and that you don't want to be bothered with the issue again. If you continue to receive calls, hang up on him and call your local better business bureau. If the creditor wants to continue to pursue the issue, you'll probably be sued. That's actually the best thing that could happen to you. It will settle the issue once and for all.

(See also credit cards, lawyers.)

BONDS

I DON'T CARE HOW GREAT the stock market is doing. Bonds should still be part of your investment portfolio.

There's no limit to how much money you can make when you invest in stocks. On the other hand, an investment in stocks can diminish in value as well. The return on a bond, however, is all but guaranteed.* When you buy a bond you're not buying ownership in a company and sinking or soaring with the company's performance or the market's perception of the company's performance. When you buy a bond, you're lending the issuer your money in return for a guaranteed rate of return over a predetermined period of time. Bonds are issued by the federal government, cities, counties, states, and corporations to raise money.

Not all bonds are equally secure. There are many different types of bonds, and they all carry some degree of risk. For example, if you were paying attention during the get-rich-quick 1980s, you'll remember the aptly named "junk bonds." Offering exceptionally high interest rates, junk

---

*The value of the bond itself, however, can go up or down depending on interest rates, affecting what you would yield if you sold the bond before maturity.

bonds were certainly high-reward. The only problem was, they were also (and still are) absurdly risky. When the junk bond market collapsed in the early 1990s, American investors, including many parts of the nation's savings and loan industry, lost billions of dollars when the issuers were unable to pay back their bond holders.

At the other end of the spectrum are bonds issued by the federal and state governments, counties, cities, and other municipalities. Backed by the financial resources of the issuing governmental bodies, they are almost risk-free. U.S. Treasury securities, in particular, are considered absolutely safe as they are backed by "the full faith and credit of the United States of America."

To help investors make informed decisions when purchasing bonds, rating services like Moody's and Standard and Poor's grade corporate and municipal bonds according to their risk. They don't bother to rate U.S. Treasury bonds because they're considered risk-free. These rating services carefully examine the financial health of the issuing corporation or municipality and then assign its bonds a grade based on the ability of the issuer to pay back the bond holders.

How Bonds Work

Bonds are most often sold in multiples of $1,000. The length of time between when a bond is issued and when it matures varies greatly. Some short-term bonds mature in a year or less. The term of intermediate bonds can be from 1 to 10 years. Long-term bonds usually mature in 30 or more years. One of the most popular bonds is the 30-year Treasury bond (often called the "long bond") issued by the U.S. Treasury.

Some bonds are sold at their face, or "par," value and pay investors interest over the life of the bond. Other bonds, such as U.S. savings bonds and zero-coupon bonds, are sold at a deep discount to their stated value. They pay nothing until they mature, at which time they return the full value to the investor.

Almost all corporate bonds and many municipal bonds are "callable." This means that if they choose, the issuers can buy back the bonds from investors before they mature. This process is called "redemption" and allows bond issuers to take advantage of falling interest rates. If rates begin to fall, the issuer can "call" its outstanding bonds, pay off the bond holders, and issue new bonds at a lower interest rate. Treasury bonds, Treasury bills, and agency bonds are not callable.

Buy for Need, Not for Growth

As I wrote earlier, the great feature of bonds is you know exactly how much money they're going to earn and when they're going to earn it. That's why they're the perfect investment vehicle for people who are going to need a certain amount of money at a fixed point in the future. If, let's say, you're saving for your child's education, you can plan ahead and know you'll have the proper amount of money available when you need it.

If you're looking for maximum investment growth, however, bonds are not the answer. Young people funding their retirement portfolios would be silly to invest in bonds. Their goal is a long way off, and they can weather the vagaries of the stock market. A 70-year-old, on the other hand, who probably doesn't have the time to ride out stock market variations, should move some of the money they've accumulated into bonds to reduce their risk.

Types of Bonds

There are many different types of bonds, each with different lengths of maturity, rates of return, and risk. Here are some of the most popular.

U.S. savings bonds. These are the bonds that were always so popular with Grandpa and Grandma for holiday and birthday gifts. The most common savings bond, the series EE bond, can be purchased in denominations of $50, $75, $200, $500, $1,000, $5,000, and $10,000. They're sold at a discount and then redeemed at maturity for their par value. When series EE bonds mature, they can be cashed in or converted to series HH bonds.

U.S. Treasury bills. Known as T-bills, these are the shortest-term of all U.S. Treasury securities. They are sold at a discounted rate and then pay their face value at maturity. T-bills require a minimum investment of $10,000 with additional purchase increments of $1,000, so they're usually not purchased by small investors.

U.S. Treasury notes and Treasury bonds. Treasury notes and Treasury bonds have longer terms to maturity than T-bills. Treasury notes have maturities of 1 to 10 years. Treasury bonds mature in 10 to 30 years. The 30-year Treasury bond is usually considered the benchmark against which all other bonds are measured.

Agency bonds. Federal agencies like the Federal Housing Administration (FHA) and the Federal Farm Credit Bank issue bonds to pay for things like mortgage loans and economic development projects. These bonds generally have higher yields than Treasury bonds and are almost as safe. Several agencies that were formerly administered by the federal government but are now public corporations also issue bonds. The best-known are the Federal National Mortgage Association (Fannie Mae), the Government National Mortgage Association (Ginnie Mae), and the Federal Home Loan Mortgage Corporation (Freddie Mac). Their bonds are backed by the pools of mortgages they issue.

Municipal bonds. Municipal bonds are issued at par values of $5,000 and up. Because these bonds are issued to pay for projects that benefit the public, the federal government exempts the interest they earn from federal taxes. They are also exempt from state taxes provided the investor is a resident of the same state in which they are issued.

Corporate bonds. Corporate bonds are available in short-term (1 to 5 years), intermediate-term (5 to 10 years), and long-term (10 to 20 years) issues and are sold in $1,000 increments. They are usually divided into four "sectors": public utilities, such as telephone companies and power companies; transportation companies, including airlines and railroads; industrial companies, including both retail and manufacturing companies; and financial institutions, such as banks and brokerage firms. Some corporate bonds allow for the investment to be converted into stock.

Zero-coupon bonds. I saved the best for last. Zero-coupon bonds pay the investor no interest while they're maturing. (The interest is paid to another investor who purchases the "coupons" off the bond entitling him or her to the interest payments, hence the name.) For this reason, they are sold at a deep discount to their par value. Zero-coupon bonds are, in my mind, the single best investment for parents saving for college. If you carefully time your zero-coupon bond purchases, you can end up owning a series of bonds that mature just as you need that exact amount of money to pay for tuition each year. No risk. Guaranteed return. Perfect timing. That's the beauty of a bond.

Smart Strategies for Buying Bonds

Buying bonds may not be as complex as buying equities, but there are still some secrets. Here are some savvy strategies.

- Buy only highly rated bonds. This virtually eliminates the possibility that issuers will default.

- Buy for the long haul. Invest in bonds with the expectation you'll keep them until they mature and for the regular income they provide.

- If you're buying bonds that are callable, make sure you know when they can be called and that the timing will not have an adverse affect on your investment goals.

- Buy the bonds of large corporations and municipalities. There is usually a good secondary market for these bonds, so if you do have to sell early, you can get a good price.

- Buy newly issued bonds. The sales commission is paid by the issuer. Buy intermediate-term bonds of 1- to 10-year maturities. They yield more than short-term bonds and are less volatile than long-term bonds. Create a diverse portfolio with different issues and with different maturity dates. This is called "laddering."

For a specialized approach consider the use of bond mutual funds. (See "Specialized Bond Funds," page 91.)

Specialized Bond Funds

These three categories of bonds can be diversified easily through the use of bond funds, and may play an important role in your portfolio.

Loan participation funds. These are funds that invest in senior floating-rate loans to the U.S. corporate market. These funds typically return above-money-market rates, with extremely low volatility of principal. Because the loans have rates that float with the market, these funds carry exceptionally low interest-rate risk. An interesting place for conservative money to be held.

Short or intermediate tax-free bond funds. Another worthwhile conservative money-parking place, these funds are winners for those in high tax brackets. Their net return will outshine the money market funds, with manageable underlying volatility (far less than the typical long-term bond fund).

Convertible bond funds. At the other end of the bond risk spectrum, these funds invest in bonds that can convert to the underlying common shares of the issuing corporation. These bonds still have guaranteed interest (although below the rates of nonconvertible bonds) and they participate in the good fortunes of the stock market. But remember, what goes up can also come down.

(See also gifts, laddering, mortgage loans, savings bonds, stocks, Treasury bills.)

BOOKKEEPERS AND BOOKKEEPING SOFTWARE

IF YOU'RE A BOOKKEEPER, find another job quick. If you employ a bookkeeper, give her a pink slip today. Technology has made bookkeeping easier to do yourself and more economical to farm out to others.

In some ways, it's a shame. For years bookkeepers have been the unsung heroes of American business. Laboring over their ledgers and worksheets, they've chronicled the financial fortunes of businesses ranging from mom-and-pop shops on city street corners to the nation's largest corporate manufacturers. Although their work was less than glamorous, it was certainly critical. A misplaced decimal or a simple mathematical error can cause disaster for any business. Good bookkeepers were worth their weight in gold.

But now they're an unnecessary business cost. Most of my small business clients have taken advantage of the many bookkeeping software programs on the market or have turned this task over to others. Some have their assistants enter the numbers in a software package. Others do the keyboarding themselves once a week. Still others, particularly those with payrolls, are outsourcing the work. The savings can be tremendous. One of my business associates, owner of a small consulting firm, parted ways with his full-time bookkeeper and hired an outside firm to handle his payroll, payables, and receivables. His accountant takes care of compliance and oversight, and he keeps all his financial records on his personal computer. It cut his annual business costs by nearly $40,000.

Delegate Responsibility to Your Accountant

The key to either outsourcing or automating your bookkeeping chores is to have your accountant do as much as possible. Let him work with the outsourcing firm to set up the logistics of passing your financial information back and forth. Have your accountant select the bookkeeping application that best suits your needs. Your accountant will still prepare periodic financial statements for you, but the bookkeeping software will allow you a quick look at the state of your business any time you wish. A good program will allow you to cut checks, print invoices, create profit-and-loss statements and balance sheets, track payables and receivables, and analyze your cash flow. It may even be able to organize all the information you need for your tax returns. Besides the general programs available, there are also some highly specific applications designed to fit the unique needs of individual businesses.

Every successful businessperson should know where he or she stands in relationship to his or her original business plan from one day to the next, so one of the most important functions of your bookkeeping system will be tracking expenses and revenues. It should be set up so you can see at any moment what your current costs are in every expense category. This allows you to track costs on a daily, weekly, monthly, and annual basis. If you see that costs in a particular area are out of line, you can make adjustments.

You can keep track of revenues in the same manner. By comparing current costs to current revenues, you'll know on a day-to-day basis how close you are to meeting your business goals for the year. If revenues are falling behind projections, you can take the appropriate action to cut costs.

How will you access this information if it's sitting in someone else's office? Again, technology comes to the rescue. Your outsourcing firm or accountant can send you daily reports via e-mail. If confidentiality is an issue, the firm can maintain a Web site on a secured server that its clients can enter using passwords. You might also be able to join an intranet—a secured network that the firm sets up for its clients. The protection of electronic data is a big business these days, so the security of your financial information will not be an issue.

There's one other advantage to using technology to take care of your bookkeeping needs. Thanks to the Internet, geographic proximity is no longer an issue in sharing information, so your outsourcing firm can be across town or across the country. If you find a firm that's perfect for your type of operation, or that offers a large cost savings but happens to be 1,000 miles away, it's not a problem. In the digital world, the firm might as well be in the next office.

(See also accountants, cash flow, e-mail, payables, receivables, Web sites.)

BOSSES

THE IDEAL BOSS is communicative and nurturing. He'll treat you with respect, acknowledge your professional expertise, and help you reach your goals. He'll also know as much about your job as you do. Unfortunately, this ideal boss is as much a fantasy as the Easter Bunny. Your boss will be all too real, and that means all too human. Knowing how to handle different kinds of bosses will be critical to your climb up the ladder.

Working for a New Supervisor

New supervisors can be the most unnerving. You have no idea what kind of person you're getting and it may take you quite some time to figure him out.

The best approach to the new-boss problem is to learn as much about him beforehand as you can. This will require a bit of sleuthing. If you're being hired for a new position, you'll get some exposure to the boss during the interview process. This will give you an opportunity to ask questions about his management style. You'll also be able to get a sense of whether the two of you can establish a rapport.

You might also ask if you can meet with some of the people you'll be working with. While I'm not suggesting they'll be completely frank with you, their reactions to your questions will provide you with some good information. It will be most telling, however, if your prospective boss refuses your request to meet people.

When the new boss is the person being hired, you'll have less chance to get information about him, unless, of course, he's being brought in from elsewhere in your company. In that case a little networking will help you track down information.

When the new boss is in place, it's critical that the two of you understand what each expects from the other. Communication is the key. Don't let questions go unasked, and make sure you understand the answers. You should also meet periodically to evaluate how things are going and to head off any problems. And work as hard as you can from the first minute he arrives. First impressions mean everything.

That's why I suggest you manipulate your first meeting. Make sure you arrive at the office before your new supervisor's secretary or assistant. Casually stop by the new boss's office to say hello and introduce yourself. Project warmth and sincerity by smiling, making eye contact, and offering a firm handshake. If he offers you a chance to say more than just a quick hello, seize the opportunity to hint at some ideas you have that you'd love to speak about when he has the chance. That should be sufficient to create a good first impression.

Working for a Micromanager

A micromanager presents a unique set of problems. The biggest is just getting your work done. If you have someone constantly watching over your shoulder or second-guessing your every move, productivity can grind to a halt. In fact, he'll create unnecessary work by giving you an

assignment and then staying so involved he ends up doing it himself.

There's not much you can do to change a micromanager's
behavior. Instead, the best tactic is the preemptive strike: Anticipate what he's going to do or say and beat him to the punch. Realize, too, that conflicts are inevitable. This means you must pick
your battles. Decide which issues are worth fighting for and let the
others slide.

Working for a Perfectionist

A perfectionist can also create needless work by never letting go of
a project. He's the one who will write six drafts of a letter or find it
impossible to take anyone's suggestions and will insist on doing
things his own way. His perfectionism may ensure a great final
product—but it will definitely come at your expense.

The best tactic with a perfectionist is to get as much information out of him as possible before beginning a task. That lessens the
likelihood that he'll make changes after the fact. It will also makes
him more confident that he's going to get what he wants. You can
also recognize his habits and adjust your behavior accordingly. For
example, if you know he's going to reject your first three or four
ideas on something, save your best ideas for last.

Working for an Absentee Superior

Having a supervisor who's totally incommunicado can be worse
than having one who constantly hangs over your shoulder. The
problem is, you never know what's expected of you. It's impossible to get critical information or approvals needed for projects.
You become paralyzed and unable to work due to a lack of
input.

Rather than waiting to be told, you need to take the initiative
and be aggressive in demanding answers from your boss. Schedule
regular meetings with him and arrive with a complete agenda. If
you're told, "I'll have to get back to you on that" when you ask certain questions, don't leave it at that. Ask for another meeting so you
can go over his response.

When you have a boss who's out in left field it's important to
establish a paper trail. If a problem arises because of his inability to
communicate with you, you need to have a record of your attempts

to get responses from him. Keep copies of memos and e-mails and a log of telephone calls. You don't want to take a fall because of his inaction.

(See also e-mail, networking.)

BRIDGE LOANS

THE UNIVERSAL FEAR of every client of mine who is selling one home and buying another is that the timing of the two events won't work out. Their nightmare is that they'll be forced to close on their new home without having the money from the sale of their prior home. I ease their anxiety by explaining that there is a solution.

If you run into this problem you can obtain what's known as a bridge loan to allow you to close on your new house while you're waiting to sell your old one. Bridge loans are issued by the same institution providing you with your new mortgage. The interest rate is anywhere from the prime rate to the prime rate plus 2 percent. Typically, the amount of the bridge loan will be sufficient to pay off your old mortgage and cover the down payment on the new home. The bridge loan will also include points, origination fees, and the first six months' interest. The lender uses your old home as collateral to secure the bridge loan.

Once you've closed on the new home, the clock starts ticking. Bridge loans are generally for six months or a year. If your old home still hasn't sold after six months, you'll begin to make interest payments on the bridge loan. (Remember, you paid the first six months' interest up front.) If you do sell your old home within the first six months, the prorated interest payments will be credited to the mortgage payments on your new home.

The Disadvantages of Bridge Loans

The biggest problem with bridge loans is their cost. In a sense, you're taking out another mortgage, albeit a very short-term one, to pay off your old house. Instead of facing one set of closing costs, you now need to pay twice—once on the bridge loan and again on your new mortgage.

As an example, let's say you take out a $90,000 bridge loan. Of that, $70,000 is used to pay off the mortgage on your old home and $4,000 is used to cover the bridge loan's origination fees and closing costs. The remaining $16,000 is put toward your new home. You've also taken out a $90,000 mortgage on your new home, with approximately the same amount of origination fees and closing costs. So the entire transaction is going to cost you around $8,000 in closing costs plus another $3,500 or so in prepaid interest on the bridge loan. If the old house doesn't sell in six months, you pay even more in interest.

Once you've closed you still need to worry about selling your old home. If you haven't sold it within six months of closing on your new one, you'll start making interest payments on the bridge loan in addition to the payments on the mortgage for the new home. That can put a lot of people on the edge of trouble. Those who don't plan for this worst-case scenario can suddenly find themselves unable to meet the payments. Then the situation gets even worse. If things get bad enough, the lender could foreclose on your old house.

You also run the risk that the person buying your new house will fail to get financing or the deal will fall through for some other reason. The bank might give you an extension on the bridge loan, but they'll only stretch it so far. If the loan comes due and you haven't sold the old home, you face foreclosure once again.

Alternatives to Bridge Loans

Because of the costs, I encourage my clients to investigate alternatives to bridge loans, such as borrowing against a 401(k) plan or against the securities in their portfolio. Some lenders also offer hybrid mortgage products that are similar to bridge loans. While they're not the perfect solutions, they do reduce your risks and your costs.

Of course, the best plan of all is to not purchase a new home until your old home has a buyer who has secured financing and established a date for closing. I realize it's not always that easy. People get transferred and need to move quickly. Or you may find your dream property and need to secure it before someone else beats you to it. Just remember: a bridge loan is a solution, albeit an expensive one. If you use it, make sure all the costs and the risks involved are worth it.

(See also closings, down payment, mortgage loans.)

BUDGETING

BUDGETING IS LIKE BROCCOLI. Everyone knows it's good for you, yet few people go to the trouble of making it part of their lives. That's too bad, for just as those who eat lots of broccoli are apt to be rewarded with a long and healthy life, so those who do lots of budgeting are likely to have a successful and rich financial life.

Budgeting is the best way to be able to meet your financial goals. It gives you control over your spending and saving. And since it's much harder to control the other side of the personal finance equation—income—it's the best way to take charge of your financial life.

Analyzing Your Spending

Budgeting begins with analyzing your spending habits. You may think you have a pretty good handle on where your money goes, but years of advising clients has taught me most people don't have a clue. I'm often astonished at people's lack of control over their spending. Young or old, single or married, working class or wealthy, most have no idea what's happening to their money.

The first step in budgeting, therefore, is to become aware of where your hard-earned dollars are going. The chart on page 98, "Analyzing Your Expenses," will help you track them down. It includes categories for the expenses most people have. If you have others, add them. After you've filled in all the appropriate amounts, total them up. Subtract that total from your monthly available income and put the result on the labeled "discrepancy." That number represents money whose final resting place is a complete mystery. Determine what percentage of your monthly income that figure represents.

I've had clients who haven't been able to account for 20 percent or more of their spending. Your goal is to get that discrepancy as close to zero as you can. You can do this by being as thorough as possible in keeping track of every cost. Keep a small pad in your pocket and write down all your expenses. Record them in a ledger in the evening. At the end of the month transfer them to the chart.

Most often, the unaccounted-for expenses are small cash expenditures, which add up to quite a bit of money in the aggregate. These expenses often include things like the cup of coffee you buy on the way to work in the morning; the beer you have after work with your coworkers; the magazine you pick up while browsing at the mall. By keeping track of these small out-of-pocket costs you'll soon see patterns.

Record every penny you spend for three or four months. Not only will you develop the habit of keeping track of expenses, you'll also become more aware of your spending tendencies. You'll see that you're spending, for example, more than $50 a month buying coffee at cafes and delis. At that point you'll be ready for the next step.

Controlling Your Spending and Saving

Once you've analyzed your spending habits, you'll be ready to establish a budget that details how much you'll spend and save each month. You can use the same chart you've been faithfully filling in for the past several months, only now you'll fill in the numbers at the *beginning* of each month. You'll have learned enough about your spending to accurately predict where your money should go and can begin planning your spending and saving rather than tracking it.

Here are a few tips.

1. *Be consistent in your budgeting effort.* One month on and three months off will get you nowhere.

2. *Keep records.* Continue to keep detailed, accurate records of what you spend money on and regularly compare the totals to what you've budgeted for the month.

3. *Eliminate impulse purchases.* Make shopping a planned event that fits within your budget. Leave the house knowing how much you can spend on clothes or books or whatever else you may have in your sights that day.

4. *Leave your ATM card at home.* Take out the cash you need for the week and use that for your expenses. If you run out of cash write yourself a check and cash it at the bank. And

next week, spend less. If you end the week with a surplus, bank your savings. If that happens regularly, start withdrawing less cash.

5. *Leave your credit cards at home.* It's okay to keep a pay-as-you-go charge card in your wallet for emergencies, but leave the rest of the plastic in your drawer. Paying cash for items makes the cost more tangible—even painful. That's okay.

6. *Write checks for your larger purchases.* The added time involved in writing a check, as opposed to using a credit card, provides a moment to think about whether you're buying something you need or just want.

7. *Be disciplined.* If you've spent the month's entertainment budget and friends ask you to dinner and a movie, ask them if they can wait a week or two. Or rather than going out, invite them to your house for dinner and a video. It will help you stay on your budget and still allow you to enjoy your friends' company.

8. *Be flexible.* If you find you need to spend more than you planned in one category, you can accommodate those expenses by cutting back in another.

9. *Give something up.* If you've spent the monthly entertainment budget but really crave that night out with your friends, decide what you can do without until next month. Some things can wait, after all. Just make sure you're spending money that was to be used for another discretionary purchase like a new sports coat, and not money that was designated for the utility bill.

Analyzing Your Expenses

Daily Living Expenses

1. Clothing   _____

2. Child Care   _____

3. Education   _____

4. Cleaning   _____

5. Cosmetics and toiletries   _____

Shelter Expenses

6. Mortgage/rent   _____

7. Homeowner's insurance   _____

8. Utilities   _____

9. Telephone   _____

10. Home furnishings   _____

11. Home improvements/repairs   _____

Medical Expenses

12. Doctor/hospital fees   _____

13. Nonprescription drugs   _____

14. Health insurance   _____

15. Prescriptions   _____

Transportation Expenses

16. Auto fuel   _____

17. Auto insurance   _____

18. Auto payments   _____

19. Auto repairs   _____

20. Parking   _____

21. Tolls   _____

22. Taxi fares   _____

23. Train/bus/air fares   _____

Entertainment Expenses

24. Books and music   _____

25. Cable television   _____

26. Video rentals   _____

27. Dining out   _____

28. Dues/memberships   _____

29. Movies/plays/concerts   _____

30. Subscriptions   _____

31. Take-out meals   _____

32. Vacations   _____

Luxury Expenses

33. Charitable Contributions   _____

34. Jewelry   _____

35. Gifts   _____

Insurance, Taxes, Etc.

36. Disability insurance   _____

37. Life insurance   _____

38. Property taxes   _____

39. Professional services   _____

40. Postage   _____

41. Banking fees   _____

42. Credit card interest   _____

43. Loan payments   _____

44. Savings   _____

45. Other expenses   _____

Totals

Total monthly expenses accounted for   _____

Discrepancy (monthly income minus
monthly expenses accounted for)   _____

Percentage of income unaccounted
for (discrepancy divided by monthly
income)   _____

10. *Maintain your savings.* Never cut back on your savings budget to make room for something else. Never.

It may take a few months to develop the discipline you'll need to stay within your budget. But once you do, you'll find it gives you a sense of accomplishment and security. Budgeting can be palatable.

_____

(See also ATMs and cash cards, credit cards.)

BUSINESS CARDS

Put a pack of entrepreneurs or marketing people together in a room for the first time and before the Palm Pilots are put away they'll immediately start handing each other their business cards. Those tiny bits of paper are a time-honored tradition of the business world, particularly among those who need to focus on promotion and publicity. Over the years I've received and handed out thousands.

The fact that they're still so popular proves their effectiveness. Although so much else in business has changed over the years, a business card is still the most effective way to begin a relationship with a new client or contact.

The basic function of a business card is to convey information about yourself: your name, title, company name, address, telephone and fax numbers, e-mail address, and so on. (If you have a business that exists only on the Web, make sure the URL is displayed prominently on your business card.) But your card will also have a much more subtle function. Its design, the quality of the paper, and the fonts you choose will say a great deal about your character and that of your business.

It's Not Just What You Say but How You Say It

Because they're such important business tools, the creation of your business cards should be given a great deal of thought. Rule number one: don't use your personal computer and office printer to create them. No matter how sophisticated your equipment, the cards will just look cheap and unprofessional. And if your cards look amateurish, so will you. This is not the image you want to present to your clients.

Your business card should be part of an overall paper package created by a professional graphic designer or an experienced print shop. In addition to your cards, the package should include letterhead, envelopes of various sizes, memo pads, invoices, and any other printed materials you use on a regular basis. They should share the same typeface, logo, and other identifiers. Their design should be creative but tasteful.

I always advise my clients to carry several different business cards. Why? Many of them are entrepreneurs who operate more than one business, and they need a separate card for each one.

Others are employed full-time by companies but also offer consulting and other professional services on the side. They obviously need a "company" card that includes all the information one would expect: name, title, company name, telephone numbers, etc. Their second card, however, just includes their name and contact information and can be handed out to clients who hire them for their freelance services. Even though these clients know they have another job, the card conveys the fact that they're equally serious about their freelance activities.

Speaking of being taken seriously, make sure that if you are doing business in a foreign country you have business cards in that nation's language. One solution is to have two-sided, bilingual cards, one side in English and the other side in the foreign language.

Alternatives to Traditional Cards

I have clients who are fond of handing out preprinted Rolodex cards as business cards. Although they're not for me, I will admit there's an admirable practicality to this strategy. Business cards are easily lost, but a Rolodex card can be taken back to the office by your clients and immediately filed away. The downside is that not everyone uses a Rolodex these days, and those who do don't all use the same size card.

Another alternative to the traditional business card is to hand out 3- by 5-inch index cards with your contact information printed at the top. The extra space on an index card allows you to include a personal message to the recipient. Writing something like "I'm looking forward to speaking with you again about your company's Internet marketing program" can dramatically increase the effectiveness of handing out your card. It also ensures that the recipient will remember who you are and what you spoke with him or her about. Finally, index cards also provide you with handy note pages for jotting down important information, and simple cards for sending messages through the mail.

One last piece of advice. Over the years, I've counseled hundreds of enthusiastic would-be entrepreneurs who had great ambitions but half-baked business plans. To a person, they all had business cards. Just remember that having a business card does not make you a successful businessperson. If you're just starting out, build your business plan first. *Then* print cards that reflects the quality of the business you've created.

(See also business plans, e-mail, equipment.)

BUSINESS INSURANCE

Yawn . . . .zzzzzz. I know. You're thinking this is probably going to be the most boring section you could imagine reading. Well, you're partly right. It's not going to leave you out of breath. However, if you're in business and you don't read it, you may end up out of business.

Business is fraught with risk. It's a simple, unavoidable fact. Fierce competitors, unpredictable markets, dishonest vendors, unexpected economic changes, and fickle consumer behavior are just a few of the factors that can lead to financial ruin. Even Mother Nature can conspire against you.

This is why insurance is so important to businesses of all sizes. Granted, it's quite expensive. But it also buys peace of mind and the ability to stay on your feet when the unexpected happens. Anyone who goes into business without the proper coverage is inviting disaster.

Still, your goal should be to spend as little on it as possible. Some large corporations actually purchase little or no insurance. Because their premiums would be higher than the damages they're likely to incur in a year, they choose to self-insure: they assume the responsibility for all damages and liabilities themselves and pay any claims out of their earnings. Large universities are also frequently self-insured.

Self-insurance is not an option for most small businesses, however. A fire, water damage from a flood, a product recall, or a lawsuit can put you out of business overnight. But you can minimize your insurance costs by selecting the highest deductibles you can afford. A deductible is the amount of an insurance claim that you agree to pay yourself. For example, if you had a property insurance policy with a $5,000 deductible, you would pay the first $5,000 of the cost of any damages. Your insurance company would pay the balance. The higher your deductible, the lower your premiums. By taking out as large a deductible as you can, you are in effect self-insuring to the fullest extent possible.

The types of business insurance and amount of coverage you require will, obviously, be determined by the nature of your product or service. For a specific analysis of your risk exposure and coverage needs you should speak with an insurance broker experienced in setting up policies for businesses similar to your own. Don't simply go to the same broker who sold you a life or homeowner's policy. Instead, ask your trade or professional association for recommendations, interview each candidate, check references, and compare price quotes and coverages. All that being said, there are some general coverage guidelines you should keep in mind.

General Guidelines

Start by protecting your assets. All businesses need property insurance coverage that protects equipment, inventory, real estate, and other property against fire, water damage from a flood, theft, and other catastrophes. You'll also need business auto insurance if you or any employees use company-owned cars.

Another necessity is business interruption insurance coverage. If your business is temporarily interrupted by a natural disaster, loss of power, or some other problem, this will cover the loss of income suffered by you and your employees, and will stay in effect until your business is able to start up again. It will also cover ongoing expenses such as rent and mortgage interest and other expenses you may incur in getting your business back on its feet.

Next is general liability insurance coverage. We live in an increasingly litigious society, so you'll need a policy to protect you and your business against lawsuits stemming from your

A Brief History of Business Insurance

As far back as 900 B.C., traders on the island of Rhodes in the Aegean Sea were insuring themselves against maritime disasters by joining together to share the risks of their profitable yet dangerous enterprise.

By the Middle Ages, Italy was the hub of European trade, and Italian shippers dominated the seas. Fragmentary historical records indicate that early forms of commercial insurance were developed in Florence and Venice as far back as the early thirteenth century. The practice later expanded to London, Antwerp, Amsterdam, and eventually the United States.

Between 1850 and 1900, industrialization resulted in the development of accident and health insurance, boiler insurance, and fidelity and surety bonds.

In 1910, the first workers' compensation law was enacted to protect the well-being of injured workers, and many companies began offering the new form of insurance. In 1911, another new idea—group insurance—was developed to provide blanket coverage for the entire workforce of a company.

New industries demanded new types of insurance. In California, Hollywood's film industry prospered and movie studios began insuring their stars and their sets during film production. Today, entertainment insurance is a critical product to producers who routinely invest tens of millions of dollars in search of the next blockbuster.

business practices. You should always have an errors and omissions or professional liability insurance policy (formerly called malpractice insurance). Although doctors and lawyers usually come to mind when malpractice is mentioned, they aren't the only people who need liability coverage. It's also critical for architects, veterinarians, engineers, nurses, accountants, and other professionals. The personal liability coverage provided by your homeowner's, auto, and any umbrella liability coverage you have as an individual will not cover your business risks. So be sure to address your business liability needs as a separate item.

A closely held small business can be devastated by the illness or death of its owner, so adequate disability insurance and life insurance is a must. In fact, since the likelihood of a short-term disability is much higher than an unexpected death, disability insurance is especially critical. Both coverages will ensure that the business doesn't go under because of the absence of its owner.

Of course, the owner of a business isn't its only critical employee. The health of many companies hinges on a few individuals with critical product or market knowledge. To protect themselves against the loss of such a person, these businesses can purchase key-person insurance. This is actually a life insurance policy, with the company named as beneficiary. The company owns the policy and pays the premiums. The benefits can be used to recruit and train a person to serve as the key person's replacement and recoup profits lost because of the person's death. There are also policies that will provide a benefit if a key person retires.

Of course, there are statutory requirements in all states with respect to workers' compensation and short-term disability policies. Some states require that employers provide both types for all employees, while others mandate just workers' compensation. Check with your broker to make sure you are in compliance.

More and more, employers are also taking out employment practice liability insurance, which provides protection against damages resulting from wrongful-termination suits, and cases of sexual harassment and age discrimination. Additionally, you may want to investigate directors and officers liability insurance, to insure your officers and board against personal liability for their actions taken on behalf of your company. Similarly, you will want to make sure that such a policy is in place for any position of this sort that you may hold, including serving on the board of a nonprofit organization.

You can also buy credit insurance to protect you against the inability of your customers to pay their bills. Businesses fail every day in the United States. If one of them owes you money, you'll likely find yourself lined up with dozens of other creditors hoping to get a few cents on the dollar. A credit insurance policy will pay you the full amount.

If you have a business that you're considering taking global, you should investigate export credit insurance. In addition to covering policyholders for their customers' insolvency, this increasingly popular coverage also covers losses caused by default as well as those caused by political events. It's not without problems, however. One of the burdens on the policyholder is making sure the debt is a legal and enforceable obligation of the buyer in the buyer's country.

If you are considering opening an office or plant overseas, you will also want to purchase foreign property and liability insurance.

An even more specialized product—political-risk insurance—is available for companies doing business in emerging nations whose governments may be somewhat shaky. Coverage is usually for overseas contracts or investments and provides protection against losses caused by the actions or inactions of a foreign government that either prevent or interfere with the performance of a contract or prevent the operations of a company's overseas interests or assets.

Survivorship Insurance

If you're the owner of a closely held business that won't automatically pass to a spouse if you die, you may want to consider survivorship insurance. The purpose of this coverage is to pay the estate tax on a business being passed to your heirs. Since it is set up outside the estate itself in an irrevocable life insurance trust, it isn't part of the taxable base of the estate and can be used to pay the tax on the portion of the estate that is taxable.

Rather than obtaining separate policies covering each of these risks, most businesses should aim to buy a combination package that comprises multiple coverages in one policy. In my experience, this not only cuts the overall cost but also makes it easier and quicker to have claims approved.

(See also business interruption insurance, disability insurance, health insurance, liability insurance, life insurance.)

BUSINESS INTERRUPTION INSURANCE

"SHIT HAPPENS." That's what the rather crude bumper sticker popular a few years ago said. Vulgar it may have been, but it is also true. And when something happens, it can wreak havoc with your business. Maybe the roof falls in. Or there's a flood or a fire. Or the city decides to close your street for two months to install new water mains, keeping clients and customers away. The list of potential catastrophes is endless. The bottom line is that your business is interrupted, and that means your income grinds to a halt.

This is why the insurance industry came up with business interruption insurance. It covers what insurance professionals call "consequential loss" and responds when your business is in peril due to an unforeseen and uncontrollable event. Business interruption policies cover the loss of income—both yours and that of your key employees—resulting from the interruption, and it can continue to pay benefits until your business is able to start up again. The policies typically cover ongoing expenses such as rent and mortgage interest. They may also cover expenses you may incur in getting your business back on its feet.

Covering a Variety of Potential Interruptions

One of the nice things about business interruption insurance is its versatility. It can be tailored to address the specific risks faced by your business. Since there are a wide variety of events that can interrupt a business, there are a number of specialized business interruption coverages.

For example, if you're a manufacturer and you have to shut down because one of your suppliers is having a problem, you can be covered by a contingent business interruption policy. If your power goes out and you have to rent generators to stay in operation, extra-expense insurance will cover the cost. If your business has to move to a new location, relocate employees, or install new telephones and computer equipment because of the interruption, those costs can be covered as well.

Customized policies are common for large corporations whose individual needs can be quite different from one another. Depending on the nature of their business, they might be interested in protection against events like a product recall, a product-tampering incident, or even the kidnapping of an executive. To obtain the required coverage, they negotiate what are essentially "scripted" policies; their insurance company's representative starts with a blank sheet of paper and crafts the terms, conditions, and exclusions that fit the expressed needs of the company. There are almost no risks that can't be covered with the proper premiums and deductibles.

But it's not just corporate behemoths that need business interruption insurance. I have clients who own a men's clothing store in Manhattan. A few years ago the restaurant next door to their business had a serious fire. Although my clients' store suffered no fire damage, the business had to be closed for almost three weeks to repair smoke and water damage. Not only was the building affected, their entire inventory had to be replaced. While other insurance policies covered the damage to the premises and the replacement of the inventory, their business interruption insurance reimbursed them for the considerable income they lost while they were unable to open their doors. They would have been in real trouble without it.

Admittedly, business interruption insurance can be expensive. Premiums will vary with the size of your business, the nature of the risks it faces, and the kinds of specialized coverages you require. But don't let the expense deter you from buying coverage. Most businesses sail along without debilitating catastrophes. But when disaster strikes, as it often does, you need to be prepared. Just remember that bumper sticker.

(See also business insurance, clothing, employees, equipment, inventory, mortgage loans.)

BUSINESS MEETINGS

E-MAIL, NO MATTER HOW WELL-COMPOSED, will never convince a balky banker to give you a loan. A telephone dialogue, no matter how tightly scripted, may never get an angry client to hire you back. There are some things that will always require personal meetings. But, because of the Internet and e-mail and cellular telephones and all the other marvelous communications technologies we now have at our disposal, I'm afraid we're losing our ability to communicate face-to-face.

Now, don't get me wrong. I certainly understand the cost-cutting benefits information technology provides. There are entries throughout this book that encourage dramatic technological measures to improve your lifestyle and bottom line. I fully realize technology lets one person do the work of many, thus reducing the cost of doing the work. For example, the telephone bills and mailing costs my coauthor and I incur being located 300 miles apart have shrunk enormously since we started using e-mail and fax machines. More than one of my clients have been able to cut their payrolls thanks to information technology.

Telephone Calls and E-mail Aren't As Effective
But despite all these positives, there's no replacement for dealing with people face-to-face. No matter what the technophiles say, in my opinion, speaker telephones and messages on computer

monitors just aren't as effective in communicating as good old-fashioned talking, listening, and observing body language. Even though it's time-consuming, there are times when I insist on scheduling a meeting with my clients rather than conducting business in a conference call.

Let's look at the downsides of e-mail and the like. First of all, effective communication depends on subtleties that electronic communication just can't provide. Our expressions, our tone of voice, and our body language are as important in communicating our feelings as the words we speak. Can you accomplish these subtleties with e-mail? Some people think so. They use "emoticons," those little facial expressions generated with keyboard characters, to express their feelings. I think they are terribly inappropriate for business communication. When a business associate sends me one of those sideways smiley faces in an e-mail, my first thought is he or she is immature. It's like receiving a business letter in which the "i" in a signature is dotted with a smiley face or a heart.

The telephone is somewhat better, and God knows I spend a great deal of time on it, but it's still no replacement for face-to-face. Granted, you can pass on emotions more effectively by using the tone of your voice than you can with words typed on a screen, and if you have a long-standing relationship with an individual, you can sense subtle changes over the telephone. But for formal business dialogues with new contacts you will still miss quite a bit relying on telephone conversations.

This is why I'm still a fan of personal meetings. I think people who don't take every advantage to conduct business face-to-face are doing themselves a disservice. You just can't connect with people as effectively any other way. You certainly can't sell your ideas, products, or services as well through e-mail or over the telephone as you can in person. See people face-to-face and you'll be more effective at getting them to see things your way.

Location and Timing Strategies

Face-to-face encounters also offer the opportunity for subtle strategies. For example, the location of a meeting can have an effect on someone's behavior. Most of us probably feel more comfortable meeting a business associate in our own office. To use a sports analogy, it gives us the home-field advantage.

But in fact, it can be more advantageous to meet on the other person's turf. First, it shows them respect. Second, it relaxes them and allows them to feel comfortable, and someone who's relaxed and comfortable is more likely to make decisions. Third, it allows you to do a little surveillance and gain information about the person and their business. And fourth, it allows you to control the speed and duration of the meeting. For example, you can begin the meeting by saying you have to leave by two o'clock to get to another appointment. Or you can arrange to have someone from your office call you at a predetermined time. If the meeting isn't going well, this will give you the opportunity to cut the meeting off by claiming an unexpected emergency needs your attention.

The time of a meeting is also important. I try to have all my meetings first thing in the morning. People are alert and there are usually fewer interruptions. I also try to avoid meetings on Mondays and Fridays. I don't want to deal with someone who's recovering from a big weekend or distracted by the anticipation of one.

When you schedule a meeting, make sure everyone attending knows the purpose of the meeting. There's nothing more frustrating than sitting at a table with a bunch of people who are operating on different wavelengths. One way to accomplish this is to draft an agenda that gets to everyone well in advance. That's a perfect use for e-mail, by the way. Make sure it spells out a clear-cut, achievable goal. That way everyone in the room will know why they're there. Even after working together for more than a decade, my coauthor, agent, and I draw up simple agendas for all of our meetings and even for most of our conference calls.

Finally, give some thought to the garb you'll wear to a meeting. Some people (myself included) believe attire is an indication of the seriousness and importance attached to the meeting. Granted, not everyone feels this way. But why take a chance. You want the others at the meeting to be concentrating on and remembering your ideas, not your khakis.

(See also cellular telephones, conference calls, e-mail, location.)

BUSINESS PLANS

IF YOU DON'T HAVE a written plan for your new business it will fail. No caveats. I don't care whether you're starting a one-woman, home-based consulting practice, or an international Web-based retail operation; without a plan you're sunk.

I've been a lawyer, a banker, a venture capitalist, and a financial adviser for almost 50 years. You'd think by now I'd have lost my capacity to be surprised. But I'm still shocked by the number of budding entrepreneurs who come to me thinking they're ready to leap into business without a business plan. They can discuss at great length and in great detail the product or service they've dreamed up. But when I ask to see their business plan the conversation usually grinds to a halt.

A Recipe for Success—or Failure

A business plan is the critical structure that underlies any successful business. It describes, in advance, every step you will take in getting your business up and running. It spells out what it will take for your business to succeed, and accurately predicts its failure.

Most people mistakenly believe the sole function of a business plan is to help obtain financing. Certainly that's part of its function. You've probably guessed that those eager entrepreneurs who came to me for venture capital with little more than an idea were politely turned down. They were, however, encouraged to create a business plan and to get back to me when they had one. Most did, and some even got the money they were looking for.

But a business plan's value as an investment hook is actually secondary. More important than what a business plan does for others is what it does for the entrepreneur.

Creating a business plan forces you to logically think through every step of the process. It includes information on your product or service, the demographic and market conditions that demonstrate a need for the product or service, and financial planning and marketing strategies. It also establishes the short- and long-term goals your business will need to reach in order to grow and make money.

A business plan can also predict failure and prevent you from throwing good money after back or taking on ill-advised projects. Once your startup costs, operating costs, and revenue projections are calculated, you may discover there's no way your idea will ever fly. That knowledge will save you a lot of time, money, and mental anguish. Your business plan can also serve as a thermometer with which to gauge the ongoing health of your business. If, for example, your revenues aren't living up to your projections, you have conclusive evidence your business simply won't make it.

The Outline of a Business Plan

A thorough business plan leaves no unanswered questions. It begins with a description of you and your strengths and competencies. You must demonstrate why you are qualified to run this business. Potential investors will look at you as carefully as they will your product or service, so this part of your business plan must be carefully crafted. As an extremely busy venture capitalist, if I wasn't impressed by an individual's profile, I wouldn't bother to even read through the rest of the document. If they couldn't sell themselves effectively, I reasoned, they couldn't be expected to sell anything else very well. For your own purposes, this a self-affirmation. When doubts creep into your mind, when fears threaten to get the better of you, when frustrations mount, reread your profile and your spirits will get a boost.

The next part of a business plan presents your product or service and demonstrates why there is a need for it in the marketplace. It describes the qualities that make it stand out from similar products or services and illustrates how it will fill customers' needs. You'll need to show how you plan to manufacture or purchase your product or deliver your service. You'll need to describe how much it will cost and how you'll be able to adjust it over time to changing market conditions.

You'll also need to discuss your competition. How many other products or services like yours are out there? What makes yours stand out? How will you capture enough of the market to be successful? You must offer data on sales and market share that support your arguments.

The next part of your business plan will describe your marketing efforts and how you'll convince consumers to buy your product or service over those of your competitors. It will include your advertising, promotion, and public relations strategies and the costs of each. Make sure you offer clear-cut strategies for reaching your goals.

Now comes the hard part—money. The last sections will provide a detailed description of how much you'll need to start your business, your ongoing operating costs, and your projected revenues. If the plan is a bad one, here is where you'll find out.

It begins with startup capital. How much will you need to set up a manufacturing or distribution system for your product? What equipment will you need to purchase or lease? Don't overlook any possible costs.

Then you'll describe your operating capital. What will it take to stay in business month after month? What will your costs be for rent, insurance, and utilities? How many employees will you need to hire and what will you pay them? How much will your salary be? What will you pay for products or materials and supplies? Again, be as thorough as possible.

Next, you'll prepare financial projections using the numbers you just described. Create an opening-day balance sheet, and projected income statements for the next three years,* including a cash flow statement for your first year. Explain when you project to break even and start making a profit.

Any potential investor or lender will expect you to validate the assumptions underlying your numbers. A savvy investor will want to see evidence you'll be able to land the number of customers you project, carve out the market share you claim, or generate the sales you predict. Proof could include things like copies of signed contracts from customers, breakdowns of existing market shares, or comparisons to similar products' performances over the same time period.

Now describe how much you can contribute to your venture. What kind of equity can you contribute to the business and how much do you need to borrow? The more you can kick in, the better you'll look to potential investors.

The final section of your plan will list all the principals involved in the business. Who are the people who will manage the business? What are their backgrounds? Create an organizational chart and show how you will meet any future personnel needs required by the growth of the business. Be sure to include any professionals you will retain, such as lawyers and accountants.

---

*Your first year's income statement should be broken down on a monthly basis. The second and third year's statements can be broken down on a quarterly basis.

Qualifying Your Idea

Solidifying your idea in a business plan is critical, but qualifying your idea in the marketplace is just as important. However, most entrepreneurs are not in a position to hold nationwide focus groups or conduct a large-scale market survey. Here are two ways that you can get some of the same information in a manageable way.

Conduct Living Room Focus Groups

Invite a group of five to eight of your friends and colleagues that fit the profile of targeted customers to meet at your house to discuss your product. Provide food, drink, and a relaxed environment.

Make sure that everyone knows you have invited them because their input is valued. (Make sure no one thinks you are trying to sell them something!) Give a full presentation on your product, including all elements of your business plan except the financial details.

First ask what they like about the concept, what they would change about it to make it better, and what they view as the most significant roadblocks standing in your way. Listen to what they have to say, don't personalize their feedback, and don't try to change their minds.

Be sure to write all their comments on a pad at the front of the room and encourage them to build on each other's ideas over the course of the discussion. After one or more of these sessions, you will have a very powerful qualitative read on both your idea and the manner in which you present it.

Go Shopping with Five Friends

Ask five of your closest friends to attempt to purchase a product or service similar to the one you are planning to sell. Ask them to describe on paper each step of their experience. What products did they find? Were the products all the same price or was there a range? Was it difficult to find any products at all? How would they rate their overall experience?

Attachments to the plan will include résumés, patents, trademarks, copyrights, contracts, letters of intent, letters of reference, and any other documents important to the business.

Tough, Time-consuming, but Necessary Labor

Business plans can be quite time-consuming to prepare. They can take months of research and writing. Some entrepreneurs, in a hurry to speed up the process, will hire outside services to prepare their plan—and spend thousands of dollars in the process.

I strongly advise against taking this route. First, it's an added cost to what will already be an expensive proposition. More importantly, it prevents you from being as intimately involved in your business as you should be. Following a stranger's plan will not give you the knowledge you'll acquire by doing it yourself. By devoting your own sweat and toil to the job, you'll be able to literally feel the pulse of your business once it's up and running. If things aren't going right, you'll know immediately and will be able to take action to correct the problem.

This leads to one last, but very important, point. Your business plan is not a document to be drafted and then filed away. It's a vital, ongoing part of business success. You'll use it to keep your business on course throughout its lifetime. It will provide you with ongoing financial goals, describe the strategies you'll undertake to adjust to changing market conditions and consumer tastes, and, hopefully, lay the groundwork for expansion. It will serve as your map to success. Without it, you will be lost.

(See also accountants, advertising, banking and bankers, cash flow, employees, equipment, lawyers, résumés.)

BUSINESS TRAVEL

I USED TO HATE business travel—until I figured out how to use the time to get work done. It took me a while to figure it out. For years I sat in airports and hotel lobbies distractedly reading paperbacks and newspapers or people watching. I'd sleep on airplanes and fidget in hotel rooms. I hated every moment of it. I was generally bored and all I could think about was the work I wasn't getting done.

Then I realized how much time I was wasting. For some reason, I was treating business trips as a few important meetings surrounded by hours of useless inactivity. Once I realized I could use all that time to work uninterrupted, my whole attitude changed.

Now I look forward to business travel. When I know I'll be flying somewhere, I spend the week before organizing work to take with me. I bought a laptop computer so I can work during flights and in hotel rooms. During the flight I catch up on professional reading or compose correspondence. It's like getting to the office early. With no one bothering me, I can accomplish an amazing amount of work.

When I'm traveling on business I usually charge clients for one-half of my costs—the trip to the event or meeting—since I'll spend that time preparing and planning. If I know I'll be working on billable matters during the flight, I often spend the extra money to upgrade to business class. I find that the extra room allows me to spread out my papers and my laptop and be more productive. The economics are simple. I just multiply my hourly fee by the length of the flight. If it's more than the cost of the upgrade my labor has more than paid for the extra cost.

I can be even more productive in hotel rooms. Now that so many hotels have data ports, I can retrieve and send e-mail and use the Internet to keep up with the market and the news. There's a telephone on my nightstand and a fax machine in the lobby. If I need to have meetings at the hotel, most have conference rooms with state-of-the-art audiovisual equipment. It's really not that different from being in my own office.

Sometimes I don't even need to check into a hotel to conduct business. Like hotels, airports are providing more and more services to businesspeople in the interest of helping them save valuable time. On more than one occasion I've flown into a city, met my clients who have also flown in from other cities, and held meetings in a conference room right at the airport. When we're finished, we board outgoing flights and are home in time for dinner. For a nominal annual fee you can join a service that allows access to the VIP lounges of various airlines. This provides you with your own "office" in almost every airport around the world.

Although I work on billable matters when I'm flying to a meeting, I never bill for my time on a return flight. I usually use the time to go over my notes from the meeting, read any material I was given, prepare correspondence related to the business that was discussed, and make plans for my part of the project. And, okay, I admit it— I sometimes sneak in a nap.

_____

(See also e-mail, equipment, reading.)

BYPASS TRUSTS

ANYTHING YOU CAN DO TO AVOID paying estate taxes is a good idea.* I think the best solution is to die broke and not leave any assets behind. But if that's too radical for you, you may want to look into bypass trusts.

When a married person dies, the surviving spouse can inherit all the deceased's assets without being hit with estate taxes. There's no ceiling on how much can be passed on. It can be literally billions.

_____

*As this book was being written Congress was debating bills to eliminate federal estate taxes, which, in an election-year ploy, were being labeled "death taxes." While there appears to be bipartisan support for some kind of change, it remains a political football. The issue may or may not be resolved by the next Congress and presidential administration.

But when that surviving spouse dies, Uncle Sam swoops in to take his cut, and it's a big one. In 2001, only the first $675,000 in an estate is exempt from estate taxes. The figure increases to $700,000 in 2002 and 2003, $850,000 in 2004, $950,000 in 2005, and $1 million in 2006. The remainder of an estate is subject to taxes, starting at 37 percent and with a ceiling of 55 percent on taxable transfers of $3 million or more. This can obviously put a serious dent in the amount that passes on to beneficiaries.

A bypass trust—also called a marital shelter trust or a credit shelter trust—can as much as double the amount that's exempt from taxes. It does this by dividing the original estate between the two spouses, thus allowing both to take advantage of the estate tax exemption. Here's how it works.

Let's say your parents have an estate that's valued at $1.5 million. If your father passes away, your mother will inherit the entire estate tax-free. But when she passes on, say in 2003, only $700,000 of the value of the estate is exempt from taxes. Of the remaining $800,000, approximately $335,000 will be eaten away in estate taxes. Of the $1.5 million value of the estate, only $1,165,000 would be passed on to you and your siblings.

But if your father has a bypass trust the entire scenario would change. A bypass trust can be created up to the estate tax exemption limit. Let's assume that before he died your father created a bypass trust worth $700,000. When he passed on, his trust will be held for your mother.

While she's still alive your mother served as cotrustee of your father's trust. She received any income generated by the trust, and she could, if she had need to, tap into the trust's principal.

When your mother died in 2003, the trust, which was worth $700,000, plus $700,000 of her remaining assets are passed down to you and your siblings free and clear of estate taxes. The only estate taxes will be around $38,000 on the $100,000 of the estate that was unprotected, meaning you and your siblings would receive $1,462,000 of the $1.5 million. By creating a bypass trust, your parents ultimately avoided $297,000 in estate taxes.

Who Could Use a Bypass Trust?

Anyone who has assets over the estate tax exemption is a candidate for a bypass trust. Admittedly, these aren't the most convenient financial vehicles. They require quite a bit of vigilance and maintenance.

To see if you're a good candidate, do an inventory of your assets. Track the value of your house, cars, and other possessions, and factor in insurance policy proceeds, investments, and everything else you own. Then subtract your debts and take a look at the bottom line. If it's more than the estate tax exemption, or even starting to get close, think about calling your lawyer. She can set up a bypass trust for around $1,500. It could be worth every penny.

Remember that for a bypass trust to work, a couple must own property separately, as community property, or as tenants-in-common without right of survivorship. A bypass trust can't be funded with property that is jointly owned. This may mean that your house, which is probably your most valuable asset, should be owned as tenants-in-common.

One last thing. There's no law that says you must leave everything to your children. Bypass trusts and other tax avoidance strategies are fine. Just don't put so much property in trust that you and your spouse are unable to live your lives the way you want to. It's your money first. Make sure you get to enjoy it.

(See also lawyers.)

CALL FORWARDING

IN THEORY, call forwarding is a wonderful idea. But so was the *Hindenberg*. If you don't use call forwarding with extreme care, it too can turn into a fiery disaster.

The concept behind call forwarding is that your telephone calls can be forwarded to you no matter where you are and no matter the hour. The idea, of course, is that critical business calls won't be missed or delayed. Your business will theoretically function better and make more money.

Most telephone companies today offer call forwarding. So do answering services. You can also purchase programmable answering machines that will forward calls to whatever number you punch into the program.

Call forwarding seems particularly useful for solo entrepreneurs. With no one back at the office to field calls, and not wanting to risk having clients leaving messages that may require immediate attention, you can be connected to your calls no matter where you are. If you're on the road, you can have your calls forwarded to your cellular telephone. If you're at a location where there's another number, the calls can be forwarded to that telephone.

But it's this very convenience that hides the problem. When calls are forwarded directly to you, you know they'll be answered in a professional manner and make your business appear professional and seamless. But when calls are forwarded to a location where someone else might be answering, all bets are off. You run the risk that the caller will be surprised when someone else answers. And if you're difficult to track down, the entire process will be confusing for both the caller and the person on the receiving end. This can make your business—and you—seem casual or, even worse, incompetent.

Let's say you're spending a long weekend at a relative's home and have arranged for your calls to be forwarded to that number. It seems like a sound enough idea—until your 3-year-old niece answers an important call from an anxious client. It's only after several confounding exchanges with the child that the telephone is given to an adult. If that adult isn't you, there will likely be more confusion until you're tracked down. If you happen to be gone, your client will end up frustrated, spinning his wheels—and possibly losing money—until you call him back.

That's why I believe call forwarding should only be used when you are absolutely certain you'll be able to answer your calls. If you have a cellular telephone or pager and don't mind annoying other people (there's nothing worse than a cellular telephone ringing in a theater), you can be reachable almost all the time. For those occasions when you are only accessible via another telephone, I suggest leaving a message on your answering machine that you can be reached at another number for emergencies only. Notified of your situation, clients won't be taken aback if someone else answers their call or if you're difficult to track down.

Sample Call Forwarding Message

When leaving nonbusiness telephone number on your answering machine as an emergency contact, make sure you stress that the caller will be reaching a personal line, not a business. Here's a sample message:

> You've reached John Smith. I'll be away from the office, attending a family function, from Monday, December 10, through Thursday, December 13. However, I'll be in constant contact with this machine. If you leave a message, I'll return your call as soon as possible. If you're experiencing an emergency, you can try reaching me at my sister's home. The number there is 516-555-1212.

(See also answering machines and services, cellular telephones, location.)

CALL WAITING

THE ONLY THING more annoying than call waiting is a Mentos commercial. This is yet another electronic marvel invented by the telecommunications industry to make our lives easier (and their bottom lines healthier), which, more often than not, actually makes communication more annoying and frustrating.

For the three individuals in the United States who haven't yet been aggravated by this technology, let me explain. If you have call waiting and you're on the telephone with someone when another party is trying to reach you, your conversation will be interrupted by a series of electronic beeps. If you wish, you can then put the first party on flash-hold while you answer the new call.

Advocates of call waiting use the same two rationalizations for it that they use for call forwarding. First, they say, rather than being stymied by a busy signal, clients will always be able to reach you when they need to. And second, it ensures you'll never miss an important call.

Maybe I've missed something, but when did receiving a busy signal become such a big problem? All businesses have periods when their telephone lines are jammed. Callers will be neither surprised nor offended if they can't get through to you on their first or second try. I've been in business for more than 40 years and I've never once had a client complain to me that she couldn't get through to my office. And I'd wager I get more telephone calls than most small businesses. If a client gets a busy signal on her first call, she just calls back. Your clients will, too.

Creates More Problems than It Solves

I think call waiting creates more problems than it solves. Let's look at the logistics of the situation. When you use call waiting, three individuals are involved: you, the person you're speaking with, and the person trying to reach you. When the call waiting signal interrupts your conversation, you're quickly forced to make an uncomfortable decision. If the person you're already speaking with is an important client, you'll be worried that you may offend her by putting her on hold. But you'll also worry that the incoming call is another important client and *she'll* be upset if she can't reach you. When you do take the second call, you'll now have two people who want your immediate attention. But one of the two must be told you'll get back to her later. In doing so, you're going to send her the message, "You're not as important to me as this other person." Do you really want to treat clients that way?

If you don't take the second call, that person may be met not with a busy signal but with a constant ring, seeming to indicate that you're not in the office and don't have an answering machine. Personally, I think that's worse than a busy signal. At least the latter indicates you're hard at work. The endless ring implies you're not only not working, but weren't sufficiently on the ball to turn on your answering machine.*

If missing calls when you're on the telephone is really a concern, there's a simple solution. Just set up your answering system so that when your primary voice line is busy, incoming calls are redirected to an unlisted second line and are answered by your answering machine. That allows the caller to leave a message rather than interrupt your call. You get your important messages as soon as you hang up, and your clients know they've passed on their important

---

*There are some answering systems, primarily those offered by telephone companies, that will accept messages while you're on another call, even if both calls are to the same line.

While I have little use
for call waiting in the
business environment, I
do think it can be use-
ful on your home tele-
phone, particularly if
you have a teenager who
keeps your telephone
line tied up. Call wait-
ing can also be of value
if you spend a great
deal of time on the
Internet and use your
telephone line for your
connection. The indus-
try is just realizing this,
and some Internet serv-
ice providers, such as
Web TV, are beginning
to offer call waiting as
part of their service.
That way, you can take
calls and then go right
back to whatever Web
site you were visiting
when you finish your
conversation.

information and will soon hear from you. Everyone will be happier
with that arrangement.

(See also answering machines and services, call forwarding, Internet service
providers, Web sites.)

CAPITAL GAINS

Not only does it take money to make money, but sometimes it costs money to make money.

When you sell an asset for a profit, the money you've made is
called a capital gain. If you buy 100 shares of a stock for $12 a
share ($1,200) and sell it for $30 a share less a $75 brokerage fee
($2,925), your capital gain is $1,725 ($2,925 − $1,200). You can
enjoy capital gains from the sale of many items besides investments,
including real estate,* art, antiques, and collectibles.

All those capital gains don't just end up in your pocket, however. Every time you sell and reap the profits of your shrewd investment decisions, Uncle Sam is there to take a piece of the proceeds
in capital gains taxes. Although the tax rate on capital gains was
lowered by the Taxpayer Relief Act of 1997, and there are perennial
efforts in Congress to eliminate the tax, it remains a painful bite.

The Advantages of Capital Gains

Despite the tax hit, capital gains are better than interest and dividends. First, you don't pay taxes until you sell the investment. Second, you decide when to sell it, take the profit, and pay the tax.
Timing can make a big difference. Let's say you want to sell a block
of stock that has appreciated favorably. If you sell it on December
31, the capital gains will be taxed for that year. But by waiting just

*There have been changes recently in the tax law regarding capital gains on real
estate. There is no longer any requirement to roll over your profit from the sale of
real estate within a certain period of time to avoid paying capital gains taxes.
Now, if you are married and filing a joint return, the first $500,000 of profit
from the sale of real estate is not taxable. If you are single, or married and filing
separately, the first $250,000 of profit is not taxable.

two days and selling it on January 2, you can defer paying the taxes for more than a year. In the meantime, the money you would have had to pay in taxes can be reinvested.

Long-Term and Short-Term Gains

Prior to the Taxpayer Relief Act of 1997, capital gains were taxed at the same rate as ordinary income—28 percent or higher for many people. Since then, they've been taxed at two different rates. Capital gains from investments that are held long-term—for more than a year—are taxed at 20 percent. People who fall into the 15 percent tax bracket pay just 10 percent. Long-term gains from collectibles have higher rates, 28 and 15 percent, respectively. Short-term capital gains—those earned from investments held a year or less—are taxed at the same rate as ordinary income.

As of January 1, 2000, profits from assets purchased after that date and held for at least five years will be taxed at just 8 percent for investors in the 15 percent bracket, and 18 percent for those in a tax bracket of 28 percent or higher.

Assets in retirement accounts, like IRAs, 401(k) plan accounts and annuities are the exceptions to the new capital gains rules. They grow tax-deferred until withdrawal. But when you begin to withdraw money from these accounts, your accumulated earnings—including capital gains—are taxed at ordinary income tax rates.

Capital Losses

Of course, not all investments or purchases are profitable. If you make an investment that performs poorly and then sell it for less than you paid for it, you experience a capital loss. Any capital losses you have in a year will be deducted from your capital gains for tax purposes. For example, if you had capital gain of $5,000 and capital losses of $1,500, you would only pay capital gains taxes on $3,500.

If you have a net capital loss for the year, you can deduct it from your ordinary income. There are limits, however. At the time of this writing, you can only deduct $3,000 a year in capital losses. Any excess has to be claimed the following year.

Capital Gains Considerations for Investors

Don't base investment decisions solely on capital gains tax issues, but do keep them in mind. Here are a few basic considerations.

- Whenever possible, try to hold on to an investment for at least a year to take advantage of lower long-term capital gains rates.

- Consider your timing. You can avoid paying capital gains on high-turnover mutual funds by putting the funds into a retirement account. Remember, however, that withdrawals from retirement accounts are taxed at ordinary income rates rather than the lower capital gains rates. If you're many years away from tapping into your retirement accounts, they may be a good place to shelter your gains. But if you're close to tapping your retirement accounts, it generally makes sense to pay capital gains taxes now rather than ordinary income taxes later.

- Offset capital gains with capital losses. If you had a good year and enjoyed substantial capital gains, offset them by selling some losing investments for a capital loss. The lowered net gain will reduce the amount of capital gains tax you pay.

(See also annuities, antiques and collectibles, IRAs, mutual funds.)

CASH FLOW

It's CASH FLOW, not profitability, that's the real life blood of any fledgling business. If your cash flow is insufficient, or stops altogether, your business is in deep trouble regardless of how profitable it may be on paper.

Just because a business is "doing well," doesn't mean it has a lot of cash on hand. For example, a business that extends credit to its customers can have sales numbers that go through the roof. Does that mean it has cash? No. Until its customers pay their bills, all it has to show for its success is a lot of accounts receivable. This is why handling receivables efficiently is so important.

To ensure that your new business will survive long enough to become profitable, you need to project your cash flow. This analysis should chart your income and expenditures, month by month, for your first 12 months of business. These figures will come from your projections of sales and expenses, and they must be carefully timed to make sure you can meet your financial obligations on schedule.

In many ways, a cash flow analysis isn't that different from budgeting your home expenses. You know how often you get paid (weekly, biweekly, monthly), so you organize paying your bills and shopping around that schedule. You do the same with your business. If your payroll is due every two weeks and you pay your creditors every two weeks, you'll need to make sure sufficient cash is there for you to meet your obligations.

You should enlist your accountant's assistance in preparing your cash flow analysis. Whatever form he chooses to use is fine, provided he follows these basic steps outlined in the cash flow worksheet on page 123. Remember, you'll be preparing a report for each month, calculating the relationship between your cash available and your cash expenditures.

If your cash available is greater than your cash expenditures, you have a positive cash flow. If your expenditures are greater than your available cash, you have a negative cash flow. Should you expect a positive cash flow every month? Not necessarily. There certainly may be months in which a large expense such as the purchase of piece of equipment or the payment of a tax bill, might keep you in the red. However, those months should be the exception, not the rule.

If you find, however, that your projections show month after month of negative cash flow, you'll know your business plan has some serious flaws. This is a perfect example of why a business plan can help you see problems before they actually occur. It can also be used as a measuring stick of your business's ongoing health.

If your cash flow analysis indicates an ongoing negative cash flow, you can try to restructure the two sides of the equation in your plan to the point where you at least break even. If you can't do that, you'll know it's time to find some other business to go into.

Once in business, you can check to see that your cash flow is meeting, or exceeding your projections. If it isn't, you'll be able to quickly see that you're on the road to potential ruin.

Cash Flow Worksheet

Step 1. Calculate your cash on hand. Enter the amount you expect to have in your accounts at the beginning of the month, whether from earnings, loans, or other sources.

_____   _____

Step 2. Calculate your cash receipts. These will include:

_____   _____

- Cash sales: Enter the amount you estimate you'll be paid in cash, check, or money order.

_____   _____

- Credit card sales: Enter the amount you expect to earn from credit card orders, less the bank or card company fee.

_____   _____

- Other cash receipts: Enter income from short-term loans or similar sources.

_____   _____

Step 3. Add lines 1 and 2 to calculate your total cash available.

_____   _____

Step 4. Calculate your loan payments. Include all monthly loan payments, including interest and principal.

_____   _____

Step 5. Calculate your capital purchases. Include any items for which you'll pay cash rather than purchase over time.

_____   _____

Step 6. Calculate purchases of inventory. Include the amount you will spend to purchase your product or products.

_____   _____

Step 7. Calculate your operating expenses. Include rent, maintenance, vehicle expenses, utility bills, professional services, insurance premiums, and other expenses incurred by the business. _____   _____

Step 8. Calculate cash withdrawals. These include the salaries you pay yourself or others, income tax payments, Social Security payments, health insurance premiums, etc. _____   _____

Step 9. Add lines 4 through 8 to calculate your total cash expenditures. _____   _____

(See also accountants, budgeting, business plans, inventory, receivables.)

CELLULAR TELEPHONES

WHOEVER CAME UP WITH the expression "too much of a good thing" must have had cellular telephones in mind. It seems half the people I see on the sidewalks of Manhattan have one hand pressed to the side of their heads, jabbering away as they briskly go about their business. An equal number are on their cellular telephones in their cars.

There's no question cellular telephones can be a great business aid. Like call waiting and call forwarding, they potentially allow you to remain constantly accessible to your clients or family. Despite their versatility, though, I don't see them as a substitute for your primary telephone system. Rather, I think they should be used only when you are unable to access your primary system.

Sensible Cellular Telephone Use

From a business point of view, it's really an issue of whether or not you have office staff. If you do, they should field your calls when you're away from the office. You can then check in periodically to get your messages. I feel it's a more professional approach to communicating with clients.

I'm a good example. I spend at least two or three hours a day on the telephone, seven days a week. Yet I rarely use my cellular telephone. During business hours, I have an administrative assistant who takes my calls. When I'm away from the office, I check in every hour or so. On the weekend, I have an answering system with remote-access capabilities, which I also check regularly. Since I'm rarely far from a telephone, I can usually return any calls I've received promptly. The rare occasions when I use a cellular telephone are when I need to speak with someone immediately and there's no other telephone nearby. Generally that means while traveling in a cab or train.

I realize, however, that not all businesspeople have office staff or easy access to telephones. If you work solo and spend a lot of time on the road outside of major cities, or if you have a business that absolutely demands that you be immediately available every second of every day, then a cellular telephone might be indispensable.

You can coordinate your cellular telephone with your other equipment to give you virtually seamless communication ability while still using only your primary office telephone number. For example, if you're on the road or otherwise out of the office, you can have call forwarding transfer incoming calls to your cellular telephone. But if you're with a client or in some other situation in which you don't want to be disturbed, you can activate your office answering machine to take all calls while you're tied up. When you've finished your meeting, you can check your messages. You can also reactivate call forwarding.

When possible, you should use your cellular telephone to just take incoming calls and wait until you're in your office to make outgoing calls. For one thing, the reception is sometimes less than perfect on a cellular telephone. You don't want an important conversation interrupted by hisses and other electronic noise. You also need to be concerned about the noise being generated in the area from which you're calling. The clamor of traffic, loud conversations, and other noises can be very disturbing. And, of course, calls from cellular telephones are usually more expensive that calls from normal telephones.*

Etiquette and Safety

No discussion of cellular telephones would be complete without a few words about etiquette. Cellular telephones are small and can be carried just about anywhere, including places where they're entirely inappropriate, such as theaters, restaurants, libraries, and (I'm told) golf courses. The ringing of a cellular telephone is incredibly annoying and just plain rude in these environments. I'm not a fan of their use in crowded trains or buses either.

Many manufacturers now offer cellular telephones that allow you to turn off the ringer and activate a silent vibrating signal to alert you to an incoming call. While these can be carried into theaters and restaurants, you should still leave your seat and go to a secluded part of the building before answering the call. And if you're anticipating a lot of calls, turn off the telephone altogether or just stay in your office. Your constant back and forth will be unfair to other people.

There are also safey issues associated with cellular telephone use. More and more automobile accidents are being attributed to distracted drivers using cellular telephones. Pedestrian

---

*Speaking of costs, never assume a cellular telephone company will immediately offer you the most economical plan. If you find your bills are more than you anticipated, give the company a call, tell them you're unhappy and are thinking of switching to another provider, but you'd like to give them another chance. Ask them to analyze your bill and see if they can come up with a cheaper plan. Most will figure out some way to save you money in an effort to keep you from defecting to a competitor.

accidents are also becoming more common as people fall off curbs and down stairs while fumbling with their telephones. If you're driving and need to use your telephone, do us all a favor and pull off to the side of the road. Likewise, find a quiet place to stand or sit when you're on foot. No telephone call is worth a sprain, a broken bone, or worse.

(See also answering machines and services, call forwarding.)

CERTIFICATES OF DEPOSIT

INVESTING MONEY in a certificate of deposit (CD) is one step removed from hiding it in your mattress. Still, there are times when these glorified piggy banks actually make sense.

Let's say you have the cash you're going to need for your son's first year of college. It's a little over a year away and you want to find a place to park your money until the bills start to arrive. You're going to need every penny, so you don't want to risk any depreciation. That rules out stocks and mutual funds. Long-term bonds, although safe, take too long to reach maturity. And short-term bonds pay very little.

The solution is a 12-month CD. It's like a savings account or money market account with a couple of important twists. In order to receive the full interest on your money, you can't touch it until the term of the CD is up. Since the institution issuing the CD is counting on having your money for a certain length of time, it will pay a higher rate of interest than a savings account or money market account. If you do withdraw funds early, you'll pay a penalty of one to six months' interest.

CDs are also favored by conservative investors who sense a storm on the financial horizon. For example, when the stock market begins a downturn, many of these investors liquidate their stock holdings and put their money in short-term CDs. When the financial weather begins to clear, they'll let their CDs mature, collect their profits, and move their money back into the market.

The ABCs of CDs

CDs are certainly easy to find. They're offered by banks, savings and loans, credit unions, and many brokerage firms. They're protected by the same FDIC insurance that protects the money you have in savings, checking, and money market accounts (up to $100,000 per bank). CDs usually require a commitment of 6 months to 10 years, though shorter terms are available. The longer the term, the higher the interest rate. Most banks offer standard terms like 6 months, 12 months, 18 months, 24 months, 36 months, etc. Some will let you decide how long you want to commit your money and then offer a corresponding interest rate.

What happens to your money when the certificate matures will be spelled out in the CD contract. Each institution handles things a bit differently. More than likely you'll be give a short grace period during which the institution will expect to receive instructions from you (the good ones will send you a letter to remind you your certificate is approaching maturity). Do you want them to send you a check? Deposit the money in another account? Reinvest it in another CD? If they don't hear from you, they'll usually do the latter. If you decide after the fact that you'd prefer to have the cash, they may or may not impose a penalty.

You may find some institutions offering CDs with rates a point or so above the average. Be careful. If the bank is making these offers because it needs to attract money to beef up a very active loan pool, it's not a problem. But some institutions may be insolvent and on the brink of being taken over by the federal government. If this should happen and the institution is then sold, you may find your interest rate reduced. Today, most of the top CD rates are being offered by online banks, which have much less overhead than brick-and-mortar banks.

Don't steer away from CDs just because you're concerned about not having access to your money. A CD is every bit as liquid as a savings account or checking account. Granted, if you withdraw money before the certificate matures, you'll lose some or all of the interest you've accumulated. But that's not the end of the world. If you're realistic about the timing of your need for the money you invest, you'll more than likely be able to keep a CD for the entire term and enjoy a healthier return on your investment than you would have gotten if you hid it under your mattress.

Special Flavors of CDs

Banks are anxious to have your money and compete viciously with one another to get it. One way they try to attract your business is to offer CDs with special terms or higher interest rates. Here are a few of them:

- *Free-ride CDs* offer reduced penalties for early withdrawal. For example, you may be able to withdraw up to half your money without penalty. Or you may be able to withdraw all your money without penalty once the term has reached its halfway point.

- *Jumbo CDs* are for big investors with more than $100,000 to invest. The downside is that if the institution fails, you may not be able to get all your money back.

- *Anytime CDs* allow you to dictate the maturity date. If you're closing on a new house in six months, you can arrange to have your CD mature the same day and pick up your check on the way to the closing.

- *Relationship CDs* are used by banks to attract new customers. When you buy a CD, the bank will provide you with a low-interest loan or free checking services.

- *Zero-coupon CDs* operate like zero-coupon bonds. You deposit an amount of money that's considerably less than the face value of the CD. At the end of the term, you collect the full face value.

- *Bump-up CDs* are designed to protect your investment against inflation. If interest rates rise, you can ask the institution to increase the return on your CD. They'll limit you to one or two such favors and put a limit on how high they'll move your rate.

- *Tax-deferral CDs* help you reduce your tax burden. You put your money into a 12-month discounted CD and the interest isn't paid until the CD matures a year later. This means you owe no taxes on your investment for the current year.

(See also bonds, inflation, money market accounts, savings accounts, zero-coupon bonds.)

CHARGE CARDS

AMERICA HAS A plastic monkey on it's back. Our credit addiction is worse than ever. During the greatest economic boom in our nation's history, credit card debt and personal bankruptcies are at an all-time high. Rather than using credit cards to avoid writing checks or carrying large sums of cash, people use their cards as loans. As a result many Americans, from the affluent to the impoverished, have amassed enormous high-interest credit card balances. Able to pay little more than the monthly minimum, regardless of income, these folks face years of payments and tens of thousands of dollars in interest charges.

This is why I'm such a fan of charge cards. They won't allow you to run up a debt. Pay your balance every month or your card will be revoked. It's that simple. Armed with this knowledge, most people are quite cautious about how they use charge cards.

Charge cards offer the same conveniences as credit cards. They're accepted at almost all the same establishments as credit cards.* Most provide you with almost unlimited purchasing power, so they're quite valuable in emergencies. You have 30 days of interest-free credit, so you have time to transfer funds to pay the bill or be reimbursed for the business expenses you charged. If you used the card for an emergency and are unable to pay the entire balance, it gives you time to

---

*Outside of the United States, however, charge cards like American Express aren't accepted in as many places as credit cards.

arrange financing. You receive consumer protection in case you have a problem when ordering goods over the telephone, through the mail, or on the Internet. Because charge card computer systems are amount-sensitive, the issuers are very good at checking up on unusually large charges, providing a further level of security. Often this will mean providing an operator with your Social Security number or some other identifying information before the charge is processed.

Most importantly, charge cards let you do all these things without running the risk of going into debt. If you want to buy airplane tickets to Hawaii for you and your spouse as an anniversary surprise, you'll only do it if you know you can pay the bill when it arrives. If you're a credit card user, you're more likely to just go ahead with the purchase and put off worrying about paying for it until the bill arrives.

Charge cards can also provide access to other accounts in an emergency, If you sign up for the American Express express-cash service, for example, you can access one of your personal accounts for up to $1,000 a week from wherever you happen to be. You can also cash personal checks at American Express offices using your card as identification and as a guarantee that the check won't bounce. (If it does, the company will just charge your account for the amount.)

Charge cards do have two disadvantages. One is they charge a fee. For example, the American Express green card charges $50 a year. If your spouse or child also has a card on the same account, they would be assessed a $40 fee. The other leading charge cards, such as Diner's Club and Carte Blanche, also charge a fee. I consider that a nominal amount for the assistance these cards can provide, not to mention the protection they provide you against yourself and your irresponsible credit card habits.

The second disadvantage is they're harder to get. Because charge card companies expect you to pay your bill in full every month, and are quite liberal in the amount they'll let you charge, their criteria for acceptance are a bit more stringent than those of credit card companies. If your income falls below a certain level, if you have a history of credit problems, or if you are already carrying a significant amount of credit card debt, you may find yourself unable to get a charge card.

If you've had a history of running up credit card debt, I suggest you follow the advice I give my wayward clients. Cut up all your credit cards except one. Put the one card away in a desk drawer and only take it out in an emergency. Then get yourself and your spouse American Express green cards.

What you don't want to do, however, is sign up for American Express gold or platinum cards. These cards play to people's vanities and egos by making them feel special, a cut above the standard cardholder. Aside from a few minor perks, I don't think these cards are worth the inflated fees they carry. If you're already an American Express customer and have a gold or platinum card, switch back to a green card. Save your money and mingle with the common folk. No one will think the less of you, I promise.

(See also bankruptcy, credit cards.)

CHARITABLE REMAINDER TRUSTS

THE CHARITABLE REMAINDER TRUST is one of those money secrets the wealthy and their advisers have kept to themselves for decades. But the time has come to let everyone in on the secret.

A charitable remainder trust is most useful when you have an asset that has appreciated a great deal in value. Maybe you jumped on the Internet bandwagon early on and bought a block of stock in an e-business that has appreciated a hundred times over. Or maybe you have a small business you started in your basement that has grown beyond your wildest expectations. Or perhaps years ago you bought a piece of cheap property that has since been zoned commercial and is now worth a small fortune.

Your concern now is how to unload your asset without getting killed by the tax man. To keep the math simple and the numbers impressive, we'll assume the asset is worth $1 million. You know that if you sell it, you'll pay a bundle in capital gains and will be lucky to have $650,000 left over. Invested at 8 percent, that will earn you $52,000 a year. If you pass away and leave the $650,000 to your kids, a second tax bite might reduce it to $325,000 or so. At that point your original $1 million asset has had nearly 70 percent of its value chewed away by taxes. You think to yourself, "There must be some other way to do this." And you're right.

Enter the charitable remainder trust. Instead of selling your asset, you call your lawyer, instruct her to set up a charitable remainder trust, and then give the trust the asset. Then, you let the trust sell the asset for $1 million and have the trust pay you 8 percent annually for the rest of your life. You also designate a charity to receive the trust's principal when you die. At this point, having avoided capital gains tax, you're receiving 8 percent of $1 million, or $80,000, instead of the $52,000 you would have received earning 8 percent of $650,000.

That sounds great. But wait. It gets even better. Since you're giving the money to a charity, you're entitled to a tax deduction for the year in which you set up the trust. Using actuarial tables, the IRS will estimate how much the trust will pay you over the rest of your lifetime and deduct that amount from the $1 million value of the trust. The result is the "remainder" value of the trust, the amount the charity will actually receive. (Of course, the charity has invested the $1 million and is paying you your 8 percent from the earnings, so the trust's principal should remain intact or even appreciate a bit.) You can then claim the "remainder" amount as a charitable contribution and receive a huge tax savings. And because you've made a substantial gift to charity, you'll be admired far and wide for your generosity.

Now I know what you're thinking: "What about my kids? After I die there won't be anything left for them." You're right. Personally, I'm a Die Broker, so I don't believe that's a problem. But if you don't share my feelings about estates, there's another trick that will solve that problem. Remember that money you saved in taxes with your charitable deduction? It can be used to pay the premium for a $1 million second-to-die insurance policy that will pay off after you and your spouse pass away.* At that point, everything will have come full circle. You'll have saved money on taxes and received a comfortable income and your kids will inherit the $1 million they would have if you hadn't sold the asset. In addition, you'll have provided $1 million to a good cause and can be assured that you'll be remembered as a shining example of selfless philanthropy. It's such a good deal for everyone concerned—except the tax man—that I can't believe it's still legal. Maybe that's why the rich have been keeping it a secret.

_____

(See also capital gains, lawyers.)

CHARITIES

I BELIEVE THAT to keep good things, you need to give them away. To remain successful at landing wealthy clients, you need to do some pro bono work. To remain financially secure, you need to give money away.

I'm not going to suggest who you should give your money to. There are more than enough worthy causes to support. What I will suggest is that you make your giving as efficient and effective as everything else you do with your money. In my mind that means finding a cause you care about, researching the charities that work for that cause, selecting one organization, and then giving the bulk of your charitable largesse to your chosen charity.

Many people have a special place in their heart for their alma maters and credit them for getting them started on successful career paths. This ongoing affection has resulted in tens of billions of dollars for the endowments of the nation's colleges and universities. Some people find giving to medical research rewarding, particularly if it's focused on a disease that has struck loved ones. Others contribute to social causes or children's groups. Still others contribute to the arts or to help animals. Whatever charities you choose to support, making a gift that helps others will provide you with a personal reward that can't be obtained any other way.

Donor Beware

Unfortunately, the philanthropic world isn't free from scams and cons. In fact, it may attract more than its share of rip-off artists hoping to prey on people's generous natures. Some fundraising organizations, while arguably not crooked, are terribly inefficient, keeping inordinate amounts of the money they raise—75 percent or more—to cover "administrative" costs. Often these include fat salaries and expensive perks for the charities' officers.

_____

*Actually, the second-to-die policy will cost only a very small portion of the income. The premiums on the policies are quite low since they cover two lives rather than one. They're very easy to obtain for the same reason.

Signs of Fraudulent Charities

Some charities are completely fraudulent. They're set up by criminals who pose as solicitors for a worthy cause but who, in fact, keep every penny for themselves. It's up to you to do your homework and confirm the legitimacy of a charity before you write a check. Here are some of the things to look out for.

- Beware of charities that sound only vaguely familiar. Many fraudulent organizations will play off the name of a legitimate charity to fool people into making donations.

- Watch out for charities that are tied to sweepstakes or that claim you've won money or some other valuable prize.

- Avoid requests to have your donation charged to your credit card. It could be a scam to obtain your card number.

- Never give money to an organization you've never heard of.

- Never make cash donations. Even if the organization is legitimate, the money may never make it out of the pocket of the solicitor. Write checks and use the full name of the organization.

- Watch out for telephone calls or mailings requesting the "pledge" you made earlier. You may have done so and it just slipped your mind. But check your records before writing a check.

By the way, don't let the guilt factor make you contribute money. While it's not a sign of fraud, many charities will send small gifts such as notecards or return address labels along with their appeal letters in a not-so-subtle effort to induce guilt. You didn't ask for these things, so there's no reason you should feel obligated to make a contribution. According to federal regulations, any unrequested items you receive through the mail are yours to keep.

Choose Your Own Charities

Competition for the philanthropic dollar is fierce. It's impossible to give to everyone. My advice is to decide what charity you want to support and initiate your own contacts. Ignore all other requests for contributions, no matter how worthy the cause. When approached, explain that you give all your donations to your favorite charity. By concentrating your giving you maximize its impact.

Before you give to a charitable organization you need to learn as much about it as possible. Just because an organization is widely known doesn't mean you'll find its practices acceptable. In fact, some of the nation's largest and best-known charities have been taken to task for having outrageous administrative costs and other errors of judgment. Here are some of the questions you need to ask:

- What percent of donations actually reach the charity after administrative costs and other costs are covered? If the answer is below 50 percent, I would eliminate the charity from my list. The most effective organizations provide between 60 and 75 percent of the money that's contributed. The worst give as little as 15 percent.

- How will the donations be used? Make sure you agree with how the funds are distributed and the activities they support.

- Are the charity's solicitors paid or are they volunteers? A charity that uses volunteers will have lower operating costs.

If the information is given to you over the telephone, be sure to get the name of the representative who spoke with you and write it down for future verification, if needed.

Ask the charity to send you annual reports and copies of its federal Form 990 for the last three years. If the charity's representative balks, end the conversation.

Checking Up on Charities

One excellent source of information on charities is the Independent Charities of America (800-477-0733; www.independentcharities.org). ICA is a tax-exempt nonprofit charitable organization that prescreens and certifies quality charitable organizations. They represent more than 400 charities in 10 different categories and include links to each one on their Web site. They maintain an emergency action alert e-mail list that will notify subscribers which certified charities are providing relief efforts when a disaster occurs. You can even make an online gift to the charity of your choice.

Another good source of information is the National Charities Information Bureau (212-929-6300; www.give.org). The NCIB can provide you with administrative costs and other information on a wide variety of charities.

(See also gifts, pro bono work.)

CHECKING ACCOUNTS

CHECKING ACCOUNTS MAY NOT make you any money, but they surely shouldn't cost you any money.

When shopping for a checking account, you need to ask yourself one important question: "How much of an average balance will I be keeping in the account?" If that number is high enough, you'll qualify for an account that pays a small amount of interest. Most banks require an average daily balance of anywhere from $1,000 to $2,500 for accounts to earn interest. On the other hand, if your balance is usually hovering in the double-digit range, you'll want to forget about looking for interest and instead find the account with the fewest fees.

Banks are very clever at finding ways to nickel-and-dime customers. You'll find flat monthly fees, fees for each check you write, fees for ATM use, and fees for debit card use. Some banks might try to fool you by offering a low monthly fee while charging exorbitant amounts for ATM transactions. Some will even charge you for using a human teller.

If you can maintain a sufficient balance, you should consider the following types of checking accounts.

Interest-paying accounts: These pay you a small amount of interest and generally don't charge monthly fees or per-check fees, provided your average daily balance stays above a certain minimum. If you fall below the minimum, you'll begin to accrue fees.

Bundled accounts: Some banks will offer you a "bundle" of services in addition to your checking account. They can include free travelers checks, a free line of credit, a credit card with no annual fee, discounted loans, and a quarter-point bonus on savings deposits. You may or may not have to pay a nominal fee.

Asset-management accounts: These accounts combine a brokerage account with an interest-paying money market account against which you can write checks. They may also include a credit card and debit card. Asset-management accounts are only offered by large banks, brokerage firms, and insurance companies, and the minimum deposit can be as high as $25,000.

Free Checking

Some banks may offer free checking under certain conditions. You may be required to open a savings or money market account or take out a loan for an automobile. Just make sure that the deal is *truly* free. You should only be assessed fees for having new checks printed, bouncing a check, and perhaps using your ATM card.

Overdraft Protection

When you write a check for an amount that's more than the amount you have in your account, your bank won't be able to pay it—it will bounce. Not only will this cost you money (your bank will charge you a penalty), but it will cost the person you wrote the check to money as well. His bank will more than likely charge him what's called a DIR (deposit-item-returned) fee. He will not be happy about it.

Bouncing a check is an embarrassing oversight that can easily be avoided with overdraft protection. You can choose to have your bank move funds from a savings account or money market account to cover your overdraft. Some banks will cover your check with a loan on which you're charged as much as 15 or 16 percent.

Overdraft protection may be offered as a free service or it may come with a small annual fee and an additional per-use charge. It won't be cheap, but it will be cheaper than bouncing a check.

Saving Money on Checks

You order new checks directly from your bank, right? They provide that convenient little order form with the last pad of checks. You just write down how many boxes of checks you want and stick it in the mail or drop it off at a teller's window. It couldn't be easier.

There's just one problem. It's costing you money. What you need to do is eliminate the middleman and save yourself a few bucks. You can bypass the bank and save money by ordering checks directly from a commercial check printer. Try Checks in the Mail (800-733-4443) or Checks Unlimited (800-533-3973).

Give Cash a Chance

Put away your checkbook, hide your debit card, and operate solely with cash. Decide how much you can spend each week, withdraw that amount from your checking account every Monday morning, and tuck it away in your wallet. Make sure it's enough for groceries, lunches, gasoline, and any other items you purchase during the course of a normal week.

Once you've taken out the money, promise yourself you won't take out any more until the following Monday. This will force you to give careful consideration to all purchases and plan ahead, two practices many of us have forgotten. If Sunday rolls around and you only have enough money for hot dogs and baked beans for dinner, so be it. The following week you'll be a bit more careful with your spending. If you run into a problem that week, you'll be even more careful the following week.

This exercise will soon begin to save you money. I guarantee it. You may even get to the point that you have money left over. If that's the case, this additional money can be put toward your children's college fund, your investment fund, or some other long-term goal.

(See also ATMs and cash cards, credit cards, debit cards, savings accounts.)

CHILD CARE

Have you ever thought that maybe it's not worth having two incomes? If you add the costs of child care to the money you spend on transportation, parking, meals, clothing, entertainment, and the other expenses that come with having a job, you just might find the cost of being at work is consuming the better part of one of your incomes.

Then add in the emotional and psychological toll of having your child in day care. And consider that when you are home, you're still not spending much time with your child because you have so many chores to catch up on. You have to begin to ask yourself, "What's the point?"

Take it from someone who often regrets that he wasn't around much when his kids were growing up. It's a privilege to be a parent, and the childhood years are fleeting. Once they're gone, you can't buy them back, no matter how much money you earn. I have four wonderful, successful children. How did they turn out so great? Don't look to me—I was preoccupied with climbing my career Mount Olympus. It's my wife Corky who deserves all the credit. I'm a late-blooming parent. Looking back, I realize how lucky we were that Corky was able to stay home with the kids for so many of their formative years.

Most of my clients today aren't as fortunate. For some, they need two incomes to maintain their lifestyle, even taking into account the costs of child care and the expenses of working. Others are on career tracks where neither parent can afford a four- or five-year hiatus. It's not surprising, then, that child care is one of the biggest concerns my clients have during their first few years as parents. Leaving your child with another person for eight or more hours a day is very traumatic, especially at first. Finding a secure, reliable child-care arrangement is critical in easing the worry.

Finding Quality Child Care

It's not always easy. In many parts of the country, child care is largely unregulated. (Hopefully, that will change soon.) And even in places where there is supposed to be some form of oversight, many businesses ignore the law and, usually in an effort to cut costs, operate without acquiring the proper certification or licensing.

So how do you find quality child care? I recommend you follow the same strategy I suggest to clients who ask me how to find a good lawyer, accountant, or banker: word of mouth. Ask people you know who have small children for the names of people they used or are currently using. Happy customers are a child-care provider's best form of advertising, and, as in any profession, the names of quality people quickly become known.

If you don't know anyone with small children, you can check with local social service agencies, community centers, schools, and churches. Some may offer child care themselves or refer you to people who do. Many excellent nursery schools advertise in the telephone directory or in community newspapers. Other people who may provide a nursery school setting in their homes also advertise.

Child-Care Options

When you're looking for child care, you'll have a number of options to sort out.

Do you want the care provider to come to your home or do you prefer to bring your child to her home? Obviously if you're searching for a situation where there will be other children present, the latter is usually your best bet.

Next you'll need to choose between a provider who cares for a limited number of children in her own home or a nursery school setting, where there are sure to be a larger number of children.

You choices might be limited if you need someone who provides care during odd hours. Some child-care professionals, particularly those who provide care in their own homes, offer overnight care for parents who work the late shift.

Investigate the Candidates

Before you decide on a child-care arrangement, make sure you investigate the person or school as thoroughly as possible. Don't cut corners. Do your due diligence. You'd automatically do this when hiring a contractor to renovate your kitchen. Your child is more important than your countertop.

- Ask for references and speak with each one.

- If your state or local municipality requires licensing or accreditation, make sure the provider has complied.

- Check the records to see if there have ever been any complaints or charges brought against the provider.

- Visit the home or school several times to observe how the children are treated. And don't make appointments—show up without notice. Any child-care professional who can't deal with the unexpected is one you should scratch off your list of candidates.

If you're among the fortunate few, you may work for a company that provides on-site child care for its employees. Parents can visit their children on breaks, have lunch with them, and even accompany them on trips. Nursing mothers can fit feeding time into their work schedules. If there's a problem, the parent is just seconds away and not across town. On-site child care takes a great deal of the worry out of the situation, for both parents and children. Unfortunately, the costs, particularly insurance, are quite high, so few employers are willing to foot the bill. Still, there's hope that more and more companies will realize that on-site child care helps attract and keep employees, and allows them to stay on the job for more hours.

(See also advertising, employees, word of mouth.)

CHILD SUPPORT

THE REAL VICTIMS of divorce are children. Regardless of which parent a child ends up with, he invariably suffers a decreased standard of living that may restrict his activities and dramatically alter the course of his life. The situation is worsened since the financial support they're supposed to receive often arrives sporadically or not at all. Collectively, deadbeat dads (and a few deadbeat moms) currently owe billions in child support. It's a disgraceful situation.

How Child Support Is Calculated

For years child support was determined by judges in their divorce rulings. It was a pretty haphazard process that relied more on the skills of the parents' lawyers than on any objective analysis of the parents' resources.

Today, however, states rely on formulas to come up with a figure. About 20 states use the "income shares" model, which examines the incomes of both parents and then uses a table of values to decide how much the noncustodial parent will contribute. Other states look only at the income of the noncustodial parent and ignore the income of the custodial parent.

Let's look at New York state as an example. The guidelines first take into consideration the incomes of both the noncustodial and custodial parent. It considers income from regular employment, self-employment, and other sources, including investments. The total is generally the same figure that appears on line 22 of IRS Form 1040. For example, the courts in New York generally prescribe a ceiling of $200,000 on which to base the amount of support, although it will certainly use a larger figure if the parent's income is a great deal higher than that. I don't think, as a hypothetical example, the court would use the $200,000 ceiling if it was confronted with calculating child-support payments from Bill Gates.

Once the noncustodial parent's income has been established, the guidelines are used to determine the amount of child support. The figure will be based on the number of children the couple has. If there's one child, the support payment will be 17 percent of the noncustodial parent's income; for two children, 25 percent; for three children, 29 percent; for four children, 31 percent; for five or more children, 35 percent. This does not include expenses for child care, medical treatment, or education. These amounts are usually prorated in proportion to both parents' incomes. In the United States child support is not considered taxable income nor can it be deducted by the payer.

These percentages are not carved in stone, however. In fact, far from it. The court may deviate from them; it may also allow the parents to set up their own payment schedule. The decision depends on a number of factors, including the financial resources of the custodial parent and the child, the physical and emotional health of the child, any special education needs of the child, the amount of time each parent spends with the child, tax consequences to the parents, the responsibilities of both parents to support children from other relationships, the educational needs of the parents, and the kind of nonmonetary contributions the parents make to the lives of their children.

Later modifications of the contract must be agreeable to both parties. They can be based on either a reduction or an increase in the noncustodial parent's income.*

Enforcement of Child Support

Deadbeat parents owe billions of dollars in unpaid child support to their ex-spouses. All the states have federally funded enforcement programs that help child-support recipients obtain court orders to enforce payment. State agencies may assist recipients in finding noncustodial parents, putting liens against their assets, or having part of their wages withheld. These agencies also have the power to revoke professional licenses and drivers licenses and attach IRS refunds. Some recipients choose to hire lawyers who will provide services based on receiving a percentage of any money that's recovered.

---

*In many states, if the amount of child support isn't working for one of the parties, he or she can go back and get it modified. This is much easier to do if the amount was set by the court. If it was set by agreement of the two parties, it's much more difficult, requiring the documentation of real hardship.

There are also private for-profit agencies that will assist recipients in tracking down their deadbeat exes. Proceed with caution in dealing with these investigation and collection agencies. Most states have no regulatory authority over these businesses and only a few even require that they be licensed. None provide any legal assistance or advice. Some simply find the ex-spouse. Once they do, it's up to the aggrieved custodial parent to obtain a court order and pay for any legal expenses. Other agencies make money by collecting the child-support payments and keeping a percentage as a fee; the rest is sent on to the custodial parent. Again, there are no guidelines determining what they can charge: It's whatever the market will bear. There are agencies that charge an application or processing fee before doing any work; some of these merely refer the case to a generic collection agency after collecting their fee.

(See also child care, divorce, lawyers.)

CLIENT AND CUSTOMER RELATIONS

IT'S NOT WHAT YOU KNOW, or even who you know, that counts in business. Expertise is easy to obtain and networks can be built in a matter of weeks. The real secret is that your clients or customers trust you.

Good client and customer relations are critical to the success of every working person. It doesn't matter whether you're one of thousands of employees of a Fortune 500 company or operating solo out of a 100-square-foot office over a pizza shop, the task is essentially the same. When it comes to dealing with clients and customers, we're all really our own, using our interpersonal abilities and intelligence to win over other people.

Fifty years of business have taught me many skills that I can bring to the table in dealing with clients and customers. A sense of humor, knowledge of my product or service, a willingness to listen and go the extra mile to meet my clients' needs—these are all extremely important in conducting business with other people. But the one element of the relationship that overrides all others is trust.

Business is, at its core, an adversarial relationship. Each party in a transaction wants to get as much out of the other party as possible. If you've earned the trust of your client or customer, it makes every part of the business process that much easier. Even when you have disagreements or arguments, the fact that you trust one another means you'll respect each another's opinions. That, in turn, makes it much easier to reach common ground.

The Shortcut to Trust

But trust isn't easy to earn. It takes time, sometimes months or even years. Only by working with you over time can a client or customer truly see evidence of your character and trustworthiness. It seems to be a natural process that can't be forced. If, over time, clients see that you respect them, operate with their interests in mind, and do what's best for them, they will learn to trust you.

But in today's hyperactive business world there isn't enough time for trust to develop naturally. You probably won't have the opportunity to earn trust. Luckily, there is a short cut: caring.

Customers, clients, coworkers, employers, employees, in fact, just about everyone in the world, will quickly trust you if you demonstrate that you care about them, not just as a client, but as an individual human being. I learned this lesson years ago from watching my friend Kenny Tillman.

Kenny owns an electronics store. He's a natural retailer. When a customer arrives at his store, Kenny or one of his staff members (who Kenny has trained) greets them as soon as they walk in the door. Kenny smiles and introduces himself and asks the customer's name. He shakes hands, and with the slightest bow from the waist, welcomes the customer to the store. He offers to take the customer's raincoat if it's raining outside. He asks if the customer wants some coffee or a glass of water or needs to use the bathroom. And then Kenny politely asks what he can do for the customer. He listens closely. He makes it clear that he is working for the customer, that he is, in fact, delighted to be working for the customer, and that he would bend over backward to provide the customer with whatever is needed. When I saw the way Kenny worked his magic with his customers, I knew I had found a role model.

Today, clients who come to my office are greeted in the same style I learned form Kenny years ago. My assistant knows to anticipate my clients' arrivals and make sure they're made comfortable while they're waiting for me. Coffee, soft drinks, water, and snacks are always offered. When I'm ready to meet with them, I greet them with a smile and let them do the talking. When we're finished, I thank them for coming to me for service. I also like to give them a small gift, if appropriate. Often I'll give them one of the books my coauthor Mark Levine and I have written. Or I'll give them the name of a nice restaurant around the corner where they might want to have lunch. At the very least, I'll walk them to the elevator. All this shows I care.

While all my manners and actions are planned, they're not an act—I really do care. My clients come to me for all sorts of reasons. Some are seeking career advice. Others need legal services. Many need financial advice in their quests to buy a home or start their children's college funds or launch a business. I'm acutely aware that the advice I give them will have an enormous impact on their lives. It's why I love what I do and what keeps me coming into the office day after day. Without them, my life would be considerably diminished.

(See also employees, networking.)

CLOSINGS

Real estate closings are almost always formalities; ritualized exchanges of checks and documents signifying the transfer of ownership of a home. Of course there are the occasional exceptions that become ritualized nightmares.

The closing is the final step in the real estate transaction. You, your lawyer, and your real estate agent will sit down with the other party and her lawyer and perhaps another real estate agent to finalize the deal. A representative of the bank that's providing the buyer's mortgage will also be there. After signing what seems like an endless number of documents, you'll leave either a proud homeowner or a much richer former homeowner.

Closings generally proceed quite quickly. When something goes wrong, however, the proceedings will grind to a halt until the problem is fixed. This can take anywhere from several minutes to several days. In the meantime, if you've already moved out of your previous home, you may find yourself without a roof over your head. This is why I always recommend to my clients that they learn about the process beforehand and not leave everything to their representatives. When a transaction involving hundreds of thousands of dollars is at stake, you can't be too careful. That's particularly true when you're the buyer.

Buyer's Preparation

If you're a buyer, the most striking thing you'll notice at the closing is that everyone will leave with a check but you. You'll be the one writing them in exchange for a set of keys. Here are the most common closing costs.

Lawyer's fees: You'll be responsible for paying your lawyer and the bank's lawyer. Sometimes the bank's lawyer's fee will be split between the buyer and seller.

Points: These are a one-time service charge sometimes assessed by the lender to cover the costs of processing the mortgage and other activities related to your loan. They could be from 1 to 3 percent of the amount of the mortgage.

Interest: You'll be responsible for the interest that will accrue on your mortgage between the closing date and the beginning of the next interest period, usually the first of the month.

Lender's inspection fee: This pays for the property inspection conducted by the bank's representative.

Survey fee: Often, when a property changes hands a survey must be conducted to ascertain the property boundaries. The buyer pays the bill. If the existing survey isn't very old, the same surveyor can be hired to "update" the survey for half the cost of having an entirely new survey done.

Purchase money insurance (PMI): Most lenders require PMI if a buyer is putting down less than 20 percent; otherwise they won't be able to sell the loan on the secondary mortgage market. This can add from $800 to more than $2,500 to your closing costs.

Taxes: If the seller has paid property taxes that cover any period of time beyond the closing date, the buyer must provide reimbursement.

Homeowner's insurance: Lenders require that they are listed as beneficiaries on your homeowner's policy. They also require that the first homeowner's insurance premium be paid at closing. This guarantees that if the property burns down an hour after they give you your mortgage they'll be able to get their money back.*

Escrow deposits: These are payments to the lender to create a reserve fund that will cover any property taxes and homeowner's insurance premiums that come due before the normal monthly escrow payments have sufficiently accrued to meet the bills. By law you'll receive interest on your escrow and a refund of any excess.

Title charges: These cover the costs of a title search and title insurance. The title search ensures there are no liens or other encumbrances that will prevent or inhibit clear title. Title insurance protects you if the title search firm makes a mistake.

Be Prepared

Make sure you arrive at your closing knowing what your costs are going to be. You can get an approximation from the good faith estimate the lender must give you within three days of applying for your mortgage. The lender should also provide you with a copy of the Department of Housing and Urban Development (HUD) guide to settlement costs. If they don't give you one, you can get one from your realtor.

The day before you close you should go over the uniform settlement statement. This will list the exact costs you'll be expected to pay. You can get this document from the lender.

When you get to the closing, make sure your lawyer has examined every document you're supposed to sign. Then examine them yourself. You'll be surprised at some of the mistakes that are made. Sometimes the interest rate on the mortgage form will be wrong (usually in the bank's favor, of course). Other times you may be asked to pay for services you already paid for. Even the address of the property can be incorrect. If you don't understand something, ask your lawyer to explain it to you. Everything becomes final once the documents are signed. If you need to correct a mistake or renegotiate any aspect of the deal, you must do it now.

---

*Actually, they invariably give you the money and their permission to rebuild.

Seller's Preparation

For a seller, closings can be a bit anticlimactic. The house is already cleaned out. The moving van is probably on the road. If you still have a mortgage, it will be paid off at the closing. Your broker and lawyer will be paid then as well. Almost all that's left is for you to collect your check for the net proceeds from the sale. The only possible holdups would be if the buyer, for some reason, doesn't have sufficient funds to pay all the fees or if you need to leave some funds to cover subsequent events, such as repairs that weren't made.

Unfortunately, you as the seller are the low man on the totem pole. If there's any problem, your lawyer and broker will end up applying pressure on you to make last-minute concessions to compensate for any buyer shortfalls. You could, in theory, refuse and let the deal collapse. In reality, the best you can do is assign the blame for not anticipating this to your lawyer and broker and ask them to take part of the hit by lowering their fees and commission. In the final analysis, if there's a problem, just do whatever it takes to get the deal closed.

(See also lawyers, mortgage loans, moving, property taxes.)

CLOTHING

CLOTHES MAKE THE MAN—and these days, the woman, too.
How we dress has an enormous impact on how other people perceive us. At the office, our attire gives subtle messages to the people we work for and with. The proper clothing provides an air of authority and commands the respect of others. It provides an unspoken message: "I'm in charge. I'm a professional. Mine is the last word."

Improper attire can do just the opposite. If you wear ill-fitting, unkempt, and unattractive clothing, you elicit some very simple unspoken responses. Employees will think: "I'm supposed to respect this person? Give me a break!" Employers will think: "I don't want this slob representing my company." Clients and customers will think: "His work is probably as poor as his fashion sense" or "He has no respect for me."

Business Attire for Men

Despite the move toward casual dress in the workplace, I still believe men should wear a jacket and tie to work. The choice between a suit and a blazer and slacks should be made based on the occasion, with the understanding that a suit conveys greater authority and is considered far more formal. An important meeting with clients or with peers from within your organization calls for a suit. For an average day with not much on the schedule, a blazer or tweed jacket is fine.

A man's business wardrobe should include several suits in conservative colors: navy blue, medium to charcoal gray, medium to dark brown. No green, please, although some subtle shades of olive are perfectly acceptable. A quiet pinstripe or pattern in the fabric can add variety. I suggest you build your way up to a minimum of five suits. This allows you to wear a different one each day of the week if necessary.

A navy blazer is another wardrobe staple. It provides enormous versatility. With a pair of dark slacks and a shirt and tie, a blazer can be almost as dressy as a suit. With a pair of khakis and a golf shirt or turtleneck, it becomes a casual outfit that can be worn almost anywhere.

Shoes, shirts, ties, and accessories should be equally conservative. I favor white and blue dress shirts, some with stripes, and ties with subtle patterns or regimental stripes. I have shoes in black, brown, and cordovan with belts that match. I'm not much for jewelry, other than a nice watch and my wedding ring. I suggest you keep it equally simple. Above all, please, no necklaces or bracelets whatsoever.

Business Attire for Women

Standard business attire for women should include a selection of suits, skirts, blazers, and conservatively cut dresses. Fortunately, the dreaded power suit with its buttoned-up blouse and little bow tie have given way to suits or blazers with open-neck blouses and jewelry or a scarf. Skirt lengths should be modest. Shoes should be equally conservative, with heels of moderate height. Keep accessories and jewelry simple and tasteful.

Women certainly have a bit more latitude than men when it comes to color, style, and fabric. I won't attempt to issue guidelines in this area other than to point out that there's a fine line between fashion and folly. When selecting clothing for the office, keep in mind the image you want to convey and select clothing that will help you convey that image.

Casual Clothing

As I mentioned earlier, the trend in the past few years has been toward more casual dress for the office. I think this is a mistake. I believe professional dress produces professional behavior. If everyone in the office looks like they're attending a Sunday afternoon barbecue, it can't help but have an effect on behavior and productivity. However, it appears I'm a voice in the wilderness.

The move to casual dress has resulted in a lot of confusion over what is and is not appropriate. Inappropriate attire includes sneakers, sandals, shorts, jeans, T-shirts, tank tops, baseball caps, sleeveless shirts and blouses, sweatshirts, running suits, and shoes without socks. Appropriate attire includes long-sleeved shirts and blouses with collars, sweaters, neatly pressed skirts and slacks, tailored jackets, hard-soled leather shoes (shined, of course), and leather belts that match your shoes.

Want to avoid confusion? Save casual dress for the weekend and put your suit back on. Regardless of whether you want to join me in the wilderness, remember that your attire should not be a distraction. When people leave a meeting, they should remember what you said, not what you were wearing.

(See also employees, jewelry.)

COBRA

THE AMERICAN HEALTH CARE SYSTEM is a travesty. Over and over again in this book you'll read chapters describing ways the informed and financially solvent can work through, over, and around the dysfunctional system that's in place. And after a while, if you're like me, you'll begin to realize how difficult things can be for the uninformed and impoverished. One of the few safety nets these folks have under them is COBRA.

COBRA is an acronym for the Consolidated Omnibus Budget Reconciliation Act, a piece of legislation passed in 1985 to allow people who have left their jobs, been laid off, or been fired to keep their group health insurance. It also covers workers whose hours have been scaled back to the point where they no longer qualify as full-time and thus lose the benefits that accompany full-time status.

COBRA allows you to keep your health insurance for up to 18 months after you leave a job (unless you're fired for cause). The difference is that now you, not your former employer, pay the premiums. There's also a 2 percent fee attached to cover administrative costs. If you decide your plan is too expensive, you have the option of choosing a different plan, as long as it's one current employees can select. Since most people who find themselves "between assignments" are interested in minimizing their expenses, this is an attractive feature, indeed.

There are a couple of catches. First, COBRA only applies in companies with 20 or more employees. Second, COBRA doesn't kick in automatically. You generally need to apply within 60 days of being notified that you have the option of signing up, or 60 days after your coverage would terminate, whichever is later. As with any health plan, a COBRA-provided plan will also cover newborns and adopted children provided you notify the plan within a certain time. Most companies require that you notify them within 30 days of the birth or the effective date of adoption.

If you work for a company with fewer than 20 employees, you're not totally out of luck. Some states have their own COBRA-like legislation. Most require that the plan keep you on for anywhere from 3 to 18 months. You may also be able to convert to an individual plan. Although this will likely be more expensive and provide fewer benefits, it's still better than being assigned to a state risk pool or, even worse, having no coverage at all.

COBRA also comes into effect in cases of death, divorce, or retirement. If a person is covered through the health insurance of a spouse, and the spouse dies or retires or the couple divorces, the person can still receive up to three years' coverage at his or her own expense and with the proper notification. Given the number of elderly the United States will see in the coming decades, this will be an important benefit to many people.

Those of you with dependent children who are older than your plan's limit will be relieved to know that COBRA will allow you to pick up the premiums after they graduate and keep the kids insured until they get started on their careers. Some companies will let you keep them on (with walloping high premiums, of course) even after COBRA expires.

COBRA coverage ends as soon as you (or your child) qualify for another group plan, usually through a new employer. Remember, though, to hold onto your COBRA coverage until the waiting period for the new plan is over. That can sometimes be as long as three months. Also, if you have an illness or other medical condition that the new plan won't cover, the old plan will continue to pay the bills.

(See also adoption, divorce, employees, health insurance.)

COLLEGE FINANCIAL AID APPLICATIONS

COLLEGE COSTS are so out of synch with the rest of the economy that about 75 percent of students now receive some form of financial aid. Monetary assistance for higher education used to be for only the poorest applicants, but today it is a middle-class entitlement.

Derived from federal, state, college, and private sources, financial aid is designed to make up the difference between what a student and his parents can pay and the actual costs of college. It can be applied to tuition, fees, books, and other academic expenses. It can also cover living costs like housing, food, and transportation. There are programs for undergraduate and graduate students, and for students attending vocational and trade schools.

Financial aid recipients are usually offered a combination of low-interest loans, grants, scholarships, and work-study programs. The awards are packaged by college financial aid officers in an amount sufficient to cover that portion of the costs that parents and students cannot afford. Grants and scholarships are highly coveted, simply because they don't need to be paid back. Loans, on the other hand, must be paid back, although most payments don't begin until a student has either graduated or left school.

Filling Out the Application

Anyone applying for financial aid of any kind must first file the Free Application for Federal Student Aid (FAFSA). The deadline for filing the FAFSA and other financial aid forms is May 1 for the school year beginning the following fall. Do not wait that long. Although loan sources are plentiful, grant and scholarship funds are limited. Once they're awarded, that's it. Applications should be filled out and submitted as early as possible during the second half of a student's senior year in high school.

Not surprisingly, financial aid applications must be accompanied by a great deal of financial information. Parents' and students' income tax returns, mortgage information, bank statements, business records, statements from investment and retirement accounts, and many other records may be requested. Be extremely careful and deliberate in filling out the applications. Mistakes will slow up the process.

About three weeks after the forms are sent in, applicants receive a confirmation report. This allows them to review the information submitted and make any corrections.

Notification of Eligibility

After another two or three weeks applicants receive a report detailing their own and their parents' expected contribution and the student's eligibility for financial assistance. The report will also go to the student's college or university and the appropriate state scholarship agency. Students who have applied for Pell grants receive a student aid report (SAR) indicating eligibility.

Most schools make financial aid decisions and send out letters notifying recipients between April and July. These indicate how much financial aid the student will receive for the school year and break the figure down by source. The letter will also stipulate how grant and scholarship funds will be distributed and whether there are any special conditions attached. The interest rate and repayment conditions for loans will be described. It will also describe any type of work-study program the student will take part in.

Important Rules to Follow

The financial aid process is time-consuming and confusing. To expedite the process it's critical to do things correctly. Here are some basic rules for applying for financial aid:

- Apply, no matter your family income. The worst that can happen is that you'll be turned down. If you are, try again next year.

- Apply early. Remember, sources of grants and scholarships are limited. Check deadlines and make sure your applications are in well ahead of schedule.

- Register for the draft. Male students have to be registered with the Selective Service to be eligible for federal assistance.

- Follow directions. Financial aid applications can be astonishingly lengthy and complex. Proceed slowly and follow directions to the letter.

- Be neat. It will speed up the processing of your application. If you write in the margins or attach sticky notes, the application may be returned to you.

- Make sure your applications are complete. Double-check that you haven't left out any information, and don't forget to sign the the forms.

- Send the originals. Only original application forms will be accepted. Keep a copy of every financial aid form you submit.

- Include your application payment if one is required.

Be Thorough and Persistent

If there's one iron-clad rule that applies to financial aid, it's this: Apply for every type of financial aid imaginable. There are thousands of grants, scholarships, low-interest loans, work-study programs, and other kinds of financial aid out there. You just may find that you fall within the eligibility guidelines of some of them.

Start investigating early, when your children are just starting high school. The standard federal and institutional sources of financial aid are easy to find. To locate the more obscure funding sources—those that may be offered by corporations, foundations, or other organizations—you'll need to do your own research, and that takes time.

Finally, be persistent. If you get turned down one year by a specific financial aid program,

Learning the Lingo

The financial aid process has its own lingo, with as many acronyms as NASA. Here are some of the most common.

College Scholarship Service (CSS): The CSS is an agency that analyzes financial need.

Expected Family Contribution (EFC): This is the amount parents will be expected to contribute for a student's college expenses.

Free Application for Federal Student Aid (FAFSA): This is the federal government's free application form, which must be filed for consideration for all Title IV financial assistance programs. It's also used to determine eligibility for all federal student loans. Separate forms are usually needed for applications for state and college financial assistance programs.

Financial Aid Form (FAF): This form is used to determine a family's financial need and ability to pay. The College Scholarship Service processes these forms and sends the results to colleges and universities. FAFs are used only when a student wishes to apply for non–Title IV funds or if a college requires supplemental data on a student.

Simplified Needs Test (SNT): This form is used by families who have adjusted gross incomes under $50,000 and who file IRS Form 1040A or 1040EZ, or who don't have to file income tax returns.

Student Aid Report (SAR): This is the official notification of federal Pell grant eligibility. The SAR usually arrives four to six weeks after an application is submitted. The report is then forwarded by the student to the appropriate colleges and universities, which then determine the amount of the Pell grant. Students who are declared ineligible for Pell grants must forward their SARs to the appropriate schools in order to qualify for other types of financial assistance.

apply again the next year. If that doesn't work out, do it again the year after that. All it takes is time and a few stamps.

_____

(See also college grants and scholarships, college loans, college planning, college selection.)

COLLEGE GRANTS AND SCHOLARSHIPS

GRANTS AND SCHOLARSHIPS are the most desirable forms of college financial aid. Why? It's simple. They don't need to be paid back.

The criteria for the two differ. *Grants* are almost always based on financial need. If they're federal or state grants, they're provided by tax dollars. Colleges and universities award grants that are supported with income from their endowments. *Scholarships* are usually given as a reward for exceptional talent in academics, the arts, or athletics. They're awarded by colleges and universities, corporations, private foundations, and other organizations. As with grants, most scholarships awarded by schools are from money generated by endowment. The exceptions are athletic scholarships, which are often supported by income generated by individual athletic departments.

It's important to understand up front that not all grants and scholarships will actually reduce the current bills you and your child are facing. Many of these awards are applied to an applicant's assessed need. (See the "The Concept of Need" on page 155.) The contribution you and your child are expected to make remains the same. It's the college that actually gets the immediate financial benefit, since the school simply takes the scholarship money and provides that much less in its own financial aid package. Still, grants and scholarships are advantageous to you and your child because they don't have to be repaid, unlike loans. They may not save you anything today, but they will save you or your child money in the future.

Federal Grant Programs

The Pell Grant Program is the federal government's largest need-based financial aid program. It's so broad, in fact, that students must apply for a Pell grant before they can be considered for any other type of federal financial assistance. When putting together financial packages, colleges often use the Pell grant as the foundation for the total aid package. The amount received is based on need and can be as much as $2,300 a year. To qualify for a Pell grant, students must:

- Demonstrate financial need.

- Have a high school diploma or GED.

- Be enrolled in or accepted by an approved school in either an undergraduate program or a certificate program.

- Attend school at least half-time.

- Maintain satisfactory academic progress.

- Be free of any grant debt and not be in default of any loans.

- Be U.S. citizens or eligible noncitizens.

- Be registered with the Selective Service (males aged 18 to 26)

- File a Statement of Educational Purpose guaranteeing that any money they receive will be used solely for educational purposes.

- Sign an Anti–Drug Abuse Act Certification.

- Be working toward their first bachelor's degree. Students working on subsequent bachelor's degrees are not eligible for Pell grants.

Supplemental Educational Opportunity Grants (SEOGs) are supplemental to Pell grants and are awarded to students with exceptional financial need. Most come from families whose annual income is below $10,000. Priority is given to students who have already received Pell grants. SEOGs can be as high as $4,000 a year. Extra money may be available if a student is enrolled in a study-abroad program.

State Grant Programs

The states also administer grant programs. Information is available from each state's department of higher education, board of regents, state scholarship commission, or similar office.

College Financial Aid

More than 85 percent of colleges and universities offer some form of financial aid to their students. Most grants and scholarships are provided with endowment income, so the higher a school's endowment per student, the greater the amount of money available.

Like federal and state grants, most college grants are need-based. The financial aid office at each school can provide you with specific requirements for eligibility.

Scholarships, however, are awarded for exceptional accomplishments or talents. High school performance, high school rank, ACT scores, SAT scores, and other academic measures can all result in a scholarship. So can athletic ability. Division I colleges and universities dole out thousands of "full-ride" scholarships every year to athletes in major sports like football and basketball. The practice pays for itself because of the enormous income these sports generate for the schools. But athletes in less popular sports like swimming, track and field, lacrosse, ice hockey, and wrestling can also earn scholarships at schools with competitive programs.

Other abilities can be rewarded as well. There are scholarships for music, art, drama, and other disciplines. There are also scholarships reserved solely for women and for various ethnic groups.

Watch Out for Scams

The demand for college scholarships has generated a number of scams. Most are run by companies that guarantee they'll find your child a grant or scholarship. In return, all you need to do is pay a modest fee. It's a practice that has increased as college expenses have continued to rise. According to the National Association of Student Financial Aid Administrators, several thousand people fall victim to these scams each year. Here are three common promises that should make you suspicious:

- The company claims to have access to information that no one else has. In fact, the same information can easily be found with a little research in high school guidance offices, in public libraries, and on the Web.

- The company promises to fill out and send in applications and do other tasks for you. This rarely happens. If it does, there's no guarantee that the deadlines will be met.

- The company guarantees to get your child a grant or scholarship. This is impossible. There are no guarantees with grants and scholarships.

There are legitimate scholarship search firms out there, but they're really just doing the work that you could do yourself. A little time with reference books in libraries and on the Internet will give you the same information they're going to sell you. There's no reason not to do it yourself.

Carefully examine scholarship offerings when researching colleges and universities. Find out how much of the total cost they cover, if they are renewable, and what you must do to renew them.

Other Sources

There are more than 300,000 individual scholarship and grant programs sponsored by organizations like Rotary International and the Elks, as well as by corporations like Coca-Cola and General Motors. To find the more obscure funding sources, you'll need to do your own research, and that takes time. But the rewards are well worth it.

While there are many books available in local libraries, I suggest you consult *Winning Scholarships for College: An Insider's Edge* by Marianne Ragins. As one of five children of a widowed mother, Ragins had enormous financial aid needs. When she reached high school, she started researching grant and scholarship sources. By the time she stopped writing letters, making telephone calls, and filling out applications, she had racked up more than enough money to completely cover her costs to attend Florida A&M University. Her book lists 100 scholarship sources and tips on how to apply for them.

(See also college financial aid applications, college loans, college planning, college selection.)

COLLEGE LOANS

D ON'T FEEL BAD. You're not the only one who can't afford the total cost of a four-year college or university education for your child. In fact, few people, regardless how diligently they save and how smartly they invest, can cover their child's complete bill. Why? Costs have soared beyond what any normal family can reasonably be expected to pay on its own, as the table on page 158 shows.

Public colleges, the state and city universities that have provided a solid education at an affordable price for years, are now averaging around $10,000 a year for undergraduate study. The cost of a year at an average private institution has risen to above $20,000. The elite schools—Harvard, Princeton, Stanford, MIT, and the like—are hovering around $30,000. With prices like that there's no more shame in taking out loans for college than there is in taking out a mortgage to buy a home.

Due to the climbing costs, millions of dollars of financial aid are now available to help students fill in the gaps, including a variety of public and private loan programs. Here are some of the most popular:

Federal Loan Programs

The Stafford Loan Program provides two types of federally insured low-interest loans to qualified students: subsidized loans based on need and unsubsidized loans. (See "The Concept of Need" on page 155.) The interest rate is pegged to the 90-day Treasury bill rate, plus 3.1 percent; it is capped at 8.25 percent. There are no limits on the total amount the program can lend, so everyone who qualifies for a loan gets one. Both undergraduate and graduate students are eligible, as are students enrolled in vocational programs and business, technical, and trade schools.

About 70 percent of Stafford loans are issued through banks, credit unions, and savings and loan associations. The remaining 30 percent are issued by colleges and universities participating in the federal Direct Student Loan Program (DSLP); in this case the lender is the U.S. Department of Education.

Repayment of the principal and interest on subsidized Stafford loans begins after a student has stopped attending school, regardless of whether he or she has graduated. There is a six-month grace period. Borrowers have up to 10 years to repay their loans, and the minimum monthly payment is $50, or $600 per year. There are certain situations in which repayment can be deferred. There are even some situations in which a loan may be forgiven. Most often this is done for teachers, nurses, and other people working for communities or people in need.

Students who fail to qualify for a need-based Stafford loan can apply for an unsubsidized Stafford loan. These differ from subsidized Staffords in two ways. First, the borrowing limit is higher. And second, the interest on unsubsidized loans begins to accrue immediately. Borrowers have the option of making monthly interest-only payments while they're still attending school.

Perkins loans carry very low interest rates and are available to eligible students enrolled in undergraduate, graduate, and professional programs. They are based on need and are derived from federal funds that are allotted to, and distributed by, college financial aid offices. Undergraduates can borrow up to $15,000 for all four years of study, and graduate students can borrow up to $30,000, including Perkins loans received for undergraduate study. Limits are increased by 20 percent for study abroad. Students do not apply directly for Perkins loans; they are distributed at the discretion of the individual college financial aid officers. Repayment begins six months after a student leaves school, and the minimum monthly payment is $40, or $480 a year. As with Stafford loans, there are circumstances in which a Perkins loan debt may be forgiven.

The Parent Loans to Undergraduate Students (PLUS) program provides financial assistance to families who don't qualify for other types of federal assistance. Families can borrow the total amount needed to pay for college less the value of any financial aid received. Interest rates vary but are capped at 10 percent. The loans are made by banks, credit unions, savings and loans, and the states.

PLUS loans frequently involve a credit check, so you may find yourself turned down or limited in the amount you can borrow. There are also origination fees and insurance fees. Still, these loans are a good source of funds should you find yourself coming up short of what you need. Repayment of PLUS loans begins 60 days after the loan is made, and the minimum annual repayment is $600. You can take up to 10 years to repay the loans. There are also conditions under which the loans can be forgiven.

DSLP loans, mentioned earlier, are made up of both Stafford loans and PLUS loans, and are obtained directly from colleges and universities.

State Loan Programs

The individual states provide a wide range of financial aid programs for college-bound students. All states offer need-based assistance. You may also find special programs that offer low-cost loans for private colleges and universities in the state, as well as loan-forgiveness programs for graduates who go into certain professions, such as teaching and health care, and who work in the state for a number of years. Information on state loan programs is available from your state department of higher education. College financial aid offices should also have plenty of information.

College Loans

Many schools have loan programs for families that don't meet federal or state loan requirements, but the interest rate is usually higher. These loans should be considered only when other sources of financial aid fall through.

Other Sources of Loans

If you don't qualify for a low-interest government loan but still must come up with some cash, there are private loan programs that can help you. Most will lend you some or all of the money you need at relatively reasonable interest rates and with long repayment schedules.

The Education Resources Institute (TERI) is the nation's largest private educational lender. You can borrow up to the total cost of your child's education and have up to 25 years for repayment. The terms vary and are dictated by the program's sponsors, most of which are banks.

The New England Loan Marketing Association (Nellie Mae) will lend you anywhere from $2,000 to the full cost of your child's education, less the value of the financial aid received. Interest rates are usually 2 to 4 percent above the prime rate, plus an initial fee of 5 percent of the amount of the loan. Repayment can be as long as 20 years.

The College Board offers two options. The Extra-Credit Loan covers all costs less financial aid for up to 4 years and gives you up to 15 years for repayment. The Extra-Time Loan allows you to borrow a year at a time. Repayment can be made over 10 years, and you can wait until your child graduates to begin repayment of the principal. Interest rates are tied to the 90-day Treasury bill plus 4.5 percent.

The College Resource Center will lend you up to $50,000. There is an application fee of 3 percent of the value of the loan and interest rates can be as low as the prime rate plus 2.5 percent. Repayment begins within 45 days, and the minimum monthly amount is $100 a month or 2 percent of the outstanding balance, whichever is greater.

The Concept of Need

The federal and state governments, as well as colleges and universities, expect you and your child to contribute to the cost of a higher education. The amount you are expected to contribute will be based on the answers you provide on a form known as the Free Application for Federal Student Aid (FAFSA).

The FAFSA form asks for the amount and sources of parents' incomes, a list of assets, parents' ages, the number of dependents parents both have, the number of children both parents have in college, and a number of other factors. The FAFSA form will also ask for information on the child's own finances. Using a standard accounting procedure approved by Congress, a financial service will then make a determination of how much parents and child should be able to contribute.

A very rough current estimate is that parents are expected to contribute 6 percent of their assets every year to meet a child's college costs. Children are expected to contribute 35 percent of their assets plus a share of any regular income. That's why, when it comes time for college, it makes sense to have your name, rather than your child's name, on a bank account.

Those expected annual contributions are then subtracted from the annual cost of attending a particular college or university. The difference, if there is any, is known as "need." That is the amount most subsidized-loan programs, financial aid, and scholarship programs focus on addressing. It is assumed you and you child will pay your expected contribution either out-of-pocket or through unsubsidized loans.

Playing the Need Game

As you've probably guessed, the fewer assets you and your child have on paper, the more "need" you'll have and the more aid you'll get. The secret to playing the need game is to understand which assets the government and colleges consider and which they ignore and to then shuffle your assets accordingly to qualify for more assistance.

The government considers the following assets as being available to pay for a child's college education:

- Employment income

- Rental property income

- Social Security income

- Business ownership income

- Bank accounts

- Investment accounts

- Stocks and bonds

- Real estate other than your principal residence

- The value of a business

On the other hand, the government, and some, but not all, colleges, ignore two major asset areas in qualifying your child's need:

- Qualified retirement accounts

- Home equity

Individuals with sufficient liquidity and foresight can dramatically increase the amount of subsidized aid their child receives by shifting their assets to areas the government and many colleges ignore. For example, someone who dissolves an investment portfolio and uses the money to further fund their retirement accounts or pay down their mortgage will boost the aid their child receives. Similarly, deferring income into a subsequent tax year can also increase aid.

(See also college financial aid applications, college grants and scholarships, college planning.)

COLLEGE PLANNING

W ITH THE COSTS of higher education rocketing upward year after year, the time has come to give serious thought to whether or not your children truly need to attend college.

I believe a child should go to college only if he is going to get out of it value comparable to what he and his parents are spending. I don't think someone should pay $100,000 or more to mature, or to meet a mate, or to have a good time for four years. There is nothing wrong with presenting your child with the option of going to college, buying a home, or starting his own business. For many people, attending college full-time might just be a waste of time. They may be better suited to entering the job market or launching their own business and, if they wish to, taking college classes during the evening. I also believe the money you have saved for a child's college education may be equally well spent helping him establish a business or buy his first home. There's no rule that says a career can't be started earlier than age 21, or that you can't go to college after having worked for a decade.

Career Tracks and College

There are four career tracks in the United States, and only one actually requires a college degree.

The nontechnical track includes those who do skilled or unskilled physical labor that doesn't require the use of advanced information technology. Examples would be carpenters, construction workers, electricians, health care aides, and housekeepers. Someone looking to pursue a nontechnical career would be better off investigating apprenticeship programs than colleges.

The technical track includes those who use, develop, and repair advanced technology. Examples include lab technicians, clerical workers, computer system operators, and electronic equipment service personnel. Careers in the technical track require vocational training, which generally doesn't come from a university.

The creative track includes individuals who use their own artistry to make a living. Examples would be visual artists, writers, chefs, entrepreneurs, designers, photographers, filmmakers, and actors. A college education would be a plus for these individuals, but not a necessity. A degree would be a safety net for them, but it won't affect their creative success.

Finally there's the professional track, which includes doctors, lawyers, dentists, accountants, financial planners, architects, nurses, bankers, teachers, journalists, and those who specialize in one of the three business disciplines: marketing, finance, or management. Anyone looking to pursue any of these professions will need a college degree.

Of course, it's crazy to start assigning your 2-year-old to a career track. Such educational decisions can't be reached until your child is close to college age. Prior to that you should be prudent financially and proceed as if college is a likelihood, because if your child does decide to go to college, every year of savings counts.

The Average Cost of a Four-Year College Education*

Year	Public College	Private College
2000	$41,600	$95,680
2001	$43,264	$99,507
2002	$44,995	$103,487
2003	$46,794	$107,627
2004	$48,666	$111,932
2005	$50,613	$116,409
2006	$52,637	$121,066
2007	$54,743	$125,908
2008	$56,932	$130,944
2009	$59,210	$136,182
2010	$61,578	$141,629
2011	$64,041	$147,295
2012	$66,603	$153,186
2013	$69,267	$159,313
2014	$72,038	$165,686
2015	$74,919	$172,314
2016	$77,916	$179,206
2017	$81,033	$186,375
2018	$84,274	$193,830

* Assuming a 4 percent annual increase.

Start Early

The cost of sending a child to college today is at an all-time high. A year at the Ivy League schools and the nation's other elite private universities like Stanford and Duke has reached the mid-$30,000 range. The average state university is more than $10,000 annually. These prices will only continue to increase. Those of you with newborns could end up paying well over $200,000 for four years at a top school. The key to even making a dent in those costs is to start saving now. The sooner you begin, the more successful you'll be in meeting the huge financial burden that awaits you.

I realize that for a young couple at the beginning of their careers, putting away a significant amount of money each month may be difficult. You have all the costs associated with your new child. You may have a mortgage and the expenses of furnishing a home. Plus you probably have some residual spending habits from your carefree single days. A child's college education seems miles away.

In a sense, it is. But don't kid yourselves. Eighteen years can suddenly become ten years, or eight or six years. By that time, it will be impossible to put enough aside to pay for college. Start early, create an investment plan, and stick to it. It may not be easy, particularly at first, but when that first tuition bill arrives, you'll be happy you went to all the trouble and sacrifice.

That being said, all you can do is your best. Don't beat yourself up if you can't save enough for a Harvard tuition. There are plenty of outstanding state colleges that cost far less and offer just as good an education as any private university. And if your child has his heart set on Harvard there are always work-study programs and loans he could take advantage of to bridge any gap in funds.

Go for Growth in the Early Years

Time mitigates investment risk. Because your goal is so far off, you can be aggressive in your investment strategies in the early years and direct the bulk of your investment dollars to stocks. Over time, stocks have provided a better return on investment than bonds and other types of security. They're also riskier. But since you have a number of years until the bills start arriving, you can weather the ups and downs of the market and still be confident in overall growth.

If you want to spread out your risk, you can diversify by purchasing stocks in different companies and different industries. The stock of some companies, like the blue chips that make up the Dow Jones Industrial Average, can be counted on for solid, if unspectacular, growth. Others, such as those of companies in the biotechnology and information technology industries, are riskier but have the potential to provide enormous returns.

Reduce Risk as College Approaches

The closer you are to your child's enrollment date, the less risk you can afford. You also need to be concerned about liquidity—your ability to turn your investments into cash when you need it.

By the time your child is five or six years away from college, you should have begun replacing the stocks in your portfolio with bonds and mutual funds. Bonds, particularly those backed by municipalities and the federal government, are virtually risk-free. Stock mutual funds carry slightly more risk but also have the potential to provide a greater return than bonds. Carefully selected, they can be a profitable and relatively safe investment. For maximum safety you should avoid aggressive growth funds or small-cap funds.

Don't forget that you're going to need access to your money. Any bonds you purchase should have maturation dates that return your money to you at the desired time. You can redeem them early, but it will cost you some or all of the interest you've earned. Mutual funds can be sold at any time.

The Beauty of Zero-Coupon Bonds

Zero-coupon bonds are perhaps the perfect investment for college. They pay no interest while they're maturing. Instead, the interest accrues and is paid to the investor at maturity. Because they delay paying interest, zero-coupon bonds are, of course, sold at a deep discount from their stated value. For example, a bond that will pay you $10,000 in 10 years might only cost you $5,000 today. The potential for paying for college is obvious. Careful timing of your bond purchases can result in a series of bonds that mature just as you need the money to pay for tuition each year. There are two downsides, however. Zero-coupon bonds are very volatile in the secondary market, so if you have to sell a bond before maturity, you could lose money. And Uncle Sam doesn't care that you're not receiving your interest every year: The IRS requires you pay taxes on the interest you would have received as if payments had actually been made.

Don't Forget Financial Aid

Don't despair if, despite your best efforts, you find you just can't save enough to meet all your children's college expenses. Colleges and universities, the federal government, state governments, and countless corporations and foundations go out of their way to make sure money is available to those who need it to meet their college expenses.

The best kind of financial aid is in the form of grants and scholarships, which don't have to be paid back. These are awarded to students who have exceptional academic, athletic, artistic, and other types of skills. The majority of financial aid, however, is made in the form of low-interest loans that don't need to be paid back until the student graduates.

Although the federal and state governments provide the bulk of financial aid dollars, there are more than 300,000 individual scholarship and grant programs sponsored by private organizations and corporations. Finding the ones that match your children's needs and talents takes time and a bit of research, but it's worth it.

(See also bonds, college grants and scholarships, college loans, mutual funds, stocks.)

COLLEGE SELECTION

IT'S CRAZY that we ask 17- or 18-year-olds to decide where they want to go to college. At that age, very few kids know what they want to do with the rest of their lives—that's one of the things they're going to college to figure out. Yet colleges are now so numerous, and many of them have become so specialized, that it can seem to young people that they they're deciding the rest of their lives by selecting a college. Nothing could be further from the truth.

Narrowing the Decision

To help young people see this, I think parents need to become actively involved in the selection process. Here are some questions you can help your child answer to prepare a list of viable candidates.

What Are Your Career Goals?   This is probably the most difficult question of all, and if it's not appropriate to ask it of your child, don't. But if you think he does know, or at least has an idea, you're both that much ahead of the game. If your child doesn't yet have career goals, he probably does have areas of interest that may turn into career options. Help him keep those interests in mind when he's evaluating different schools.

What Size School Is Right for You?   U.S. colleges and universities range in size from a few hundred students to tens of thousands of students. Generally, smaller schools offer smaller class sizes and more of a sense of community than large universities. There's less competition for resources, and its usually easier to get the help you need if you have academic or personal problems.

Large schools, on the other hand, have more resources: bigger and better labs, more sophisticated computer networks, more athletic facilities and intramural sports programs, bigger libraries, and increased opportunities for off-campus study like semester-abroad programs and internships.

You may have your own thoughts as to which type of school would be best for your child, but help him come to decisions of his own. Did he go to a large or small high school? Did he enjoy the experience or not? Is he a self-starter or does he sometimes need a push? Self-starters will do well at big schools, while the occasionally apathetic will get lost. But self-starters might feel limited at a small school, while those in need of motivation will be more apt to get it.

What Kind of Academic Offerings Are You Looking For?   The big choice here is between a liberal arts curriculum and a more specialized program with intense concentration in a certain field. A liberal arts background is excellent preparation for graduate school or professional training in law, medicine, or business. A more specialized program will prepare for immediate entry after graduation into either a specific profession (like engineering or teaching) or business.

When in doubt it's usually best to opt for a liberal arts program, which will expose your child to many more potential fields. If, after a couple of years at a liberal arts school, it's clear a more specialized path would be better, your child can always transfer.

What Kind of Academic Environment Do You Prefer?   Some colleges and universities have higher academic standards than others. If your child wants to get all he can out of college academically and intellectually, then a school with a tough academic reputation may be better for him. But if he's interested in a balance of school work, social events, and other activities, he may be happier at a school with less pressure.

Do You Prefer a Coed or a Single-Sex Campus?   Yes, there are still single-sex colleges in the United States. Most are for women, and for some they're the perfect environment. Women who attend women-only colleges generally become more interested in their courses, have more confidence in their intellectual abilities, and go on to graduate school more often than women in coeducational schools.

Do You Want to Stay Near Home?　For some young people, the most traumatic part of going to college isn't the academic load, it's moving away from home. It's easy for kids to be pressured into "going away" because all their friends are attending distant schools. Sometimes, however, staying at or near home is a better choice for children who still have some growing up to do. A compromise might be attending a school close enough that weekend trips home are easy and inexpensive.

Do You Want a School Where Fraternities and Sororities Are Active?　Greek life, as it's called, dominates the social scene at some colleges and universities. For students who like a busy social whirl, fraternity and sorority life is often a wonderful part of the college experience. There's more to Greek life than parties, however. Many are active with community organizations or involved in other public service activities. Greeks also study. At many schools the average GPA of fraternity and sorority members is higher than that of the rest of the student population.

Will the Availability of Financial Aid Affect Your Choice?　Here's one question you can definitely help your child answer. Very few students today come from families who can afford the entire cost of a four-year education. If you're relying on financial aid, you'll want him to get some idea of what's available from each school.

Research Your Candidates

The college research process can't begin too soon. Here are some of the best sources of information:

Guidance counselors. A good guidance counselor can help match students' interests, goals, and talents with the proper college.

Outside counselors. Independent college counselors can also be useful in making recommendations. They're expensive, however, and may be beyond the reach of many families. My advice is to work with your high school staff first. If you feel you're not getting the information you need, then start looking for an independent. One word of caution. If you run into a counselor who guarantees he can get you into a particular school, thank him politely and walk away—fast.

College representatives. Most colleges have admissions officers who travel around the country to meet with high school students and their parents. They often are recent graduates of the colleges they represent, and they do an excellent job of describing what their schools have to offer.

Alumni. Alumni are often a college's best ambassadors. Just keep in mind that the longer they've been away from school, the less accurate their knowledge will be. The younger they are, the more accurate the report you'll get.

Guidebooks. There are dozens of college guidebooks on the market offering unbiased, carefully researched information.

The JUCO Option

JUCOs, or junior colleges, offer two-year associate degrees. They generally fall into two categories: community colleges, which offer varied liberal arts programs; and agricultural and technical colleges, which offer more specialized, pre- or paraprofessional programs. These two-year schools can serve as the basis of a couple of very savvy college strategies.

Students who underachieved in high school can attend a junior college for one or two years, demonstrate improved academic performance, and get into a better college than they would have directly out of high school.

Students who can't afford four years at an expensive university can save money by attending junior college for two years, then transferring to the expensive school. They'll receive the same degree as if they'd attended for four years for much less money.

College recruiting material. Colleges and universities go to great pains—and expense—to create handsome and informative materials to send to prospective students.

The Internet. The sophistication of college and university Web sites varies. The best will take you on a virtual tour of a campus, even letting you apply online. The worst will offer little more than the text and photos from their brochures.

(See also Web sites.)

The Safety School

The safety school is the insurance policy of the college application process. While it's certainly admirable for your child to set his sights high and apply to the best schools he can find, you don't want him finding the mailbox jammed with nothing but rejection notices in the spring.

This is where the safety school comes into play. He should pick at least one college that he knows he'll be able to get into. Many students will use a branch of their state university as a safety school. It may not be a first choice, but it guarantees they won't find themselves working at the car wash or daycare center come fall.

COMMODITIES

DON'T BE A FOOL. I don't care who you are, commodities aren't for you. They're extremely risky investments that can cause you to lose your shirt almost overnight. Only experienced, confident, knowledgeable investors who can afford to lose a great deal of money should even think about commodities.

Of course, human nature being what it is you haven't flipped to the next chapter. Greed is, after all a more integral part of human nature than humility. So in a further effort to shake you of any interest commodity investing, let me explain what it's all about.

At the heart of the commodity market are the raw materials—the commodities—we use every day of our lives: wheat, barley, sugar, orange juice, crude oil for gasoline and fuel oil, precious metals like silver, and many other products. They have in common a built-in volatility because of the many unforeseeable factors that affect their prices. For example, the price of wheat and other crops is directly affected by the weather: A summer drought can severely reduce the harvest and cause prices to skyrocket. The price of crude oil is affected by supply restrictions imposed by oil-producing countries in the Middle East.

Trading in commodities is expensive, regardless of whether you win or lose. First you need to open an account with a broker. With your broker's advice, you can trade individual commodities, and your broker will keep as much as 20 percent of your profits. You can also invest in a commodities fund, for which you'll pay an up-front commission and exorbitant management fees. It's hardly worth the trouble. Although commodities funds, like mutual funds, reduce risk, they usually return only 5 to 10 percent per year.

Many people choose to put their money in commodities futures. These are contracts that require the holder to buy or sell a commodity at a specific price at a certain date in the future. A contract to buy is called a "long position" and is a gamble that the price of the commodity will increase. A contract to sell is a "short position" and speculates that its value will decrease.

Commodities futures have a very practical use for farmers, manufacturers, food processors, and people in other industries. They allow the price of the materials produced or purchased to be locked in. A wheat farmer can protect himself against falling wheat prices by securing a contract to sell his crop at a certain price, for example.

But for investors, commodities futures represent one thing: the ability to make huge profits. This is because they provide investors with a great deal of leverage—the ability to buy a contract for only a fraction of its value. Let's say you enter into a futures contract to buy September wheat for $3 a bushel. (All futures contracts expire on the third Friday of the specified month, so if you hold on to it, your order to buy wheat would be executed on the third Friday in September.) A single wheat contract is worth 5,000 bushels, so the contract would be worth $15,000. But you're only required to pay 10 percent, or $1,500, for the contract. This payment is called the "margin."

But you have no intention of actually buying wheat. You're gambling that wheat prices will rise and you'll be able to make a tidy profit. It could easily happen. Let's say that a few months later wheat prices have risen to $4 a bushel. This means your contract is now worth $20,000. To cash in and collect your profit (which will be diluted by commissions and other costs, by the way), you cancel your obligation to buy September wheat by entering a second contract to sell it. (Conversely, if you originally enter a futures contract to sell a commodity, you enter a buy contract to get out of it.)

But let's take a look at the opposite scenario. Rather than increasing, wheat prices have fallen to $2 a bushel. The contract that was once worth $15,000 is now only worth $10,000. At this point you'll receive a margin call from your broker notifying you that you must put more money in your account to make up the difference. To get out of the deal altogether, you can again enter a contract to sell September wheat. Then you stagger off to count your losses.

If you hold on to a futures contract until it reaches its execution date, you'll have to live up to your obligation. If you have a long position, you'll be responsible for buying the commodity in question at the designated price. If you're short, you'll be expected to come up with the commodity you're obligated to sell. Only 2 or 3 percent of futures contracts are actually carried through, however. Most investors close out their positions long before they reach the execution date.

If nothing else in this chapter has convinced you of the absurdly risky nature of commodities trading, maybe this will: The risk is so high that most brokerage firms go out of their way to protect you from yourself. They'll carefully examine your financial situation before they allow you to invest in commodities. When an industry that's known for gleefully taking your money for almost any other kind of investment suddenly balks, you should take heed. If that's not a warning sign I don't know what is.

(See also futures, gambling, precious metals.)

CONDOMINIUMS AND COOPERATIVES

WHILE MOST PEOPLE THINK that condominiums and cooperatives are interchangeable names for apartments and attached townhouses that are owned rather than rented, they are actually two different forms of real estate ownership.

When you buy a *condominium*, you actually own your living space, which is the apartment or townhouse you occupy. But you share ownership of the rest of the property—the hallways, elevators, lobbies, grounds, swimming pool, tennis courts, and any other amenities or common areas—with other condominium owners. Everyone pays a monthly common charge to cover the upkeep of the jointly owned areas. This can also cover heating and air conditioning, groundskeeping, trash collection, and maintenance and improvements to the building. Mortgage payments (if any) and taxes are often included in these payments. Owners of condominiums generally receive the same tax benefits as they would if they owned a single-family house. Condominiums are usually governed by an owners' association, which is headed by an elected board of directors. The association makes decisions regarding the property.

Owners of *cooperatives*, on the other hand, have purchased shares in a corporation that owns the real estate or buildings, property, and other facilities that make up the cooperative. When the cooperative is formed, shares are allocated to each unit based on its size and location. Rather than taking out a mortgage, as you would to buy a condominium, you take out a personal loan that's secured by the value of your shares. The interest is tax-deductible. The monthly fees assessed to coop owners is called maintenance.

The Advantages of Condos and Coops

Condos and coops have a number of advantages over traditional fee-simple homes. One is the extras that usually accompany them, such as swimming pools, tennis courts, and game rooms. In Florida, Arizona, and other retirement hot spots, it's not uncommon to walk out your door and step onto a golf course.

But an even greater attraction is the fact that someone else is responsible for the maintenance of the property. There's no grass to mow or snow to shovel. The shrubs are trimmed and the pool gets cleaned. All you need to do is take care of your living space.

A financial advantage is that interest and taxes that are part of the common charges is tax-deductible.

The Disadvantages of Condos and Coops

The biggest downside is the monthly maintenance or common charge. Sure, you don't have to take care of the property, but it costs money to hire someone else to do it. Often these fees turn out to be more of a burden than purchasers expect. And if the property's governing board decides that the fees must increase because of rising costs of maintaining the property, there's little you can do about it. And if one of the other shareholders defaults, the remaining shareholders will have to shoulder that share of the building's expenses.

Coop owners can sometimes run into difficulties selling their properties. Buyers must be approved by the coop board, which is made up of other stockholders, and they can reject potential buyers for almost any reason that doesn't smack of outright racial, sexual, or religious discrimination. (And don't kid yourself that such discrimination doesn't occur.) This can hold up a sale for an inordinate period of time. Coop boards have been known to turn down investment bankers because the board members think the bankers' fortunes will be short-lived and actors because they think they'll be too noisy.

Condo owners, on the other hand, have much more freedom in selling or leasing their properties. The condo board doesn't have to approve the buyers of the property. To protect itself, however, most boards retain the right of first refusal to purchase any unit that goes onto the market.

Considerations in Purchasing a Condo or Coop

Purchasing a condo or coop requires special considerations not found when purchasing a fee-simple home. Here are some of the most important:

Understand the Fees.   Make sure you know what the maintenance and common charges will be, not just today but five and ten years down the road. If there are major repairs to be made or the association is planning to expand its facilities, that's a good sign the fees will increase. Also, if the building is being converted from a rental property to a condo or coop, make sure the developer has set aside sufficient funds for major repairs. If not, they'll eventually fall on you and the other owners.*

Check Minutes and Talk to Other Owners.   Ask to see the minutes of previous board meetings to find out what kinds of problems may be facing the coop or condo. Visit with current owners as well.

Find Out If You're Allowed to Sublet The Property.   If you own a condo you're free to sublet. A coop may restrict this right, however. This could become problematic if you're having trouble selling your unit and need to find a tenant until the property is sold.

Have an Inspection.   Coops are inspected by a municipal building department, and since the coop is responsible for most repairs, it's generally in good condition. Condo units, on the other hand, should be inspected prior to purchase, since most repairs are taken care of by the individual owners.

Hire a Lawyer.   The paperwork attached to a condo or coop purchase can be lengthy and confusing. Hire a lawyer who's experienced with condos and coops and have her look for potential problems. She'll want to compare the expenses for the past few years, looking for any increases. Unusual jumps in legal fees could mean there's ongoing litigation. Dramatic changes in labor costs means there has been excessive hiring or firing. If the accounts receivable represent more than one-twelfth of the coop's revenues, it means some of the owners aren't paying on time. Only after your lawyer gives you the green light should you proceed with the purchase.

(See also discrimination, mortgage loans.)

CONFERENCE CALLS

CONFERENCE CALLS ARE NEVER a replacement for face-to-face meetings. Sitting around a conference table directing your conversation at a device that resembles a miniature UFO just doesn't cut it.

During a one-on-one telephone conversation it's difficult to convey the subtle tones of voice, facial expressions, and body language that are critical to effective communication. On a conference call it's impossible. Some people even find it difficult to pay attention or stay on the subject. I've found that as the number of people involved in a conference call increases, the ability to accomplish anything meaningful decreases. (Of course, sometimes the same thing is true

---

*When the owner of an apartment building or development wants to "cash out," he can convert his property into a cooperative. To encourage sales, current tenants are offered an "inside price," which is usually cheaper than the market value.

of meetings in general.) There are times when it becomes hard to determine who is speaking, and the conversations often end up as fruitless searches for consensus.

It won't be long before it will be possible to conduct conference calls over the Internet. If everyone has the proper software and an inexpensive video camera hooked to their computers, all the participants will be able to see each other on their monitors as they converse. Whether this will be an improvement over the current technology remains to be seen, however. Nonetheless, conference calls are, and will continue to be, part of conducting business. So here's my advice on making them as useful as possible.

The Mechanics

Rather than rifling through your files to find the owners manual to your telephone and then trying to set the conference call up yourself, contact your telephone company's conference call service center. For what I think is a very reasonable fee a conference call operator will get all the individual parties on line and will remain available throughout the call in case there's a problem. If one party gets disconnected, you can hit the star (*) or pound (#) key; the operator will then get back on the line and take care of the reconnection.

When to Use and Not to Use

Conference calls are most useful when you need to get a group of people together quickly to deal with an unexpected issue or an emergency. Conference calls also make a lot of sense for a group of people who are working on a project as a team. Let's say several members of your team are on the West Coast, several are in New York, and others are scattered around the country. Logistics and expense considerations make getting together regularly out of the question. Regular conference calls, however, allow everyone to stay abreast of the others' progress and make decisions about how to proceed. Since everyone has a high level of knowledge about the topic at hand, fruitful communication is possible.

But as soon as you introduce an outsider into the mix, conference calls become problematic and face-to-face meetings become essential. Let's say the team decides to bring in a consultant to work on one part of the project. That person needs to meet the people she'll be working with, be brought up to speed on the project, and clearly understand what's expected of her. A conference call places severe time restrions on everyone, reduces the ability to thoroughly convey information, and may result in crucial questions going unasked or imperfectly answered. As a result, your consultant may not receive the information she needs to be effective.

There are people who believe conference calls can be effective if you need to quickly close a deal that's near deadline. The pressure of so many people being on the line may force fence-sitters into making a decision. But it might also set back the cause. That's why I'd be very careful about using them to try to close a deal. Try to arrange a face-to-face meeting first. If that's impossible and time is of the essence, a conference call may be worth the risk, but I'd be very nervous about the outcome.

I most often use conference calls to introduce people who won't necessarily be working together, but should at least have the opportunity to exchange a few words. This is particularly valuable when I retain the services of a consultant to help out on a client's project. I'll call the client and tell him that this person will be providing some services on her behalf. Then I'll have my assistant patch a call through to the consultant so I can introduce them to each other. This serves several purposes. First, it shows respect to my client by keeping him informed. It also allows the consultant to ask any questions she may have of my client, and vice versa. Chances are they'll merely exchange pleasantries, but the fact that they've spoken will reassure my client that his project is in the hands of people who care about him.

CONSUMER ELECTRONICS

CONSUMER ELECTRONICS PRODUCTS REMAIN state of the art just long enough for them to be unpacked and installed. By the time you're familiar with the features and controls a new, more advanced system or unit is on the market.

The secret to buying consumer electronics is to use the incredible speed of technological advancement to your advantage. How do you do that? In a word, patience. Never buy the newest technology. Wait a year, or better yet, two years, and you'll obtain yesterday's cutting-edge products for bargain-basement prices. The longer you can wait, the more bang you'll get for your buck.

For example, when CD players first hit the market, it was impossible to find one for less than $1,000. Today you can buy a perfectly serviceable CD player for less than $150. Granted, it won't have the bells and whistles that accompany the most advanced players. But it will accomplish its basic task—reading the digital information encoded on a disc—quite effectively. Besides, it's those bells and whistles that break most often.

Decide what features and equipment best meet your needs and your budget, wait for the price to drop, buy it, and plan on living with it for the long haul.

Let's consider a stereo system. The most important component in any system is the speakers, so the bulk of your budget should go toward finding a pair you love. Don't get tricked into buying an amplifier that has more power than you need or a CD player that has a 10-disc changer and other unnecessary features. Save on the bells and whistles and put the money toward the speakers.

At the same time, don't get too carried away with the speakers. You can get a perfectly good set for well under $1,000. Beyond that, the sky's the limit. There are speakers on the market for $50,000 and more. The problem with some of this high-end equipment is that we as consumers reach the point of diminishing return pretty quickly. Does a $50,000 pair of speakers sound 50 times better than a $1,000 pair? Of course not. In fact, much of the measurable "quality" afforded by expensive speakers is often inaudible to the average person. If we had the hearing of dogs, it might be worth it. But to a 71-year-old man like me, it's immaterial.

I believe you should also seek simplicity when purchasing a VCR. Many people spend a lot of extra money for features they never learn to use. It's become a national joke that most of us can't even figure out how to set the clocks on our VCRs, much less the more complicated features that allow us to record on a certain day or at a certain time.

Televisions should be selected for picture quality first and screen size second. The bigger the screen gets, the better the chance that the image quality will suffer. In my opinion the industry has only recently begun to produce big-screen projection televisions that are worth their cost. Up until now, most have produced grainy pictures and have appealed more to the ego than to the eyes.

One product on which people often overspend is a camera. Above all else, a camera should be easy to use. If you've been a "point and shoot" person all your life, an expensive camera and a set of lenses isn't going to make you a better photographer. Most cameras today produce quality images. Unless you're a serious shooter, you should opt for the smallest, lightest, cheapest, and easiest-to-use camera you can find.

By the way, digital cameras may be the product of the future, but unless you have some reason to digitize a photo, traditional silver halide film cameras are a much better buy. If you do need to digitize an image, you can always have it done by the photo lab or scan it yourself at home or at a neighborhood copy shop.

Keep in mind that it's a buyer's market out there. These days consumer electronics products are better and less expensive than ever before. Do your research before you buy and comparison-shop to get the best deal you can, And once you make your purchase, plan on keeping it for a while. When it comes to consumer electronics, trying to keep up with the technology is a futile and foolish task.

(See also equipment.)

CONSUMER FRAUD

CONSUMER FRAUD IS a multibillion-dollar industry in the United States, so you can bet that eventually someone will set their sights on you. To cover every con game out there would require a book unto itself. Absent that book, here are few of the most commons frauds perpetrated time and again on people from all walks of life. Consider yourself forewarned.

Home Improvement Scams

People lose money every year to dishonest contractors. One of the simplest scams is the unusually low estimate accompanied by a request for partial or full payment in advance to "pay for materials." The only problem is, the work never gets done. Once they have your money, you'll never hear from them again.

Others will offer free inspections that turn up work that really doesn't need to be done. Or they'll "just happen to be in the neighborhood" and notice as they're driving by that one thing or another needs to be repaired. Some will offer to do the job right away. Sometimes it's done correctly, but there will always be a big bill to pay.

To protect yourself against home improvement scams, follow these suggestions.

- Never hire anyone who shows up claiming your home needs work.

- Always get several estimates before selecting a contractor. Ask ahead of time if there's a charge for the estimate.

- Ask for references and actually check them out.

- Have a contract that specifies completion dates for various portions of the project and how much the job will cost, including a detailed list of materials. Insist on a clause that deducts a certain amount from the bill for every day the job is late.

- Never pay for a job in advance. Agree to a schedule that pays incrementally as the work is being done, saving the largest portion for when the job is completed.

- Make sure work is continuous.

- Never pay with cash. Always use a check. If the job is unsatisfactory, you can issue a stop-payment order.

Unsolicited-Merchandise Scams

If an individual or business sends you something in the mail that you didn't ask for, it's yours to keep, no matter what it is. If it's accompanied by an invoice, you don't have to pay it. If it's accompanied by a plea for a contribution, you don't have to make one.

There are only two situations in which unsolicited merchandise can be sent to you legally through the mail. One is when a company is distributing free samples of a product, which must be clearly labeled as such. The other is merchandise from a nonprofit organization that's seeking a charitable donation.

If you receive anything else, you have three options. Keep in mind you have no obligation to the sender.

1. Write "Return to Sender" on the package. The post office will return it with no additional postage charged to you.

2. Open the package. If you don't like what you find, throw it away or give it to someone else.

3. Open the package, If you do like what you find, you can keep it with no obligation to anyone.

If you receive unsolicited merchandise and are then plagued with bills or telephone calls demanding payment, contact your local postmaster. The sender is breaking the law and can be prosecuted.

Credit Card Scams

People with poor credit ratings are commonly targeted by con artists. What appears to be a legitimate credit offer can end up costing you a great deal of money.

They usually work like this. You'll receive a telephone call or a letter offering you a preapproved credit card. There's just one catch. You need to pay a fee, anywhere from $15 to $50. The problem is that when you get the card, you discover it can only be used with one particular business. And, surprise, the business is owned by the company that issued you the credit card. To make matters worse, the merchandise offered by the business is usually inferior-quality junk that no one would ever buy.

If you have poor credit, you should be highly skeptical if someone contacts you out of the blue to offer you a credit card. Get as much information as you can, including written material, and make sure that the solicitation is for a conventional Visa or MasterCard and that it's being issued by a reputable bank. If that's the case, you're likely being offered a debit card or a secured credit card requiring a deposit in the bank. If you're still not satisfied, contact your local better business bureau or state attorney general's office.

Loan Scams

People with poor credit are also targeted by con artists offering "guaranteed" loans. But—you guessed it—there's a fee up front to have the loan "processed." The fee is often a percentage of the amount of the loan. For example, if the fee is 5 percent, you'd have to pay $250 to obtain a $5,000 loan. When you do, your money and the person who guaranteed to get you your loan will quickly disappear. If he doesn't, he'll put you off until he can get you your $5,000, which will come from the fees paid from other people he's conned. In this case, he may be using a kind of pyramid scheme to gather and distribute money. But it won't last long. When the pyramid starts to collapse, he'll disappear along with a lot of people's cash.

Here's how to avoid being taken by a loan scam.

- Get the loan representative's name, address, and telephone number.

- Ask what lending institution the loan representative is from and contact the institution for verification.

- Verify all the oral and written representations made by the loan representative with the lender.

- Ask for the names and telephone numbers of other customers who have applied for loans with the representative. Call them to make sure they received their money.

Legitimate lending institutions don't require up-front fees for personal loans. If you're asked for one, the offer is more than likely a scam.

(See also contractors, credit cards, personal loans.)

CONTINUING EDUCATION

THE PACE OF CHANGE in all fields today is so rapid that if you don't keep up you'll quickly find yourself not only out of touch but out of a job. Whatever your age, experience, or rank, you must be proactive about finding classes and seminars that will improve your skills and help you keep pace with developments in your profession.

If you live near a college or university, find out what kinds of evening or weekend classes are offered. Investigate certificate programs offered by the graduate schools and local universities. If you don't already belong to one, join a professional association. Most sponsor a wide selection of classes and seminars to help their members improve their skills. Membership also allows you to broaden your professional contacts by introducing you to other people in your field. This can lead to new business and employment opportunities.

You should also look online. The Internet has eliminated distance and geographic and political boundaries as barriers to the dissemination of knowledge. As a result, it has spawned an entirely new concept in higher education: the virtual university. One of the pioneers in online education is UCLA. Through an arrangement with a private company, OnlineLearning.net, the university offers dozens of courses in business studies, human resources, education, journalism and writing, and computers and information systems.

There are also several regionally based consortia of universities that provide classes and degree programs over the Internet. One, the Western Governors University, is financed by 17 states and Guam and has an impressive list of corporate partners, including Microsoft, IBM, Apple, and AT&T. It expects to have more than 100,000 students by 2006.

One of the great things about online classes is that you decide when to "attend" class. Because the schedules and assignments are posted on the course Web sites, you can log on anytime from any place you have access to a computer. This makes it the perfect medium for the busy professional. Is early morning the best time of the day for you to get in you classwork? You can log on before the sun comes up. If you want to wait until the kids are in bed and the dishes are done to do your work, that's fine, too.

Virtual universities also mean you can enroll anywhere. UCLA's online classrooms are just as accessible to someone who lives in New Jersey as they are to someone in Los Angeles. Your choices will continue to grow as more and more universities come online.

What should you study? That depends on where your interests lie and what skills you want to improve. Obviously, courses directly related to changes in your profession will be beneficial. But you might also want to improve your general knowledge in areas such as business, finance, accounting, marketing, and management. Look at basic communication classes such as writing, public speaking, and foreign languages. These are skills that will help anyone.

Finally, consider taking courses that can prepare you for the future of your profession, not just the present. Continuing education is the best way for a working professional to position herself on the cutting edge of a field.

It's also to indulge yourself. If you have an interest in something and have the time and money to take classes, it really doesn't matter whether it's related to your profession or not. Learning never stops. It keeps the mind fresh and adds immensely to the quality of life. It could also help secure and improve your stream of income.

(See also Web sites.)

CONTRACTORS

Need a contractor? Just open the telephone directory and call the first name you see. After you get off the telephone, call a lawyer. You'll probably need her next.

After car repairs, shoddy work by contractors is the most frequent source of complaints to consumer advocacy groups. It's not surprising. Anyone can call himself a contractor. There's little oversight in the industry and fly-by-night operators are a dime a dozen. If you're not careful, you could be one of their victims.

Finding Skilled Professionals

Even the smallest building project will cost you a few hundred dollars. From there, the sky is the limit. Tens of thousands of dollars can be at stake. When you're spending that kind of money, you need to take the time to find skilled, reliable professionals. Here's how to do it.

Ask for Recommendations. This is rule number one for hiring a contractor. As with other talented professionals, good contractors develop reputations in their communities. If you ask around for recommendations, their names will quickly come up.

If you can't come up with your own recommendations, call the National Association of Home Builders at 800-368-5242 and ask for a list of member contractors in your area.

Never hire someone from an ad or because they called you on the telephone or stopped by your house. If a contractor needs to solicit business, he's not very good. The best contractors are too busy to have to worry about drumming up business.

Get Estimates. After you've found a few candidates, get written estimates from each one. Each estimate should be based on the same job specifications and should include detailed information on labor and materials charges. It should also include an estimate of how long the job will take to complete. Don't automatically hire the contractor who gives you the lowest estimate, particularly if all the others are close to each other. That's often just a strategy to get the job. Later you'll find that the amount on the estimate and the amount on the bill are two different things altogether.

Another option is to ask for flat or firm prices rather than estimates. To provide a firm price, most contractors will bump their fees up in order to protect themselves. Sometimes, however, I've found the certainty is worth the increased cost.

Ask for References. Ask each candidate for references from both his three most recent customers (rather than his favorites) and from suppliers (to see that he pays his bills). Ask the contractor about his training and experience and whether he has affiliations with any professional groups.

Interview Each Candidate. This a good way to find out if the two of you can work well together. A good contractor will have a lot of questions for you, too.

Check Licenses. Most states and numerous local jurisdictions require that contractors be licensed. It's not always a guarantee that the person is particularly skilled. Some states merely require that a form be filled out and a fee paid. Others, such as California, have a rigorous testing program that a contractor must pass before being licensed.

Check Insurance. Make sure your contractor has personal liability insurance, business liability insurance, and disability insurance. Otherwise you could be sued if someone is injured while working on your property. Insist on receiving a certificate of insurance that states that you are covered under the contractor's policy.

Signing the Contract

Once you've selected a contractor, the two of you should draw up a contract. I advise you to always get a contract, regardless of the size of the job: it protects you both. (Many contractors use the boilerplate American Institute of Architects contract. While it's not a terrible agreement there are some modifications you need to make. See "Amending the AIA Contract," page 179.)

Your contract should include the following:

A description of the work to be performed. This should include a detailed description of the materials that will be used.

A timetable. This should include a starting date, dates for completion of various phases of the job, a clause stating work will be continuous, and a final completion date. An able contractor will agree to a provision giving you an agreed-upon penalty for every day the job is late.

The fee. You can either agree to pay a flat rate or time and materials. I often advise choosing the former. It puts more pressure on the contractor to finish the job in a timely manner.

A payment schedule. It should include a down payment and several payments to be made at various points during the job. The final—and biggest—payment should only be made when the job is completed to your satisfaction. It should also be conditional on receiving signed letters indicating all subcontractors have been paid.

Compliance responsibilities. The contractor should be responsible for obtaining building permits and any other legal documents that are necessary for the job, as well as arranging for inspections during and after the project.

Guarantees and warranties. Any good contractor will stand by his work. He should guarantee both materials and labor against defects for at least a year and agree to perform any needed repairs during that time free of charge.

Cleanup responsibilities. Don't forget this one. Cleaning up a building site is a big job and an important one, owing to environmental concerns. The contract should specify that cleanup will occur at regular intervals during the project and that the contractor is responsible for the removal and disposal of all excess materials and debris.

Judging Contractor Work

One good way of judging the professional skill of a contractor is to examine similar work he has done for others. Of course, if you were an expert on quality work, you'd probably be doing it yourself. Rather than foregoing inspections of prior jobs, use the following tips to help judge candidate contractors' work. Contractors whose skills can't be determined on sight, such as electricians and plumbers, aren't included. In those cases you'll need to rely on references.

Awning and Canopy Installers   Check on both the product and the installation. Problems with framing or mounting hardware can be traced to the installation; problems with the canvas itself should be blamed on the manufacturer.

Cabinet Refacers and Refinishers   Since you don't know what the cabinets looked like before, you can't rely on a visual inspection of a previous job to get an accurate reading on the workers' skill. That's why pros will have a book of before-and-after photos. If they don't, either they're rookies or they have something to hide.

Carpenters' Framing   Sills should be made of pressure-treated lumber. There should be a continuous sill sealer between the wood and the foundation wall. Studs should be 2 × 6s, toe-nailed into the plate or beam. Floor joists should be at least 2 × 10s. Subflooring should be either ¾-inch tongue-and-groove plywood or two layers of at least ½-inch plywood, installed perpendicular to the floor joists with the seams staggered.

Carpenters' Finish Work   Look for neat, clean cuts and tight joints. You shouldn't see any saw or hammer marks. The margins between doors and their frames should be even all around. Cabinets should be screwed, not nailed, into the wall.

Carpet Installers   Check around walls and door jambs, looking to see that the carpet is flat rather than bunched up. Patterns should be parallel to the most visible adjacent wall. If you can easily spot a seam, the job wasn't done well.

Ceiling Installers   The edge rows of panels should all be at least half a tile.

Central Audiovisual System Installers   The telltale sign of skill is how well wiring is hidden.

Deck Builders   Check that boards are straight and no more than ¼-inch to ⅜-inch apart, nail heads are flush, and there are no split ends. There should also be no rough edges that could cause splinters on railings or benches. Check the ledger—the board installed against the house to which all the joists are then attached. Pros will remove the siding and bolt the ledger directly to the structural framing through the exterior sheathing. Flashing should be installed around the ledger to prevent moisture from getting to the sheathing. The original siding should then be reinstalled to fit neatly around the ledger. Joists should be attached to the ledger using U-shaped galvanized steel connectors.

Driveway Contractors   Look for driveways that are as straight and perpendicular to the roadway as possible. Check if the driveway is either pitched or crowned to allow for proper drainage. Every concrete drive should have 4-inch-wide asphalt expansion strips at least every 20 feet. There should also be a final asphalt extension strip where the garage floor meets the driveway.

Drywall Installers   Sheets should be installed perpendicular to the direction of the framing members. Butt joints, where two 4-foot edges meet, should be staggered. Outside corners should be finished with metal corner beads that are nailed into place. Expert tapers will form joints approximately 8 inches wide along the longer side of the sheet, and 10 to 12 inches wide along the shorter side.

Exterminators   Pros will immediately ask whether you have young children or pets, and will explain whether or not you'll need to leave the premises. Most experienced exterminators base their fee on time and materials, so they will be hesitant to give anything other than a ballpark estimate over the telephone.

Garage Builders   The best way to check craftsmanship is to examine prior jobs, paying particular attention to the detail work where high-speed, specialized contractors such as these might cut a few corners. Be wary of any garage builder whose concrete slab floors exhibit cracking.

Gutter and Downspout Contractors   A real pro will examine the drainage around the house and suggest solutions to any problems, rather than simply replacing the existing system. They will also have their own portable gutter-forming machine, which can custom-fit continuous lengths of gutter to your home.

House Painters   The best way to tell the difference between a summer moonlighter and a full-time professional is to see him at work. A professional will use heavy fabric drop cloths, long-handled brushes, and large 2-gallon buckets of paint. When preparing the exterior of a house he'll cover all landscaping with drop cloths; use scaffolding if working in a crew; use power sprayers, scrub brushes, scrapers, and disk sanders to remove dirt, mildew, and old paint;

and work only in the shade when the temperature is above 70°. If you can't see him on the job, look for these signs of quality work: even coats with no signs of brush marks or roller nap; no visible repairs; even lines where the gloss paint on trim meets the matte paint on walls or ceilings or where two different colors meet; and neatly painted window frames with paint in the joint where glass meets wood, but not on the pane itself.

Insulation Contractors   One sign of an experienced insulator is that he removes siding before drilling holes into the cavity, and then replaces it so there are no visible signs of the job.

Masons   When examining masonry work look for aesthetics first and craftsmanship second. Check if the mortar has been cleaned out to an equal depth and if there's discoloration from mortar spilling out of joints. Obviously, watch out for large cracks in foundations or slabs. Small cracks are to be expected in older work, but sizable gaps indicate poor preparation and workmanship.

Paperhangers   Pros will have their own portable pasteup tables and will often use strap-on stilts to help them reach up to the ceiling. If you don't get a chance to see him on the job, look for how he handled light switch and outlet plates. Skilled paperhangers will cover the plates with scrap paper, making sure the pattern matches the wall.

Porcelain Refinishers   The sign of good workmanship is simple: If the job is a few months old and you can't tell it was done, it was done well. A poorly done job will blister and peel rather quickly.

Resilient-Floor Layers   Look for a centrally located pattern; equal borders on all sides; no gaps between walls or cabinets and the flooring; even margins around obstructions like radiator pipes; flooring that extends under major appliances; and tight, flat, straight seams in unobtrusive areas.

Roofing Contractors   Since it's next to impossible for homeowners to see what has been done to a roof, it's necessary to see a roofing contractor on the job. Pros wear sneakers while working on granulated roofs, use copper flashing sealed with solder around chimneys and vents, and use ladders with a mechanical lift to hoist shingles.

Security System Installers   One sign of good workmanship is how well wiring is concealed.

Siding Contractors   Pay particular attention to the trim areas around doors and windows. They should be neat and tight. Look at the corners of the house. A good siding contractor will try to make sure the horizontal courses line up where walls meet. In a good job, sliding joints will be placed in inconspicuous places, such as above doors and windows. Aluminum siding should be tight to the house, while vinyl siding should hang in place so there is room for it to expand and contract.

Sun Space and Greenhouse Builders   All hardware and fasteners should be rust-resistant. The wooden framing should be pressure-treated lumber. Glazing should be insulated, tempered, or laminated safety glass.

Tile Layers   The signs of good workmanship are symmetrical layouts in which the outside tiles are all approximately the same size; even spacing between tiles; a level surface; and untracked and sealed grout that's between, not on the surface of, the tiles.

Wooden Floor Sanders, Refinishers, and Installers   Professional refinishing jobs involve sinking exposed nails; multiple passes with various size machines and grades of sandpaper followed by vacuuming; two coats of oil; and finally two coats of polyurethane. Most experienced workers use plastic to seal off the room from the rest of the house. Professional installers will use a special tool that allows them to avoid nailing through the face of boards—a technique known as "blind nailing." Those few nails that do need to hammered through the face of boards will be countersunk and filled with wood putty.

Amending the AIA Contract

While it is fairly evenhanded for a form contract, the AIA contract has three areas that I believe need to be expanded on.

Timing, Penalties, and Premiums

The AIA form is lax about stating exactly when jobs will be started and finished. Firm commencement and substantial completion dates should be added. A clause imposing penalties of a specified amount for each day beyond the completion date should also be added. In compensation, a clause providing for a specified premium for early completion can be added as well.

Payment Schedule

The AIA form should be amended so that, aside from a down payment, the owner doesn't pay the contractor until specified stages in the project are finished. Exceptions can be made if the contractor must make a sizable payment for materials to be delivered to the job site. Progress payments should be structured so they equal the value of the work completed, less 10 percent held back until the entire job is done.

Periodic Inspections

The AIA form doesn't contain a provision stipulating interim inspections, either by the building department or by a third-party job supervisor. A clause should be added that before payments are made, all work must be approved by the building inspector.

(See also consumer fraud, disability insurance, home improvements, liability insurance, suppliers and vendors.)

CORPORATIONS

ANYONE WHO RUNS A BUSINESS today should consider incorporating. While most people associate incorporation with big business, even a one-person, jack-of-all-trades marketing firm should be incorporated. Why? Simple: protection from personal liability.

The Advantages of Incorporation

Think of a corporation as a shield protecting your personal assets. If someone sues a corporation, he or she can only attack corporate assets, not the private property of its shareholders. Let's say you're an online retailer who buys computer equipment from a major manufacturer. If you bought the equipment through a corporation and the business fails and is unable to pay the bill, the manufacturer won't be able to sue you personally. But if you signed your contract for the materials as a sole proprietor or representative of a partnership, the manufacturer can come after your personal assets and those of your partners.

Another advantage of incorporation, particularly for medium-sized and large businesses, is the ability to raise capital as needed by selling additional stock. Investors would rather buy stock than become partners since a stockholder's potential liability is much less than a partner's. Although this spreads ownership of the business among more people, you can still control your company by carefully drafting the stockholders agreement to ensure that you retain decision-making power or by creating voting and nonvoting classes of stock.

Incorporation also has a certain cachet for most people, and many businesses will incorporate simply to have that "Inc." after their name. Corporations are perceived as being larger, more stable, and more substantial than other forms of business. They have a greater air of professionalism. I don't believe there's sufficient added prestige for it to be the sole reason for incorporating. Instead, look at it as an added bonus.

The Basics of Incorporation

How do you incorporate? It's simple. Call your lawyer. She will apply to the secretary of state of whichever state will be the legal home of your corporation. All 50 states recognize corporations but since corporate laws, taxes, and regulations vary greatly from state to state, some research is needed before you decide where to incorporate. To keep it simple and inexpensive, you should consider incorporating in the state where your business will be located; otherwise you may incur duplicate filing fees and other unnecessary expenses. Once you apply, the secretary of state issues you a charter—a license allowing you to form the corporation and state that you are incorporated.

A corporation is owned by its stockholders. In a large, publicly held corporation, the stock may be owned by thousands of investors and can be bought or sold through one of the nation's securities exchanges. In a small, privately held company, however, the stock might be owned by just a few individuals and will not be publicly bought or sold.

In theory, incorporation protects your personal property from business creditors, but that doesn't mean a determined creditor and his lawyer won't try to come after you in a pinch. Creditors may attempt to prove you're actually operating your business as a sole proprietorship or a partnership rather than a corporation. This is sometimes called "piercing the corporate veil." In order to protect yourself against such efforts, it's critical that you follow your state's corporate laws and regulations to the letter and keep your personal and corporate affairs separate.

Sophisticated lenders and suppliers will often eliminate the corporate shield by requiring you or other stockholders of the business to personally guarantee payment for loans or supplies. They may name both you and the corporation on their invoices.

The Downside . . . and a Solution

There is one downside to operating as a corporation, and that's taxes. Corporate taxation is too complex to be covered in detail, but here's the basic problem. Corporations are treated like individuals for federal income tax purposes and their tax rates can be higher than personal rates, which is what you would pay if your business was a sole proprietorship or partnership. Corporate profits can also be taxed twice. The corporation pays a tax on its profits before it distributes them to its shareholders, which reduces the amount being distributed. Then the shareholders must pay a second tax on the profits (dividends) as personal income. If the shareholders also receive a salary from the corporation, they have to pay a tax on that as well.

One way to avoid double taxation is to elect to be treated as an S corporation (previously called a subchapter S corporation). This allows the corporation, at the request of the shareholders, to set aside the corporate entity and pass profits and losses directly through to the shareholders. A corporation must meet the following requirements to qualify for S status.

- It must be incorporated in one of the 50 states.

- All shareholders must be citizens or resident aliens.

- The shareholders must be persons, estates, or trusts, not partnerships or corporations.

- The corporation cannot have preferred stock, and while it may have different classes of common stock, they all must have identical economic rights. The only difference can be voting rights.

- There must be no more than 35 shareholders.

All this complex tax work will mean higher fees for your accountant. But you can counter your despair over spending the extra money with the knowledge that, as a corporation, your business is far less likely to be audited than if it were a sole proprietorship or partnership. Since S corporation returns report little or no profits—the profits are passed directly on to the shareholders each year—they're rarely audited. The shareholders of an S corporation will

The Case against Incorporating

Incorporation will not make sense if you're operating a one-person home based service business, in which clients or customers never visit your office, since your exposure to liability is almost nil. Instead, make sure you take out an umbrella liability package from the insurer that issues your homeowner's policy.

report their income as regular salary. Individual returns that have regular salary as their only source of income are also rarely audited. Income from sole proprietorships and partnerships, on the other hand, is reported on a tax form called a Schedule C, which is believed to be a big red flag for the IRS.

Incorporation requires the assistance of an experienced lawyer. There are how-to manuals on the market that come with preprinted forms as well as services that will help you file and prepare the paperwork. But I believe there's too much at stake to take shortcuts. Incorporation is serious business. It will cost you a bit more to do it right, but it's money well spent.

The Limited-Liability Company

Within the past few years a popular alternative to the S corporation has developed: the limited-liability company. The limited-liability company must be formed within one of the 50 states, but need not meet any of the other requirements of an S corporation. In a limited-liability company, the participants enjoy rights that are equivalent to those of partners in a partnership, except that they have limited-liability much as if they did business through a corporation. A limited-liability company can be managed by its members or by managers elected by the members. In most states, the manager can assume titles usually associated with a corporation, such as director or president. A limited-liability company provides greater flexibility: It can have corporate or foreign members; it can pay one member a preferred return or a return disproportionate with his or her capital contribution. In most states the cost of forming a limited-liability company is comparable to that of forming an S corporation. In New York, however, there is an additional requirement of publication, which can greatly increase the cost of forming the entity.

(See also partnerships, sole proprietorships.)

CREDIT CARDS

THE CREDIT CARD is the bane of personal finance. Nothing has caused more harm or misery than those little pieces of plastic.

Don't get me wrong: Credit cards are indeed a convenience. If you're going shopping and don't want to carry a lot of cash, they're wonderful. If you're traveling, they're even more convenient. And those that offer buyer protection plans or frequent-flier miles can be excellent tools.* But even those cards should only be used if you're sure you have the money to pay the bills when they arrive.

Unfortunately, few people are that careful. They get into trouble because they use credit cards as loans of 30 days or more, rather than as short-term loans payable as soon as the bill arrives. These folks see something they want, and because they don't have the money to buy it, they pay for it with a credit card. This behavior goes on for years until one day they suddenly come to the realization, either on their own or by coming to see me or a credit counselor, that because of the size of their balances and the rate they're being charged, their monthly credit card payments have begun to take up an enormous part of their net income.

I've seen the powerful spell these cards can cast on people. Clients of mine with incomes of well over six figures have skirted bankruptcy because their minimum monthly payments alone amounted to thousands of dollars each month. Like drug dealers, the credit card companies feed the sickness by constantly increasing lines of credit and sending preapproved cards to those already in debt. And like any addict, the credit card junkie eventually self-destructs.

Types of Credit Cards

Credit cards fall into two categories.

Bank cards are those issued by banks and other organizations in cooperation with companies like Visa, MasterCard, and Discover. Many come with an annual fee—although some banks drop the fee in an effort to entice new customers—and begin to incur interest on their account balances 20 to 30 days after the bill arrives. Interest rates can range anywhere from 9 percent to 22 percent depending on the state in which the issuing institution is located. Some cards may also charge transaction fees or other fees.

Many bank cards also offer a cash advance option and will send cardholders checks they can use to make purchases. Don't use them. They're nothing more than extremely expensive loans and should be avoided except in emergencies. Interest on cash advances usually begins to accrue

---

*I received a great many e-mail messages from readers about my anti-credit-card statements in *Die Broke.* The best arguments I received for tempering my absolutist stance were from individuals who charged purchases on their credit cards in order to receive frequent-flier miles but who then paid the bill in full when it arrived. After some investigation I'm now convinced: If you have the discipline to pay the bills in full when they arrive, using your credit cards to accumulate air travel miles is an excellent idea.

the moment the money changes hands. In addition, many banks will charge a fee for the transaction.

Travel and entertainment or charge cards, such as American Express, Diner's Club, and Carte Blanche, generally don't have preset spending limits and the entire balance is due each month. Rather than charging interest after 30 days, they charge a late fee. They're also quick to cancel your account if you become unacceptably delinquent with your payments. Some cards offer the option of paying some charges, such as airline ticket fees, over time. Of course, interest fees are added on.

I think charge cards make a lot more sense than bank cards simply because you must pay your bill each month. Armed with that knowledge, people are likely to pay more attention to what they're spending. There is one catch, however. Because they want their money every month, travel and entertainment card companies are a bit more choosy than banks about whom they issue cards to. An adequate income and a solid credit record are critical if you hope to get one.

Finding Low-Interest Credit Cards

Credit card annual fees and interest rates vary greatly. For information and advice on obtaining no-fee or low-interest credit cards, you should join the Bankcard Holders of America. This non-profit organization charges $18 for a membership, an amount that can pay for itself with the savings on just a purchase or two. Write or call them at Bankcard Holders of America, 560 Herndon Parkway, Suite 120, Herndon, VA 22070; 703-481-1110. Another good source for information is *Barron's,* which provides a list of low-interest cards each week.

Using Credit Cards Responsibly

Banks love people who carry enormous credit card debt. The 18 or 20 or 22 percent interest that banks charge their credit card holders would make anyone quite happy.

Consumers get themselves into these precarious financial positions because, to some, plastic isn't like real money. Falling victim to the great American tradition of instant gratification, they buy whatever they want and defer the issue of payment until the bill comes. Soon, they are staggering under an unbearable financial burden—too many purchases, too many monthly payments, and too much interest.

The only way to use credit cards responsibly is to pay off your card balances every month. To do that, you must carefully monitor your purchases and make sure the money to pay for them will be there when the bills arrive. If you're using your credit cards for purchases you can't afford, you're on a road that can only lead to financial disaster.

If you're already using credit cards strictly for convenience and are in the habit of paying off your entire balance each month, make sure you have a card with no annual fee, even if it carries high interest charges.

On the other hand, if you've taken the antiplastic pledge but are still carrying balances from your free-spending days, look for a card with a low interest rate and be willing to pay a higher annual fee.

If you simply can't manage to control your credit card use, put your cards away in a drawer and pay cash for everything. If you have a financial emergency in which you truly have nowhere else to turn, take the cards out of the drawer and use them. But for everything else, save your money and buy the item with cash when you've put enough aside.

Avoiding Credit Card Fraud

Credit card holders can fall prey to all sorts of scams. That short series of numbers on your card has quite a bit of monetary value, and there are lots of crooks out there who would like to use them for their own gain. Here are some tips for avoiding credit card problems and scams.

1. Never give your credit card number to someone over the telephone unless you initiated the call and the other party is well-known and reputable. Anyone who finds out your credit card number and expiration date and knows your address and telephone number can go on a telephone shopping spree.

2. Tear up the carbon paper from credit card receipts. By scouring through trash bins and copying valid credit card numbers from these carbons, thieves can charge purchases to your account.

3. Keep all your credit card receipts and check them against your monthly billing statement. If you find you're being billed for a purchase you didn't make, or the amount is incorrect, contact the credit card company immediately and contest the charge. If the problem recurs, cancel the card.

4. Report the loss or theft of a credit card immediately. Your liability for charges made to lost or stolen card numbers is limited, as long as you report the situation quickly.

5. Carefully dispose of any preapproved credit card offers you receive in the mail. If these should fall into the wrong hands, they can be used to fraudulently open credit card accounts in your name.

6. Cut old credit cards in half before throwing them away. Not all retail clerks bother to check the expiration date on a card, so an old card in the wrong hands can cause the real cardholder a great deal of trouble.

7. Don't apply for affinity credit cards. These are cards that bear the logo or emblem of an organization and donate a certain percentage of your purchase dollars to the organization. These cards are becoming very popular with colleges and universities, among others. The problem is,

they charge you very high interest rates and annual fees while actually contributing very little to the organization. If you want to help out your alma mater, do it the old-fashioned way. Send a check.

8. Beware of secured credit cards. These cards require you to make a minimum deposit with a bank, which then issues you a credit line equal to the amount you deposit. You don't really have a credit card, you have a debit card—and you're also losing interest on the money you've deposited with the bank.

(See also ATMs and cash cards, bankruptcy, charge cards, debit cards.)

CREDIT REPORTS

A CREDIT REPORT IS LIKE AN ADULT REPORT CARD. It carries coded information that reveals a great deal about your finances and your lifestyle, and it uses that information to actually grade your financial character through a method called "scoring." That's why it's being consulted, not only by potential lenders but by potential landlords, employers, and others who make material decisions that can influence your life.

What's in a Report?

A credit report begins with demographic characteristics: your name, address, birth date, and Social Security number, as well as information such as education, employment record, and marital status.

Most reports include information on credit cards and charge cards like Visa, American Express, and MasterCard, and charge accounts with large national retailers such as Sears and J. C. Penney. Home mortgage records are now being reported to credit bureaus more and more often. Any judgment against you from a court action is likely to appear. Debts that won't appear on your credit report include your utility bill, telephone bill, cable bill, rent payments, magazine subscriptions, and dental and medical bills.

Whenever you apply for a loan, and the creditor inquires about your credit, it's recorded in your credit report. Too many such inquiries can create a negative perception. Almost every credit card balance is recorded. Your payment records for the various credit cards, accounts, and loans tracked are recorded. If you pay off your bills in full every month, that fact is included. If you're frequently late with payments or sometimes miss them altogether, that information is included as well.

Obtaining Copies of Your Credit Reports

Most people whose reports are in error usually don't discover this fact until they're turned down for a loan. It's not a pleasant way to find out. Checking your credit report in advance will allow you to avoid such a predicament.

Getting a copy of your credit report is simple. The first step is to locate the credit bureaus in your area. While hundreds of such firms specialize in regional markets, it should be sufficient to contact the three large nationwide credit bureaus:

1. **Equifax Information Services:** PO Box 4091, Atlanta, GA 30302; *404-885-8000*

2. **TRW Information Services:** Customer Assistance, PO Box 749029, Dallas, TX 74374-9029; *214-235-1200*

3. **Trans-Union Credit Information Company:** Eastern Region, PO Box 360, Philadelphia, PA 19105; *215-569-4582*; Midwestern Region, 222 South First Street, Suite 201, Louisville, KY 40202; *502-584-0121*; Western Region, PO Box 3110, Fullerton, CA 92634; *714-738-3800*

Credit bureaus are required by law to let you see a copy of your credit report for free—if you show up at their offices. They will mail you a copy for a fee of around $25. To obtain a copy of your report, write or call the credit bureau and give them your name, Social Security number, and the addresses you have used during the previous five years. If you've been turned down for credit recently, you can obtain a copy free of charge.

Reading the Reports

Once you have the report in hand, you'll probably find it a bit difficult to decipher. There are lots of codes and symbols that can be interpreted only by reading the fine print. Once you've figured out the language, you'll see the report contains the credit limit for each of your accounts, your account balances, any late payments or current payments past due, the date the information was last updated, and so on. Some credit reports are updated once a month. Others every two or three months.

Some of the larger credit bureaus have created credit checking clubs. For an annual fee, they'll provide periodic updates and notify you when someone has checked your file. Although it's a tempting service (we all like to know who's checking us out, after all), it's hardly worth the money. There's really no reason you need to know every time someone checks your credit. It's cheaper just to pay for a copy of your report once a year, or when you're anticipating a major purchase, to make sure it's accurate.

Errors in Your Credit Report

Like other large organizations, credit bureaus are prone to making mistakes. That means there's a good chance your credit report may not be accurate. In fact, some studies have found that nearly 50 percent of reports contain at least one error. These mistakes can be caused by something as simple as someone hitting the wrong number on a keyboard. They can also result from a situation in which you returned a purchase that was unsatisfactory but the charge remained reported on your credit report as an unpaid bill.

Correcting an inaccurate credit report can be done, but it's often time-consuming and aggravating. You do have some clout on your side, however. The Fair Credit Reporting Act requires that any incorrect information in a credit report be corrected. The burden for proving a disputed fact lies with the credit bureau, which must confirm the information within 30 days. If the bureau can't confirm you paid your Visa bill late, then it must change the information and report that change to anyone who has recently requested your report.

The problem is that credit bureaus only correct mistakes for which they are responsible. If the problem is incorrect information supplied by a creditor—say, Visa mistakenly tells them you've paid late—then you need to go after the creditor to correct the information.

Let's say your credit report indicates that you haven't been making payments to a department store charge account, even though you've been quite diligent in getting those payments off to the store each month. You may only discover this problem when you're turned down for a loan. To correct the report, you need to deal directly with the store itself. This usually requires a letter or two to the company's credit manager pointing out the mistake and asking that it be rectified. Mention in your letters that you are writing under the provisions of the Fair Credit Reporting Act (or the Fair Credit Billing Act if it's a billing issue). That will get their attention. If the store fails to respond within 90 days, it's in violation of the law.

Explaining Problems

By law you are entitled to add a 100-word statement to your credit report, placing any potentially troublesome information in context. For instance, let's say you failed to pay the charge for a set of dishes you ordered form a department store because they arrived broken. The department store is demanding payment since it claims the damage was the shipping company's responsibility. While you're busy trying to clear up the situation, the store's credit department makes credit bureaus aware of the matter, but says only that you're delinquent in paying you bill. To place the issue in context you can send a concise statement to the credit bureau, explaining the matter from your point of view, and insist that it be made part of your permanent credit report.

Such statements can be very effective in mitigating potential damage from a single blemish on an otherwise spotless credit report. However, if your file has repeated negative judgments, or the problem is major—say, a bankruptcy—100 words, no matter how well chosen, aren't going to change any creditor's mind.

(See also bankruptcy, mortgage loans.)

CREDITOR RELATIONS

Borrowing money can be like lying. It's very easy at first, but unless you come clean it gets harder as you go along. At a certain point your lie will be revealed or your credit will "maxed out."

Insuring sufficient and affordable credit is as important to personal finance as it is in running a business. The secret is to establish good relations with your creditors.

Dealing with Banks

Let's begin with banks. Banks want nothing to do with small start-up businesses. The best you can do will probably be a personally guaranteed or secured passbook loan. But banks love consumers. That's because the money they give us is often protected by tangible assets they can take from us if we're unable to pay our debts. The payments you send your bank each month on your mortgage, car loan, personal loans, credit card bills, and other debts keep them quite profitable. The more the banks can extract from your pockets, the happier they are.

Your job is to keep that amount to a minimum, and that means paying as little for the money you borrow as possible. Since banks don't have any particular loyalty to you, you shouldn't feel any loyalty to them. Follow your nose to the best credit terms you can find. If, after a time, you find better terms somewhere else, pull up stakes and move again. I call this being a "serial debtor." Banks are very competitive and anxious to have your business, and the credit application process is quick and painless, so why not take advantage of the situation? If it can save you a few bucks a month, it's well worth your time.

Dealing with Suppliers

As a businessperson, you will find that your most important creditors won't be banks—they'll be your suppliers. Maintain good relations with them, let them know how important they are to your business, and give them credit for your successes. Since you're all in the same industry, they can act as your partners and provide you with advice about your business. After all, your success will be important to them (if you fail, they don't get paid), so they'll do whatever they can to help you succeed.

Keep in mind, too, that your suppliers generally will be much easier to deal with than any bank when it comes to credit. They'll be much more willing to provide extended terms, deferred-payment plans, consignment programs, and other creative devices that will help you improve your cash flow.

This isn't to say they won't get tough if push comes to shove and you fall far behind in your promises. But business is often cyclical. Any seasoned supplier will acknowledge that and will work with you to get you through the tough times. In the final analysis, that's the kind of consideration you want from any creditor.

Secrets of Dealing with Cranky Creditors

Don't let creditors intimidate you. There are no debtor's prisons in the United States. You have far more power than you realize. Demonstrate your willingness to use the power you have and you'll turn the most aggressive creditor into a pussy cat.

If you realize you'll need more time from a creditor, launch a preemptive strike. Rather than waiting until the bill comes due, call the creditor right away, demonstrate you're willingness to pay your obligation, but explain that you need additional time and would like to either make a partial payment or skip one payment. You'll be pushed a bit, but if you stick to your guns you'll be able to reach a compromise.

If you're threatened with collection, don't panic. The last thing a creditor wants to do is hand your account over to someone else. That insures he will only get back a portion of his debt.

If you've been turned down for credit, ask for the specific reason for the rejection. Then, rather than debating the decision, ask for a reconsideration based on new facts. For instance, if you're told you don't have sufficient income, come back with documentation of additional income streams you overlooked, such as reasonable expectations. Make sure you present this appeal to someone with the power to make a decision, not just a clerk.

(See also banking and bankers, cash flow, suppliers and vendors.)

DEBIT CARDS

RATHER THAN WRITE checks for groceries, the dry cleaning, and other day-to-day purchases, most of my clients now pay for them with debit cards. These debit cards, which also serve as ATM cards, look and are treated by merchants just like credit cards. They have the Visa or MasterCard logo and they're accepted anyplace that accepts Visa or MasterCard. The difference is that when you make a purchase with a debit card the amount is deducted immediately from your checking account.

That's the downside to debit cards. If you used a credit card for the same purchase you wouldn't get a bill for the purchase until the end of the month and you'd then have another 20 to 30 days to pay the bill without any interest being tacked on. Because the amount of a purchase is immediately deducted from a checking account, you lose interest on the money you spend. That's why most people use debit cards only for purchases that they would previously have paid for by check.

It's ironic that most of my relatively affluent clients now use debit cards so frequently; 20 years ago only people who couldn't get credit cards used them. Banks would only issue them such a card if they paid several hundred dollars in advance to cover their purchases.

But with the advent of electronic banking, the use of debit cards began to make a great deal of sense. They cut down on expenses for banks, who don't have to process as many checks, and for consumers, who don't have to pay for as many checks. They're simply more efficient.

Most banks will issue you a debit card linked to one or more of your accounts for no charge. Their use does require a bit of vigilance, however. Since you won't be making entries in a checkbook when you make purchases, you need to be careful to put receipts in your wallet and enter the deductions in your checkbook when you get home. Debit cards can also be used to make cash withdrawals at ATM machines, so you need to treat them as carefully as you do cash cards.

If you have a debit card you need to keep careful track of it. If you report the loss of your debit card or any fraudulent charges within two to four days, you'll only be responsible for a maximum of $50 in fraudulent charges. If you wait any longer you could be responsible for up to $500 in fraudulent charges. If you're really out of it and don't make a report for 60 to 90 days, you could be entirely responsible for all subsequent charges.

DEBT CONSOLIDATION LOANS

I WISH I DIDN'T NEED to include this section. The fact that it's necessary is indicative of the irresponsible manner with which most Americans handle credit. At this writing, personal debt and bankruptcies were both at an all-time high, at a time when the economy is more vibrant than ever before.

The chief culprit? Those credit cards—the bane of personal finance. It's not unusual for me to discover that new clients of mine have credit card debt in the tens of thousands of dollars. By the time I shock them to their senses and force them to recognize the hole they've dug themselves into, it's sometimes too late to undo the mess. Even when I get them to stop using their cards, if they're unable to afford more than the minimum monthly payment on each credit card account, they're faced with years and years of payments and thousands of dollars of interest.

This is where debt consolidation loans come into play. A debt consolidation loan is used to pay off all your individual debts. The lender then presents you with a monthly payment that's theoretically lower than the sum of the payments you were making on those debts. Is it a good deal? It can be, but only under the right conditions.

Personal Loans

The key to a debt consolidation loan is its interest rate. The lower it is, the better. This is where personal loans often fall short. If you take out a personal loan from a lender who specializes in debt consolidation loans, chances are the interest rate will be close to or even higher than what you're already paying on your individual credit card debts. The lender, however, structures the loan so that the repayment term is much longer than that on your credit cards. As a result, your single monthly payment to the lender is lower than the cumulative payments you were making before.

On the surface this reduces some of the pain. But over the long haul, you end up paying much more in interest than you would have if you had whittled away at your card debts individually. It will still be years before you're free of debt. The only difference is, your monthly payment is a bit more palatable. And if you should suddenly have the means to pay off the loan ahead of schedule, you'll usually find the lender has included a heavy prepayment penalty in the loan agreement to ensure maximum profit.

Home Equity Loans

A home equity loan is a much more sensible means of consolidating your debt and it's the option I first suggest to my clients. The interest rate will be much lower than the interest on your credit card debt, and the interest you pay is largely tax-deductible. You can both lower your monthly payment and decrease the amount of time it will take you to pay off your debt.

Most lenders allow you to borrow up to 70 percent of the equity in your home. Let's say you're home is worth $150,000 and you have $80,000 left on your mortgage. That means you have $70,000 worth of equity in the home and can therefore borrow as much as $49,000.

The major downside to home equity loans is that you're literally betting your house that you'll be able to pay off the loan. If you should lose your job or suffer some other financial calamity that makes it impossible to meet that monthly payment, the lender could quite legally seize your house and sell it to get his money back. If that happens, you and your family will find yourselves without a roof over your heads.

Borrowing from Retirement Accounts

You may be able to borrow money from your 401(k) account to pay off your debt. Some employers will allow you to borrow up to 50 percent of the money you have contributed to your account at an interest rate that's about 2 percent above the prime rate. You have five years to pay back the loan.

The main attraction of borrowing from your retirement fund is that because you're borrowing money from yourself, the interest you pay on the loan goes back into the account. The downside is that by taking out a loan you're reducing the pretax earning potential of the money you borrow. But faced with credit card debt at 20 or 21 percent, I think it's a wise use of your money. When clients of mine faced with huge credit card debt, and don't have home equity to borrow against, I suggest they tap into their retirement funds.

There is another negative to borrowing against your retirement account: If you leave your job, you must repay the balance immediately. If you don't, you'll have to pay taxes on the amount as if it were ordinary income. And if you're not yet age 59 ½, you'll also pay a 10 percent penalty.

Learn Your Lesson

Regardless of which strategy you choose, a debt consolidation loan is pointless if you don't learn something from the experience. Once all your credit card debts have been paid with the loan, cancel your cards and cut them into pieces. If you feel you need to keep one card for emergencies, stick it away in a desk drawer and leave it there. Even better, stick to an American

Express or Diners Club card. These cards require payment in full every month. Armed with that knowledge, I guarantee you'll be much more attentive to your spending habits.

(See also ATMs and cash cards, banking and bankers, checking accounts, credit cards.)

DISABILITY INSURANCE

IF THE ENTRIES IN THIS BOOK were in order of importance rather than alphabetical, you'd be starting right here. It is scandalous how few of my clients—and how few of my readers— carry adequate disability insurance.

People today are, rightly in my view, focusing on their streams of income rather than their assets and liabilities. But at the same time, saving is down, spending is up, and personal debt is at an all-time high. If you couldn't work because of illness or injury, would you be able to make ends meet? If you're anything like most of my clients, the answer is no.

During my years of advising people from all walks of life I've discovered that most overinsure their lives and fail to adequately prepare for a disability. It just doesn't make sense. Statistically, your chances of being unable to work due to a long-term illness or disabling injury are much higher than dying young. A misstep on the stairs can result in injuries that keep you laid up for months. Without disability insurance, financial disaster lies just around the corner.

I speak from firsthand experience. At the age of 48, I was diagnosed with tuberculosis. I lost my banking job and was unable to work for two years. I had two children in college, two in high school, two mortgages, and very little set aside for an emergency. Because I had disability insurance, and the most wonderful wife in the world, my family was able to stay afloat until I recovered sufficiently to launch a consulting business. Without it, I don't know what would have happened.

I'm sure some of you are dismissing my harangue because you have some disability coverage through your job and you assume workers' compensation or Social Security will pay for any disability. Those are the kind of foolish assumptions upon which disasters are built. Most employer-sponsored disability plans offer minimal benefits, for very short periods of time. Workers' compensation only covers job-related injuries and disabilities. And Social Security makes it very tough to qualify for benefits. In effect, you have to be unable to do any job whatsoever in order to collect the pittance they offer. If a former brain surgeon is disabled but still capable of sorting glass at a recycling plant, she won't qualify for Social Security disability. In my opinion, if you don't have your own disability coverage, you don't have any disability coverage.

There are several factors to consider when evaluating your own disability insurance needs and options.

How Much Do You Need?

Most people assume they should have enough disability coverage to replace their current income. That's just not possible. No insurer will provide benefits equal to 100 percent coverage since it is a disincentive to return to work. Benefits are usually limited to 60 percent of your income. But even if they did offer 100 percent coverage, it wouldn't be necessary. The fact is, some of your expenses will decline if you're disabled. Because you're not working, you won't have the often considerable expenses of going to work each day. You may find yourself spending less on entertainment and dining out. Keep that in mind when calculating your needs. Also, if you're paying the premiums for your policy, the benefits are tax-free. The secret to determining how much of a benefit you need is to base it around your expenses, not your income. Assume you won't get any workers' compensation or Social Security.

Renewability

You need a policy that's "guaranteed renewable" or "guaranteed renewable and noncancelable." The former means your insurance can't be taken away so long as you continue to pay your premiums. The latter means your insurance can't be taken away and your premiums cannot be increased. Avoid any policy that's "class-cancelable." That means the insurer can cancel all policies that fall into a particular category, such as policies held by mimes, Alaska residents, and everyone born in 1969.

When Should It Start?

The longer you wait for payments to begin after you become disabled, the lower your premiums will be. If you can wait to receive your first payment for 90 to 120 days—until any other sources of short-term disability payments, perhaps from your employer, have ended and your personal emergency funds are just about exhausted—your premiums will be considerably lowered.

How Long Should It Last?

Your premiums will be even lower if you elect to receive benefits for a short length of time. Keep in mind that 90 percent of disabilities last less than two years. If you elect to purchase short-term coverage, you're gambling you won't be one of the 10 percent who suffer longer-term disabilities, including the few who become permanently disabled. Personally, I think this is too big a gamble. On the other hand, I think lifelong benefits are too expensive and unnecessary. I advise my clients to have sufficient coverage to get them to age 65. At that point, Social Security and Medicare benefits will kick in. You can also opt for a "retirement rider," which will provide for partial payments after age 65.

Defining Your Disability

Insurers are never anxious to pay an insurance claim. It cuts into their bottom line. So their definition of a disability might not necessarily jive with yours. They may argue that although you might not be able to go back to work in your former profession, you can still hold a job. Under

Gender Bias

A woman will pay more for the same level of disability coverage than a man. Why? The insurance companies claim that all the actuarial data shows that women are more likely to become disabled than men. So just as a coal miner pays for more coverage than an accountant, so a woman pays more than a man in the same job category. Is this discrimination? Not according to state insurance commissioners. Every state in the union has accepted the insurer data as a valid reason for having gender-specific rates.

this kind of definition, a rocket scientist who suffers a head injury can conceivably go back to work pushing a broom down at the donut shop. You can protect yourself against this problem by purchasing "own occupation" coverage. It provides full benefits if you are disabled to the point that you can't go back to the same kind of work you did prior to becoming sick or injured. This type of coverage is very expensive, however, so I advise clients to take out the less expensive "income replacement" coverage. This kind of policy considers you disabled if your income drops because of an illness or injury.

Partial and Intermittent Benefits

Only consider policies that pay residual or recovery benefits. *Residual benefits* are partial payments made to those who go back to their job but for less than full-time at first. *Recovery benefits* are for self-employed individuals who need time to rebuild their customer base or workload. You want a policy that will pay intermittent benefits, not requiring you to go through a second waiting period if, for instance, your illness or problem recurs within six months.

Waiver of Premiums

Better policies will, while requiring you to keep paying your premium for the first few months you're collecting benefits, refund those premiums and waive future ones if your disability continues longer than those few months.

Two Incomes, Two Policies

If your family relies on two incomes, both you and your partner need disability coverage. It's that simple.

Get Coverage While You're Still Employed

If you're planning on going into business for yourself, make sure you obtain disability insurance while you're still employed. Self-employed individuals do all they legally can to minimize their income to cut their tax bills. That becomes problematic when applying for disability insurance since it becomes difficult to document actual income.

If you're unable to find traditional disability insurance that both meets your needs and is affordable, and you're under age 50, investigate annually renewable disability insurance (ARDI) polices. These are new products being offered by a handful of life insurance companies, including Guardian and Equitable. Unlike most disability policies, which have level premiums, ARDI policies begin with low premiums that increase every year over the life of the policy. The policies are a bargain when you're younger, but become expensive as you grow older. I think these are great products since they make disability coverage affordable for those consumers who have been least likely to get them even though they have the greatest long-term risk. My suggestion is when you reach the point when the premium becomes too steep, opt for a traditional policy. By that time, hopefully, you'll be better able to afford the cost.

(See also health insurance, Social Security.)

DISCRIMINATION

AS FAR AS I'M CONCERNED, the only color anyone should be concerned with is green. Unfortunately, not everyone agrees. Even though we live in the most enlightened nation on the planet, people are denied jobs, housing, credit, and other critical life tools simply because of the color of their skin or some other personal characteristic or belief.

Discrimination is an immoral and illegal act committed by stupid people. And it's bad business too. Engaging in those kinds of discriminatory acts can only hurt your reputation and your bottom line.

Legal Definitions and Protections

Both employers and employees need to be conversant with the legal definitions of discrimination and the laws that protect people from it. Illegal discrimination occurs when an employee or group of employees are treated less favorably than employees of a different race, religion, sex, sexual orientation, age, or national origin. Discriminatory acts include blatant behaviors such as name-calling, slurs, and jokes, but in the workplace discrimination can be, and often is, more subtle behavior, like not being given important assignments or promotions.

There are three major federal laws that cover discrimination. The Civil Rights Act of 1964 makes it illegal to discriminate against an employee on the basis of race, sex, religion, or national origin. It was expanded and strengthened by the Civil Rights Act of 1991. The Age Discrimination in Employment Act of 1967 makes it illegal to discriminate against an employee because of age. And the Americans with Disability Act of 1990 makes it illegal to discriminate against employees who have a disability.

What has been missing is a law that protects people from discrimination due to their sexual orientation. The Employment Non-Discrimination Act (ENDA), introduced to Congress in 1999, should change that by guaranteeing fair employment practices to homosexuals, bisexuals, and heterosexuals. Although this type of protection is provided in 11 states and the District of Columbia, this will be the first federal legislation that addresses the issue.

State and federal laws treat discrimination very seriously, as a violation of what's known as a "clear mandate of public policy." The penalties for violations are severe, providing fines, jail time, and compensation for victims, including the restoration of employment if they have been unjustly fired from their jobs.*

Employer Responsibilities

If you're an employer, you have a responsibility to prevent harassment or discrimination of any kind, including retaliation against employees who have filed complaints. If you find discrimination, you must take steps to correct the situation. If you don't, the employee or employees who feel discriminated against can file a complaint with the federal Equal Employment Opportunity Commission (EEOC). That could result in legal action against you as the employer.

There are a number of steps you can take to make sure your employees work in a environment free of discriminatory behavior. The first is to be tough and establish a zero-tolerance policy. Make sure the policy is widely disseminated. Tell all new employees that you will not stand for discrimination, sexual harassment, or retaliation and include the policy in your employee handbooks and other literature. If appropriate, post the policy in prominent locations in the workplace.

You also need to make it easy for employees to voice complaints. They should have someone other than their supervisor to turn to (supervisors are often the source of complaints). In a small company it should be you, even though it's best to have someone who has no direct authority over the employee. If your organization is large enough, it should be a human resources professional or a company ombudsman.

When you do have a complaint, investigate it promptly but objectively. If you find the complaint is a valid one, take action against those who are guilty of violating the policy. This could

---

*It's important to realize that gaps in federal legislation against discrimination may or may not be covered by state and even municipal legislation. If you have any questions about your rights and protections, check with someone knowledgeable about local statutes.

include anything from a written warning to suspension without pay. If the offense is serious enough, it can, and should, result in termination.

Once you've dealt with an incident, you'll need to take appropriate action to avoid a reccurrence. Monitor employees who have been warned to discontinue their offensive behavior. Make sure they've stopped and that no retaliatory action is being taken against the person who filed the complaint. If the inappropriate behavior continues, more severe action will need to be taken. Again, this could include termination.

Lodging a Complaint

If you feel you're a victim of discrimination in the workplace, keep careful documentation. Report the incidents in writing to the person designated to receive complaints. Include the dates, times, and nature of the incidents, including the treatment you received and verbal encounters. Get witnesses to these incidents, if possible. Keep copies of your performance evaluations. If you feel your situation is being ignored or is not being sufficiently addressed, you can enlist the assistance of the EEOC. I guarantee that will get everyone's attention.

There is simply no place for discrimination in the workplace. It's degrading, demoralizing, and destructive to a person's self-esteem. It can have a devastating effect on employee morale and productivity and poison the workplace environment.

(See also age discrimination, employees, promotions and lateral moves, terminations.)

DIVERSIFICATION

THE BEST WAY to take prudent investment risks is to diversify. Put all your money in a single investment, whether it's a stock, a mutual fund, a bond fund, or some other security, and your financial future is totally linked to the strength of that investment. Even the most brilliant investment will fluctuate in value, often quite dramatically. If it's at a low point when you need to liquidate it, you'll have lost a great deal of the appreciation it may have demonstrated earlier. By diversifying you mitigate investment risk. While some of your investments may lose money, others are meeting expectations, and others will exceed anticipated yields. With a properly diverse portfolio, you'll maximize overall growth without taking undo risk.

Look for Balance

A diverse investment portfolio should be well-balanced. For example, you may have some of your money in fixed income securities like corporate or municipal bonds. You know what the return will be and that creates a certain amount of security. But it fails to take advantage of the better returns that can be provided by other kinds of investments.

To balance your fixed-income investments, you should also put money into equity investments like stocks and stock mutual funds. In doing so, you're assuming a certain amount of risk; equity investments can lose money. But you're also positioning yourself to take advantage of the fact that they can provide much higher returns that your fixed-income investments.

You also need to pursue diversification within each category of security. You don't want to own just one or two stocks. Nor do you want to own stock in companies that are all in the same industry. You should own a variety of stocks in a variety of industries. That way, if the high-tech stocks in your portfolio take a tumble but your health care and utility stocks are on the rise, you still enjoy overall growth. Your mutual funds should also be spread among different categories.

You can also achieve diversific ation in your fixed-income investments. If you're going to buy municipal bonds, make sure they're from a variety of states. Your corporate bonds should display the same industry diversification you've achieved in your equity investments.

Don't overlook international investments. We now live in a world economy. Putting some of your investment dollars in overseas markets is a good way to balance the investments you've made in the U.S. economy. To reduce risk, I'd suggest investing in international mutual funds. Not only do you gain a degree of protection; the funds' management take care of all the currency and taxation hassles that accompany international investing.

The Beauty of Mutual Funds

If you want to achieve the highest degree of diversification, you should put the bulk of your money in mutual funds. Because mutual funds are diverse to begin with—they invest in a wide variety of stocks and bonds—there's a very desirable multiplier effect. For example, if you own shares in just a dozen different funds, your fortunes are actually tied to hundreds of different stocks and bonds. You're achieving a degree of diversification you could never accomplish otherwise unless you were extremely wealthy.

Interestingly, the need to diversify doesn't change with age or goals. While you might want to shift your asset allocation from equities to debt vehicles as you get older, you'll still need to diversify within the individual categories. For instance, the proceeds from the sale of stocks and stock funds shouldn't be poured into one type of bond or a single bond fund. They should be put into different types of bonds and bond funds to mitigate risk.

(See also asset allocation.)

DIVORCE AND MEDIATION

I'VE BEEN PRACTICING LAW and counseling clients for more than 40 years and I haven't seen an amicable divorce yet.

Divorce is always a gut-wrenching, traumatic, and generally miserable experience. Granted, there have been some changes that make it a little easier: no-fault divorce, equitable distribution, and community property. Still, divorce remains one of the most difficult experiences a person can go through.

Money: The Root of Many Problems

The most vexing issue in a divorce is often money. When there are no children involved money is always the most contentious issue. This isn't surprising, since poor communication over financial issues is usually cited as one of the main causes of divorce. Each year around 5 million Americans head for the altar, many for the second or even third time. Yet many have never discussed their basic money styles with their soon-to-be spouses. When this happens, it doesn't take long for conflicts to arise.

It stems from our society's taboo against discussing money. I doubt that your parents shared information about their income, debts, and so on with you and you siblings—and I bet you don't share such information with your own children. We also attach a whole range of personal values to money, The emotions and anxieties we experience over money relate to our own identities, our sense of ourselves and our own self-worth. When we join our finances with those of another person through marriage, in many ways we are putting our identities and self-worth at risk. In effect, love and money become hopelessly intertwined.

I've counseled a great many couples about how to avoid this trap. I believe the key is to keep their financial and emotional lives separate, but this only works when both parties play an active role in managing the family finances. This gives each person a sense of equal responsibility and equal power.

For a young couple with few financial assets, it's easier to start with a blank slate and develop healthy strategies to handle financial matters together. For a couple who are each bringing considerable assets to a marriage, like many of my clients, a prenuptial agreement can spell out the disposition of their individual assets while they craft a strategy for handing their joint finances after the marriage.

For couples who have spent years embroiled in unhealthy financial relationships, however, the separation of money and emotion can be more difficult. It almost always requires the help of a marriage counselor or a financial adviser. It also requires a total commitment from each person to change. If it doesn't work, the next step is divorce.

This is when open warfare usually breaks out. All the hostilities that have been bubbling beneath the surface for years quickly erupt when divorce proceedings are initiated. Even if the hostilities aren't all based on money, the stage that's set for the inevitable money showdown includes plenty of room for anger that's spilling over from other areas. And each individual's lawyer will be fanning the flames by dwelling on money issues, only making things worse.

Mediate the Financial Issues

This is where people like me come in. Although I don't handle divorces in my law practice, I do provide mediation services. My suggestion is that divorcing couples should mediate their money issues and divorce their emotional issues.

You can find the names of professional mediators in the Yellow Pages, but I'd suggest you instead contact the local bar association and ask for the names of lawyers who do divorce mediation. It's not that lawyers know any more about the process than mediation specialists, it's just that they know more about the psychology of other lawyers, who will of necessity become involved in the process.

As a mediator, my role is to help the two sides reach a mutually acceptable agreement. I remain a completely neutral third party. The couple presents me with their individual and joint financial holdings as well as their individual and joint liabilities. They also each describe their financial needs and wants. Once I've learned as much as possible about their financial situations I prepare a plan that separates their finances equitably. If they agree to the plan, they sign an agreement, which is then given to their lawyers. The lawyers then proceed to handle the nonfinancial aspects of the divorce. With one of the most contentious issues out of the way, the rest of the divorce usually proceeds quite smoothly.

Now I'll be the first to confess that this approach doesn't always work. Sometimes there will be such anger between the two parties or they'll be so far apart in their demands that no amount of mediation will help. Even when I feel I have come up with a fair and reasonable plan, it will sometimes be sabotaged by lawyers who, sometimes in the interests of their own wallets, want to keep the financial issue alive.

When mediation does work, however, it can make a divorce much less taxing emotionally. I'm not promising it will become amicable, mind you. I'm not that much of an optimist. But it will reduce animosity and speed up the entire process.

(See also child support, lawyers, pre- and postnuptial agreements.)

Two Warnings to Women

I'd be remiss if I didn't take a moment to offer some warnings to women about the divorce process. As an observer of more divorces than I care to recall, I've noticed some definite trends.

Many women focus too much on speed. They correctly see divorce as a lose-lose issue and just want to get the whole thing behind them. Men, on the other hand, often view divorce as a competition—and they want to win. In their minds, victory is measured in dollars. As a result, women often end up trading money for speed.

Men have an incredible ability to mentally separate financial issues from child support issues. I've seen otherwise devoted and caring fathers dive into denial and fail to recognize that their financial haggling is hurting their children as much as their ex-spouse. A man who once didn't think twice about spending money on his children may suddenly become a penny-pincher when those dollars are being spent by his ex-wife on his children.

Sample Mediation Agreement

The following is a sample boilerplate mediation agreement of the kind typically used by a mediator to draft a customized agreement. I strongly urge you to have your own mediator draft an agreement specifically for your needs.

Mediation Agreement

_____ and _____
_____ (collectively, the "Parties"), intend through mediation to resolve the controversies arising out of _____. and to enter into an agreement that (i) settles major areas of dispute (including, but not necessarily limited to _____, and (ii) is in their mutual interest, and (iii) is fair to both Parties.

Therefore, the parties agree to the following:

1. **Role of the Mediator.** The mediation shall be conducted by _____
_____ (hereafter the "Mediator"). Neither of the Parties has had any prior personal or business relationship with the Mediator. (The Parties are aware that the Mediator is an attorney as well as a mediator, and understand that he will be acting in this process exclusively as mediator and not as their mutual attorney.)

2. **Cost of Mediation.** The Mediator's fee for the mediation will be based on the time expended by the Mediator. The Mediator's hourly rate is $_____. The Mediator will be charging an hourly fee for time spent with the Parties, as well as for time which he may spend preparing for the mediation, reviewing documents, consulting with consultants or experts, and preparing his written recommendations. The Parties have agreed to pay the Mediator a retainer of $_____. The Mediator is authorized to apply the retainer to reimburse himself for his services as Mediator and for disbursements as they are incurred. The Mediator will render statements to the Parties on a monthly basis, which to the extent applicable will reflect any retainer applied to the services rendered. In addition to paying the Mediator for his services, the Parties will reimburse the Mediator for out-of-pocket disbursements, such as photocopies, messengers, and the like. In the event that any single disbursement may exceed $_____. same will not be expended unless that Parties agree thereto.

3. **Confidentiality.** The Mediator will treat all information provided during the mediation process, whether by the Parties or by any third party, as confidential as to any third party,

including but not limited to counsel to the Parties. No information obtained during mediation will be given to any third party unless (i) both Parties concur in writing, or (ii) disclosure is compelled by subpoena or other lawful process; in which event the Mediator will give the Parties prompt notice thereof. The Mediator will not hold information confidential as between the Parties. The Parties will (i) to treat the mediation process, in the spirit of negotiation and compromise, as confidential and free from the threat of later adversarial use of any statements made or materials supplied during the process, (ii) whether or not the mediation process is completed, not use, or attempt to use, in any court or other proceeding statements made in the mediation process by either of them or by the Mediator, and (iii) not call, or attempt to call, the Mediator or any other person who participated in the mediation (other than the Parties) as a witness or subpoena the records of the Mediator or any such other participant (other than one of the Parties).

4. Consultants. Persons other than the Mediator (such as therapists, accountants, business evaluators, actuaries, and the like) may be consulted by the Mediator if in his sole judgment he believes that such consultation is necessary for the effective progress of the mediation. The Parties shall be responsible for paying the consultants directly, and will be required to agree in writing to the rate of compensation and payment arrangements prior to any such consultation services being provided.

5. Attendance at Mediation Sessions and Disclosure. Mediation sessions will be scheduled at the convenience of the Parties insofar as practical. The Parties will be expected to arrange their business and personal affairs so as to enable them to attend mediation sessions as scheduled. Notice of cancellation of appointments with the Mediator must be given by the Parties not less than one full business day in advance of the appointment. Third persons having a direct interest in the mediation may participate in the mediation sessions relating to their interests if the Mediator finds that their participation may facilitate settlement, provided, however, that both Parties concur. Each of the Parties is expected to fully disclose all _____, and provide _____ as may be requested by the Mediator, and all information requested by the opposite party, if the Mediator finds that the disclosure may aid the mediation process. The Parties understand that the mediation process depends on candor, honesty, and full disclosure and that any failure to disclose financial information (including without limitation _____) may render the process useless and any agreement reached voidable.

6. Personal Counsel. The Parties understand that it is not the Mediator's role to serve as attorney, therapist, or marital counselor, and agree that for legal advice and representation each will retain separate legal counsel of his or her own respective choice (and any other consultants as required) during and at the conclusion of the mediation process. Each of the Parties shall advise his or her counsel that he or she has agreed to mediation, as is herein provided. The Parties agree to identify, upon request of the mediator or other party, such counsel and hereby release the Mediator to communicate with the such counsel (except as is otherwise precluded by Section 3 of this Agreement), and agree to authorize such counsel and consultants to communicate with the mediator for purposes of the mediation process.

7. Impasses; Termination of Mediation. If the Parties are unable to reach an agreement about any or all issues, the Parties and the Mediator will discuss options for resolution of the issues. These options may include separate sessions with the Mediator, referral of particular issues to other professionals, or suspension or termination of mediation. Mediation is a voluntary process, and either of the Parties may terminate the process by notice to the other party and the Mediator.

Name: _____

Date _____

Name: _____

Date: _____

Name: _____, Mediator _____

Date: _____

DOCTORS

PEOPLE SHOULD spend as much time interviewing and checking up on their doctors as they do researching the background and skill of their plumbers. When clients of mine have renovation work done they interview craftspeople, ask for references, check on insurance, and contact the better business bureau. Yet these same people would never dream of going through the same exercise when selecting a doctor.

Our culture has always treated physicians as demigods or infallible sorcerers whose professional competence is beyond question. This image is perpetuated by the medical industry's own public relations efforts. They do a remarkably good job of holding their best and brightest up for public acclaim while keeping their incompetents under wraps.

Years ago, most of us inherited our physician from our parents. This wasn't necessarily a bad thing. The relationship between family and physician can transcend the normal relationships between professionals and their clients. Over the years, the physician demonstrates the competence needed to gain the family's trust. At that point, he or she becomes a member of the family, treating three or four generations before retiring. When a health problem arose in the family, there was no crisis over who to call. If the physician felt that additional expertise was needed, the family had the utmost trust in the recommendations that were made.

Today, however, few of us return to our childhood communities after college. Moving to new communities, if not new states, many times in our lives, we need to select physicians on our own. To make an informed, rational decision, you need to knock physicians off their pedestals and conduct a search using the same criteria you would use for any other professional.

I believe the best approach is to start with the medical community itself. Find the best hospital in your area. I recommend teaching hospitals that are associated with major universities. The next best bets are state or regional hospitals.

Telephone the hospital's head of internal or family medicine. Tell the doctor you're new to the community and are looking for recommendations for a family physician. If you or a member of your family have any special medical conditions, make sure you mention them.

Telephone the offices of the doctors whose names you're given and explain your situation. Tell the receptionists who referred you and explain that you would like five or ten minutes to meet with the doctor at any time that's convenient. You may be told the doctor isn't accepting new patients, in which case you can move on to the next name on the list. But you should also move on if you're told the doctor can't meet with you. If a doctor can't or won't set aside ten minutes to speak with a potential patient, she won't have time to provide the kind of care you want and deserve.

When you do make an appointment, stick to the time frame you asked for. Granted, five or ten minutes won't allow you to learn everything you need to know, but it will provide you with a valuable first impression. First of all, it's a good sign that the doctor has agreed to take the time to meet you. It means that her ego is in check. And when you get to her office, you can make some quick observations about the staff and the practice in general. Here are some things to look for.

The age of the doctor. I have nothing against youth, but when it comes to doctors and pilots, I like to see a little gray around the temples. Medical training today is better than ever, but some knowledge can only be gained with experience. Don't be afraid to ask the doctor how long she has been in practice.

The doctor's personality. Look for someone who is serious and businesslike. There's nothing wrong with a sense of humor, mind you. But we're dealing with your health here. I'll opt for exceptional technical expertise over an exceptional bedside manner any day.

The doctor's appearance. If the doctor obviously doesn't take care of herself—perhaps she's obese or smells of cigarettes—why would you expect your health to be of concern to her.

Ease of scheduling appointments. Ask the receptionist how long the typical wait is for an appointment and whether the doctor can squeeze in patients who have emergencies.

Keep in mind, too, that there's a lot more public information about doctors than there used to be. Health care consumers are gradually getting over our culturally ingrained habit of considering doctors as demigods. In certain cities and regions consumer groups have begun to make lists of physicians that include information about malpractice suits and other formal complaints. Take advantage of these and other sources of information to find a physician who is as good as your plumber.

DOLLAR COST AVERAGING

Only fools try to time the stock market. No one, not even Warren Buffet, has ever been able to consistently predict market swings. Trying to time your buys for when the market is down and your sales for when the market is up is an exercise in futility. You'll have as much luck turning seawater into gold.

Historically, the stock market has been the best place to invest your long-term savings. Over the short term, the market—like individual stocks—goes up and down. But over the long term, the market goes up. Rather than trying to time your investments, practice dollar cost averaging. That's just a sophisticated name for the simple practice of investing a set amount of money at regular intervals.

Let's say you want to invest $6,000 a year in a mutual fund. There are two ways to accomplish this. You could try to time the market and buy in all at once. Or you can invest $500 each month over the course of the year. Let's look at what happens when you do the latter.

At the end of the year, your $500 a month investment has purchased 269.42 shares of the mutual fund at an average price of $22.27 a share. Since the fund rallied at the end of the year to $27 a share, your shares are worth $7,274.34, which gives you a 21 percent return on your investment.

But what would have happened if you had invested your $6,000 at the beginning of the year? You would have purchased 240 shares in the mutual fund for $25 a share and would have finished the year with $6,480, a return of 8 percent.

This serves to show you the wisdom of slow but steady investing. Granted, you can track the share price and buy in when you think it has reached a low point. In fact, you could have made your $6,000 investment during 7 of the 12 months and achieved a lower per-share price and a greater return on investment than with your monthly payments.

But what if the fund had started to move upward rather than downward in March? Most likely you'd have been wracked by indecision and done nothing, waiting for it to reverse direction. The price might move a few dollars higher before you take action and invest. At that point, it might continue upward or it might take a dive, taking the value of your investment with it.

That's the point of dollar cost averaging. No one knows what's going to happen to share prices, so for people who are investing for the long term, it's the best strategy for achieving the best average purchase price. You'll be buying on the upside and buying on the downside, but when all is said and done, you'll have made out better than 99.9 percent of investors who try to be clairvoyant and act when they think the time is right. Don't get greedy. Try to beat the market and you'll end up a loser.

Month	Amount Invested	Share Price	Shares Purchased
January	$500	$25	20
February	$500	$25	20
March	$500	$22	22.73
April	$500	$21	23.81
May	$500	$20	25
June	$500	$20	25
July	$500	$21	23.81
August	$500	$20	25
September	$500	$21	23.81
October	$500	$23	21.74
November	$500	$25	20
December	$500	$27	18.52
Totals	$6,000	$22.27	269.42

DOMESTIC PARTNERS

LIKE IT OR NOT, the world is still largely structured for "conventional" couples: heterosexual partners who have married one another in a legal ceremony.

Personally, I believe all couples, whatever their sexual orientation or marital status, should be looked upon equally in financial and legal matters. But the simple fact is, they're not, particularly in legal matters. And until they are, they need to approach things differently.

At the moment, domestic partners are gaining some ground in the financial arena. They can be named as beneficiaries in one another's life insurance policies. They can buy joint-and-survivor annuities. They're also gradually being acknowledged by employers and provided with the same health insurance benefits given to married couples. (While this book was being written, General Motors, one of the largest and most traditional U.S. employers, decided to extend health benefits to domestic partners.)

From a legal perspective, however, domestic partners still have a way to go. While they have gained recognition in Vermont, domestic partners cannot file joint federal tax returns. They don't automatically inherit one another's estates. They can't recover damages due to injuries to the other partner. They don't qualify for Social Security survivor benefits. They can't obtain residency for a foreign-born partner or make medical decisions for an incapacitated partner.

Some careful planning can solve some of these problems. Here are a few suggestions:

Make wills. Have a lawyer draw up wills for each of you naming each other as beneficiary of your estates. Without wills, your property will automatically go to you parents or siblings. Wills are especially important if you think your relatives will fail to honor your verbal wishes and will try to seize control of your property if you die.

Use trusts. Even a properly drawn will is easy to contest (although not necessarily easy to contest successfully). If your lifestyle or choice of partner provokes a strong emotional response from your family, you may wish to further protect your wishes regarding estate disposition by transferring some of your assets to a very carefully drafted trust. This trust can remain revocable, allowing you complete control while adding a strong barrier between your assets and angry relatives.

Create living wills and health care proxies. Your lawyer can also draw up living wills and health care proxies. Your living wills will spell out what kind of medical treatment you wish to receive if you become gravely ill and unable to speak for yourself. Your health care proxies allow you to each make sure the wishes of the other are carried out.

Sign a partnership agreement. A partnership agreement will allow you to establish joint ownership of property and other assets. It also specifies the disposition of the property should you split up or when one of you passes away.

Accomplishing all the above will require the services of a good lawyer. Select someone who is experienced in these areas and make sure he or she clearly understands your wishes. It will take some time and money, but with the proper legal documents in place, the two of you can rest assured that your wishes will be carried out.

Finally, to any degree you can, you should also push the envelope in getting equal treatment in other areas. For example, if your employer doesn't offer health insurance to domestic partners, start lobbying for it. Recruit other employees who are in domestic partnerships. The fact that more and more employers are starting to provide such coverage is in your favor. But without some prodding, it's easy for an employer to avoid the issue.

(See also benefits, health care proxies, living wills, partnerships, wills.)

DOWN PAYMENTS

FOR YEARS, down payments were the biggest stumbling blocks for most first-time home buyers. These often young families have sufficient income to make mortgage payments, but not enough to save up a down payment.

The traditional way, obviously, is to skimp and save and wait until you've set aside enough. But that's become more and more difficult. For a young family just starting out, possibly with a child or two, the ever-increasing costs of rent, groceries, car payments, child care, and other expenses make it difficult to put much, if any, money aside.

In response to this increasing difficulty, I encourage my young clients to borrow a down payment from their parents. Many parents are happy to lend the money with very generous terms. Even better, some may just give it to you and consider it an advance on your inheritance.

If parents aren't a possibility, I suggest you consider other relatives and friends. And rather than a loan, I suggest you make it a business arrangement. Perhaps you can offer part ownership in the house in exchange for the down payment. You get to live in the house, but when it's sold, the person gets the down payment back plus an agreed-upon percentage of the profit. Or you can offer to buy out the other person after a fixed period of time. If you don't have all the cash you need, you can take out a loan against the equity you've built up in the home.

Don't overlook your own possessions. Do a home inventory. You'll be amazed at the amount of stuff that's up in the attic gathering dust or tucked away in the basement and the garage. Much of it can be turned into cash with a yard sale, garage sale, or visit to a thrift shop. You may have some other possession you can live without, as well. Perhaps the old set of china you inherited from your grandmother would be more valuable as part of a down payment for your house.

Generally speaking, the larger the down payment, the more house you can afford. I don't believe, however, that you need to, or should, buy the most expensive home that you can. A wiser move is to make the down payment cover a larger percentage of the purchase price and take out a more affordable and shorter-term mortgage.

This becomes especially true after you've sold your first or second home and have amassed a considerable chunk of cash. Let's say you've made a tidy profit on your previous homes and now have $75,000 to put toward the purchase of your next home. Your lender requires a minimum down payment of 20 percent. This means that, assuming you can afford the monthly payments, you could take out a $300,000 mortgage and purchase a $375,000 home.

But do you really need to spend that much? I realize that bigger and more expensive is the American way, but sometimes I think it's silly. In most parts of the country, $375,000 buys more house than most of us really need. Rather than spending $375,000 simply because you can, see if you can find something that might meet your needs for, say, $250,000. That means you'll only need to borrow $175,000. The money you save on your monthly mortgage can be invested. Or you can choose a 15-year mortgage, reduce your interest costs, and pay off the house that much quicker.

(See also mortgage loans.)

DREAD-DISEASE INSURANCE

DREAD-DISEASE INSURANCE MAKES ME SICK. It's probably the most egregious example of insurers taking advantage of our fears. These are policies allegedly designed to cover the exceptionally high costs associated with specific serious, long-term diseases. They provide coverage for different categories of expenses, such as hospital bills, doctor bills, surgery, radiation, and other therapies.

Of course, the one disease insurers all trot out in their sales literature is cancer. Their sales pitches sound reasonable. Statistics indicate that a significant percentage of the population will be stricken with cancer some day, so the demographics are huge. It can also be a frighteningly expensive disease to battle. Many people receive treatment for years. Coverage against heart attacks and strokes is also heavily marketed. Not surprisingly, the public's response to insurance companies' ominous advertising and scare tactics has been quite active.

My advice: Don't even think about purchasing dread-disease insurance. If an agent suggests it to you, show him or her the door. If you think I'm just being overly opinionated, consider this: A number of states have severely restricted or banned its sale altogether. For one thing, it's overpriced. There are strict limitations on the procedures that are covered and the dollar amounts that will be provided to cover them. Consumers get very little for their dollar. The sales and administrative fees are also excessively high.

Dread-disease policies also often don't hold up when they're needed. Cancer insurance, by far the most popular coverage, usually doesn't include coverage for the many complications that

**Other Types of
Insurance to
Avoid**

Dread-disease coverage
isn't the only foolish
product being sold by
the insurance industry.
Some others to avoid
are:

• Double-indemnity
clauses

• Flight insurance

• Any life insurance
offered as part of a
loan

• Any life insurance
offered by a car rental
company

can occur from cancer. This means that once a patient's immune system is weakened from the effects of radiation and chemotherapy, any additional illnesses that a person may suffer will not be covered. If a person loses a limb from the cancer, the cost of a prosthetic device and physical therapy may not be covered.

The states have also reacted to the grossly misleading scare tactics used by companies promoting dread-disease insurance. They target seniors, who are understandably concerned about both their health and their finances. On the face of it, dread-disease insurance makes a great deal of sense. It promises to defray the exorbitant costs of a long-term illness that many are likely to suffer at some point in the near future. But as with all scams, the product itself doesn't deliver.

If you're really concerned about the costs associated with a long-term illness, you'd be far better off augmenting the health insurance coverage you already have. That way you're protected across the board. No matter what calamity strikes—cancer, heart disease, stroke—you'll be covered.

(See also health insurance.)

DURABLE POWERS OF ATTORNEY FOR HEALTH CARE

IF YOU DON'T WANT to end up a vegetable, with your ultimate fate in the hands of uncaring hospital bureaucrats or a politically motivated judge, you'll make sure you have a durable power of attorney for health care.

Granting power of attorney is giving someone the right to act on your behalf. In most cases, powers of attorney are limited to specific spheres of action. A good example is the transfer of real estate. If a seller moves to a new location before the house is sold, returning to the area for the contract signing and closing is usually an inconvenience. In this case the seller may grant someone power of attorney to act in his stead in this particular real estate transaction. In this example, the person usually is an attorney. She will represent the seller during negotiations and at the closing and make any decisions on the seller's behalf.

A power of attorney is considered "durable" if it remains in effect even if the person granting the authority is no longer competent. Therefore, a durable power of attorney for health care (sometimes known as a health care proxy) has a very specific function. It assigns a person of your choosing the responsibility and authority to make decisions about your medical care and health care if you become incapable of making decisions on your own.

Durable powers of attorney for health care are different from living wills. A living will is a document signed by you that spells out your wishes if your life can only be prolonged by extraordinary measures. If you don't want to be kept alive by artificial means, the document will state as much. A durable power of attorney for health care, on the other hand, oversees all aspects of your health care. The person you name to have durable power of attorney for health care will make decisions about surgical procedures, physical therapy, nursing home care, and even the kind of prescription medicines you are given.

Technically, if you grant someone durable power of attorney for health care, you don't need a living will. If life support becomes an issue, the decision is just a logical extension of your health care and your medical care. If your representative knows and understands your wishes regarding life support, he or she can make the decision for you.

My advice, however, is to have both. This is because it's one thing for your representative to decide what kind of treatment you should receive for an illness or disease; it's quite another to decide whether you live or die. The availability of a living will removes the responsibility and

Who Should You Appoint?

Your representative will have awesome responsibility. It should be someone who passes these three tests:

1. *Sensitivity:* Your representative should be sensitive to your wishes and concerns. Have a frank discussion with this person, who should be able to question you about all possible health crises and your general direction of response.

2. *Strength:* Knowing your wishes is one thing, carrying them out is another. Many medical professionals have their own views and perspective, so it's important that your representative has the ability to keep your wishes paramount.

3. *Objectivity:* One of my clients refused to name a son as representative. She explained most eloquently that she was not going to have the one who would gain the most by her death have his hand on the plug when the time came to make that decision. In the other extreme, guilt might prevent them from acting as you'd wish. Children may be the right choice for you, but try to put yourself in their shoes before making your selection.

Sample Durable Power of Attorney for Health Care

I strongly urge you to have a lawyer draft your durable power of attorney for health care. This sample is intended solely for informational purposes and shouldn't be used as a template.

Health Care Proxy

I, _____, residing at _____

_____, hereby appoint

   (Name) _____,

   (Address) _____,

   (Telephone number) _____,

as my health care agent to make any and all health care decisions for me, except to the extent I state otherwise.

This health care proxy shall take effect in the event I become unable to make my own health care decisions. Although not necessary, you may wish to state specific instructions or wishes, or limit your agent's authority. In addition, unless your agent knows your wishes about artificial nutrition and hydration, your agent will not have authority to decide such issues. It is therefore advisable to state your wishes. If you choose to state instructions, wishes, or limits, please do so below by inserting your initials in any of the applicable boxes and adding any additional material.

I wish all life-sustaining treatment be withheld from me and no cardiopulmonary resuscitation shall be administered to me if I have an incurable or irreversible condition that is likely to cause my death within a relatively short time.

I wish all life-sustaining treatment be withheld from me and no cardiopulmonary resuscitation shall be administered to me if I am in a coma or persistent vegetative state that is reasonably concluded to be irreversible.

The withholding of life-sustaining treatment *shall* include the withholding or withdrawal of administration of artificial hydration or nourishment.

Other instructions: _____

_____

I direct my agent to make health care decisions in accordance with my wishes as stated above or otherwise known to him or her. I also direct my agent to abide by any limitations on his or her authority as stated above or as otherwise known to him or her.

In the event the person I have appointed above is unable, unwilling, or unavailable to act as my health care agent, I hereby appoint

   (Name) _____,

   (Address) _____,

   (Telephone number) _____,

as my health care agent.

I understand that unless I revoke it, this health care proxy will remain in effect indefinitely or until the date or occurrence of the condition I have stated below: (Complete the following if you don't want this proxy to be in effect indefinitely.)

This health care proxy shall expire:

   (Date) _____

   (Condition)_____

This health care proxy shall revoke all prior health care proxies made by me.

   (Date) _____, 2000

   (Signature) _____

I declare that the person who signed or asked another to sign this document for him or her is personally known to me and appears to be of sound mind and acting willingly and free from duress. He or she signed (or asked another to sign for him or her) this document in my presence. I am not the person appointed as agent by this document.

Witness: _____

Address: _____

Witness: _____

Address: _____

Witness: _____

Address: _____

saves your representative from a great deal of emotional and psychological distress. It also provides support for your surrogate's decisions if they're called into question. It's really in your best interest to have both documents.

If you have a life partner and are unmarried, it's absolutely essential you each have durable powers of attorney for health care that name each other as representatives. Most state laws don't recognize unmarried life partners (whether same or different gender) in their "substituted judgment" statutes. State laws usually automatically pass authority on to parents, siblings, or children. While the person appointed by the court may adhere to the wishes you made on behalf of your partner, there's no guarantee. The only way to ensure you both get what you wish is to have the documents drawn up. Once you have them, they're foolproof, No one can intercede, regardless of who they are.

I recommend you have a lawyer draw up a durable power of attorney and a living will at the same time. It's not an expensive service and can be accomplished in tandem with other legal work, such as preparing your will. Copies should be given to the person you've named as your representative and any friends or family members who may be concerned about your care. Your lawyer should keep copies on file in her office as well.

EARTHQUAKE INSURANCE

Here's a fact that could shake you up: Earthquake damage isn't covered by conventional homeowners policies. It can only be obtained as a rider to an existing policy or as totally separate coverage.

Earthquake insurance premiums are determined differently by each insurance company and can vary widely depending on several rating factors. Older homes are more expensive to insure than newer homes. Wood homes get better rates than brick homes because they withstand the stresses of a quake better. Regions of the country are given a rating of 1 to 5 for likelihood of quakes. Your rating will be reflected in your premium.

Why Buy Earthquake Insurance?

The potential for earthquakes is greater than most of us realize: 39 states experienced earthquakes during the twentieth century; 90 percent of the American population live in areas considered seismically active.

Of course, everyone knows California is the most likely spot to suffer an earthquake. Small tremors are a daily occurrence there, and the U.S. Geological Survey predicts there is a 70 percent chance that the San Francisco Bay area will be hit by one or more quakes measuring 6.7 or higher on the Richter scale in the next 30 years. The last magnitude 7 quake to hit the state, the Northridge quake of 1994, caused more than $12 billion in damage.

Despite the risk, only about 20 percent of California homeowners have earthquake insurance. One reason is the cost. Depending on where they live, Californians can pay as much as five times what the rest of the country pays for coverage. In addition, deductibles are generally 10 percent of the value of the property. In other words, if your home is valued at $200,000, your deductible would be $20,000.

Many homeowners decide to take the chance and remain uninsured. They figure that unless the "big one" hits, the amount of damage they'd suffer would be less than their deductible. Still, Californians did shell out more than $386 million for earthquake insurance in 1988, representing more than half of all the premiums in the country; Washington ranked second, and Missouri third.

The rest of us will pay more reasonable premiums for earthquake insurance. An exception might be parts of Missouri that lie along the New Madrid fault. Relatively inactive for decades, and much less celebrated than the San Andreas fault in California, it was the source of a catastrophic quake during the nineteenth century. Experts agree that it has the potential to repeat history.

Your decision to buy earthquake insurance should be based on a number of factors. How likely is an earthquake to occur where you live? If one did occur, how strong would it likely be? How much damage would it cause? How much can you afford to lose? You might be interested to know that there are active earthquake insurance policies in all 50 states, including the 11 that have never experienced a quake.

What Does Earthquake Insurance Cover?

Because of their wide degrees of severity, the damage from an earthquake can range from a few broken dishes to a totally collapsed house. Any earthquake insurance policy should cover the cost to repair or replace any property damaged in a quake. Here are some of the critical questions to ask when considering various coverages.

1. Will the policy cover both the value of your house and its contents?

2. Does the policy have guaranteed replacement cost coverage?

3. Does the policy cover your car, boat, motorcycle, or other vehicles?

4. Does the policy cover structures other than your house, such as your garage, barn, or other outbuildings.

5. How will the deductible be applied in the event of a loss? Will there be separate deductibles for your house, your garage, and other structures or will there be just one deductible applied to your total loss?

6. If you have to leave your home, will the policy cover the cost of a hotel or other temporary housing?

7. What if there are aftershocks following the initial quake and after your property has received a damage appraisal? Will your deductible go into effect all over again for the new damage?

8. Does the construction of your house (brick as opposed to wood frame, for example) affect your premium?

E-MAIL

E-MAIL IS THE PERFECT TOOL for business communications. It's easy, cheap, convenient, effective, and incredibly fast. With the push of a button you can fire off a message to a person around the corner or around the globe. If the recipient isn't there when the message arrives, it will be waiting for him when he returns. If he wants to respond, he pushes the reply button, types in his message, and sends it on its way. And you never have to be out of touch because the world is becoming more wired every day. If you travel with a laptop or electronic organizer, you can plug in at hotels and other businesses to retrieve and send messages. It won't be long before wireless technology eliminates the need to plug into anything at all. For these reasons, e-mail is going to be the business communication method of choice—at least until something better comes along.

The way you approach e-mail correspondence should reflect the type of communication you're involved in and your relationship with the person you're communicating with. If you're chatting with friends, it's perfectly acceptable to be informal and not worry about misspellings and grammar. E-mail's primary virtue is speed, after all. You can carry on a virtual conversation that consists of short back-and-forth notes that almost resemble face-to-face conversation. (E-mail fosters such a feeling of intimacy that it has spawned romances and even marriages.) Banging out your messages as fast as possible is not a problem.

But for business messages, you should exercise almost the same care you would with a conventional business letter or other forms of written communication. Spell-check your messages before you send them to your clients and customers. If your e-mail program doesn't have a spell-check feature, switch to one that does.

You also need to format your messages. Forget about indenting paragraphs. The tab features on most e-mail programs seem to operate differently. Instead, begin each paragraph flush left

Sample E-mail Signature

Think of email signatures as the equivalent of the letterhead on traditional stationery. It needn't be dramatic or graphic, simply informational. Here's a good example:

Third Millennium Press, Inc.
555 Washington Avenue
Oneida, NY 14871
Voice: 716-555-1212
Fax: 716-555-1213
Net: http://www.tmp.com

and leave a space between paragraphs. That will give your messages a neat appearance and make them easy to read.

You don't need to use letterheads and dates, either. But be sure to use a formal "signature" at the end of each message. Most e-mail programs allow you to create a signature that will automatically appear at the end of each message. It should include your name, title, company name, mailing address, and telephone and fax numbers. If your business has a Web site, you can create a hyperlink that will allow your customer to go directly to the site with a click of his mouse.

Many e-mail programs allow you to select a font and font size. For regular correspondence, I suggest you use a serif font such as New York or Palatino and a font size of 12 or 14. For other types of messages, like a notice of a new product or service or an announcement of a meeting or seminar, you can make use of some of your program's other features. Use larger font sizes for headlines and bold or italicized type to call attention to important information. You may even be able to select different colors for your text. But do so judiciously. It's easy to get carried away and end up with a message that looks more like a holiday card than a business communication.

Respond to e-mail messages as quickly as possible. This is particularly important if you have a business that sells merchandise over the Web. It's just good customer service. I have a client who has a Web-based compact disc business and ships merchandise to customers around the world. He learned very early on that if he didn't respond quickly to their questions, they would take their business elsewhere.

Don't forget the telephone as a business tool. It's not obsolete yet. In fact, it's still superior to e-mail in allowing two people to have a fruitful discussion. E-mail is great for sending messages and asking questions that require a simple answer. But for more complex communications requiring serious discussion, the telephone allows the voice inflections that we all rely on to get our message across. The telephone also allows for more effective use of humor, sarcasm, and other emotions that are often difficult to translate into type. And remember, just because you receive an e-mail message doesn't mean you can't respond by telephone.

Here's a word of caution. E-mail makes it very easy to pass on jokes and other missives that people may or may not find funny. Don't run the risk of offending your clients and customers. If you receive a joke you like, forward it to your friends and family if you must, but keep your business communications businesslike.

You should also double-check to make sure your messages are addressed to the proper people before you hit the send button. Most e-mail programs have an address book feature that allows you to preprogram the e-mail addresses of individuals and groups. That way, you can just click on a name and that person's e-mail address will automatically appear as the recipient of your message.

But it's easy to accidentally hit the wrong name, so be careful. The results could be embarrassing to you and harmful to your business. You don't want your request for a job interview ending up on your current boss's computer screen. The same ease and speed that makes e-mail a dream for business communication could also lead to a business nightmare.

EMPLOYEES

I F YOU HAVE MORE than one employee working for you, fire someone. If you have just one employee, see if you can turn her into a part-time person or an independent contractor. Your mission as an employer should be to have as few employees as you possibly can. The ultimate goal is to have none.

It may sound heartless, but employees are expenses. In addition to their salaries, you may need to pay for their health and disability insurance, and possibly contribute to a retirement plan. At the very least you'll be forced to deal with payroll returns, FICA, and withholding taxes. In effect, every employee you have on staff who doesn't generate her own profits reduces the health of your bottom line.

Going Solo

If you can operate your business with no employees at all, by all means do it. I believe the perfect small business form for the twenty-first century isn't a pyramid with an executive, a handful of middle managers, and a number of employees, but a solo entrepreneur at the center of a hub linked to independent contractors, outsourcing firms, and other entrepreneurs.

Achieving this solo status may be easier than you think, for two reasons: technology and outsourcing. Many business tasks today can be performed by computer systems, which are much cheaper to acquire and maintain than employees. Many other tasks can be farmed out to independent contractors. Temps are another solution, since you're only responsible for their salaries and don't need to worry about insurance and retirement costs.

If You Can't Go It Alone

The reality, however, is that not every entrepreneur will be able to operate as a one-person show and will, instead, require a few employees. The key to maximizing employees' effectiveness is making sure they're as flexible in their skills as possible. Businesses today need to be able to turn on a dime to react to market conditions and competition. Your employees need to be equally pliable. They should be able to field calls, deal with customers, provide accurate information on your product or service, and generally cover as many tasks as possible. They need to be generalists, not specialists.

What Makes a Good Employee

The demand for flexibility means you need employees with intelligence, of course. But there are a couple other characteristics that are equally important: candor and humility. This is because you're going to be expecting a lot from your employees, so you need to hire people who will admit when they don't know how to do something or when they make a mistake. People with high intelligence or inflated egos are often reluctant to admit they don't understand something or they've made a mistake.

You also need people who are reliable and who have a sense of urgency. Frankly, I'd rather have an employee whose talents are average, but who is honest, shows up every morning, and is dogged and determined in the pursuit of her assignments, than a talented superstar, who isn't totally candid and whose day-to-day status is always a mystery.

The New Workplace Relationship

All this may sound rather callous, but the hard fact is that the employer-employee relationship has changed over the last decade or so. There was a time when people would go to work for a company right out of high school or college and spend their entire careers there. They would have complete loyalty to the company and in return would receive fair compensation, valuable benefits, and a comfortable pension.

But American business has changed. Rather than being an industrial economy, we now work in an economy based on technology and the provision of services. Businesses in these industries are smaller and more numerous. This, in turn, has created more employment opportunities for people, and they switch jobs at the drop of a hat. It's common now for people to work for five or six companies during the course of their careers. As an employer, you can expect your employees to stay with you for three to five years. Loyalty is no longer an issue; the workplace relationship is now totally mercenary. (See my books *Die Broke* and *Live Rich* to learn more about how to prosper in this new paradigm.)

All this means that healthy workplace relationships today are based on honesty. You'll know that even though they're working for you, your employees are going to be keeping an eye on the horizon for better opportunities. And they'll know you expect the best performances they have to offer. They'll also know that if your business begins to fall off, they can expect to be handed a pink slip (the smartest of them will see the storm clouds gathering and bail out long before that day arrives). As long as everyone understands and acknowledges this relationship, no one has reason to complain.

The best way to ensure this understanding is to be frank with your employees when you hire them. Make sure they know their continued employment is contingent upon their satisfactory performance and the financial health of the business. You should also acknowledge that you understand they will be looking for new opportunities.

You can even take the situation a step further and discuss beforehand how your employees' departures will be handled. In the event you have to lay them off, you can agree to how much notice they'll be given and what kind of compensation package they'll receive. They, in turn, can agree to give you a certain number of weeks' notice if they choose to leave voluntarily. In today's business climate, you can be sure one or the other circumstance will arise. You'll be better off if all parties are prepared for it.

I realize I've painted a pretty grim picture of the workplace. You might think that being a boss is pretty unpleasant, but that couldn't be further from the truth. We're all individual entrepreneurs today, looking out for number one. It's just the nature of the world we live in. As long as everyone understands this, there's no reason you and your employees can't have fun and enjoy one another's successes together. The key is to be honest, acknowledge the nature of the relationship, and not expect to give or receive more than you owe each other.

_____

(See also independent contractors, outsourcing, temps.)

EMPLOYEE STOCK OWNERSHIP PLANS

I DON'T CARE HOW MANY Microsoft millionaires there are, for the average American, stock options are no replacement for a pension.

Employee stock ownership plans (ESOPs) are increasingly popular with companies as an alternative to pension plans. On the surface they do seem like a great way to build your retirement fund. You acquire stock on a regular basis at no cost. Over time, as the company grows and becomes more successful, the value of your stock increases. By the time you're ready to retire, you have a nice little nest egg sitting there. Who knows, maybe you'll be one of those millionaires next door.

Well, maybe—but then again, maybe not. If your company does grow, you could be quite comfortable when you walk out the door. But what if it doesn't do well? Perhaps the company falls on hard times and the value of your stock becomes static or steadily decreases. In a worst-case scenario, your company could go out of business, taking your retirement fund with it.

One problem with an ESOP is that you have no control over the stock you've accumulated until you either quit or retire. Until then the stock is held by a trustee and you have no voting rights. This means that even though your retirement fund is intimately linked to the success of the company, you have no say in how the company is run.

Another problem is calculating what your shares are worth when you retire. If you work for a publicly held company, you'll know exactly where you stand. But if you work for a privately held firm, the stock's value is a little more nebulous. Basically, you're at the mercy of an appraiser when the time comes to cash in.

This is why it's not to an employee's advantage for a company to make an ESOP the only form of retirement fund available to its employees. Remember that ESOPs are usually a better deal for the company than for the employee. Companies offering their employees ESOPs gain certain tax advantages. They can also help a company fight off a takeover.

If you do remain with your company, the law provides one option you can exercise to protect yourself. When you reach age 55, you can ask that 25 percent of your ESOP be liquidated and put in other investments. You can specify that the transfer occur all at once or over five years. Five years later you can repeat the process.

If the stock is doing well, you may be tempted to wait. Don't do it. If you're in an ESOP, your goal should be to diversify as much as possible as soon as possible. If your company has an adequate defined contribution plan, you can consider transferring the money there. Or you can have it transferred into an IRA. The important thing is that you not have all your eggs in one basket. If you do, you're gambling with money you can't afford to lose.

(See also pension plans.)

EMPLOYMENT AGENCIES

THE ENTREPRENEUR WHO DOES HIS OWN hiring has a fool for a human resources director. If you're like most entrepreneurs, you're probably tempted to try to do everything yourself. After all, no one can do something better than you can, right? Wrong. When it comes to hiring employees, stick to doing what you know best—running you business—and hire experts to take care of the recruitment and interviewing of candidates.

Better for Both Employers and Employees

Employment agencies are professional matchmakers. They're much better at wording and placing ads, interviewing, checking references, gauging skills, and assessing personalities than the average businessperson. This gives them the ability to weed out bad matches, which saves you valuable time. If you've ever had to sit through an hour-long interview with a prospective employee who you realized was wrong for the job the moment she walked in the door, you know what I'm talking about. You sit there in agony fretting about all the time you're wasting while you go through the motions of trying to appear interested.

Because an employment agency eliminates any unqualified people beforehand, you know they'll send you only viable candidates.* If you were to take care of the process yourself, you might have to go through six or seven interviews just to find someone who barely qualifies for the position. And if you worded the ad wrong you might not get anyone who's qualified.

It works the same way for the prospective employee. Rather than going on countless interviews in which the mismatch quickly becomes apparent, you see only employers who are seeking people with your particular experiences and skills. Employment agencies also help job seekers avoid those dreaded situations in which someone—usually an internal candidate—has already been selected to fill the position but other people must still be interviewed to meet some political or legal quota.

Fees and Mitigating Costs

Like all good business services, employment agencies can be expensive. A fee of 10 percent of the position's salary is common. Some agencies charge the employer, others the employee. Some charge both. I personally feel it's money well spent. If you're hiring someone for a $40,000-a-year position, you have to ask yourself if the results and the countless hours you save aren't worth the $4,000 it costs you.

Of course, it may not cost you a cent. It's not uncommon for an employer to require a new employee to reimburse all or part of the fee once she begins work. The employer won't demand it all at once, of course; usually he'll just withhold a certain amount from the person's paycheck for the first year or two until the fee is paid off. The ability to do this depends on the size of the market for the position. If competition is fierce, chances are the person who is ultimately offered the job will agree to the reimbursement. If it's a position that requires rare skills and therefore attracts few good candidates, it's unlikely that the employer will make such a request.

The opposite is also true. If an employee is expected to pay the agency fee, she may be able to get her new employer to cover the cost. Once again, it comes down to how anxious the employer is to have the person join the firm.

---

*To make the matchmaking even more efficient, I usually advocate the use of employment agencies that specialize in a particular profession, industry, or position.

Looking for a Job through an Employment Agency

If you're using an employment agency in your job search you need to watch out for unscrupulous operations. Here are some ways to protect yourself:

Always visit an agency to make sure it's legitimate. If you just deal with the agency over the telephone, you could fall victim to a boiler-room operation that's set up solely to scam people. You can also check out the agency with the National Association of Personnel Services, the American Management Association, or the Society for Human Resource Managers.

Watch out for advance fees. If it's gong to cost you money just to walk in the door, my advice is to walk away. Once an employment agency has your money, its motivation to help you decreases significantly. You should only pay a fee if you land a job.

Beware of any agency that wants to charge you to take aptitude tests. Find out who pays the fee. When an employment agency's efforts result in a job, someone pays the fee. Some firms charge the employer. Others charge the job seeker. Some may try to charge both. If you're expected to pay, find out the timing of the payment. Do you pay when you're hired? After some time in the job? What happens if you don't like the job? Can you get a refund?

Watch out for classified ads that are placed by agencies. The ad will look like it's been placed by an employer. In fact, it's just a way to get you to call. If you take the job, you'll be charged a fee. More often, the ad is just bait to lure you in. The job itself may be pure fiction. Don't respond to job offers with 900 numbers, either. All you'll end up with is a big phone bill.

Don't sign a contract until you've read it thoroughly. Some employment agencies will present you with a contract almost as an aside. "It's just a standard form," they tell you. In fact, it could commit you to all sorts of charges. Take it home and read it carefully. If the terms are acceptable, sign it and return it the next day.

Regardless of who pays the fee, I believe they should negotiate a payment plan with the employment agency that's tied to the employee's tenure with her new employer. After all, in today's business climate, it's quite possible the person will leave the position before a year is up. So rather than a lump sum payable up front, ask to pay the fee in 12 monthly installments. But stipulate that if the employee should leave within the year, the balance of the payments are canceled or you'll get a replacement employee.

Will the agency agree to your requests? If nothing else, most will give you at least a 90-day guarantee. Think about it. Every vacancy on your staff means more work for the agency. If the employee leaves early, you'll quickly be on the telephone asking the agency to start a new search. One way or another, the agency ends up getting its money.

EMPLOYMENT CONTRACTS

THE ONLY WAY an employee can have even a modicum of security in today's workplace is to have an employment contract. Anyone who doesn't try to get one from his or her employer is making a big mistake.

Although there are no boilerplate employment contracts, they all include compensation figures and describe an agreed-upon term of employment. Beyond that, everything and anything can be included. Benefits, bonuses, raises, vacations, severance pay, duties, place in the hierarchy, termination provisions, and other items can and should be included.

Successful Scenarios

Admittedly, employment contracts are difficult for the average person to pull off. The clients of mine who have been most successful at getting employment contracts have used one of three strategies. Some have turned raise discussions into employment contract discussions; some have used job offers from other firms as leverage to get contracts with their current employers; and some have asked for and received termination agreements that spell out how much money they'll get, and for how long, if they are terminated without cause. (See "The Backhanded Contract," page 228.)

The other thing clients who get employment contracts have in common is they're all key employees whose departures would cause their companies a great deal of discomfort. This is why employment contracts are often initiated by employers who want to make sure their key employees remain with the company. This is a particular concern when a company is up for sale. Any potential buyer is going to want assurances that the company's key executives will remain if the company changes hands. Employment contracts allow the sellers to make sure these people are included as part of the deal.

Negotiating the Terms

Employment contracts can be for any length of time. For this reason they have something of a catch-22 quality. A shorter term provides less security but allows greater flexibility to look for a better and higher-paying job. A longer term, on the other hand, provides greater security but makes it difficult to act on new opportunities. I feel most people should aim for a term of three years.

In addition to salary and term of employment, an employment contract should spell out in detail your responsibilities, who you report to, and the performance benchmarks that will trigger raises or bonuses. It should include a clause stating that if your responsibilities are significantly

The Backhanded Contract

Many company executives, when approached about an employment contract, respond by saying, "The company doesn't issue contracts." Rather than letting that put an end to your efforts, try to negotiate what I call the "backhanded contract": a termination agreement. When told the company doesn't issue contracts, explain that your primary concern is being terminated without cause. Invariably, the executive will say, "We never terminate people without cause." Respond by noting that you, of course, have perfect trust in your superior, but you're worried about a change in management. Since you both know the current company would never terminate you without cause, drawing up a termination agreement would just be for your own emotional comfort and, therefore, nothing that could raise objections. Since the most important provision in any employment contract is the severance package, having a termination agreement that covers just that is almost as good.

Sample Annotated Employment Contract

Your employer or the company's lawyer has undoubtedly negotiated a lot more employment contracts than you ever will. To help even the odds you should hire a lawyer experienced in employment law. As a head start, here's a sample contract along with some provision-by-provision pointers I usually provide my own clients.

1. Term
   The term of Employee's employment shall commence on the first day of December, 1998, and continue for thirty-six (36) consecutive months thereafter (the "Expiration Date"), unless sooner terminated pursuant to Article 5 (Reasons for Termination) hereof.

   This section defines the length of the contract—one year, two years, etc. Its inclusion is more than a bookkeeping detail. In most states employers can terminate an employee for any reason at any time and without further compensation (unless civil rights or discrimination laws apply). However, if your contract specifies a of employment, you'll be entitled to receive the balance due if your employer fires you without cause, as defined in Article 5.

2. Duties
   During the Term, Employee shall devote all his business time, attention, and energies to the business of Employer. Employee will be executive vice president and Employee will perform such duties and such other duties as may be assigned by the president or such other individual as may be designated by the Chief Executive Officer.

Many employment contracts are far too vague or sketchy when it comes to defining the employee's job. There's nothing wrong with flexibility, of course—so long as everyone's happy. But if the relationship sours, latitude makes it possible for an employer to give an employee loathsome or even humiliating work assignments, perhaps in a deliberate effort to persuade the employee to quit. Remember, you and your employer can always agree to make changes in a contract. So if your pride can't stand emptying the trash or having your desk moved to the stairwell, make sure your contract says something about what you'll be doing and where you will be doing it. Get as specific a description of your duties and responsibilities as possible. If that's not possible, at least make sure this section includes a clause saying that your duties will be restricted to those that are "reasonable and customary" to the position you hold.

3. Compensation

(a) *Salary compensation:* For all the services rendered by Employee, Employer shall pay to Employee the sum of one hundred fifteen thousand dollars ($115,000) per annum ("Salary"), payable in accordance with Employer's then-effective payroll practices.

(b) *Bonus compensation:* In addition to Employee's Salary, Employee shall be entitled to receive bonus compensation in such amount as may be deined by the Employer in its sole discretion.

(c) *Benefits:* Employee shall be entitled to participate in such vacation, medical, dental, life insurance, 401(k), pension, and other plans as Employer may have or establish from time to time and in which Employee would be entitled to participate pursuant to the terms thereof.

(d) *Expenses:* During the Term, Employee shall be reimbursed for such reasonable travel and other expenses incurred in the performance of Employee's duties hereunder as are customarily reimbursed to other employees of Employer.

The rule here: If it ain't written down, it won't end up in your pocket. Everything that could be remotely considered compensation—from vacation days and special perks to salary and stock options—should be detailed in this section. Unless you don't expect a raise during the time period covered by the agreement, this section should also spell out the procedure for determining pay increases. If nothing else, insist on a yearly salary review or a minimum annual increase at least equal to the cost of living.

4. Exclusive Employment, Confidential Information, No Employee Solicitation, Return of Property

(a) *Non-competition:* Employee agrees that Employee's employment hereunder is on an exclusive basis and that during the Term and for three (3) years thereafter (the "Noncompete Period"), Employee will not engage in any other business activity that is in conflict with his duties and obligations hereunder. Employee agrees that during the Noncompete Period he shall not directly or indirectly engage in or participate as an officer, director, shareholder, member, agent, or consultant for any business directly competitive with Employer.

(b) *Confidential information:* Employee agrees that Employee shall not, during the Term or at any time thereafter, use for Employee's own purposes, or disclose to or for the benefit of any third party, any trade secret or confidential information of Employer (except as may be required by law or in the performance of Employee's duties hereunder). Confidential information shall be deemed to include all customer lists and pricing strategies of Employer. Notwithstanding the foregoing, confidential information shall not be deemed to include information that (i) is or becomes generally available to the public other than as a result of a disclosure by Employee or any person who directly or indirectly receives such information from Employee or at Employee's direction, or (ii) is or becomes available to Employee on a nonconfidential basis from a source that is entitled to disclose same to Employee.

(c) *No employee solicitation:* Employee agrees that during the and for three (3) years thereafter, he shall not, directly or indirectly, engage, employ, or solicit the employment of any person who is then or has been within three (3) years prior thereto, an employee of Employer.

(d) *Return of property:* All property, whether tangible or intangible, including all information stored in electronic form, obtained or prepared by or for Employee and utilized in the course of Employee's employment with Employer shall remain the exclusive property of Employer. In the event of the termination of Employee's employment for any reason, Employer reserves the right, to the extent permitted by law and in addition to any other remedy Employer may have, to deduct from any monies otherwise payable to Employee, the following: (i) the full amount of any debt Employee owes to Employer and (ii) the value of the Employer's property which Employee retains in his possession after termination of Employee's employment.

(e)   The provisions of this Article 4 shall survive the expiration or sooner termination of this Agreement.

Many companies today are offering employment contracts precisely because they want their charges to sign a document restricting their ability to jump to a competitor—or take proprietary information with them when they do. The covenants contained in this section are where employers seek to obtain this protection. In other words: watch your flanks. Your objective should be to give yourself as much flexibility as possible. Do not simply accept boilerplate language. Employers like to push for extreme limits on who you can work for and when. In a sense, they'd just as soon you dropped off the face of the earth forever if you're not going to be toiling to their benefit.

In examining the validity of the exclusions contained in this section of an employment contract, courts weigh the employer's legitimate business interests against the ability of an employee to earn a livelihood. For instance, a court might agree to bar the employee of a cable television channel that specializes in children's programming from working for another children's television channel for a year or two, But the court might let the employee work for another cable channel that occupies a different niche, say cooking.

While there's no requirement for employers to offer employees compensation for these covenants, such payments have sometimes helped courts overcome their problems with employee livelihood. In other words, if you can't eliminate or soften restrictions on where you can earn a living, try to shorten the period or get compensation for them. You can also work to subtly undermine exclusions you can't negotiate away through your choice of the law governing the agreement (Article 7).

Employers understandably try to keep all internal information confidential. Nevertheless, courts have ruled that there are limits to confidentiality. Client lists, for instance, are protected only if the information can't be obtained elsewhere. Similarly, publicly known or previously published key contracts, pricing policies, and buying habits aren't protected. That doesn't mean the provisions don't have some teeth: courts have held employees liable for the disclosure of confidential information whether or not it was willful.

5. Reasons for Termination

This Agreement may be terminated:

(a)   By Employer "for cause" in the event of Employee's (i)   embezzlement, fraud, or any other conduct which would constitute a felony; (ii)   conviction of, a plea of guilty to, or a plea of nolo contendere to a felony; (iii)   willful unauthorized disclosure of confidential information; or (iv)   a material breach of this Agreement, or

(b)   By Employee in the event that Employer shall have materially breached this Agreement, and such material breach is not cured within thirty (30) days after written notice is given to Employer.

> A paragraph should be added that provides for a "cure period" during which, after a warning, you are given an opportunity to address your employer's complaints about your work. This should apply to performance issues—such as your not producing promised results—rather than, say, your being convicted for insider trading. If your employer balks at such language, explain that it also benefits him by limiting his potential exposure to litigation. An additional reason for termination, "change of control or ownership," should be included to allow for it to be specifically discussed in the subsequent section. Finally, some provision should be included to provide ample notice (such as six months) to you if your contract isn't going to be renewed for another. Obviously, the more notice you can get, the better. If they won't promise notice, ask for severance pay instead.

6. Results of Termination

Upon termination of this Agreement pursuant to subsections 5 (a), (b) or (c) hereof, Employer shall pay to Employee any amounts of Salary or Bonus that have accrued but were unpaid prior to the date of termination. Upon termination of this Agreement pursuant to subsections 5 (b) and (c) hereof, Employer shall pay to Employee Employee's Salary and Bonus for six (6) months following the date of termination; provided, however, that Employee will be required to mitigate the amount of any payment provided for in this paragraph by seeking other employment and the amount of any such payment provided for in this paragraph shall be reduced by any compensation earned by Employee from a third person.

> Ask for full payment of your contracted salary if you're terminated without cause or if your employer breaches the agreement. But be prepared to cut a

deal. By expanding the reasons for termination in the previous section, you can include language here outlining your rights to compensation after a change in management or ownership. Strive for such compensation to be the same as if you were terminated without cause, but settle for the best you can get.

7. Governing Law, Jurisdiction

This Agreement and all matters or issues relating thereto shall be governed by the laws of the State of New York applicable to contracts entered into and performed entirely therein. Any action to enforce this Agreement shall be brought in the state or federal courts located in the City of New York.

This may seem like neutral boilerplate, but it's more important than you might think. The common-law obligations of employers and employees vary from state to state. So, too, does the way local courts interpret and enforce the covenants outlined in Article 4. The choice of governing law and jurisdiction in the agreement will ultimately deine what elements of Article 4 can be enforced and how strenuously they will be enforced. You should try to use the state law most beneficial to you. If, for example, you work in the California office of a corporation headquartered in Alabama, your employer will want Alabama law to govern the contract, since it's considered employer-friendly. But you should push for interpretation under California law, since it's considered employee-friendly.

It also makes sense to try to insert an arbitration clause in the agreement since that will cut the time and cost of settling any disputes. Speedy, cheap resolution is advantageous to employees and robs employers of some leverage.

8. No Modification, Entire Agreement

This Agreement may not be modified except in a writing signed by both parties hereto. This Agreement contains the entire understanding of the parties hereto relating to the subject matter herein contained.

9. Void Provisions

If any provision of this Agreement, as applied to either party or to any circumstances, shall be adjudged by a court to be void or unenforceable, the same shall be deemed stricken from this Agreement and shall in no way affect any other provision of this Agreement or the validity and enforceability of this Agreement.

10. Captions and Headings
    The captions and headings hereof are for convenience only and shall not be construed or interpreted as part of the agreement.

    IN WITNESS WHEREOF, the parties hereto have signed this Agreement as of the date first above written.

_____

Employer

_____

Employee

changed, or if the chain of command changes, you have the right to terminate the contract upon due notice. And don't forget a signing bonus, a lump sum payable upon signing, or a "staying" bonus payable at an agreed-upon point during the contract. Companies today are anxious to recruit and retain talented people and are often quite generous to those employees they value highly.

You'll also need to negotiate benefits such as health and life insurance, retirement contributions, vacation days, sick days, and personal leave. You may think this level of detail is unnecessary, but if these items aren't spelled out in the contract, your employer doesn't have to give them to you. Don't assume anything is "understood."

Make sure any employment contract spells out when discussions for renewal of your contract will begin. Make sure it's as far from the expiration date of the existing contract as possible. This let's you accomplish two things. First, if your employer wants to keep you on, it gives you a great deal of time to negotiate the terms of your new contract. But perhaps more importantly, if he doesn't intend to rehire you, it gives you more time to look for a new job.

Employers will want to include restrictive covenants in the agreement, limiting your ability to work for competitors. Some of these restrictions can seem quite daunting. However, the more restrictions imposed on you by a contract, the less likely it will hold up in court. What a judge may do, however, is rule that you cannot work in a certain geographic area or for a direct competitor of your former employer or you cannot start a company in the same business for a certain length of time. Rather than trying to weaken the restrictive covenants themselves, it's often savvy to negotiate as short a time as possible that they will remain in effect; alternatively, negotiate more pay during the period.

It also makes sense to try to have an arbitration provision in the contract since it can lead to inexpensive and speedy resolution of disputes. That's an advantage to employees who don't have the deep pockets of the employer.

Don't let issues of perceived fairness cloud your negotiating. If you or your representative negotiate intelligently, you might end up making twice as much as someone who's already working for the company and doing a comparable task. But that's not your problem. We're all free agents in today's business climate and you deserve whatever you can get. At the same time you need to remember that the person or people on the other side of the negotiating table will have the same attitude. The bottom line is to get as much as possible. Once you signed your name on the dotted line, however, live up to the terms of the contract and do the best job you can. But remember to keep one eye on the horizon in case something better should appear.

(See also terminations.)

ENTERTAINMENT

FUN SEEMS TO COST far too much money these days.

The cost of tickets for movies and concerts, the theater, sporting events, and just about every other form of entertainment is going through the roof. When you add up admission, food, souvenirs, and parking, an evening at the ball park for a family of four can easily exceed $200. Court-side seats at professional basketball games are more than $1,000 in some cities. Theater tickets in New York City crossed the $100 threshold several years ago.

Even amusing ourselves at home is expensive. Cable television can cost $400 or more a year, depending on the level of service you receive. Video and DVD rentals save money on going to the movies but can still cost $3 to $5 per rental. The electronic equipment we need to view them is also expensive.

There are ways to have fun that don't cost an arm and a leg, however. Here are some ways you can save on entertainment costs.

Rehearsals

Many theater groups, dance troupes, and orchestras welcome visitors to their rehearsals. They can often be more interesting than the real performances. You get to see and hear how the creative process is fine-tuned behind the scenes.

Festivals

During the summer months there are weekend festivals of all types throughout the United States. Some are community-based. Others are organized around music or food or the arts. Admission is often free and any associated costs are usually quite modest.

Factory Tours

Many companies conduct free tours of their manufacturing plants. To them, it's good public relations and a way to increase their customer base. Breweries, distilleries, and candy factories are traditional favorites. The wine-producing regions of California and New York have dozens of wineries that are open to the public. In Vermont, Ben & Jerry's ice cream plant has become the state's largest tourist attraction.

Museums

It's hard to find museums that don't charge admission anymore, but most give out free passes to schools and libraries. If they're not being used, these institutions will usually be more than happy to pass them on to you.

Videos

Go to the library. Most libraries these days have fairly extensive video collections that are free to library members.

Inexpensive Theater Tickets

There are several tricks to getting discount theater tickets. One is to attend previews, for which seats are often discounted. If you're a real theater buff, buying a series subscription will save you up to a third off the regular ticket price. Some plans allow you to select a portion of the season's offerings. Others require you to buy a subscription for the full season. You can also go after "rush" tickets, the unsold tickets that theaters discount heavily a half-hour or so before the scheduled performance.

Cheap Movies

The best way to save money on movie tickets is to relive your youth and sneak in. Just kidding. However, you can attend matinees, which are usually 20 to 30 percent cheaper than evening shows. Many theater chains sell discounted passbooks that offer considerable savings. And don't forget senior citizen and student discounts.

Bargain Sporting Events

The cost of professional sporting events has become a thorn in the side of sports fans everywhere. One way to keep the cost down is to invest in a season ticket with a group of other fans and then divvy up the games. Group discounts are still offered, so organizing an office trip will save everyone a few bucks. You can also pass on the big leagues and watch the minors. There are minor-league baseball and hockey teams throughout the country. Not only will you pay a fraction of the big-league price, you'll get to see tomorrow's stars in action.

Read a Book

Here's a novel idea. Rather than frantically trying to entertain yourself with expensive trips to movies and ball games and concerts, go to the library and take out a few books. Then spend some quiet evenings at home reading. For my money, that's still the best form of entertainment.

EQUIPMENT

DON'T TRY TO SAVE MONEY by purchasing less than top-notch equipment. If you have a full-time need for a particular piece of equipment and the cost of buying a high-quality unit is beyond your reach, lease it instead. If you have a part-time need for a piece of equipment and cost is an issue, rent time on it instead of leasing or buying it.

Equipment is a major expense for any size business. I have a client who owns a large printing firm. A new state-of-the-art offset press costs him more than $1 million. I also have clients who run small consulting practices form their homes. Outfitting their home offices with a computer, printer, fax machine, telephone, and other essentials can easily be between $5,000 and $15,000. That's a lot of money when you're operating a one-person shop.

Some people are tempted to cut corners and get the cheapest equipment they can find. I disagree. Think of yourself as a craftsperson. I believe a craftsperson should have the best tools available. These are the tools you use to do your work. The better your tools, the better your product. The better your product, the happier your customers will be.

Your goal should be to have every piece of equipment you use in your business as close to state of the art as possible. For that reason, I suggest you take two approaches to acquiring equipment. If a piece of equipment will remain adequate for the job you expect it to do for at least five years, buy it. When you buy a piece of equipment, you can depreciate the cost over a period of time, usually five years.* During that time you'll be setting aside enough money to replace it when that depreciation period is up.

But if a piece of equipment is likely to become quickly obsolete because of advances in technology, lease it. Look for short-term leases—12 to 18 months. That will give you the flexibility to stay abreast of technology. When the lease is up on a piece of equipment, you can replace it with an improved model. If the technology hasn't changed appreciably, you can renew the lease, usually for a reduced price. If your needs have changed and you no longer need the equipment, you can return it.

---

*One-time deductions of the full cost are also possible, with some limitations.

If you can't obtain a short-term lease, insist on a clause that will allow you to periodically upgrade the piece of equipment after 18 months. That way you're still able to keep abreast of the technology.

Keep in mind that whatever route you take, buying or leasing, your equipment costs are a deductible business expense. And although leasing is usually more expensive long-term than buying, it provides you with a flexibility you lose when you own a piece of equipment that has become obsolete. In today's business world, flexibility is a key to success. I think increased flexibility is worth the extra expense.

Of course, you should first ask yourself whether you need to invest in equipment at all. Have you been to a Kinko's or Staples lately? Those well-known chains and others like them are now offering in-store workstations that businesspeople can use to conduct their work. With the latest in computers, printers, copiers, scanners, fax machines, and Internet access, these mini- offices have become a home away from home for people in all sorts of businesses. You can walk in, roll up your sleeves, and get to work. When you're finished, you pay for your time and head out the door. For a piece of equipment you only need occasionally, you may find buying time at Kinko's is the best solution.

(See also home offices.)

EXECUTORS

O NE OF THE FEW up sides of dying is you won't be around to see if there are any knock-down, drag-out brawls over your estate.

That thankless task goes to your executor, the person you designate to make sure your will is carried out. It's time-consuming, emotionally draining, and generally not a whole lot of fun. Insurance companies and creditors must be notified of your demise. All your property has to be located and inventoried. All your bills and taxes must be paid. Your investments have to be managed until the estate is settled. Professionals must be hired. And there are always your heirs to deal with. Even though they'll be mourning your departure, we can also assume that, human nature being what it is, they'll be more than a little anxious to find out what's coming to them.

At best, things will proceed smoothly, you'll have taken my advice and died broke, and your executor will just have to deal with the emotional distress of dismantling your life. That's bad enough. But if arguments start over who gets the Mr. Coffee and the Salad Shooter, it could drive him or her straight into therapy.

Naming an Executor

Most people name an heir or a close friend to serve as the executor of their estates. Although it is comforting to know that someone close to you will be handling things, it's also important that the person you choose be reliable, honest, and sensitive to the situation.

It's even more important that he or she be willing, so don't forget to ask. I know a woman I'll call Sally who lost an old friend quite suddenly from a heart attack. Sally discovered at the funeral she had been named executor of her friend's estate. The news came as a shock to her; she only vaguely remembered the subject being discussed in a brief conversation years earlier.

It was a complicated estate involving an ex-husband, a son, a long-term domestic partner, numerous brothers and sisters and nieces and nephews, and considerable assets, including ongoing royalties from several books her friend had written. Nonetheless, Sally dutifully carried out the job, although it required her to take a leave of absence from work and to travel several states away on more than one occasion. It was also upsetting enough to affect her health. Fortunately for Sally, her friend left her a generous sum of money that more than made up for the lost wages and travel expenses.

Unless different arrangements are made, executors receive a standard commission as allowed by law. If you want your executor to receive either no commission or more commission, you need to have a separate agreement drawn up. Executors can also elect not to accept the commission.

You can also choose a lawyer to serve as executor, but you should arrange in advance what the charges will be. She will then hire herself as the estate's attorney and, in addition to the executor's commission, she will either charge by the hour, charge a set fee, or charge a percentage of the value of the estate. Just remember that every penny your estate is billed is money that's being taken from your heirs. Unless your estate is unusually large or complicated, I see no reason why it can't be handled by an executor who is a friend or family member. The probate process is much simpler today than it used to be. If you stay on top of things and are clear about how you want your assets distributed, the task can be done by a nonlawyer who is willing to spend the necessary time.

If you do hire a lawyer, appoint a friend or heir as coexecutor to make sure the process is taken care of in a timely manner. And shop around for price and experience before you make a decision. You'll be surprised at the range of quotes you receive and also the differences in a lawyer's qualifications.

(See also lawyers, probate and settlement, wills.)

FAMILY LEAVE

BALANCING WORK AND FAMILY during a personal crisis is impossible. One or both will suffer from divided attention.

The Family and Medical Leave Act (FMLA) of 1993 was an effort to change that. The act allows you to take as much as 12 weeks of unpaid leave every year for specified family and medical reasons. They include the birth and care of a child, the placement of a child into foster care or adoption, the care of an immediate family member who is seriously ill, or the serious illness of the employee himself. Leave for the birth and care of a child, or the adoption or foster placement of a child, must be taken within 12 months of the birth or placement.

Nearly 70 million workers are covered by the act, and about 17 percent of those covered have taken advantage of it every year since it has been law. Employees of public organizations, and most private companies that have 50 or more workers, are covered. To be eligible, you need to have worked for your employer for at least a year and must have worked at least 1,250 hours during the previous 12 months. There is one glitch to the system, however. If you and your spouse work for the same employer, you're entitled to a combined 12 weeks of leave, not 12 weeks apiece.

Workers requesting FMLA leave must apply for it at least 30 days in advance, although exceptions are made at the employer's discretion for emergency situations. If you're requesting the leave for health reasons—either yours or a family member's—you may be required to provide medical certification of the illness. You may also be required to check in with your supervisor from time to time.

When you take FMLA leave, your employer is required to maintain your health insurance coverage, although under certain circumstances you may be required to contribute to the premiums. Many employers will also allow you to take the time off intermittently rather than all at once.

The intermittent-leave option is tailormade for working couples whose individual responsibilities may make taking 12 weeks at one time impossible. Let's say you have a sick child and you and your spouse want to make sure one of you is with her every day. You could arrange a staggered two weeks off, two weeks on, arrangement that would let you accomplish this and still keep your professional lives somewhat under control.

If your position is critical to your company's operation, you may have a problem taking all the leave you want. The act recognizes the economic hardships a company may suffer from the absence of a salaried key employee and provides the company with some protection. It stipulates that if your salary is among the top 10 percent in the company, you must be notified that you're considered a key employee when you apply for leave. Then, during your leave, the company can force you back to work by informing you that you won't be given your old job unless you return within a certain time frame.

Could you call their bluff, take the entire 12 weeks, and still have a job? Sure, if they really need you. But I'd make sure I really held all the cards before I tried anything that bold. Otherwise you might find yourself visiting the unemployment office.

If you don't return to work at the end of the leave (about 6 percent of employees don't), most employers will terminate you. You'll also likely be required to reimburse your former employer for the health insurance premiums that the employer paid during your leave.

Of course, the biggest problem with FMLA is the economic aspect. Being given the freedom to take 12 weeks off is one thing. Being able to survive without 12 weeks worth of wages is something else altogether. Some employers will ease the burden by letting employees combine accrued vacation, personal, and sick time with the leave to make up the 12 weeks. Some low-wage earners are even allowed to use public assistance to supplement their incomes while on leave.

Most people, however, just bite the bullet and either live off their savings or take out a modest loan to pay the bills while they're on leave. If you decide to take advantage of FMLA, I advise you to sit down beforehand and work out the financial details to make sure you can afford to take the entire time off. If you can afford it, count yourself lucky. If not, take as much time as you can afford or try to slide by, borrowing as little as possible. And if you do borrow, use a home equity loan or personal loan, not credit cards. Otherwise you will have another crisis on your hands.

FAMILY LIMITED PARTNERSHIPS

FAMILY LIMITED PARTNERSHIPS ARE FOR THOSE people who don't trust their kids but still want to give them money anyway.

The traditional method of avoiding taxes on the transfer of assets has been to take advantage of the $10,000 gift exclusion. This allows you to gradually divest yourself of wealth by giving up to $10,000 annually ($20,000 if the gifts come from both you and your spouse) in cash or other assets to each of your children, grandchildren, or other family members. The gifts are tax-free.

This type of gifting can be a problem when the assets represent shares of ownership in a business or commercial real estate. The issue becomes control of the assets that are transferred. For example, if you gradually give your kids a portion of your business, you're also giving them the right to make decisions concerning the business. Depending on your kids, this may not be such a good idea.

This problem can be avoided by transferring your assets into a family limited partnership. Under this arrangement you are able to transfer assets to your heirs while retaining control of the assets. You and your spouse assume the role of general partners and your children are considered limited partners. As general partners, you make all the decisions regarding the assets of the partnership, including those you've already transferred. Your children have no voice in how the assets are handled. This includes how the assets are to be invested or managed and how income generated by the assets will be distributed. You only have to give enough money to the limited partners to allow them to meet their tax liabilities.

Upon creation of the family limited partnership you, as general partner, give each of your heirs or limited partners a percentage of ownership which counts toward the $10,000 annual gift allowance. Each year you give the limited partners additional ownership shares, always valued within the $10,000 limit. Eventually you may give up 99 percent ownership of the business entirely, effectively removing it from your estate while still retaining complete control.

Another advantage of family limited partnerships is that your children or other limited partners are unable to transfer their interests without your permission. Also, unlike gifts of cash or securities, the transfer of a limited partnership interest could be valued at 20 to 30 percent below its real value for gift-tax purposes. This is because Uncle Sam considers the value of a limited partnership interest to be the price an outside investor would pay for the partnership. Because such a third-party investor would have no say in how things are run, he would never be willing to pay the true value of the partnership. Thanks to this convenient little calculation, business and property owners are able to give away more of their assets to their children and grandchildren and suffer a less painful gift-tax bite.

Family limited partnerships are considered good options for people with taxable estates. Over time, you may transfer the majority of your assets to your heirs. The law only requires that you retain I percent of general partnership interest.

Creating a family limited partnership is accompanied by some legal and appraisal expenses. Your biggest cost will be for an independent, written appraisal of the value of the partnership interests in order to substantiate their discounted value with the IRS. This figure will be examined very carefully, so you want to make sure it's carefully calculated.

_____

(See also gifts, gifting.)

FINANCIAL PLANNERS

Is your butcher offering stock tips while cutting your roast? I wouldn't be surprised. It seems like everyone, including accountants, lawyers, insurance agents, brokerage firms, investment banks, and even real estate brokers, thinks they're qualified to offer financial planning advice. With a record number of individual investors in the stock market and more companies requiring employees to take an active role in their own retirement planning, the average person today has more than just a passing interest in both making his money grow and preserving it. This has made financial planning a big business. Some professionals who are trying to cash in on this trend are actually competent at the task, but they're the exception. Most should stick to their main areas of expertise and leave financial planning to the trained financial planners. I urge my clients to use fee-only, or fee-plus-commission planners who have earned the designation CFP.

What Can a Financial Planner Do for You?

A good financial planner can make your life much more secure. She can help you define your financial goals and risk aversion and then devise a plan that fits both. Meeting college costs, funding your retirement, and reducing your tax burden are all a lot easier with the help of a professional.

A good financial planner will also be a listener. When you've finished talking, she'll ask a lot of questions. And she'll move slowly and carefully in helping you make investment decisions, making sure you understand them completely before taking the plunge. Above all, she will put your interests above her own.

But a bad financial planner, and there are a lot out there, will be more interested in padding her own bottom line than in helping you reach your goals. This is often a problem when dealing with stockbrokers, who may be under pressure to sell you certain financial products, and who encourage action of any kind since they make money both when you buy and when you sell. (Such unnecessary activity is called "churning.") If your planner is incompetent to boot, you can quickly find yourself in trouble.

Choose Carefully

The biggest problem facing consumers is that financial planners are basically unregulated. You don't need to be a member of the ICFP to call yourself a financial planner. Your butcher could hang out a shingle if he chose to.

The best way to find a good financial planner is through word of mouth. Talk to people you respect and find out who they use. Choose people whose economic situation is similar to your own. That way you'll know that the planner has experience in dealing with clients with similar needs and goals.

Look for people who are members of the Institute of Certified Financial Planners, which requires its members to meet the highest standards of ethical conduct and professional competence. Although other professional organizations will argue that their members are equally competent, I think the ICFP is still the best when it comes to finding unbiased advice. Another good source is *Worth's* annual survey of the nation's top financial advisers.

Ask the Right Questions

Once you've found a few candidates, you'll need to interview each one. If any of your candidates say they're too busy to meet with you or are vague in answering your questions, cross them off your list and find other candidates. If they try to sell you something during your first visit, you should end the conversation immediately and move on to someone else. By the way, your initial meeting should be free of all fees and obligations.

Here are some of the questions you'll need to ask:

- How long have you been a financial planner?

- What is your educational background?

- Are you registered with the Securities and Exchange Commission?

- What are your investment, insurance, retirement, and estate philosophies?

- What is your area of expertise?

- What professional affiliations do you maintain?

- How long have you been with your current firm?

- How long has the firm been in business?

- Do you work part-time or full-time?

- Are you a C.F.P.?

- How many clients do you have?

- Do you have clients whose financial situations are similar to mine?

- Do you personally research the investments you recommend?

- Do you develop customized plans or use an electronic profiling program?

- What kinds of ongoing professional training do you receive?

- What other services do you provide?*

- How are you compensated?

You'll also want to get the names of two or three references. Just remember you'll be given the names of people who the candidate knows will give you a good report. For that reason, make sure you ask questions that are quantitative ("What has the average return been on your portfolio since working with this person? How quickly does she respond to your telephone calls?") rather than just asking if they're happy with the service they've received.

Get What You Pay For

Financial planners aren't cheap. Here are the four most common ways in which they are compensated.

Fee only: The financial planner may charge a flat fee or be paid by the hour. Hourly fees can range from $75 to $300.

Commission only: The financial planner will receive compensation from the sale of financial products you purchase as part of implementing your financial plan.

Fee and commission: The financial planner will receive a fee for her advice and consultation services. It may be a flat fee or an hourly charge. If you choose to purchase investment products through her, she will also receive a commission on the sale.

Salary: Some financial planners work for banks and other financial institutions and are paid a salary by their employer. The fee you pay goes to the institution and not to the planner.

Planners who receive a flat fee regardless of the investment decisions you make, are, I believe, most likely to dispense objective and unbiased advice. Those whose compensations are tied entirely to commissions, on the other hand, will always have the pressure of selling you products hanging over their heads. That's a built-in conflict of interest that makes me very uncomfortable. That being said, I have worked with excellent planners who charge a fee but also take commissions in an effort to keep their fees manageable. Some have even offered to waive commissions when I balked, in exchange for charging a slightly higher hourly fee.

Follow Your Instincts

As with most professionals, you'll need to establish a level of comfort and trust with the financial planner you select. This is often as much a gut feeling as anything else. Remember that the

---

*Top-flight financial planners should be knowledgeable about insurance as well as investing since they'll be dealing with estate planning issues.

best financial planners are good listeners who won't act until they have a thorough understanding of your needs and goals. The best will work with you for several months before beginning to develop an investment strategy. If you get the feeling that the planner you've selected is moving too quickly, you may want to reconsider your choice.

Also remember that the financial planner works for you and must put your needs first. The financial planner–client relationship is fraught with potential conflicts of interest. If you get the feeling that the planner is more interested in what she's going to make out of the relationship than she is with your own fortunes, find someone else to work with.

———————————

(See also word of mouth.)

FINANCIAL RATIOS

ENTREPRENEURS LOVE EXCITEMENT. Financial ratios aren't the most exciting aspect of running a business. That's why most entrepreneurs wouldn't know a financial ratio if it turned around and bit them on the bottom line. But such ignorance is a big mistake. Financial ratios serve as gauges of the health of your business. If you want to be a successful businessperson rather than just an adrenaline junkie, you'll need to carefully monitor them, understand what they mean, and take corrective action if they're not what they should be.

A ratio is simply a relationship between two or more numbers. A financial ratio means there are dollar signs in front of the numbers, which should make them quite worthy of your attention.

The Quick Ratio

One of the most critical for any business is the quick ratio. This is really a measure of cash flow sufficiency, and answers a very simple question: Do I have enough cash on hand to meet my current liabilities?

To determine your quick ratio, you need to calculate all the assets you have on hand that can be quickly turned into cash and compare them with your liabilities. You won't include assets such as inventory, real estate, machinery, and supplies since converting them to cash would take time. If you find you have a quick ratio of 1:1, you know that if all your creditors requested payment tomorrow, you'd be able to meet their demands.

If your quick ratio is less than 1:1, it's not the end of the world. You know that, if pressed, you could request a little time to sell off some of your other assets to pay your bills. But if it remains less than 1:1 for some period of time, it's an indication that your business may be in a precarious situation.

Working Capital Ratio

The quick ratio is part of a larger financial picture that compares all your current assets to your current liabilities. In this case, inventory, real estate, and other assets are included. The difference between your assets and your liabilities is considered your working capital. If you have assets of $50,000 and liabilities of $25,000, you have $25,000 in working capital and your ratio is 2:1. This ratio is generally considered safe for most businesses. But you may want a larger ratio, as much as 4:1, if your business is seasonal or if you are currently carrying a large amount of debt. On the other hand, if your business is very predictable and your debts are low, a ratio of 1.5:1 may suffice.

Collection Period Ratio

Another important financial ratio is the collection period ratio, which tells you how long your cash is being tied up by customer credit. Obviously, the sooner your customers pay their bills, the better your cash flow. Calculating your collection period ratio is a bit more complicated. Let's say you have sales of $250,000 and your accounts receivable are $25,000. If you divide your sales by your receivables you get a result of 10.

Now you have to factor in time. Most financial analysts assume that, for simplicity's sake, there are 360 days in a year rather than 365. If you divide 360 by 10—your sales-to-receivables ratio—you get 36. This tells you your customers are taking an average of 36 days to pay their bills.

This number by itself is fairly meaningless. What makes it meaningful is comparing it to how many days your suppliers are giving you to pay your bills. Most suppliers require payment within 30 days. If you subtract your suppliers' payment window—30 days—from the one you extend your customers—36 days—the result is 6. A business is generally considered healthy when this number is below 15. Any more than that, and you can see the problem. You'll be writing checks faster than you'll be receiving them. That results in a poor cash flow. If your collection period ratio is too high, you'll need to correct it by either negotiating longer payment terms from your creditors or tightening up your own credit policies. If you don't, your business will slowly wither.

Stock-to-Sales Ratio

All businesses need to keep careful track of the movement of their inventory. This is accomplished with the stock-to-sales ratio. It's simple. Just compare your annual net sales to the value of your monthly inventory. If your annual sales are $100,000 and your monthly inventory is $10,000, your ratio is 10:1. This means your inventory turns over 10 times a year. Since inventory is money, the less time inventory spends on the shelf, the better. I always recommend to my retail clients that, other than big-ticket items, they turn over their inventory as close to 12 times a year as possible.

Profit Margin

Another number critical to your bottom line will be your profit margin, the ratio between your net income and your net sales. If you have $100,000 in net income on $200,000 of net sales, your profit margin is 1:2, or 50 percent. You pocket 50 cents for every dollar of sales. Different industries have different standards for healthy profit margins. Some are as high as 100 percent. Others are only 10 or 15 percent. Comparing yours to your industry's average will tell you whether you're doing well or not.

Return on Investment

Finally, there's the big ratio: your return on investment. The whole purpose of being in business is to earn as much money as possible. Calculating your return on investment will tell you whether you're wasting your time running your business and can earn more with your money doing something else, including investing in securities.

There are many formulas used to calculate return on investment, but for small businesses the easiest is to divide your net income by the equity you have in the business.* For example, if your net income is $20,000 and your equity is $500,000, your return on investment is only 4 percent. This is a no-brainer. These days, you can put that equity in an index fund designed to mimic the stock market and earn much more than that. Meanwhile, you could be lying around the pool and not worrying about inventory and customers and bills.

On the other hand, if you earned $100,000 on equity of $500,000, your return on investment would be 20 percent. In that case, your efforts are paying off handsomely. In fact, you might start getting calls to see if you need a partner.

What constitutes a satisfactory return on investment is really a personal decision. If you're a savvy investor and have historically earned 10 or 12 percent with your money, anything less than that will seem like a waste of time and effort. On the other hand, if you're a conservative investor with little stomach for risk, a business that chugs along and predictably returns 6 or 7 percent may suit you just fine.

(See also cash flow, working capital.)

FLEX TIME AND TELECOMMUTING

Business magazines are filled with stories about cutting-edge companies with new ideas about worker comfort and productivity. These innovators have done away with the regimented, cubicle-infested environment that has been so familiar for so long. Instead, they pro-

---

*If your business is a subchapter S corporation your balance sheet may show that the company has no capital, since it is paid out at the end of every year. In that case the best way to determine whether your business is worth the investment you've made in it is to compare the salary you're taking from the business to the salary you would be earning if you were employed by someone else.

> ## Employees versus Freelancers
>
> If you're an entrepreneur, you need to minimize expenses as much as possible. So ask yourself a question: If it doesn't matter *where* a person works, why do you need him on your payroll? I believe that if people are able to carry out their jobs for you from home or some other location, you should make them consultants, not employees. If you find the savings on real estate and furniture attractive, the additional savings from no longer having to pay for benefits will make you positively ecstatic.
>
> Am I saying you should have no employees? Perhaps. If it's possible, I would suggest exactly that. But I know it rarely is. What I'm really saying is that in today's business environment there are two kinds of people you need to run your business. The first are those who are absolutely critical to your operation and who you need to know will be there—in the flesh—when you need them. The second are those who perform important functions but whose physical proximity really doesn't matter. The first group you make employees. The second you hire as freelancers. Knowing the distinction between the two will make you more successful.

vide comfortable chairs and couches, computers that can be moved about on wheeled tables, and even pool tables and pinball games that make many of their offices look more like clubhouses than workplaces. The idea is to stimulate happiness and creativity and, in turn, profitability, by making work more like home. It all sounds great, especially for the vast majority of us who are still working in those sterile Dilbert-like cubicles or assembly-line operations. But rather than holding out for your employer to adapt such cutting-edge ideas, become proactive. Instead of waiting for your office to become more like home, start working from home rather than from the office.

Quite a few employers (far more than have adopted innovative office designs) have instituted formal flex-time policies or informally allow staff members to telecommute from home or on the road part or even all of the time. Some do both.

The Flex-Time Option

In the flex-time model, all that matters is that the work gets done each day. *When* it gets done is immaterial. This option is wonderful for employees with growing families. Flex-time allows them to organize work around their family schedules rather than vice versa. For a two-income couple with children or elderly parents, it provides the opportunity for at least one person to be home during the majority of the day. One partner may choose to leave for work very early in the morning and come home by midafternoon. The other partner can wait until late morning or noon to head into the office and then stay there through the evening. This arrangement not only increases family stability, it lowers child-care and elder-care expenses.

Flex-time also allows employees to enjoy more of their time away from work. If someone wants to leave in the middle of the afternoon to play golf or go boating, she just comes in early. Conversely, if she has appointments in the morning, she can arrive at work late and stay late. Of course, the family stability argument is far more acceptable. I wouldn't advise using your golf game or love of matinees as a reason to shift to a flex-time schedule.

The Telecommuting Option

Telecommuting goes a step further. It allows employees to come in to the office only rarely, or even not at all. This phenomenon is really a product of the electronic age. Computers, the Internet, e-mail, cellular telephones, fax machines, and the like have given us the ability to work from almost anywhere. Who needs to get all dressed up and spend 45 minutes in traffic every morning when you can sit at home in your bathrobe and get your work done?

The ability to telecommute has also created many long-distance work relationships. Many people who work in Web-related industries work for companies based on the other side of the country. The work they do can be delivered over the Web and they can communicate electronically with their supervisors and coworkers. Face-to-face meetings are rare.

Bucking Tradition

For employers, flex-time and telecommuting are a double-edged sword. Since the dawn of the industrial age, there's been a hidebound tradition in this country: Managers and supervisors have strict control over their employees. The idea of having employees out of sight while doing their jobs is difficult for many companies to swallow. And, granted, their concerns do have merit. Human nature being what it is, some employees no doubt take advantage of the situation and goof off or even spend some of their time doing work for other people.

But employers' eyes begin to sparkle when they look at what flex-time and telecommuting do to the expense line in their monthly financial reports. When employees work at home, less money is spent on office space, furniture, and other items. The difference to the bottom line can be significant. This has spawned one of the new concepts in modern office design: the shared workstation.

In companies where many employees telecommute at least part of the time, fewer individual workstations are needed at the office. When employees do come in for meetings or other business, they use whatever workstation happens to be available. Using this approach, one of the nation's major consulting firms reduced the office-to-employee ratio in its San Francisco office from 1:1 to 1:5 a few years ago. That's a lot of money saved.

FLOOD INSURANCE

YOU DON'T HAVE to live on the banks of the Mississippi to benefit from flood insurance. Floods cause more damage and deaths than any other natural disaster. And they don't just happen in areas with a lot of water.

Take Arizona, for example. With no coastline and one of the most arid climates in the nation, it would seem an unlikely place to find flooding. But from 1978 to 1999, more than 3,000 Arizonans filed insurance claims for more than $21.5 million in flood damage. At the other end of the spectrum was hurricane-prone Louisiana, with more than 150,000 claims and nearly $1.5 billion in losses.

The lesson? Flooding can occur most anywhere. But unless you live in an identified flood plain or some other area where the risk of flooding is high, you've probably given the subject little or no thought. You're not alone. Every year, thousands of homeowners and business owners learn their lessons the hard way when their properties suffer severe damage from unexpected flooding. Nationwide, it's estimated that only 1 in 4 households in special flood-hazard areas have flood insurance. In areas in which the risk is lower, the numbers drop to 1 in 10.

How to Buy Flood Insurance

There are a lot of misconceptions about flood insurance. Here are some of the basic facts:

1. Your homeowner's policy does not cover your property against flood damage.

2. Anyone can buy a flood insurance policy, regardless of where they live and regardless of their level of risk.

3. You can purchase flood insurance at any time, although there is usually a 30-day waiting period for it to go into effect.

4. Flood insurance is affordable. The average policy is around $320 a year for $100,000 of coverage. You can insure your home for up to $250,000. Contents coverage is often sold separately and is available to renters and owners.

5. Nonresidential buildings and their contents can be insured for up to $500,000 each (business owners take note).

6. You can't count on federal disaster assistance if your property is damaged by flooding. Less than 10 percent of floods are declared federal disasters by the president.

Flood insurance can be purchased from many private insurance companies. Some companies offer coverage through the National Flood Insurance Program (NFIP). This federal program, which is administered by the Federal Emergency Management Authority (FEMA), has nearly 19,000 participating communities, all of which qualify for membership by agreeing to adopt certain flood-plain management practices. If you own a home in one of those communities, you can purchase NFIP-sponsored insurance.

Flood insurance premiums are tied directly to risk. For example, properties located near the ocean, where they are vulnerable to storm surges and hurricanes, are considered the worst risks. These coastal areas are called V zones. Flood insurance for homes in V zones can be as high as $1,000 a year for $100,000 in coverage.

Many of these areas are designated special flood hazard areas (SFHAs). Lenders in these areas are required to make mortgage customers purchase flood insurance before they agree to finance their homes.

Homes that are near lakes and rivers are less risky and are considered to be in A zones. The same coverage in an A zone would be around $600. Other properties, those that run the least amount of risk, fall into B, C, X, and A-99 zones. An annual policy with $100,000 worth of coverage in these zones can be less than $300.

I recommend you buy your flood insurance from the same company you use for your home-owners and automobile insurance. That way, no matter what kind of a claim you have, you'll be working with just one company. You may also be able to save some money by having your agent create a "package" of coverages with a lower combined premium.

If you're still skeptical of your need for flood insurance, just consider the following. If your home suffered $50,000 in flood damage and you were uninsured, you'd have two choices. You could pay for the damage out of your own pocket and be out $50,000. Or you could take out a $50,000 loan and pay it back with interest. Either way, you've suffered a severe financial disaster, wiping out or seriously depleting savings you were planning to use to pay for your children's' education or to fund your retirement.

What could have prevented all this trauma? A check for a few hundred dollars. My advice? Call your insurance agent today. Or you can call the NFIP at 1-888-CALL-FLOOD, extension 445.

FOCUS GROUPS

IF OUR POLITICAL LEADERS can base our nation's policies on the findings from focus groups, then they're certainly good enough to use to get feedback on your business ideas.

To be effective, a focus group must represent your target demographic market. Let's say you're thinking of marketing a new line of "designer" kitchen gadgets that utilize the latest in contemporary product design. They're going to be relatively expensive and will be sold in upscale department stores, specialty cookware shops, and through high-end catalogs.

You can assume a number of things about your customers. They'll be largely female. They'll be cooking enthusiasts. They'll represent all ethnic groups and will have relatively high incomes. Most will be between 30 to 60 years of age. To be effective, your focus group should be a portrait of the characteristics I just described.

You should never ask friends or family members to participate in a focus group. You need to have as unbiased an audience as possible when seeking feedback on your product, and you're not going to get unbiased answers from people who know you. Either they're going to be overly critical out of concern for your well-being, or they're going to be overly positive because they're afraid of hurting your feelings. If the members of your focus group don't know you, they'll be much more likely to give you objective feedback about your products.

Conducting a Focus Group

If you want to insure accurate results, it's important to hire a firm with expertise in setting up focus groups. Focus group members may come together to analyze a product or use the product in their own homes. In the latter case, user feedback will be tallied via a mail-in questionnaire or a telephone survey.

If you plan to meet with your focus group in person but know that using the product at the meeting will be impractical, you should distribute it to the group beforehand so they can use it before they meet. If you're going to do a mail or telephone survey, make sure you send out the product well ahead of time. You should always let your focus group members keep the product samples to show your appreciation for their time.

There are several other ways to use less formal focus groups, perhaps on your own. If you have a product with fairly universal appeal, you might consider setting up a small table at a mall or some other location with a lot of pedestrian traffic. The idea is to get as much consumer response as possible. Put up a sign offering free samples of your product. Let people try out the product and talk to them to get some feedback. Have them respond to a short questionnaire—one that they can fill out on the spot in just a minute or two.

One bit of advice: Often you'll see people handing out questionnaires with postage-paid return envelopes so the questionnaires can be filled out later and mailed in. Don't waste your money. Once they're out of your sight, most people are going to forget all about you. Your questionnaire—and your expensive return envelope—are just going to end up in the trash.

Ask the Right Questions

You need to know beforehand exactly what you want your focus group to tell you. Here are some questions you might want to ask.

- How often do they buy this type of product?

- How much do they usually pay for this type of product?

- Where do they usually purchase this type of product?

- Do they buy whatever they happen to run across or do they stick to a particular product brand or source?

- Would they be comfortable purchasing this type of product via mail order or would they prefer to purchase it in person?

- Does your product meet their expectations for quality and performance?

- Is your product reasonably priced?

- How can your product be improved?

Use Your Information

Pay careful attention to the answers you receive. When people know they're being asked for an honest opinion, they usually won't hesitate to give you one. If they tell you your product or service is poor, find out why. If they think it's too expensive or could be improved, investigate the required adjustments. You also want to find out if they think it's a real bargain for the money. That means you might be able to charge more. Once you've fine-tuned the product or service, conduct a new round of focus groups to learn if the problems have been solved.

Remember that a focus group is designed to tell whether your business has a chance of succeeding. Take the results seriously. If you find that the product or service generates consistently negative comments, you must ignore your own feelings and opinions. Cut your losses and move on to your next idea. If you don't, you stand to lose a lot more money.

FRANCHISES

IN BUSINESS, familiarity breeds cash not contempt. And nothing breeds more familiarity than franchises. They provide customers with known products and services. Given a choice, most consumers or businesses will spend their money on that which is familiar to them.

Entrepreneurs looking for a competitive edge find that franchises offer them a greater chance of success than starting a business from scratch or buying an existing business. When you buy a franchise, you're buying a proven business system: products, services, trade name, marketing strategy, trademarks, advertising strategies, and business procedures. You're also buying the ongoing support and expertise of the franchisor, the company that sells you the franchise. Of course, in exchange you're giving up some of your autonomy. An entrepreneur who owns a franchise is more like a sergeant than a general. But he's often a very successful sergeant.

The numbers tell the story. While four out of five small businesses fail within five years, more than 95 percent of franchises survive to their fifth anniversary, and the vast majority are still operated by their original owners. Over the last 30 years, franchising has grown steadily regardless of the overall condition of the economy.

You Still Need to Be Careful

Franchises aren't foolproof, however. They can still fall victim to the downturns in local economies and shifting demographics that can doom any business to failure. You also must be wary of the motives and actions of the franchisor. It's not uncommon for franchisors to spend too much effort selling franchises and not enough effort developing the infrastructure needed to support the network of businesses they're creating. When that happens, the entire system can quickly collapse.

Questions You Need to Ask

Investing in a franchise requires the same careful research, market analysis, and business planning that you'd give any new business venture. While many of your questions will be answered by the federal disclosure documents the franchise company is legally required to give you, you'll need to get a lot of information yourself by investigation and interviewing other franchisees. Here are some of the critical questions to ask of the franchise company.

- *How long has the company been selling franchises?* The longer, the better. If you find you're one of the first to invest, proceed with extreme caution. It doesn't mean it won't be a good deal. It just means there's less of a track record for you to evaluate.

- *What kind of financial shape is the company in?* Ask for financial reports. Don't hesitate to hire an accountant to help you analyze them.

- *Do you like and trust the company's management?* Success in franchising depends on a harmonious relationship between franchisor and franchisee. If you don't feel you can work together constructively you should look elsewhere.

- *Is the company involved in any litigation?* If there are lawsuits, it's a sign that there are some people out there who aren't too happy with the company's business practices. It also means that the company won't be able to give its full attention to its franchisees.

- *How quickly has the company grown?* Beware of rapid growth. It may be a sign that there are too many franchises and not enough of a support system.

- *Are you confident that the company can come up with new products or services?* The company should place a high priority on market analysis and research and development.

Next, you need to evaluate the company's products and services.

- *Does the product or service have a recognizable trade name?* The recognition factor is the most valuable asset of a franchise company. If the company and its products or services aren't immediately recognizable to consumers, there's no reason to buy the franchise.

- *Is the product or service marketable in your area?* Many products and services have regional markets. Evaluate your market to make sure there will be sufficient demand to support the business.

- *Is the product or service marketable over the long haul?* Avoid trends and fads. You need to make sure there will be an ongoing demand for what you're selling.

Finally, you need to examine the franchise system. Your best source of information will be the company's other franchisees. Don't just talk to the people the company sends you to. You know you'll get good reports from them. Look up others on your own.

- *Are the current franchisees happy with the company?* If they're not, they'll be happy to tell you all about it.

- *Has the company lived up to its promises?* Are the franchisees getting the support and expertise they were told would be provided them?

- *Does the company provide training?* Don't even consider a franchise company unless it provides training. It should be ongoing, not just at the beginning of the relationship.

- *Do the franchisees belong to an association?* Franchisee associations give franchisee owners more clout in dealing with the parent company.

- *Do franchisees have to purchase their supplies and inventory from the parent company?* If they do, the company may not be giving them as good a deal as they could get on the open market. On the other hand, the company may be purchasing in bulk and passing on the savings to its franchisees.

- *How many franchisees have left the company?* Contact some of them and find out why they left. You may see a pattern that sends up a red flag.

Examine Your Own Abilities

Buying a franchise can be an excellent investment, but franchises require an incredible amount of work and flexibility. Forget the tidy 9 to 5, Monday to Friday corporate routine; you'll be working six or seven days a week and often 10 or more hours a day. When you're not working, you'll be worrying.

In addition, franchising won't offer all the chances for creativity and freedom that you'd get from starting your own independent business. Even though the word "franchise" means freedom, franchise owners are always constrained by the need of the collective to maintain that degree of familiarity that makes the business attractive to customers.

I tell my clients that they should look at buying a franchise as they would at buying an annuity: You're investing money up front in return for what amounts to a guaranteed income stream. If you can accept some degree of control and you're willing to work hard, I highly recommend franchising. But if you have a problem with authority and are looking for creative as well as financial independence, you won't last very long as a franchisee.

FRANCHISING YOUR BUSINESS

SELLING A FRANCHISE is as close to providing a guarantee as you can get in small business. The seller of a franchise—the franchisor—sells the buyer—the franchisee—a complete business system. It includes the business's name, trademark, slogan, business practices, inventory system, advertising and marketing concepts, and all other factors unique to the business.

The franchisee pays the franchisor an initial fee, called a franchise fee, and then monthly royalty payments. These can range anywhere from 5 to 10 percent of the franchise's gross revenues. Many franchisors also charge a smaller monthly fee to support advertising and marketing efforts.

Businesses that have enjoyed steady success in a local or regional market will often begin to sell franchises as a way of expanding even further. Franchising allows them to expand with minimal investment and provides a steady cash flow from fees and royalties paid by franchisees. Because the cost of setting up a franchise falls to the franchisee, the franchisor has little financial risk. The larger risk to the franchisor is that the franchise will fail. This will reduce the revenue stream and damage the reputation of the company.

What Makes a Business "Franchiseable"?

Perhaps you're a business owner and have considered expanding by selling franchises. You need to realize that just because you've been successful in one location doesn't mean you're ready to become a franchisor. To be successfully franchised, your business must have the following:

- A well-recognized name and image

- A trademark that can be registered

- A product or service that's in demand

- A distinctive method of doing business

- An established market niche

- A record of consistent growth and success

- Clear opportunities for future expansion

Of these, the most important elements are a well-recognized name, image, and trademark. Franchising is successful because people like to patronize businesses that are familiar. They know what products or services they'll receive, how much they'll have to spend, and how they'll be treated. If you're business doesn't have a high level of consumer recognition, it's not ready to be franchised.

If you choose to sell franchises, you have to engage in careful planning. You need to determine the long-range marketability of your product or service and select markets where you feel your franchises will perform best. You need to analyze how factors such as competition, demographics, societal trends, government regulations, technology, and the availability of suppliers will affect your business.

Once you've selected the markets you want to enter, you need to develop a marketing plan to attract potential franchisees. The projected income and costs of each franchise must be calculated and a lot of legal documents will need to be prepared.

The Relationship between Franchisor and Franchisee

As a franchisor, you'll be selling your franchisees more than just your business concept. You'll also be selling them an ongoing support system, including the following:

- Assistance in site selection

- Product research and development

- An operations manual

- Continuous training

- Advertising and marketing support

- General advice and counsel

It's not uncommon for differences to arise between franchisor and franchisee. The most common conflicts are over advertising support and royalty payments. Failure to provide your franchisees with the support they need can jeopardize the entire franchise organization.

Legal Documentation

Before you begin offering franchises, you'll need to prepare the following two legal documents. Their preparation requires the assistance of a lawyer experienced in franchise law.

The franchise-offering circular discloses information about you, your company, its management, its financial history, and its business practices. This information must be given to all potential franchisees when you first meet with them. To give them ample time to inspect the information, you may not accept any money from them for at least 10 business days after they receive it. Depending on the state in which you're selling the franchise, you must use either an FTC-approved circular or a uniform franchise-offering circular (UFOC).

The franchise agreement is the binding contract that describes the responsibilities of both parties in the franchise arrangement. It serves as the rule book governing the franchisor-franchisee relationship and should be thoroughly examined and understood by both parties before it is signed.

FUNERALS

SPENDING LOTS OF MONEY on a funeral is crazy. Why throw a huge party when the star of the show can't appreciate all the hoopla?

Way back in 1963 Jessica Mitford first exposed the shocking abuses and shady practices of the funeral industry in her best-selling book *The American Way of Death*. The resulting public outcry and congressional hearings piqued the interest of the Federal Trade Commission, which began investigating the practices of the funeral industry. After more than a decade of interviews, visits, reports, and comments, followed by presentations, hearings, court cases, and appeals, the FTC reached some conclusions.

Government Efforts at Reform

The government found that the purchase of a funeral is unlike any other transaction. There's an incredible imbalance of knowledge between the buyer, who has probably never arranged a funeral, and the funeral director, who's trying to sell as much as he can. The buyer is suffering from shock or feelings of guilt. There are tremendous time constraints, requiring the buyer to select a funeral home within 24 hours of death. The buyer is facing a major expense, perhaps after losing the family's primary earner. And finally, the buyer is often embarrassed to discuss price.

And price is a major issue. Consider all the elements of a traditional funeral. First, the body must be picked up from its place of death, prepared, and dressed. A cemetery plot, a casket, and perhaps a grave liner must be purchased. If the family chooses to have calling hours, they'll pay a rental fee for the funeral home. They'll also pay the mortician for the use of at least one limousine to carry mourners. They'll write a check to the clergyman or his church for his services and to the cemetery owners for preparation of the grave site. Then, once everyone has gone home and the grave has been filled in, they'll need to purchase a gravestone. Even the most modest of funerals can cost $4,000. It's not uncommon for people to spend $10,000 or more.

In an effort to mitigate these factors and keep consumers from being gouged, the FTC enacted its Regulation-Rule Funeral Industry Practices, commonly referred to as "the funeral rule," which require "the disclosure of itemized price information both over the telephone and in writing" and prohibit "misrepresentations about legal, crematory and cemetery requirements pertaining to disposition of human remains." Certain "unfair practices" were also prohibited: embalming without prior permission; requiring caskets for cremations; and conditioning the purchase of some goods and services on the purchase of other goods and services.

Industry Efforts and Consumer Hesitancy Counter Reforms

But despite these efforts, the purchase of funerals remains problematic. Funeral homes that have no nearby competitors, like other monopolistic small businesses, continue to charge whatever the traffic will bear. Funeral homes that share markets, often choose to implicitly divide up the pie by affiliating with specific ethnic or religious groups, becoming minimonopolies rather than competing on price.* Funeral homes have been able to avoid price competition because the average consumer has no desire to comparison-shop for funeral goods or services. Even individuals who know about the funeral rule and its provisions don't seem to take advantage of them. Instead, they continue to choose a funeral home based on proximity and the past experiences of family members and friends.

Once having chosen a funeral home, most people leave matters up to the funeral director. Of course, the funeral director is usually in an excellent position to make a judgment on just how much money is available. He graciously asks about the deceased and may even help prepare the obituary: "What did he do for a living? Did he belong to any clubs or organizations?" The funeral director may even help prepare insurance claims, thus getting an inside look at the finances available. And while most are far from villains, they have the ethics of any other small businesspeople—no more and no less.

And like any other businesspeople, funeral directors have an arsenal of sales techniques at their disposal. Guilt, an almost universal response to the death of someone close, is subtley fanned by comments about this being "the last thing you will be able to do for your loved one." The arrangement of caskets and the prices assigned to them follow rules that would be familiar to the most aggressive auto salesperson. Since most Americans opt for the middle item in any good-better-best purchase choice, funeral directors typically tailor their selection so as to create as high a middle range as possible. Lower-priced items, if displayed at all, are shown in the least popular colors. Despite the FTC regulation, false claims are still made about the abilities of some caskets and vaults to preserve remains and the minimum requirements for embalming and cremation.

---

*In New York City, for example, many Jews choose Riverside Memorial Chapel, while Protestants select the Frank E. Campbell Funeral Chapel. Neither is in any way sectarian—rabbis can officiate at Campbell's and ministers can preside at Riverside—but tradition and marketing have given them ethnic identities.

Demographics to the Rescue?

Despite the failure of the FTC funeral rule to completely clean up the industry, and the willingness of most Americans to completely avoid the topic, the business of dying is slowly changing, thanks to demographics. Older Americans, forced to confront death more often are being forced to make decisions about their funerals. Those who prearrange their funerals usually attempt to remove survivor guilt from the transaction and seize control of the process. In most cases, those who preplan specify much simpler, less expensive arrangements than a survivor would.

The population shift to the sun belt states—principally Florida, Arizona, and California—has also made for changes in the funeral process. Often, transplants are not as settled in their new homes—they may not belong to a church or feel like a part of the community—so they may feel less of a need for a formalized public good-bye. Many are opting for immediate cremation.

The funeral industry, however, has also shown an extraordinary ability to adapt to these social changes, jumping on the bandwagon and developing new sales and marketing strategies to capitalize on them.

The trend toward prearrangement has spawned an entirely new branch of the funeral industry: "preneed" sales. Not unlike the early life insurance industry in its techniques, preneed companies are using door-to-door salespeople and telemarketers to target demographically promising areas. Some consumer activists complain that the purchase of a preneed plan is an even more dangerous transaction than the purchase of a regular funeral, since it combines the emotions of the latter with financial legerdemain. The worst offenders offer plans with no provisions for moving from one location to another, no guarantee on prices, and no assurances on the integrity of the trust fund where the money is placed for safekeeping.

Cremation, by its very nature, is a simple process. That's why it costs substantially less than burial. The funeral industry, however, has been busy complicating cremation in an attempt to bring up its costs and their profits. Deluxe cremation containers, rivaling caskets in their cost and ornamentation, are pushed as replacements for the standard low-cost containers by funeral directors looking to make more money. Hand-painted, designer-crafted urns—some with gold trimming—costing more than $2,000, are also being offered to those who opt for cremation. Memorial plaques, urn niches, and 1-foot-square graves are also available, since, as funeral industry promotional literature puts it, "those whose loved ones are cremated are left with no place to memorialize them."

It's Up to the Individual

The failure of regulation to create competition and clean up abuses, the refusal of the average consumer to comparison-shop for funeral goods and services, and the ever-adaptable funeral industry's ability to come up with a new arsenal of sales techniques doesn't bode well for industrywide reform.

I'm afraid the only solution is for individuals to take charge of their own deaths. I believe that when it comes to funerals, we should all adopt the do-it-yourself approach. No, I'm not suggesting you bury Granddad in the back yard next to the perennial bed. But just as you plan for all the other major events of your life, I think you should make your funeral plans in advance.

Make sure everyone knows your wishes. Personally, I believe they should include a gathering of family and friends and then a quick burial or cremation. Later on, when the dust has settled, a memorial service can be held to allow all your friends and associates the chance to come together and celebrate your life. By having plans in place beforehand, you save your family members from the ordeal of organizing your funeral and throwing a lot of money away needlessly.

The most affordable and, to my mind, sensible funerals are "direct cremation" and "immediate burial." In a direct cremation the body is brought from its place of death to the place of cremation and then, within a short period of time, privately cremated. Caskets aren't necessary. Immediate burials once again involve the quick transport of the body from place of death to cemetery with only the briefest of stops at a funeral home to prepare it for burial. The reason these arrangements are less expensive is that the body is not placed on public viewing. Almost all the exorbitant costs associated with funerals—embalming, caskets, room rental, limousine, flowers—center on the care and appearance of the body and its display.

You should also take care of the financial end of things so your family doesn't need to worry about writing a slew of checks. Make funeral arrangements with the mortician beforehand and pay him either in a lump sum or in installments. You can select and pay for your own casket and headstone if you want to go the traditional route. If you plan on being cremated, you can also take care of that arrangement. If you don't have the cash to pay up front, you might consider taking out a modest whole life insurance policy and earmark the proceeds to be used to pay for your funeral expenses.

Let's face it, when it comes to funerals, we're literally throwing our money into a hole in the ground. By making all the arrangements beforehand, you're taking care of your loved ones rather than forcing them to take care of you. Freed of the tasks of organizing everything, they can do what they really need to do—spend their time mourning and focusing on their feelings. And you'll go to your reward secure in the knowledge that you've spared them from a wasteful expense.

FURNITURE

IF YOU'RE ABOUT TO START a business, *do not*, I repeat, *do not*, go to an office furniture store. Time and time again I see my fledgling entrepreneur clients, after spending months or years meticulously crafting bare-bones business plans and scraping together seed money, run out and spend thousands of dollars on office furniture.

The psychology behind this misguided behavior is obvious. If they look successful, they think to themselves, they can't help but be successful. The problem is, this behavior also violates one of the most important rules of any business: Don't spend any more money than necessary. Money not spent is money added to your bottom line at the end of the year.

If you have a business in which you won't be dealing with customers and clients in your office, you don't need brand-new, expensive office furniture. We live in a throwaway society. The world is full of secondhand chairs, filing cabinets, and other used office furnishings that are perfectly serviceable.

If you do need a place to meet with customers and clients, I suggest finding a nice nearby restaurant or hotel lobby to serve as your office away from the office. If that's not possible, create an area in your office solely for the purpose of meeting clients. It should consist of several comfortable chairs, and possibly a sofa and coffee table. Functionality is the key word. Pick furnishings that are comfortable but that won't break the bank.

Creating a separate conference room accomplishes a couple of things. It allows you to minimize your furnishings expense because it can be used by everyone who works in the office, eliminating the need to spend a lot of money on individual offices. And it creates an atmosphere that I think most visitors find more comfortable and inviting. A conference room lends an air of neutrality to meetings, whereas a client or customer may feel intimidated in your individual office, especially if you're sitting behind a massive wooden desk and they're seated in front.

Don't get me wrong. I'm not suggesting that you and your employees must sit on crates. Just be careful how you spend your money. You can find bargains from firms that are going out of business and liquidating their inventory and equipment. And don't forget to pay attention to corporations, universities, and other large organizations. They commonly get rid of perfectly acceptable office furniture that you can buy for very little. Often it will be offered at auction or by bid.

When you are considering furniture for your offices, pay particular attention to chairs and lighting for employees who spend all day at their computers. Ergonomics research has found the modern computer workstation to be the cause of a number of chronic musculoskeletal disorders. Adjustable chairs and lighting systems will allow employees to individualize their work areas for maximum comfort. And that translates into maximum productivity. A good chair and a good lamp can make an old door on a couple of saw horses quite acceptable.

(See also auctions, equipment, inventory.)

FUTURES

EVERY AUTUMN I hear the same ad on radio. "*Invest in heating oil futures!*" the announcer fairly screams. He then goes on to excitedly explain that with winter just around the corner, the demand for heating oil will soon push prices through the roof. The opportunity for returns of 50 percent or even 100 percent are ours for the taking. All we have to do is give him our money. It's only at the end of the spot in the barely audible high-speed tones of a sleazily carnival barker that the pitch man says, "Any investment carries with it the risk of losing money," and then whispers, "This offer is accompanied by no guarantees." Of course, by that point the suckers have already called the toll-free telephone number and are mortgaging their homes to take advantage of those 100 percent returns.

Pigs Get Slaughtered

One of my favorite Wall Street sayings is: "Bears make money. Bulls make money. Pigs get slaughtered." The futures market is the biggest slaughterhouse of them all.

The annual commercial I just described takes advantage of one the most unfortunate and enduring of human traits: greed. By dangling the lure of huge quick profits before our eyes, the weasels behind these ads lure in an amazing number of people who can't resist the promise of easy money. And while some of them are naive in addition to being greedy, others are experienced enough to know better.

Granted, some of these folks do make money. It just so happens that as I write this there has been a heating oil shortage and prices have indeed risen dramatically. But most of the people who get into futures will see their hard-earned dollars evaporate before their eyes. Do not kid yourself. Futures are a high-risk game that should be played by only the most knowledgeable and skilled investors. This does not include you or me.

How Futures Work

A futures contract is an agreement to buy or sell something at a certain price at a certain date in the future. The biggest futures markets in the United States deal in commodities: sugar, fuel oil, soybeans, corn, cotton, wheat, pork bellies, and the like. There are futures on foreign currency. There are futures on gold and silver and platinum. There are even futures on U.S. Treasury notes.

Futures do have a logical function for manufacturers of products and commodities producers. A wheat farmer, for example, can protect himself against falling prices by purchasing future contracts to sell his wheat at a certain price. On the other side of the deal might be a huge producer of bread and other wheat-based products. They buy contracts to purchase wheat at a certain price. Knowing what they'll pay for their raw materials makes it easier for them to create a business plan and set prices.

But investors who buy futures are gambling that the price of the underlying commodity will move in the proper direction and allow them to execute their contracts for a huge profit. And the profits can be huge. This is because when you invest in futures you have a great deal of leverage. For a relatively small investment, you control a commodity worth many times the investment. When you win, you win big. When you lose . . . well, believe me, you don't even want to think about that.

Options on Futures

Options on futures are for investors who just want to stick a toe in the futures pond and check the temperature. When you enter into a futures contract, you're obligated to execute the contract if it reaches its execution date. An option on futures, however, gives you the choice of entering into a futures contract.

There are two kinds of options. A call option is an option to buy a futures contract and is a bet that prices will rise. A put option gives you the choice of selling a futures contract and is a bet that prices will fall. If market conditions look advantageous, you exercise the option and enter into the underlying futures contract. If conditions don't look good, you let the option expire. At that point, all you've lost is the premium you paid for it.

Don't Even Think about It

I hope this chapter has convinced you to stay away from futures. If you find yourself tempted, say, by the idea of options on futures, just remember that three out of four speculators in futures lose money. And most of them are professionals who—in theory, anyway—know what they're doing. The poor saps who respond to ads promising instant wealth do even worse.

Also consider this: Brokers will actually evaluate your financial situation before they'll agree to execute commodities and commodities futures contracts for you. They're trying to protect you against yourself because they know how risky it is and don't want to leave themselves open to a lawsuit when you lose your shirt. If that doesn't convince you to head the other way, I don't know what will.

———————————

(See also commodities, gambling, options.)

GAMBLING

THE IDEA OF WALKING into a casino with $500 and leaving an hour later with nothing makes me weak in the knees. I think it's insane. I'd rather spend the money or give it away than gamble it. Sure, it's possible I could also walk out an hour later with $1,000. That, after all, is why people gamble, even though they know that they're likely to lose.

Games of Chance

Casinos offer gamblers any number of games of chance. The favorite seems to be the slot machine. Others include roulette, craps, keno, and blackjack. People do sometimes win money at all these games. Slot machines in Las Vegas, for example, return around 95 percent of the money that's put into them.

Just remember that the casino always has the edge. If it's 5 percent, as in the Las Vegas slots, it means the casino will keep $5 out of every $100 that's bet. The casino's edge varies from game to game and on the kind of bet that's made. There are bets in craps, for example, that will return almost 17 percent to the casino. Others will return only 1 percent. The best deal for casinos, and the worst for gamblers, is keno. The casino keeps anywhere from 25 to 50 percent.

The one game in which you can gain an edge over the casino is blackjack, but it requires you to keep track of all the cards that have been played and to know when to increase your bets.*

---

*This practice is called "card counting" and is frowned on by casinos. In fact, if a casino suspects someone of being a professional card counter, it will throw the individual out and place him on a blacklist that is circulated to other casinos.

Most people don't have the discipline, concentration, or practice time to accomplish this. But by following simple rules of strategy, you can conceivably reduce the casino's edge to about 1 percent.

Sports Gambling

Do you know if the Broncos are going to beat the Steelers by more than 10 points? I sure don't. But if we want to, we can make bets that they will.

In theory, sports gambling is less risky than games of chance. You think all you'd need to do is pick the winner or loser of a game. The reality is a bit more complicated than that. You also have to beat the "spread"—the predicted difference between the favored team's score and the losing team's score.

For example, if you bet that the Broncos are going to beat the Steelers, and the spread is 10 points, the Broncos will have to win by 11 points or more for you to win. If you bet on the Steelers, and the Broncos lose or win by less than 10 points, you also win. If the game ends with a 10-point difference, say, 24–14, it's a tie and you neither win nor lose.

Some sporting events, such as baseball, boxing, and horse racing, use odds rather than point spreads. If you bet $2 to win on a horse that had 3-to-1 odds, for example, you would win $6 if the horse actually won. If you bet $200, you'd win $600.

I suppose sports gambling can be entertaining for obsessive fans, but you'll still probably lose in the long run. If you do play, make your own bets. Don't rely on the so-called experts who will sell you a tout sheet with recommended picks. If you do, you're just throwing more money away.

Lotteries

Lotteries, which are operated by many states, are the biggest swindle of them all. They're also an enormous business. Promising multimillion-dollar payoffs on a $1 bet, they rake in billions. Granted, much of the profit goes to support education and programs for senior citizens. (At least that's where the money is *supposed* to go.) If that's your rationale for playing, let me suggest you give half the money you lose playing the lottery every year to charity and put the other half in mutual funds. Everyone will be a lot better off.

On average, lotteries pay out 54 cents on every dollar played in prize money and keep the rest. The profits are enormous. Of course, so are the jackpots—for the handful of bettors who win. In New York, for example, jackpots of $10 to $20 million are common. The biggest game of all, the multistate Powerball lottery, has offered jackpots in excess of $100 million. These huge payoffs are why people play. Few wouldn't risk $1 on the chance they could spend the rest of their lives on Easy Street.

The chances of that happening are pretty slim, however. Statistically, lottery players are more likely to be struck by lightning than they are to hit the jackpot. In New York, for example, where you have to pick six winning numbers between 1 and 51, the odds of hitting the jackpot are 18,009,460 to 1.

If you insist on buying lottery tickets, let me give you one piece of advice. Let the computer pick your numbers for you. This is because the computer's selection, just like the winning numbers, will be completely random. The numbers selected by many players aren't. They often choose birthdays, anniversaries, and other important dates and thus limit their selections to the numbers one through 31. Because they ignore numbers higher than 31, they don't get a true random sampling.

GARB AND HYGIENE

Appearance counts. Perhaps in an idyllic world what you looked (and smelled) like wouldn't matter as long as you did your job. Well, we're not living and working in a utopia. We're all interacting in a small world in which we have little time to make judgments, forcing us to rely on our senses, not just our intellect. Because of that, people who are physically attractive have a definite advantage in the business world. The rest of us, who are average-looking, can mitigate that advantage by being as well-dressed and groomed as possible. I may not look like Richard Gere, but I can do everything possible to ensure that my appearance and persona won't be disconcerting to anyone else.

Dress for Success

Let's start with the art of dressing for business—and I do mean art. When you get dressed for work, you're creating an image that will dictate the way people respond to you. If you do it right, you'll be perceived as sophisticated, knowledgeable, trustworthy, and understanding. If you do it wrong, you'll give the exact opposite impression.

Proper business attire should be quiet and conservative and, above all, appropriate. That makes it easier for your clients and customers to focus on you. Anything that distracts them from what you're saying and doing makes it that much harder for you to do your job. When you leave, the only thing they should remember is what you told them or did for them. Your appearance should be exactly what they expect. If your boss is reeling around the office doubled over in laughter at your suit there's little chance he'll remember much of what you had to say.

Office attire for men should almost always include a jacket and tie and shined leather shoes. Dress-down day should mean a less formal shirt, pants, and blazer and perhaps an open neck. It shouldn't mean jeans and a T-shirt. When you meet with clients, customers, or superiors, make sure your jacket is on and your tie is snugly knotted. To do otherwise is to show them disrespect. If you're fond of working with your sleeves rolled up and your tie loosened, make sure your jacket is carefully hung in a closet. When you're notified that a client or customer has arrived, spend a minute or two in front of the mirror straightening up before you open the door of your office or go out to greet them. Similarly, if you're heading to the executive suite, make sure you look like you belong there. If your superior visits you in your office, it's okay to remain as you are.

For women, standard business attire should include suits or a blouse and blazer with slacks or a skirt. Skirt lengths should be modest, as should the neckline of blouses. Shoes should be equally conservative, with heels of moderate height. Keep accessories and jewelry simple and tasteful.

Business clothing is expensive for both men and women. It often makes sense to stick with classic styles that will see you through the endless changes the fashion industry tries to impose upon us. It will save you a lot of money. On the other hand, if you're in a field where creativity and artistry counts, stylish garb is important. That could run into quite a bit of money, but consider it a cost of doing business.

Speaking of costs, whether you're dressing for style or tradition, don't scrimp on your clothing. Quality clothing is expensive, but it will last much longer and retain its appearance much better than cheaper garments. Also, take care of your clothing. Keep garments clean and pressed and have your shoes shined regularly.

Invisible Hygiene

Just as with your attire, your hygiene should be invisible. I don't think I need to tell anyone of the importance of bathing every morning. But many people do need to be reminded to rein in their cologne and perfume. First of all, strong scents can be very distracting. (I once had a colleague whose visits to my office almost made the air shimmer. I finally had to—very diplomatically—speak to him about it.) Secondly, many people have sensitivities to fragrances. If you're drenched in cologne, some people may find meeting with you physically uncomfortable.

What do you do when a coworker's garb or hygiene is a problem? The secret to dealing with these uncomfortable situations is to lead by example. Assume your coworker is unaware of the problem. Drop some subtle hints, such as suggestions about where you go for sales on business clothes. Offer a breath mint after lunch and comment that you use one every day. If hints aren't sufficient, you'll need to be more direct. Just stress that it's in the person's own interest.

The same modesty should extend to the deodorant and mouthwash you use. Keep hairstyles and makeup conservative and keep your nails clean and trimmed. And make it a habit to brush your teeth and spend a bit of time touching up your hair and makeup after lunch. If you have a heavy beard consider bringing a portable electric shaver with you to the office for an afternoon touch-up. This is all part of the package that will influence how you're perceived by your superiors, customers, and clients.

Remember, when meeting with superiors, clients, and customers, you are as much a part of your business as your product or service. If your appearance sends the wrong message, you'll be operating with one strike against you before you even open your mouth. If it sends the right message, you'll have already achieved a step toward your goal.

(See also clothing, jewelry.)

GIFTS

Today, having a job is gift enough; there's no need to give your employees little holiday presents. If you want to do something special, give people a year-end bonus.

When I first started in business, it was accepted practice for employers to give their employees baskets of fruit, bottles of Scotch, pens, scarves, ties, even frozen turkeys during the holidays. Even the smallest firms would spend astonishing amounts of money on such items. It was thought to reflect the sense of family that was common in the work environment in those days.

Today, every employee should be working with one eye on the horizon watching for that better job to appear. Employers are less concerned with their employees' long-term welfare and more concerned with their short-term performance. It's a purely mercenary relationship that lasts as long as both parties feel they're getting what they want. As soon as one feels he no longer needs the other, the relationship ends.

This has led to changes in the workplace culture. It's become a nomadic environment, with managers and staff people often coming and going like baseball managers. As a result, relationships are shorter and more impersonal. Concerns about sexual harassment and discrimination have also served to keep relationships more formal. Many small companies these days will instead throw a holiday luncheon or dinner for their employees. This takes care of the issue with minimal fuss on management's part.

I think the best way to handle the gift issue these days is to give people the one thing everyone is really interested in—money. But rather than make it a fait accompli, treat it as a bonus that's tied to each individual's effort and the overall financial health of the business. If a person performs well and business is good, it's reflected in their holiday bonus. If the opposite is true, the cash reward might pay for little more than a stocking and a lump of coal.

While the majority of employers have stopped giving gifts to employees, most vendors still routinely send gifts to their customers in appreciation for past business and the hope of future consideration. That makes a bit more sense since it can be seen as a marketing device.

Rather than giving gifts to clients or customers you might consider taking the money you would have spent on gifts and making a contribution to charity instead. For example, my office makes a donation to a shelter for homeless children each year. We tell our clients about the gift in our end-of-year letter and thank them for their part in enabling us to continue to make such a donation. It's a tradition we all feel is more in keeping with the season. It also makes us feel better about ourselves.

The Gift That Keeps on Giving

If it is standard practice in your business or industry to give gifts to clients or customers, I'd suggest giving a recurring gift rather than a one-shot deal. "Clubs" like those that offer fruit, nuts, cheese, or coffee every month may seem corny, but they ensure that your generosity will be remembered for an entire year, not just for a week.

GIFTING

For years I've advised my clients to plan to die broke by distributing their wealth to their heirs while they're still alive. Not only does this reduce estate taxes when they do pass on, it helps their children and grandchildren with educational costs, house purchases, and building their own nest eggs. The ability to do this provides my clients with great joy and satisfaction.

This doesn't mean just writing checks indiscriminately, however. There are laws regulating gift giving and strategies you can follow to make the most of those laws. Here are some of them.

Giving Tax-free Gifts

As you probably know, one person can give any other person up to $10,000 a year in cash tax-free. Neither you nor the recipient will owe taxes on the gift and the gift does not have to be reported to the IRS.

Cash gifts of more than $10,000 are taxable and must be reported to the IRS on Form 709, which is filed with your income tax. The excess gift over $10,000 reduces your lifetime estate tax exemption, which is currently $675,000.*

Because each $10,000 gift is considered a discrete transaction between two individuals, it's a simple matter to avoid gift taxes. Let's say you and your spouse want to give your son and his family $40,000 a year in cash. You begin by each making a $10,000 gift to your son. There's $20,000. Then you each make $10,000 gifts to your daughter-in-law to get the amount up to $40,000. If you wanted to give their family unit more money, you could each give $10,000 gifts to their individual children. In theory, by moving each $10,000 increment through its own unique channel, you could give them as much money as you have channels.

There are a couple of situations in which gifts of more than $10,000 are not taxable or reportable. One is when money is given directly to a school in payment for any tuition. (It can't be applied to room and board.) The other is when medical, dental, or hospital bills are paid directly to the provider. The gifts are technically known as "qualified transfers." The great thing is you can still give the person whose bill you paid a $10,000 tax-free gift if you choose to.

You can also, obviously, make noncash gifts, though these too are supposed to be included in calculating the $10,000 limit. Let's say you want to buy your son a new car that costs more than $10,000. The IRS relies on either you or your son notifying it that the purchase took place and that it was a gift of over $10,000.

---

*This, of course, may change. Congress is working toward eliminating estate taxes. And while the current administration has threatened a veto, there's no telling how or when the issue will be resolved.

Giving Gifts to Minors

If you wanted to give $10,000 a year to each of your grandchildren, there's no reason you couldn't just write them each a check. But let's face it, letting a minor handle a chunk of money that size might not be the best idea. The money you intend for college might end up funding the world's biggest collection of video games or Pokémon cards.

You could put the money in an investment account with the child named as beneficiary. The problem is, the child wouldn't get the money until you pass away, and I'm assuming you expect to still be around when the child reaches college age. You would also be responsible for taxes on the interest the account earns. Another option would be to put both your names on the account. But then you'd need the child's signature to gain access to the funds. The account would also be considered part of your estate when you pass away.

To give kids money and still retain some control over its destiny, I suggest you take advantage of either the Uniform Gifts to Minors Act (UGMA) or the Uniform Transfers to Minors Act (UTMA). These allow you to name a custodian for the money who will manage it until the child reaches maturity. At that point, the money becomes the property of the child, who at this point (we hope, anyway) has reached a level of maturity to handle it with some responsibility. If not, expect postcards from his trip around the world.

Another downside to UGMAs and UTMAs is that, because the money is in the minor's name, colleges will expect most of it to be used to pay tuition, reducing the amount of any financial aid they will offer.

For more substantive gifts there are various trusts that can be utilized, such as 2503(b) and 2503(c) trusts. Speak with a qualified estate lawyer to find out how these trusts might be able to help you accomplish your gifting goals.

GRATUITIES

TIPPING IS ABSURD. Why is it some employers are allowed to get by with paying substandard wages, relying on their customers to adequately compensate their staff? And why is it good service isn't considered standard, but is instead something so exceptional it needs to be rewarded? Of course, I'm just tilting at windmills. Tipping may be absurd, but it's an accepted part of the consumer landscape. Still, there are problems.

There are no real rules on how much is appropriate. And what are the standards of performance? Do you automatically give every waitperson the same percentage of the bill, or should you penalize them if you feel they've been less attentive than they should have been. In an effort to mitigate, if not eliminate, the problems, here are a few general guidelines for tipping in different situations.

Restaurants

If the service has been good, a tip of between 15 and 20 percent is considered the going rate. If it has been bad, 10 percent or less will let the waitperson know your displeasure. Leaving absolutely nothing should be reserved for staff who are openly hostile. It should also be followed by a few words with the manager or maitre d'. If you've been waited on by several people—captain, wine steward, busboy, etc.—leave a tip of 20 to 25 percent and let them divide it up however they wish.

If you're drinking at the bar, a 15 percent tip is appropriate. If you're asked to wait in the bar while you wait for your table, however, you aren't obligated to order a drink. If you do, ask the bartender to put it on your dinner bill.

If you check your coat, $1 is a sufficient tip for the attendant hanging and retrieving one or two coats. That's also appropriate for a valet parker. Fifty cents is sufficient for a bathroom attendant who simply hands you a towel.

If you know that the maitre d' is also the owner of the restaurant, a tip is inappropriate. If you aren't sure and you're not likely to be returning any time soon, there's no need to tip him. But if you know the maitre d' isn't the owner and you could be back, a small token of your appreciation—say $5—will probably get you a good table. If you do end up visiting frequently, the occasional $20 bill will go a long way to ensuring you're treated as an old and valued friend.

Hotels

Sometimes it seems that hotels are lined with people with their palms out. It starts at the front door, where the bellhop takes your bags. When you reach your room a tip of $1 per bag is usually appropriate. The standard for exclusive hotels is a bit more. I'd tip $1.50 per bag.

Room service personnel should be given a 15 percent tip. Maids should get $1 or $2 a night, but only if you stay for more than one night. And don't forget the concierge if you plan on using the service. A $20 tip when you first arrive will guarantee attentive service.

Apartments

Tips for apartment building personnel are usually made at holiday time. The amount of the tip will depend on the size and quality of the building. Superintendents generally receive between $100 and $200. If they do special jobs during the year, $10 to $20 per job is usually appropriate. Doormen receive between $50 and $100. They may also occasionally perform additional favors that merit a $5 tip such as helping with packages. If your building staff turns over often, you my want to tip quarterly rather than just once a year.

Other Services

Here are some tipping suggestions for other service providers:

- *Skycaps:* $1 per bag, more if the bags are exceptionally large or heavy. Never tip flight personnel.

- *Take-out food delivery persons:* 10 to 15 percent of the bill.

- *Taxi drivers:* 10 to 15 percent of the charge. If they're unfriendly or uncooperative, drive dangerously, or refuse to help you with your bags, stiff them.

- *Garage attendants:* $1 is usually sufficient unless you live in a major city; in that case, $2 is more appropriate.

- *Newspaper delivery people:* A $10 to $20 tip at holiday time is appropriate.

- *Beauty parlors and barbershops:* It depends on how exclusive the shop is. Haircutters usually get 10 to 20 percent. If they own the shop, you need not tip them. Consider a Christmas gift, though. A manicurist or pedicurist will get 15 to 20 percent. Colorists get 10 percent and hairwashers get $2 or $3.

- *Cruise personnel:* On a cruise your total gratuity should be 15 percent of the fare. Of that total, 4 percent should go to the cabin steward, 4 percent to the dining steward, and 7 percent can be split among all the other service personnel.

Remember that a gratuity is just that—an expression of gratitude. It should only be given for competent and friendly service. You should never feel intimidated into giving a tip. Nor should you feel badly about not leaving a tip if the service was horrible. That's the only way the service provider will learn that tips aren't automatic.

GROCERY SHOPPING

GROCERY STORES ARE the most manipulative retailers in the country. From the moment you walk through the doors, everything is designed to get you to spend as much money as possible. The store's layout and the positioning of its merchandise are strategically—almost scientifically—planned to steer you to items they want you to buy.

Once you're aware of the manipulation you can actually stand back and admire how clever grocers can be. It can be fun to go into a supermarket and try to analyze the way shopper traffic has been routed and different products have been placed where it's impossible to miss them.

The consumer in me, however, hates being manipulated this way. I don't like to spend any more for groceries than I have to. Here are some tricks to help you keep the grocery bill to an acceptable level and still eat nutritiously and enjoy the foods you like.

Shop for Nutrition

Let's look at nutrition first. You don't want to sacrifice your health in the interest of saving money, so you want to buy the most nutritious foods you can find.

Steer clear of "health" foods. You'll pay more for something that's likely to be no more nutritious than ordinary food. "Natural" foods are also of questionable value. And although "organic" foods—those grown without chemical fertilizers or pesticides—may be better for us, they're also quite expensive. And, frankly, I'm cynical enough to question whether everything labeled "organic" is as pure as the stores would have you believe. I think you get equally healthy foods buying the regular foods; after all it's not like they're inorganic.

For nutrition information you can read the "nutrition facts" label that's now required by law to be on almost every food item sold in the United States. The label will tell you the per-serving quantity of total fat and saturated fat, cholesterol, sodium, total carbohydrates, and protein. It also tells what percentage of the recommended daily intake of vitamin A, vitamin C, calcium, and iron are in each serving. Armed with this knowledge you can make you own decisions about what's healthy and what's not.

Beyond that, I believe if you follow the recommended dietary guidelines—eat lots of fruits, vegetables, and grains and go easy on red meat—you'll be fine. There's too much nutrition information available these days to be ignorant on the subject.

Shop for Savings

Now let's see how you can keep the grocery bill down. Here are some ways to cut costs:

- Buy fruits and vegetables in season. When supplies are plentiful, prices are lower. Plus the produce is fresher and tastes better.

- Be wary of juices and drinks in bottles and cans. Buy frozen juices. The bottled and canned juices are often made from the same concentrate that's in the frozen cans.

- Make your own iced tea and skip the powdered mix.

- Buy in bulk. Generally, the larger the package, the better the deal. It's no coincidence that no-frills wholesale shopping clubs have become so popular. If you have one near your home, by all means join.

- Avoid impulse purchases. Make a list and stick to it.

- Don't bring children with you unless you have no choice. If you must, look for a candy-free checkout aisle.

- Buy generic products. Those anonymous products in plain white wrappers can cost up to 30 percent less than their name-brand counterparts.

- Buy store-brand products. All major grocery store chains market a wide variety of products under their own label. Although they're not as cheap as generic products, they're still cheaper than the name brands. In almost every case they are, in fact, one of the name brands under a different label.

- Buy bread by weight, not by the size of the loaf. Many breads are puffed up with air to make you think you're getting a lot for your money.

- Don't buy bottled water. If you're concerned about contaminants in your tap water, buy a water filter. It will pay for itself in no time at all.

- Buy what's on sale. If you can tailor your shopping list to the week's specials, you'll save a bundle.

- Use coupons. It's a no-brainer, but it's also time-consuming and requires some organizational skills.

When and How to Shop

This one's easy. If you can find the time to shop midweek you'll have far fewer people to deal with. Thursdays through Sundays are the busiest times in most grocery stores, but on Mondays and Tuesdays they're like ghost towns. If you can organize your life to do your shopping on those days you'll save a lot of time.

Finally, here's the ultimate challenge. Organize your shopping list to match the layout of the grocery store. In other words, if you hit the produce aisle first, all your fruits and vegetables will be at the top of your list. If the paper products are in the last aisle, they'll be last on your list. Then see if you can get everything on your list on one pass through the store. If you can, you're a lot more efficient at grocery shopping than I am.

HEADHUNTERS

Headhunters are a necessary evil. Almost every corporation large enough to have a human resources department chooses to bypass that department and use outside search firms to hunt and bag upper-level executives. That means if you want to eventually move into a corner office, or shift from your present corner office to the board room, you'll need to deal with these poachers of the corporate world and learn how to play their game.

The Public Case for Headhunting

Clearly, headhunters have their uses. For the corporation with an opening, a headhunter saves time: about 20 percent. There's no sorting through reams of résumés or conducting repetitive rounds of interviews. After about three months of searching, the headhunter presents the corporation with three to five prescreened candidates for their upper-level opening. They are all qualified, interested, and ostensibly willing to accept the kind of compensation package being offered. The headhunter may even express a preference from among the finalists, and then negotiate and close the deal, using the intimacy he's developed with a candidate to bring him in as cheaply as possible. Finally, some search firms—those that work on contingency—guarantee their work. No in-house human resources department would ever do that. Makes headhunters sound downright wholesome, doesn't it? Well they would be, if that was as far as it went.

The Real Case for Headhunting

The real reason almost all corporations use headhunters to fill their upper-level executive positions is that it lets them steal people from their competitors. Headhunters have not only legitimized staff-jacking, they've institutionalized it. Most headhunters won't seriously look at an out-of-work executive. Sure, they may chat with a former rising star who's now falling. And they might even use an "independent consultant" or two to flesh out their group of candidates. But they'll never offer one up as the prime nominee. It's not because unemployment bears a stigma—layoffs stopped carrying the mark of Cain when downsizing shifted from the factory floor to the front office. But the unemployed just aren't as attractive as the employed: hiring them won't hurt a competitor or generate publicity.

Corporate executives are eager to tout the time and money savings that result from using executive search firms. They're quick to point to the expertise and skill of the search firms they use. Right. The guy who fixes the office copier has more training than most headhunters. Sure, there are a handful of professional, experienced recruiters out there, most of whom work on retainer rather than contingency. But all you need to enter the business is a business card, a telephone, and chutzpah. When the tape recorder gets turned off, corporate executives admit the real lure of headhunters is their ability to steal someone good from a rival.

Search firms have at least one simple but distinct advantage in poaching. A call from some unknown person who won't or can't leave the name of his or her company ends up at the bottom of the message pile, whereas a headhunter's call to an actively employed executive is returned immediately since the executive knows who is calling and why. Just how powerful is a headhunter's telephone call? One well-known executive searcher boasted to me that he had his secretary telephone the Pentagon and ask for a high-ranking general on the verge of retirement. The general speedily returned the call—from inside a tank on maneuvers in West Germany, using the army's satellite communications system.

Of course, it's this larcenous element that has given executive recruiting its nom de guerre. Headhunters, like the celebrated Jivaro of Ecuador, raid neighboring villages and keep the heads of their victims, not just as trophies but because taking heads is believed to strengthen their own tribe while weakening the enemy. The practice is thought to be a variation on cannibalism.

A Corporate Climbing Tool

Distasteful as this larceny may seem, headhunters offer real opportunities for the astute careerist as well as for the corporation.

Headhunters are, and will probably remain, the only route into the upper level of corporate management. You're not going to fill a prime slot at a Fortune 500 company by answering a classified ad. You're not going to become a candidate by flooding human resources departments with your curriculum vitae. And you're surely not going to get to the top through the ranks: today's messiahs all come from out of town. You enter the running for a top spot by being on a headhunter's shortlist.

Headhunters also offer the best way to boost your income at your current job. In my more than two decades of advising employees I've never failed at turning a headhunter's solicitation into a pay raise. There's really no secret to it: you just need to carefully couch your blackmail. (See "Subtle Extortion" on page 280.)

Subtle Extortion

Using contact with a headhunter to boost your income or accelerate a promotion at your current job is like playing the stock market: There are unavoidable risks, but you need to do it if you want to succeed.

March in yourself and proclaim you've been approached and you may indeed get an immediate increase or promotion. However, such blatant blackmail may also instantly put a big bull's-eye on your back. I've found that the best way of mitigating the risk while maximizing the gain is to have a third party inform on you. Either casually let the office snitch know of the headhunter's approach or use a trusted colleague or contact—a client or the chairperson's assistant—to pass along the message.

When your superior confronts you with the story, act nonchalant. Stress that it was nothing out of the ordinary and therefore you didn't think it merited bringing it to her attention: "I get calls from headhunters every four or five months." Then add some superficially reassuring words that carry a subtext: "You know I'm not happy with the money here, but don't worry, I don't want to leave." Odds are, you'll get an increase or a promotion within four months.

The indirect approach may take a bit longer to pay off than blatant extortion, but it will keep you from rising to number one on the hit list. If it doesn't yield the results you want, you were already living on borrowed time. Call back the headhunter, tell him you've reconsidered and are eager for other offers, and then grab the first good one to come your way.

Getting into a Headhunter's Rolodex

How do you become a party to this legitimized and mutually profitable larceny? Forget the direct approach. The headhunter motto is "Don't call us, we'll call you." They're not looking to find jobs for people, they're looking to find people for jobs. Their client is the corporation, not the candidate.

One way to enter the loop is to simply show up on their radar screen. Try to network with prominent individuals in your profession and industry—the folks who headhunters call for leads. Of course, that's no simple task.

There is a quicker, if less noble, way into the game. If you get a call from a headhunter for information, become an informant. Name names and provide organizational charts. And once you've become a source, keep the pipeline active by staying in touch and providing goodies whenever you can. Headhunters always say one hand washes the other. Clearly, there's a need for frequent ablution.

There's No Turning Back

Personal ethics aside, getting into bed with headhunters has repercussions: You will forever be regarded as a hired gun. Land a corner office with the help of a headhunter and you'll never quite win your board's total faith. If they could successfully woo you away, so could someone else. You'll be marked as a maverick: useful and effective, but not really part of the team. Use a headhunter's offer as leverage to increase your income from your current job and your bigger paycheck will come with the label of potential defector. If heads need to roll, yours will now be the first on the chopping block. Once you start to work with headhunters, you can't stop. Never again will you be seen as the selfless company man or woman. You are now and forever a mercenary: a skilled rogue, to be used but not fully trusted.

Am I suggesting you shouldn't cross this career Rubicon? Not at all. It's the demise of corporate loyalty—boards' unwillingness to promote from within and their desire to poach—that has created this new landscape. The only way for you to get to the top, financially or politically, is to play the game by today's rules and become a mercenary. Know the dangers, but take prudent risks. After all, it's better to be a rogue than a fool.

———————

(See also networking.)

HEALTH CLUBS

JOINING A HEALTH CLUB is like buying a diet book. It's a wise investment—if you use it. A lot of people don't.

Many people join health clubs as part of a wonderful new self-improvement plan. Sometimes the decision is a knee-jerk reaction to their reflection in a full-length mirror. Or perhaps their doctor told them they need to lose 15 or 20 pounds. Often it's their own response to a sudden weight gain. It's no coincidence that a lot of health club memberships are taken out in January.

A handful of those people become regular health club attendees. But a lot of those New Year's resolutions don't pan out. Some people never even go to the club; buying the membership was enough of an effort for them. Others are religious about visiting the health club—for a few weeks. But then the novelty wears off and they slowly begin to fall back into their old habits. Within a few months they've stopped going altogether.

But what about that $500 to $1,000 they paid when they signed up? The most practical of them might approach the health club management to cancel their memberships and ask for a prorated refund. But guess what. Few, if any, are going to receive a dime. Few health clubs will refund membership fees for any reason. The two exceptions are if your job takes you to another town or you suffer an injury or illness that prevents you from exercising. Other than that, you're stuck.

This is why I suggest you start with a short-term membership. Many clubs allow you to pay by the month or by the quarter. That should be a sufficient length of time to decide if you're willing to make the commitment to a new exercise regimen. If you are, then you can buy an annual membership, which will be your most cost-efficient option.

Check the Fees Carefully

Most health clubs have a variety of membership options. Some offer a basic membership, which will include use of the exercise machines, weight room, steam room, Jacuzzi, and locker facilities and the freedom to enroll in any of the club's exercise classes. But they might charge an extra fee for "court use." If you're a squash player or racquetball player, you're going to pay a premium to join the club.

Watch out for hidden fees. One of the most onerous is the "towel fee." Yes, they'll charge you extra for a towel so you can take a shower. There may also be fees levied for certain classes.

When you visit the club you're thinking of joining (always visit before you join—some clubs pay less attention to cleanliness than others), sit down with a representative and discuss the various membership options. There's no point in paying for things you're not going to use. And make sure to ask if there are any special enrollment periods coming up. Many clubs have them from time to time. They can save you some money.

Be sure to ask if your membership fee remains constant year after year or whether you'll have to pay increases along with new members. Some clubs will "grandfather" your membership as an incentive to keep your business. But the moment you let your membership lapse, you'll have to pay the current fee to rejoin.

Here's another way to save money. If you work for a company, ask your boss if the company will invest in a corporate membership. This will subsidize your membership or even cover it completely. More and more companies are recognizing the value of encouraging their employees to exercise. It reduces stress, cuts medical bills and sick days, and improves productivity. To them, it's an investment with a proven return.

Do It Yourself

Before you sign on the dotted line, ask yourself if you can't accomplish your physical fitness goals without the expense of a health club. If you want to lose weight, how about a good pair of walking shoes and a book on nutrition? Even a visit to a good nutritionist will be a fraction of what you pay for a health club membership.

You might also look into a home gym. There are a variety of exercise machines on the market that will provide a workout for just about every part of your body. Many can be purchased for about what you'd pay for a year's membership at some health clubs. Over time, you can purchase additional pieces of equipment with the money you save on memberships. Plus you won't need to pay for towels.

If you prefer the health club, though, I see no reason to deny yourself the pleasure of membership. Anything you can do to improve your health is a worthy investment. Again, just make sure you use it. Otherwise you're just wasting your money.

HEALTH INSURANCE

THE UNITED STATES MAY HAVE the best-quality medical care in the world, but its value is another question. You can go to the best doctor in the world, and maybe afford a checkup, but God forbid she finds something wrong with you. A serious illness or injury requiring lengthy hospitalization could cost more than you paid for your house. Lots more. Those individuals and families who don't have health insurance—and there are tens of millions of Americans who fall into this category—are literally a serious illness away from financial disaster.

Only health insurance can take some of the sting out of medical costs. The better policies will cover most of the expenses of physician visits, tests, lab work, x-rays, hospitalization, and other medical treatments. A few, though not enough in my opinion, are even paying for preventative care.

Employer-Provided Health Insurance

The best and most common way to get health insurance is through your employer. The company may foot the bill for all or a portion of the premium, withholding your contribution from your paycheck. Few companies today provide the kind of inexpensive, comprehensive, individualized coverage they did 10 to 15 years ago. Most have shifted from the more expensive fee-for-service plans, which offered policyholders almost unlimited choice, to health maintenance organizations (HMOs) or preferred provider organizations (PPOs), which offer fewer choices but lower premiums. Still, most employers provide enough coverage that a serious illness won't cause you to lose your home.

If you lose your job, you can take your policy with you. COBRA (Consolidated Omnibus Budget Reconciliation Act) allows you to keep your health insurance for up to 18 months after you leave a job. You pay the premiums plus a 2 percent administrative fee. You can also switch to a different plan, as long as it's one that current employees can select. By the way, COBRA also allows you to pick up the premiums of children who are graduating from college and are no longer covered by your policy. This ensures that they are covered while they're looking for a job.

Selecting Your Own Health Insurance

If you are self-employed or your employer doesn't provide health insurance, you have three options: fee-for-service coverage, an HMO, or a PPO.

In a fee-for-service plan you choose your own doctors and hospitals. Your benefits kick in after you meet a certain deductible, either per person covered or as a family. The insurer then pays either (1) a predetermined rate (the reasonable and customary charge) for specific covered services and procedures or (2) more likely a percentage of that rate, leaving you to pay the coinsurance charge. Some expenses may not be covered at all; other expenses may be subject to annual ceilings. It's essential that you investigate the details to make sure your family's needs are covered. Fee-for-service plans are available for hospitalization expenses only, for nonhospital expenses only, or for both types of expense. The advantage of a fee-for-service plan is that you are in control: You decide what doctor to go to, when, or what hospital to use. You insurer may require second opinions or limit its reimbursements, but it won't stand in the way of your obtaining the care you want. The disadvantage of a fee-for-service plan is the cost: It is the most expensive of the three options.

Health maintenance organizations are organizations comprised of health care providers and facilities. In exchange for a premium they provide comprehensive medical coverage, often requiring a nominal out-of-pocket payment—say, $10—for each office visit. Instead of choosing all your doctors and hospitals, you select or are assigned a single primary-care physician who then refers you to other member specialists or facilities as needed. The advantage of an HMO is its lower cost. The disadvantage of an HMO is the lack of control. It's in the HMO's financial interest to limit use of medical service. While in many cases HMO refusals are made on medically sound grounds, there have been enough well-reported refusals that seem to be based on financial rather than medical grounds to earn them a poor reputation. It's important to remember that people covered by an HMO can always go to a nonmember doctor or hospital. They just have to cover most, if not all, of the cost themselves.

PPOs are the middle ground between fee-for-service plans and HMOs. They're usually a loosely affiliated group of medical providers in a particular geographic area. Premiums entitle members to inexpensive care from any provider in the group. Patients can go to nonmember doctors or facilities, but it will cost a great deal more. PPOs are more expensive and less controlling than HMOs, less expensive and more controlling than fee-for-service plans.

Buy the Best Coverage You Can Afford

What's the best type of coverage? In my opinion there's no question: fee-for-service plans. They provide the highest-quality health care and the most personal control. Granted, premiums are high, but they can be reduced if you opt for a high deductible, in effect becoming as much of a self-insurer as possible. Your major concern, after all, is protection from catastrophic costs that could disrupt your finances. There are also scores of professional associations, trade groups, and social organizations that offer their members less expensive group coverage. There are even artificial groups, formed by nonprofit health insurers like Blue Cross/Blue Shield, that offer group coverage to the self-employed.

I don't think PPOs are as good as fee-for-service plans, but they do provide better care than HMOs. If you still can't afford fee-for-service coverage even after opting for a high deductible and joining a group, opt for a PPO.

HMOs should be your last resort. While the best of them may give you all the care you need, that might not be all the care you want. If you have no other choice, make sure you select an HMO that lets you "go out of group" and still get some reimbursement.

(See also benefits, COBRA.)

Questions to Ask When Purchasing Your Own Health Insurance

1. Is the policy guaranteed renewable? You don't want your coverage canceled if you develop a serious illness or have a lot of bills. Once you lose coverage, it can be difficult to find replacement coverage. Is there a waiting period before the policy goes into effect, or does coverage begin immediately?

2. What is the insurer's policy on preexisting conditions? Some companies will refuse to insure you if you already have a serious illness. Others may require a waiting period of as long as 18 months.

3. Does hospitalization coverage begin the day you're admitted? Some policies will not cover procedures done on your first day in the hospital.

4. Does the policy only cover procedures done at approved hospitals? If so, are the hospitals you prefer to use on the list?

5. Do you need to obtain a second opinion and preapproval before undergoing a nonemergency surgical procedure? Does the policy require that you see certain physicians for a second opinion?

6. Are the policy's benefits adjusted to keep pace with inflation?

7. Are newborn children automatically covered by the policy?

8. At what age does coverage stop for children? Are they covered if they are full-time students? Some companies continue to cover children up to age 24 or 25, as long as they're in school.

9. Is your premium waived if you become disabled?

Tips on Choosing an HMO

Many companies today offer employees a choice between a number of competing HMO plans. Here are some tips on suggesting which is best for you:

- Obtain the full terms of coverage for each plan. Make sure you have information on premiums, copay, deductibles, and exclusions.

- Rule out plans without a point-of-service (POS) option, which means it will at least partially reimburse you for visits to nonparticipating providers.

- If possible, talk to someone who has used the plan.

- Call the state insurance department to check for complaints against each plan.

- Ask the insurance department what percentage of each plan's premium is paid out in claims.

- Check to see how many specialists of various kinds are included in each plan.

- Check which local hospitals are under contract with each plan.

- Check whether emergency care must be approved in advance.

- Find out the limits if any, on psychotherapy visits.

- Check into each plan's grievance procedures.

- Find out about coverage for emergency and nonemergency travel illnesses.

- Find out what percentage of the plan's primary-care physicians are board-certified.

- Check whether any of your current physicians participate in any of the plans.

HOBBIES

I'M A REFORMED WORKAHOLIC. Ten or fifteen years ago I wouldn't have been able to say much on this topic. Weekday or weekend, morning or evening, if I wasn't working, I was filled with anxiety and guilt.

But today I spend much of my spare time listening to classical music and opera. My wife, Corky, and I are also regulars at Lincoln Center and other Manhattan theaters. My devotion to music has made my busy life much richer. My hobby helps me relax and relieves the tension of a hectic day. It has made me a more rounded person and expanded my social circle. I've made many new friends through our subscription concert series.

I've also discovered that hobbies can be an asset in conducting business. It's not unusual for me to end up in a business-related conversation during intermissions at the theater. I've even been introduced to prospective clients by my opera-loving friends.

Hobbies also provide other people with some insight into who you are, providing a common ground for conversation and broadening relationships beyond just business. When I meet new clients, I always try to find out what they do away from work. Most people are excited to talk about their hobbies, and see related questions as a true expression of your inter-

Using Hobbies to Send Subtle Signals

Mentioning your hobbies or interests, either on a résumé or during a job interview, can send subtle but important signals about you as a person and a job candidate. For example, interviewers can't ask about your health, but noting that you're a marathon runner or an avid racquetball player lets them know you're in good aerobic health and almost certainly not a smoker. Hobbies such as bridge and chess imply you're an analytical person. Participating in an adult ice hockey league says you're aggressive and a good team player. Try to be as specific about your interests as possible. Instead of writing that you love historical fiction, note that you're a fan of Patrick O'Brian's novels. Specificity makes you appear a more interesting person, and if by chance an interviewer shares your specific interest, you'll have a leg up on the competition.

est in them as a human being, not just as a source of income. For example, I discovered that one of my clients, a very conservative, button-downed executive, is also an accomplished amateur violinist. Now when we get together, I always make a point of steering the conversation to her music. As soon as I do, her eyes brighten and she starts gushing over her trio's latest efforts.

Knowledge of a person's hobbies can also smooth the path to a successful business negotiation. Years ago when I was in the banking business, I was frequently called upon to close important deals for my employer. I would prepare for these meetings by learning as much as possible beforehand about my counterparts. During our initial meeting, after we concluded our business and were making small talk, I would ask them about their hobbies. Invariably, this helped us connect and served as a foundation for future conversations.

Once I subtly used my information about an adversary's gourmet cooking hobby as a way to warm up what could have been a difficult negotiation. During a break in conversation I asked if there were any gourmet cookware shops in the city where we were meeting, explaining that my wife was a gourmet cook (she actually is). The change in the other party was visible, as he softened into a lover of fine cooking and dining. When we got back down to business, it was clear that he had shed some of his corporate armor.

HOME-BASED BUSINESSES

"LOCATION, LOCATION, LOCATION," was the mantra for predicting small business success in the twentieth century. I think in the twenty-first century the new maxim for entrepreneurs will be "There's no place like home."

There are more home-based businesses today than ever before. Traditionally these have included specialized mail order, accounting and tax preparation, telemarketing, graphic design, financial advisement, and other services. In the last five or six years a new breed of home-based entrepreneur has joined the ranks: the cyberworker. The Internet has made the concept of "location" obsolete for many American businesses. No matter where he lives, the cyberworker can be employed by a company based across the country (or across the world, for that matter). Connected over the Internet, he can work on projects with his coworkers, wherever they are. They can each be looking at the same thing on their monitors. If they choose, they can have audio and video connections that allow them to see and speak to one another. About the only thing they can't do is go out for lunch together (but as far as I'm concerned, that's okay). At the end of the day, he turns off his machine and navigates the five-second commute out of his office to join his family for the evening.

Advantages

A home-based business has many advantages. Here are those most often cited by the home-business owner:

- It saves money. Not paying rent and utilities removes a great deal of the overhead from your business.

- It gives you complete autonomy. You can choose the hours you work. You can decide how your office is laid out. You can choose how you dress for work each day. Plus, if you don't have clients visiting, you save a great deal of money by not having to purchase an office wardrobe.

- It eliminates commuting, saving you time and money and protecting the environment from unnecessary air pollution.

- You can claim a portion of your rent or mortgage as a business expense on your taxes. Likewise, a portion of many of your home expenses is deductible.

- It removes a great deal of risk from the process. If your business doesn't work out, you're not tied into an expensive lease. You can just turn your home office back into an extra bedroom.

- It's now considered entirely respectable. In some industries it even has a certain cachet.

Disadvantages

The home-based business isn't perfect. Granted, you can't operate a business more cheaply, but you're also alone a lot of the time. And you have the television, the kitchen, and all the other temptations of home just a few steps away. Here are some of the most frequent complaints I hear from my clients who work at home:

- Loneliness. Many go the entire day without interacting face-to-face with another person. Some love it, but those who don't usually list it as their biggest complaint.

- Your personal life can be disrupted. If your family is home during the day, it can be very distracting. And because the office is just a few steps away, a lot of people tend to become workaholics; this can cause a great deal of domestic stress.

- Lack of a support system. When you work in an office you can usually get help from coworkers if it's needed. When you're by yourself, all the responsibilities fall on your shoulders.

- Your space may be limited. Although most people can generally find some space in their home to use as an office or workplace, it's not always as big or as comfortable as they'd like.

- You may run into zoning problems—especially if you're in an apartment—that make it difficult to have a business in your home. Some home-business operators have run into problems when a sign on their lawn or a steady parade of clients tipped off authorities about their business.

- If you rent your home or are a member of a condominium or community association, there may be clauses in your lease or association agreement forbidding the operation of a business on the premises.

- Customers may find it uncomfortable or inconvenient to come to your home, particularly if you live far out of town or in a neighborhood where parking is difficult to find.

Setting Up a Home-Based Business

Home-based businesses fall into two categories: those that have clients visiting and those that don't. If you fall into the second category, you don't need to worry about appearances and can set up your work space exactly as you want. But if you have clients coming through the door, you need to create an environment that's both comfortable and professional.

As you set things up, keep in mind that the ideal home office has several characteristics:

- It needs ample room for your basic equipment plus any other tools or materials needed for your business.

- It should be far enough removed from the rest of your home to protect you from the bustle and noise of your family and ensure your privacy.

- It should be used exclusively for your business and not have a secondary function as a storage room, a playroom for the kids, or a hobby room for your spouse.

- It must have its own door, preferably one that opens to the outside.

- It should provide you with ample room for all your day-to-day activities as well as for storage and record keeping.

- It must be well-lit and well-ventilated and have a window that opens.

Perhaps the most important of these characteristics is privacy. It's critical to your happiness and satisfaction. If you don't feel adequately separated from the noise and activity in the rest of the house, you'll find it extremely difficult to give your full attention to the matters at hand. Constant interruptions from children or your spouse will have a terribly negative effect on your productivity.

It's also important that the room function solely as your office. It shouldn't be an after-hours playroom for the kids or a family room. Running a business requires organization, and if you have people playing on your computer, rearranging your files, and shuffling through your papers, you'll quickly become quite disorganized.

Don't Forget to Have a Life

In my opinion, there are two significant downsides to home-based businesses. The first is that home-based workers usually work alone. Isolation can make it difficult to cultivate the kind of friendships that most people develop at the office. The second is that they can easily become workaholics. With the office just a few feet away, it's easy to think about work 24 hours a day and neglect your family (and yourself).

It's important for people who work at home to get involved in activities away from home. Join a health club or become active in your church. Follow your interests to others who share the same interests. Create a schedule of activities that forces you out of the house. There's a lot more to life than work, you know. Make sure you take advantage of it.

(See also equipment, home offices.)

HOME EQUITY LOANS

TAKING OUT A SECOND MORTGAGE on a home used to be considered a sign of financial distress. It was something done as a last resort when cash was desperately needed and there was no other access to credit.

What a difference a name has made. Once the second mortgage was rechristened the "home equity loan" the disgrace vanished. Rather than being viewed as the Last Chance Saloon of personal solvency, it's being touted by financial institutions as a logical and desirable method to finance all sorts of things, from new cars to college educations.

My advice? Tread this area of credit *very* carefully—it's full of potential pitfalls. Yes, home equity loans do have some very desirable characteristics. They're easy to get, the interest rate is usually quite reasonable, and the interest is often tax-deductible. But the downside can be disastrous. When you take out a home equity loan, you're using your home as collateral. If you can't make the payments, you could find yourself without a roof over your head.

Granted, the odds of that happening may be slim. However, continuing to borrow against your home's equity robs you of the advantage that a paid-off mortgage could bring to your life: the ability to direct your stream of income to other more financially or emotionally rewarding areas. Alternatively, if you are mortgage-free, you don't have to generate as much income and can spend more time doing things that you enjoy, whether that's working for Literacy Volunteers or golfing.

Why Lenders Love Home Equity Loans

Home equity loans became popular with lenders for one simple reason. They provide them with a decent return and virtually no risk. Back in the 1960s and early 1970s, financial institutions lent out billions of dollars in home mortgages at relatively low interest rates. As rates began to rise from the single digits into the double digits, they grew frustrated at the amount of money they had tied up in low-interest loans. The answer was to offer home equity loans at higher rates. As bait, lenders touted all the wonderful things borrowers could do with the money. Today the home equity loan is the easiest and most available source of financing available to Americans. Since Americans will do most anything to keep their homes, the default rate on home equity loans is quite low.

How Home Equity Loans Work

The amount of money homeowners can borrow in a home equity loan depends on the value of their home and the balance of their mortgage. Let's say your home is worth $150,000 and your mortgage balance is $50,000. That means you have $100,000 worth of equity in your home. You can borrow against that equity—usually up to 70 percent of it—and use the money however you wish.

If you own a home, you've no doubt received literature from banks inviting you to "put your money to work" by taking out a home equity loan. That new addition on your home, a trip to Europe, a new car—all that can be financed by signing a few forms, they say. What they don't mention, of course, is that once you sign on the dotted line you're basically starting over again, taking out a 30-year obligation.

Banks also don't mention the up-front fees that may be required. To make sure you keep such costs to a minimum, you should approach your search for a home equity loan just like you did for your first mortgage. Call the commercial banks, credit unions, and savings and loans in your area to shop around for interest rates. Are they offering fixed-rate or variable-rate loans? If they're variable-rate, how is the rate adjusted and what is the cap? Are there additional up-front fees you'll have to pay? Will you have to pay "points," sometimes 1 to 3 percent of the principal, at the beginning of the loan? Remember to include any fees paid at the beginning of the loan to your total start-up costs.

When a Home Equity Loan Makes Sense

I believe there are four situations in which a home equity loan makes sense.

To make repairs or improvements to your home that add to its value. In this case, you're borrowing money to make an additional investment in your home and increasing its value. I would not encourage you to take out a home equity loan for a renovation that doesn't add to the home's value, however.

To finance college educations for your children. As recently as 10 years ago I probably would not have included this as a valid use of home equity loans. But today, with college costs increasing at two and three times the rate of inflation, it makes a great deal of sense. If you don't have the cash on hand to pay for your share of your child's education, compare the impact of taking out a student loan versus using a home equity loan.

To pay off credit card debt. While there's no such thing as good debt, some debt is worse than others. Far and away the worst debt is from high-interest credit cards. I've counseled enough debt-ridden young couples to recognize true desperation when I see it. If you can consolidate credit card balances on which you're paying 20 or 21 percent interest into a single payment at 8 or 9 percent interest, which is also tax-deductible, you should be able to pay off the loan in a few years. This will only be successful, of course, if you then throw away your cards and consider the entire episode a painful lesson learned.

To provide seed money for a business. If you have a solid business plan and know what you're doing, and are unable to raise the money you need through any other means, a home equity loan is an acceptable way of launching your entrepreneurial career. Just remember, four out of five small businesses fail within five years, usually from undercapitalization.

To use a home equity loan for any other purpose is, in my opinion, just plain stupid. If you want to take a vacation to Europe or need a new car, wait until you've saved enough money to pay for it.

(See also credit cards, mortgage loans.)

HOME FURNISHINGS

THERE'S SOMETHING TERRIBLY WRONG with the furniture industry. It offers expensive products and, in general, terrible service. It's a good thing furniture is a necessity; otherwise, most of these manufacturers and retailers would be out of business.

The first problem in buying home furnishings is the difficulty in comparison-shopping. When you're buying a particular brand and model of television, for example, you'll usually have at least a half-dozen retailers in the vicinity whose prices you can check. But if you find a couch or a chair you like, it's usually the only one of its kind around. You never really know when a price is fair and when you're being overcharged.

Then there's the waiting game. Most furniture and carpeting has to be ordered from the manufacturer. The retailer usually has a sample and no inventory. If you're lucky, your furniture will arrive on time. If you're even luckier, it will be what you ordered and won't be damaged. If you're unlucky, the item that arrives will be wrong or damaged, it will arrive late, and then it will have to go back to the manufacturer, forcing you to wait all over again, perhaps for another damaged or wrong item.

Getting the Best Deal

Here are some tips to make shopping for home furnishings as painless as possible:

Know what you're after. If you're looking for a couch, for example, make sure you know how long you want it to be. Always bring a tape measure with you. If you have certain color requirements, bring paint and carpet samples. If you're buying a rug or carpet runner, know how big the area is you want to cover. If you're looking for carpeting, have a fairly good idea how many square yards you'll need. That will allow you to calculate prices.

Read the labels. All furnishings should have labels describing the type of wood they're made from or the content of the fabric. They should also tell you if the fabric is fireproof. Descriptions of the wood should tell you whether it's solid wood, veneer, or an imitation surface. The same information should appear for leather furniture. If a nation of origin is indicated ("Real Italian Leather!") it must be exactly that.

Examine each item carefully. Don't be satisfied with just appearances. If you're looking at a piece of furniture, check its construction. Frames should be screwed rather than nailed. Joints should be smooth, with no glue or fasteners sticking out. Make sure all moving parts operate smoothly. Check the density and pile of carpets. And don't forget the ultimate test—comfort. Sit down and sprawl around on couches and chairs. Lie down on mattresses and try different positions.

Bring samples home. The true test is how something looks in your home, not in the store. Bring home carpet samples and fabric swatches to see how they'll look against your existing furnishings.

Negotiate the price. Most furniture stores have a fair amount of flexibility when it comes to price. If you're buying more than one piece, offer a single price for the entire selection rather than separate prices for each item.

Don't pay up front. Leave as small a deposit as possible and don't pay the balance until the item or items are in your possession and you've checked them thoroughly for damage.

Get an itemized receipt. This is very important to avoid confusion later on. The receipt should describe in detail each item you've purchased. It should include the manufacturer, the model number, the color and size, the material, and the price. If the item is on sale, both the sale price and the retail price should be included.

Get a firm delivery date. This should also appear on the receipt. Insist on a day and time, not an approximate date. If the day and time arrive and no delivery has been made, call the store immediately for an explanation. If the problem continues, negotiate an added discount. If they refuse, complain to your local better business bureau or consumer affairs office.

Travel to the best furniture deals. If you don't mind a little travel—perhaps you can make it double as a vacation—rent a big van and take a trip to North Carolina, the furniture capital of the United States, with hundreds of manufacturers of everything from dining room and bedroom sets to couches and chairs to bureaus and bookcases. Most are in or near the cities of High Point and Hickory. Many of these manufacturers operate enormous outlets where you can save up to 50 percent. By driving your purchases home yourself you can also save hundreds of dollars in shipping costs.

Do It Yourself

If you want to save money and don't mind a little work, you might consider buying unfinished or unassembled furniture. *Unfinished furniture* is usually made of maple, pine, or oak. It's completely assembled, but the wood hasn't been stained or finished. This gives you the ability to pick the exact stain you want, a choice you're unlikely to have if you buy a finished piece of furniture.

Unassembled furniture can usually be put together with a screwdriver, hammer, allen wrenches, or a few other common tools. Most major department stores carry unassembled furniture. So do some specialty stores like the Ikea chain. The quality is usually good and the instructions are quite detailed. Of course, if you wish, you can pay to have the pieces assembled by store employees.

(See also furniture.)

HOME IMPROVEMENTS

Most of the $100 billion American homeowners invest in home improvements every year is wasted.

Not only is the home improvement business plagued with poorly trained and incompetent craftspeople who do shoddy work, overcharge, and generally make the entire experience a nightmare for their customers, but many homeowners spend a great deal of money on work that decreases rather than increases the value of their homes.

It generally makes sense to renovate when you want to have more space but can't afford to buy another home, add character to a generic home, boost the value of your home, increase the pleasure you get from your home, or make your home more functional.

The Case against Doing It Yourself

You may think that one solution would be to do the work yourself. Wrong! Despite what the how-to books, genial television hosts, and reassuring clerks at the home center say, you won't be able to do as good a job on your own as a professional would.

Nearly every man who has hung a shelf thinks he can build a deck. Don't get me wrong, this isn't just a case of excessive machismo. While men are probably worse in this regard, women can be just as foolish. While the woman may not have delusions of grandeur revolving around hammers and nails, if she have successfully started and managed her own company, she may think managing a minor renovation project will be a piece of cake.

Lack of actual skill isn't the only obstacle to doing it yourself. Those who think they should do home renovation work themselves often fail to realize there's an added cost involved: their time. If you earn $40 an hour at a job, it makes sense to pay a contractor $30 an hour to do it for you and concentrate on what you do for a living.

Hiring professional help isn't a panacea. There are terrible general contractors and architects out there: Some are incompetent, some are corrupt, and some are both. The secret is to ensure that they're not working on *your* job and take steps to guarantee that the process is as smooth as possible and the inevitable cost overruns and scheduling delays are kept to a minimum.

That's where you should be concentrating your efforts. Rather than trying to take the place of someone else, you should instead try to play your part to the best of their abilities. That means functioning as the chief executive officer of the project: overseeing the planning, making policy decisions, delegating authority to implement those decisions, making sure the project stays on course, and paying the bills.

What Makes Financial Sense?

The decision to renovate involves both financial and emotional elements. Financially, renovations can add to or detract from the value of a home. The entire cost of the renovation may be easy to recoup right away or may never be recoverable. That's because real estate values are based more on location than on the size or quality of the dwelling itself.

For example, low-end homes in a given location may be in poor condition and have only two bedrooms and one bathroom. Midrange homes in the same location may be in good condition and have three bedrooms and two bathrooms. Houses in the high end may be in excellent condition and have skylights, fireplaces, fencing, landscaping, and other amenities setting them apart.

In order for a renovation to make financial sense, it should bring a home from one part of the range up to another. If your home is in the low end of the range and you add a third bedroom and second bath, or if you put on a new roof and upgrade the heating, electrical, and plumbing systems, it will pay off. If your home is in the midprice range, a renovation would make financial sense if the condition of the home is improved or if popular luxury features and amenities are added. If your home is already at the high end of the price range, the cost of any changes may never be recouped, and if the improvement is too eccentric it may actually reduce your home's value.

Here's another way to look at it: generally, the cost of renovations that improve a home's comfort and convenience, while less dramatic, are more recoverable than the cost of those that increase its size or make it more modern.

In addition to affecting value, certain renovations will affect how quickly you can sell the home. In real estate, time equals money. Any cosmetic renovation that reflects neutral or traditional taste will speed the sale of a home, while anything that reflects personal taste will slow the sale.

For a fee of $150 to $300 a knowledgeable local appraiser should be able to give you an estimate of how a proposed renovation will affect the home's value. For a fee of from $100 to $200 a real estate broker can make an educated guess as to whether the renovation will speed or delay an eventual sale.

What Makes Emotional Sense?

If you're a purely pragmatic individual, you will only make renovations that add to the value of a home, improve its salability, or enable you to recoup the cost. But that's not how most of us live our lives, nor should it be. A home is more than a financial investment. It's where you eat, sleep, work, make love, fight, laugh, cry, play, relax, raise your children, celebrate your holidays, and mourn your losses. While its financial importance cannot be overestimated, neither can its emotional power. A home can be a refuge, a safe haven, a protective umbrella from the storms of the outside world for ourselves and our family. And the more wonderful you make your home, the more comforting and rewarding your life becomes. Having a magnificent home won't turn your life around, but it will make you happier.

After calculating the financial return on a proposed renovation, and its effect on the home's salability, you must factor into the equation the emotional or psychological benefits it offers. How will the renovation affect your life? How much pleasure will it bring you? If it will improve your life and bring you a great deal of pleasure then the money that's not recouped isn't wasted—it has been invested in you and your life.

You must ask yourself whether a potentially nonrecoverable renovation will bring enough pleasure to your life to justify the cost. The answer usually depends on how long you intend to remain in this particular home. Think in terms of 5-year increments. How soon do you envision selling this home? If you were to sell within 5 years, would the emotional and psychological benefits from a renovation still outweigh its nonrecoverable cost? How about if you sold in 10 or 15 years? The shorter the length of time you see yourself remaining in a home, the more you should stress the financial elements of a renovation.

Types of Renovations

Home renovations fall into one of five categories: cosmetic face-lifts, system upgrades, space additions, luxury additions, or remodeling.

1. *Cosmetic face-lifts* are projects that improve the appearance of the home: for example, painting the exterior or interior; landscaping the yard and grounds; replacing or refinishing the floors; replacing appliances; replacing, refacing, or restoring cabinets; replacing or refinishing bathroom fixtures. Most face-lifts are less expensive than other types of renovations. They offer the most immediate but least enduring return on investment.

2. *System upgrades* are renovations that improve the functional quality of a home: replacing or improving the electrical, plumbing, heating, and cooling systems; replacing windows and doors; repairing or replacing the roof; completely insulating and weather-stripping the entire home. System upgrades aren't very glamorous and won't offer much emotional return on your investment. However, they can add immeasurably to your comfort and happiness in subtle ways. They offer a good return on investment, especially in the short term, but they can be complex and costly.

3. *Space additions* are projects that add to the actual living space of a home: for example, finishing a basement, finishing or expanding an attic, expanding dormers into additional rooms, converting a garage into living space, building an extension on the home. Space additions can be reasonable or very costly, simple or complex, valuable or nearly worthless. That's why it pays to be very thoughtful and deliberate when contemplating a space addition.

4. *Luxury additions* involve incorporating an amenity into the home that adds to the comfort or pleasure of the occupants: for example, adding fireplaces, darkrooms, workshops, skylights, swimming pools, tennis courts, central air conditioning, central vacuuming, security systems, greenhouses, decks, hot tubs, central audiovideo systems. This is the one type of renovation where people must usually come down on one side or the other—sound investment or emotional enjoyment. With a couple of notable exceptions—fireplaces and skylights—you may not be able to recoup the money you put into adding an amenity to a home.

5. *Remodeling* involves anything that alters the floor plan of a home: for example, entirely redoing a kitchen or bathroom or combining two bedrooms and a bathroom into a master bedroom suite with a dressing room and two bathrooms. Remodeling projects are usually expensive and complex. They can be a great investment if they add something to a home that other homes in the area have—a well-designed, eat-in kitchen, for instance. However, they may also destroy the flow or character of a home, dramatically reducing its value.

Financing Options

Once you've decided to go ahead, you need to figure out how to finance your project. Here are three options:

Installment Loans Projects costing between $3,000 and $10,000 are best financed with installment loans. Typically unsecured, these loans rely solely on your income and credit history. The payments for these loans last from one to three years. Installment loans are fairly easy to obtain. Banks are aggressive in issuing them, since the short-terms and high-interest rates make them very profitable.

Borrowing on Equity If your renovation work will cost more than $10,000 it is best to borrow against the equity you have in your home. Your equity is equal to the difference between your home's current market value and the balance of your mortgage. If your home is worth $200,000, and you have a balance of $150,000 left to pay off, you have $50,000 worth of equity. Banks will generally lend you up to 70 percent of your equity.

If you opt to simply receive a check for the amount, interest will accrue on the entire sum immediately. If you decide you'd rather draw the money as you need it, interest will accrue only on what you draw out. The former is better if you want a set monthly payment, and if your project is scheduled to last only a short period of time. If you'll be involved in a long project stretching out months rather than weeks, or if you intend to renovate your home through a series of separate smaller projects over an extended period of time, the latter may be more convenient and end up costing less in interest.

Refinancing Your Mortgage   Another financing option would be to refinance your first mortgage. Most people think of mortgage refinancing as a way to decrease monthly payments, but it can also be used to pull your equity money back out of the house. The concept is called "cashing out." Let's say that 10 years ago you bought your home for $100,000. You put $20,000 down and took out a 30-year, $80,000 mortgage. Today your home is worth $130,000 and you've paid your mortgage down to $70,000. If you turned to a bank and asked it to refinance your mortgage, it may offer to lend you up to 75 percent of its value in a refinanced mortgage. That means it will let you borrow up to $97,500. After paying off the remaining $70,000 on your previous mortgage you'd be left with $27,500 (less any application, processing, and financing charges), which could be used to finance a home renovation.

Get a Set of Plans

In order for a home renovation to work smoothly you'll need a description of the renovation project—a blueprint for the job. A comprehensive set of plans and specifications ensures that your wants and needs—not those of the general contractor's—are expressed in the design; it reasonably ensures that bids won't be out of line with your budget; it allows competitive bids to be compared, analyzed, and validated; and it guarantees that attention will be paid to the aesthetic sense of the structure.

Who you commission to draft these plans and supervise your project depends on what type of job you're having done. If you are remodeling or adding space to your home, you'll need to hire an architect to prepare your specifications. If your project is a cosmetic face-lift, you should hire an interior designer. And if you are upgrading a home system or adding an amenity, a home inspector or general contractor can provide specifications and supervision.

Hiring a Contractor

Selecting a general contractor to execute your plans isn't simply a matter of soliciting bids from a handful of candidates and then choosing the low bidder. Selecting a general contractor for your job should be a studied process made up of five distinct steps.

1. Determine what type of general contractor is right for the job.

2. Find at least three qualified candidates.

3. Carefully investigate the craftsmanship, character, and financial stability of each candidate.

4. Scrupulously analyze each bid.

5. Negotiate an air-tight contract with the general contractor you select for the job.

General contractors fall into two major categories: traditionalists and specialists. The traditional general contractor is able, or at least claims to be able, to do any type of work. A specialist is, like a medical specialist, someone who concentrates on one particular type of project. If all you're looking for is someone to build a deck, then it makes sense to hire someone who specializes in building decks. But if you're adding a deck and redoing your kitchen, you need to look for a generalist.

The best way to develop a list of candidates is to get some expert advice from your architect or designer, a construction manager, a space planner, or a home inspector. Stress that you're looking for the *right* contractor for the job, not the cheapest, then run the recommended names past the local building department, a member of your co-op board or homeowners' association, or a representative of the managing agent. Using a general contractor who has been okayed by a bureaucracy that you need to deal with later on could be an added insurance against potential problems.

(See also contractors, location, mortgage loans.)

Buy Your Own Materials

One way to save money on a renovation project may be to buy the materials yourself. Most people aren't aware that contractors mark up the price of materials to their clients. If you do the purchasing, you may be able to eliminate the markup. You might even be able to negotiate a substantial discount if the purchase is large enough. Your contractor may not be too happy about it, but you can save a considerable amount of money. Just make sure you get a specific and exact list of materials from the contractor before you head over to Home Depot.

Get Paperwork

It's important to insist that your home improvement professionals obtain all the necessary building permits and have their work inspected by the appropriate municipal authorities. If all this paperwork isn't in place when it comes time to sell your home, you won't have a valid certificate of occupancy and won't be able to sell the property. Savvy buyers will ask about the legality of any obvious improvements.

Avoiding Scams

Scams are all too common in the home renovation field. Elderly men and women living on fixed incomes are particularly vulnerable to fast-talking con artists. Here are some of the most common scams. Avoid them and you'll save a lot of money and heartache.

- You're offered "free" home improvements if you tell your friends and neighbors about the contractor's product or service. In fact, the convoluted fine print in the contract requires you to pay in full for all work done and offers you a rebate only if your referrals lead to work for the contractor.

- A contractor shows up at your door claiming that some part of your property "isn't up to code" or is otherwise unsafe and should be replaced.

- A contractor claims the material he uses is "maintenance-free" or will "last forever." No such materials exist.

- A contractor claims to have a special relationship with the manufacturers of certain "name-brand" building products. The fact is, any contractor can buy any product he chooses. Using high-quality material means nothing if the quality of the work is below par.

HOME OFFICES

EVERYONE LOVES HOME OFFICES—everyone except the IRS. To them, a home office is a fraud waiting to happen.

In order to claim a home office as a business expense, the IRS says it must be your "principal place of business." There is constant debate between tax preparers and the IRS over exactly what that phrase means. Because of this ongoing debate, some have felt that claiming home office expenses on your income tax return is a good way to trigger an audit. In my experience, however, a home office claim is only an audit trigger if the taxpayer has another office somewhere outside the home or if the office isn't used exclusively for the business.

For example, you might use your study from time to time to do work that you bring home from the office. But you also use it for personal business and for entertainment. Under the IRS definition, that does not qualify as a deductible home business expense.

The definition of a principal place of business has always been a bit murky. For years, the IRS would examine the importance of your home office to your business in deciding whether or not it qualified. For example, if you spent most of your time visiting clients and only used your home office a few hours a week to do paperwork and make telephone calls, your claim would more than likely have been denied. The fact that it may have been your only office didn't matter. But if clients came to visit you in your home office, then it would qualify.

The Taxpayer Relief Act of 1997 changed all that. Under the act's new provisions, you can claim your home office as a business expense as long as it is used for administrative or managerial functions that are not performed at some other fixed location. Whether you travel to meet your clients or they come to you no longer matters. There are a lot of home-based salespeople and service providers who are benefiting from this change of interpretation.

If you are going to claim a business deduction for your home office expenses, make sure it's clear you use the room solely for your business. It should have a separate telephone line from the rest of your house. Don't put a television or a bed in the room. Don't decide to have the room do double duty as a home gymnasium. If the office only occupies part of a larger area, a common situation with basement offices, make sure the boundaries of the office are defined by bookcases or filing cabinets.

You have some accounting responsibilities when you set up a home office. One task is figuring out what percentage of your mortgage, utilities, property taxes, and maintenance can be included in the cost of your home office. If your office takes up 13 percent of the square footage of your house, then you need to calculate 13 percent of all those individual expenses. Total those numbers and the result becomes your base home office expense. Of course, you can also add other expenses such as stationery, pens, staples, and paper, and you can deduct any furnishings you purchase for the office. Again, just make sure they're used solely for the office.

You can deduct the cost of your computer, even if it's not used solely for your business. You are allowed to keep investment information on it or use it for other personal business. If you do, you need to keep a log to document the proportion of business use and personal use. If business activities constitute more than 50 percent of the computer's use, you have the option of depreciating it over five years or claiming the entire expense in a single year.

If you work for someone else you can claim the cost of the computer as long as you can show that the computer is for the convenience of the employer and that it is a condition of employment. I recommend you obtain a letter from your employer that confirms these conditions. You can never be too careful with the IRS.

(See also audits, home-based businesses.)

HOME OWNERSHIP

Home ownership can still be the road to riches in the United States. But today those riches are often more spiritual than financial.

To understand home ownership it's important to look at it from two perspectives: the spiritual and the financial. The two are so different that I use separate terms to distinguish them. I think of the spiritual dwelling as the *home*—that ideal environment we create where we and our families can live out our lives. But when I apply my financial perspective I refer to the *house*—that bundle of wood, brick, shingle, and mortar into which we sink such large sums of money and, hopefully, get back even more when we sell it.

The Home

We'll begin with home. It's the one piece of the world we can truly shape to our own desires. Unlike a rental property, which leaves you vulnerable to sudden displacement, your home represents security. Pay the mortgage and taxes and you can stay there the rest of your life if you choose.

Home ownership allows you to create an environment that reflects your tastes and interests. Some paint and carpet, comfortable furniture, a little carpentry and plumbing, and you've created your own kingdom. You also control the property that surrounds your home. If you have a green thumb, you can derive countless hours of pleasure creating gardens or growing vegetables.

We also equate home with family. Over time, a home takes on the character of the people who reside within its walls. They dictate its appearance, the objects it contains, and even the way it sounds and smells. The home also has an organic quality that allows it to change over time. My wife and I still live in the same home in which we raised several of our children. But it certainly has taken on different feelings than it did when we had several teenagers and their friends running through the place. For a few years it was much quieter—with only my wife and me in residence and an occasional visit from children and their spouses. But lately, with grandchildren running down the hallways, the pace has picked up again.

The House

Now let's be pragmatic and look at things from a dollars-and-cents point of view. A house is an asset. Buying one is almost always a sound financial move. First, it can provide some tax relief, since the interest on a mortgage is tax-deductible. More importantly, a house will often appreciate over time. Most people can count on their houses increasing in value at a pace at least equal to inflation. The lucky ones will enjoy an appreciation that outpaces inflation. Even if your house doesn't outpace inflation, it still represents a form of savings that can often be the foundation for financial security later in life.

The parents of the baby boomer generation are perfect examples of what can happen when you buy well. Buying houses in the 1950s and 1960s, they started selling them in the 1970s and 1980s as their children reached adulthood and headed out on their own. It was a seller's market, flooded with house-hungry boomers looking to buy their first houses and start families of their own. The result? Prices were pushed through the roof. Houses that had sold for $20,000 in the 1960s were selling for $200,000 by the 1980s.

The oldest of the boomers also made out well. Taking advantage of rising prices, and the horde of younger boomers following in their footsteps, they became serial house owners. They would start with a modest house, hold onto it for a year or two, and then sell it for a handsome profit, then repeat the process with a second house. Many ended up with houses worth hundreds of thousands of dollars that were largely financed through profits made from the sale of their previous houses.

By the late 1980s, however, the excitement was over. The demographics shifted and sellers began to outnumber buyers. Prices stagnated and sometimes even declined. Unlucky buyers who bought houses around this time watched in horror as the value of their homes dropped below the balances on their mortgages. Those who were forced to sell to accommodate career moves or family needs often lost thousands of dollars.

Home Ownership Today

The economic forces that fueled the great real estate boom of the 1970s and 1980s won't happen again unless another great demographic bulge comes along. Instead, some areas of the country are experiencing a real estate boom based on the surging economy. Those who today enjoy great gains in the value of their houses are residents of booming economic areas like Silicon Valley outside San Francisco, where a modest ranchhouse might set you back $400,000 and offers above the asking price are now the norm. Other winners nationwide are those who own higher-priced homes and apartments. Those who have experienced increases in wealth from the stock market boom are shopping for larger, more expensive homes, driving prices up in the top end of markets all across the country.

If you're not one of the lucky ones whose house is soaring in value, take heart in the fact that when you make that last mortgage payment, you'll be the owner of a valuable asset that has kept pace with inflation and, if need be, will go a long way toward funding your later years.

(See also inflation, location.)

HOME SALES

IN MOST OF THE UNITED STATES, selling a house is hard work. Still, there are few other areas of our lives where a little bit of dedication can make such a difference in how much money ends up in our pockets. My advice is to approach the sale of your home as you would a similar sale in your business. How much time and effort would you put into closing a sale that would yield you a $200,000 bonus? Put that same amount of energy into selling your $200,000 home.

Get the Timing Right

When it comes to selling your house the first thing to do is think baseball. Just like our national pastime, the prime home sales season kicks off in the spring and ends in the fall. Sure, houses are sold and bought all year long, but to get top dollar you need to sell in season. People start looking in the spring because they are anxious to make their moves over the summer so they can be settled and have their kids ready for school by the fall. Also, houses look their best in the spring with the plants in bloom and the sun shining. To take advantage of market demand, you should be putting your For Sale sign in the lawn by April 1.

Get Your House Looking Its Best

If your house is going to hit the market when baseball season opens, you need to conduct your own version of spring training. That means you'll spend February and March cleaning, painting, and repairing. First impressions mean everything in home selling, both inside and out. If buyers drive up to your house and it doesn't look inviting, they won't even walk in the door. And if they walk into your house and the place is filthy or things are in disrepair, you're going to have one strike against you before they've gotten past the front hallway.

Here's a little tip to help you get ready: Have a friend do a thorough tour of your house and tell you what needs to be done. She'll be able to spot all the little things most of us are oblivious to after we've lived in a place for some length of time.

Building Your Team

Are you going to hire a real estate agent or try to sell your home yourself? If you do the latter, you'll become a Fisbo (For Sale by Owner), the scourge of the real estate industry. Every realtor in town will glare at your property when they drive by and see your sign. Of course, that doesn't mean they won't call you constantly to see if they can list your property.

In my opinion you should hire a broker. Yes, they do cost money, usually from 6 to 8 percent of the selling price of your house. But I think they're worth every penny. It takes a lot of time and flexibility to sell a house, and those are two things most of us have very little of. If you have potential buyers who call and want to see your house in an hour, are you going to be able to leave the office to meet them? I doubt it. But a broker will be there.

That's the main downside of being a Fisbo. Unless you or your spouse can be available at the drop of a hat to meet potential buyers, you're doing yourself a great disservice. Besides, once people realize you're selling your house yourself, they'll automatically reduce their offers by the 6 or 7 percent you'd have paid a broker, so there's often no real savings.

Your lawyer will be the second member of your team. While the legal work attached to sale of a home is relatively simple, you should still find someone with a sense of urgency. You want a lawyer who will be able to have a contract ready within 12 hours of your call. You also want someone experienced. Odd, unexpected things can happen during a home sale. Title problems can crop up or an inspection will turn up previously unnoticed damage. And of course these crises usually occur just before you're scheduled to close the deal. When the unexpected happens, you'll be a lot happier if you have a lawyer who has been down that road before.

Setting Your Price Range

The asking price of your house will be tied to the recent selling prices of other homes in your community. Your broker will present you with a list of "comps," properties comparable to yours that have recently changed hands. They will be the barometer of what the market will bear. Make a list and note the highest and lowest selling prices in the group. You'll probably end up accepting a price somewhere between the two. You may be disappointed or you may be pleasantly surprised, but do be realistic. If you set a price that's too high, you're only kidding yourself and delaying the inevitable.

But don't be too conservative, either. Home buying is a negotiating process. It's almost certain that you'll end up accepting less than your asking price, so you'll want to start somewhat high. Keep in mind that these days the average difference between asking price and selling price of homes is about 7 percent. Of course, this will change depending on market conditions. If you live in a seller's market, it will likely be less. If you're in a buyer's market, it might be more.

Marketing Your Product

Selling a home requires the same marketing strategies that accompany the sale of any product. Your first step will be to work with your broker to describe the property in the real estate listings that go out to all the brokers in your area. (That's another plus in hiring a broker. Once a home is listed, any licensed broker can sell it. You'll have dozens of people working on your behalf, not just one.) You'll want to list all its desirable features—central air conditioning, a game room, a secluded lot—as well as any appliances and other items that will "convey," meaning they'll be part of the sale.

The next step is to make buyers aware of your product. Newspaper real estate listings are a traditional method, as are free real estate guides that are distributed in supermarkets and other locations. You should also use the Internet. Make sure your broker has a Web site and that photos of your home, inside and out, will be prominently displayed.

Once your house is on the market, you'll need to be ready for potential buyers who might show up with little notice. That means keeping the place neat and clean. You may or may not be there when they come through, so keep jewelry and other valuables in a safe place. If you are home when they show up, go take a walk or run some errands. Your presence will make it an uncomfortable visit for everyone.

Negotiating the Sale

With any luck, you'll have an offer soon after your house hits the market. Just remember, home buying is a negotiation. Any offers you receive will likely be considerably below your asking

Home-Selling Tips

Real estate brokers have turned the marketing and packaging of homes into a science. Here are some of their secrets for getting top dollar for a home:

- Focus first on curb appeal.

- Look for anything that detracts from the home's look or distinguishing features.

- Empty closets of unwanted clothes.

- Thin out furniture, giving away, selling, or storing the excess.

- Give the home a thorough cleaning, sprucing up floors, washing windows, and painting wherever needed.

- Consider having your own inspection done. It will tip you off to any defects and may even lead a naive buyer to go without their own.

- If improvements or renovations have been made without the required permits, clear the matter up with local authorities, insuring your home is completely legal.

- Add flowering plants in season outside.

- Keep fresh flowers on the table.

- Make sure shades or curtains are open and lights are on whenever the house is shown.

- Agree on the minimum notification you require for buyer visits. Insist on a telephone call before someone is brought to the home.

- If the house will always be open to potential buyers, keep it looking its best, with prompt cleanup after meals.

price. But the buyers will expect you to counter with a new asking price. This back-and-forth will continue until you've reached a price that's acceptable to both or it becomes apparent that your numbers are just too far apart.

Take your time and don't be pressured into accepting less money than you feel is fair. If you eventually become convinced that the buyer has reached his top offer, you have to either accept or wait for a new buyer to come along.

The other side of the coin is to have two or more parties interested in your house. In that case, the world is your oyster. Multiple buyers may end up bidding against each other and possibly even drive the final price above your initial asking price.

(See also closings, negotiating.)

HOME SECURITY

Here's the dirty little secret about home security: it's all about making your home harder to break into than your neighbor's.

Burglary always has been and always will be one of the most common crimes. A break-in occurs every 10 seconds in the United States. That's more than 3 million a year. It doesn't take long; a skilled burglar can get inside most homes in 60 seconds or less, regardless of how secure the locks are.

This is why the best approach to home security is to deter a burglar in the first place. If he really wants to get in, he'll get in. Your job is to make the job appear too difficult, so he goes elsewhere.

Lock Up

Home security begins with securing the home. Locking doors and windows seems like a no-brainer, but you'd be surprised how many people will leave the house without locking up. "I'll just be gone for an hour," they tell themselves. A burglar only needs a fraction of that time to be in and out. One-quarter of all burglaries occur because of unlocked doors and windows.

Don't assume you're safer during the day. Most break-ins occur between 9 A.M. and 4 P.M., when most people are at work and school. It makes sense. A burglar is more comfortable entering a vacant home than one in which people are present, even if they are sleeping.

Don't let the house look vacant when you're away on business trips or vacations. Alert the neighbors that you'll be gone. Install timers for inside lamps to make it appear that someone is home at night. Make sure the newspapers don't pile up on the porch and the mail is collected. Have someone keep the grass mowed.

Remove Hiding Places

Trim any trees and shrubs that might provide cover around doors and windows. Install floodlights that are activated by motion detectors. If a burglar feels exposed, he's less likely to pick your house. And while high fences and walls may add to your privacy, they also make it easier for a burglar to go about his work undetected.

Hide the Goods

Burglars will frequently spend a few moments peering in your windows before they decide to break in. If they don't see anything tempting, they may decide to move on. Use a cabinet for your electronic equipment and keep your valuables locked up. But don't hide them in the bedroom. That's the first place most burglars head for.

Improve Your Locks

Most burglars enter on the first floor, so you need to install the best locks you can find. The best door lock is a dead bolt, but even these can be kicked in with the proper effort. It's not the lock that's at fault; it's that everything else around the door is made of wood. You can add additional protection by buying a heavy-duty strike plate, the metal plate that receives the door latch. You can also set the strike plate with extra-long screws.

Window locks are even more problematic. Most are worthless. The best way to secure your windows is to drill a hole through the upper and lower sashes and screw them together. Of course, this means you can't open your windows either, so you only want to do this when you're going to be away for a length of time. Keep in mind, too, that if a burglar wants in badly enough, he'll just break out the glass. If you're home is secluded, the noise probably won't be a problem. For ultimate protection, install metal bars over your windows.

Alarm Systems

Alarm systems provide the best—and the most expensive—home security. A good system can cost $1,500 or more. If it's tied into a dispatch center or wired to your local police department, there will also be a service charge. False alarms can be a problem, bringing the police to your home unnecessarily and annoying the neighbors. Still, statistics show that alarm systems reduce burglaries by as much as 80 percent. They can also reduce your homeowner's insurance premiums.

Keeping Them Out versus Scaring Them Away

There are two schools of thought when it comes to home security systems: one is to keep the burglars from getting access to the home through perimeter protection; the other is to scare a burglar away after he has entered the home. Perimeter protection, such as wired doors and windows, is a more visible deterrent, but it tends to be less aesthetic and more prone to false alarms. Interior protection, such as motion and sound detectors, is a less obvious deterrent, but it is also less obtrusive or accident-prone. Alarm companies push for a system combining both. Personally, I'd advise you to opt for the perimeter protection. If security is an important enough issue for you to buy an alarm system, you should be willing to compromise on aesthetics.

The best alarm systems are those that cause the most racket. There's nothing like a screaming alarm inside and outside the house to send a burglar packing. Some systems now come with strobe lights as well. Not only do they confuse and frighten the burglar, they make it easy for the police to find your house.

Make it apparent that you have an alarm system. Security companies have little signs you can put in your yard and decals for your windows. If you don't have an alarm system, use them anyway. It's okay to lie to criminals.

Get a Dog
Of course, if you want to take the low-tech approach, buy a dog. The sound of a barking dog is enough to scare off most burglars. For one thing, they don't relish the idea of being bitten. They also worry that the dog's barking will alert neighbors to their presence. You get an inexpensive alarm system and a great companion all wrapped up in one package.

Before You Buy
Before you make any home security decisions, I suggest you consult your local police department. Most will come to your house and do a free crime-prevention audit. They'll point out vulnerable areas and make suggestions on how you can improve them. They'll also give you some idea of how prevalent break-ins are in your neighborhood and when they're most likely to occur.

HOMEOWNER'S INSURANCE

Do YOU KNOW how much homeowner's insurance you have? If you're like most people you haven't the foggiest idea. Considering that your policy could be all that's standing between your family and homelessness, you should be paying a bit more attention.

Don't feel too bad. Obviously you're not alone. Homeowner's insurance probably gets less consumer attention than any other form of insurance. That's because it's usually a last-minute purchase during the frantic days leading up to the closing on your home. Often it's the result of a quick call to the broker who handles your other coverage, or a name plucked from a telephone book. At that point, you're not that interested in the details. Your only real concern is that the policy meet the requirements of your lender.

For most people, that level of ignorance continues long after they move into their new home. The premiums are usually included in their monthly mortgage payment, so they're not even aware of when their policies expire and are renewed. The bill goes to the bank and a copy of the policy goes to the homeowner. In most cases, it's thrown into a drawer or filing cabinet with the policies from past years.

Analyze Your Needs

Homeowner's insurance deserves more attention than that. After all, if your home is damaged or destroyed, if you have a burglary, or if someone slips and falls on your property, your homeowner's coverage will suddenly become very important. Don't wait until something happens to find out whether or not it's adequate.

If you do, more than likely you'll discover that all or part of your coverage is not exactly what you need. Basic homeowner policies are just a starting point for coverage. We all have different situations, and our homeowner's coverage needs to be tailored to those situations. If you rely on a generic policy, the time may come when you'll regret that you didn't pay more attention.

Types of Homeowner's Insurance

Homeowners of relatively new homes have three types of progressively expensive coverage to pick from. In the industry, they're referred to as HO-1, HO-2, and HO-3. A fourth, HO-6, covers "unit" dwellers—people who own condominiums, coops, and lofts—and a fifth, HO-8, covers older homes.

Considering the value of what it protects, homeowner's insurance is relatively inexpensive. That's why I recommend my clients purchase HO-3 coverage. A good HO-3 homeowner's policy protects your home and possessions against just about everything. It will protect you from loss due to fire, lightning, wind and hail, smoke, vandalism, vehicle collision, theft, snow and ice, exploding appliances, burst pipes, and surges of electrical current. It even covers damage caused by civil disturbances.

An HO-3 policy won't cover damage from flood, earthquake, war, nuclear accident, and any other exclusion that may be specified. Home-business operators should note that it more than likely won't cover any business-related property that's in the house. Earthquake and flood damage protection can be purchased as separate policies. Unfortunately, there aren't any insurers out there who are willing to insure you against damage from war. If your house gets nailed by a Scud missile, you're on your own, and if there's a nuclear war, no one will be around to worry about rebuilding.

Your personal possessions are covered by an HO-3 policy, regardless of whether they're in your home or temporarily away from home. This includes items that may be in your car or in the possession of your children away at college.

An HO-3 policy also provides liability protection if someone other than a family member should be injured on your property or elsewhere because of unintentional acts or damage by you, your family, or your pets. It also covers intentional damage by children younger than 13.

Remember, too, that HO-3 coverage is only for newer dwellings. If you're one of those lucky people who owns a really old home—one that's loaded with charm but may be a little creaky in the rafters—you'll be relegated to HO-8 status. That means you may have trouble finding coverage against things like ice and snow damage, burst pipes, and the other calamities that frequently befall older houses.

Inventory Your Possessions

If your house burns down, are you going to be able to remember everything that was in it? Not likely. This is why making an inventory of your possessions is so important. Write down the serial numbers of your televisions, stereo, computers, and other electronic devices. Take photographs of your furniture, appliances, and other items. Even better, do a videotaping session of the entire house, room by room, closet by closet, and drawer by drawer. Don't forget the basement, attic, and garage.

Once you've completed your inventory, keep it stored in a safe deposit box or other secure location *outside your home.* And keep it updated as you make new purchases by adding the receipts to the file.

Floater Policies

If you have certain possessions for which your standard policy doesn't provide adequate protection, you can add layers of protection with floater policies. For example, most homeowner's policies limit coverage for silverware to no more than $2,000. If you need more, you can buy additional coverage for about $5 per $1,000 worth of silver. The same holds true for jewelry and other valuables. Be aware, though, that some companies may require sales slips or professional appraisals of your property before they'll agree to insure it under a floater policy. It's understandable. The potential for all sorts of scams is obvious.

If you have special equipment for a business operated from your home you should have floater coverage as well. You may want to investigate to see if you can buy special home office packages which cover equipment as well as liability claims by clients visiting your home.

Make sure your floater policies will pay off under all circumstances, including just plain losing things. (The insurance industry calls this "mysterious loss.")

Review Your Policy Regularly

Your homeowner's policy isn't doing you much good if it doesn't cover the real value of your possessions and the replacement cost of your home. The latter requires particular attention.

If you live in an area where home prices are rising sharply, and construction costs are on the increase, the replacement cost of your home could be increasing each year. Your coverage needs to increase right along with it. You also need to consider the value of an addition or other improvements to your home.

Make sure the policy provides you with "guaranteed replacement cost" coverage. With this the insurer promises to completely replace your house and any other structures that are on the property. It even includes replacement of landscaping and specimen trees.

If your home is valued at over $200,000, put your homeowner's insurance out for bid every

(See also earthquake insurance, flood insurance.)

year. High-end policies such as these are very attractive to insurers and you may be able to save premium dollars by finding a hungry insurer.

HOTEL RESERVATIONS

FORGET THOSE PRINTED RATE CARDS. Hotel room rates vary almost as much as air fares. Just as few people on airplanes pay the same fare, few people in hotels are paying the same room rate. That's why I'm always amazed at how people who will search high and low for the cheapest travel arrangements or the best deal on a new car will just make a hotel reservation and pay whatever they're asked to pay.

When making a hotel reservation, you should be prepared to bargain over the price. Hotel personnel are trained to quote the highest rate and then work downward. You need to use every trick you can to get their absolute bottom-line price.

Don't call a company's toll-free number to make a reservation. That will just connect you to a national reservation office. The person you speak to will have no authority to offer you anything other than the prescribed price, which is called the "rack rate" in the industry. Central reservation offices are useful for getting information on the locations and telephone numbers of hotels that fit your itinerary and on amenities such as swimming pools, restaurants, and health clubs.

When you're ready to make a reservation, you should call the hotel directly and ask to speak to the desk manager. He has the authority to bargain over prices. He also has the responsibility of keeping the hotel full, which will make him even more likely to give you a deal.

He'll begin, of course, by quoting you the highest price. Nothing ventured, nothing gained, right? You, in turn, will immediately ask if there are any special weekday or weekend rates, senior-citizen rates, or discount options available. If you're a member of the American Automobile Association or the American Association of Retired Persons, ask if you qualify for a discount. If the hotel has special corporate rates, use your employer's name when making the reservation. You can also ask if the hotel gives special rates to state or federal government employees.

Scout Before You Sign

If you've made a reservation, insist on seeing your room before you offer up your credit card. Many hotels try to hold onto their most desirable rooms as long as possible and fill up their mediocre facilities with guests who reserved in advance. If you don't like the room you've been assigned, ask for a better one when you return to the front desk. Odds are you'll be accommodated immediately.

The desk manager's willingness to bargain will be tied to his occupancy rate. Like seats on an airplane, rooms in a hotel are a perishable commodity. If the manager doesn't book a room for a particular night, he loses that money forever. If things are slow, he'll be more than happy to give you a discount. But if there's a convention in town, forget it. If he has any rooms left at all, he'll more than likely hold out for the full rate. If you don't take it, someone else will.

Some travelers have begun using the services of hotel brokers or discount programs. Brokers guarantee to fill a certain percentage of a hotel's rooms in exchange for a deep discount, sometimes even purchasing a block of rooms in advance. They then sell the rooms to the public at a discount. Some brokers require that you pay them directly. Others require you to pay the hotel.

A discount program can save you even more money. Typically, they use coupon books that you can purchase for $30 to $50. The coupons are good for 12 to 18 months. You can use the coupons to save up to 50 percent on the price of a room. Of course, that's 50 percent of the highest rate. Still, the savings are substantial. Most discount programs require that you reserve your room 30 days in advance, and they are only required to give you the discount if their occupancy rate during the time you intend to stay there is less than 80 percent.

The other way to save money is to participate in a "frequent-stay" program with one of the major hotel chains. They work like a frequent-flier program. You accrue points with every visit and eventually earn enough for a free night's lodging. Some also have arrangements with American Express or some other credit card company. In this case, the credit card company awards you points both for lodging fees and for the purchase of other services.

Here's one final tip. Once you've made a reservation and agreed upon a price, check back with the hotel every few days. Remember, hotel room prices are like air fares. They can change from day to day, or even hour to hour. If you find that the rate has dropped below what you were promised, grab it.

INDEPENDENT CONTRACTORS

I BELIEVE that people who work for small businesses should either be temps who actually work for an outside agency or independent contractors who, in theory, work for themselves. The reason is simple: employees cost more.

When you hire an employee, she comes with a built-in set of expenses over and above her salary. As her employer, you're responsible for half her Social Security taxes. You must also pay her worker's compensation and disability insurance premiums. You may need to pay her health insurance premiums, vacation pay, and other benefits. You may even have to contribute to her retirement plan. Besides costing more money, employees cost more time. There's a great deal of paperwork involved in having employees. For example, you'll need to withhold federal and state income taxes from her paychecks and make sure they get sent in to the proper offices at the proper times.

Hire a temp and the agency does all that. Independent contractors, on the other hand, are independent workers hired to perform specific tasks over a finite period of time. A good example of the employer–independent contractor relationship is the general contractor who builds homes. He doesn't have an army of masons, carpenters, plumbers, electricians, roofers, tile setters, and other tradespeople on staff. He hires them as he needs them. Because they're not his employees, he doesn't have to worry about their taxes and benefits. They show up when he calls them, he pays them when they're finished, and they go on to the next job.

There are other advantages to independent contractors. Because they're self-employed and generally work on a fee-for-service basis, they're more efficient. You won't find them hanging around the water cooler or taking long lunches or engaging in gossip. Time is money to them, so

Employee or Independent Contractor?

There isn't any one characteristic the IRS believes sets employees and independent contractors apart. Instead, the IRS looks at the preponderance of the evidence. The IRS considers workers to be employees if they generally:

- Are required to comply with instructions about when, where, and how they are to work

- Are trained by other employees and are required to attend meetings and other company-functions

- Provide services that are integrated into company functions

- Are required to render their services personally

- Work a schedule that's determined by the person hiring them

- Devote full time to the work, are told how much time they must spend working, and are told whether or not they can do work

- Perform their work on the premises of the person who is paying for the work

- Are told in what order their services must be performed

- Submit regular or written reports

- Are paid by the hour, week, or month

- Receive reimbursement for their business and travel expenses

- Are furnished with tools, materials, and other equipment

- Can quit without incurring any liability

- Can be fired

- Have a continuing relationship with the person hiring them

The IRS considers workers to be independent contractors if they generally:

- Pay for the facilities and equipment used in performing their service

- Realize profits and losses

- Perform services for two or more unrelated firms at the same time

• **Make their services available to the general public on a regular basis**

Obviously, these criteria aren't carved in stone. After just a brief reading I'm sure you can come up with many exceptions to them. Don't worry. These criteria are just offered to give you an idea of how the IRS will make judgments. Remember, its goal is to classify workers as employees. The burden of proving someone is an independent contractor will fall on you.

they operate with a greater sense of urgency than a full-time employee. The sooner they're finished with their job, the sooner they can move on to the next project.

Finding independent contractors is easy. Most are members of trade and professional associations and advertise in association publications. I've also found that, as with all professionals, good independent contractors quickly earn reputations in their industries and benefit enormously from word-of-mouth recommendations. Putting out a few queries among your colleagues can often put you in touch with a whole lineup of talented people.

Some independent contractors will find you before you realize you need them. Many are experts at helping businesses improve their efficiency and sell themselves with that strength. The most talented among them can help reduce your payroll while increasing your business's productivity at the same time. That's a hard combination to beat.

A good independent contractor is worth her weight in gold, so you should go out of your way to maintain a mutually beneficial relationship. If she performs a task that arises regularly, consider signing her to a long-term contract. One of the downsides of being an independent contractor is the constant search for employment. A regular assignment with a known client can be very reassuring.

Not surprisingly, the IRS has paid close attention to independent contractors over the years. To determine whether someone is an independent contractor or an employee, the IRS has developed a series of questions about the relationship between the worker and the employer. (See "Employee or Independent Contractor?" page 316.)

Without the IRS's criteria, employers would no doubt switch as many of their employees as possible over to independent contractor status and save a bundle. Trust me, it's not worth the risk. If the IRS determines that a person you've claimed is an independent contractor is indeed an employee, it can cost you a great deal of money.

The trick, then, is to carefully examine your business to determine how a legitimate independent contractor can save you money. In an ideal world, you'll operate just like the building contractor I mentioned earlier. When it's time for a task to be performed, you bring in the expert. When they're finished, you pay them. Result? No extra paperwork, no extra costs, and more money in your pocket.

_____

(See also employees.)

INFLATION

Put two economists in a room and you'll end up with three conflicting theories. The only thing economists agree on is that inflation is very bad. What is it that is so vile it can inspire consensus from the most disputatious bunch in the world? Inflation is, simply enough, the yearly increase in the cost of goods and services. Historically, the average increase in the Consumer Price Index, which is what the government uses to measure inflation, has been about 4 percent a year. This means that an item that costs $10 today will cost $10.40 next year. In two years it will cost $10.83. In five years, $12.17.

At first glance, this seems fairly tame. Why would it inspire such universal loathing? Take a look at what inflation does to the prices of real consumer items over time and you'll see why. Let's say the average price of a new car in 1998 was $20,000. By 2010, if inflation averages 4 percent, that same new car will cost $32,020. A house that cost $175,000 to build in 1998 will cost $280,181 to build in 2010.

Concerns over inflation can have enormous economic consequences. The mere mention of the "i word" by the Federal Reserve chairman can send markets into a tizzy. Many businesses will put off plans for expansion if they think the economy is headed into an inflationary period. It makes it difficult for them to plan for the costs of materials, labor, and other costs. They may also find it difficult to decide what to charge for their products in the future. This reduced investment slows economic growth.

Economists have debated the causes of inflation for years. Some believe that it happens because we _expect_ it to happen. Look at it this way. You no doubt look forward to a raise every year. One reason you expect that salary increase is your anticipation of an increase in the price of food, clothing, energy, and the other costs of living. Because your boss has to increase your salary and those of your coworkers, he has to charge more for the products or services he provides. That, in turn, raises the price of things once they reach the store shelves. So inflation, once entrenched in an economy, tends to be self-perpetuating.

Economists also recognize that inflation is characterized by a large money supply and relatively few goods. (The opposite of this, small money supply and a large inventory of goods, is deflation.) This means that the price of goods increases during times of high inflation. As dollars grow less valuable, the best hedges against inflation are real property—your house, jewelry, and other assets.

Here's an example of how inflation erodes the buying power of your money. If you have

$100 in cash sitting in your sock drawer and inflation is 4 percent, it will be worth only $96 in a year. In 10 years, it will be worth only $66. People whose incomes are indexed to inflation know their salaries will be adjusted upward to keep pace with inflation. They're assured the buying power of their incomes will not go down. (Social Security payments are adjusted for inflation, so you can rest assured that part of your retirement income will maintain its buying power.) But most people's incomes are not adjusted for inflation. Many fail to keep pace, particularly when inflation is high, and lose buying power. People on fixed incomes are especially vulnerable.

To investors, inflation represents an erosion of earnings. Let's say you have $1,000 in an investment. If it returns 10 percent, and inflation is 4 percent, you've realized a real return of 6 percent. If the investment returns 4 percent, however, all you've done is keep up with inflation. Even though your $1,000 investment is worth $1,040 after a year, its buying power is the same as it was a year ago. If the fund only returns 2 percent, the buying power of your money has actually decreased. An investment can only be considered profitable if it returns more than the rate of inflation.

Inflation is a critical factor for people investing for retirement. This is why conventional wisdom suggests that the further away you are from retirement, the more aggressive you should be in your investment strategies. Stocks and mutual funds, although risky, have the potential to provide returns that leave inflation in the dust. If retirement is many years away, you can afford to ride out the short-term ups and downs of the market in order to make sure in the long term you'll outpace inflation.

INFORMATIONAL INTERVIEWS

THE INFORMATIONAL INTERVIEW is a charade, yet it's a pretense that benefits everyone involved. In fact, the informational interview is one of the more useful business tools.

By cloaking what amounts to a job search in the garb of a fact-finding mission, the person looking for an opportunity increases the odds of getting to speak with someone, lowers expectations so success can be measured by more than just a job offer, and begins creating a network.

This camouflage works for the person who is approached for the interview as well. It reduces the pressure dramatically: Having the meeting means you're doing something for this person, who may have been referred by someone whose continued goodwill is prized. It also allows the "applicant" to become a resource, directly or indirectly: you may not have an opening, but you may know someone who does.

The key to getting the most from informational interviews is understanding and accepting the rules of the game. Remember, it's not a job interview; it's a fact-finding mission and an information-gathering tactic. It provides information that may lead to new business opportunities and projects, both inside and outside your particular industry. It's also a networking strategy, a method of building an eclectic list of business contacts.

Your primary goal in these interviews is to establish a connection. You need to go in with no expectations. Down the road it could lead to a job offer, a request for a service you provide, a purchase of a product you may be selling, or a reference to someone who can use your service or product. Of course, nothing may ever come of it. The important thing is that you're getting your name and your product or service in front of as many people as possible. And the more people you know, the more business opportunities you have.

The best way to get an informational interview is through people you already know. Perhaps you have a business associate with connections at a company you'd like to learn more about. If you ask him to arrange a meeting with the company, he'll be more than happy to do it. For one thing, he knows that you'll do the same for him down the line. And if, by chance, the meeting leads to a profitable business arrangement, everyone will be extremely grateful to him for his role as matchmaker.

You don't have to rely on business associates alone. Your friends are also potential links to informational interviews. Each has a wide social and business network you can tap into. Sometimes the best connections come from the most unexpected sources.

If you don't have a personal connection, your only option is to make an approach on your own. You can call and ask for an appointment with the person you'd like to meet. Or you may be more comfortable sending a cover letter or e-mail with some promotional material and then follow up with a telephone call. Whatever you do, don't just show up at the person's office unannounced with the excuse that you "just happened to be in the neighborhood." That shows great disrespect and you risk being regarded as more of an annoyance than anything else.

In your telephone call or letter, explain that you understand how busy the person is but that you would greatly appreciate just a few minutes of his time. Don't underestimate the power of a little flattery. Telling him that you've heard a great deal about him can't hurt. Nor can intimating that you think of him as someone from whom you can learn a great deal.

Once you've set up the interview, take time to prepare for it. Know what it is you want to accomplish. Since you requested the meeting, it will be up to you to set the tone. Make a list of questions to ask and items you want to discuss. Arriving unprepared is as bad as arriving unexpectedly. It shows enormous disrespect and will guarantee that you'll be perceived as a lightweight.

Arrive at the interview at the appointed time. Once you've sat down, remember that time is money. You've been given a piece of the person's day and he will expect you to put it to good use. Again, preparation is the key. Tell him why you wanted to meet. Explain what you do and that you're interested in learning more about his business and exploring whether there may be opportunities for you both.

An informational interview calls for a bit more humility than a job interview. You're on his turf and his time, so you need to act like it. Ask him how he got in the business and what has brought him his success. Encourage him to talk about himself and listen attentively. If the conversation turns away from business, listen for opportunities to forge a social relationship. Perhaps you'll find he's an avid golfer or a fan of a certain author. Make a note to invite him for a round at your club or send him a book.

Keep an eye on the clock while you talk. If you've asked for 30 minutes of his time, start to wrap things up when the half-hour is over. If he wants to keep things going, he'll let you know. And if you see that the conversation has run out of steam after 15 minutes, thank him for his time and leave. Forcing him to sit there for another 15 minutes and watch you spin your wheels is not going to make a very good impression. Before you leave, ask him if he can suggest other people you might want to visit to discuss your business.

After your meeting, send a note thanking him for his time and touching on a few of the key points that came up during your discussion. This is also your chance to mention that round of golf or send that book. A small personal gesture like that can cement a new business relationship.

(See also job interviews, networking.)

INITIAL PUBLIC OFFERINGS

ONE MORNING during the spring of 2000, when the Nasdaq and its arsenal of tech stocks was going through the roof, I heard a radio commentator report that there were an average of 63 new millionaires being created every day in Silicon Valley. I'll bet that everyone of those folks was riding the wave of an IPO.

An IPO, or initial public offering, is just what it says—a public offering of stock in a company that had previously been privately held. Companies that have reached a certain size and level of success usually "go public" by selling shares in themselves to anyone who wants to buy. They then use the large infusion of cash they receive to finance the new buildings, equipment, and employees they need to continue growing.

The 63 new Silicon Valley millionaires referred to on the radio were no doubt employees of Internet start-ups who had been issued large quantities of company stock in lieu of pay. The day their companies went public, they woke up just average folks with a whole lot of stock worth very little money; by the time they went to bed, they were very wealthy people (on paper, anyway).

Investing in IPOs

For investors, IPOs carry a great deal of risk and an equal amount of potential reward. Investors who buy in on the first day (or "get in on the ground floor," to use Wall Street jargon) almost always fall into one of two groups. The first group are *short-term speculators* who hope to make a quick profit on the volatile price shifts that often accompany an IPO. The price of a stock that's being offered in an IPO is set by the company and the investment bankers who agree to underwrite the IPO and sell all the public shares.

When trading begins, the price can be bid through the roof by investors anxious to have a piece of the company. The IPOs of some of the better-known technology companies have seen opening prices increase fourfold or more by the end of the day. (Of course, the opposite can also happen. Sometimes the public will be far less enamored of a stock than the investment bankers, and its price can actually decrease.)

After that, it's often anybody's guess as to what will happen. Prices can move crazily in any direction. Speculators, if they didn't get in and out in the first frenzied moments of trading, will watch the price carefully for the next few days or weeks, waiting to sell their stock and get out at the right moment. But when is the right moment? It's impossible to say. In an IPO, prices have virtually nothing to do with a company's performance and everything to do with investor demand.

The second group of IPO investors are *people looking for long-term growth and profit.* They examine the financial health and prospects of the company issuing the IPO, just as they would any other company they were considering investing in. They consider the growth potential of the company's industry and examine its current and potential market share. They are interested in the history of the company: some successful businesses have operated privately for years before going public. They consider the reputation of the investment banking firm that's underwriting the IPO. If they make the decision to invest, you can bet they're planning on holding onto their stock for a long time.

Invest Carefully

My advice is to follow the approach of the latter group. I advise my clients to treat an IPO just as they would any other stock: research before you buy. Any company that's planning to go public will issue a prospectus with a detailed analysis of its finances, its products, or services, and the background and experience of its management.

If you're interested in IPOs, a good broker will have plenty for you to pick from. Just make sure you do your homework and ask the right questions before you part with your money.

One more thing: If you become interested in a really hot IPO, it will help if you know somebody. The best issues can attract so much investor demand that brokers actually have to ration the shares they're allotted. Unless you're one of your broker's better customers, you might find yourself out of luck.

INSURANCE SALESPEOPLE

Insurance salespeople are like fleas: once they get into your home you can't get rid of them. While there are exceptions, as a rule, insurance salespeople are overly aggressive, annoyingly upbeat, cloyingly solicitous, and, far too frequently, unscrupulous. Few are motivated by providing service to their clients. Most focus on accumulating commissions, which can be as high as the customer's first annual premium bill. That's why it's common for insurance salespeople to try to resell to customers a few years after they purchased a policy: the commission on the original sale has run out and the salesperson is hungry for more.

Insurance salespeople also offer a dizzying array of products. If you have ever had the misfortune of inviting an insurance salesperson into your home you know how confusing it can be. You will be asked to wade through a seemingly endless assortment of coverages. Your kitchen table will quickly covered with brochures and charts and graphs illustrating how premiums and benefits will change along with your life circumstances. And, if you're looking for life insurance, you'll get the hard sell to purchase whole life coverage—which the salesman will call "permanent insurance"—rather than term coverage. Perhaps that's because a whole life policy pays 10 times the commission of a term policy,

Still, insurance is a valuable and much needed tool of modern life. It provides peace of mind and protects our families and assets. And, despite the stereotype, there are some knowledgeable professionals out there who are very good at what they do. The secret is finding them.

Agents and Brokers

There are two types of insurance salespeople. Knowing the differences between them is critical if you plan on getting the best insurance coverage at the cheapest price.

The first kind of insurance salesman is the agent. He's a man on a mission: to sell you a policy at all costs. He's also apt to know a lot more about the art of selling than he is about the fine points of insurance.

This is because, as an agent, he represents a single insurance company, and because he represents just one company, he's limited to that company's products. They may be entirely inappropriate for your particular needs, but that doesn't matter. He's a salesman. He can and will do everything he can to leave with a signed contract. If he doesn't get one the first time around, he'll keep on trying. The telephone will continue to ring and letters will continue to arrive in the mail. As you might guess, he has trouble taking no for an answer.

A broker, on the other hand, works for her clients. Rather than selling the products of a single company, she will represent many products from many companies. Unlike her agent counterpart, she will have been required to pass a licensing exam and will therefore have a good understanding of your needs and the products that can meet them. She will be a good listener and will work hard to match you with the kinds of insurance products that meet your needs and your budget.

Don't let down your guard, however. A broker will be just as interested in getting you to sign a contract as an agent. After all, this is how they make their living. But a broker will be better trained, better informed, less biased, and able to offer you a much greater selection of products than an agent. In my opinion, they're the only people to deal with when buying insurance.

Look For Certification

Good insurance brokers take every opportunity to hone their professional skills. The more they know, the more they can offer you. When looking for life insurance, for example, you should only deal with brokers who are designated as certified life underwriters (CLUs) and certified insurance consultants (CICs). These designations mean they have passed rigorous training and testing. Although these designations are no guarantee of professional ethics, they do mean the brokers have received some of the best training in the industry.

Where to Find Insurance Brokers

Insurance brokers aren't difficult to find. You can find dozens in the Yellow Pages. Professional associations are another source of names. But just as I do when advising my clients on selecting other professionals, I recommend word of mouth. Ask friends and business associates for recommendations. People whose life situations are similar to yours are particularly useful. If they have someone they like, they'll be more than happy to share the name with you. That way you'll have some security in knowing that others have benefited from the broker's advice.

I recommend that you select someone who has been in business a minimum of five years. Consider a broker with a medium-sized firm that may have its own claims department, perhaps speeding up settlement of any claims you file. When you first meet with the broker, let her know what coverage you need and ask her to give you four or five options for each. Take your time to inspect each one and compare them with each other. If you're not satisfied with the choices she has given you, find another broker to deal with.

(See also life insurance, word of mouth.)

INTERNET SERVICE PROVIDERS

EVERY BUSINESS, no matter how large or how small, whether it sells to other business or to consumers, regardless of what it does, needs to be an e-business. And every individual, no matter how old, and whatever their profession or location, needs to be online. The Internet is the most powerful communication tool ever invented. After the invention of radio, it was 50 years before there were 50 million radio users. Television was much quicker, taking only 10 years to attract 50 million users. But the Internet outpaced them both. It hit the 50 million mark only four short years after its birth. Online commerce, increasing called e-commerce, is already measured in billions of dollars annually. Many believe the trillion-dollar mark isn't far off.

No matter what you use the Internet for, you need to be connected by an Internet service provider, or ISP. You have a number of options, each offering increasing speed at increasing prices. The least expensive, a dial-up service, will link you through a modem and the same copper wires used by the telephone companies. It might cost as little as $20 a month. But it's also the slowest.

The next option, and the one I think will become most popular with small businesses and home consumers in the near term, is a cable connection. For the past 25 years, cable television companies have been creating the perfect infrastructure for transmitting data. For $40 or $50 a month, you can have an Internet connection 100 times faster than the fastest dial-up service.

At the other end of the spectrum are several state-of-the-art connections that provide lightning-fast data transfer at premium prices. One option is an integrated services digital network (ISDN) line. Like dial-up access, it uses regular telephone lines, but it's completely digital, which means you won't need a modem. An even faster solution is an asymmetrical digital subscriber line (ASDL). With a speed of 1.5 million bytes per second delivered over regular telephone lines, ASDL is being touted as the first national standard.

Of course, if you want to be really wired, you can get a direct connection to the Internet via a T-1, T-2, or T-3 line. These use fiber-optic cables that send data at literally the speed of light.

Of course, unless you're running a business the size of Amazon.com, it's unlikely you'll need that capacity (or expense).

If you decide to create a Web site for yourself or your business, you'll probably want your ISP to maintain your site on one of its servers. When you do this, you're renting memory on the machine's hard drive, much as you'd rent a storefront for a conventional business. The more memory you need, the more you pay each month. If your site is large enough and has enough traffic, you may need to have your own dedicated server.

You may also want your ISP to be in charge of maintaining your site—updating information, adding new pages, and deleting outdated ones. This is often the easiest option for small business owners who don't have the budget to hire a full-time webmaster. Not all ISPs offer complete services, though, so you'll need to shop around carefully before you make a decision. Here are a few of the questions you need to ask:

- Does the ISP provide round-the-clock technical support?

- What percentage of the ISP's connection capacity is used?

- What kind of server will house your Web site?

- How many other clients will share your server?

- Is the server secure?

- Does the ISP have a backup system?

- Does the ISP offer all the technical expertise you'll need?

- Does the ISP charge transaction-based fees?

- Is the ISP willing to contract month-to-month?

- What, if anything, will the ISP expect you to do?

If you choose to have your ISP host and maintain your Web site, you need to determine what sort of server arrangement you need. Most small businesses and individuals make out just fine sharing a server with other businesses, individuals, and organizations. Traffic to the sites is modest enough that access doesn't become an issue and all the residents on the server manage to carry out their activities without getting in one another's way. But if your site is quite large with a great deal of interactivity, you may need your own exclusive server.

One last thing: e-commerce and everything else connected with the Internet is evolving at a furious pace. What's state-of-the-art today could be completely obsolete a month from now. This means that anyone who hopes to be successful in this brave new world must be extremely vigilant. Granted, your ISP should be monitoring changes in order to provide you with the best service possible. But don't assume anything. Become a student of the technology and do your homework. To do otherwise is to miss opportunities.

(See also e-mail, Web sites.)

INVENTORY

THE BEST INVENTORY IS NO INVENTORY. This is because inventory costs money. When you have a ton of goods sitting on your shelves, it's like having your money sitting there. This is not where your money should be. Your money should be sitting fat and happy somewhere it can earn you some interest.

If you purchased the inventory with borrowed money, the situation is even worse. Not only are you losing out on the profits the money could generate in an investment account, you're paying interest on it as well. This is a double whammy that can cut deeply into your bottom line.

Savvy entrepreneurs in all industries realize you should only have enough inventory on hand to meet your immediate needs. In fact, the concept has a name: "just-in-time inventory." Auto makers take delivery of parts just in time to slap them on vehicles that are rolling down the assembly line. Retailers schedule the arrival of merchandise just in time for the beginning of a new season or a big sale. The producers of that merchandise receive the raw materials for production just in time to craft it into product and fill orders.

The key to keeping inventory to a minimum is to turn it over as quickly as possible after you receive it. If you're a retailer, for example, you should only keep enough inventory on hand to meet projected sales for a short period of time—maybe two or three weeks—while timing orders of new merchandise to arrive just as the old merchandise is headed out the door. The more times you can turn over your stock each year, the less money you'll have tied up in inventory. (This is called "stock-to-sales ratio.")

If you're in mail order or operate a retail business on the Internet, you might be able to eliminate inventory altogether. One of the great things about mail-order and Internet retailing is that, unlike a retail storefront, you don't always need to have merchandise on hand to make a sale. You just need to be able to get it to your customers within the promised time frame.

The first way to accomplish this is to have items drop-shipped when you receive an order. Under this arrangement, when you receive an order you notify the manufacturer, who bills you and then ships the merchandise directly to the customer. It never passes through your hands.

If you can't arrange for drop-shipping, you can take advantage of the window of time between when you receive an order and when you ship the merchandise. The shorter the time frame for delivery, the greater the need to keep inventory on hand. For example, if you promise shipment immediately, you'll need to have a certain amount of inventory on hand when orders arrive.

But if your customers expect to wait a week or two for their purchases to arrive, you may be able to wait until you've amassed a week's worth of orders and then purchase the merchandise needed to fill them. You've already been paid for the merchandise by your customers and you'll use this money rather than your own to pay for the merchandise. When it arrives, you ship it right out to them. It's about as fast an inventory turnover as you could ask for.

The key to this approach is finding suppliers who can guarantee shipment of your merchandise in time for you to fulfill your own delivery commitments to your customers. With the good selection of next-day and second-day delivery options available this should not be a problem. (Keep in mind that there are strict Federal Trade Commission regulations regarding timely delivery of merchandise. They're not to be fooled with.)

The faster you can get inventory from a supplier, the more options you have in filling your orders. For example, if you have a reliable supplier who can promise delivery within a week, and you promise delivery to your customers within two to three weeks, you can wait until you have a week's worth of orders before you purchase the inventory to fill them. When the merchandise arrives, you still have plenty of time to get it to your customers within the promised time frame.

Having said all this, I should also point out that juggling orders and inventory in this manner can be hard to do. First of all, depending on what you're selling and the type of people you're selling to, a two- to three-week wait may just not be acceptable. This will certainly be the case if they can get the same item more quickly from someone else. And finding suppliers who can get merchandise to you in the requisite time frame is not always possible. Nevertheless, if you can find the right customers, the right products, and the right suppliers, it's a fantastic way to do business.

(See also suppliers and vendors.)

INVESTMENT CLUBS

INVESTMENT CLUBS ARE PERFECT for people uncomfortable with making independent investment decisions. These clubs are small groups of people who pool their money to make modest investments in the stock market. They get together periodically, usually once a month. They all put in the same amount of money each month and then decide jointly what stocks to purchase.

Even the most risk-aversive individuals find investment clubs palatable. There are more than 8,000 investment clubs in the United States, and with the market performing the way it has for the last decade, more are no doubt starting every week. The most famous club is undoubtedly the Beardstown Ladies, a group of women from Beardstown, Illinois, whose alleged investing prowess was the topic of a best-selling book a few years ago.

Some investment clubs have as few as 15 members and require an investment of as little as $10 a month. Others have monthly contributions of $100 or more. Members are asked to find potential investments, conduct research on their picks, and present the findings to the rest of the club members. After some discussion, the members vote on whether or not to purchase the stock in question. They can also vote to sell a stock if they agree they're unhappy with its performance.

In a way, investment clubs are like mutual funds in which the members together play the role of fund manager. Most clubs have 15 to 30 stocks in their portfolio. Club members buy shares in the club with their monthly contributions, and each person's current holdings in the portfolio are measured by the number of shares they own and the value of each share. I know people who have been in investment clubs for decades and have amassed tens of thousands of dollars with their modest monthly deposits.

I think investment clubs are excellent ways to learn the basics of investing. Because each member has the responsibility of scouting out candidate stocks, they learn how to read stock tables and prospectuses, how to evaluate such markers as earnings per share and price-earnings ratio, and how to use other analytical tools. They become avid readers of *Barron's, Fortune, The Wall Street Journal,* and other financial publications. Many eventually become confident enough to make substantial investments on their own in the same stocks their club has invested in.

Although I've never seen data from a formal study, my own experience with investment club members leads me to believe that they generally do well. One client of mine who puts $30 each month into her club's coffers, reports that the value of the club's portfolio grew 91 percent in 1999. Of course, much of that was on the coattails of one stock that quadrupled in value in the few months the club owned it. Still, when she showed me the club's year-end statement, it showed that only 2 of the 18 stocks in its portfolio had lost money. Many mutual fund managers would love to be able to make the same claim.

(See also mutual funds, stocks.)

IRAS

I F YOU'RE RELYING SOLELY on individual retirement accounts, or IRAs, to fund your golden years you're in a lot of trouble. While designed as retirement devices, today they're more realistically viewed as tax-avoidance tools.

If you and your spouse both work you can each invest up to $2,000 each year in your own individual retirement account. If only one of you works outside the home, you can contribute up to $2,000 a year in your own IRA and deposit $2,000 a year in a spousal IRA. If your employer doesn't offer a retirement plan, you are almost always allowed to deduct the full IRA contribution from your taxable income, and not pay taxes on the money until you begin to withdraw from your account many years down the road. There's also a nice break in the timing of contributions. You can open an IRA anytime up to April 15 and claim a deduction against the previous year's taxes.

Things get a bit more complicated if you or your spouse are eligible for employer-sponsored retirement plans. In this case you can deduct the full $2,000 annually only if you are single and have an adjusted gross income (that's a line on your federal tax return) of $32,000 or less or if you are married, filing jointly, with a combined adjusted gross income of $52,000 or less.* If you aren't eligible for your company's retirement plan, but you are married to someone who is eligible under an employer's plan, you can make the full $2,000 annual contribution only if you file a joint tax return and your combined adjusted gross income is $150,000 or less. If you have any questions about how the complex rules impact your eligibility, speak with an accountant.

What Can IRAs Be Invested In?

IRA money can be put into just about anything you can imagine. If you're not a risk taker, you can put your IRA money into a certificate of deposit. If you want to be more aggressive, your IRA can invest in mutual funds, stocks, bonds, gold and silver coins, or even real estate. You can switch investments if you choose, depending on the rules of the bank or brokerage. You can also have an IRA with one institution switched to an IRA with another institution.

Traditional IRAs

A traditional IRA is the plain vanilla version of the plan. The numbers are simple. You can contribute up to $2,000 a year to your account ($4,000 if you're married and your spouse doesn't work) and deduct that amount from that year's taxes. Your contributions and earnings grow interest-free until you begin to withdraw them. Like most retirement plans, you can't begin to take money out until age 59½ and you must begin by age 70½.† If you dip into the account before you turn 59½, you'll pay a penalty of 10 percent of the amount you withdraw unless:

1. You're a first-time home buyer. If you are buying your first house, you can make a limited one-time withdrawal from your IRA or your spouse's IRA to put toward the down payment. You can also use the money to help a child or grandchild buy their first house.

---

*These limitations increase each year: to $33,000 and $53,000 in 2001, to $34,000 and $54,000 in 2002, to $40,000 and $60,000 in 2003, to $45,000 and $65,000 in 2004, to $50,000 and $70,000 in 2005, to $50,000 and $75,000 in 2006, and to $50,000 and $80,000 in 2007 and thereafter.

†There's an interesting loophole in the rules about mandatory withdrawals from IRAs, Keoghs, and SEPs. You can stretch out the withdrawals by naming a beneficiary younger than yourself. When you do that, the calculation involves using a joint life-expectancy table rather than a single-life table. If you name a younger beneficiary who is female the withdrawals will be stretched out further still since female life expectancy is longer than male.

2. You have higher-education expenses. You can also use money from your IRA to pay "qualified" higher-education expenses for yourself, your spouse, or your children and grandchildren.

You are also allowed to borrow from an IRA once a year for up to 60 days without paying any interest, making it a possible source of short-term emergency funds. However, if the money isn't returned within 60 days, the withdrawal is subject to tax and penalties.

Roth IRAs

The Roth IRA (named after Delaware senator William Roth) has become the IRA of choice for two simple reasons. One, you pay no taxes on your money when you withdraw it. And two, within certain guidelines, you can withdraw money any time you want to. However, you can't begin to withdraw earnings until your account is five years old. If you take any earnings out of the account before that time, you pay a 10 percent penalty. Like a traditional IRA, you can also withdraw money without penalty for a first-time home purchase.

Of course, there is a catch. Because you pay no taxes on your withdrawals, your contributions aren't tax-deductible. There are also limitations on who can start a Roth IRA. Single taxpayers earning less than $95,000 are eligible, as are married taxpayers (filing jointly) who earn less than $150,000. Apparently, the government feels that anyone earning more than that doesn't need the tax break.

Converting to a Roth IRA

People whose adjusted gross incomes are less than $100,000 can, if they wish, switch their traditional IRAs into Roth IRAs. Although you won't be assessed a 10 percent penalty for early withdrawal, you will be expected to pay income tax on the money you're moving. People who made the switch prior to 1999 were given four years to pay the taxes. Unfortunately, if you're just learning about your ability to switch to a Roth, you won't be extended the same courtesy.

But it might not matter. Transferring your traditional IRA into a Roth is not always a great move, particularly if it's an IRA that you've been contributing to for years. The big issue is the income tax. If you have to cover it from the money in your account, you're negating years of growth and substantially reducing the value of the account. So if you can't cover the taxes from current income, leave your money where it is.

It doesn't take a rocket scientist to figure out if a conversion makes sense or not. Still, if you're not comfortable running the numbers yourself, my advice is to visit an good financial planner or accountant and let him crunch the numbers for you. There are also a number of Web sites that allow you to plug in the figures and do the calculations yourself.

JEWELRY

Aʟʟ ᴛʜᴀᴛ ɢʟɪᴛᴛᴇʀs is not gold.

That, in a nutshell, describes the problem with buying jewelry. It's extremely easy for the unwary to get taken. Poor-quality, fake gemstones and questionable metals abound in the jewelry marketplace. To protect yourself, you need to know how to distinguish quality from junk.

It begins with buying from a reputable jeweler. A flagship retailer like Tiffany's or Cartier, for example, is not going to rip you off. Neither are other established stores. Good reputations in the jewelry business are hard to earn and easy to lose. All it takes is one "incident" for a jeweler's credibility to vanish. They're all well aware of this, and they won't knowingly misrepresent pieces to their customers.

Notice I said "knowingly." Even trustworthy jewelers can sometimes be taken. If they are, and a poor-quality or fake piece somehow gets passed on to you, you can be sure they'll settle the matter quickly and to your satisfaction. Again, they have too much to lose.

You also need to educate yourself before you buy.

Evaluating Precious Metals

When evaluating gold, silver, and other precious metals, you should look for the quality mark. This mark is required by law. It identifies the manufacturer and describes the percentage of precious metal that's alloyed with other metals. Sterling silver, for example, must have at least 92.5 percent silver. Gold jewelry uses karats (k) to designate quality. The higher the number of karats, the greater the gold content. The best gold jewelry has a quality mark of 14k (58.5 percent gold) or 18k (75 percent gold). No jewelry is made from pure (24k) gold. It's too soft.

332

To qualify as gold, a piece of jewelry must be made from at least 10k (41.6 percent) gold. Some pieces are "gold-filled." This means that 10k gold has been bonded to the surface of another metal. The gold must account for at least 20 percent of the weight and have a quality mark. Other pieces are electroplated with a thin layer of gold. They, too, must have a quality mark.

Don't be fooled by the term "solid gold." All it means is that a piece hasn't been hollowed out. It can still be made from 10k gold. The quality mark will tell you.

Evaluating Gemstones

Evaluating gemstones involves four criteria: cut, color, clarity, and carats. The cut of a stone affects both its shape and its brilliance. The color of diamonds is graded from D (flawless and completely clear) to Z (tinged with yellow or brown). Other stones are also evaluated for their color. Clarity is also graded, from FI (flawless) to I (imperfect). Finally, carats are used to indicate weight. A carat weighs 200 milligrams. All else being equal, the heavier a stone, the more expensive it is.

You also need to know the difference between the terms "natural," "synthetic," and "imitation." Natural gems are found in nature. Synthetic gems have the same composition as natural gems but are made in laboratories. Imitations are just that. They look like real stones but have just a fraction of their value.

Shopping Tips

Once you're in the store, pay attention to a few things. Make sure that any piece you're considering has a quality mark on both the clasp and the jewelry itself. Otherwise you might end up with a quality clasp attached to real piece of junk.

Don't pay attention to wholesale offers or discounts. Wholesale prices are given to dealers. You're not a dealer. And the term "discount" is meaningless. Discounted from what? More than likely, it's discounted from an exorbitant price down to what it's really worth.

Unless you have the utmost faith in the jeweler, you should always have gemstones evaluated by an independent appraiser. If the jeweler is legitimate and honest, he won't be offended by your request. Don't use an appraiser recommended by the jeweler. Find someone who is certified by the National Association of Jewelry Appraisers or some other professional association. Offer the jeweler your credit card number as security while you have the stone in your possession. If the appraiser feels the stone is of poor quality or overpriced, return it to the jeweler and thank him for his time.

If you do buy, make sure to get a detailed receipt. It should include the type of setting used, the quality of the gold or silver, and the ratings and weight of the gemstones. Ask for a money-back guarantee if the descriptions of the piece turn out to be in error. If the jeweler is honest, he'll give you one without protest.

Here's one final piece of advice: Don't overspend. Have a budget when you begin shopping for a piece of jewelry and stay within it. It might not be easy. A good salesperson and a display case full of glittering baubles (you'll never find better lighting than in a jewelry store) can cause your head to spin—and your wallet to open. Most jewelers aren't required to put prices on their pieces, and that can make it even more difficult. The only reason to move beyond your budget is if you can't find what you want for that price. At that point, either move up in price or leave the store.

JOB INTERVIEWS

IRONICALLY, YOU'LL ALWAYS come across best in interviews for jobs you don't really want. Why? Because unconsciously you've become the buyer rather than the seller.

In every interview there's a seller and a buyer. Most applicants approach job interviews as if they're the seller, and a desperate seller at that. They come in eager to convince the interviewer that they're the right person for the job. They give total control over to the interviewer. That's why job interviews are incredibly nerve-racking for most people. They feel there's so much at stake, they have so little time to make an impression, and they have no control over their fate.

When you consciously approach the interview as if you're the buyer, there's an incredible transformation. It's only human nature that if you act like the buyer, the interviewer will start acting like the seller. Suddenly you're in control of your own destiny; you're deciding whether this is the right job for you, rather than the interviewer deciding whether you're right for the job. The interviewer actually begins to recruit you.

Obviously, approaching a job interview this way takes a great deal of confidence and self-assurance. If you've been out of work for months and you're worried about hungry mouths at home, that degree of aplomb can be tough to come by. Still, it's essential you appear that confident, even if you're not.

Years of advising job-hunting clients have led me to arrive at the following eight points as the keys to turning the job interview around and getting an offer.

Look for the Offer, not the Job

Don't clutter your mind with internal debates about whether or not you want the job. Don't start worrying about how you'll fit in or what the commute will be like. Your objective in a job interview should be to land a job offer, not a job itself. Do everything you can to impress and dazzle the interviewer. Only after receiving an offer should you even start to think about whether or not you really want the job.

Exude Confidence

I don't mean that you should be smart-alecky or cocky, I mean being self assured. Studies have shown that the most critical time in an interview is the first three minutes. Often the decision to hire or not hire will be made within that short a time frame. After all, your résumé has already been reviewed and passed scrutiny.

The importance of first impressions amplifies the need for self-assurance. Arrive on time, with a smile, shake hands firmly, and make eye contact. Your dress and grooming should be impeccable, and your perfume or cologne should be understated. When you leave the interview, you don't want your interviewers to smell you for the next hour while they discuss your merits.

Don't forget the power of body language. Lean forward when making a point or answering a question. Sit back, break eye contact to indicate you're thinking, and take your time when pondering a question. When you're ready to answer, reestablish eye contact. Don't slouch or cross your arms or legs, and try to keep your hands from fluttering about. I once interviewed a job candidate who had an annoying habit of constantly putting her hands in front of her face and making "quote" signs with her fingers to emphasize what she was saying. She "didn't" get the job.

Have a Sense of Humor

Humor takes the edge off any situation. I'm not suggesting you go in and do a stand-up routine. I'm just pointing out that you need to relax, enjoy yourself, and let your personality show through. If you're stiff as a board, the interviewer can only assume that you're always that way. That is not an assumption that works in your favor. You want to show her that you're good company in addition to being qualified for the job. A good sense of humor is a well-known sign of intelligence. What if the interviewer is humorless? In that case you probably wouldn't want to work there anyway.

Know Who You're Speaking With

An interview is like any other semiadversarial situation: the more you know about your opponent, the stronger your position. You can research the company by going through recent annual reports and product literature and visiting its Web site. Look up articles about the company to get a sense of its position within the industry and learn of any issues it might be facing. The more knowledge you can naturally demonstrate during your interview, the better an impression you'll make. Even if all your knowledge isn't made manifest, it will boost your confidence, and that will be obvious.

You should also try to learn as much as possible about your interviewers. It makes it much easier to make small talk. It also allows you to have meaningful discussions about their relationship to the position you're interviewing for. Granted, it's not always possible to get much information, particularly if you have no mutual acquaintances. But if you're interviewing for another position within the company you already work for, if the company is in the same industry as you're currently working in, or if the company is local, you should be able to get plenty of information on any individual interviewer simply by tapping into your network. No man or woman is an island.

Be Prepared

Job interviews can be like roller-coaster rides, quickly going from the predictable to the unexpected. The better prepared you are, the more at ease you'll be. One way to prepare is to make a list of all the questions you can think of that you're likely to be asked. Many of them will be easy to predict—and equally easy to answer. "Why do want to work here?" "Where do you see yourself in five years?" "Describe the most difficult problem you've had to deal with and tell us how you solved it."*

Other questions, however, might come out of the blue and catch you off guard. Sometimes these are designed more to gauge your reaction than anything else. Don't get flustered. After all, if they weren't interested, they wouldn't be talking to you. And don't pretend you know an answer. If you're at a loss, admit it. The worst thing you can do is try to wing it and risk talking yourself right into a corner.

Make a list of questions for your interviewer, as well. This makes you appear motivated and interested. It also keep the meeting from being an inquisition. Make the interviewer sell you on the company and the job. Don't let her assume you're automatically going take the job if it's offered to you.

Know Your Business

The skills and knowledge required to stay on top in many professions change at breakneck speed these days. Make sure you're up to date in the latest changes in your profession. If you've let things pass you by, it won't take the interviewer long to figure that out.

If you're applying for a position in a different industry, be prepared to make the case for why your skills will fit. And be prepared to make it over and over again. Having an applicant who doesn't fit the mold often sends up a red flag, particularly in a large corporation where an interviewer's ability to think creatively can be stifled by a long-standing and inflexible corporate culture. This may require you to do an end run of sorts, so plan accordingly.

Know Your Value

Your salary will certainly be a critical factor in deciding whether or not to accept the job. Make sure you know what people in your position are making, not only in the industry you're in but in the geographic region you'll be in. The cost of living varies widely around the country. If you're moving from an area that's been economically static to a boom town where the cost of housing and other necessities are going through the roof, you'll need a salary that will allow you to maintain, if not improve on, your former lifestyle.

Negotiate the Salary

Salary negotiations start with one party putting a number on the table. My advice? Keep your mouth shut. If you play your hand first, the rest of the conversation will be centered on lower-

---

*My favorite question is, "What is your biggest flaw?" Of course, the proper answer is, "I'm a workaholic."

ing the figure. If the interviewer is the first to throw out a number, the conversation will be about increasing it.

Here are two things to keep in mind. First, employers will always come to the table with a salary range, not a specific figure, that they're willing to pay. It will usually be centered on what the last person in the job was making. For example, if the person you're replacing was making $80,000, they'll probably have a range of about $70,000 to $90,000.

Second, if they really want you, they'll move out of that range. It's basic supply and demand. The more skills you offer, and the harder it is to find those skills, the more they'll be willing to pay. It's no accident that still-wet-behind-the-ears kids with exceptional information technology skills are being paid six-figure salaries right out of college. Some haven't even finished college. It's their skills that make them marketable, not a degree.

Play Hard to Get

It's unlikely you'll be offered the position and a salary on the spot unless you're meeting with the actual decision maker. If you are, thank the interviewer profusely. Say you're flattered by the job offer but you need time to think about it. If you're pressed for a reason for your hesitancy, tell the interviewer the salary is less than you had hoped for and once again ask for some time to think over the offer. You also might intimate that you're engaged in other interviews or considering other offers. Ask when an answer is expected and thank your interviewer for her time.

Your goal, of course, is to set the hook even deeper and squeeze as much money out of the company as possible. The largest salary increases come when you take a new job, not when you're given an increase by a current employer. And you will never be so powerful as you are before you are hired. At this point you are all potential. You are the unblemished possible messiah. If the interviewer is anxious to get things settled, she may increase the offer right then and there in an effort to get you to sign on at once. Or they may wait a day or two. Just don't overplay your hand and make things too difficult. You want to be hard to get, not impossible to get.

(See also annual reports, networking.)

JOINT OWNERSHIP

JUST AS THERE ARE NO SET RULES for remaining happily married, there are no ironclad principles for approaching finance as a couple. Some split everything fifty-fifty, regardless of who paid for what. Others divide things according to their relative incomes. For example, if one partner earns two-thirds of the couple's combined income, she will cover two-thirds of property costs and will also own two-thirds of all property. Some couples pool all their resources and their property. Others manage to create a hybrid of the three.

The Case for Joint Ownership

Most married couples—and a surprising number of unmarried couples—choose joint ownership (with right of survivorship) of their assets. They do this for a number of reasons. For many, it's a matter of commitment. It makes the marriage or relationship more of a partnership. It also streamlines the inheritance process. When one partner dies, the surviving partner gets everything, pure and simple. Another advantage is that property owned out of state passes to the survivor without probate in that state, further streamlining things.

Joint ownership protects both parties when things turn bad and divorce or a split-up is the only solution. Even though marital assets are supposed to be divided fairly, the fact that each party has their name attached to all the assets—the house, the investments, the cars—provides them with some degree of insurance.

Joint ownership is particularly useful for same-sex couples. Let's say two partners own a house jointly and one dies. The other partner gets the house automatically, regardless of whether or not there is a will involved. If there were only a will, the family of the partner who died could challenge it in court.

Joint ownership also has advantages for people who aren't romantically connected. If your mother is ill or infirm, for example, a bank account with both your names on it will make life—and death—much easier. You can pay her bills and taxes, purchase her groceries, and meet all her other living expenses.

To jointly own something, both names must be on the deed, title, or other ownership document. The term "with right of survivorship" is important. Without it, it can be argued that you held the property as tenants in common. This is a form of ownership in which property is divided into shares.

The Case Against Joint Ownership

You might think the issue is clear-cut: joint ownership is the way to go. But actually there are some areas for concern.

One of the biggest downsides to joint ownership is that it makes each partner financially vulnerable to the other. If you have a jointly owned bank account or a safe deposit box, either one of you can clean it out and head for Las Vegas (or anywhere else, for that matter) without the other's permission.

Investment accounts are also somewhat vulnerable. Mutual funds and brokerage accounts usually allow either party to buy and sell securities, so one party can sell all the assets in the account. The fact that the check will be made out to both parties is supposed to prevent one from making off with all the cash. But it still happens when one partner forges the name of the other on the check.

Selling property can be a problem, too. If one partner is too ill to sign the papers, or is just angry at the other and refuses to sign, trying to sell a house or any other piece of jointly owned property can be a real headache. This is why divorces can go on for so long. Even though both parties are protected by joint ownership, they can also each drag their feet when the time comes to dispose of jointly owned property.

Children can be hurt by joint ownership when a parent remarries and puts all his or her property in joint ownership with the new spouse. If the parent should pass away, all the property goes to the spouse. The kids get nothing. (One solution is a prenuptial agreement.)

Beneficiaries can be accidentally overlooked in other ways. Let's say the account held jointly by you and your ill mother had a significant portion of her assets in it. When she dies, all the assets in the account would go to you, even though she intended them to be divided equally between you and your siblings. The solution to this problem is to have a will or for all the names to go on the account. Joint ownership isn't limited to two people.

Unmarried couples can have a problem trying to divide joint property when a relationship ends. Even if one buys the other out—one partner might purchase the other partner's interest in a house, for example—the partner who sells his or her share will still be listed on the mortgage and therefore legally responsible for the debt.

Joint accounts may also interfere with your estate-planning strategies. The most carefully worded wills and trusts may be bypassed completely if your property is all owned with rights of survivorship. Make sure your legal advisers are fully aware of the registration of your assets.

What to Do?

My advice is to make the allocation and assignment of assets a conscious, rather than reflexive, decision. If there are no extenuating circumstances, joint ownership probably does make sense in many situations. But certainly consider making different arrangements if you're in a second marriage with children from prior relationships, or if you're at all uncertain about the relationship's future. Admittedly, it may not be easy to work out a different division of assets. Still, it will be a lot easier dividing them up now, when you're together, than it will be if the relationship breaks up.

(See also divorce and mediation, pre- and postnuptial agreements, probate and settlement.)

KEOGH PLANS

KEOGH PLANS ARE ONE OF THE BEST ways for the self-employed person with an average to large income to accelerate retirement savings.

Keoghs are named after the congressman who shepherded them into existence in 1964. Contributions are tax-deductible and you don't pay any taxes until you begin to withdraw funds. As long as you establish a Keogh by December 31, any additional contributions you make between then and April 15 can be deducted from the previous year's income. There is a ceiling on contributions based on your earned income, so check with your tax preparer.

In fact, that leads directly to the downside of Keoghs: their complexity. There are some rather odd formulas you must use to figure your contributions. They're so odd, in fact, that unless you have a love of numbers or a real masochistic streak, I suggest you allow your accountant to figure them out for you. The basic problem has a kind of catch-22 aspect to it: the income figure on which you calculate your contribution must have the amount of the contribution itself subtracted from it before you make the calculation. You also need to subtract half your Social Security tax. Your accountant will know how to figure this out, however, so let him take care of it.

There are several different flavors of Keogh designed for various financial situations.

Profit-Sharing Keoghs

These are usually the most flexible plans and best for the average saver. You can contribute up to 15 percent of your annual income but there is no minimum required. If you have a bad year you don't have to contribute a cent.

Money-Purchase Keoghs

Money-purchase Keoghs allow a contribution of up to 25 percent of your self-employment income every year, up to a ceiling of $30,000. There's just one catch. Once you pick a percentage, you have to contribute at least that amount every year. If you don't, the IRS will assess you a penalty.

Because you must be able to contribute a certain amount year after year, money-purchase Keoghs should only be considered by people with substantial and reliable incomes. If you do start a money-purchase Keogh and discover you can't keep up the contributions, you should abandon the plan and start a profit-sharing Keogh or some other plan.

If you have a variable income and are worried about committing to a large money-purchase contribution, you might consider starting both a profit-sharing plan and a money-purchase plan. When you have a good year you can make the maximum contribution to the money-purchase Keogh and direct any excess contributions to the profit-sharing Keogh.

Defined-Benefit Keoghs

As the name implies, defined-benefit Keoghs provide you with a guaranteed income after retirement. They are designed for high-income people who are nearing retirement and want to set aside a large amount of money in a short period of time. You decide how much money you want to receive each year beginning at age 65. An actuary will meet with you annually to calculate how much you need to contribute that year (yes, the contributions are tax-deductible) and also make adjustments to your plan to keep it compliant with any changes in the law.

Do You Have Employees?

If you do, you must also start Keoghs for them. This makes it imperative that you consult with your accountant before making any retirement account decisions.

Investing Your Contributions

You can set up a Keogh with a stockbroker, mutual fund company, bank, or financial adviser. It really depends on how you choose to invest. The best investments for Keogh contributions are, I believe, stocks, bonds, and mutual funds. Make sure you select a large, reputable company that has a proven track record. You don't want to start your retirement by discovering that your years of contributions have disappeared.

Withdrawing Your Contributions

Like most other retirement plans, you can begin withdrawing from a Keogh at age 59½. Take funds out any earlier and you will pay a penalty. You must begin to withdraw funds by age 70½, although if you're still working you can continue to make contributions. You can withdraw the entire amount in one lump sum or have it paid out in installments.

When you begin to make withdrawals, you'll need to structure them so that the account is drained by the time you die. Of course, no one knows when that will be, so the IRS lets you use actuarial tables. If your life expectancy is 18 years when you begin to tap the account, you must set up a withdrawal schedule that takes out enough money each year to empty the account in 18 years. Don't fail to pay attention to this detail. If you don't take out enough, you can be socked with a penalty of up to 50 percent of the amount you failed to withdraw. That is one reason why it's important to have a named beneficiary on all your retirement accounts.

(See also IRAs.)

LADDERING

INVESTING IN FIXED-INCOME VEHICLES can make you feel like either a genius or an idiot. For example, if you make a sizable investment in bonds and interest rates start to drop, you'll think you're brilliant and be happy with your higher rate of return. If they start to rise, however, you'll feel like a fool and be unhappy knowing your money is earning less than it could.

Laddering can mitigate interest rate risks and mollify your self-image. To ladder investments, you purchase securities with different maturation dates and then keep reinvesting the money as the securities mature. It works like this. Let's say you decide to put a certain amount of money into bonds. You invest an equal amount in each of three different series of bonds, all earning around 8 percent. One series matures in 5 years; the second matures in 7 years; the third matures in 10 years.

In five years interest rates have fallen to around 5 percent. You get your principal back and immediately reinvest in a new series of bonds. Yes, you're stuck with a lower interest rate, but you're only forced to reinvest a third of your original investment. The other two-thirds is still paying you 8 percent.

Two years later your second series of bonds matures. But by now interest rates have climbed back to 8 percent. You reinvest the principal and continue to earn 8 percent. Three years later, when the final series matures, interest rates have reached 9 percent. You reinvest at 9 percent and then watch as rates drop back down to nearly 6 percent again.

Let's look at how laddering has protected you. Interest rates are now around 6 percent. If you had originally invested all your money in the series of bonds that matured in five years and then reinvested the money when they matured, your investment would now be earning around 5 percent. But because you laddered your investments, a third of your money is returning two points more than the current interest rates and another third is returning three points more.

So laddering protects you from having to invest all your money when interest rates are low. It's a similar strategy to dollar cost averaging, which protects you against fluctuations in the price of equity investments like stocks and mutual funds.

Laddering provides one other important benefit. Since your fixed-income investments are staggered, they provide you with regular and predictable source of income. When they come due, you can reinvest all of your money if you wish or you can put it into more liquid forms of investments. Careful planning allows you to avoid selling off other investments like stocks and mutual funds.

For all the above reasons I recommend laddering as a strategy for people who are either approaching a traditional retirement or are simply anticipating a reduction in their earned income. By gradually switching your equity investments into less risky fixed-income investments, laddering those investments will reduce your risk and provide a regular cash flow. To me, those are two worthwhile goals.

——————————

(See also asset allocation, dollar cost averaging.)

LAND

IF YOU THINK VACANT LAND is a great investment, I have a few acres in Florida I'd like to speak to you about.

I shouldn't be so flip. Land can be good investment *if* you buy the right piece of property and *if* you hold on to it for a long period of time. Land isn't the kind of investment you can rely on, nor is it going to pay off quickly.

You also need to be aware of the cost of owning vacant land. At the very least you'll need to pay property taxes. If you buy a piece of land with the intention of selling it in 10 or 20 years, you'll need to factor in your annual taxes. If the land doesn't appreciate sufficiently to at least cover the cost of taxes, you'll actually lose money when you sell it. Depending on the land's location, you may have other costs as well. For example, it may need to be fenced in, and there may be ongoing landscaping costs for keeping grass mowed or trees trimmed.

Another problem is that the value of land is difficult to establish. Unlike a dwelling, whose value can be determined by looking at the recent selling prices of other homes in the neighborhood or apartments in the building, a piece of land is unique. Its real value will be determined by its future use, and there's no real way of determining exactly what that might be.

How to Buy Land

I believe you should always be thinking one step ahead when you buy land. That means you need to have a clear idea of what the potential of the land is and who you're going to sell it to down the road. For land to have commercial potential it should be a flat piece of property that's on a major or soon-to-be-major thoroughfare and near expanding residential areas. For land to have industrial potential it should be flat and near major transportation hubs, such as highways, railroads, seaports, or airports. The best potential residential property, on the other hand, will be well served by rolling property and beautiful scenery. A water view or waterfront location is particularly valuable. Don't be tempted by the occasional empty lot in areas that are already developed. Some pieces of property have the kiss of death about them and no amount of time or money will turn them into successful investments.

Here's another tip. Buy the land; don't have it sold to you. Initiate your own search and find a piece of property you want by doing your own research. Find an area that interests you and start asking questions. Talk to real estate brokers and local bankers. Once you find a piece of property you're interested in, approach the owners yourself and make them an offer. If they haven't been considering selling, they may decide to take advantage of the sudden opportunity and sell the property to you.

Whatever piece of property you decide to buy, just remember that land is a long-term commitment. If you're looking for a quick return, you need to look to other investments. Granted, you may get lucky and experience events that increase the value of the property quite rapidly. But that type of thing is entirely unpredictable. Accept the fact that you're in it for the long term. But don't make it too long. You want to be around to enjoy the big payoff.

LAWN CARE

I WAS ONCE A LAWN REBEL. When living in a Long Island suburb of New York City many years ago, I grew tired of my neighbors' obsessions with their little patches of nature. They spent hours fertilizing and trimming and mowing and expected everyone else to do the same. I had better things to do.

I did what I suspect millions of homeowners secretly yearn to do: I let my lawn go natural. In a few weeks I had a great crop of grasses, clovers, and wildflowers that I thought was quite lovely. My neighbors hated it and began to complain bitterly. So I got out my Toro, fired it up— and mowed my initials into my front yard. Of course, this only made the neighbors angrier. After a few more days of letting them stew, I relented and gave my property a crew cut.

Although I didn't realize it at the time, my actions were predating a movement that's gaining some credence today. Environmental concerns have prompted many homeowners to begin looking at their yards from a new perspective. They're more aware of the risks posed by chemical fertilizers and herbicides and have stopped using them altogether or have cut back considerably.

They've also become attuned to the amount of water that's being used to keep lawns green. It's a practice that's both wasteful and expensive. It's the latter problem that accounts for this entry in the book. People spend hundreds of dollars and, worse yet, hundreds of hours, a year taking care of their lawns. In my opinion, that's time and money better spent on other things.

A few have even followed my back-to-nature approach and let their yards do what they will. (Who would have thought that I'd be an environmental trend setter?)

I realize that such a practice is not practical for most of us. Still, there's a lot you can do to practice environmentally sound lawn care and save money in the process.*

Watering

Many homeowners overwater their lawns. Most lawns only need an average of 1 inch of water a week, an amount that's usually produced by Mother Nature in many parts of the country. But all too frequently the sprinklers will come out after just a few dry days. That's too soon. If two weeks go by without any substantial rainfall, then it's time to start watering.

Make sure you water enough to soak the soil and not just the grass. And water first thing in the morning or in the evening. Watering during the day will result in much of the water evaporating before it reaches the roots.

If you're on a municipal water system and concerned about your bill, you may decide you can't afford to water your lawn. Similarly, people with wells must be concerned about maintaining adequate water supplies, particularly during dry periods. If you don't water your lawn, the grass won't die. It will go dormant, however, and turn brown. The next good rainfall will green it back up again.

Fertilizer

The overuse of fertilizer is a serious environmental concern. Any fertilizer that's not taken up by your grass will run off into streams and groundwater, where it can pose a health threat. If you have a well as your water supply, you should be doubly concerned.

Keep fertilizer applications to a minimum. Most lawns need just a moderate dose, once in late spring and again in the fall. You can also minimize the chances of polluting the groundwater by using organic fertilizers rather than chemical products.

Herbicides and Pesticides

Nowhere in nature will you find just one kind of plant living exclusively on a piece of ground. But that's what we expect in our lawns. The sudden appearance of a patch of clover or some other intruder absolutely panics some homeowners.

The only way to make sure that grass is the only thing growing in your yard is to apply her-

---

*I've never really gotten over being a lawn rebel, so for this entry I'm relying on the wisdom of my son, Michael Pollan, the author of *Second Nature* and *A Place of My Own.*

bicides. But there's a price for perfection. Some of these chemicals have been proven deadly to animals and potentially deadly to humans and have been taken off the market. The long-term effects of some that are still being used are uncertain. The chemicals used to battle insects can also be problematic.

If you do apply herbicides and pesticides, use them only where and when needed rather than a giving general application to the entire lawn. Make sure you wear proper protective clothing and only apply them on a calm day. Post the area that's been treated with signs and keep pets and people away from the area until the treatment has dried.

Mowing

A lawn always looks best right after it's mowed. To mow as little as possible, many people tend to have their mowers set too low and risk harming the grass. The ideal mowing length is 2 to 3 inches. The higher length allows the blades to smother weeds. The grass also requires less water.

If you use a mulching mower, the clippings will remain on the lawn and help feed it, reducing the need for fertilizer. They also help retain moisture and reduce the need for watering. Mower blades should be kept sharp to avoid ripping the grass, which can invite disease. Sharp blades also make the grass look better.

Go Natural

Here's some advice from a former suburban lawn rebel. Let Mother Nature have her way, and enjoy whatever grows. Keep it mowed to appease the neighbors, but beyond that, live with what you have. If you're really concerned about appearances, plant ground cover and shrubs. The important thing is to reduce water use and chemical applications. The health of the environment and your wallet is more important than having a perfect lawn.

LAWSUITS

A PLASTIC SURGEON CLIENT of mine says he feels he's walking around with a target on his back. He has good reason to feel this way. Americans' propensity for suing one another at the drop of a hat has reached the point of absurdity. One reason might be the equally absurd settlements they're winning.

Keep in mind, however, that many lawsuits are filed as part of an overall strategy to win a dispute. The person filing the suit often has no intention of having the case actually reach a courtroom. Many times the lawsuit is a scare tactic designed to leverage a desired response from the person being sued.

Don't Panic

If you're sued, you should receive a summons. This is a formal notification that you're being sued and either an order to appear in court on a specific date or, more likely, a request to answer the suit.

If you receive a summons, don't panic. On the face of it, a summons is meaningless. Anyone can sue anyone over anything. All a summons means is that someone has found a lawyer who's willing to pursue the matter on his behalf—and perhaps collect a nice fee. It doesn't necessarily mean the lawyer thinks her new client has a chance of winning or that the lawsuit even has any merit, for that matter.

Before you do anything, make sure what you've received is indeed a summons. Collection agencies are not above sending threatening letters designed to look like a summons. Read the document carefully. If there is no mention of a court appearance, then it's not a summons. You may have received a subpoena, not a summons. A subpoena is an order to appear in court as a witness in a case involving someone else. It does not mean you're being sued.

Don't worry about going to jail or losing all your assets, either. Granted, you may have to pay someone some money. In most instances, lawsuits in this country seek monetary compensation for damages, either physical or financial. Just remember, most lawsuits are settled for only a portion of what's specified in the actual complaint.

Let's say that you're in a dispute over $10,000. The other party may sue you for $100,000, throwing in the extra $90,000 for emotional distress, punitive damages, loss of consortium, and anything else his lawyer can dream up. He doesn't expect to get $100,000. He's just hoping the big number will scare you into paying the $10,000 without a fight.

Hire a Lawyer

Here's the real downside to being sued. If you receive a summons you need to hire a lawyer, which is going to cost you money regardless of the merits of the suit.* This is necessary because you can't ignore a summons. By law, you are required to respond to it within a certain number of days from the date you received it, or the other party will receive a default judgment. You'll need a lawyer to help you.

Your lawyer will first need to look over the facts of the case. This will require a bit of legwork on your part. You'll need to gather together all documents, correspondence, and other records pertaining to the case, including canceled checks and receipts. Once your lawyer has reviewed everything, she'll advise you on a course of action.

If she decides the suit is without merit, she may advise you to go to trial, if you're willing to pay the bills. Fighting a lawsuit is expensive, so you may find that her next suggestion makes more sense. That would be to settle the suit out of court by offering the other party a percentage of what he's seeking in damages. If the other person's lawyer recognizes the weakness of the case, she will more than likely recommend that her client take the money and drop the whole

---

*Unless of course you're being sued in small-claims court, which doesn't allow lawyers.

thing. While this will be a hard nut for you to swallow, it will be far cheaper than going into litigation, which could take months or even years.

If you're in the wrong, however, you'll likely need to pay an amount that's closer to the figure in dispute. It really becomes a game of numbers. Everyone involved will be interested in getting as much as possible out of the exercise. For you, that will probably mean paying the other party the money and minimizing your legal fees. Your opponent will be interested in getting as much as possible while minimizing his legal fees. That's why so many lawsuits are settled out of court.

Here's a way to avoid lawyers altogether. It's a long shot, but it just might work. If you receive a summons, call the other party and make one last attempt at settling your dispute amicably. Point out that the involvement of lawyers is going to cost you both money and ask if there isn't some way to reach an agreement without involving the legal system. If you can show that the numbers work out better in everyone's favor by avoiding legal action, you just might be able to work a deal.

(See also lawyers, liability insurance.)

LAWYERS

AT THE RISK OF SOUNDING SELF-SERVING, I believe your lawyer is the single most important professional in your life. Think about it. Unlike your doctor or your accountant, your lawyer plays a role in many major events during the entire course of your lifetime. She'll draw up your will, work on your adoptions, help you create business plans and contracts, incorporate your business, represent you in real estate transactions and civil and criminal trials, help you write a prenuptial agreement, handle your divorce, and manage your affairs if you become incapacitated. Finally, when you're dead, she may serve as executor of your estate or provide assistance to the person you choose as executor.

That's why you need a lawyer in whom you have implicit trust and with whom you have a personal rapport. As a lawyer, I'm acutely aware of the role I play in my clients' lives. I consider myself on call 24 hours a day, 7 days a week. Clients have my home telephone number, and when the telephone rings on a Sunday morning at 8 A.M. or on a Tuesday night at 10 P.M. I pick it up. Often it's just a client agonizing over a business transaction or some other worrisome event. Granted, it's often nothing that couldn't wait until morning, but my job is to be there when they need me. If a 10-minute chat makes them feel better, then I've done my job.

You also need a lawyer who is extremely knowledgeable in a host of areas. The best lawyers are good businesspeople. They understand their own businesses as well as those of their clients. They also have contacts. A lawyer with colleagues in a variety of fields will be much more useful to you than someone whose contacts are largely in a single industry. Among those colleagues should be a stable of other lawyers representing many legal specialties. They will serve as backups if you need legal advice in an area in which your lawyer is not particularly well versed.

How to Hire a Lawyer

I think the best way to find the right lawyer is through word of mouth. Ask friends and business associates for recommendations. Ideally, you should seek the advice of people whose personal and professional lives have some parallel to your own. If they have a recommendation, ask as many questions as you can think of. You want to know as much about any candidate you're thinking of contacting before your first meeting with her.

I feel most people are best served by hiring an experienced lawyer from a midsized firm. Big firms with big reputations have equally big expenses and fees. A lawyer from a midsized firm should be able to take care of your most frequently requested legal needs. Ideally, there will be a sufficient number of partners and associates in the firm to deal with anything your lawyer can't take care of. And if there isn't someone in the firm who can help you, she will be able to recommend someone outside the firm.

Once you've established a list of candidates, you can begin to meet each one. Describe the kind of services you're most likely to need and let your candidates describe what they and their firms can provide you. Make sure you understand which services each candidate will perform personally and which ones will be passed on to associates and paralegals. Make sure you get a roster of all the lawyers associated with the firm, including detailed biographical information. And don't be shy about asking for references.

You'll also need to discuss fees. Most lawyers charge by the hour, but there is no average rate. They vary from city to city and firm to firm. Again, a partner in a large, well-known firm will certainly be the most expensive. You may even find that the older and more experienced lawyers in a firm charge more than the younger ones. Keep in mind that fees can be negotiable. Rather than reducing her hourly charge, a lawyer will work to lower your bill by having other, lower-priced staff work on your matter or by asking you to do more work yourself. Even if your lawyer can't reduce her fee, she may be able to offer you a payment plan that spreads your fees out over an agreed-upon period of time. It's also okay to ask her to establish a budget for the project and warn you if you're close to reaching your limit. Whatever the billing pattern you agree to, ask for monthly invoices.

Hiring Lawyers Who Advertise

In retrospect it seems kind of silly, but for years there was an unwritten rule in the legal community that lawyers wouldn't advertise their services. Of course, there were always some who did, and they, of course, were looked upon as bottom feeders by the entire industry.

That's all gone by the wayside. Law firms advertise heavily these days. But don't take anything you read or hear too seriously. Advertising can serve as another method of finding candidate lawyers, but you still need to go through the steps I just described to find one who's a good fit. Interview all your candidates in person and look for the one who can give you the services you need and also become a confidant and adviser.

And don't ignore your gut feelings. You can usually tell pretty quickly whether you can form a bond with someone. Don't hire a lawyer who acts like she's doing you a favor by taking your money. If you find a candidate who just feels right, she probably is.

LAYOFFS

BEING LAID OFF is like getting punched in the stomach: It knocks the wind out of you and disrupts your sense of equilibrium. But just like a blow to the gut, the pain will soon pass.

A layoff isn't the end of the world, although it sure feels like it at the time. In an instant you and your family have gone from being safe and secure to facing an uncertain and frightening future. The shock and sense of betrayal can be overwhelming.

The first thing to realize is, it's not your fault. It probably had nothing to with you at all. Layoffs are the result of economic conditions beyond your control. When times are tough, one of the first things a business has to do to survive is cut payroll costs. Unfortunately, that means you.

But rest assured that you'll land on your feet. It may take a while, and it will definitely be emotionally and financially difficult. But if you persevere, use your contacts, and follow up on every lead you'll eventually find a new position.

In order to speed that transition you need to move into active mode as quickly as you can. Taking even the most rudimentary actions will empower you. Sitting around, being depressed, doing nothing, will weaken you.

Talk to Your Family

The first thing you need to do if you're laid off is talk to your family. Explain to them what happened, why it happened, and how it will affect them. Your income stream will be significantly lessened, so there will no doubt be some belt-tightening. That will mean fewer luxuries for everyone. There could even be the possibility of a move if you think you might have to relocate for a new position. Try to get as many of the possibilities on the table at once to minimize surprises down the road,

Do not keep this to yourself. Show your trust and faith in your family and friends by making yourself vulnerable to them and asking for help and understanding. That demonstration of your respect for them will guarantee supportive responses.

You still need to be prepared for some emotional upheaval. A layoff exacts a toll on the entire family. Tempers may eventually become short and behaviors may become a bit erratic. Self-esteem issues can certainly come to the fore as well. If things get bad enough, you may want to consult a clergyman or family counselor.

Review Your Finances

The next thing you need to do is review your finances. It begins with redoing your spending plan. Trim every unnecessary expense you can think of. Forget restaurants, movies, new clothes, and other purchases. You're retrenching and going into crisis mode. Your goal is to make sure the bills get paid and there's food on the table. Everything else is secondary.

Consider Your Options

A layoff is the perfect opportunity for a serious career check. Are you really that happy with the work you do? Are you in an industry that's in decline or on the ascent? Sixty percent of people who lose their jobs consider moving into a new career. Granted, you might think it's really not the time to be picky, that anyone who is jobless should be grateful for anything that's offered them. But you may decide after some reflection that you'd like to try something completely new.

Take the time to do a little research about other fields. Analyze the working conditions, the salaries, the future of the industry, and the kinds of qualifications that are needed. Determine how your skills can be transferred to new fields. Don't hesitate to contact people who work in industries you're interested in. You can also conduct research at the library.

Don't Burn Your Bridges

Anger is a common and understandable emotion for someone who has been laid off. Don't take it out on your former boss or the company. As I mentioned earlier, layoffs are usually beyond anyone's control. What happened wasn't personal. It was business.

You're going to need good references from your former employer, so it's important to remain on good terms. Keep him appraised of your progress in searching for a new position. Let him know when he can expect to hear from potential employers. If there's any particular aspect of your performance you would like him to emphasize, ask him to do it. He'll be as anxious for you to find a job as you are, so he'll be happy to help you out.

Package Yourself

Once you've set your sights on a certain industry or industries, you need to package yourself. The most important thing is to make yourself appear as valuable as possible. Your job is to show potential employers what you can do for them, not ask them what they can do for you.

The best way to do this is to focus on your accomplishments and skills. Remember that employers are impressed by productivity and innovation. Keep this in mind when you prepare your résumé and write cover letters. Make those two qualities the focus of all your personal contacts with potential employers, including interviews.

Use Your Networks

Two-thirds of job openings are never advertised. This means that for every job you see advertised in the newspaper or professional publications, there are two others you're missing out on.

The only way to find them is to talk to everyone you can think of—professional contacts, neighbors, friends, relatives, former college classmates. They'll be the best source of leads. Keep notes from all your conversations and follow up on every lead, no matter how unlikely. That's the best way to keep the odds in your favor.

If you keep working your network you'll eventually find a new job. Once you do, resolve to keep one toe in the job market at all times; looking for your next job, even when you're gainfully employed, and maybe even jumping ship if it's for more security or money. That's the only way to guarantee you'll never be blindsided by a layoff again.

(See also job interviews, networking.)

LEVERAGE

LEVERAGE IS ONE of the great tools of capitalism. It allows us to borrow against money we will earn in the future to purchase something today. Without it, most of us would be unable to purchase homes, automobiles, and other big-ticket items.

As an example of the power of leveraging, let's look at the most common item for which people use leverage—their homes. Few of us can afford the total purchase price of a house out of pocket, so we leverage our future incomes by taking out a mortgage.

Let's say you're buying a $200,000 home. Most lenders will require you to put up 20 percent of the purchase price and they'll lend your the rest. So for $40,000, you leverage a $200,000 purchase. In doing so, you're guaranteeing the lender that you will repay the amount of the loan, plus interest, over an agreed-upon length of time.

The Dangers of Leverage

Having pointed out the advantages of leverage, I'm now going to spend the rest of this chapter giving a sermon on its dangers. This is because the more pedestrian term for leveraging is "borrowing." And too many people in the United States have leveraged themselves right into the poor house, mainly by overusing credit cards.

The constant danger with leveraging is that you will find yourself in a position where you can no longer pay your debts. Leverage must be constantly supported by an income stream large enough to support both interest payments and amortization payments. If your stream of income is interrupted—you are be laid off or suffer some other financial catastrophe—you're going to have a severe problem. In a worst-case scenario you could lose your home or your car or be pushed straight into bankruptcy.

Using leverage correctly requires a delicate balancing act. It's not easy to do. Most people either err on the side of caution or leverage themselves right into trouble. Here are some of the basic principles of leveraging. Following them will help you avoid financial trouble.

Don't use leverage in place of cash. You should only use leverage in certain situations. I've listed them at the end of this chapter.

Don't assume tomorrow's income will be greater than today's. Borrowing on the assumption that your income will increase could get you into a financial bind. I used to feel otherwise, but then corporate loyalty was thrown out the window. Since then, every year tens of thousands of middle-aged Americans find themselves forced to take a lower-paying job just to get reemployed. Today I think you're better off acting as if your income will stay the same, or perhaps even decrease.

Keep track of what percentage of your income is leveraged. If you're devoting too much of your income to pay off leveraged purchases, any interruption of your stream of income will instantly put you in a crisis situation.

Don't use leverage compulsively. Use leverage for needs, not wants. If you want a new set of golf clubs or a Caribbean vacation, wait until you've saved up the cash. If you need a heart transplant, use your leverage.

When to Use Leverage

I believe you should only use leverage in the following situations:

- **To buy a home**

- **To start a business**

- **To buy an automobile** (Just don't get carried away; see "Automobiles"; page 55.)

- **To cover the costs of an illness, including hospitalization, surgery, and physician's bills**

- **To cover the cost of a detoxification program or psychiatric treatment**

- **To pay college tuition**

- **To pay for home improvements that will add to the value of your home**

How Much Is Too Much?

The answer is simple. If you're having trouble paying your monthly bills, you're overleveraged.

Lenders look at the issue more mathematically. They feel that if you're using more than 36 percent of your gross income to pay off leveraged debt, you're in the danger zone. Personally, I feel that most people can carry as much as 40 percent if some of that debt is for low-interest student loans.

The bottom line, however, is your own comfort level. I know people who shudder at the idea of debt and use leverage sparingly, if at all. I also know people who cheerfully write out thousands of dollars worth of checks every month to pay off leveraged debt. They all seem to sleep well at night.

LIABILITY INSURANCE

T HE NICE OLD WIDOW who walks her dog past your house every morning suddenly trips over a rock one day, falls, and breaks a hip. Before you know what's hit you, she's claiming your poor maintenance of your property caused her to fall and is suing you for everything you're worth.

Can't happen, you say? Well, you're wrong. People sue each other every day for all sorts of things. And they win outrageous settlements. You may recall the case of a woman who sued McDonald's some years ago because she was burned by a spilled cup of coffee. No one disputed she was burned. But McDonald's lawyers argued she was burned because she was driving down the highway holding the cup between her thighs when her car hit a bump. When it was reported she'd been awarded $5 million in damages, insurance companies began getting lots of calls about liability coverage.

Excess Personal Liability Insurance

If you're sued, you'll need liability insurance to protect you. You'll have some coverage through your automobile, homeowner's, or renter's policies. There's just one problem. Even the best homeowner's policies only provide $300,000 in liability coverage, and people are being awarded settlements for many times that amount these days. If you lose a liability case, any amount over your $300,000 in coverage will have to be paid out of your personal assets.

You could increase your protection by purchasing additional liability coverage through your homeowner's and automobile policies. But I think your best move is to purchase an umbrella liability policy. Depending on your circumstances, a $1 million policy can be obtained for as little as $150 a year. However, the company that issues the policy may still require that you beef up your homeowner's coverage as well. This is because umbrella insurance takes over when you've exhausted your homeowner's benefits.

It's called umbrella insurance because it covers a wide range of potential calamities. It protects you from home-and auto-related accidents, of course, but it also protects you against accidents involving aircraft, watercraft, motor vehicles owned by other parties, and rental properties. Personal-injury suits, such as libel, slander, and defamation of character are included. And not only are damages covered; legal costs are also covered, regardless of whether you win or lose.

Professional Liability Insurance

If you own your own business, neither your homeowner's policy nor your umbrella policy will provide protection against liabilities related to your professional activities. This means you'll need to purchase separate business liability coverage.

Depending on your business, your first reaction might be to scoff at this notion. Most people associate professional liability insurance with doctors and lawyers. But the fact is, anyone who owns her own business should be covered. Let's say you own a catering business. It's a fairly safe endeavor, right? But what happens if people get food poisoning at an event you cater and are hospitalized or, even worse, die? You're suddenly going to be looking at multiple-lawsuits.

The bottom line is anyone whose professional activities could make them liable for personal or financial injury should have liability coverage, also known as "errors and omissions insurance." Even if you work for someone else, you should evaluate your individual liability risk and find out how much coverage your employer provides. If it's not enough, get more. It's expensive, but it's absolutely essential.

Shopping for Coverage

The best place to start looking for business liability insurance is through an agent specializing in small business coverage. Trade and professional associations are also good sources of information. You may even be able to purchase coverage through an association. And make sure any policy you're considering covers both your professional activities and your place of business. If a client falls off a chair in your office and is injured, your professional liability policy alone won't protect you.

You also should evaluate your liability if you serve on the board of a company or charity. If you're on the board of directors, or even just donate your time, with an organization or company that's sued, it could end up costing you plenty. Neither your umbrella policy or your professional liability policy will protect you. Find out what kind of liability you're exposed to and what kind of protection, if any, the organization or company provides its officers and volunteers.

(See also lawsuits.)

LIFE INSURANCE

ONLY DUPES BUY WHOLE LIFE INSURANCE. Forget all the sales spin about term insurance being "only temporary" and about its escalating premiums. If you're looking for plain vanilla coverage, look no further than term.

Unfortunately most don't listen to this advice. I think that's because they have a totally inappropriate approach to life insurance. Taken in by legions of clever salespeople, they have come to regard it as one or more of the following:

- A measure of their personal worth

- A great investment

- An indication of their love for their families

- A lifetime source of revenue for their beneficiaries

As a result, most have too much coverage and the wrong types of coverage, and they're paying through the nose for it.

How Much Life Insurance?

The real question is how much money will your survivors need. Life insurance should accomplish just two things. First, it should pay any outstanding debts of the deceased that would place an undue burden on survivors. And second, it should replace the deceased's income for a finite period of time, during which survivors will be able to make necessary lifestyle changes.

If you have no dependents, you don't need life insurance. That means young single people don't need it. Neither do most older married people whose children are grown and who have sufficient assets and income from investments, Social Security, and pensions to provide for a sole survivor for the rest of his or her life.

If you have dependents, however, you may need life insurance. But the amount you need should just be enough to cover your debts and obligations—including the cost of your funeral—and buy time for your dependents to make adjustments to their new situation.

Your coverage should be sufficient to temporarily pick up the slack on anything they can't afford on their own. Life insurance should not be treated like the lottery. Your payout should allow your heirs to briefly maintain their lifestyle while making adjustments, not improve it or even maintain it forever.

While it's a generalization, in my experience it takes a surviving spouse and dependents about three years to make the necessary financial and lifestyle adjustments.

I don't think it's necessary to buy enough insurance to pay off your mortgage. Instead, buy enough to replace your contribution to the payments for three years. During that time your survivors can either develop new streams of income or sell the home and move someplace smaller and less expensive.

It may not be necessary to buy enough insurance to pay your children's college tuition. If they're currently in college, I'd say yes, cover the bill. But if they're not, I'd suggest you simply provide enough to maintain contributions to your current savings and investment plan for three years. During that time adjustments can be made both in finances and expectations. In addition, the time can be used to investigate alternative funding sources, such as loans, scholarships, and financial aid packages.

Should you buy enough insurance so your stay-at-home spouse never has to work outside the home? If your spouse is five years or less from collecting Social Security, it might be wise to provide enough to carry her until benefits begin. However, if she's younger, I think it's sufficient to provide her with three years to prepare for a work life outside the home.

By the way, make sure you buy life insurance on *both* spouses, even if one works as a full-time homemaker. Insurance on the stay-at-home spouse's life should cover the costs of full-time child care and homemaking services for at least three years.

What Kind of Life Insurance?

You already know my feeling on this issue. But let me back up and explain. Insurance shoppers have two basic choices: cash-value life insurance (whole life insurance, universal life insurance, and variable life insurance are the most common) or term life insurance.

Cash-value insurance consists of two elements: an insurance portion and an investment portion. While your premiums are level throughout your ownership of the policy, in the early years most of your money goes toward the investment portion. As you get older, more and more of your money goes toward the insurance portion instead. Policies generally yield from 4 to 7 percent. Premiums on cash-value policies are higher than on term policies, and pay higher commissions. As a result, they're heavily pushed as investments by salespeople. The policy stays in effect as long as you pay the premiums. If you should eventually cancel the policy, you'll receive the money the policy has accrued over the years. You may also be able to borrow from the equity in the policy to pay for college costs or other expenses.

Term insurance, on the other hand, is strictly pay-as-you-go. You write a check for your insurance premium and that's it. At the end of each subsequent year you can renew the coverage for what will probably be steadily increasing premiums. If you pass away while a term policy is in effect, it pays off. But there's no equity or any other sort of financial benefit involved.

Despite what salespeople will tell you, cash-value life insurance is a lousy and expensive investment. If you want a good investment, take the money you save with the less expensive term premiums and buy shares in a selection of mutual funds. That's the real way to build equity. If you want insurance, buy term.

What Kind of Term Insurance?

Eliminating all the cash-value options makes life insurance shopping a lot simpler. You still need to make some choices, however. The most important is whether to buy an annually renewable or a level-premium (also called reentry term) policy.

The premiums on annually renewable term policies start out low and increase steadily every one, three, or five years. You only need to take a medical exam and fill out a questionnaire only when you first apply for the policy. Whatever your health, you'll be able to continue to renew the policy up until about age 70. Most companies won't sell term insurance to people over that age.

The premiums on level-premium policies start out higher than those on annually renewable policies. However, they stay the same for 10 or more years, resulting in a lower total bill than for a comparable annually renewable term policy. When that period runs out you will be required to take another medical exam and fill out another questionnaire. If you bought a guaranteed-renewable policy, as I advise, you won't be denied continued coverage. But your premiums could jump dramatically owing to changes in your health.

I usually suggest level-premium term to clients who already have an established savings and investment plan and are confident they'll be able to become more of a self-insurer in 10 years. On the other hand, I advise younger clients, who are just starting out and who don't yet have a firm financial foundation, to get an annually renewable term policy.

Shopping for Term Life Insurance

Term life insurance has become a commodity purchase, with shoppers able to compare costs on the telephone or the Internet as well as through a broker. The differences in premiums today are based on different insurers' administrative costs, fees, and profit margins. Here are a few of the things to look for when comparing term policies:

- Compare policy costs by asking for the interest-adjusted net-cost index. It sounds complicated but it's really just the cost per $100 of coverage. The lower the number, the better the deal. Insurers are required by law to provide you with this figure if you ask for it.

- Make sure the policies are guaranteed renewable for as long as you want and can't be canceled because of poor health.

- Premiums on annually renewable term will steadily increase over time. Ask for a list of premiums for at least the first 5 to 10 years.

- Don't buy a policy which you have been offered unsolicited through the mail, over the telephone, via e-mail, or in response to a television or magazine ad. These are almost always ripoffs.

- Avoid policies that pay more if you die in a certain manner, such as in an airplane accident. The premiums will be higher and your survivors' needs remain the same however you die.

The Big Exception to the Term Rule

There's always an exception that proves the rule. In the case of life insurance, the exception to choosing term over a cash-value policy is if you're over age 70. Most insurers simply won't write policies on individuals over that age. If at that point you still have a need for insurance, you'll need to buy a whole-life policy instead.

Many of my clients who are Die Brokers opt to take out a whole-life policy that pays just enough to cover their funeral costs, thus ensuring that they can spend every last penny while they're still alive without burdening their survivors with any bills.

A Brief History of Life Insurance

Life insurance is actually quite interesting from a historical perspective. It has its roots in ancient Rome. Citizens from the lower classes formed *collegia*, associations to which they would regularly contribute a nominal sum and from which they could draw for burial expenses when a family member passed away. Later, merchant and craft guilds formed in Europe and maintained funds for those members and their families who fell upon misfortune. Another common structure was the burial society. The residents of a village or town would agree to share in the burial costs of residents, insuring that individual families would not have to bear the costs by themselves.

By the seventeenth century, life insurance was becoming a more sophisticated strategy for providing financial security. The primary reason was the advent of statistics. Mathematicians began to develop mortality tables to which insurance rates could be linked.

A number of well-known scholars—including Pascal, Descartes, Newton, and Leibniz—all contributed to the mathematical breakthroughs of the time. But it was the Swiss mathematician Jacob Bernoulli who made the most important contribution to insurance. His "law of large numbers," which states that the risk of error in predicting the outcome of an event decreases as the number of observations increases, is still the basis of modern insurance.

In 1759, the Presbyterians founded the widows-and-orphans life insurance company in the American colonies, the Presbyterian Ministers Fund. The Episcopalians soon followed suit. Yet, for a variety of reasons, many of which were ethical and religious, the idea was slow to catch on.

By the early nineteenth century, however, life insurance was immensely popular. Charles Dickens took time from his writings to publish laudatory articles on the industry, pointing out that "if you lose your life, your fellow men provide something for those who may be left to mourn you." By midcentury, many of today's biggest insurance companies had been formed. Mutual of New York, New York Life, Aetna Life, Massachusetts Mutual, and several others were all founded between 1840 and 1851. Today they are among the premier insurers in the country.

- Avoid policies that offer partial payment for certain injuries. Again, the premiums will be higher. This coverage should be provided by health insurance and disability insurance.

- Ask whether a "living-benefit option" is available. This allows benefits to be paid out while you are still alive and provides you with money that can be used for nursing home care or hospice care.

LIMITED-PARTNERSHIP INVESTMENTS

LIMITED PARTNERSHIPS ARE BETTER in theory than in reality. In theory, they work like this. You and other investors pool your money in an investment, most commonly real estate. If it's a private limited partnership, you and just a handful of other investors who meet certain asset requirements—such as having hundreds of thousands if not millions of dollars to invest—put your money into a single specific project, say an office building. Today private limited partnerships in many instances have been replaced by limited liability companies. In these situations, the role of the former general partner (who is responsible for management) is delegated to a particular class of members or to managers elected by a particular class of members.

If it's a public limited partnership, you and many other small investors have stakes in the partnership, which directs the money toward a variety of projects. Public limited partnerships are registered with the Securities and Exchange Commission and often with state agencies. Whether it's public or private, the limited partnership requires a financial commitment of 10 years or more. During that time you'll receive some cash return and some tax benefits. But the big payoff is supposed to come at the end, when—again, in theory—the investment is sold and everyone gets his or her initial investment back plus a tidy profit.

In reality, limited partnerships have proven to be a lot less profitable. There are many people—some quite affluent—who invested in limited partnerships in the 1980s and today would happily accept 50 cents on the dollar to unload their membership shares. Instead, they're stuck with shares that have been producing little or no income. In many cases they aren't even salable.

Judging Limited Partnerships

As an investor, you need to recognize that limited partnerships are extremely risky investments that require a good deal of knowledge about real estate in different parts of the country and the ability to read a prospectus and ask the right questions. They're not all bad investments. You just need to be able to spot the good ones. Here are some of the rules to follow:

- Pay attention to up-front costs. Brokerage fees and other costs can be exorbitant in limited partnerships. If the fees are more than 15 or 16 percent of the investment, look elsewhere.

- Make sure the prospectus states that the sponsor of the partnership will not receive any profits from the sale of the investment until all the limited partners have received their initial investment plus an agreed-upon share of the profits.

- Make sure that the prospectus identifies the property or properties to be purchased and developed. Get an independent appraisal of the property or properties and the prices that are being asked for them.

- Read the fine print. The prospectus will have a section on "risk factors." Go over them carefully. It's not a bad idea to have your lawyer and accountant take a look at them as well.

Getting Out of a Limited Partnership

If you have shares in a limited partnership that has proven a poor investment, you have a few options to get rid of them. One is to try selling them through the secondary market. There are a dozen or so firms that buy and sell shares of existing partnerships. One way to find them is on the American Partnership Board (www.apboard.com or 800-736-9797), an online market that posts units for sale, recent prices, and other data. I think you'll be shocked at how little people will be willing to pay.

In a worst-case scenario, you may simply want to abandon your holdings altogether. You can usually do this by simply notifying the general partner by certified letter that you abandon your interest in the partnership and that he is free to do what he wishes with your shares. That action should at least provide you with a capital loss you can claim on your income taxes. Check with your accountant first, though. The last thing you need is a penalty from the IRS when all you're trying to do is get rid of a poor investment.

LISTENING

A FEW YEARS AGO my son Michael asked my wife, Corky, and I, if he could bring Marc Danner, an old college friend, to our home for Thanksgiving dinner.* Marc was from California and would otherwise be spending the holiday alone. We, of course, agreed. To outsiders, a holiday dinner at our home can be quite daunting. Such events usually include my wife and me, our son and three daughters, their four spouses, and our nine grandchildren—19 people in all. All of my children and their spouses are intelligent (they get that from my wife), opinionated (they get that from me), and accomplished (they did that on their own). Sometimes even I have a hard time getting a word in edgewise. Realizing this, Corky and I made

---

*Marc, later a winner of a MacArthur "genius" grant, is currently a tenured professor at the University of California at Berkeley.

mental notes to do what we could to make sure Marc would feel comfortable. We needn't have worried.

From the moment he walked in the door, Marc was an integral part of the day. Far from being intimidated or overwhelmed, Marc was almost the center of attention. The way he accomplished this taught me a lesson I've never forgotten. He asked questions of everyone and then he listened—intently.

I've always found that people think they need to be talkers to be successful. You see examples of it constantly. How many times have you left a meeting where one individual tried to dominate the proceedings by talking the most. Yet when the meeting was over you couldn't remember a single thing he said.

We're taught, incorrectly, that we need to talk to be successful. There are endless courses and books on how to talk, how to use the proper body language when you talk, and what to wear when you talk. There are even age-old homilies—"The squeaky wheel gets the grease," for example—that point out the importance of flapping your gums.

But I find the most important communication tool is listening. If you learn how to listen, everyone, from your business contacts to your family members, will find you to be a more empathetic and caring individual. This means that they'll be more likely to come to you first, both in business and in personal matters. I honestly believe that becoming a good listener can dramatically increase your income.

I have a little exercise I recommend to my clients who are interested in improving their communication skills. I tell them to concentrate solely on listening the next time they're in a one-on-one meeting with someone. Forget about body language and facial expressions and all the other strategies too many of us think about when we're in a conversation. Forget about formulating a response while the other person is talking. All that just takes away from our ability to listen. Instead, I tell them, put all your mental energy into understanding what the other person is saying.

When the person has finished, I tell my clients to repeat back to them, in their own words, what the person said. If they're corrected, I tell them to apologize and then once again repeat the other person's point in their own words. Then, I suggest that, instead of coming up with a response, they ask another question, based on what the other person said. And once again, I tell them to listen closely.

My clients are usually astonished at the results. By repeating what the other person said, you're confirming that you understand him. And once a person learns that you really understand what he's saying, he'll be much more willing to make an effort to hear and understand what you have to say. It takes a conversation to an entirely new level.

I also ask them to go back and think about what their unconscious mannerisms and body language were like. They usually report that they found themselves making eye contact and leaning forward a bit in their chairs in their efforts to concentrate. They also report that not having to strategize a response to what the other person was saying made it much easier to pay attention.

It's important to make a point here. Listening doesn't mean being told what to do. Nor does it mean giving in to the other person's point of view. Too many of us think that the only way we can get what we want out of another person is to dominate a conversation. In effect, we think we can talk him into whatever it is we want to accomplish. Salespeopale, in particular, have this model of communication drummed into them from the very beginning of their careers.

But if you learn to be a listener, you'll find you can turn a conversation with even the most aggressive talker to your advantage. By demonstrating that you've heard and understood exactly what another person is saying, you force him to give more weight to your response. If you repeat what the other person has said, ask a follow-up question, and then give a carefully measured response to his point, he has no choice but to to give you the same courtesy and acknowledge what you're saying. The whole pace of conversation changes and it becomes impossible for the other person to bully you into a corner by the sheer weight of his words.

I believe that if you make it a practice to listen carefully to your clients, family, and friends, you'll find that you become more successful in all aspects of your life. The simple practice of listening is more valuable than all the fancy communication techniques that are out there on the market. If you learn to really hear what others are saying, your business practices will improve and your personal relationships will become richer. Like my son's friend Marc, you'll be able to walk into potentially uncomfortable social or business situations and shine.

LIVING TRUSTS

L IVING TRUSTS ARE SCAMS. They're usually pitched to fearful elderly people by oppor-tunistic lawyers who claim that without a living trust, the seniors' hard-earned estates will fall into the black hole of probate. Once there, warn the shady professionals, their assets will be mired for years in a morass of legal entanglements and will never make it into the hands of their children and and grandchildren. A living trust, these snake-oil salespeople claim, will allow heirs to bypass probate altogether and take possession of assets without the involvement of the court. The sales pitch might also imply that a living trust will help avoid taxes.

Here are the facts. First, probate is not the mess it's made out to be. Most states have simpli-fied the process.* Second, even with a living trust your estate may still need to be probated. That's because for it to be effective, a living trust must be backed up by what's called a pour-over will, which—you guessed it—must be probated. And third, a living trust offers no tax benefits. With very few exceptions, the only people who benefit from living trusts are the lawyers, who make a lot of money setting them up. And every penny the lawyer makes decreases the value of the estate.

---

*All that being said, there remain a handful of counties, including one large one in Florida, that still make probate difficult enough for it to be worth exploring the living trust option.

How a Living Trust Works

A living trust is a legal sleight-of-hand that creates a degree of separation between you and your assets. When you set up a living trust, you transfer all the assets you want the trust to control into the trust and then name yourself as trustee. Depending on the state you live in, you may need to name a cotrustee. You'll also need to name a successor trustee to manage things if you become incapacitated and to oversee the distribution of your assets after you've passed away.

Once the trust is established, all the assets it holds belong to the trust and not to you. If you buy a new car that's to be held by the trust, you sign the check as the trustee, not as the purchaser and owner of the vehicle. The same holds true for real estate or any other asset that's designated for the trust.

As trustee, you control the assets of the trust and the management of the trust. If you and your cotrustee or successor trustee disagree on how matters should be handled, you have the option of firing them and appointing someone to take their place.

Maintaining A Living Trust

When you die, property will go directly to named beneficiaries, if you remembered to place the property in the trust. Herein lies a major problem. When a trust is set up, your assets aren't automatically moved into it. You must designate which ones are to be made part of the trust. If you miss something, its disposition is determined by your will, which requires probate.

Similarly, as you acquire assets after the trust is established, you must remember to have them purchased by the trust, or moved into the trust at a later date. Many people who create living trusts are unaware of this requirement. As a result, they end up with some possessions going through probate and others being distributed through their living trusts when they pass on. This is why maintaining a living trust is so expensive. It requires *constant legal attention.*

Rather than relying on constant updates, the way to back up a living trust is to draft a pour-over will. This will state that assets of the individual not held by the trust become property of the trust upon the individual's death.

Revoking a Living Trust

Most living trusts are revocable, meaning they can be dismantled and all their assets can return to your possession, or their terms can be changed by you. It's not a big deal, but once again, who do you think benefits from it? You guessed it: the lawyer, who needs to file the proper papers and have all the property held by the trust retitled to the appropriate party or parties. Then she'll send you a bill.

When Does a Living Trust Make Sense?

In my opinion there are three legitimate rationales for setting up a living trust. The first is for privacy. When you go through probate you're engaging in a public process. There will be records of the action filed with the court that are open to the public. Anyone can see what assets were being transferred, what they were worth, and who inherited them. This is not a concern for most of us. But for the rich and famous, who are dogged by the press at every turn, it can be a real problem. If you have realistic privacy concerns about your estate, then a living trust makes sense. In addition, if you think that your will may be contested, or that you may become incompetent, a living trust makes sense.

LIVING WILLS

A NYONE WHO DOESN'T have a living will doesn't really care about his or her loved ones. None of us like to think about becoming incapacitated by illness or injury, but we are all vulnerable to unspeakable calamities. One second we can be fine, and the next barely holding on to life. When this happens we may be comatose or otherwise unable to communicate our wishes about the extent of treatment we wish to receive during our final days. Often this gut-wrenching task will fall to a spouse, child, sibling, or other relative. Physicians can decide to ignore family wishes, unless a court or court-appointed guardian backs up the family. This means that rather than being allowed to die with dignity, you could face weeks or months of being connected to machines that keep you alive against your wishes; conversely, you could be allowed to die through inaction when you wish every effort to be made to preserve your life.

A living will can take care of this problem. It is a legal document that instructs your doctors in advance on what kinds of medical treatment you want to receive. Living wills are accompanied by a durable power of attorney, or health-care proxy, that names a person who can act on your behalf to make sure the terms of the living will are carried out. This includes the decision to cease all forms of care and allow you to die. Some people choose a relative to act on their behalf. Other people choose their lawyer. It's not a bad idea to select more than one person to serve in this capacity in the event that one of them is not around when critical decisions need to be made quickly. Each should have the authority to make a decision in the absence of the other.

Living wills can also have a considerable effect on the value of your estate. Without one, your assets may be seriously depleted by excessive and unwanted treatment. The cost of a final extended hospital stay for a patient without a living will can be many times that of a patient who has left instructions "that extreme measures not be used to prolong my life." Every dollar spent on your care is one less dollar you'll leave your heirs. This situation is so common that social workers have a name for it: a million-dollar death. Medical professionals, dedicated to preserving life whatever the emotional or financial costs, can spend a good portion of the dying person's life savings by scheduling every possible test or treatment.

Living wills should be signed in front of two impartial witnesses. This means they should not be in a position to inherit anything from your estate, play a role in your financial affairs, or be an employee of your health care provider. Once signed in the presence of witnesses, the living will overrides all other opinions on what kinds of treatment you should receive. If you draw the line at being connected to machines, for example, it will state just that. It can also specify that your organs be donated and outline other directives.

Most states have boilerplate language your lawyer can use to fashion a living will and durable power of attorney for health care. Among other things, it may require the provision of "comfort care," making sure the patient is given nourishment and fluids. Because the withdrawal of such care is usually the final step in allowing a patient to die, this issue should be carefully addressed in the living will. Most states require a separate section in the document stating your wishes to have nourishment and fluids withheld. A living will or durable power of attorney for health care must also be signed by you and two witnesses. If you spend time in more than one state, you should have a living will prepared for each one.

You should also make sure your living will addresses the issue of stopping treatment. If you've been receiving a certain treatment for a period of time, let's say a medication that enhances heart function, your health care provider may be concerned about liability if the treatment is stopped. Make sure your living will specifies that your representative has the authority to approve the withdrawal of all forms of such treatment.

Living wills should be reviewed regularly to make sure they reflect your current best interests and those of your family. Some states require they be updated or reaffirmed every five to seven years. Even then, there's no guarantee they'll be enforced when a real crisis hits. If your daughter argues that, despite what's in the will, you really would want to receive treatment, chances are a physician will abide by her wishes. Some physicians may even choose on their own to ignore the provisions of the document and the efforts of your representative to have them carried out. At that point it can become a legal battle that will drag your family through hell. A durable power of attorney health care, if recognized by your state, can prevent this from happening.

Remarkably, despite the agony and money they save, living wills are used by only about 20 percent of Americans. If you do become terminally ill and don't have a living will, some states will recognize the right of family members or a legal guardian to make decisions on your behalf. Other states are less predictable and may require a court decision or a hearing before a hospital ethics committee to decide your fate. A few states will ignore all surrogates unless there is clear evidence that you expressed your wishes not to be kept alive by artificial means while you were still functioning.

My advice is to avoid all this and take the time to have a living will prepared. Your lawyer can do it in no time at all. And once you have it, make sure your wishes are known by your friends, family members, and doctors in advance. Your living will should not appear unexpectedly out of the blue at the last moment.

(See also Durable Powers of Attorney for Health Care.)

Sample Living Will

Here's a sample living will that illustrates the kind of boilerplate form most lawyers will use to craft a custom document. I strongly urge you to have your own lawyer draft a document specifically for you.

Living Will

I, _____, residing at _____

_____, declare that if I become unable to make my own health care decisions, as determined by my attending physician, such decisions, including those to accept or refuse any treatment, service, or procedure used to diagnose, treat, or care for me, and to withhold or withdraw life-sustaining measures, shall be made in accordance with my wishes, which follow.

I do not want my life prolonged by life-sustaining measures, but want to be allowed to die naturally and to be given all care necessary to make me comfortable and to relieve pain:

1. If I am diagnosed to have an incurable or irreversible condition which is likely to cause my death within a relatively short time; or

2. If I am in a coma or persistent vegetative state which is reasonably concluded to be irreversible; or

3. (Other): _____

_____

In the circumstances described:

1. Artificial hydration and nutrition shall be withheld or withdrawn.

2. No cardiopulmonary resuscitation shall be administered to me.

3. Any other medicines or medical procedures that may be available to prolong my life should not be used.

4. (Other): _____

_____

Any invalid or unenforceable direction shall not affect my other directions.

This document shall not limit the powers given to any existing or future health care agent designated by me.

I understand the purpose and effect of this document and sign it after careful deliberation on

Date _____, 2000.

Signature _____

LOCATION

OCATION MAY OR MAY NOT still be the key to business success, but the term definitely no longer implies a old-fashioned brick-and-mortar site in a commercial district.

These days location can mean several things. Sure, the traditional retail storefront, manufacturing plant, and office suite are still staples of the American economy. But two other models are becoming increasingly important. One is cyberspace, the home to an increasing number of online businesses. The other is the home, which is proving to be a popular option for more and more Americans who are interested in simplifying their lives and having time to spend with their families.

Retail Locations

For any retail business that depends on people coming through the door, location is the critical factor for success. Regardless of the quality of your product, if you're not doing business in the right place, you'll be in trouble from the day you open.

If you own a retail business, you must weigh downtown locations against suburban shopping centers, strip malls against free-standing stores, and expensive spaces against cheaper ones.

Your decision should be based on a location's proximity to your target demographic, the volume of foot and auto traffic it experiences, the hours you intend to be open for business, and the economic fortunes of the surrounding area.

Think about whether you're a "destination merchant"—a specialty store that customers will make a special trip to visit—or a "convenience merchant"—one consumers will want to frequent only if it's near their other needs.

Obviously, you also need to consider cost. Monthly leases will vary with the nature and location of a space. Most retail landlords will charge based on frontage feet. Others might charge a percentage of your monthly gross. A few will charge a base rent with percentages of other costs tacked on, allowing the landlord to pass along some of his own cost increases.

You also need to consider security. Is the location in an area where people feel safe? Can they leave their cars without worrying about theft or vandalism? Can they walk around without feeling threatened? Is there adequate lighting at night? This is an extremely important consideration. People are reluctant to visit a neighborhood in which they feel vulnerable to danger. Even light plays a part; the shady side of the street is often better than the sunny side.

There's one critical question a lot of retailers fail to ask when evaluating a potential location for their business: How many businesses have been in the location over the past 10 or 15 years? The fact is, some retail locations have the kiss of death and are haunted by the ghosts of failed businesses. When that happens, consumers begin to associate the location with failure and refuse to stop in even though they know there's a brand-new business there.

Service Locations

There are two types of service businesses: Those where you go to the customer and those where the customer comes to you. If you travel to clients' homes or businesses to provide your service, your main requirements for a location are accessibility to your customers and space for any inventory you need to keep on hand. In that case, I believe you should consider operating out of your home. You can't get your overhead much lower than that.

If you have a service business where the customer comes to you, however, convenience for your customers becomes paramount. Your needs are really quite similar to those of any other retail business. Let's say you own a dry-cleaning business. People come to you for your service, so you need to be in a location that's highly visible and easy and convenient to get to. Stopping at the dry cleaner is an errand, so you should be in area where customers travel to do their other errands, like grocery shopping or getting a prescription filled or renting a video. That's why throughout the country you see one strip mall after another containing the same mix of supermarket, dry cleaner, drugstore, one-hour photo lab, and video rental store.

Cyberspace

I've become a big fan of online businesses, and not just the Amazon.coms and eBays of the world. Frankly, I'm like a lot of other people in that I believe many large online businesses are going to die relatively quick deaths once the venture capitalists and other investors come to their senses and stop throwing handfuls of money at them.

But I think the small specialty retailer is a perfect match for the Internet environment. A small business owner can establish a Web presence for a fraction of the cost of opening a real-world storefront. Granted, it's a bit more difficult to attract customers when you're operating with a modest budget. But over time, as people discover your online business, they'll become repeat visitors and let others know about you. In the meantime, you'll be enjoying minimal overhead and, if you structure your business correctly, little or no outlay for inventory.

Home-Based Businesses

I know quite a few cybermerchants who operate from their homes. They're just the tip of the iceberg. Computers, the Internet, e-mail, voice mail, and fax machines have made this a possibility for millions of people. Even the most buttoned-down corporations have seen the cost benefits of having some employees operate from home and are saving millions of dollars in real estate costs. When they need to meet a client, the home-based worker uses restaurants, hotel lobbies, or the client's office as a meeting place.

For an entrepreneur the advantages of a home location are enormous. Not only are costs cut to the bone, but there's little time wasted on travel or commuting. Work can be conducted at almost any hour of the day or night. And just as important, that time can also be spent on family interaction. Not only can the home-based entrepreneur hold a conference call at 9 P.M. on a Tuesday night, he can also catch his son's 4 P.M. Little League game.

(See also inventory, home-based businesses.)

LOGOS

Your business's logo can be more important than its name. What television network comes to mind when you see a multicolored peacock? Whose athletic footwear can be immediately identified by the "swoosh"? And don't forget a certain burger chain and its golden arches, perhaps the most recognized logo in the world.

Logos are effective because they're universal and unique. American businesses have long understood that the creation of an identity and a graphic personality helps them distinguish their products and services from those of their competitors. The next time you're driving down a commercial strip, take a moment to look at all the logos that call for your attention. I guarantee that you'll be able to name each company and describe its product or service at a glance.

That's why I believe almost every business should have a logo. Some companies choose to create a logo using their name: Kodak and Xerox are two prime examples, both following the same formula of an invented five-letter, two-syllable word, beginning and ending with the same, unusual consonant. Others, like McDonald's with its famous golden arches, use their initials. Still others use a graphic representation that's linked to their product or service. Nike's "swoosh," for example, gives the impression of speed and grace. A good designer can provide you with variations on all three approaches.

How Much Will a Logo Cost?

More than you'd like. Although the final result often seems modest, even minimal, it's usually the result of many hours of brainstorming and the development of dozens of prototypes. A designer can spend hours and hours working on ideas. You can spend an equal amount of time trying to make a decision.

Of course, sometimes you might wonder what all the expense was for. An amusing incident occurred back in the 1980s when, totally independent of one another, the NBC television network and the state of Nebraska adopted the same logo. It was a fat, hard-edged, blocky N. But even more amusing was that NBC reportedly spent more than $100,000 developing their logo, while Nebraska spent about $300.

The trick to not overspending on a logo is to create a budget and stick to it. Let your designer know how much you have to spend and ask her to work within your budget. Create a production schedule with dates for each stage of the process. Allow for some back-and-forth between you and the designer and give her sufficient room to put her imagination to work. Graphic designers do not function well with clients breathing down their necks.

There are a few shortcuts you can take to keep your costs down. One is to hire a student. If you live near a college or university with a graphic design program, it may be possible to find a talented student who will do the job for much less than you'd pay a professional. Just make sure to see samples of their work, including, of course, any logos they've designed. You might be pleasantly surprised by what they produce.

The other strategy is to do it yourself. But I only recommend this if you have some proven design talent and a bit of experience. Otherwise, leave it to a professional.

Using Your Logo Effectively

The ultimate goal of your logo is to make the printed version of your business's name superfluous. Once people can identify you solely by your logo, it has done its job.

To accomplish this you need to take every opportunity to keep your logo in front of consumers. It should appear anywhere your company's name appears. It should be on every piece of advertising, whether print or electronic. It should be on your stationery, business cards, invoices, brochures, and all other literature. If you have business vehicles, it should be prominently displayed on their doors. It should be on your Web site. You might have T-shirts or hats printed with your logo as handouts to clients. If you sponsor a Little League team, your logo will appear on their uniforms.

This kind of saturation is guaranteed to produce results. Eventually, the sight of your logo will cause consumers to think of your business, even if only subconsciously. The more aware consumers are of your business, the more likely they are to come to you when they need your product or service.

(See also advertising.)

LONG-TERM CARE INSURANCE

LONG-TERM CARE in the United States is a nightmare. There's something terribly wrong with a system that leaves the poor helpless, forces the middle class to fake poverty, and requires the affluent to play Russian roulette. And it's not like the problem isn't common. Forty-three percent of Americans who reach age 65 will at some point spend time in a nursing home. Of those, 25 percent will stay in the home for at least a year, at an annual cost of anywhere from $30,000 to $50,000. A few unfortunate souls—approximately 10 percent—will spend five or more years in the home.

How do families pay this bill? Someone who's poor—really poor—will be covered by Medicaid. But since nursing homes receive so little from that federal program, they're hesitant to take in any more than the minimum number of Medicaid recipients they're required to accept. That means the poor person must wait for an opening and then take the first available bed in any facility. Basically, the impoverished individual loses control over his or her own life.

I know, some of you are thinking, "Beggars can't be choosers." Isn't it ironic, then, that so many middle-class and affluent individuals facing the need for long-term care try to artificially impoverish themselves in order to qualify for Medicaid. Why? So their accumulated assets will go to their families rather than the nursing home operator. Medicaid planning, in a nutshell, involves the maintenance of just enough assets, but no more than are needed to buy a private place in a nursing home of your choice. Remaining assets are given to others. After gaining entry, the resident is shifted onto Medicaid as quickly as possible to qualify for government assistance.

There's nothing illegal about Medicaid planning. In fact, it's most often done with the assistance of an elder-care lawyer. However, even its most ardent supporters admit the process is ethically troubling. The alternative to this financial shell game is long-term care insurance. Unfortunately, it's an imperfect option with a steep price tag and questionable success.

The long-term care insurance industry is as much of a mess as the nursing home industry. It's plagued with high-pressure salespeople and poor products whose fine print is often incomprehensible.

Who Needs It?

If you're somewhat affluent, but you're not so wealthy that the cost of care isn't a problem, long-term care insurance makes a great deal of sense. Unfortunately, not everyone who can afford it can get long-term care insurance. Some companies will refuse to sell you a policy if you've had a stroke, cancer, high blood pressure, asthma, eye problems, or hip replacement surgery. Those that will sell you coverage may put you on absurdly long waiting lists and then charge you exorbitant premiums.

What's Covered?

There are really three different kinds of long-term care coverage. The first type covers stays in nursing homes, the second covers care provided in the home, and the third covers both.

You need to be very careful when you examine policies that the terms "nursing home" and "home health care" are clearly defined. Otherwise you may find yourself getting into a battle with the insurance company over what kinds of facilities are eligible.

You should also be clear on when you're considered eligible for benefits. Is your doctor's opinion that you need care enough for you to receive benefits, or must care be medically necessary due to illness or injury? And who decides what "medical necessity" is, your doctor or the insurance company? You'll also find that some policies require that you spend time in a hospital before being admitted to a nursing home. I can't emphasize how important it is to wade through the fine print that covers all these questions.

How Much Coverage Do You Need?

The simplest approach to this question is to determine how much you're willing to spend out of pocket for nursing home care each year and then ensure yourself for the balance. If you want to leave every penny you have to your spouse and the kids, you'll need full coverage.

The next question is, how long do you want your policy to last? To have all the bases covered, you can purchase a lifetime benefit, which will cover your nursing home costs until you die. Five-year, three-year, and one-year benefits are cheaper but will force you to pick up the costs if you outlive the benefits. Some policies, rather than having a maximum time-period benefit, will have a maximum dollar benefit. If you're going to engage in Medicaid planning, opt for a benefit that lasts long enough so you can get into the facility of your choice, legally transfer all your assets, and then apply for Medicaid.

You also need to choose how long you're willing to wait for coverage to start after you enter a nursing home. (You pick up the bill during the waiting period.) If you choose a 30-day waiting period, for example, your premiums will be much higher than if you select a 100-day waiting period.

Riders that increase benefits in an effort to keep pace with inflation are an excellent idea. Unfortunately they're very expensive. A compromise choice is to forego the inflation rider but make sure it remains possible to increase benefits over time by buying more coverage.

How Much Does Coverage Cost?

Prices vary dramatically, depending on your age, which of the many options you decide to select, and the profit margins of the individual insurer. To give you some idea, however, I'll use some basic figures. If you're 55, a policy that provides you with $100 a day for nursing home care and $50 a day for at-home care* for four years, with a 30-day waiting period, will cost around $700 a year. At 65, the same coverage will cost approximately $1,400 year. At 75, it will be almost $3,000 a year. Shorter waiting periods, longer benefit times, and increased benefits will result in higher premiums.

When Should You Buy It?

The younger you are when you purchase a policy, the lower the premiums will be. For example, a policy that's purchased at age 55 and not used until age 85 will be cheaper than one that's purchased at 75 and then used 10 years later. Policies aren't sold to anyone under 55. Keep in mind, too, that if you become ill, you might not be able to get coverage at all. This is another good argument to buy it when you're still relatively young.

Despite all that, I advise my clients who are not yet 65 to wait and see what happens to the industry. Long-term care insurance is currently such a mess that I believe the government will

---

*These numbers are just to illustrate the cost of obtaining certain benefits. Care itself will cost far more.

soon be forced to develop regulations and standards. (Some states have already done so.) If they do, the coverage can only get better and, hopefully, less expensive.

I advise my clients who are 65 to find the most highly rated company they can and buy a policy with the longest possible waiting period, inflation protection, a sizable daily benefit, and a year's worth of coverage. Most people don't require long-term care for any longer than that. If they do, that will give their family time to make the necessary financial and lifestyle changes, or asset manipulations. In effect, if you can afford it, buy a year's worth of effective coverage and if you need more, set your ethics aside, hire an elder-care lawyer, and engage in Medicaid planning.

(See also Medicaid planning, nursing homes.)

LUMP-SUM DISTRIBUTIONS

IT'S A COMMON DREAM: to suddenly receive a huge chunk of cash. Some people buy lottery tickets. Others dream of an inheritance from a wealthy relative. Others visit Las Vegas or Atlantic City. The harsh reality is, you're unlikely to hit the big one unless you wait until retirement. The only realistic source of a huge chunk of cash is your pension: You may have the option of taking it in one lump sum and then investing it yourself.

It seems to make a lot of sense. If you take out your money you save yourself worry over the health of your company's pension plan. If it goes under or there's an unpleasant policy change, you won't have to worry about losing some or all of your retirement pension. The downside, of course, is that you now have to manage the money yourself. It's a big responsibility. That money is supposed to help support you for the rest of your life. If you make a mistake, your golden years can quickly become tarnished.

How Much Will You Get?

When you take a lump-sum distribution, your employer first figures out how much of an income the money would have paid you over your projected life span. Then he calculates the "discount rate"—the interest the money would have earned the company over that time if it had remained in the pension fund. The difference between the two is the amount you'll receive as your lump-sum distribution. When interest rates are high, discount rates are also high, so your distribution will be less than when rates are lower.

Once you've received the money, your job is to make it last through your lifetime by making intelligent investment decisions. That does not mean running out and buying a boat or taking a trip around the world. It means planning for the long haul. Because you've given up the interest the money would have earned had it stayed with your employer, it now becomes your job to make sure the investments you select earn at least as much. The discount rate therefore becomes the benchmark by which you gauge your success. If you earn less than the discount rate, your decision to take the distribution will cost you money. If you earn more, you'll be able to give yourself a pat on the back.

Before you make any investment decisions, however, you need to pay tax on your distribution. If you're 59½ or older you can take advantage of "forward averaging." This allows you to pay taxes on the money as if had been received over five years rather than in one year. For example, if your distribution was $400,000, you would pay tax on $80,000 a year for five years. The tax savings can be considerable—as much as 30 percent. If you were born before 1936, you may be able to use 10-year forward averaging.

If you choose, you can roll your lump-sum distribution over into an IRA rather than take it in cash. There's just one catch. The money can only come from pretax contributions and the earnings from those contributions. Money on which you already paid taxes cannot be included.

Rolling your distribution into an IRA has several advantages over taking it in cash. One is that you won't pay taxes until you withdraw money from the account, and the interest the account earns continues to grow tax-deferred. Taxes on a cash dispersal, on the other hand, are due immediately. You'll also owe annual taxes on your investment gains.

Another advantage of IRAs is that because you are limited in how much you can withdraw each year, you'll be prevented from spending down your money too fast. That's one of the real dangers of taking a lump-sum distribution in cash, so such control measures shouldn't be overlooked.

Regardless of whether you choose a cash distribution or a rollover into an IRA, remember that a lump-sum distribution is your future security, not fun money. Examine each option carefully to determine how much income you'll receive, compare the tax implications, and then make your decision. It may be the one time in your life you'll have a big pot of money to invest. Don't treat it foolishly.

MAGAZINE AND JOURNAL ARTICLES

I DON'T THINK THERE'S A BETTER WAY to promote a personal-service business than writing a magazine or journal article.

Write an article on a topic and everyone thinks you're the expert. We live in a culture that bestows enormous authority and credibility on the written word. Setting aside the merits of this perception, you can use it to your advantage to promote yourself or your business by authoring magazine or journal articles. It's one of the most effective ways to get your name in front of potential employers, clients, and others in your industry. It establishes you as an expert in your field and boosts your credibility enormously.

You'll find the best results will come from articles that are relevant to your work and are read by potential employers, customers, and clients in professional publications. If you own or work for a business that services the hotel industry, for example, you might write an article on the benefits of your service for one of the industry's trade publications. By doing so, you've managed to plug yourself, your company, and the service. With any luck, you or your company will receive a few telephone calls from people wanting to know more about the service.

Some publications are more difficult to break into than others. Placing an article in most consumer magazines and newspapers, for example, requires a great deal of persistence. It sometimes helps to know a few people in the right places, so it's a good time to take a stroll through your Rolodex. You might also consider teaming up with a professional journalist. That allows you to contribute the professional expertise while she provides the communications skills and publishing contacts.

Other publications, such as trade magazines and business journals, can be surprisingly easy to get into. With small, overworked, underpaid staffs and tight deadlines, editors welcome ideas from outside contributors. Frankly, it makes their job easier. Any idea you come up with is one less idea they need to dream up. Any article you can write is one less they need to write. Sometimes getting published in your industry magazine is as simple as calling the editor and asking what he needs.

If you are fortunate enough to get an assignment, be ready to give it your full attention. For one thing, you're being asked to create something for a professional publication. You owe it to the editor to be professional in your approach to the project. More importantly, it's going to have your name on it.

When you begin your research, you will find that with the journalist's badge on your chest, you suddenly have access to people you previously had trouble meeting. Take advantage of the situation. Most people are flattered when told their expertise is needed for a magazine article, so you shouldn't have any trouble getting your foot in the door. Later, you may be able to use that meeting as a springboard to other interactions. You should also interview current clients, your boss, and any other people with whom you want to curry favor.

If at all possible, try to get the editor to include a brief paragraph about you and your business at the end of the article. Even better, check to see if the publication has a contributors page. That should earn you a photo as well as a brief biography.

Once the article is published, don't expect the magazine to get the word out about your article. You need to toot your own horn. Ask for as many free copies as you can get and make sure they're distributed to all the people you interviewed for the article, to your current and prospective clients, and to influential people in your company and industry. If you need more copies, buy them.

Here's what will happen. Everyone you interviewed will be thrilled; people love seeing their name in print. Your current clients will be impressed that they have an associate whose expertise is deemed worthy of publication. This will make it more likely that they'll remain your clients. And potential clients and others in the industry will have a better idea of who you are. Your boss will think you're a go-getter, and so will those who could be your boss in the future. All things considered, that's not a bad return on an investment of a little bit of time and effort.

MAILING LISTS

JUNK MAIL MIGHT BE ANNOYING to receive, but it works. That's why mailing lists are one of the most popular ways of reaching target audiences. A mailing list is a compilation of qualified buyers for your product or service. A qualified buyer is a consumer with a documented interest in what you're selling and the ability to pay for it. When you buy or rent a well-prepared mailing list, every name on it is a qualified buyer who could end up sending you some money.

Using List Brokers

List brokers compile lists of people who purchase goods and services, many through the mail. They group the names by product category and make the lists available to whoever is interested in reaching those groups. Prices usually start at around $50 per 1,000 names. Some companies will require you to purchase a minimum of 5,000 names.

The better a list is prepared, the more useful it will be to your business. For example, let's say you you're interested in reaching people who are avid cooks. A list broker might sell you a list of names compiled from food magazine subscription lists and other businesses selling cooking products.

Most of the country's major list brokers are in New York City and Chicago. Write for information and prices. Ask how they obtain their lists and how up-to-date they keep them. Legitimate firms will be more than happy to give you whatever information you need. If they're reluctant to discuss their practices with you, find another broker.

When considering buying from a list broker, make sure to ask yourself the following questions:

- What is the broker's reputation in the industry?

- Has the broker been forthcoming with answers to all your questions?

- How old is the broker's list?

- Has the broker kept names and addresses up-to-date?

- How does the rental or purchase price compare to what other brokers charge for similar lists?

- Have other businesses had positive results with the broker's lists?

- Do the demographic and socioeconomic characteristics of the people on the list match your product or service?

- When was the last time the broker sold the list to someone selling an item similar to what you're selling?

Should You Buy or Rent Your Lists?

I believe it makes more sense to rent a mailing list. To ensure maximum response, a mailing list must be constantly monitored to make sure it reflects changes of address, name changes, and people who have passed away. It's a time-consuming job. If you buy a list, you're responsible for doing it. I think it's easier to let the broker worry about keeping it up-to-date.

Buyer Beware

A list is only as good as the firm that prepared it. If you're dealing with a broker who's sloppy in putting his lists together or doesn't keep his list current, you're not going to get very good results with your mailing.

Mailing lists don't come with guarantees. A poor-quality list may cost you hundreds, if not thousands, of dollars in wasted mailings. But if you're unhappy with its performance, you'll have little recourse other than to complain to the broker. You're not going to get your money back, much less any financial consideration for the losses he may have caused you. This is why it's so important to check out a firm before you purchase its list.

Using Zip Code Mailings

Mail-order firms whose customers fall within a defined socioeconomic group will frequently use zip codes to direct their mailings. This is because people of similar economic means tend to cluster together in the same neighborhoods.

Let's say you have a product that is affordable only to people with fairly substantial incomes. If the wealthier neighborhoods in your target market are defined with their own zip codes, you can direct your mailing to addresses within those zip codes. By doing this, you'll reach the type of people who can afford your product.

This tactic really only works in fairly large cities that are subdivided by zip code. In smaller cities or towns, where there may be just a single zip code, it's impossible to differentiate between neighborhoods.

Creating Your Own Mailing List

Of course, the best list you can ask for is the one you create with the names and addresses of the people who buy from you. This list will grow steadily over time and, since its made up of past customers, should always be your best performer.

As the owner of the list, however, you'll need to work hard to keep it current. The best way to do this is to always include a change-of-address form with your literature. When people move, the post office will only forward mail from their old address for a few months. After that, if you haven't obtained their new address, you'll lose them.

MALPRACTICE INSURANCE

If your professional miscues have the potential to harm another person you must be covered by malpractice insurance, now called professional liability insurance, either on your own or by your employer.

Anyone can bring a malpractice suit against you for just about any reason. Regardless of the grounds for the suit, or its plausibility, you must defend yourself. This involves lawyers' fees and court costs, which can add up quite quickly. If you lose, you also have to pay whatever judgment is levied against you. Since many malpractice cases are tried before juries, who are often quick to identify with plaintiffs, the chances of losing a malpractice case are considerable.

Although most of us think of doctors when we talk about medical malpractice insurance, anyone who works in the health care industry should have coverage. Nurses can find themselves at the center of a malpractice suit just as quickly as doctors. So can dentists.

Doctors and other medical professionals are commonly sued for malpractice when their actions harm or result in the death of a patient. We've all heard stories of doctors operating on the wrong knee or nurses giving the wrong medicine or dose. But malpractice suits can be brought for almost any slight, whether real or perceived. Plastic surgeons, for instance, have been sued for malpractice by patients who claim the results of their surgeries failed to live up to the surgeons' preoperative promises.

Lawyers are sued for malpractice when clients feel they have failed to provide reasonably competent representation or have violated their fiduciary obligations. Plaintiffs have the responsibility of proving damages, which, in the case of legal work, is usually more difficult than in a medical malpractice suit.

When selecting professional liability insurance, professionals typically must choose between claims-made coverage and occurrence coverage.

Claims-Made Coverage

When you purchase a claims-made policy, the initial premiums are discounted and then gradually rise over the next few years. As long as the policy is in effect, you're protected.

The big decision comes when you decide to cancel your policy. A malpractice suit can be brought at any time. If you're sued over an incident that occurred while you were covered by a claims-made policy that has since been canceled, you will have no protection. For example, let's say the policy was in effect from 1994 through 1997. Eighteen months after the policy is canceled, in June 1999, you're sued over an incident that took place in 1996. Since your policy is no longer active, you have no coverage.

To maintain coverage for the four years the claims-made policy was in effect, you must purchase a "tail." Coverage will then remain in place as long as you continue to pay the premiums, which, by the way, will be two to three times those of the original policy. Your choices are simple: You can pay the inflated premiums and sleep well at night or save your money and take the chance that nothing you did will come back to haunt you.

Occurrence Coverage

To me, claims-made coverage is an obvious gamble, and not a very intelligent one. I believe professionals should only consider an occurrence policy. It's straightforward coverage. You pay the premiums company actuaries determine are appropriate for the policy period. While they'll be higher than for a claims-made policy, when you cancel the policy you'll always remain covered for the time period the policy was in effect.

Depending on the company that issues your professional liability policy, you may or may not have to pay for several additional coverages. One, "defense for regulatory investigation" coverage, covers the cost of a lawyer if you're called before a regulatory authority. "Billing error and omissions" coverage pays for your legal costs and any civil fines that may arise out of billing errors. You should also make sure that the policy has a "written consent to settle" clause. This requires your insurer to get your written consent to settle any claim made against you.

(See also liability insurance.)

MANNERS AND MANNERISMS

BE POLITE AND YOU'LL EARN MORE MONEY.
Politeness seems like such a basic rule of behavior that I shouldn't have to mention it. But, frankly, based on what I sometimes encounter in the business world, there are many people who could stand a few lessons in etiquette.

Let's begin with the act of being introduced to someone. Always remember to smile. First impressions mean everything, and if you have a dour look on your face, you're going to be instantly perceived as unfriendly and unpleasant. It could take a lot of time and effort to undo the damage.

If you're busy with something when you're introduced, stop what you're doing and take the time to greet the person cordially. All too often I'm introduced to people who, busy with an important task, merely glance up, extend their hand, and give a perfunctory and dismissive "How ya doin" and then return to their task. I understand they're busy, but that shouldn't prevent them from taking 20 seconds to be civil. Later on, if I'm considering candidates for a service that person provides, he's not going to be very high on my list.

When you're speaking to someone look her right in the eye. Maintaining eye contact suggests interest and sincerity. If meeting people's eyes makes you nervous, concentrate on their foreheads or the tips of their noses. During meetings, avoid yawning (I know it's difficult sometimes), blowing or picking your nose, fussing with your hair, licking you lips, or touching your face. Don't fidget, either. Constantly shifting in your seat or crossing and recrossing your arms and legs makes you appear bored and inattentive.

Here's another piece of advice: Don't swear. I'm not claiming to have the most pristine mouth in the world. I can let go with an angry epithet now and then. But I never do it in front of clients or in the company of people I don't know well. Many people are deeply offended by swearing, and you can cause serious damage to both your professional and personal reputations if you make it a habit.

Some of us have to curb our natural tendencies. Perhaps you're a talker. While there's nothing wrong with that, it can become a problem in some social and business settings. People who dominate conversations can easily be perceived as abrasive and bullying. If you have a loud and unpleasant speaking voice, that can only add to the problem. Pay attention to your behavior during conversations and make sure you give others a chance to speak. Spend more time listening than speaking.

You may also need to rein in your sense of humor. Don't get me wrong. I think a sense of humor is one of the most valuable personal qualities anyone can have. But if you have a tendency to be "on" all the time, it can be quite wearing on people. On the other hand, if you have a quieter, more self-deprecating sense of humor, it can be a real asset.

Finally, always remember that everything you do and say in the company of others colors their opinion of you. Over time, those opinions get distilled into very distinct positive or negative feelings. Once you're in disfavor with someone, you might never be able to regain his or her respect. Every person you meet has the potential to be a client, customer, or employer or the conduit to a new business or career opportunity. Treat everyone you meet the way you expect to be treated.

(See also listening.)

MARGIN LOANS

MAKING MARGIN LOANS available to the average consumer is like putting a loaded gun in the hands of at 12-year-old. Yet I'm afraid that's just what is going to happen. As the surge in personal stock investing wanes with market stabilization, many of the new brokerage firms that have been riding the wave of interest will look to new sources of revenue. The first place they'll turn is to margin loans. That is going to result, I believe, in a whole new round of consumer credit trouble.

When you have an account with a securities firm, you have more than just stocks and bonds and mutual funds sitting there. You also have a source of low-interest loans. You can borrow against the value of the securities in your account to take out a margin loan.

If you know what you're doing, margin loans can be a great deal. You can't beat the interest. It's usually near the prime rate. You can borrow up to 50 percent of the value of some of the stocks in your account. You can borrow up to 50 percent of the value of your mutual funds, selected convertible bonds, and even some over-the-counter stocks. You can also borrow up to 75 percent of the value of your corporate bonds, 85 percent of the value of your municipal bonds, and 95 percent of the value of your Treasury securities.

Another advantage of margin loans is that you don't need to make loan payments. The interest compounds in your account and slowly increases the amount of your loan. You can eventually either pay back the loan with cash or sell the securities you borrowed against to cover your debt.

Most savvy investors use margin loans to buy additional securities. That's why most brokerage firms love customers who use them: they earn commissions on the purchase of other securities. When loans are used to purchase additional securities, the interest is usually tax-deductible. If you use the loan to buy tax-free bonds or municipal bond funds, however, you will be responsible for taxes on the interest. You're also usually limited to deducting margin loan interest up to the amount of interest and dividend income you receive in a year. In other words, if you earn $3,000 in interest and dividends and owe $3,500 in margin loan interest, $500 of your margin loan interest will not be deductible. Of course, you can also use margin loans to buy a new car, take a vacation, or for another personal use.

But before you rush to the telephone to call your broker and start planning a trip to Tahiti or your takeover of Microsoft, let's look at the downsides of margin loans. The problem is, you're borrowing against securities that may decrease in value. That changes the entire equation. If you borrow against stocks, for example, and their value starts to plummet, you may receive a telephone call from your broker informing you that you need to repay part of your loan. This is known as a "margin call." If you don't have the cash, your broker will sell some of the stocks in your account to cover the debt. This means your little jaunt to the South Seas suddenly got a lot more expensive.

Margin loans can also be expensive if the securities you purchase with the money don't perform up to expectation. The cost of a margin loan is the sum of the interest and the brokerage commission. Let's say you borrow $5,000 to buy 100 shares of stock at $50 a share. Your broker charges a $100 commission and 8 percent interest. If the stock you purchased performs well—let's say it increases to $60 a share after a year—you'll have made $1,000 less the $100 commission and $400 in interest, or a net profit of $500. That's a 10 percent return on your investment.

But what if the stock only goes up to $52 a share? In that case your investment has returned $200 but your costs are $500. You've lost $300. And if the stock you buy decreases in value, say to $47 a share, the combination of your investment loss, $300, coupled with the $500 in interest and commission charges translates into a $800 loss. At that point, there's a very good chance you'll hear from your broker.

For all these reasons, I believe margin loans are only for experienced, sophisticated investors who know how to use the money to increase the value of their portfolios. Margin loans should be paid off quickly, within a few months at most. Otherwise the interest can quickly eat up any profit. You need to know what the expenses of the loan are and weigh them against your potential to make a profit. You also need to recognize when you've made a losing transaction and get out of it quickly rather than hoping things will reverse themselves. They usually won't.

Finally, don't take out a margin loan for spending money. If you need to borrow money for a new car, go to your bank or credit union and get an auto loan. At least you'll know exactly what the money you're borrowing is going to cost you.

MARKETING AN IDEA

Almost everyone experiences that moment of enlightenment at one time or another. After years of thinking and tinkering, you've finally hit upon the idea that's going to make you a bundle.

But now what? If you're like most people, coming up with the idea for a new product or service was easy, but when it comes to getting your idea off paper and into the stores, it's a whole different ball game.

For your idea to be more than a pipe dream, you need to develop a detailed, systematic, step-by-step strategy designed to bridge the gulf between you and your customers. Here are the key steps.

Conducting Market Research

The first step in bringing any product or service to the market is determining if there is a market. There's no point in spending a lot of time and money to create something nobody wants. The answers to the following questions will tell you whether or not if your product or service is viable.

1. Does the product or service fill a need? There's a big difference between a great idea and a great idea that people will buy. If there's no existing need or demand for your product or service, you'll be doomed to failure.

2. Are the merits of the product or service easily recognized or will it need a great deal of promotion? A product or service that "sells itself" is a lot cheaper to bring to market than one that needs a lot of advertising and promotion.

3. Is the market for the product or service sizable enough to warrant the investment in development and marketing? You must have a large enough customer base to generate ongoing sales and revenues.

4. Is the market easy to reach? Markets are determined by geography, demographics, socioeconomic conditions, and a variety of other factors. An analysis of the costs of reaching your market will need to take all these factors into consideration.

5. Are development costs low enough that the product or service can be sold at a reasonable profit? You won't make money if they're not.

Creating a Marketing, Advertising, and Promotional Plan

Your market research will serve as the foundation of a marketing plan. This will involve advertising, packaging, logos, promotions, public relations, and any other technique to spread the word about you product or service.

Your plan will also include a strategy to reach your customers and clients. You may choose to buy mailing lists from other businesses or target mailings to certain zip codes that include your target socioeconomic groups. You may select different advertising venues, including radio and television if you have a sufficient budget. I also suggest having someone design a Web site so that you can provide consumers with information about your product or service on the Internet. Down the road you might begin using it to conduct e-commerce.

Finally, make sure you decide what sets your product or service apart from the competition. That becomes your selling point. Those special qualities should be articulated and communicated in every bit of advertising and every promotional activity you carry out.

Let Someone Else Do It

Although manufacturing and marketing a product yourself is potentially very lucrative, it can also be extremely expensive and very risky. Most businesses founded on a single good idea or product fail after three or four years unless they can come up with additional products.

Many individuals make money by coming up with an idea and, rather than trying to market it themselves, sell it or license it to others. To sell a product or an idea, you should find a company that's interested, negotiate the best price you can, and take the money and run. It's the safest strategy, but obviously it can be the least profitable. If the product takes off, you're left with just a fraction of the profit you could have earned.

Another approach is to license a company to manufacture and market your product in return for an initial fee and an ongoing percentage of sales. It's a bit more risky than selling your idea: if the product falters, you'll earn little more than your fee. But if it does well, you'll enjoy monthly royalty checks the entire time the product is on the market. Most licensing agreements pay the creator of a product anywhere from 5 to 10 percent of sales.

Protecting Your Idea

An important consideration in selling new products or services is legal protection of the idea. Otherwise, your idea is fair game. If you can protect your concept with a patent, you'll have gone a long way toward locking in your market, at least temporarily. Just as important, it also provides you with added leverage in selling or licensing your product.

There are several types of patents. *Utility patents* provide the best protection. But obtaining one is time-consuming and, because it requires the services of a patent lawyer, expensive. If you have a novelty product with a limited market life, it probably doesn't need a utility patent. If it's a more substantial product with years of lucrative sales potential, a utility patent is probably worth the cost. *Design patents* protect the appearance of a product, but not its function. *Trademarks* are the name, logo, design, slogan, or any other identifier you use to distinguish your product from others on the market. *Copyrights* are issued by the Library of Congress and protect creative works like books, films, plays, and paintings.

(See also advertising, logos, mailing lists, Web sites.)

MEDICAID

MEDICAID HASN'T TURNED OUT the way its authors intended. Medicaid and Medicare were created by the federal government in 1965. The strategy was quite clear and simple. While Medicare would provide health insurance coverage for all Americans over 65, Medicaid would cover the costs of medical and nursing home care for those who were too poor to pay for it themselves.

As with a lot of great ideas, there's the concept and then there's the reality. The problem with Medicaid has been the arguably necessary ongoing manipulation of the system by seniors who artificially impoverish themselves in order to have the program pay for their nursing home care while their assets go to their children. (This process is called Medicaid planning.)

Nonetheless, the program has indeed helped millions of people who literally had no other place to turn. Assuming the government continues to fund it, it will continue to assist millions more. Thankfully, most Americans will only come in contact with Medicaid when they or their parents are in need of long-term nursing home care. Here's how the system works for those who aren't artificially impoverishing themselves.

When a senior needs skilled rehabilitation care after 3 or more days in a hospital, Medicare will pay 100 percent of the cost up to the first 20 days. From day 21 to day 80, Medicare will pay a portion of the care, but there is a copayment at $97 per day. Ordinarily, a Medicare supplement, or medigap policy, will take care of the copayment. Seniors who don't have medigap policies must cover the copayment amounts privately. After day 80 the patients are on their own. If they need to stay in the nursing home, they must begin to use their own assets to pay the bill. If they can't afford it, they can turn to Medicaid for assistance.

Here's the first problem seniors may encounter. The more desirable nursing homes aren't eager to accept Medicaid patients and those who cannot pay privately will probably be forced to settle for a second-rate establishment. Those who have sufficient assets to pay for at least the initial part of a stay, however, will be able to lock in their residency at a facility. Once persons are accepted in a Nursing home, they cannot be kicked out, even if they eventually run out of funds and need to switch over to Medicaid.

Although Medicaid is paid for by the federal government, it is administered at the state level. Every state has different criteria that people must meet to qualify for assistance. Although recipients will be required to spend down assets before they qualify, they will be allowed to keep a few things. Spouses of Medicaid recipients will be allowed to keep some of a couple's joint assets, including a home, so they aren't forced to suffer because of their spouse's medical needs. It's quite possible, however, that after both spouses pass away the state may go after the estate to recoup some of the money it spent on care. (For a fuller explanation of Medicaid asset exceptions see the entry on Medicaid planning.)

Medicaid will pay for daily visits to an adult day-care center, including transportation, if a recipient doesn't need full-time nursing home care. This enables many impoverished and ailing seniors to continue to live in their own home. If therapy or some other form of attention is necessary, the program may pay for visits from an in-home health care worker. Because adult day care is much cheaper than nursing home residency, seniors are allowed to keep some of their Social Security benefits and other pension income.

Medicaid is the final resort for someone who is ill and impoverished. It's not perfect—entitlement programs never are—but given the alternative, it's a great program.

(See also long-term care insurance, Medicaid planning, Medicare, medigap insurance.)

MEDICAID PLANNING

MEDICAID PLANNING is one of the most shameful practices of those who know their way around the world of personal finance. It's also, unfortunately, one of the most necessary. I help my clients do it, but I wish I didn't have to.

Medicaid is a taxpayer-funded program designed to guarantee medical treatment for the indigent. It's funded by the federal government and administered by the states. Since its creation in 1965 (along with Medicare), it has provided medical care to millions.

On the surface, it's hard to imagine a more worthwhile endeavor, but in fact Medicaid has become an ethical and legal morass and one of the most abused entitlement programs in history. The problem is the legions of seniors who, quite legally, artificially impoverish themselves to qualify for the program and avoid having to use their assets to pay for medical care, particularly long-term care in a nursing home. They accomplish this by transferring their assets (usually to their children) and sinking into "paper poverty." For example, 36 months after signing over $1 million worth of stocks, bonds, and other assets to her son and his wife, a 70-year-old widow can appear poor enough to bureaucratic eyes to receive benefits.

The way this financial sleight-of-hand takes place is one of the most complex stories in the world of personal finance.

Exempt Assets

Medicaid permits recipients to keep certain "exempt" or noncountable assets and still be eligible to qualify. The amounts differ state by state, but for a single person they generally include these items:

- A home, regardless of its value

- Countable assets of $2,000

- Burial funds of $5,000

- Personal property, such as a car and household furnishings

- Retirement accounts, such as IRAs

- Some types of income-producing property

- Some types of life insurance

If the person applying for Medicaid is married and the spouse is going to remain in the community, the exempt assets generally include the following:

- A home, regardless of its value

- Countable assets of $2,000 for the spouse residing in a nursing home

- Countable assets of $84,120 for the spouse remaining in the community

- Burial funds of $5,000 for each spouse, ($10,000 total)

- Personal property, such as a car and household furnishings

- Retirement accounts, such as IRAs, if they belong to the spouse residing in a nursing home

- Some types of income-producing property

- Some types of life insurance

Asset Transfers

When someone applies for Medicaid, the government looks back to see if any assets were transferred outright within the past 36 months. If there were assets transferred, it will result in time penalties delaying eligibility for Medicaid. Transfers to irrevocable trusts must take place more than 60 months prior to the application for Medicaid to be considered valid. Time penalties vary by state, but are generally determined by dividing the fair-market value of the asset transferred by the monthly cost of nursing home care.

Let's say that in January your mother transfers all of her Medicaid countable assets—a securities portfolio—to you. It has a fair-market value of $100,000. One year (12 months) later she applies for Medicaid. Since it took place less than 36 months prior to her application, the outright transfer, will delay her qualification for Medicaid. The delay is determined by dividing the fair-market value of the asset—in this case $100,000—by the monthly cost of nursing home care—for example, $2,000. The result is a penalty of 50 months.

Penalty periods may begin the month the transfer takes place, not the month the application is filed, depending on the timing of the application. However, there won't be a penalty if

- The transfer is between spouses

- The transfer is from a parent to a disabled child

- The parent "intended" to receive fair-market value in exchange for the asset transferred

- The reason for the transfer was for a purpose exclusively other than to qualify for Medicaid

- The imposition of the penalty would cause "undue hardship" on the applicant for Medicaid

- The transfer was a home and the home was transferred to a spouse, minor, blind or disabled child, sibling who owns an interest in the property, or adult child who provided care for the applicant, providing the child resided in the home two years immediately prior to the admission to a nursing home, and the care provided allowed the parent to delay nursing home admission

- The transfer was made to a d4 trust, discussed in the next section

Estate Recovery and Trusts

As if the process wasn't complex enough, in 1993 Congress complicated Medicaid rules even further in an effort to cut back on artificial impoverishment.

The new laws require that states have estate recovery programs to try to recoup Medicaid dollars spent for long-term nursing home, home, and community care. While the rules vary by state, basically they involve Medicaid liens being placed on real estate and personal property that remain in Medicaid recipients' estates at the time of their death. Congress gave the states broad discretion about deciding what may or may not be included in an individual's estate, including jointly held property and "life estates" in real estate.

In addition, Congress tried to crack down on the use of trusts to transfer assets in an effort to speed up Medicaid eligibility. Today, trusts are largely unavailable for Medicaid planning and involve a 60-month, rather than a 36-month "look-back" period. But, being Medicaid, there were exceptions written into the crackdown for third-party and d4 trusts.

Third-party trusts are those that established by one person for the benefit of another. If someone establishes a trust, during your lifetime or through a will for your benefit, with their own assets, and the trust is available to pay for items and services not covered under the Medicaid program, the trust will not be countable as an asset for Medicaid purposes. If, however, the terms of the trust require distributions to you of income or "corpus" (principal), the distributions will count as income for Medicaid purposes.

The other trust exemptions are for *d4 trusts*. A d4-A trust is one established by a parent, grandparent, legal guardian, or court of competent jurisdiction for a person under age 65, which includes a payback provision to the state Medicaid agency upon the death of the beneficiary. A d4-B trust is an "income trust," which can used in Medicaid "income cap" states, where income from a pension or Social Security is transferred that would otherwise cause the beneficiary to be "over income" for Medicaid. The income trust must include a payback provision.

Finally, a d4-C trust is a "pooled-asset trust," which contains the assets of disabled individuals and is established and maintained by a nonprofit organization. Once again, it must contain a payback provision.

Expert Assistance is a Must

This description of the process should convince you of the need to enlist the expert professional assistance of lawyers who specialize in Medicaid planning.

Medicaid is the most complex and complicated program I have ever explored, filled with contradictory state and federal laws, arcane exceptions, and obscure provisions. Despite the scorn heaped on elder-law practitioners who specialize in this area, and the families who engage in it, Medicaid planning can allow you to preserve some assets for the benefit of the nursing home resident, the spouse living at home or in assisted living, or disabled children. It can also help people avoid costly catastrophic mistakes, such as needlessly selling a home.

Despite the rhetoric coming out of Congress (and from the nursing home industry) about Medicaid planners "fleecing the public," the exceptions written into the law clearly show an acknowledgment of the need to not penalize spouses, caregivers, or disabled children.

Downsides and Alternatives to Paper Poverty

Aside from the complexity of the process and the resulting need for costly expert advice, there is another downside to creating paper poverty. Let's say your widowed mother transfers all her assets to you and your spouse in anticipation of taking advantage of Medicaid in a few years. She must then rely on you to use those assets to maintain her quality of life in her remaining years. While I'm not suggesting you would do anything that wasn't in her best interests, it's not unheard of for children to start spending down a parent's assets on cars, vacations, and other luxuries while the parent sits by helplessly, unable to do anything about it. In fact, it's often the children who pressure their parents into switching over their assets.

There are a couple of alternatives to paper poverty that don't require parents to turn over their assets to the kids. One is to take out a reverse mortgage that will provide them with an income for the rest of their lives. Reverse-mortgage income is overlooked when establishing Medicaid eligibility (It's not really income, but the proceeds of a loan.)

Another strategy is to have Mom and Dad pay off the remaining mortgage on the property and perhaps have some home improvements made to the property with their excess assets. Mom can then transfer her interest in the home to Dad before she enters the nursing home. Once she is qualified for Medicaid, Dad can keep the house in his name or gift all or part of the house to the children. The gifts to Dad and to the children won't cause Mom to lose her Medicaid and the house won't be subject to estate recovery. Dad can then engage in planning of his own.

Avoiding the Issue Altogether

With adequate planning, and sufficient income, most people can arrange for long-term medical care without artificial impoverishment. If you establish adequate health, disability, long-term care, and medigap coverage, you shouldn't have to worry about becoming poor enough (whether artificially or naturally) to need Medicaid.

Your comprehensive major medical plan will see you through until age 65. At that point Medicare coverage goes into effect and can be augmented by medigap coverage. This will enable you to pay any doctor and hospital bills. While you're still working, disability insurance will make sure you're able to continue to pay your insurance premiums if you should become ill or injured.

While they're currently quite expensive and riddled with loopholes, long-term care insurance can be used to provide for any potential nursing home care. With any luck, we'll soon have more effective long-term care insurance plans in place. As the baby boomers inch closer to retirement, their sheer numbers and economic clout will undoubtedly force the issue, lead to reforms in long-term care policies, force full funding of more efficient and cost-effective alternatives to nursing homes, and, as a result, eliminate the need for Medicaid planning. Until then, however, we all need to do whatever we think best to take care of our loved ones, and I that means consulting with a lawyer who specializes in Medicaid planning if you suspect nursing home care may become necessary.

(See also long-term care planning, Medicare, medigap insurance.)

MEDICARE

Medicare, like most federal programs, hasn't performed as well as intended. It was created, along with Medicaid, in 1965 as the first national health insurance plan. While it still does a pretty good job of covering the costs of acute illnesses, such as heart attacks and strokes, it has fallen far behind in providing preventative and custodial care. It hasn't kept up with rising costs, either. After adjusting for inflation, today's senior citizens spend twice as much as the first batch of Medicare recipients in out-of-pocket medical expenses. They also have to spend $1,000 or more on supplemental coverage to cover those services that Medicare misses.

Don't Forget to Sign Up

Medicare coverage starts at age 65, but it's not automatic. You need to sign up during a 7-month window surrounding your sixty-fifth birthday. You can apply as early as 3 months before you turn 65, in which case coverage will begin on your birthday. If you apply during the month you turn 65, coverage will begin on the first day of the following month. If you apply during the 3 months following the month of your sixty-fifth birthday, coverage will begin in 2 months. If you procrastinate too long and miss the 7-month window altogether, you need to wait until the next year's general enrollment period—January through March—to apply. In that case, coverage won't begin until July.

Anyone who has met the work qualifications to receive Social Security benefits also qualifies for Medicare, as do people who are named in their Social Security accounts—spouses, surviving spouses, unmarried ex-spouses (if the marriage lasted at least 10 years), and parents who received at least half their income from a Social Security–eligible child who died or became disabled. This includes the vast majority of Americans. The small percentage who don't qualify can purchase Medicare coverage just as they would any other form of insurance.

If you started receiving Social Security retirement benefits early, you'll be enrolled in Medicare automatically when you turn 65. People who receive Social Security payments because of a disability automatically get Medicare coverage two years after the payments begin. You also automatically qualify for Medicare if your kidneys fail and you need to begin dialysis treatments.

A Two-Part Plan

Medicare has two parts. *Plan A* is free and includes, with some limitations, coverage for hospital stays, skilled nursing home care, hospice care, some home health care, and blood transfusions. *Plan B* is optional and carries a monthly premium of about $50. If you're still working for a company that provides a comprehensive health care plan, you don't need to sign up for plan B. Some people who have retired have the option of continuing their employer's plan at their own expense and might not select plan B for this reason. But most insurance companies begin to really ratchet up their premiums at age 65, so it's likely that plan B will be a lot cheaper than continuing your old plan. Also, if you sign up just for plan A upon turning 65 but then decide to sign up for plan B at a later date, your premium will be 10 percent higher for every year you delayed.

Plan B provides the equivalent of conventional major medical coverage and adds additional medical expenses to the menu of services. These include lab work, x-rays, screenings for certain medical conditions, hardware such as wheelchairs and hospital beds, physical therapy, emergency room care, some home health care, and outpatient hospital treatment. If you're receiving Social Security payments and opt for plan B, the premiums will be deducted from your monthly check. Again, as with plan A, there are limitations on coverage.

How extensive are these limitations? Well, not surprisingly, it's a nightmarish list of copays, conditions, assignments, and approved costs that can be quite lengthy and confusing. It's certainly much too long to include in this book. Your local Social Security office can provide you with literature with detailed descriptions of both plans; the toll-free number is 800-772-1213. The American Association of Retired Persons (AARP) can also provide you with literature, call 800-424-3410.

You'll Need Additional Coverage

As you've probably guessed by now, Medicare will not cover all your heath care needs. Some retirees are able to supplement Medicare with low-cost coverage through their former employers. Everyone has the option of signing up for a Medicare HMO or a medigap plan, and the truly or artificially poor will be able to take advantage of Medicaid.

It is unforgivable that health insurance coverage for seniors is such a mess, but it could be worse. At least we have coverage. The good news is that the combined premiums for Medicare plan B and a medigap policy are a lot cheaper than pre-65 coverage cost.

MEDIGAP INSURANCE

I T'S INDICATIVE OF HOW SCREWED UP Medicare is, that a specific insurance product has been developed to fix its problems. Medigap insurance is private supplemental coverage tailored specifically to fill the gaps in Medicare coverage. Acceptance is guaranteed, no matter the state of your health, as long as you apply within 6 months of turning 65 and signing up for Medicare plan B. Medigap insurers can, however, refuse coverage for preexisting conditions for the first 6 months of coverage. They also can refuse to sell it to you or limit your choices of coverage if you don't apply within 6 months. But once you've obtained coverage, it can never be canceled as long as you continue to pay the premiums.

The rules allow you to be a little indecisive. You're guaranteed medigap coverage if you opt for a managed-care plan at 65 but then switch to Medicare/medigap coverage within a year. You can also go from Medicare/medigap to managed care and then back to Medicare/medigap, as long as the entire process occurs within a year of turning 65.

What Medigap Covers

Although it's offered by private companies, medigap insurance is tightly regulated by the federal and state governments. In 1992, 10 basic levels of coverage, labeled A through J, were introduced. Plan A costs around $400 a year and plan J costs around $2,000. Not all states offer all 10 plans, although they're all required to offer plan A. Here's what it provides:

- All the copayments you're required to make if you're hospitalized for more than 60 days

- All the copayments you have to pay for nonhospital care

- The first three pints of blood you receive, whether in or out of a hospital

The most expensive coverage, Plan J, provides the following additional coverage:

- Deductibles for all hospital expenses

- All deductibles you have to pay for nonhospital care

- Copayments for days 21 through 100 in a skilled-nursing facility

- All doctor's fees above the approved Medicare amounts

- Emergency medical care received in foreign countries (good news for the word traveler)

- Short-term in-home care if you're recovering from an illness or injury

- Prescription drugs

Plans B through H offer coverages that fall between these two extremes. To help you decide which is best for you, insurers who sell medigap policies must provide you with a chart that allows you to compare coverages and prices. (A table of coverages appears on page 397.)

Where to Look For Medigap Insurance

The medigap plan you select will be dictated by your particular needs. Take time to compare your current situation and decide on one or two plans that best match up. Keep in mind that your needs will more than likely change over time and that it's expensive to switch coverage down the road; therefore, whatever you select should see you through the rest of your life. If you decide the policy you've purchased is inadequate, you have 30 days to cancel it and get your money back.

The next step is to shop around and compare different offerings. You'll find quite a variety of prices. Some states require that prices be the same for everyone. Others allow prices to be set according to the age of the purchaser. Still others allow escalating premiums that rise steeply with age. You should only consider policies with a set premium and make sure the cost of the premium is clearly spelled out in the contract.

Good sources of medigap insurance include Blue Cross/Blue Shield, the American Association of Retired Persons, Medicare HMOs, and independent insurance agents. My advice is to get a quote from each, but be careful. There are a lot of dishonest insurance agents out there who try to prey on the fears of the elderly. If your agent tries to sell you more than one medigap policy, he's breaking the law. And if he tries to claim that his products are tied in with Medicare or Social Security, he's lying. Medigap policies are *completely independent of the government.*

You should do a little of your own research to compare policies. Your local Social Security office can provide you with a copy of their free brochure, "Guide to Health Insurance for People with Medicare." Call your state's Department of Aging to find out which of the 10 plans are available in your state. The United Seniors Health Cooperative in Washington, D.C. has free analyses of medigap policies. Contact them at 1331 H Street, NW, Suite 500, Washington, D.C. 20005; 202-393-6222.

Medigap Insurance Policy Plans

	A	B	C	D	E	F	G	H	I	J
Hospital coinsurance, days 21–60	x	x	x	x	x	x	x	x	x	x
Lifetime reserve coinsurance days	x	x	x	x	x	x	x	x	x	x
100% of 365 hospital days	x	x	x	x	x	x	x	x	x	x
Blood, Medicare A & B	x	x	x	x	x	x	x	x	x	x
Coinsurance, Medicare B	x	x	x	x	x	x	x	x	x	x
SNF (skilled nursing facility) coinsurance, days 21–100			x	x	x	x	x	x	x	x
Medicare A deductibles		x	x	x	x	x	x	x	x	x
Medicare B deductibles			x			x				x
% of Medicare B excess charges	100						100	80		100
Emergency foreign care			x	x	x	x	x	x	x	x
At-home recovery				x			x			x
Prescription drugs								x	x	x
Preventative care					x					x

Alternatives to Medigap Insurance

Medigap isn't the only way to augment Medicare coverage. Some retirees are able to change the coverage they've had through their employers into a supplementary plan. There's also a Medicare Select program available in some states. It provides comparable coverage for less money than most medigap policies by requiring policyholders to use certain doctors or hospitals. Finally, some states offer their own medigap plans. Again, compare coverages and premiums and match them to your needs.

(See also Medicaid, Medicare, Social Security.)

MEMBERSHIPS

Sometimes it's who you know, not what you know. For better or worse, the path to success often runs through your personal life, rather than your business life. That's what gives those Rockefellers, Kennedys, Bushs, and Gores a leg up on the rest of us. The best way for us to compensate for our lowly births is to become members in various organizations.

Memberships are clearly invaluable for making business contacts. Professional and industry associations, business groups like the Rotary Club, and even social organizations like country clubs, are full of people who may present you with business opportunities or serve as conduits to business opportunities. They can also lead to new employment opportunities.

Your professional skills may benefit from membership in industry organizations. Many sponsor educational programs or publish material that can keep you up to date on changes within your particular business or industry. Just having the opportunity to chat with other people in the business can keep you informed.

Membership in a nonprofit service organization can also have its benefits. In addition to the personal satisfaction of contributing to a good cause, your activities can serve to raise your profile within your company and community. This can lead to promotions and entry into desirable social groups.

When you volunteer for the public good you often are doing so as a representative of your company. This, in turn, reflects well on the company, which becomes viewed as benevolent and civic-minded. Let's face it, that kind of a reputation never hurt anyone's business. Why do you think there are so many corporate sponsors for activities than benefit medical research and other good causes?

Make it Part of Your Job

The benefits of membership in a variety of organizations are obvious. Yet I'm always amazed at how few of my younger clients have any affiliations outside the office. They come to me for advice on how to become more successful professionally, and yet somehow they've missed this most obvious strategies. Many are so caught up in the cultures of their own companies that it has never occurred to them to join outside groups of fellow professionals.

At first, many balk at the idea. They work hard, and they really don't want to take any more time away from their families. That's understandable. But it needn't be a choice between organization and family. They are representatives of their companies, and it's entirely reasonable to use company time to participate in these activities. Employee contributions to these organizations reflects positively on their employers. This goes for activities in both professional associations and service organizations.

Getting Accepted

Depending on the organization you want to join, you may need to go through an application process. Membership in many professional and industry associations is open to anyone, but other organizations, including country clubs, require an application. Some are accessible only by invitation.

It can be an intimidating exercise. Some of these groups are deliberately discriminatory. There are social organizations that will exclude all but the "right" kind of people. In these cases, the boundary lines are easy to identify. The boudaries of some professional organizations, that admit only those who are considered to have attained a certain level of accomplishment, are a little harder to spot.

But if you aspire to membership in these organizations, you're going to have to play the game. It begins with the membership application. These can get surprisingly personal, delving into your financial and social situations. You may be asked to submit a statement of your net worth, including possessions such as artwork and collectibles.

You'll also be asked to include a list of other organizations you belong to. I find that membership in arts and cultural organizations always look good. You can legitimately claim membership to many museums and other cultural institutions with a modest $25 or $50 donation. Affiliations with charitable organizations are also looked on positively.

Some organizations will ask for several letters of reference that attest to your good character and professional accomplishments. The sources of these letters will be dictated by the organization you're joining. If it's a professional group you'll want to use others in your industry. If it's a social organization, letters from prominent members of your community are in order. You might ask your lawyer, physician, or banker.

When asking people for a personal letter of reference, provide them with a sample you've written yourself, stressing that you're offering it only as a form to follow. Most will be happy to have the job taken care of for them. If they wish, they can tailor it to reflect their own opinions. But these things are such boilerplate documents that 9 out of 10 will simply sign their names and hand it back to you.

One last thing: When preparing documents for a membership application, bear in mind that you want to appear as uncontroversial as possible. If you belong to organizations or participate in activities that might raise eyebrows in the organization you want to join, keep that information to yourself.

MENTORING

Success isn't a solo act. Every successful businessperson I know had a mentor who helped guide them through one or more of the crucial phases of their life.

I've had several mentors myself. One was David Osler, who was in the roofing and siding business. A second was the real estate developer Sam Fox. Then there was Manny Zimmer, my partner in my first law practice. Although their interest in me was completely selfless—they gave me advice out of the goodness of their hearts—I must confess that our associations weren't accidental. I actively sought out each of these men because I recognized they had knowledge that could be of benefit to me.

I believe anyone can benefit from mentoring. Perhaps the biggest service a mentor provides is a crash course in the school of hard knocks. While education and training and theory can prepare you for your chosen craft or field, it takes someone who has been in the trenches to really show you the ropes. With your mentor at your side, you can avoid many of the stumbling blocks that might befall your less fortunate peers.*

For example, I have a client who is an executive in a stock options trading firm. Options, while potentially enormously profitable, are a risky business. One of my client's mentors is an older man who has been on the floor of the nation's exchanges most of his adult life. The man's experience has taught him to be wary of the fickle nature of markets. He learned the hard way that one or two good years doesn't guarantee that more good years will follow. He taught my client early on that nothing is guaranteed in their line of work, and that you should only spend money you've earned.

My client has taken that to heart. Unlike a lot of successful young executives, he has no debt. Rather than leveraging his potential earning power to mortgage fancy homes and cars, he has always waited until he had the cash to buy these things. He tells me he has watched in horror as several of his colleagues who had gotten heavily into debt were forced to abruptly sell their homes and uproot their families because their businesses took a turn for the worse. My client concedes that had he not had the wisdom of his mentor to guide him, he could easily have ended up suffering the same fate.

While some mentoring relationships occur by chance, I think you'll do best to seek out your own mentors. They're easy to spot. Just look for people who have accomplished what you hope to accomplish. Once you find them, seek them out and explain that you've admired their success and would like to emulate it. Then ask them how they did it. Unless the person sees you as a competitor, a situation you should know enough to avoid, they'll be happy to tell you. In my experience, most people who have achieved great things in life are eager to help those following in their footsteps.

That leads me to another point. I've found that serving as a mentor yourself is a good way to honor the people who extended the same kindnesses to you. As you move through your career, you'll gain knowledge that can only be had through experience. Using that knowledge to help younger people in their business or personal lives can be immensely rewarding. I think you'll find that not only do you create a meaningful professional relationship, you also create a lasting friendship.

---

*Your mentors needn't be older than you. I frequently turn to my son, Michael Pollan, and my coauthor, Mark Levine, for mentoring.

You can also mentor as a volunteer in any number of service organizations. One good example is the Service Corps of Retired Executives (SCORE), whose members volunteer their skills and knowledge to small businesses that are just getting off the ground. Keep in mind, too, that you have more than just business acumen to offer. As someone who has led a full and successful life, you have knowledge in many areas that can be passed on. You could just as easily become a mentor to a school-age child as to an adult following your own career path.

Whoever you choose to work with, I guarantee that sharing your life experiences to improve the lives of others will make your own life more rewarding.

MONEY MARKET ACCOUNTS

MONEY MARKET ACCOUNTS ARE the best kept secret of banking. Everyone who has more than a couple of thousand dollars to their name should have one. Yet few average Americans know about them. Money market accounts are a cross between certificates of deposit and checking accounts. They earn less interest than CDs but more than checking accounts. And unlike CDs or savings accounts, you can write checks against them. This makes them the perfect place for you to keep emergency cash or money that you may be holding between investments. You can open a money market account with most banks, savings and loans, and credit unions. Like traditional savings accounts, they're insured by the FDIC.

Money market accounts are a direct result of the inflationary 1970s. In droves, depositors were pulling their money out of banks in favor of high-yield money market mutual funds. Desperate, banks sought and were granted permission to begin offering money market accounts. Although they didn't offer as high a rate of return as their mutual fund cousins, they were federally insured. They also offered more liquidity.

Today, the interest rate and check-writing privileges offered by a money market account are usually tied to the minimum balance that's required. The higher the balance, the greater the interest. Most banks and S&Ls offer money market accounts with minimum required balances of from $1,000 to $2,500. If your balance falls below the minimum, it will earn a lower rate of interest. When it's above the minimum, it earns the higher "market" rate. You can keep as much money in your account as you like. However, at a certain level it becomes more profitable to move funds to a higher-yielding, if less liquid, type of instrument.

You can write checks against a money market account, although you'll usually be limited to three a month. The checks also have to be for a minimum amount, from $250 to $500. If you write more than three checks in a month, you'll pay a steep fee for each one. This is the bank's way of insuring you don't just use the money market account as a replacement for a checking account.

Unlike traditional savings accounts or CDs, the interest in a money market account can vary slightly from month to month. When you're comparing money market accounts be sure to ask how the banks compute their interest rates. Some will use the tiered method, which pays the same amount of interest for your entire account, depending on its balance. For example, if you have $10,000 in a money market fund that requires a $2,500 minimum, you'll earn the higher market rate on the entire amount. If you had only $2,000 in the account, you'd earn the lower rate. But if the bank uses what's called the blended method, it will pay a lower rate of interest for the first $2,500 and the market rate for the balance. Opt for banks that use the tiered method if you have a choice.

There's no limit on the interest rate a bank can pay on a money market account. If it's interested in attracting new customers, it might offer a half a point or so more than its competitors. If you find a bank halfway across the country that's offering an exceptionally high rate on its money market accounts, there's no reason you can't open an account there. Just be prepared for a bit more hassle in making deposits.

Obviously, money market accounts are not places to keep the money you're counting on for long-term appreciation. Those dollars should be invested in stocks and mutual funds and then gradually switched over to bonds and Treasury securities as you approach your investment goal.

My advice is to keep enough money in your money market account (or better, a money market fund, see below) to cover three to six months of living expenses.

Money Market Funds

The alternative to a bank's money market account is a brokerage firm's money market fund. These are mutual funds that invest in short-term, very secure instruments and offer check-writing privileges to shareholders. These money market funds pay much higher interest than bank money market accounts, while placing fewer limitations on check-writing privileges. They're offered by brokerage firms, including those affiliated with banks. Your checks might still need to be for amounts of over $250, but there will likely be no limit to how many you can write each month. However, your deposits aren't insured, and making deposits and transfers won't be as convenient.

A good compromise might be a money market mutual fund offered by the securities firm affiliated with your bank. Because of federal banking regulations, banks cannot be in the securities brokerage business. To work around these restrictions, most banks have affiliated with their own securities firms. While you may not be able to physically make deposits into your money market mutual fund down at your local branch, or access it from your bank's ATM, the customer service personnel at the bank will have provisions and procedures that make the necessary "work-arounds" as convenient as possible. In a few years, when banking regulations are inevitably changed, the only remaining downside will be the lack of federal insurance. Personally, I think that's often outweighed by the higher interest rate.

MORTGAGE LOANS

MORE THAN ANY OTHER financial instrument, the mortgage loan is responsible for creating the American middle class.

The type of mortgages commonly used today has only been around for the past 50 years or so. Prior to that, people either paid cash for a home or took out balloon mortgages—short-term loans on which they paid only interest for a few years; when the loan came due, they paid the entire principal in one big "balloon" payment.

After World War II, as a way to thank the GIs who saved the world for democracy, the federal government began offering veterans mortgages that could be slowly paid off over 30 years. The concept was so successful that commercial lenders began to offer the same types of loans. Today, mortgages are among the most profitable and safest loans offered by lenders. Only 4 percent or so default each year, and when they do, the lender has a very tangible asset—the home purchased with the mortgage—that it can sell to get its money back.

Types of Mortgages

Over the years, lenders have developed a mortgage for almost every conceivable financial situation; there are nearly 200 different mortgages out there, including the old balloon mortgage. Choosing one that's right for you depends on your present and future income, the assets you have, and the amount of debt you're carrying. Here are the most common types of mortgage. Note that the majority of mortgages are variations on one of them.

Fixed-rate mortgages: These are the most common type of mortgage. They charge the same rate of interest over the entire term of the loan and the borrower pays the same amount each month until the mortgage is paid off. In the early years of the loan the payments are primarily interest rather than principle. Over time the ratio moves more toward principle so that in the final few years payments are almost entirely principle. The traditional fixed-rate loan has a term of 15 or 30 years and an amortization of the same length.*

Adjustable-rate mortgages: ARMs have interest rates that fluctuate and are indexed to instruments such as one-year Treasury bills. To protect borrowers (and lenders), there are limits on how far the interest rate can move in a year. There is also a lifetime cap on how far the rate can rise from its original number.

---

*One of the recent mortgage techniques that my clients have been using is obtaining a a very short-term mortgage loan, say 3 to 7 years, which is amortized over 30 years, so the payments are the same as a loan of a 30-year term. When the term expires a balloon payment comes due, but this can then be refinanced, perhaps with the same lender. The advantage of this is that borrowers get the benefit of lower payments with the flexibility of being able to shift to a more advantageous interest rate in a few years.

Two-step mortgages: These mortgages offer one interest rate for an initial number of years, usually 5 or 7, and then a higher rate for the balance of the term. The second step can be either a fixed-rate or an adjustable-rate mortgage.

Farm Home Administration mortgages: FHA mortgages are designed to help lower-income home buyers.* They require down payments as low as 5 percent (as opposed to the usual minimum of 20 percent) and have borrowing limits based on the median home price in different areas of the country. The downside of FHA mortgages is the expensive mortgage insurance premium that accompanies them.

Veterans Administration mortgages: VA mortgages are available to qualified veterans with no money down and no points (percentage points of interest that are often paid up front), although there may be other loan fees. They require a certificate of eligibility from the Department of Veterans Affairs.

Balloon mortgages: The one constant characteristic of balloon mortgages is that the entire principal comes due after a certain number of years, usually 10 or less. Until then, your monthly payments may consist solely of interest, or they may include both principal and interest. It's typical today for mortgagees to refinance when a balloon loan comes due.

Graduated-payment mortgages: GPMs recognize the fact that most people's income increases over time. The response is to increase the monthly payments over time. They are designed for young, first-time homeowners. They're less common today, chiefly because of the paperwork involved, and have been replaced by the more popular two-step mortgage.

Shared-appreciation mortgages: These also offer young home buyers the chance to get more with their money. The lender will provide a mortgage at a below-market interest rate in exchange for part of the appreciation when the home is sold. They are commonly used by nonprofit organizations to help low-income people buy their first home.

Where to Obtain a Mortgage

Mortgages are available from commercial banks, savings and loans, credit unions, and some government agencies. Depending on where you turn, you may deal with a mortgage broker or a mortgage banker. A broker will take your application and then find a lender willing to give you the money. A mortgage banker, on the other hand, represents the institution that is lending you the money.

Because of the wide variety of contacts he has, a mortgage broker can be useful for people who might have difficulty getting a mortgage. He can also be useful for average borrowers who

---

*Actual FHA mortgages are pretty rare these days since they're limited to small amounts. Insttead, the FHA's primary role now is to serve as guarantor.

may not have the time for an extensive investigation of their mortgage options. Mortgage brokers have much closer relationships with lenders than consumers. Lenders like working with them because they know borrowers will be prequalified and applications will be prepared professionally. Because of their special relationship, brokers often get special rates and services that can compensate for your having to pay a fee.

You don't have to go through a broker or commercial lender to get a mortgage. Sometimes your parents or another relative or friend can be a source of financing. It could be a great deal for both borrower and lender. For instance, your parents might lend you the money below the rates offered by commercial lenders but above what they could earn by putting their money in a certificate of deposit or some other relatively safe investment. If they're financially comfortable they may even make the mortgage interest-free.

MOVING

ONLY NOMADS MOVE MORE than Americans. Every year, 20 percent of the families in the United States change addresses. One of three people in their twenties moves every year.

Moving may be common, but it's rarely pleasant. The trauma of leaving friends and family, combined with the anxiety over a new job or life situation, can send the blood pressure soaring. The fact that your every possession is being trucked away by strangers makes matters even worse. You won't rest easy until you see them all sitting safely in your new home.

Then, of course, there's the cost. The bill for moving the contents of the average three-bedroom house across the country is more than $6,000. It's no wonder most rankings of stressful life events place moving right behind the death of a loved one and divorce.

Selecting a Moving Company

We've all heard horror stories about moving companies that show up late, arrive late, or both. Then there are the tales of broken or missing property.

Many people put themselves at risk by failing to carefully select a moving company. Too many people simply open the Yellow Pages and call the first name they see or call several companies and go with the lowest bid. The next thing you know, they're sitting on boxes in the living room wondering where their furniture is.

The two most important factors in selecting a moving company are reliability and price. Your best sources of recommendations are friends, colleagues at work, and family members. Ask what companies they have used and what kinds of problems they had. If one company stands out, give them a call.

Begin your conversation by making sure the mover is licensed. Interstate movers must be licensed by the Federal Highway Administration. Movers who operate within a state fall under the jurisdiction of that state. State regulations are very inconsistent, so you need to be doubly careful when selecting a local company.

You can check on an interstate moving company's reliability be asking for its annual performance report. This document, required by the FHA, lists the number of claims the company received for damaged property, the number of shipments it delivered late, and how often the final bill exceeded their estimate. If the company can't—or won't—provide you with the document, cross it off your list.

Once you've investigated a number of companies, narrow your list to three, and ask each for an estimate—in writing. The price of interstate moves is generally determined by the weight of the shipment and the distance to the new location. The price of in-state moves may be based on personnel needs and time.

You can choose between two kinds of estimates. A binding estimate is a guaranteed price. To make it stick, however, you need to inform the company of every problem they're going to encounter. If they have to take apart a piano to get it through a doorway or navigate 10 flights of stairs with a half-ton piece of sculpture and you haven't told them beforehand, the estimate will be voided. A binding estimate may be accompanied by a charge. It's the mover's way of protecting himself.

A nonbinding estimate is just that—a guess at what the mover thinks the job will cost. An experienced and reliable mover will be able to give you a fairly accurate estimate. An inexperienced mover may or may not be accurate. An unscrupulous mover will lure you in with a low estimate and then hit you with a shocker of a bill at the other end—before he unloads the truck. With your possessions held hostage, you'll be more likely to pay.

Delivery and Payment

When you move, you'll receive a contract from the mover called a bill of lading. It will include the estimate, the pickup and delivery dates, and the time and place of delivery. It should also include the company's liability policy. Most movers will give you a window of several days for delivery rather than a specific day. If they're going to miss the window, they're required to notify you. If the delay causes you to incur expenses, such as a hotel stay, you're entitled to compensation.

Most movers will require payment before they unload the truck. Few will take a personal check, so plan on making other arrangements. If you asked for a nonbinding estimate and the bill ends up being higher, you only need to pay the estimate plus 10 percent of the excess charge at the time of delivery. You have 30 days to pay the balance. If you dispute the bill and refuse to pay, the mover can put your possessions in storage—at your expense.

Damages and losses are commonplace in moves; nearly 50 percent of moves result in a claim. If you discover damaged or missing property, you have 9 months to fill out a claim form and return it to the company. The company has 30 days to acknowledge receipt of the claim and must either deny it or offer a settlement within 120 days. Reputable moving companies settle much more quickly than that. If a company refuses to pay, you'll end up in court.

MULTILEVEL MARKETING

IF YOU'RE EVER AT A PARTY and are confronted by an acquaintance who won't stop pitching you about some new program he's involved with, one that you too should become involved with, you're face-to-face with either a cult group member or with someone who's into multilevel marketing. Actually, sometimes I think they're both the same.

Also known as "matrix" and "network" marketing, multilevel marketing is a method of selling goods or services through distributors. The most famous names in the business are Amway, Avon, and Mary Kay. The products are usually sold over the telephone or through visits to customers' homes. As a distributor, you receive a commission on all the merchandise you sell. If you recruit enough other people to be distributors, you also get a commission from their sales. The more people you recruit, the more money you can make. I suppose the goal is for everyone on earth to become a distributor.

It's important to distinguish multilevel marketing, which is perfectly legal, from pyramid schemes, which are not. While on the surface the two can be virtually indistinguishable, there is one very important difference. Multilevel marketers make their money by selling products. Pyramid-scheme promoters make their money by recruiting other people to join the organization and then extracting a hefty fee from them. The product, if there even is one, is secondary to the recruitment. Pyramid schemes are illegal because they are impossible to sustain. Their collapse is guaranteed, and when it happens, many people lose a lot of money.

What's Sold?

Multilevel marketers sell a wide variety of products and services, but the two most popular seem to be health supplies and beauty supplies. You may have a friend who has tried to sell you vitamins, nutritional supplements, weight-loss products, homeopathic remedies, or some other product designed to improve your health. Often, these people become distributors of a product they've tried and found effective. Their motives are usually twofold: to pass on their wonderful discovery to friends and others and to provide themselves with a free supply of something they've become dependent on. Whether they make any money is sometimes secondary.

That's probably a good thing, because most multilevel marketers don't make a whole lot of money. According to one major multilevel marketer's 1998 business review, the average distributor earned $88 a month in net revenues (gross sales minus the cost of the merchandise). Only 41 percent of its distributors of record were active. That's a good indication that a lot of people who give multilevel marketing a try don't find it worth the effort.

Those who do make real money in multilevel marketing are the ones who are successful at recruiting new salespeople. In addition to the earnings from their own sales, they derive revenue from the sales of the people they recruit.

Becoming a multilevel marketer is easy. In fact, they're quite happy to have you. Since distributors are sources of revenue for the parent company, the more distributors they have, the greater their potential income. Distributors don't have to have any special knowledge of the product they sell. Most receive a sales kit at the outset that provides them with information about the product and a few sales tips. Then they're ready to go.

Investigate Before You Join

As I mentioned earlier, there's a fine line between multilevel marketing and a pyramid scheme. If you're considering becoming an independent distributor with such a business, you need to investigate it carefully.

Research the company. Find out how long it has been in business and check with your local better business bureau or your attorney general's office to find out if there have been any consumer complaints about the company. Does it belong to the Direct Selling Association or other recognized professional groups? Ask for copies of its business and financial statements.

- Investigate the product. What will it cost you and what can you sell it for? What kinds of products does it compete against? Can it compete successfully from both a quality and cost standpoint?

- How big is the market for the product? Many promoters overstate the potential market and distributors find themselves unable to attract enough customers.

- Determine up-front fees. Do they pay for training, sample products, sales literature, or display materials?

- Can you return unsold products to the parent company? If not, you run the risk of losing money.

- How many other distributors are there in your area? If there are too many, it will be impossible to find enough customers. A legitimate company will not allow an area to become saturated with distributors.

- How much money can you *really* make? Many companies exaggerate the earnings potential of their distributors. Sometimes they hold up one exceptionally successful person as an example when, in fact, the majority of their distributors enjoy only modest success.

- Most importantly, does the company encourage you to recruit others in return for a commission? If it does, you've likely stumbled upon a pyramid scheme. If you become involved, you risk both financial loss and legal problems. Walk—no, run—from the deal and don't look back.

One last thing, if they ask you to attend a meeting don't take off your shoes or drink the Kool-Aid.

(See also pyramid schemes.)

MUTUAL FUNDS

THE EMERGENCE OF THE MUTUAL FUND has been the single most important factor in democratizing the stock market. Prior to mutual funds, stock market investing was limited to the very wealthy. Only they had sufficient funds to purchase a balanced portfolio, in effect, not putting all their eggs in one basket. The mutual fund allows someone with limited funds the same opportunity to invest as the affluent.

Mutual funds take the "strength in numbers" approach to investing. The idea is that by grouping a large number of stocks or other securities in a single fund, and selling investors shares in the fund, they improve investors' chances to make a profit.

It's really a very sensible premise. When you buy an individual stock, your fortunes rise and fall with the stock's performance. If it goes up, you make money. If it goes down, you lose. But if you group 30 or 40 or more carefully selected stocks together, chances are that the majority will do well and the overall value of the fund's holdings will increase.

Selection is the key. That's why mutual funds are run by talented fund managers who are backed by well-armed research staffs. Their sole mission in life is to search the horizon for promising places to put your money. The best of them become legends on Wall Street. The most famous is probably Fidelity's Peter Lynch, whose Magellan Fund averaged an astonishing 30.5 percent return during the 15 years he managed it.

Mutual funds earn income for their investors in three ways: payment of dividends received from the securities held by the fund, payment of capital gains realized from trading securities in the fund, and increases in the price of their shares. The sum of these three is the total return on a fund.

Dividends are paid either as cash or as additional shares in the fund. Dividend income, whether received in cash or reinvested in additional shares, is considered taxable income.

Capital gains are the net profits realized during the year by fund managers buying and selling securities in a mutual fund. They are usually paid out to investors at the end of each calendar year. As with dividends, capital gains can be received either as cash or as additional shares in the fund. The price of the shares in the fund will decrease to offset the capital gains distribution, and they are taxable whether received as cash or as additional shares.

A fund's share prices fluctuate with dividend and capital gains payouts and with the infusion of capital from new investors into the fund. At some point, the share price may be less than what you paid, although this will be offset by profit in the form of dividend and capital gains payouts. At other times it may be more than you paid.

The Advantages
Mutual funds offer a number of advantages over individual stocks and bonds, including:

- Different funds are structured to achieve different investment goals, so you can select a level of risk that you're comfortable with.

- The securities in the fund are selected by a professional manager.

- The mutual fund market is carefully documented, so you can research a fund's past performance record before you buy.

- Mutual funds provide a diversity that is almost impossible for the average investor to accomplish otherwise.

- You can buy in with a minimal investment, sometimes as little as $500.

- They're inexpensive to own. A good stock mutual fund should cost you no more than 1 percent of the value of your investment every year in service fees.

- You can reinvest your dividends and capital gains.

Choices

There are currently more than 6,000 mutual funds available to investors. Most invest in stocks. Others invest in bonds and money markets. A few invest in real estate, gold, and just about every other kind of security you can imagine. Here are some of the most common:

Stock funds, also called equity funds, invest in stocks and are usually categorized by the type of stocks they invest in. Because stock prices are inherently volatile, stock funds are generally considered to be the riskiest type of mutual funds.

Bond funds invest in a variety of bonds that have similar maturities. They can be short- (2 to 3 years), intermediate- (5 to 10 years), or long-term (20 years or more). Bond fund managers constantly shift the bonds they manage to maintain the fund's desired average maturity. Those of you who are allergic to risk will be happy to know that, because bond interest rates are set, shorter-term bond mutual funds carry much less risk than stock funds.

Money-market funds are virtually risk-free. The fund assets are put in short-term money market investments. Like a savings account, you get back your investment plus whatever interest it earns.

Hybrid funds invest in both stocks and bonds. This is done to minimize risk in times of economic downturn. Bond interest rates are guaranteed, so the bonds in a fund help the fund maintain its value if the stock market goes into decline. Of course, the other side of the coin is that the bonds can hold the fund back somewhat when the stock market is booming.

Index funds are structured to mimic an existing market index, without trying to outperform it. For example, one of the most popular index funds is based on the Standard and Poor's 500, an index of 500 large U.S. companies. Sounds kind of pedestrian? Well, keep in mind that for every mutual fund that enjoys a 20 or 25 percent rate of return, there are a bunch earning only 4 or 5 or 6 percent. There are also some that are actually losing money. So matching the market is not that bad a deal in the overall scheme of things. In fact, over periods of 10 or more years, index funds outperform 75 percent of all other mutual funds.

Tax-free funds pay tax-free distributions. They accomplish this by investing in things like tax-free municipal bonds and selling the mutual funds created with those bonds to residents of the states in which the bonds are issued.

Security funds, also known as sector funds, invest in securities in specific industries such as communications or manufacturing. They're odd ducks in a way because they seem to fly in the face of the whole rationale behind mutual funds. Rather than pursue diversification to reduce risk, they put all their eggs into one basket in the hope that the industry they've chosen will enjoy a boom period. Still, they mitigate risk by letting you invest in an industry, rather than a single company. They are also excellent tools in allocating your assets among specific industries or sectors.

Questions to Ask about Individual Mutual Funds

One of the great things about mutual funds is that they're easy to research and understand. Here are some of the questions you need to ask:

1. *What's the reputation of the fund manager and the fund family?* Different companies have strengths in different types of mutual funds.

2. *What does the fund invest in?* This will determine the fund's risk and potential return.

3. *How is the fund operated?* As an investor, you get to vote on the policies and procedures governing the management of the fund.

4. *How can shares be bought and sold?* If you do all your own research, you can buy directly from the company offering the fund.

5. *What's the minimum investment required by the fund?* It may be as little as $500.

6. *What are the costs associated with the fund?* Investigate the transaction fees and service fees. These charges can put a big dent in the income you receive.

7. *Is it a load or a no-load fund?* No-load funds don't charge you a commission (a load) when you buy in. It's the only way to go for the investor with research abilities and discipline.

8. *How has the fund performed over time?* Look at its performance over a 5-to-10 year period. This will give you some idea of how the fund matches up to your investment goals.

9. *Is it an open-end or close-end fund?* An open-end fund is allowed to grow by selling as many shares as the market will bear. Close-end funds are created with a predetermined number of shares.

10. *What's the fund's turnover rate?* The shares of open-end mutual funds are bought and sold just like stocks. High turnovers generally mean higher costs and less tax efficiency.

11. *What are the tax implications of the fund?* Some mutual funds produce more taxable gains than others, and the taxes on those gains diminish the actual return.

NAMES

A ROSE BY ANY OTHER NAME may indeed smell as sweet, but if it's called stink weed, not too many people would care to know it. The same is true of business names, which can run the gamut from the ultraserious to the totally frivolous. If they're appropriately selected, they can send an accurate message about the nature of the business itself. If they're inappropriate, I believe they can do your business a great deal of harm.

Somber Service Businesses

Let's begin with people who run their own white-collar or professional service businesses. Obviously, the simplest approach is to use your own name. This is clearly the best strategy for those who provide a service aimed at the more sober aspects of people's lives. You are your business, so you may as well name it after yourself.

Make sure you use your full name (William rather than Bill, for example) and always use your middle initial (or your first initial if you're commonly known by your middle name). It creates an air of dignity and seriousness. These are two characteristics you'll want to promote as much as possible. If you have a nickname—perhaps all your pals know you as "Bubbah"—keep it to yourself. Bubbah and similar monikers will not inspire a whole lot of confidence in people who are looking for serious guidance on vital areas of their lives.

People who have service partnerships should simply use their last names—Lewis and Clark, for example, or Tinkers, Evans, and Chance. Full names can be included on business cards, advertising, stationery, and other business literature.

If you have employees and feel this fact may be important to clients, consider adding "and

Associates" to your name. Many potential clients are put off by professionals who appear to be flying solo. It raises questions about how successful and competent they are. By making it clear that you have a professional staff, you can make your business seem larger and more formidable than it might actually be.

Sadly, there may be some occasions when using your name is not a good idea. One of the hard facts of life is that we live in a society in which discrimination against certain racial, ethnic, and religious groups still exists. You need to ask yourself if your name might cause your business to be discriminated against. If this is a possibility, you could choose to use your initials or just a first or last name. Or you could use the name of your neighborhood or community. A name like Oak Valley Legal Services certainly resonates dignity and professionalism.*

Descriptive Names

People who own blue-collar service businesses, retail stores, restaurants, and other kinds of businesses often have a bit more fun with names. Many choose to select a name connected to their product or service. In upstate New York there's a septic tank service called Stinky's. That makes it crystal clear what the business is all about. Names like Rent-A-Wreck, Jiffy Lube, U-Haul, Terminix, and Roto-Rooter all give a clear indication of what kinds of services those businesses offer.

You might come up with a name that's a stylized version of your own. One of the best examples of this is Adidas, the athletic shoe company, which is named after its founder, Adi Dassler. Or you might choose a name that is symbolic of the nature of your product. Nike, another major athletic shoe manufacturer, chose this strategy by naming itself after the Greek goddess of victory.

Some businesses create unforgettable names by using the most tried-and-true approach of all—sex. Take the Hooters restaurant chain, for example. By combining its owl logo with a clever double entendre, the company has managed to turn another basic burgers, chicken, and fries emporium into a national success. Okay, the scantily clad waitresses may have had something to do with it, too. My point is that it's the kind of name people only have to hear once to remember.

Finally, once you come up with a name, check to see if it has already been registered by another business. If it has, you may be precluded from using it. Of course, subtle variations of the name which aren't registered may be just as effective. If the name isn't registered, and you feel it's particularly effective, consider registering it yourself.

---

*Discrimination might not be the only reason to avoid using your own name on your business. One afternoon when driving around, my wife and I stumbled across a lovely restaurant not far from our weekend home. It's name was, apparently, the last name of the proprietor. There were "x"s and "z"s in the name and, unfortunately, I forgot to take a business card. A few weeks later we wanted to return, but the name was so unusual that neither of us could remember enough of it to even look for it in the telephone directory. We haven't been back.

NEGOTIATING

I'VE NEGOTIATED HUNDREDS OF DEALS during my career, from fairly modest real estate transactions to multimillion-dollar compensation packages. There have been hundreds of books written on complex systems, strategies, and philosophies of negotiation. Since I'm something of a professional negotiator, I think I've read them all. Yet, despite the wide range of money at stake, the different natures of the negotiations, and the varied philosophies, I always come back to the same seven basic rules when I prepare to sit down with my opponent. I'll discuss them in a moment. First, I want to talk about negotiating in general.

A lot of people are uncomfortable with negotiating. There's an inherent adversarial quality to it that they find offensive. But guess what. That delicate sensibility can cost you thousands of dollars. Even setting aside the opportunities for making more money through business and career negotiations, think of all the big-ticket consumer items you'll spend money on during the course of your lifetime—cars, boats, appliances, furniture, electronic equipment, sporting goods, and, of course, houses. Depending on the asking price of the item being purchased, a little haggling can save you anywhere from a few dollars to a few thousand dollars. Believe me, negotiating is a talent we should all cultivate for our personal as well as business life.

It doesn't have to be an unpleasant experience. In fact, negotiating can be fun. This is particularly true when both parties treat it as a normal part of the process. Do you think a car salesman expects you to come in and simply write a check for the full sticker price of a car? Of course not. He expects you to negotiate. It can be done without any ill feelings at all. If he doesn't get what he wants, it's his fault, not yours. Nobody is twisting his arm to make him accept your offer.

Seven Rules for Successful Negotiating

As I mentioned earlier, I have some basic rules I follow when preparing to enter into a negotiation. Granted, they're not the only tactics I use. As a professional negotiator, I have a few more tricks up my sleeve than the average Joe who might be haggling over the price of a car. But for most people, these seven rules should be more than adequate to get them through any negotiation:

1. *Have a reasonable, clearly defined goal.* Know exactly what it is you want to accomplish in the negotiation process. If you're buying a house, determine how much you're willing to pay beforehand. If you can't reach that price, walk away from the deal.

2. *Knowledge is power.* Learn everything you can about your opponent and the issue being negotiated. If you're negotiating your salary with a new employer, for example, you need to know what others in similar positions are making, both in the company and in your industry.

If you're buying a car, find out what the dealer paid for it and use that figure, not the sticker price, as the basis for your negotiations,

3. *Don't mess with the pros.* If your opponent hires a professional negotiator, you need to hire one, too. Don't try to operate over your head. If you see me sitting across the table when you walk into the room, head straight for the telephone.

4. *Don't waste time and effort.* Negotiate only with people who have the authority to give you what you want. If you want to streamline the purchase process of an item, bypass the salesperson and ask to deal directly with the sales manager. Better yet, ask to speak to the owner of the business.

5. *Be civil, businesslike, and straightforward.* Don't spend time trying to be your opponent's friend. He's no more interested in becoming buddies than you are. And try to negotiate face-to-face. Negotiating over the telephone tends to make people braver than they really are. This can get them into trouble. Negotiating in person creates a more positive environment and fosters better communication.

6. *Be content to achieve your goal.* Don't worry about "winning." The negotiation process is not about winning. It's about reaching the goal you set for yourself. This leads to a basic fact of negotiating. I think the most effective negotiations are those in which both parties are successful in getting what they want. If they can't reach a deal, then the negotiation should come to an end. If one party agrees to a deal but doesn't get what he wants, he has no one to blame but himself.

7. *Have patience.* Remember that negotiating requires patience. Despite all the books that come out on the subject every year and all the self-proclaimed experts who conduct seminars on the "latest" in negotiation strategies, negotiating remains, at its core, a very simple act. It's just two parties, one wanting to accomplish one thing and the other wanting to accomplish something else. Their little dance can go on for weeks or months until they either reach common ground or give up and look for someone else who can give them what they want.

NEIGHBOR DISPUTES

IF GOOD FENCES MAKE GOOD NEIGHBORS, then electric fences make even better neighbors. People who live next door to each other don't always get along. They differ over how they care for their properties. They argue over barking dogs and loud music. They complain when their leaves blow onto each other's properties. Frankly, it can get a little ridiculous and more than a little costly.

I'm something of an expert on ridiculous neighbor disputes, having been at the center of one a couple of decades ago. At the time, my wife and I and our young children were living in Farmingdale, a suburb of New York City. The community consisted of lots of young families, just like ours. However, many of the residents wanted to ensure that uniformity covered more than just demographics. All the men in the community commuted to work during the week, and on summer weekends it was expected that they'd spend their time tending their lawns so the entire neighborhood would look like a golf course. That wasn't my idea of relaxation, however. As a result, our lawn—or meadow, as I preferred to call it—stood out from the rest. Subtle hints were, admittedly, ignored. Pleas to spouse and children were shrugged off. Finally, a posse was dispatched for a direct confrontation. My response was to mow my initials in the meadow.

It doesn't have to be this way. I have clients who have great relationships with their neighbors. They'll get together with two or three other couples for dinner or a night at the theater. They have great times with one another's children and grandchildren. Sometimes they'll even vacation together.

But they're all very similar to each other. They have the same kinds of lifestyles and share the same values. Their neighborhoods are picture-perfect, with manicured lawns and well-maintained houses. Everything is just so, created with a cookie-cutter precision that breeds contentment and civility. Their unwritten, but very much understood, rules of behavior ensure that they will not tread on one another's sensibilities.

It wouldn't take much to upset their apple carts. If the wrong person with the wrong lifestyle moved next door—me, for example—most of them would hit the ceiling. And with the benefit of hindsight, I can see they might be right in getting upset. Although we think of our homes as the one place on earth where we can do what we damn well please, the fact is that we all have an impact on our neighbors' quality of life, and they on ours. Coexisting peacefully requires more than a little courtesy and thoughtfulness.

But let's be realistic. There are a lot of people out there who just don't possess these qualities. If one of them ends up living next door to you, you're bound to have some differences at one time or another. If you do, it's important to know what to do to resolve your differences.

If you have a dispute with your neighbor, your first tactic should be to try to settle your differences amicably. Give him a call, tell him you have something you'd like to discuss, and ask if you can stop over. When you make your visit, explain your problem as diplomatically as possible and ask if he would consider taking appropriate action to change the situation.

If he does, that's that. If he doesn't, you need to resort to stronger action. Your options will depend on the nature of the problem. If it's noise, you can file a complaint with the police. Most communities have ordinances governing noise in residential areas. If it's the condition of the neighbor's property, you may be able to complain to your local government officials. If the appearance of the property is bad enough, you'll probably be able to recruit other neighbors to your cause. A shoddy property can affect the values of all the homes in a neighborhood, so they'll be as concerned as you are.

The worst problems can end up requiring legal action and some time in court. But before you resort to such drastic action, I suggest you try mediation. According to the American Bar Association, there are more than 22,000 mediators in the United States trained to deal specifically with disputes between neighbors. Unlike arbitration, in which the arbitrator's decision is final, mediators don't decide who is right and wrong. They merely help two sides come to an agreement. A good mediator is a facilitator. She'll know what facts are pertinent to the dispute and which to ignore. She'll also remain impartial and help each side see the other's point of view.

It may become necessary to seek expert advice during mediation. The mediator may direct either or both parties to obtain expert advice at any time during the mediation session. Likewise, the mediator may also contact experts directly. Again, their opinions will only be used to help you and your neighbor come to some sort of an agreement. You can't be told what to do.

The mediation process requires a good-faith effort on the part of both parties and full disclosure of the facts. It also requires a willingness to listen. If one or the other of you has your heels dug in so deep that no amount of mediation can make you budge, the effort will be pointless.

If mediation fails, you really have no other recourse than to turn to the legal system, but only if you have a case. Frankly, some disputes between neighbors can't be solved by legal means. People have the freedom to do whatever they want with their property, as long as they're not creating a hazard for their neighbors. If your neighbor paints his house purple or has five or six cars in the driveway or does something else you find horribly offensive, your only choice may be to live with it. If you can't live with it, you'll have to move.

Or, who knows, the offensive neighbor might move. Not that long after I immortalized my initials in our lawn we moved to another, less stuffy, community.

(See also mediation.)

NET WORTH

NET WORTH STATEMENTS ARE the adult scorecard. Many membership applications—such as for country clubs, co-ops, and condominiums—ask for this information. I agree that it's often an obnoxious practice—we all know a person's character has nothing to do with the amount of money he or she has in the bank—but like it or not, people will be making important judgments of you based on your net worth, so it's important to learn how best to present your information.

At its most basic, a net worth statement tabulates the difference between your assets and liabilities and says to the world, "Here's how much money I have, and here's how much money I owe." You can get that from your accountant, but that approach can be limiting. To be as useful as possible, your net worth statement needs to be more than just a simple black-and-white financial listing of assets and liabilities. The job of your net worth statement is, frankly, to impress people. To do that, you need to go into more detail, highlighting areas of particular merit or interest, maximizing the value of your assets, and minimizing your liabilities.

You should begin by attaching as much value as possible to your personal property. Many items you've acquired over the years have appreciated in value. At the very least, they've increased at the rate of inflation. The value of some has no doubt outpaced inflation. This should be reflected in your personal property calculations. For example, the dining room set you and your spouse purchased 15 years ago could be valued at today's cost, not at what you paid for it. That applies to all your other personal property as well.

Collectibles are always impressive additions to net worth statements. Perhaps you collect antiques, art, or rare Chinese porcelain. I suggest listing these collections separately from your other personal property. Once again, make sure you value them at today's market prices, not by what you paid for them. If necessary, you can have them appraised and attach the appraiser's letter to your statement. Keep in mind, too, that collectibles can increase in value unpredictably. You should have them appraised regularly and make the proper adjustments to your net worth statement.

Another way to enhance your asset line is to include any monies owed you or that you can reasonably expect. If you've lent money to your children or parents, be sure to include those amounts (even if you're not so sure you'll ever be repaid). Also include any cash gifts you receive regularly. For example, perhaps your parents or some other relative gives you a sizable cash gift every year for your birthday or some other occasion. You can include that gift as an asset and include a note describing the gift and the likelihood of it's being a recurring event. Obviously, if you're owed any money for work done, include it as accounts receivable.

Many applications will ask that you include the original cost of any real estate you own. Just make sure you include its current market value as well. That's the figure indicative of your net worth.

The liability side of your net worth statement will be a little more concrete than the asset side. Debts are debts, after all. There's not much you can do to couch them in a particular light, unless they have some contingencies attached. A good example is a loan for which you've acted as guarantor. Perhaps you cosigned a car loan for your son or daughter. Add a note to your statement that shows it's quite unlikely the debt will actually fall to you because of the net worth and income of the primary borrower. If you owe money to a relative or friend, ask if you can list it as a subordinated debt. That means in the case of bankruptcy, they'll be last in line. You certainly don't intend to declare bankruptcy, you simply want to minimize the potential negative impact of these debts on your creditworthiness in the eyes of other potential lenders.

Keep in mind that all these strategies are ethical and legal. A net worth statement is often the key to accomplishing something that means a great deal. If those who are judging you attach a great deal of weigh to your net worth, you have every justification to present yourself in the best possible light.

Sample Net Worth Statement

Assets

Cash in bank _____

Securities _____

Investment in personal business _____

Real estate owned _____

Automobiles _____

Collectibles

Personal property _____

Life insurance (cash surrender value) _____

Other _____

Expectations (explain in footnote) _____

    Total Assets

Liabilities

Notes payable

    To banks _____

    To relatives (subordinated) _____

    To others _____

Installment accounts payable

    Auto _____

    Other _____

Mortgage balances _____

Unpaid real estate taxes _____

Unpaid income taxes _____

Loans on life insurance policies _____

Other debts _____

    Total Liabilities _____

Net worth (total assets minus total liabilities) _____

NETWORKING

THE BEST WAY TO GET A JOB is networking. In some industries, it's the only way. The old saw is truer today than ever before: it's not what you know, it's who you know. Successful job hunting in this era of workplace free agency doesn't come through faithfully scouring the classified ads. It comes from establishing an extensive multidisciplinary network. Since you're not tying your future to a particular company, profession, or industry, your network will need to include people at various levels in a variety of businesses.

Networking requires constant effort. You can't not network for a year and then expect your contacts to be active when you get a pink slip. Make it a practice to save the business cards of everyone you meet. Take the time to make a few notes about each person and keep them in a file in your desk or on your computer. The more you know about someone, the easier it is to reestablish a relationship. Take a cue from the better salespeople who establish databases containing all sorts of information on each of their possible clients or customers. A good salesperson will be able to quickly find out the names of a potential customer's spouse and children, maybe even their birthdays. The good salesperson will know what a client likes to drink with dinner and what football team he follows. Like the good salesperson, you should follow up on all your meetings, even if it's just with a note or e-mail saying how much you enjoyed meeting them.

Networks need not be limited to people you've met. If you read an article about someone who might someday be a valuable contact, clip the article and file it away. Keep an eye out for changes in the upper-level management of the leading companies in your industry. Track the moves of key industry executives from company to company. Such changes can often be a sign of major shifts in the fortunes of individual companies or even in the industry itself. In addition, no man or woman is an island. The concept of six degrees of separation actually works. Diligently look for ways to establish contact with someone—say, a CEO you've read about—and you'll probably be successful.

Add to you personal network through your activities in professional associations and community organizations. Becoming involved in local politics, service organizations, and other local clubs provides a chance to meet people from many different industries. Joining a church or synagogue can expand your network even further.

I'm also an advocate of what I call "Rolodex renting." All the people you know will have their own extensive network of business contacts. By contacting them, explaining that you're looking for mentoring, and then gently asking them for the names of people who may be able to help you in your search for a job, in essence you're borrowing their Rolodex.

Remember that you're trying to cast as wide a net as possible. Don't limit your network to coworkers and business associates. Talk to your friends and neighbors. Call old college classmates. Ask members of your church or temple for names. Explain your general interests and intentions and that you're hoping they might be able to recommend some friends or business associates who can point you in interesting directions. As you compile a list of leads, be sure to write down the name of the person who gave them to you. That name will be your ticket to an initial contact.

As you mine your network of names, you'll be able to schedule a number of informational interviews. These are casual information-gathering meetings with contacts in which you can discuss general opportunities. Although the primary reason for these meetings is to create a professional relationship, it's okay to use them for a little additional networking as well. It's perfectly appropriate at the end of such a meeting to ask your host if she can suggest anyone else you might talk to about the topic under discussion. If your meeting with her went well she'll be more than happy to help you.

Keep in mind that networking is important for more than just job hunting or business start-ups. It's also critical for the success of your current career or business. No one can succeed in a vacuum.

Businesses need to have relationships with other businesses that may become clients or customers. Your company might also become involved with another business in joint ventures providing services to shared clients. Often a business relationship is critical in having reliable access to products or services. If you have a manufacturing business, for example, it's critical that you have a network of reliable suppliers who can provide you with materials when you need them. Otherwise, any glitch in your production schedule can cause you to lose customers and valuable revenues.

For your current career to continue in a positive direction you need to remain on top of trends inside and outside your company and industry. Just as you'll get better dirt at the company water cooler than from the employee newsletter, you'll get better industry information from personal contacts than from a trade journal.

—————————

(See also business cards, informational interviews, memberships.)

NEWSLETTERS

IF YOU'RE IN BUSINESS for yourself and you're not sending out regular newsletters, in one form or another, to your customers or clients, you're not going to succeed. In today's information economy, with even the largest of businesses using technology to personalize its relationships with customers, the business that doesn't maintain contact will soon be forgotten.

The traditional method of maintaining contact is, of course, advertising. But advertising is expensive and often poorly targeted. As a result, it's often difficult to determine if you're getting any return on you advertising dollar.

I prefer, and encourage my clients, to use the cheaper, more accurate, and more personal form of contact: the newsletter. I send a newsletter to all my current and former clients every quarter.

What's in a Newsletter?
It is, quite literally, a news letter: a personal letter from me to them, reporting on what has transpired in the past three months and what is likely to happen in the near future.

At times I include short articles describing recent legal and financial developments that may be important to them. Often this includes changes in the tax laws or recent trends in the job or real estate markets.

I also include news about my practice, such as the names and backgrounds of new associates and any other personnel changes. I also include personal news, like the arrival of new children and grandchildren, weddings, and anniversaries. My practice is small and my clients get to know everyone who works for me on a first-name basis. They enjoy keeping up with what's going on in our lives.

Cheap and Simple Is the Best Approach

My newsletter isn't fancy. It has no photographs and it's not in color. It's just black copy on off-white paper, printed on the laser printer in my office, and mailed out by my office manager. It's bare-bones simple, but it's sufficient to get my information across.

By contrast, I have several clients who are in the habit of distributing fancy newsletters with four-color photography and lots of graphics. These are printed by commercial printers and cost a dollar or two apiece to produce. Yet I'd be surprised if these slick productions ever had any more impact with their audiences than my modest little effort (which costs me pennies apiece to produce, by the way).

I tell these clients they're wasting their money producing such fancy newsletters. I explain that they've failed to distinguish between a marketing piece, which is worthy of some financial commitment, and an informational piece, which isn't. A newsletter is the latter. It doesn't need to be fancy. It's not designed to reel in new customers. It's purpose is to give information to the customers you already have and to reinforce your relationship with them.* What I advise my clients to do is cut back on their newsletter costs and redirect that money to their marketing and advertising budgets. It's a much more effective use of precious dollars.

Newsletter Dos and Don'ts

There are several things to keep in mind when producing a newsletter. The first is legibility. Let's start with type sizes. Keep in mind that you have customers of all ages. The type must be large enough that aging eyes can read your newsletter without difficulty. The type style is equally important. I recommend a serif font, such as Times. Sans serif fonts, such as Helvetica, are more difficult to read, particularly in copy-dense pages, though they might be good for headlines.

Paper color is another important consideration. A lot of people make the mistake of thinking that a bright color will make their newsletter stand out from the rest of the mail. It may. But it also might make it impossible to read. Stay away from colors and stick with white or off-white stock. You don't need fancy colors. Your name alone should be sufficient to get your customers' attention.

---

*I also discourage the use of generic newsletters you buy and to which you attach your name or logo. It's an obvious piece of marketing and the effect is the opposite of what you intend.

Internet Newsletters

The popularity of the Internet has created new opportunities to keep in touch with customers—but only if your customers are accustomed to receiving information this way. One way to send out your newsletter electronically is to create a listserv, a kind of electronic mailing list. With your listserv in place, you can reach hundreds or even thousands of people with one click of your mouse. If you have a Web site, you might also consider keeping your newsletter on that section of the site that's devoted to customer service.

NURSING HOMES

N URSING HOMES ARE a big business that's about to get bigger. The fastest growing demographic group in the United States is its oldest: those above 80. It won't be too long before the oldest and sickest among them are tottering off to a long-term care facility of some sort.

Evaluating Nursing Homes

Selecting a nursing home is a difficult decision. Unfortunately, it's often done in haste when an elderly parent is struck down by a major illness. If she's released from the hospital, she may be unable to return home and care for herself. This puts pressure on her family to find a nursing home as quickly as possible.

The best nursing homes offer a complete selection of nursing and personal care. This includes therapeutic services, dietary services, and social and recreational activities. Residents' meals will be prepared, housekeeping and laundry services will be provided, and medical care will be available.

For some residents—particularly those who enter at an advanced age—the nursing home will be their last home, so no matter how nice the home is, it's a difficult adjustment for both the senior and her family. Here are some important considerations for choosing a nursing home:

Certification: The nursing home should have a current operating license from the state. The administrator should also be certified.

Medicare and Medicaid acceptance: If you're planning on either program to help finance the cost, either now or in the future, make sure they're accepted. Most homes maintain a limited number of rooms for Medicare and Medicaid residents. (See "Check Admissions Agreements Carefully" on page 427.)

Location: It should be close to family members so they can visit frequently. It should also be near stores, restaurants, and other places that are appropriate for short trips.

Facilities: Inspect the facilities carefully. They should be clean and orderly. Pay particular attention to kitchens and bathrooms. Living areas and recreation areas should be bright and inviting. Furnishings should be comfortable and in good repair. Look for handrails in hallways and bathrooms and room for wheelchairs to navigate. Bedrooms should open into the hallway and have windows that open. There should be a secure garden or patio area that residents can visit for sunshine and fresh air. Watch out for any areas from which you're excluded.

Personnel: All nursing homes should have a physician on call for emergencies. The staff should be friendly, caring, and experienced. Ask if the home has a volunteer program.

Philosophy: Speak extensively with the administrator to determine the nursing home's philosophy on things like the use of physical restraints and medications. Ask if it has posted a patients' bill of rights or some other statement that acts on the residents' behalf.

Religious or cultural affiliations: Some nonprofit nursing homes are affiliated with religious and cultural groups.

I also advise my clients to seek out a long-term care advocates for assistance. There are more than 500 patient advocate programs throughout the United States. Advocates visit nursing homes to investigate complaints and mediate disputes. They're an excellent source of information on the quality of care in the homes in their areas. They aren't permitted to recommend one nursing home over another, but they can provide you with objective information on surveys, complaint rates, and the results of complaint investigations. Then it's up to you to make your own decisions.

Another source of information can be the official Medicare Web site at http://www.medicare.gov. The site has a feature called Nursing Home Compare, which lets visitors view the most recent state surveys for any nursing home that participates in Medicare and Medicaid. These surveys are conducted once a year to make sure homes are complying with federal regulations. If a home fails to meet a particular regulation, a "deficiency" will be noted. While it's difficult for even the best of homes to remain entirely deficiency-free, it is possible. You'll certainly want to steer clear of homes with many deficiencies in the resident care and resident rights categories.

Nursing Home Costs

Nursing homes aren't cheap. The daily fee at a skilled-nursing facility varies from state to state but can be $200 or more a day. In some areas of the country annual care runs as high as $96,000. Meeting the costs of nursing home care is an enormous concern for all families.

About half of all nursing home residents use savings, investments, and other private resources to pay for their care. A growing number of residents are using long-term care insurance. These products are still quite complex, however, and should be approached with caution. Other people get nursing home benefits from managed-care plans or employer benefit packages.

Another option for payment is a limited benefit from Medicare. Everyone who receives

Medicare part A benefits has available to them a skilled-nursing facility (SNF) benefit. This means that Medicare will pay for up to 80 days of a stay in a qualified nursing home facility. However, Medicare only pays under certain circumstances.

First, you must have spent at least a 3-day stay in a hospital during the past 30 days. If you go right from home or any other facility into a nursing home without spending three days in the hospital, Medicare won't pay. Medicare will pay 100 percent of the cost for the first 20 days you're in the skilled nursing facility. From days 21 to 80, Medicare will pay everything except $97 per day. (If you have a Medigap policy that will pick up the $97 difference.)

The second catch is that you must need skilled care, as Medicare defines it. For instance, physical therapy to help you recover from a broken hip is considered skilled care. But once it's determined that you can no longer benefit from therapy, Medicare stops paying.

People with very limited resources will have their care covered by Medicaid. Medicaid will also take over when people using private funds to pay for their care deplete their resources and are no longer able to pay for the nursing home on their own.

The Secret to Admission

But people who qualify for Medicaid will find it very difficult to get into a quality nursing home. That's because states actually allow nursing homes to practice what's called Medicaid discrimination.

When searching for a nursing home for your family member, the admissions coordinator for the home will ask who will be paying. If you say Medicaid, you'll most likely be told there's a long waiting list—perhaps as long as two years. But if you tell the admissions coordinator your family or the senior herself will be paying, you'll be told there are several beds open for immediate occupancy.

Nursing homes are allowed to maintain a set percentage of Medicaid residents. In other words, they set aside a limited number of beds for individuals who qualify for Medicaid. Once that quota is full they're permitted to turn other Medicaid-eligible applicants away.

The secret to getting around this is planning. Since nursing homes will give admissions priority to potential residents who can pay for themselves, the answer is for your mother to be able to pay the full fee for at least a little while. If she can pay her own way, for say, six months, after which she'll qualify for Medicaid, she'll have a much easier time gaining admission into the nursing home of her choice.

Don't allow an admissions coordinator to pressure you into making a time commitment about how long your mother will be paying privately. Similarly, don't stand for any pressure to sign a third-party guarantee requiring you or another family member to guarantee payment as a condition of your mother's admission. Both tactics are illegal.

(See also long-term care insurance, Medicaid, Medicare, medigap insurance.)

Check Admissions Agreements Carefully

Hospitals aren't in the business of long-term care. Sometimes, discharge planners will say an elderly patient must leave the hospital within 24 hours and simply hand family members a list of names and telephone numbers of area nursing homes. Under pressure to act quickly, patients and family members may rush to sign admissions contracts, unknowingly agreeing to illegal terms. Despite the time pressure, it's essential to examine admissions agreements and make sure they don't violate residents' rights.

Nursing home admissions contracts may include terms that expand the basis on which a resident may be discharged beyond the legal reasons, for example:

- The transfer or discharge is necessary for the resident's welfare

- There has been nonpayment of allowable charges

- The resident no longer requires a nursing home level of care

- The resident's needs can't be met in the facility

- The resident hasn't paid for care, either privately or through Medicare or Medicaid

Nursing homes cannot require residents to waive their right to apply for Medicare or Medicaid as a condition for admission. Any duration-of-stay clauses requiring residents or their families to pay privately for a given period of time are illegal.

Nursing homes cannot require a third-party guarantee of payment as a condition of admission. Unfortunately, that hasn't stopped some from trying.

Any contractual or verbal demands for special payments or contributions in exchange for admission or continued stay are illegal.

Nursing home admissions agreements sometimes include provisions limiting the rights of residents. Alternatively, some agreements provide incorrect or incomplete information about residents' rights.

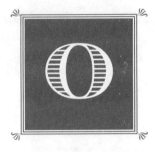

OFFICE POLITICS

IT WAS HENRY ADAMS who said politics is the systematic organization of hatreds. That holds true in office buildings as well as in capital buildings. Any time you have a group of people who spend a great deal of time together, factions evolve. Nowhere is this more true than in the office. Depending on the size of the staff, you may find the office divided into half a dozen or more little cliques. Sometimes it's simply based on job description. Managers may only hobnob with managers, and secretaries with secretaries. The marketing people and the folks from accounting may rarely get together. And if the anecdotes I hear from most workplaces these days are true, no one seems to see much of the people who work on the Web site.

Now I'm not saying this kind of workplace fracture is always a negative. There is a natural tendency to form alliances with people who do the same kind of work you do. Sometimes the nature of work itself will drive certain people together. The results can be both constructive and profitable.

But just as often the behavior can be destructive. We've all seen it. So-and-so doesn't get along with so-and-so because of some perceived slight that goes back years. This person is mad at that person because he or she has a nicer stapler. These are the kinds of petty differences that result in backbiting, gossip, and barely contained hostility. It's the kind of behavior that can affect everyone, regardless of how few people are involved.

Play It Straight

Office politics are unprofessional and a waste of time and energy. I believe the workplace is for work, that socializing should be kept to a minimum, and that people should keep their personal lives personal. I don't have much use for the desperate-for-attention single woman who feels compelled to share every detail of her love life with anyone who will listen. I'm equally repulsed by the weekend warrior who comes in every Monday and spends an entire morning boring everyone with a shot-by-shot description of the two rounds of golf he played over the weekend. And I certainly won't put up with behind-the-back gossip about coworkers.

Don't be a part of it. Be civil to everyone. Don't gossip. Remain neutral if someone attempts to have you take sides in a squabble. If you have nothing nice to say about someone, say nothing at all. If pressed for an opinion about someone, remain noncommittal, even if it makes you seem out of touch.

When problems are chronic, some companies will hold "gripe sessions" to clear the air or even bring in consultants in workplace dynamics. In my experience these only serve to worsen the situation. Let's be frank: these specialists aren't just there to conduct group therapy. They'll be presenting a report to management, and the names of those employees who are the most voluble will come up. You can be sure that will earn them reputations as complainers. The fact is, managers don't like employees who stir things up, regardless of the validity of their complaints. It makes the managers' jobs harder. Frankly, when it comes to personnel problems, they'd prefer not to hear about it.

The Role of the Manager

That attitude is wrong. I believe managers are responsible for making expectations known and for setting the proper tone in the office. They need to make sure that every employee is expected to be aware and in charge of their own behavior.

Shortcuts to Cut Short Office Politics

If politics in your office gets out of hand and you're forced, as manager, to step in and clean up the mess, here are a couple of strategies that can make the task a bit less odious.

To put an end to backstabbing, you need to do some independent investigation. Interview all the affected workers, including the alleged perpetrator. Demonstrate in words and deed that continued backstabbing won't be tolerated. Often the investigation alone is enough to resolve the issue. If not, determine who is the cause of the problem and tell him, in no uncertain terms, that his behavior is unacceptable and has put his job at risk.

Gossip can be as harmful as backstabbing. Because of the elusive nature of rumors and innuendo, getting substantive proof of who's responsible can be difficult. Instead, try to create a sense that it's the practice in general that you're targeting. If you delay taking any action because of lack of proof you demonstrate acceptance. Instead, act quickly. Make it clear in dialogues with all your subordinates that gossip will not be tolerated. Ask for help from everyone, including those you believe responsible, to put an end to gossip.

I used several strategies to keep such nonsense at bay when I had my own office. First of all, I kept office socializing to a minimum by eliminating the traditional office gathering spots. There was no "watering hole" where people could gather comfortably. The water cooler, copy machine, and fax machine were all in a converted galley kitchen that was only big enough for one person.

I also made sure everyone knew I'd hired them to do a job and that I expected them to adhere to strict professional behavior. Don't get the wrong idea. I didn't have an office where people were chained to their desks for eight hours a day. Most everyone got along and there was the normal amount of banter about this or that. But everyone knew where the boundary lines were. If groups gathered a little too long, I could walk by and, with just a glance, send them scurrying back to work. I encouraged my staff to take pride in being part of a professional office and in being well-compensated.

This isn't to say I didn't have problems. Like any other employer, I occasionally had to deal with petty feuds. Each time I called all the people involved into my office and presented them with two options: change your behavior immediately or be fired. Suffice it to say, most changed their behavior, and those who didn't changed jobs.

OPTIONS

Do not invest in options. I could leave it at that but I realize some of you might need a bit more persuading, and others might just be intellectually curious.

Options are contracts that allow you to buy or sell a specific security at a specific price within a certain period of time, usually five months or less. They are high-risk investments that can make you a bundle but also cause painful losses. The market mechanisms affecting them are complex and must be well understood before investing. Even if you do become an expert, only a small portion of your overall portfolio should be put at risk. If you win, it's great fun. If you lose, it's not.

Options are similar to futures contracts except for one big difference. When you own a futures contract, you must carry out the transaction on a specified date. With an option, you only carry out, or exercise, the option if you choose to. Hence the name. Also, you can exercise it within a specified period rather than on a specific date. If you don't exercise the option by the end of that period, the option expires.

Options are most useful in helping sophisticated professional investors hedge, or reduce risk in other investments. Let's say you purchase 100 shares of a stock for $25 a share. Your risk is that the price of the stock will drop and you'll lose money. To protect yourself, you can buy an option to sell the stock for $25 a share (the strike price) within a certain period of time. You'll pay the seller of the option a premium, but if the stock should fall through the floor, it'll be worth every penny. You can exercise the option, get back your original investment, and limit your losses to the money you paid for the option.

I know what some of you are thinking. Why not buy an option to sell the stock at $35 or $40 a share and lock in a profit? You can, but there's a catch. The cost of the premium to buy the option will be higher than the profit you would make.

Options as an Investment

Investors who specialize in options aren't as interested in the hedging function of options as they are in the fluctuating value of the options themselves. They see high-risk investment opportunities that can produce enormous profits. Such gains are possible because trading options is characterized by enormous leverage. With a relatively small cash outlay, you can make an investment of much greater value.

The value of an option is tied to the price of the underlying security. If the price of the security—they can be stocks, Treasury bills or bonds, currency, stock or bond market indexes, and even futures—moves in the direction you hope it will, you make money. Options to buy securities are known as calls, and options to sell are known as puts.

The price, or premium, paid for an option is determined by how far away the strike price is from the actual price of the security at the time you buy the option, and how far away the option is from expiration. During the life of the option, its value rises and falls with fluctuations in the price of the underlying security. When a security's value rises, calls also increase in value while puts decrease in value. When the price of a security decreases, the opposite occurs. This fluctuation allows people to make money simply through buying and selling options rather than the securities themselves.

Buying Options

People who buy calls are betting the price of the underlying security will increase. For example, if you buy a call to purchase 100 shares of stock for $20 a share and the price increases to $25, you can exercise the option, buy the stock at $20 and immediately sell it at $25. Your profit is $5 a share, less the premium you paid for the option.

People who buy puts, on the other hand, are hoping for a decrease in the value of the underlying security. Let's say you buy a put option to sell 100 shares at $25 a share and the price drops to $20. You buy the stock at $20 and immediately sell it for $25. Again, your profit is $5 a share, less the cost of the option.

Selling Options

Investors can also take the other side of the deal and be a seller, or writer, of options. The idea is to collect the premium and have the price of the underlying security move in such a direction that the buyer allows the option to expire. If the buyer decides to execute the option, however, you have the obligation to carry out the transaction.

It can be quite painful. Sellers of calls are either covered, meaning they actually own the securities in question, or naked, meaning they don't. Naked sellers are extremely vulnerable to a big move in the price of the underlying security.

Here's a good example of how much suffering options can cause. Let's say a stock is trading at $20 a share and you sell a call option to sell it at $25. One option contract is equivalent to 100 shares of stock, so you're promising to sell the buyer of the call 100 shares for $25 a share. You collect the premium and hope the price doesn't start to rise. As long as it stays below $25, the buyer won't exercise the option.

But then the unthinkable happens. The stock takes off and soon reaches $35 a share. At this point, the holder of the call understandably decides to exercise the option and make a lot of money. What happens next depends on whether or not you actually own the stock you promised to sell.

If you do, you have a few choices. One is to sell your stock to the buyer at $25 a share. If you purchased the stock for less than that, you'll make some profit but will miss out on the extra $10 a share. A second choice is to hold on to your stock and buy a call option to buy 100 shares at $25 (at an astronomical premium). You then exercise the option and immediately sell the shares for $25 to the holder of the call. The other choice is to sell stock on the market at $35 a share to cover the premium you'll pay to purchase the call option you'll then exercise to meet your obligation. You'll end up selecting the strategy that's least painful financially.*

If you're a naked seller of options, on the other hand, and don't own the stock, you're in for big trouble. You have two methods of coming up with the stock. You can buy the 100 shares on the market at $35 a share and sell them to the buyer for $25 a share to meet your obligation. In this case, you lose $1,000 less whatever you received as the premium. Or you can buy a call to buy the stock at $25 a share (with that astronomical premium), exercise the option and then turn right around and sell the stock at $25 to meet your obligation. In this case, you lose the difference between the two premiums. In both cases, you lose your shirt.

Leave It to the Professionals

As you can see, the options market would be appropriately headquartered in Las Vegas or Atlantic City. The examples I just mentioned are options trading at its most basic. Professional options traders use sophisticated strategies that involve buying and selling both calls and puts as well as shares of the underlying security. And even then they often lose money.

Options clearly have no place in the portfolio of the average investor. Only if a client had a huge nest egg and a taste for risk, and could afford to lose it all, would I let them take the plunge. Even then, I would encourage them to be very conservative and only play with money they can afford to lose—the same advice I give to my clients who go to Las Vegas to shoot craps. It's hard enough knowing if a stock will go up at all, let alone by a set amount before an expiration date.

---

*This approach only makes sense if you bought the stock at a much lower price, and chose this price as a target for sale. Now, at least, you will earn extra money while waiting for the price to reach your target.

OUTSOURCING

I F YOU OWN YOUR OWN BUSINESS, outsource every function you possibly can. If you're an employee, always keep one eye open to make sure you're not about to be outsourced out of a job. And if you start picking up some hints, look for a new job—perhaps as a consultant with an outsourcing firm.

By farming out noncore functions to outsourcing companies business owners can save on labor costs, real estate costs, and equipment costs. You gain efficiency and speed. Perhaps most importantly, if the relationship doesn't work out, you can end it in an instant and look for someone new.

I began to see the first major moves toward outsourcing back in the early 1980s when a client of mine abruptly lost his job as a graphic designer with a midsized corporation. He was a member of a 30-person in-house advertising team that arrived at work one morning to find out they'd all been terminated. The company had turned its advertising needs over to an outside agency. The move saved the corporation several hundred thousand dollars a year.

That was just an early example. Today, many businesses outsource payroll, accounting, data management, and Web site functions. One major investment media company I'm familiar with turned over all its financial functions to a midsize outsourcing firm. It's not uncommon to find company cafeterias run by outside vendors. Many hire independent businesses to take care of their grounds and facilities management needs. Most now hire outside public relations and advertising agencies. By farming out all these functions, the companies not only eliminate the personnel needed to do the work, but they strip away an entire level of management. The savings can be enormous. When I had my own office I eventually outsourced my bookkeeping function. I was able to replace a bookkeeper who earned $60,000 in salary and another $15,000 in benefits with a financial services firm that charged $48,000 and did a better job.

Hiring an Outsourcing Company

The key to outsourcing is to find reliable and talented service providers. That's why it's not surprising that a lot of companies that downsize by eliminating positions or entire departments end up hiring as consultants the same people they've just let go. They're getting the same talent and, because the former employee is now responsible for his or her own taxes, equipment, and other costs, they save money in the process.

If you're not hiring former employees you need to make sure you're hiring professionals with experience in your business or industry. My advice is to look for companies that specialize in servicing businesses like yours. As specialists they'll be able to quickly adjust to your way of doing things and hit the ground running. They may also provide unexpected benefits.

One client of mine, who uses an outside financial firm to handle her small public relations agency's payables and receivables, received an interesting call one day. The executive that handles her accounts noticed that her telephone costs were twice those of comparable businesses. My friend looked into it and was able to make the necessary adjustments. Had she had a staff book-keeper handling the bills it's unlikely she would ever have known her expenses were so out of whack. By having the advantage of comparison, the accounting firm picked right up on it.

Approach the hiring of a service provider just as you would that of any professional. Ask for references and take the time to talk to the people whose names you're given. Ideally they should be businesses that are currently using the service provider. Keep in mind, too, that down the road the two of you can compare notes and look for problem areas.

You also need to carefully calculate the cost of each potential service provider. The costs of all the services your interested in receiving should be laid out contractually with no wiggle room for unexpected increases. After all, the reason you're doing this is to save money. Crunch the numbers to make sure you'll actually be saving as much as you expect to.

Finally, keep confidentiality in mind. One of the dangers of outsourcing is that you may be sharing information about sensitive issues. Certainly anything having to do with money—payroll costs or payables and receivables—should be kept confidential. Personnel issues should also be kept off-limits to prying eyes. Some information, such as product specifications or anything else that's critical to keeping your business competitive and profitable, should not be shared at all. Make sure your contract with the service provider is quite clear about confidentiality issues. If the provider fails to live up to the terms of the contact, you have the grounds for a lawsuit.

PAGERS

PAGERS MAY NOT just be for drug dealers anymore, but that doesn't mean they're for every-one. My ambivalence over pagers has to do with their ubiquitousness. There's no question they serve an important function. Anyone in the health care field certainly needs a pager to be alerted to emergencies. And any business owner can certainly validate carrying one in case some-one at the office needs to get in touch with him. Parents have made good use of them as a method for their children to reach them in a pinch. I just sense there's a bit of fashion and van-ity involved in a lot of pager use, and that, frankly, I find somewhat annoying.

Now I won't get into a debate over whether or not you need a pager. If you think you do, that's reason enough to get one. What I will suggest, however, is that you purchase a pager than can be set to vibrate rather than beep. There's nothing more annoying than having someone's pager go off in the theater. It's plain rude and there's no call for it. This is why many theaters now request that cellular telephones and pagers be checked before performances begin.

If you're considering getting a pager, keep this in mind, too. What you intend to be a serv-ice to your customers and clients can turn out to be a disservice to you. By having a pager you're agreeing to extend a courtesy to people. You're in effect saying, "Don't hesitate to contact me at any hour of the day or night. You're that important to me." Just make sure you mean it. Ask yourself if you really want to be bothered by a call in the middle of a movie or a round of golf or while you're out sailing—a call that may well turn out to be about something that could wait until later. If you have a pager, it doesn't matter what your opinion is of the situation. If a client or friend feels that it's of sufficient importance to page you, you have no choice but to respond.

If you still insist you need a pager, be judicious about who you give the number to. Your spouse and children certainly qualify, as do business partners and certain key people within your organization. But when it comes to clients and customers, think long and hard. It really depends on the kind of business you're in and your individual client relationships.

One more personal note. I don't think there's a professional in the world who is more service-oriented than I am. I've held telephone client consultations on Sunday mornings, on my vacation in Europe, even while I'm in an airplane. I check my answering machine regularly and call people back from home or while I'm on the road if it's necessary. Without giving out my cellular telephone number, and without having a pager, I think I'm doing just fine, thank you.

PARTNERSHIPS

A PARTNERSHIP SHOULD EQUAL more than the sum of its parts. For their relationship to be worthwhile, business partners should each bring unique talents to the job—talents the other partner or partners lack. If you have a partner who's basically a clone of yourself, you're duplicating rather than expanding effort. What you need is a partner whose skills fill the gaps created by your weaknesses. A partnership that works in this manner will generate more profit than a sole proprietorship.

Partners can also be sources of additional capital, an important consideration when you're considering strategies to start or expand the business. Generally, the creditors of an individual partner cannot come after property owned by the partnership. They can only attach the interest and income of the individual partner.

An investor in a business can be what's called a "limited partner." This type of partnership provides special tax advantages and limited liability and is usually found in real estate development and international business deals. Being recognized as a limited partner requires some legal hoop jumping and therefore the assistance of your lawyer.

Partners are extremely vulnerable to one another, so they should be chosen with great care. For example, one partner can commit the partnership to all sorts of legally binding arrangements without the knowledge or consent of the other partners. This is why trust and communication between partners is so important. It's a lot like being married. There are many decisions to share and disagreements to work out. Anger and resentment can quickly become overwhelming if the partners are unable to communicate and resolve their differences.

Lack of autonomy can be a disadvantage in a partnership. Decisions are no longer made based on what's best for you, they're made based on what's best for the organization. They also must be made jointly, and this may slow down the speed with which things happen.

It's important to recognize that a partnership is a business relationship first and a personal relationship second. Or it may not be a personal relationship at all. I know many people in productive and profitable partnerships who almost never see their partners outside the office. It's not that they don't get along. They just have different interests and different social circles. If you and your partners have such an arrangement, that's just fine. What matters is the success of the business.

Partners' Rights and Obligations

The rights and obligations of each individual in a partnership are spelled out in the Uniform Partnership Act. This is a model partnership law adopted in its entirety or in part by most states. You should have your lawyer check your state's interpretation of the act before you create a partnership. The act states that each partner has the right to:

- Share in the management and conduct of the business

- Share in the profits of the firm

- Receive repayment of contributions

- Receive indemnification for, or return of, payments made on behalf of the partnership

- Receive interest on additional advances made to the business

- Have access to the books and records of the partnership,

- Have formal accounting of partnership affairs

The act also states that each partner has the obligation to

- Contribute toward losses sustained by the partnership

- Work for the partnership without pay in the traditional sense, but rather for a share of the profits

- Submit to majority vote, or arbitration, when differences arise about the conduct or affairs of the business

- Give other partners any information known personally about partnership affairs

- Account to the partnership for all profits coming from any partnership transaction, or from the use of partnership property

When you enter into a partnership, lawyers for the individual partners should negotiate a formal partnership agreement. Without one, problems can arise if one partner dies or leaves the partnership. The agreement should include:

- Each partner's salary and duties

- A strategy for solving disputes

- A description of the process used to establish the value of the partnership at the time the agreement was drawn up

- Buy-back and buy-out provisions for partners who die or choose to leave the business

- Negative covenants restricting the activities of retiring partners (for example, the retiring partner can't start a similar business within the same city for 10 years)

When a Partnership Can Be a Trap

It's not uncommon for a company to offer a valued employee a partnership stake—and the accompanying corporate profits—as an inducement to stay with the company. Not surprisingly, there's usually a negative covenant attached that restricts the employee from going to work for a competitor.

If you're offered such an arrangement, give serious thought to the pros and cons of the situation before you sign the agreement. If you're happy with your employer and decide the extra money is a fair tradeoff for losing some autonomy, then by all means take up the offer. Keep in mind, too, that there will be a time limit on the period during which you can't work for a competitor. You might be happy leaving and taking some time off before starting a new position. But if you want to keep all your options open and have the freedom to leave whenever you choose, don't sign anything. You may well end up trapped if you do.

Instead, you might want to use the offer of an ownership interest as the opening you need to begin discussing an employment contract or termination agreement. This could provide you and your employer with the security you both want, without limiting your freedom to leave.

PASSPORTS

IF PASSPORT APPLICATIONS ARE any indication, Americans are traveling overseas more than ever before. From 1989 to 1999, the number of passports issued each year increased more than 80 percent.

Hopefully, all these new travelers applied for their passports well before their scheduled departure dates. If not, they more than likely experienced some anxious moments. Getting a passport has become one of the most drawn-out bureaucratic processes. Although the government advertises a 25-day turnaround (which in itself seems unnecessarily long), many people have horror stories of waiting 8 to 10 weeks for their passports to arrive.

Part of the problem are the numbers involved. As applications increased over the last decade, the number of federal employees assigned to passport services remained fairly static. In order to deal with the increasing numbers of applications, the government reassigned many workers to process applications and took them away from jobs answering phones and fielding questions. In fact, not only is it harder to get through to a clerk to get a question answered; you now have to pay for it. All the numbers are 900 numbers, which means you're assessed a fee each time you call.

Start Early

This means you should apply for your passport as soon as you know you'll need one. In fact, to play it safe it might not be a bad idea to get one now, whether you plan on traveling overseas soon or not, just to eliminate any worry down the road. They're not expensive—$60 for people 16 and older and $40 for those younger than 16—so preplanning is a sound investment.

If you're applying for a passport for the first time, you must apply in person. Application forms are available at more than 4,500 passport acceptance facilities around the country. These include post offices, federal and state office buildings, and many county and municipal offices.

You'll need proof of U.S. citizenship. You can present a certified birth certificate, a naturalization certificate, a certificate of citizenship, or a consular report of birth abroad. You'll also need a proof of identity such as a driver's license, a work or student ID, a military ID, or a government ID. You also need a Social Security number.

You need to provide two photos of yourself. The rules are fairly strict. They must be 2 inches square, identical to one another, and have been taken within the previous six months. They must be full face and can be color or black-and-white. Backgrounds must be plain white or off-white. Hats can not be worn. Vending-machine photos will not be accepted. Many photography stores offer passport photo services. In fact, it's a good bet that there's a shop of some type within walking distance of every passport office in the country that provides passport photo services.

If you're applying for a passport for a child 12 or under, the child does not need to appear in person, although the passport agent can require that the child appear if there is reason for such an appearance. You must show a current form of identification. Children older than 12 must appear in person.

Passport Renewals

If you already have a passport, you don't need to appear in person to have it renewed. You send your expired passport along with an application form and a $40 fee in the mail. If your name has changed

> ### Try a Passport Service
>
> There are a number of passport expediting services advertising on the Internet that "guarantee" they can have your passport delivered to you within a week or less after receiving all your documentation. Of course, they charge a hefty fee, as much as $150, in addition to the $95 federal rush fees. But if you're in a bind, it may be worth the money.

since the first passport was issued, you need to include a copy of the court order, marriage certificate, or other legal document that specifies your new name. When your new passport is issued, your old one will also be returned to you.

Expedited Applications

If you need your passport in a hurry, you can expedite the process by paying a $35 fee. Sending your application in overnight mail with a second postage-paid return overnight mail envelope inside will help you get the passport as soon as possible. The Passport Agency will process expedited applications in 3 working days after they've received the forms and will send you your passport in 7 to 10 working days.

PAYABLES

IT TAKES YEARS TO ESTABLISH a good reputation in the business world. And it takes no time at all to ruin one. One guaranteed method to destroy your credibility is to become a late payer. It's a small world out there. If you don't pay your bills on time, that fact will quickly become known among the vendors and suppliers in your industry.

I'm not suggesting you shouldn't put off paying bills as long as ethically possible. If the terms for payment are 30 days, take advantage of every second. That's not being a deadbeat—it's being a savvy businessperson. As long as that money is in your accounts, it can be earning interest.

But the line between deadbeat and savvy businessperson is often a fine one. In business it's important to treat people the same way you expect to be treated. The moment you begin to stretch your payments past their due date you begin to cause financial difficulties for your creditors. That's not fair to them, and it's not fair to you. The damage you do to yourself and your business will far outweighed a few extra days' interest.

Of course, given the fickle nature of business, there will likely be occasions when you may have problems paying your bills on time. It's your responsibility to be prepared for such emergencies. One strategy is to establish a line of credit with a bank. Although banks aren't generally great sources of startup capital, they may be willing to give your business a line of credit as long as it's secured by fresh inventory, accounts receivable, or some other kind of relatively liquid asset. If they're not willing to provide a line of credit to your business, they may be willing to extend one to you personally in the form of an installment or bullet loan.*

As an entrepreneur you must be willing to put your own assets on the line to get through the tough times. I have a very successful client who owns a chain of franchised weight-loss centers

---

*A bullet loan is a loan that comes due in one shot.

in the Midwest. The early going was tough for her. At one point during her first year of business, she took out a loan using her Mercedes as collateral just so she could pay her employees.

Asking for an Extension

There may come a time when, for very legitimate reasons and despite your best efforts, you just can't meet your payments on time. If that happens, you should immediately call your creditors and inform them. By contacting them first, you're showing that you're aware of your obligations and are willing to make a good-faith effort to solve the problem. The more warning you give creditors, the more flexible they'll be.

You don't need to go into great detail about the reasons for your inability to pay. If you're having problems with your own receivables, you can inform your creditors that you are expecting the money you need to pay them to arrive very soon. In the meantime, you tell them, you would like an extension on your current bill, perhaps 60 days rather than 30. If you can give them a date when they can expect payment it will make the process go that much more smoothly. I think you'll find that most vendors and suppliers will be quite reasonable if you're honest with them.

If you really fall into financial trouble, you need to ask for a longer period of time to pay off your creditors. Offer them all the same payment plan and agree to pay all your obligations without interest. Don't worry if they play hardball and threaten to turn your account over to a collection agency. If they do, they won't receive the full amount since collection fees are quite high. And they don't want you to go out of business and declare bankruptcy. In that case, they'll lose a customer and likely get even less.

One last thing: You may have to wade through a few levels of bureaucracy before you get to a person who can help you. Your first contact is likely to be a powerless clerk who will merely recite the party line. Ask to speak to a supervisor and repeat your request. If that doesn't work, ask for the next level of supervision. Eventually you'll find someone capable of creative thought who has the power to make exceptions to rules. When you find that person you'll be able to hammer out a workable plan.

PENNY STOCKS

THERE'S A RECURRING BELIEF among some investors that the cheaper the price of a stock, the easier it will be to make money. That's why penny stocks—stocks selling for $1 or less—have been so appealing for so long.

Unfortunately, they've been losers for just as long. Any company, regardless of the price of its stock, must grow and make money in order for its stock to appreciate. Just because a stock is selling for $1 a share and not $50 a share doesn't make it any more likely that its price will increase. In fact, it's more likely the opposite will happen. Most penny stocks are issued by small companies that are constantly teetering on the edge of bankruptcy. Many will eventually tip over the edge, taking investors' money with them.

Of course, penny stock promoters, who subscribe to the P. T. Barnum approach to selling securities ("There's a sucker born every minute"), won't tell you of this danger. They'll only point out the enormous opportunity for profits—and there are indeed a few examples—that penny stocks can provide. One of their favorite stories is the rise of the Tandy Corporation, which owns the Radio Shack chain. If you had purchased 500 shares in the early 1960s for 60 cents a share—an investment of $300—you would have seen your investment grow to nearly $400,000. This is all many investors need to hear.

Penny stocks are usually sold over the counter. While many are legitimate, others are often promoted by boiler-room operations that pitch stocks by making cold calls over the telephone. Here are a few of the ways you can be taken:

There is no company behind the stock. Sometimes a penny stock scheme will sell shares in a non-operating company, or shell. When enough cash has been solicited from guileless investors, the promoters will look for a cheap business to buy. It may be legitimate. It may not. Regardless, it won't be the kind of business you thought you were investing in.

The price is exaggerated. Once promoters have a company to pitch, they exaggerate its performance and its price. Sometimes all the information they provide investors is completely fabricated. As they artificially drive up the price, the promoters make more and more money.

You get trapped. Once you invest in a penny stock, you may see the share price rise for a while, courtesy of the broker who's manipulating things behind the scenes. But when you try to sell the stock you may be told you have to reinvest the proceeds in other stocks. Eventually, the promoters stop pitching the stocks you've bought, prices return to their true value, and your holdings drop through the floor.

If there's any advantage to penny stocks, it's that the big fish of the investment world—banks, pension funds, insurance companies, and the like—ignore them. They're generally not interested in stocks that sell for less than $10 a share. If you invest carefully, deal with a reputable broker, and find a legitimate winner, the big institutions may eventually discover it, too. At that point you might enjoy a quick ride to the top. Statistically, however, you're more likely to get burned. My advice is to stay away from penny stocks. As I've pointed out elsewhere in this book, if something seems to be too good to be true, it usually is.

PENSION PLANS

THE TRADITIONAL DEFINED-BENEFIT PENSION plan is like a liberal Republican. There are still a few around, but they're hard to find and their days are numbered. It wasn't always this way.

Defined-benefit pensions plans (those that provide a fixed income, based on how long you worked for the company and how much you earned, that begins at retirement and lasts until you die) began to catch on in the early years of the twentieth century and grew popular during the 1920s after tax legislation made them advantageous for employers. In the 1930s Social Security was created to provide what amounted to a pension for everyone. Then, in the 1940s and 1950s, private pensions expanded once again as compensation for organized labor's acceptance of wage controls during World War II.

Things began to change in the 1980s and 1990s. Retirees were living longer than anticipated. Medical costs were soaring. The economy was bouncing in and out of recession. Employers realized they could no longer afford to provide a defined benefit to their employees. More than 50,000 companies dropped their defined-benefit pension plans altogether over the last decade.

The result? Most workers need to take care of it themselves. What most employers now offer are defined-contribution retirement plans that employees must at least partially fund themselves. The most common investment vehicle for these plans are 401(k) accounts (nonprofit companies have their own version, the 403(b) account). Money is deposited to these accounts through payroll deduction plans and grows, tax-deferred, until the employee chooses to start drawing on the funds at age 59½ or later. At that point he pays taxes on the money he draws out. Money withdrawn before age 59½ is not only taxed; it is also subject to a 10 percent penalty.

A defined-contribution plan requires that the employer put a predetermined amount of money into your retirement account. It can be a percentage of your salary or a fixed share of the company profits and can be in cash or stock. You can also make contributions of your own. Employers prefer defined-contribution plans because they only have to pay out whatever was put into the account, plus earnings, during your career. There are no guaranteed lifetime benefits. If the money runs out before you pass away, that's your problem.

You also need to be prepared to make some decisions about how your money is invested. Most employers offer a menu of investment options, ranging from nearly risk-free money market funds to aggressive-growth mutual funds. Many people find this a lot of fun and become quite engrossed in the fortunes of their accounts, regularly moving funds from one account to another. But others panic at the responsibility. If you're the latter, the services of a good financial planner are a must.

You may have some other decisions to make. Some companies offer employees an employee stock ownership plan (ESOP) as their defined-contribution plan. The risk is obvious. If the company does well, so do you. But if the company performs so poorly that the stock decreases in value—or worse, goes bankrupt—you have nothing. When you invest in an ESOP plan, you're really putting all your eggs in one basket: not only your current income, but your future income as well, depends on the health of one company.

While you're analyzing your plan, check into its safety as well. It's not inconceivable that your employer has been strapped for cash at one time or another and dipped into the kitty to bail the company out of trouble. An estimated 25 percent of corporate pension funds are believed to be underfunded, and nearly 2,000 funds have completely collapsed over the last 25 years. While that's a small number given the number of businesses in the United States, it still illustrates the fact that your retirement funds are extremely vulnerable. You can check the health of your plan by asking the employee benefits office for a copy of Form 5500, which all companies must file each year with the Department of Labor. The report will contain an actuarial analysis that will tell you everything you need to know.

If disaster does occur, a federal agency called the Pension Benefit Guaranty Corporation (PBGC) provides some assistance to people whose pensions have disappeared. But it's rare that all the money an individual is entitled to is recovered. The biggest problem is that the PBGC doesn't guarantee 401(k) accounts or other defined-contribution plans. Plus there's a ceiling on the maximum benefit it's allowed to pay out. So if your fund does fold, you'll probably end up getting pennies on the dollar and will end up being involved in a class-action lawsuit to try to get your savings.

Perhaps you're fortunate enough to have an employer who contributes to a pension plan. Or maybe you're doing it all yourself. Regardless, it's important to take advantage of retirement plans. Even if, like me, you don't believe in retirement, the tax advantages of putting money away in these accounts is irresistible. Start as early as possible and put as much money as you can afford into retirement plans. The earlier you start saving and the more you put away, the sooner you can wake up each morning and spend the day doing what you want to do, not what someone else tells you to do.

PERFORMANCE REVIEWS

ONLY SADISTS AND MASOCHISTS look forward to performance reviews. An employee who knows he has been underperforming can rightfully expect a wrist slap. But even employees who think they're doing a good job are often beset by doubt and arrive at their performance reviews quaking in their boots.

Some supervisors, too, can be made anxious by performance reviews. Uncomfortable with criticism or confrontation, they hate having to point out people's faults. As a result, they may fail to get the needed message across when they meet with an employee whose performance is lacking. That, in turn, just leads to more of the same problematic behavior from the employee.

It also reduces the supervisor's credibility if and when she finally does choose to bring up problematic behavior. The employee can quite rightly question why something that's gone undiscussed for so long is suddenly being made an issue.

Receiving a Performance Review

I believe the best way to approach a performance review, regardless of whether it's positive or negative, is to get to the point before your supervisor does. This requires a bit of subtlety. For example, if you know you're going to be faulted for various transgressions, present your plans for improvement right away, before your supervisor can even bring up the subject. If you know your review is going to be positive, start a discussion that focuses on your goals and challenges for the coming year. In both cases you've made the future the focus of the conversation.

Remember that a performance review is your supervisor's forum, not yours. That means it's a very subjective exercise. If she feels you're doing poorly in some areas, don't argue with her criticisms unless you know them to be based on hearsay. Since it's her show, it's also not a good time to bring up money. Asking for a raise during your performance review can actually cause your supervisor to backpedal and come up with reasons why your performance is negative and undeserving of a raise.

It's important that you let your supervisor know you understand the points she's made. Ask her for advice on how you can improve. This accomplishes two things. First, it flatters her, which never hurts. Second, it encourages her to pay more attention to your progress. To show her how serious you are to improve, ask to have another performance review in a month or two to see if she feels the changes are working.

You should also use a performance review to get a sense of your status within your company. If you receive a negative review, it may mean your future with the company is limited and it's a good time to start job hunting. But even a good review can set off alarms. If you're told you're doing a good job but not presented with new opportunities, it may be a sign you're being shelved. Unless you look forward to years of doing the same thing day after day, you should start sending out your résumé and mining your network of business contacts.

Giving a Performance Review

As a supervisor, you need to treat performance reviews with the utmost seriousness. Your job is to promote behavior that is in the best interests of your company, not win a popularity contest. If you have bad news to deliver, do so frankly and matter-of-factly. If your criticisms are well-founded, the employee has no right to become angry or upset. If he does, you need to present specific examples of negative behavior or poor performance.

Your job is also to help the employee. Suggest ways he can improve his performance and offer to meet with him on a regular basis to review his progress. You also must be sensitive to the causes of his poor performance. If you suspect it may be due to personal problems—a substance abuse or a marital crisis, for example—you might diplomatically broach the subject. If he concedes that there are problems in his life at the moment, it's your job to help him get assistance.

Your company may have in-house counselors. If not, your health insurance provider should be able to refer him to someone.

To be most effective, I think performance reviews should be conducted every six months. New employees should be reviewed after three months. Criticisms and suggestions on how to improve should be presented in writing to the employee. When the meeting is over, you should have the employee sign the performance review and give him a copy. The original should be kept in your own files. The idea is to create a paper trail that documents the issues discussed and your requests for improvement.

Ultimately these documents will become stepping stones to termination if you need to fire an employee. They are proof that the employee was made aware of his shortcomings, was asked to improve his performance, and was given suggestions on how to do it. If, after a number of conversations, he fails to improve, you're entirely justified in letting him go. It may not be easy. Just remember that incompetent employees are a drain on your business—and your wallet.

(See also promotions and lateral moves, terminations.)

PERSONAL LOANS

YOU DON'T HEAR MUCH about personal loans anymore. Why? Because banks don't want to encourage them. Not because they're dangerous. They'd just prefer you use your credit cards because of the higher interest you'll pay on the debt.

A personal loan is usually unsecured. As a a result it will carry a higher rate of interest than automobile loans or home mortgages, which are secured. Still, the rate on a personal loan will probably be about two points below the average credit card rate.

Another possible advantage of personal loans is that they could prevent impulse spending. Let's say you and your spouse are out shopping one day and wander into a furniture store. There you spy a couch you both fall in love with. It also happens to have a $3,000 price tag. A credit card allows you to buy it on the spot, without careful consideration of the debt you're taking on.

But if you were going to use a personal loan, you'd need to leave the store, visit the bank, fill out forms, talk to a loan officer, and possibly wait a day or two for the loan to be processed. That would give you time to consider what you're doing. You might decide you're making a mistake and should wait until you have the cash to make such a purchase.

A personal loan also comes with a firm payment schedule. You'll know exactly how may months it will take to pay off the loan, how much your monthly payments will be, and the total you'll pay in interest. By contrast, a credit card debt can drag on for years. As long as you're making your minimum payment each month, most of which will be interest, the bank will be quite delighted. The longer you take to pay off the debt, the more interest the bank collects.

Personal loans require the same kind of comparison shopping as an automobile loan. In fact, since personal loan rates differ even more than automobile loan rates it's really essential you call several area banks to obtain quotes. You'll probably get the best rate at a credit union, although you may need to join by opening a checking or savings account. In your shopping you might find some lenders offering variable-rate loans with low initial rates. These can be dangerous over the long term, however. As with any variable loan, you really need to do the math and calculate what the highest rate might be during the term of the loan.

You may be able to get a reduced interest rate by authorizing the bank to make direct deductions from your checking or savings accounts. Banks like this arrangement for a number of reasons. One is convenience. They just shift the money from your account to one of their own accounts. Another is that the lack of correspondence makes serving the loan less costly. But the banker's main reason for favoring direct deductions is what's called "right of offset." This means that if you default on the loan the bank can seize the funds in your accounts. Keep that in mind when deciding what kinds of payment arrangements you're most comfortable with.

If you're dealing with the same bank with whom you have your checking and savings accounts, they may offer you a savings-secured or passbook loan. Because the loan is secured by your account the interest will be lower—perhaps two or three points above what they're paying you on your savings account. But there is a catch. You might think you're in effect only paying two or three points in interest, but you're not. You don't earn interest on the collateral account while the loan is active.

Personally, I think that if the amount in your savings account is larger than the amount of the loan, you shouldn't even bother taking out the loan. You're better off depleting the account and then saving and depositing the money you'd have used to pay off the loan.

PETS

Buying and owning a pet can be extraordinarily expensive, but it probably provides a greater return on investment than any other purchase you could make. Pets can provide companionship, comfort, entertainment, protection, and unconditional love and affection. They can even improve your health. Medical studies have linked pet ownership to lowered blood pressure and reduced incidence of heart attack.

You may already know this from firsthand experience. More than 60 percent of the households in the United States have at least one pet. Many have two or more. But if you've never had a pet and think you might like one, read this chapter carefully.

Are You Ready for Pet Ownership?

The decision to get a pet should not be entered into lightly. Pets require both time and money. They must be fed, walked, and provided with medical care. They also require a lot of attention. If you're not willing to make the commitment, you won't be successful.

Let's look at the cost first. The American Kennel Club estimates that caring for the average dog over 11 years will cost as much as $13,000. Caring for a cat over 15 years will cost around $6,000. A serious illness can add a lot more to the cost.

The time factor must also be considered. Cats are fairly independent and don't require a lot of time. Dogs, on the other hand, require a great deal of attention. First, they must be trained. They also love walks and playing with toys. Some breeds will pester you endlessly to play. If you don't give them enough attention, they may develop behavioral or even health problems.

Choosing the Correct Pet

The type of pet you choose will be determined by the amount of money you want to spend, the time you have to devote to the animal, and your living situation. If you're living in a rural area, for example, you can have as many pets as you want, as long as you have the time and money. But if you live in a studio apartment in the middle of Manhattan, your options are limited. A small dog might work, if you don't mind taking it out several times a day. A cat is probably a better choice. A bird or some fish might be better yet.

You also have to be concerned about rules and regulations. If you live in a co-op or condo, there may be restrictions on the type of pet you can own, Many retirement communities also have rules governing pets. Some ban them altogether. Other require that dogs be within a certain size and weight or that cats be kept indoors.

Where to Get Pets

For a dog or cat, start with you local humane society or the ASPCA. More than 8 million unwanted animals are euthanized every year in the United States. By bringing home a dog or cat from the pound, you're more than likely saving it from the same fate.

There are other advantages. Most of the animals have already been neutered or spayed, received their vaccinations, and been examined by a vet to make sure they're healthy. The cost to adopt is usually less than $50.

The disadvantage of bring a pet home from the animal shelter is you're not sure what you're getting into. That tiny little friendly puppy could grow into an enormous, aggressive dog. The only way to ensure you're getting a pet with a particular set of characteristics is to buy a pure-bred animal.

If you're interested in a particular breed, buy the animal from a reputable breeder rather than a pet store. Breeders pay better attention to their animals and are concerned with maintaining the positive traits and health of a particular breed. Many pet stores buy their animals from "puppy farms" where there is no concern about inbreeding and the resulting genetic conditions. Breeders will also provide information on the parents and bloodlines of an animal, so you can get an idea of exactly what your pet will be like.

Purebred cats and dogs can be costly. Popular breeds of dogs that don't come from "champion" blood lines may cost as little as $100. Rarer breeds or those whose blood lines are sprinkled with award winners can cost well over $1,000.

For other kinds of pets—fish, birds, turtles, hamsters, gerbils, ferrets, and the like—you're usually limited to a pet store. There are dealers, however, who specialize in exotic fish and birds. There are also dealers specializing in snakes and other reptiles. Make sure, however, that such dealers aren't selling illegal or endangered animals.

Training

If you don't want to train your pet, get a fish or some other animal that's kept in a cage or tank. If you want to minimize training, get a cat. Once they have the litter box and scratching post down, which takes no time at all, you're set. But if you get a dog, be prepared to put in some time.

Some people buy a book and attempt to train their dogs themselves. Those who fail usually end up in obedience class with a professional trainer. Just remember that the dog-training field is entirely unregulated. Ask around for recommendations.

(See also pet insurance.)

PET INSURANCE

ADVANCES IN VETERINARY SCIENCE and the increasing cost of pet care will, I think, make pet insurance ubiquitous by the end of the decade. Americans currently spend hundreds of millions of dollars every year on pet food, toys, veterinarians and other pet-related items. Pet insurance, available in the United States only since the late 1980s, is already as common here as it is in England and Sweden, the two nations in which it first became popular.

While it might seem a bit extreme, from an economic point of view, pet insurance isn't a bad investment. A serious injury or illness to a pet can result in several thousand dollars in vet fees and medicines. These are costs that few people anticipated when they brought home a puppy or kitten. When a health crisis arises, however, even though they're shocked at what it will cost to save their beloved companion, most pet owners bite the bullet and spend the money.

Buying pet insurance is a project. There's very little uniformity among the policies offered. Some only cover certain kinds of pets, dogs and cats being the most common, of course. Others only offer certain kinds of coverages. Premiums vary dramatically and are often tied to the breed of the animal, as well as its age. This means you need to spend some time comparison-shopping.

Since pet insurance is relatively new, it's also not always easy to find. My advice is to start with your veterinarian. Although pet insurance was viewed with some skepticism by the veterinary industry when it was first introduced in this country, more and more vets have come to see it as a viable option for their clients. You might also contact one of the following companies:

- Veterinary Pet Insurance Group: 800-USA-PETS; usapets@veterinarypetins.com
- Pet Wellness Plans: 800-645-2939
- VetSmart Pet Hospital and Health Center: 800-785-0557
- Preferred Pet Health Plus: www.pethealthplus.com

Questions to Ask

Here are some of the questions you should ask when evaluating pet insurance policies:

1. *Does the company insure my kind of pet?* Some companies insure just about every kind of domestic animal. Others only cover a few.

2. *Can I get a discount if I insure more than one pet?* Most pet insurance companies offer discounts if three or more pets are on the same policy.

3. *Am I required to use certain veterinarians?* Fortunately, pet health insurance gives us a lot more freedom in choosing a care provider than do most human health care companies. Generally, you can use any veterinarian you want.

4. *What does the policy cover?* Most policies cover treatment for illness or injury, x-rays, surgeries (including neutering and spaying), lab tests, and prescriptions. Some will also cover annual checkups, dental care, euthanasia and burial expenses. Some even cover acupuncture, herbal medicines, chiropractic treatment, and homeopathy. Pet insurers have accepted alternative treatment much quicker than human insurers.

5. *What doesn't the policy cover?* Common exclusions are pre-existing conditions, hereditary conditions, vaccinations, behavioral problems requiring therapy, special diets or nutritional supplements, grooming products, and elective treatments. Many of these coverages can be purchased as add-ons for an additional premium, however.

6. *Are there age limits?* Some companies won't insure animals beyond a certain age. Some, for example, won't insure dogs and cats over 10 years of age. Others will insure older animals, but with correspondingly high premiums, of course. Similarly, most companies require that a pet be 8 to 12 weeks of age before it's eligible for insurance.

7. *How much is the deductible?* Most deductibles are in the $100 to $200 range. Like human health care plans, pet insurance plans only pay a portion of the costs of treatment after the deductible has been met. Also, the insurance company will not assume any responsibility for paying the veterinarian. You must send in a form to the company to be reimbursed after you pay the vet yourself.

8. *What is the basis for reimbursement?* Make sure the company bases payment on your real out-of-pocket expenses, not on "reasonable and customary" charges.

9. *What will my premium be?* It will depend on the type of pet you own, its age and breed, and its environment—indoor or outdoor, for example. It will also depend on how extensive you want the coverage to be.

Is Pet Insurance a Good Deal?

If you would pay whatever it costs to save the life of your pet, it probably is. It won't necessarily break the bank. You can buy a basic illness and injury policy for several hundred dollars a year. After that, you can add extended coverage for almost any condition or situation. The amount of coverage you think you need and the premiums you're willing to pay are entirely personal. But if you're like most of the pet owners I know, you'll be willing to pay quite a bit.

PRE- AND POSTNUPTIAL AGREEMENTS

ANYONE GETTING MARRIED for the second time should insist on a prenuptial agreement. Any single affluent woman should insist on a prenuptial or postnuptial agreement. (A prenuptial is worked out prior to a marriage and a postnuptial is signed after the marriage takes place.) And any woman or man whose family owns a lucrative business should insist on a prenuptial or postnuptial agreement.

Second-Marriage Prenuptials

Second marriages are on the increase. One reason is that Americans divorce each another at the drop of a hat, and statistics show that most remarry, many with astonishing speed. But a second reason is that our elderly population is growing, and many men and women are entering second marriages after losing a spouse. This trend will grow as the first wave of baby boomers begins to topple over.

These are the people for whom prenuptials make the most sense. Let's face it, the longer you've been around the more wealth you've acquired. Those entering second marriages often have grown children from previous marriages and don't intend to have any children together. They have possessions, cash, investments, and other assets that they want to leave to their children or nieces and nephews and not to their second spouse. A prenuptial makes the disposition of all these assets quite clear. Since both parties generally have the same goal with regard to their respective families, creating the agreement is easy. Hopefully, they've gotten together for companionship, not for material gain.

Most second-marriage prenuptials divide assets into three categories: those brought to the union by the wife, those brought by the husband, and those acquired while they are together. Those assets each person brought to the marriage go to surviving children or other designated heirs upon their respective deaths. Should the couple divorce (statistically quite likely, by the way), each one walks away with whatever they had before the marriage. Jointly acquired possessions are usually left to the surviving spouse or, in a divorce, split between the couple.

Single Rich Female Prenuptials

It's been a long time since women went to college to get their Mrs. degrees. Women today are enjoying careers and waiting much longer to marry than their mothers and grandmothers. As a result, they often arrive at the altar with significant assets. They may own a house or an apartment. Because they've worked for some time, they're likely to have established an investment portfolio. They may have put money into art or antiques. They're not going to want to risk losing them through a failed marriage.

You may think this is a bit paranoid, but the fact is that women are much more vulnerable than men to financial crises after a divorce. One reason is the ongoing inequity between the salaries of men and women. Another is that when women leave their jobs to stay home and raise children, they are often unable to find jobs with the same salaries if they have to reenter the workforce. Working women are also often awarded reduced support by judges, even when they have custody of the children. The financial security blankets they worked hard to create before marrying can go a long way toward easing the financial strain that can accompany being single again.

Protecting the Family Business

Anyone who owns part of a family business should unquestionably have a prenuptial. Without one, his or her spouse can be entitled to as much as one-half of the interest in the business if

Bringing Up The Prenuptial Issue

Accept that this is not apt to be an easy discussion. There are ways, however, to mitigate the pain and potential for disaster. Bring this up soon after deciding to marry, not just before the wedding. Never frame it as a requirement for the marriage to take place. Be matter-of-fact about it. Try to bring the subject up as part of a general conversation about finances. Suggesting the idea came from a third party—family business partners, lawyer, accountant—can be helpful. Give a specific reason—family business, children—and frame the matter as mutual protection. Be sure to hold the dialogue someplace private. After making your case, try to get the matter in the hands of the lawyers as soon as possible.

What Should Be Covered By A Prenuptial Agreement

Prenuptial agreements are necessarily complex, and *must* be based on full disclosure. Here are some questions that should be addressed:

- What happens to premarital property?

- What happens to appreciation on premarital property, whether passive appreciation (market factors) or active appreciation (through efforts of either spouse)?

- What happens to property inherited or received by gift from a third party during the marriage?

- What happens to property accumulated during the marriage, including property kept in separate names and property placed in joint names?

The other areas that need to be discussed include:

The marital home: Will the funds used to buy it most likely be premarital (say, from sale of a premarital home or premarital savings)? What are the ramifications if the couple plans to reside in the premarital home of one spouse? What funds that will be used to maintain it and pay the mortgage, and what will become of it in the event of divorce? Will one person have first choice of staying there? How will the children be impacted? If the home belongs to one person and the other has to move out, what finances will be involved in obtaining alternate housing for the nontitled spouse (consider the time that may pass, the possibility that housing will cost much more by the time that person has to obtain it, and the loss, if any, of the nontitled spouse's premarital housing)? In the case of older couples, or couples with premarital children, who inherits the home?

Alimony: Sometimes it is appropriate to waive it, while other times there is a specific provision for how much, how long, and so forth. Sometimes this is a formula. Factors that may be built in include how long the couple is married, whether they are both self-supporting, whether they have children, what their expectations are about career interruptions or changes made to have children.

Estate planning: Should the rights of inheritance that each spouse would have under the laws of the particular state be waived? (Some agreements do this, others don't.) Who are the beneficiaries on retirement plans, life insurance, and so forth?

Separation: Will announcing the desire to separate trigger the terms of the agreement automatically?

they should divorce. I think we can assume this is a situation the other family members would not be too happy about. In addition, the family may not wish business ownership to pass out of the family even in the case of death. In that case, a financial settlement is often agreed to ahead of time, in a prenuptial.

Be Careful Before You Sign

Take it from someone whose been part of the process, negotiating a pre- or postnuptial agreement can be a delicate matter. Handled incorrectly, it can take a serious toll on a marriage before the union is even completed. But it must be taken seriously and prepared with a great deal of thought and impeccable honesty. Both lawyers (each party needs their own lawyer) will need to examine the document to make sure it conforms with your state's laws.

Beware of future spouses who spring a prenuptial agreement on you two weeks before the wedding. Not only is it unfair, but courts are apt to feel that any such agreement was signed under duress.

Once you sign a prenuptial agreement it's very difficult to get the terms modified. Unless you can prove you were lied to by your spouse or coerced into signing the agreement against your will, it's unlikely a judge will see things your way. You can claim the agreement treats you unfairly, but, in many states, as long as it was fair when it was made, and it's not unconscionable when incorporated in a divorce decree, there's nothing you can do.

PRECIOUS METALS

B Y ALL MEANS wear precious metals. Just don't invest in them.
Gold and silver have always held a special power over people. Virtually every culture in history has bestowed great value upon them. Thieves have gone to great lengths to steal them. Artists and writers have spent countless hours praising them. But as investments? Frankly, they're really not that great.

Gold did have one outstanding decade, the 1970s, when it rose in price from less than $50 to more than $800 an ounce before falling back into the $300 to $400 range. During most of that run-up, however, it was illegal for Americans to own gold coins or bars. Since ownership became legal, gold has basically increased in value at about the rate of inflation.

Still, gold, silver, and other precious metals have a fascination for many investors. Admittedly there is a certain elemental thrill to holding a pure gold coin or bar in your hand. Some people see precious metals, gold in particular, as a hedge against the collapse of currency systems. Of course, the only way we'll find out if that theory holds up is to experience some cataclysmic event. In the meantime, the prices of precious metals will continue to be determined like those of other commodities—by their availability and the demand for the products made from them. If you can't resist the temptation to throw some money their way, however, here are some of the ways you can invest in precious metals.

Gold

The federal government has piles and piles of 25-pound gold bars stacked in vaults in places like Fort Knox in Kentucky. If you've never seen them, it's quite an impressive sight. Unfortunately, investors have to settle for more mundane 1-ounce gold coins and wafers. The South African Krugerrand, the American Eagle and the Canadian Maple Leaf are the most popular gold coins on the market. At this writing, they were trading in the $300 to $325 range.

Some people also invest in gold jewelry, which is not always a bad move. At the very least, a piece of jewelry is "worth its weight in gold," to put an old saying in perspective. Its value will be enhanced by its worth as a piece of ornamentation and the precious stones and other materials that are used in its design.

Silver

Silver is also most common in coins like the Canadian Silver Maple Leaf, the U.S. Silver Eagle, and the Australian Kookaburra. Also, like gold, products made from silver, especially antique silverware, have value over and above their weight. At the end of 1999, the Silver Eagle was trading in the $8.50 to $9.00 range.

Platinum

Because of its relative scarcity, platinum is worth much more than gold or silver. Investors purchase 1-ounce coins such as the Canadian Platinum Maple Leaf and the U.S. Platinum Eagle. The latter was trading in the $425 to $475 range at the end of the 1990s.

Certificates and Accounts

If you don't care to physically own handfuls of gold and silver coins, you can purchase an interest in the holdings of a bank or securities firm. The nice thing about these is that you can direct a regular amount to the institution each month rather than hand over a big chunk of cash all at once. That way you can gradually build up your stake. Some firms will give you a certificate for the precious metals you own. Others will send you a monthly statement.

This kind of investment solves a problem that a lot of investors would rather avoid: If you do own precious metals you'll need to find a secure place to keep them. That means renting a safe deposit box or buying a safe.

Stocks

Rather than buying precious metals, you might want to invest in the stocks of publicly traded mining companies. Although mining company stocks offer a potentially higher return on investment, they are extremely volatile. In fact, their prices move more widely than those of the metals they produce. There are also political considerations. Many of the world's most productive gold-mining companies are in South Africa, a country whose turn away from apartheid and toward representative democracy is still a work-in-progress. Investments in North American and Australian companies are usually more stable, although not as profitable.

Mutual Funds

Mutual funds composed of mining company stocks reduce investor risk, although they're still more volatile than the metals themselves. Also, because they invest in companies in a single industry, they don't offer as much protection as a regular mutual fund that holds a wide variety of stocks. As with any mutual fund, investors benefit from the expertise of professional fund managers. Mutual funds also allow you to have money tied up in foreign companies that you might find difficult to obtain on your own.

Should You Buy Precious Metals?

I say no, although many investment counselors still advise their clients to put a small percentage of their portfolios, maybe 5 percent, into gold, silver, or platinum. As far as I'm concerned, the only precious metals you own should be the kind you can wear.

However, if the ability to roll a few gold coins around your palm gives you a certain erotic thrill, a small investment can't really hurt. Just make sure you buy your metals from a reputable dealer and have a safe place to keep them. They may not be the best investments in the world, but they're still very popular with thieves.

PREPAID TUITION PLANS

I'M GLAD MY FOUR CHILDREN aren't college age today. I have some clients with two, three, or even four or more children to educate and, regardless how affluent they may be, they're all tearing their hair out trying to figure out how to afford college. Their concerns are well-founded. For years, college tuition increased at about the rate of inflation. Since 1980, however, it has increased at more than three times the rate of inflation. This has outpaced even medical care by about 50 percent.

This increase has been particularly threatening to the middle class. While tuition has been going through the roof, the middle class has had to contend with a shifting economy that for many has resulted in downward economic mobility and sporadic unemployment. At the same time, they've had to continue to pay for significant portions of their children's college expenses.

A mid-1990s study by the National Institute of Independent Colleges and Universities showed how difficult it has become for people to save for college: 62 percent of respondents planned to use personal savings for college, but only 50 percent reported saving on a regular basis; 23 percent were unable to save and didn't expect to be able to start in the immediate future; and of those who were able to save, the average amount put aside was just over $500 a year.

The Advantages

Most of these people might want to investigate prepaid tuition plans. They're the reverse of the old buy now, pay later approach to purchasing something. Even though your child may be 5 or 10 or even 15 years away from college, you can lock in the average current tuition at your state's public institutions by giving the money to the state while your child is growing up. More than 30 states currently offer prepaid tuition plans or have legislation pending to implement programs.

How does the state afford such an offer? Simple. It invests the money you and other parents have given it and uses the earnings to cover the difference between the rate you locked in and the actual tuition at the time your child enters college. If it earns more than that, the state makes a profit, since it's only guaranteeing you the cost of tuition when your child enrolls in college.

The biggest advantage of prepaid tuition plans is that they operate like forced savings plans. Contributors don't have to pay the money in one lump sum. If they wish, they can make weekly or monthly contributions. They can even have the money deducted from their paychecks so they never even see it. At that point, saving for college becomes something they really don't even have to worry about anymore. The money's being put away, and they know it will be there when they need it.

Another advantage is that the money put into a prepaid tuition plan is tax-deductible when your child redeems it to pay for tuition. It's also backed by the full faith and credit of the state, so there's virtually no chance you'll lose it.

Most states allow participants to enroll in the in-state college or university of their choice, regardless of whether it's public or private. Of course, if your child chooses a private college or university, you'll have to pay the extra tuition over and above the cost of the public school.

The Disadvantages

The strongest argument against prepaid tuition plans is that they're a poor investment. By giving your money to the state, you're guaranteed only that it will appreciate at the same rate as tuition. In the meantime, you'll miss out on all the appreciation it could have earned in mutual funds, stocks, or other investments. Those profits will belong to the state, which will have a number of years to invest your money before it needs to be used for tuition.

Another problem is that some states hedge their bets and only guarantee to pay an estimated tuition, determined at the outset of the plan. If their estimate is low, you pay the difference. And remember, the guaranteed tuition is that of state institutions. If your child wants to attend a private college or university, you're going to have to come up with a lot more money.

Refunds can be a problem, too. If your child decides not to attend college, you'll only get a very small portion of the interest or yield that the money has earned. In some states, unless you fall within a set of often absurd guidelines, you might not receive any interest on your money.

Do Your Own Investing

Personally, I think prepaid tuition plans take advantage of people's weaknesses. If you have the discipline to contribute money to a prepaid tuition plan while your child is growing up, you should have the discipline to put the same money into zero-coupon bonds, stocks, or mutual funds, where it will appreciate much faster than the increase in tuition. If you give your money to the state, you're simply letting the state do your work for you and paying a big premium for the service.

***

(See also college planning.)

PRESCRIPTION DRUGS

WE MUST be the most heavily medicated society on the face of the earth. Every year Americans spend more than $50 billion on prescription drugs and more than $10 billion on over-the-counter medications.

For the elderly, many of whom are living on fixed incomes and suffering from a number of chronic ailments, prescription drugs can represent a significant part of their disposable income. The cost can also add up for younger people with chronic conditions like high blood pressure or asthma. Of course, considering the alternative, it's money well spent.

Still, no one wants to spend more than they need to. Here are some of the best ways to save money on prescription drugs.

Buy Generics

Generics are usually about half the price of brand-name medications. Why the big difference? When a drug first hits the market, it's given a name by the company that developed it. The product is expensive because the company has to recoup the money it spent on research and marketing in addition to making a profit.

After a certain number of years, the patent on the drug expires and other companies are free to market the same drug with a generic name. Generics require the same approval by the Food and Drug Administration and work just as well as their better-known counterparts. Around 40 percent of prescriptions today are filled with generic drugs.

When you take a prescription to be filled, ask the pharmacist to fill it with a generic. Chances are your doctor will have written down the name brand. Of course, you may not have to ask. Some states require that generic drugs be used unless the doctor or patient requests otherwise.

Ask for Samples

If cheap is good, free is even better. Keep in mind that pharmaceutical companies give away nearly $3 billion worth of free samples to doctors every year. Most doctors are happy to pass them on to their patients. All you need to do is ask.

Buy at Discount Stores

Discount chains like Wal-mart and Kmart offer the same discounts on prescription drugs that they do on everything else. The difference between a discount store price and a drugstore price can be as much as 35 percent. These stores can offer low prices because of the huge volumes they purchase.

Buy in Volume

If the discount chain is buying in volume and then you buy in volume from the discount chain, you can save even more. This is because all prescription charges include a fee for the pharmacist. The size of the prescription doesn't matter. The charge will be the same whether it's for 20 pills or 200 pills. If you have a chronic condition requiring daily medications, it's much cheaper to buy several months' worth with one prescription than it is to run to the pharmacy every week or two. Not only will you save on those extra pharmacist fees, you may be given a discount for buying in bulk. Ask your doctor to write the prescription so you can purchase in bulk.

Try Mail Order

Mail order can save you up to 30 percent on drugstore prices and 10 percent on some discount chain prices. One of the most popular mail-order sources is the pharmacy service run by the

American Association of Retired Persons in Alexandria, Virginia. And it's not popular just for getting prescriptions filled. The service carries more than 12,000 items. Even better, you don't have to be an AARP member to order, although if you are you'll get a discount on some items. Call 800-456-2277 to order a catalog.

Count Your Order

Prescription drugs are expensive. When you have a prescription filled, count the pills to make sure you got what you paid for. I'm not suggesting the pharmacist would try to take advantage of you. I'm just pointing out that some people don't count very well or might use faulty machines.

The Safety Factor

I mentioned earlier that Americans spend $50 billion a year on prescription drugs. That's a lot of pills. Many elderly people have five, six, or even more prescriptions to battle a variety of ailments.

If you have multiple prescriptions, be sure to speak with your doctor and your pharmacist about possible drug interactions. Otherwise you're risking a severe reaction that could threaten your life. Ideally, your pharmacist should always counsel you when you have a prescription filled. In fact, more than 40 states require her to. But don't wait to be counseled. Tell her what other drugs you're taking and ask her if there could be a problem.

Once you have a prescription, follow the directions to the letter and make sure you finish the complete course. Don't operate on the theory that if the doctor says to take one a day that three a day will work even better. You're taking the drug to get better, not to make yourself even sicker.

PRESS RELEASES

MOST PRESS RELEASES SENT to the media end up in the wastebasket. They almost always land on the desks of low-level editors or editorial assistants whose job is to weed out important news from the mountain of material the media receive every day. That means a press release is going to get just a second or two of inspection by someone with little or no experience. Unless there's something in it that immediately grabs the attention of the poor soul who has to wade through all that paper, it's going to get tossed.

How do you get the attention of this overworked screener? Unfortunately, there is no magic formula. The best thing you can do is make sure the release works as effectively as possible during the few seconds it's going to be looked at. To do that, it needs to immediately convey three pieces of information. The first is the name of your company or business. Use your standard letterhead and stationery. If designed correctly, your company's name and logo will be the first thing the editor's eye is drawn to, so he'll know right away who the press release is from.

The second element is your headline. It must be tailored to fit the needs of the publication and also appear newsworthy. Remember, the junior editor who will be reading your press release has one goal in mind—to look for information pertinent to the publication's audience. Keep that in mind when preparing the headline.

The third element is the contact information. If you manage to pique the junior editor's interest and he wants to contact someone for more information, that person's name, telephone number, and e-mail address must be included. Don't assume he's simply going to call the number on your letterhead. Even though he's a junior employee, he'll know that that could just lead to a receptionist, who may or may not know who he needs to speak to. He won't have time for that. You need to put the contact information in large bold print in a prominent location at the top of the press release.

The success of your press release will also depend on the kind of information you're trying to place. If it's something that will go into a calendar or some other standard informational column, it will probably be accepted as a matter of course as long as it's sent early enough. But if it's information you're trying to place elsewhere in the publication—perhaps you're trying to attract the interest of a reporter and hope to have a news article written—your chances diminish enormously. You'll have better success if you follow your press release with a telephone call to a reporter. Even then, you're likely to encounter a receptionist or administrative assistant, who may or may not pass on your message to the reporter.

Frankly, the best way to get a press release into a publication is to know the right people or scratch the right backs. Most press releases that make it into print have a little leverage behind them. Perhaps the editor owes the person behind the press release a favor. Or maybe the press release was accompanied by a "sample" product. Or, surprise, perhaps there's a prominent paid advertisement elsewhere in the publication for the same company that issued the press release.

The bottom line is that the space in a publication is valuable real estate. You're going to have to use your wiles, and perhaps your checkbook, to grab a few inches of it. Just treat it as you would any other investment. If it provides the desired return, it's worth the time, effort, and money.

PRO BONO WORK AND VOLUNTEERISM

I BELIEVE THAT if you've been successful in your life, you must help others who have been less fortunate. Not only is it good for society, it's good for the soul. Selflessness provides rare benefits. There's a special kind of satisfaction that can only come from doing something for the benefit of others. I honestly feel that in order to keep your good fortune, you have to give some of it away.

The easiest way to contribute to a good cause is to write a check. There's nothing wrong with that. Money makes things happen. Just make sure that the charity you give your money to isn't plagued with astronomical administrative fees.

But I believe real satisfaction comes from giving away a far more valuable commodity—your time. When you write a check, it's almost immediately forgotten. But when you give your time to a project or organization, you gain a much more tangible sense of having contributed. You work with other people who are also contributing their time and effort. You often get to interact with the people who benefit from your efforts.

Pro bono work (the term means "for good" in Latin) and volunteerism can take many forms. Some people choose to serve on the boards of directors of charitable or nonprofit organizations. Others volunteer to do work that takes them right into the trenches. The options are endless. Youth groups, homeless shelters, soup kitchens, nursing homes, churches and synagogues, libraries, hospice centers, hospitals, and Big Brother and Big Sister programs are just a few of the organizations that depend on volunteers.

If you're a professional, you can contribute a great deal by donating your services to benefit an organization. Most charitable organizations have legal and accounting needs, for example. Many have lawyers on their boards to provide legal expertise. Accountants are often most valuable serving as the treasurer of an organization.

While I heartily encourage you to give your time, I also urge you to draw distinctions between giving your personal time and your professional time. When you're giving your personal time and resources to a worthy cause, your main return will be emotional. But when you devote work time, I believe you're entitled to a return, albeit not directly financial.*

The fact is, pro bono work and volunteerism can benefit you professionally, and I believe you should make the most of your efforts. If you or your business contributes time or services to a charitable organization, make sure that fact is widely know. It can heighten your image and, potentially, bring you new business. If you sponsor a charitable event, make sure your name is on all the literature and signage for the event. It's a remarkably effective way to advertise yourself and your business. Think about it. Many of the nation's large corporations sponsor events that contribute money to charity. Their names are on everything that's associated with the event, from advertising to programs to T-shirts. You need to do the same.

Don't feel you're being callous by expecting some promotional return from your efforts. Business is business; every penny and every minute of your business resources should be devoted to making money. Gaining some favorable publicity and a few new customers from your charitable efforts is hardly asking a lot. It doesn't diminish the work you do on behalf of an organization. If anything, I feel you both benefit by being associated with each other. If you have any qualms about promoting your pro bono work, simply volunteer to do things outside your profession. What you do matters less than that you do something.

---

*Obviously, you can deduct contributions to charities. However, you cannot deduct your professional fee for services as a charitable contribution. You can, however, deduct any out-of-pocket and travel expenses you incur while volunteering either as a professional or as just another set of hands.

PROBATE AND SETTLEMENT

Probate, for generations a potential nightmare for heirs, is today a paper tiger. The settling of the estate of a deceased should be a simple task. The purpose of the process is to make sure that the will was valid—the word "probate" means "prove."* Settlement means that the assets have been passed on to the right people. If Uncle Marty wanted you to have his antique walking stick after he died, the probate process was supposed to make sure you got it quickly and without any fuss.

Unfortunately, that was not always the case. Probate hearings all too often turned into lengthy court battles that dragged on for years. While lawyers padded their wallets with sometimes exorbitant hourly fees and judges moved cases to the back of their dockets, the assets in question—often investment portfolios rather than walking sticks—went unmanaged. As things dragged on, those waiting for bequests watched in helpless horror as the estates were bled dry. There were also many scandals involving surrogate courts indulging in judicial patronage by appointing political cronies as guardians.

Recently, however, individual states have gotten involved and passed probate laws that streamline the process, especially when everything is going to a spouse, the estate is relatively small, and the will is uncontested. The transfer of tangible property, such as a car or jewelry, is usually agreed upon informally by family members or by other means, like a letter, rather than through probate. Bank accounts, homes, and other assets whose ownership is held jointly are transferred immediately outside of the probate process. So are assets for which there is a named beneficiary, such as IRAs and the payouts from life insurance policies.†

The process of settling an estate can be so easy you can handle it yourself. It may be as simple as going to the probate court and following the directions of the court clerk. Of course, when things become complicated you can also hire a lawyer and have her guide you through the process. She should be able to do it with a minimum of effort and an equally minimal fee. In most states, an uncontested will that dictates the disposal of a relatively modest estate to just a few heirs can be settled in 30 to 90 days after papers are filed.

More time will be needed for larger estates that involve many heirs and have a variety of assets, although, again, the transfer of bank accounts and tangible property can be done immediately. Even then, all but the largest of estates should be fully settled and the assets distributed within six months to a year.

Avoiding Probate with a Revocable Living Trust

Back when probate was still the stuff of Dickens novels, some in the legal community saw an opportunity for new products that would allow people to bypass probate altogether. The result

---

*What is being proved is that the will was not coerced, not a forgery, and that it was done by a competent person.
†Just remember, even though these assets transfer immediately they are still part of an estate and could be taxable.

To Make Things Easier for Your Heirs

If you want to make probate and settlement easy for your heirs you should:

• Make sure your will is properly prepared and up to date

• Have a current inventory of your assets available for your heirs and executor

• Try to simplify your assets, keeping portfolios or bank accounts to a minimum

was the revocable living trust, a rather cumbersome arrangement in which you put all your assets in a trust and then name yourself as the trustee. If your state requires another trustee, you can name your spouse or someone else. You also need to name a successor trustee to manage things if you become incapacitated and to distribute the assets of the trust when you die.

When you pass away, all assets in the trust are immediately transferred to the beneficiaries. If you have assets that weren't placed in trust prior to your death, their distribution will be dictated by a pour-over will that states that such assets should be added to the trust.

Living trusts are expensive to create and to maintain. You need to carefully consider whether your financial situation would benefit from having one set up. Most people are fine with a conventional will and the probate process, as long as they follow some simple advice.*

Planning and Communication Are Key

The key to avoiding problems in settling an estate is to make sure your will is as complete as possible and to discuss your wishes with your heirs and make sure everyone understands them. Make sure that beneficiaries are specifically named for all your assets. If you want your spouse to get the house and the bank accounts, the two of you should be named as joint owners. If Billy gets the car and Bobby gets the boat and Eddie gets the lawn tractor, that should be spelled out in the will. The trick is to avoid gray areas that can become ammunition for those who want to contest things. With a little planning and communication, the process will be a breeze.

(See also living trusts.)

---

*As I note in the entry on living trusts, they only really make sense for individuals who want or need to maintain privacy after death, who expect their will to be contested, who anticipate their own incompetency, or who live in the handful of counties in which probate is still a nightmare.

PROMOTIONAL KITS

Businesspeople can learn a lot from actors and politicians. In today's competitive world you can't wait for potential customers or clients to find out about you. You need to actively tell them about yourself, making sure your story is presented in the best light possible.

The best way to tell your business's story is with a promotional kit. These are similar to the media kits public relations firms send out to publicize their clients. Traditionally used to increase the visibility of people in the public eye, promotional kits are becoming popular with lawyers, accountants, and other professionals people as a strategy to market themselves and their products and services. I think every businessperson, from plumbers to pottery shop owners, should be doing the same.

Your promotional kit material will be presented in a pocket folder or narrow three-ring binder. Your name or business name and your logo should be printed on the outside, along with any slogans or other identifiers you use for your business. The inside of the folder should have slots for your business card and a Rolodex card. If you've developed a color scheme as part of your business identity program, the folder or binder should be printed in those colors.

Standard elements of every promotional kit include short biographies of you and your business. You should include a formal "studio" photograph and a résumé with information on your education, job history, and professional accomplishments. If you send out a business newsletter or other publication to your clients and customers, be sure to include one or two copies. They can provide a more informal perspective on your business.

Include information sheets on your products or services. Each product or service should have its own page, with appropriate backup such as photographs, technical specifications, schedules, and prices. Another option is to create a separate brochure or booklet with all your product information. Don't forget to include copies of industry and consumer reviews. A favorable evaluation of your product from an impartial organization or publication is a very valuable marketing tool. Glowing letters of thanks from customers or clients should be included too. Awards and honors should be noted. Finally, it can't hurt to offers some personal information, including hobbies and other interests.

The other contents of your promotional kit will be dictated by your profession and your goals in preparing the kit. Artists, writers, actors, and musicians should include lists of all their publications, exhibits, performances, and any reviews of their work. Awards and prizes should be given special recognition. Artists should include a list of any public or prominent private collections that include their work, as well as prints or slides of selected works. Actors and musicians should include a videotape, audiotape or CD-ROM with recordings of their performances.

It's important to customize your promotional kit to fit individual situations. For example, if you have a wide product line, it's unlikely that each product you offer will be appropriate for every customer. In this case, it would be wise to keep a supply of generic promotional kits on hand and then add the appropriate product information when preparing to visit customers.

Similarly, if you have a service business, you might have one set of information for commercial clients and another for homeowners.

Preparing a professional promotional kit will require some investment. You may want to hire a freelance writer or technical writer to help you prepare your material. You should definitely work with professional photographers, illustrators, and graphic designers to have your package designed. Use quality paper and use at least one other color in addition to black. Again, if you have a color scheme that's part of your business identity, it should be used throughout the kit.

The bulk of printing costs are up-front labor charges for setting up the presses and fine-tuning colors and registrations. Paper and ink are actually quite inexpensive. Once the presses are running you're better off printing as many copies as possible to reduce your cost per unit. If you think you can go for two years without making any changes to the kit, have two years' worth printed.

Save where you can, but don't be penny-wise and pound-foolish. Your promotional kit is a business investment. If it's poorly designed and haphazard in its organization, customers can only assume that you and your business are equally unprofessional. Prepare it correctly and use it wisely and you'll enjoy a healthy return on your investment.

PROMOTIONS AND LATERAL MOVES

PAST SUCCESSES ARE as likely to hurt as help you in getting a promotion. Savvy managers don't view prior performance in one job as being indicative of future performance in another job. If you've done a great job, they'll reward you monetarily. If they need to fill a position, they're more concerned with the potential of the candidates to do the new job, not what the candidates did last year or the year before that. If you're a great salesperson, it just means you're a great salesperson. It doesn't mean you'll be a great vice president of marketing. In fact, you may be so good at your current job that your manager might not want to risk losing your production by shifting you. That's one reason why so many opening are filled by people coming from outside of organizations and companies.

To be seriously considered for an in-house promotion you need to demonstrate what you will do for the company in the future. And you need to do that better than every outsider who's also looking for the job. I suggest you accompany your promotion request with a written plan outlining your strategic plan for the new position and how you would assist the person who takes over your old job.*

The second part of the memo is every bit as important as the first. When a company pro-

---

*Depending on the circumstances you may even want to note that you can retain some of the responsibilities of your current position.

motes someone, a new void is created that must be filled. As I warned earlier, some people will be left in their current position because they would be too hard to replace.

Don't make money part of your proposal. Sure, you expect a salary increase to be part of the promotion. Your employer knows it as well. But if you make it an issue, you may draw your employer's attention away from your potential and refocus it on what the promotion would do to the bottom line. That could work against you. If the promotion is not accompanied by an immediate raise, and there's a good chance it won't be, your performance will soon result in one.

Lateral Moves

A lateral move can be just as good as, if not better than, a promotion if it positions you for a better career track. A salary increase may be involved, but that shouldn't be your goal. If you succeed in getting on a clearer path to where you want to go, the financial rewards will appear down the road.

Let's say, for example, that your current job is in a department with a traditional function, like sales or marketing. The career path is clear, but also crowded. You may not care to spend the coming years trying to scramble over others by meeting sales goals. And you just might be ready for something new and fresh.*

Let's then say your company decides to join the e-commerce fray by starting up a Web marketing division. It presents you with an entirely new career direction that would take advantage of your marketing expertise and potentially provide enormous revenues for the company. As part of the team designated to lead the company down this exciting new path, you can count on being handsomely compensated if it proves successful.

The most important consideration in making a lateral move is making sure there's a position available to move into. Stay in contact with the management of the department you're interested in joining. Treat your pursuit of a transfer like you would the pursuit of a brand new job. Make management aware of your interest and qualifications. Stay abreast of the department's activities. Perhaps you'll discover they have an important project starting soon that could benefit from your participation. The fact that you can step in and immediately be productive will become a major selling point when you present your request for a transfer.

When the right opportunity does present itself, you need to move swiftly. You're likely to be just one of many who are interested in the job. This is when the groundwork you've laid over the previous weeks or months will pay off. If you've played your cards correctly, the managers of your new department just might be waiting to greet you with open arms.

Keep in mind that in your attempt to accomplish a lateral move, you could earn the ire of your current supervisor. That could threaten your current position if you fail to accomplish a transfer. You could also be putting yourself in jeopardy if you transfer into a position for which you might not be totally qualified. Once you talk the talk, you have to be able to walk the walk. If you don't, your only walk might be a one-way trip out the door.

---

*Of course, never say you're tired of your current position: don't burn your bridges.

PROPERTY TAXES

WHAT'S THE SALES TAX RATE in your community? What's the property tax rate? I bet you can answer the first question off the top of your head but need to do some research to answer the second.

Sales tax is easy to remember since we see it every time we look at a receipt. But property taxes? They're easy to forget about. First of all, the bills only come twice a year. Second, many of us don't even see them. They often go right to our mortgage holders and are paid out of our escrow accounts.

That's one reason why local governments often turn to property taxes first when they need to raise additional revenues. It's simply more palatable to the citizenry. And it's not just that we seldom get billed. There's also a certain amount of fiscal sleight-of-hand that makes the process seem more benign than it actually is.

The Hidden Equation

It works like this. Property taxes are determined by multiplying two numbers, the property tax rate and the assessed value of the property. For example, if the property tax rate is 1.5 percent (the national average) and a home is assessed at $100,000, the homeowner will pay a property tax of $1,500. While there is a national trend to 100 percent assessment, some local governments get creative by changing the figure they use for assessed value. Some communities might consider the assessed value of a property to be only 50 percent of the market value. Others might consider it to be 75 or 80 percent of market value. There was one infamous case where assessed value was based on the 1938 replacement cost. In any case, by leaving the tax rate alone and increasing a home's assessed value, governments can dramatically increase revenues.

Let's go back to the example I just used. If the $100,000 assessment had been based on 50 percent of the market value, the home in question would have a market value of $200,000. To increase taxes, the local tax assessor will leave the 1.5 percent tax rate in place but increase the assessment to, say, 75 percent of market value. The assessed value then becomes $150,000 and the poor homeowner sees his property tax bill increase to $2,250. It's a neat trick and one that's becoming increasingly popular in cities and towns across the country.

How to Fight Back

When you get your property tax bill remember one thing—it's merely the opening move in a negotiation with your local tax office. More and more people are appealing their assessments and, depending on the state, anywhere from 50 to 75 percent are winning and having their assessments reduced.

How do you appeal? Most communities have a designated period during the year when property owners can come before the assessment board and argue their case. It's not as intimidating as you might think. They're generally very informal and reasonable procedures. Reasonable arguments will be carefully considered and you'll be treated fairly.

Here are some of the situations in which you might appeal your assessment:

- There's an error in your bill. It happens more often than you'd think. The square footage of your home or the size of your lot may be incorrectly recorded, for example. The assessor will correct it and there will be no need for a hearing.

- You find that your assessment is higher than those of properties comparable to yours.

- You just bought your home and it's assessed for more than the purchase price.

- There's a legal problem. For example, the property might be classified incorrectly.

If you feel you have grounds for an appeal, you should first call the assessor's office to find out when the appeals period is scheduled and what the process entails. The appeals period is usually fairly short—three to six weeks in most towns—so you need to act quickly. If you miss

The Power of Assessments

Need proof that it's assessments rather than tax rates that count when it comes to property taxes? Just take a look at this chart, listing the U.S. cities with the 10 highest property tax rates back in 1996.

Newark may have had the highest tax rate in the country, 4.02 percent, but when that was coupled with an assessment level of only 17.6 percent, the taxes on a property with a market value of $100,000 came out to a minuscule $707.52. Portland, Maine, had a significantly lower tax rate, 2.46 percent, but its 100 percent assessment policy led to a tax bill of $2,460 on that same $100,000 property. But even that pales next to another New England city: Manchester, New Hampshire, is proof of what happens when you couple a high tax rate, 3.48 percent, with a high assessment rate, 113 percent. That added up to an annual tax bill of $3,932.40.

City	Tax Rate per $100 of Assessed Value	Assessment Level, % of Market Value	Total Taxes on $100k property
1. Newark, NJ	4.02%	17.6%	$707.52
2. Bridgeport, CT	3.96%	58.6%	$2,320.56
3. Manchester, NH	3.48%	113%	$3,932.40
4. Milwaukee, WI	3.32%	94.9%	$3,150.68
5. Providence, RI	3.04%	100%	$3,040.00
6. Des Moines, IA	3.95%	68%	$2,686.00
7. Detroit, MI	2.76%	46.9%	$1,294.44
8. Philadelphia, PA	2.64%	32%	$844.80
9. Houston, TX	2.61%	100%	$2,610.00
10. Portland, ME	2.46%	100%	$2,460.00

Source: U.S. Department of Commerce, 1996.

the window, there's a good chance your assessment will be considered final, no matter what your argument may be.

Winning Your Case

When you meet with the tax department, your arguments will be heard and, if necessary, passed on to an appeals officer. There's usually a filing fee of between $5 and $25. If your claim is based on an obvious mistake, it will be corrected, usually by the assessor, and the hearing can be avoided. If you're appealing on the grounds of illegality, you may want to hire a lawyer, who will be better prepared to argue the fine points. Fees are usually on a contingency basis, with a modest guaranteed payment that the lawyer will keep whether you win or lose.

Facts are the key to winning a property tax appeal, so do your research. Bring copies of all documents that support your argument. And don't be afraid to ask beforehand what information the assessor wants from you. Hearing officers aren't out to beat you out of your money. They just want to be fair. They'll be happy to tell you what you need.

You may find that you're offered a compromise settlement, somewhere between the original assessment and your proposed reduction. If you choose not to accept it, the next step will likely be a judicial hearing involving lawyer's fees and a lot of time and hassles. My advice is to accept the compromise figure and just be glad you achieved a partial victory. But don't forget to check your assessment the following year. If you want to continue to fight, look for a lawyer who specializes in tax certiorari (property tax appeals) proceedings.

PROPERTY TITLES

TITLE PROBLEMS—something in the history of the property that might prevent ownership being transferred—are more common that most people think. That's why an entire industry, title insurance, has sprung up to deal with them.

You'd be surprised at some of the problems that can occur. One of the most common in urban and suburban areas is a lien against the property by the IRS or a state or local government for failure to pay taxes. In rural areas, sometimes special rights to the property, such as a right-of-way or access to a pond or stream, may have been granted to a third party. Often these will have existed for decades. Although the responsibility to provide clear title to the property falls on the seller, a buyer's lender will require a title search.

Title problems are almost always caused by lawyer error. That's why the buyer's lawyer will hire a title insurance company to conduct the search. The company's researcher will go through previous deeds on the property and compile a short history of the passage of title. Her report will then be given to both the buyer's and seller's lawyers. If she has unearthed some problems, the seller's lawyer has the responsibility to clear them up. At the closing, another representative of the title insurance company will be present to make sure the seller's mortgage has been satisfied and record the new deed.

The title insurance company will also present the buyer with a bill at the closing. This will cover the insurance fee, title search fee, building department and municipal agency search fee, survey inspection, if any, and recording and transfer fees.

To protect itself against title problems, your lender will require that you provide it with title insurance. This is a one-time expense that is usually paid at the closing. For a small additional premium, you can provide title insurance coverage for yourself as well as your lender. The fees for title insurance are regulated in many states. Where they are not regulated, they

Pay Attention to Your Deed

The type of deed that will be passed on to you by the seller will be specified in the contract. Different deeds are accompanied by different responsibilities on the part of the seller. Here are the most common:

- *Quit claim:* These absolve the seller of responsibility for any title problems that may crop up. The title they had is what you get. These deeds should be avoided at all costs.

- *Bargain and sale with covenants against grantors acts:* In this case the seller guarantees that he did nothing to create claims against the property by others. However, he makes no such claims on behalf of previous owners of the property. That becomes the responsibility of your title search company.

- *Full covenant and warranty:* These provide you with the most protection. The seller takes responsibility for the entire series of ownerships up to and including his own.

vary widely. Have your lawyer shop around for the best deal with a reputable, experienced firm.

You should also protect yourself against title problems in the purchase contract. You might try inserting a clause in your contract stating that if the title search turns up a material problem, you have a right to back out of the deal and get your deposit back. It should also specify that the seller is responsible for any costs you may have incurred up to that point, including legal fees and the title search. If the problems are minor, it's reasonable to expect the seller to take care of them. For example, you might include a clause that says if the title problems can be solved for a certain amount of money—let's say up to $3,000—the seller should be responsible for paying that amount and setting things right.

(See also closings.)

PUNCTUALITY

WASTE YOUR OWN TIME and you cost yourself money. Waste a client's time and you may cost yourself a client.

Be on time. Be on time for work, for appointments, for meetings, to make and receive telephone calls, for teleconferences, and for any other activity for which your presence is necessary.

When you're on time, the money-making machine keeps churning. When you're late, it grinds to a halt.

Take punctuality an extra step and show up early. I can speak from experience that getting to the office before the rest of your coworkers will provide you with the most productive time of your day. I'm in my office by 8 A.M. at the latest and usually have at least an hour to myself before the next person shows up. I often accomplish more work in that single hour than I do the rest of the morning. It's completely quiet. No one is sticking his head in my door with questions, no one is calling on the telephone. And my mental energy is at its highest point of the day.

I use my early morning time to plan my day and prepare notes for any meetings I may have. I also use the time to make telephone calls to people I know I'll have trouble reaching later in the day. Many executives arrive at the office as early as I do. Until their secretaries show up, there's no one to field calls for them. Most have trouble ignoring a ringing telephone, so I'm usually successful at reaching the person I need to speak to.

For an employee there are also certain political benefits to being at work early. If your boss sees you in the office before the rest of the crew, she can't help but notice. You'll also have more opportunity to visit with her. This may well improve your relationship. She may come to expect to spend a few minutes with you every morning, which can't help but boost your image. Even if she doesn't, you still stand out from the rest of your coworkers.

Some offices these days have moved to a flex-time arrangement in which you're free to set your own hours. While I certainly recognize the rationale behind this kind of flexibility, I don't think you're doing yourself any favors by waltzing in to the office at 9:30 or 10 o'clock every morning. Yes, your boss will be aware that you'll be there well into the evening to compensate. And yes, she may know that your work will be done before you leave. But there will still be some subconscious residual feeling that you're somehow slacking off and less committed to the job than people who come in early.

Coming in early, I believe, is far better than staying late. Since most upper-level managers come in early, chances are they won't be burning the midnight oil as well. If your superior leaves while you're still sitting there, it may generate some subconscious concern that you're somehow not being as efficient as you should be. And no matter how late you stay, she won't be there to witness your hard work. The bottom line is that managers are always a bit leery of what goes on when they're not around to keep tabs on things. I realize it's not a fair situation, but this is the way the world works sometimes.*

One last thing: You can't be punctual without being organized. When you make an appointment or schedule a meeting, write it down immediately in your daybook or planner. When you get to the office the first thing you should do is review your appointments for the day. You may have committed yourself to a meeting weeks earlier and forgotten all about it. In the meantime, you'll

---

*By the way, do yourself a favor and don't make obvious preparations to leave and then walk out the door at exactly 5 P.M. That will only irritate your boss.

have excluded it from your mental lineup for the day. We all live at a hectic pace these days. The better organized you are, the better the chances you'll show up when and where you're expected.

PYRAMID SCHEMES

EVERY PYRAMID SCHEME is a scam. If you start one or recruit others to join one, you can be prosecuted. And if you invest in one, you will lose all your money.

Pyramid schemes are illegal business structures that operate just like chain letters. The person who starts the pyramid recruits several people, each of whom pays him money to join. They in turn, recruit new people who pay them money, a percentage of which they pass on to the person at the top. As new people join, the money they pay filters all the way to the top of the pyramid, with each person taking a small piece of it as it passes through them. In theory, the closer you are to the top of the pyramid, the more money you make.

Pyramid schemes are usually disguised as games, buying clubs, mail-order opportunities, or investment companies. Many appear to be structured around a product. Recruitment meetings are led by talented promoters who create a frenzied, enthusiastic atmosphere that centers on one thing—easy money. The money people pay to join buys them a certain amount of inventory and covers certain "fees."

Pyramid schemes eventually collapse because they run out of new people to recruit. It's simple mathematics. As the pyramid grows, each succeeding generation of members becomes larger and larger. In order for the pyramid to survive, it needs to have an infinite supply of new investors. But the chances of each new generation of participants recruiting new members becomes less and less. Eventually, the pyramid collapses, the money stops flowing, and the participants, many of whom are friends and family, become locked in bitter financial dispute.

The diagram on the next page illustrates how unrealistic pyramid schemes really are and how quickly they can collapse. It's based on an organization that requires each member to recruit 5 new members.

As you can see, by the thirteenth level, the pyramid would need to have signed up most of the American population to survive. By the fifteenth level, it has exceeded the population of the entire world.

There's a fine line between an illegal pyramid scheme and a legal multilevel marketing business. Like a pyramid, multilevel marketing involves many people marketing a product. The difference is, members are independent distributors who earn money solely through the sale of the product. They don't need to pay fees or recruit new members to participate in the organization. Consumers don't need to join the organization to purchase its products.

If you're considering investing in a business that has a distribution structure, you must investigate it as thoroughly as possible. The Federal Trade Commission investigates pyramid schemes and offers the following advice:

- Avoid any marketing proposal or distributorship that gives little or no mention to a product.

- Avoid any plan that offers commissions to recruit new distributors.

- Beware of plans that require new distributors to spend money on high-priced inventory.

- Be cautious of plans that claim you'll make money through the continued growth of your "down line," the commissions on sales made by members you recruit, rather than from your own sales.

- Be wary of promises of high earnings or "miracle" products.

- Be cautious about the references they give you. They could be acting in concert with the promoter.

- Don't pay money or sign contracts in a high-pressure situation or during your first week of visits to an online offer. Take your time to think through a decision to join. Discuss it with your spouse, accountant, lawyer, or a knowledgeable friend who isn't in the business.

- Check with your local better business bureau or attorney general's office to see if they have any knowledge of problems with the business.

- Report any suspicious offers or Web sites to the authorities.

Just remember that any offer that seems too good to be true probably is. Pyramid schemes prey on the greedy and the naive by promising quick and easy money. What they really bring is financial disaster and legal problems.

1

5

25

125

625

3,125

15,625

78,125

390,625

1,953,125

9,765,625

48,828,125

244,140,625

1,220,703,125

6,103,515,625

(See also franchises, multilevel marketing.)

READING

MY NAME IS STEPHEN and I'm an infoholic.
I suspect many of you share my problem and are familiar with the warning signs. Piles of partially read magazines and newspapers by your side of the bed, in your office, and in the bathroom. You try to catch up on weekends, but just can't seem to make it through the backlog. You tell yourself you won't renew subscriptions and you stop making impulse purchases at newstands, but you can't quite pull it off. The guy at the recycling center knows you by name. You feel overwhelmed by all the reading material that's available these days. It seems every year there are more and more publications that fall within your areas of interest. If you indulged your addiction, you could spend hours every day just leafing through newspapers and magazines. While that might be enjoyable, it would also wreak havoc with your business and personal life.

You Need to Prioritize

There's only one way around the problem. You need to prioritize your reading and abide by some self-imposed rules.

First, you need to surrender and admit you can't read everything and that when reading begins to replace doing it becomes a waste of valuable time. Then you need to decide which magazines and newspapers are most important to you. Let's start with newspapers. I think they're the single best source of news and recommend that you subscribe to a daily paper. If you don't have access to a good local daily, get a subscription to the nation's "paper of record," *The*

New York Times. If you can't get it delivered, get subscriptions to both *USA Today* and *The Wall Street Journal* instead.*

Next you need to decide what weekly newsmagazine to read. *Time, Newsweek,* and *U.S. News and World Report* are the old standbys, but ask yourself if you really need one of these magazines. If you have a good daily newspaper, these newsmagazines will just be a rehash of the stories you read during the previous week. My advice is to forgo a subscription and just leaf through issues on the newsstand. If you see a feature or two that interest you, buy the magazine and take it home. If you feel the need for a weekly newsmagazine, I suggest *The Economist.* Because it truly is an international magazine, it provides a different perspective than you'll get from your newspaper. It also devotes less space to entertainment and more space to business and finance than the American newsweeklies.

The next category is professional reading. You should subscribe to whatever publication is considered the bible of your industry and take the time to scour it for information that is useful to you. You might also want to read one or two other publications, either in your industry or in a related industry. Don't bother with newsletters or bulletins. They'll just be condensed versions of information you have already received elsewhere.

The last category includes publications you want to read for enjoyment. They might include magazines about sports or culture or other subjects in which you have an intense interest. These are the publications that make you a well-rounded person and an interesting conversationalist, so don't hesitate to indulge yourself. Go to the library or newsstand once or twice a month and just browse for articles that catch your interest. You'll find the practice both rewarding and educational. If you find yourself routinely grabbing the same magazine every month, opt for a subscription. Otherwise indulge your whims.

These days we information junkies also have the Internet. More and more magazines are creating online editions of themselves. There are also many publications ("zines") that exist only in cyberspace. It's worth your while to spend some time browsing, but be careful to monitor yourself. It's very easy to get carried away. Consider devoting one afternoon a month to browsing the online journals. Any more than that and you'll be taking time away from other important parts of your life.

Finally, there are books. Try to read a combination of fiction and nonfiction. Books on history, business, science, and other topics not only spark your imagination, they add to your general store of knowledge. Reading about different fields, people, time periods, and places gives you a broader perspective on the world. That will make you a more creative and innovative person. Reading good fiction—whether serious, genre, or mainstream—can be mind-expanding and a wonderful escape.

---

*Make sure you read the morning newspaper prior to any job interviews. There are some interviewers, like me, who ask candidates questions about current events to see if they're aware of the world. Even if you're not quizzed, the morning newspaper may give you material for discussions you initiate. It could even provide you with last-minute insight into the company you're visiting.

Making Time to Read

It's hard for busy people to find time to read. I recommend making it a part of your daily schedule. For example, when I get to the office every morning, I first check my messages and schedule, then I pull out *The New York Times* and *The Wall Street Journal.* I skim through them and dog-ear those pages that have articles I want to read. Later, sometimes over lunch at my desk or during the afternoon, I'll go back and read those articles. I also use my afternoon reading time to keep up with my local bar association journal. In the evening I read for enjoyment. Novels and nonfiction books and my favorite magazine are on my bedside table.

I also look for other opportunities to read. Weekends allow me to catch up on what I've missed during the week. Vacations include piles of reading material. I also plan what I'll read during airplane flights. Do I get to read everything I'd like? No. But I make sure that what I read contributes to my knowledge, my professional acumen, and my enjoyment of life. I suggest you do the same.

REAL ESTATE INVESTMENT TRUSTS

IF YOU'D LIKE TO INVEST IN real estate beyond just owning your own home, yet have no desire to be either a landlord or a professional renovator, real estate investments trusts (REITs) are your best bet.

When you invest in an REIT, you pool your money with other investors to back the development or join in the ownership of shopping malls, hotels, apartment complexes, resorts, and other large projects.

REITs are popular for several reasons. Like a mutual fund, they reduce risk by allowing you to invest in a variety of properties rather than putting all your investment eggs in one shopping center, for instance. REITs also offer the small investor a chance to get into an investment market—real estate development—that's usually only open to big investors. REITs also have the potential to provide enormous returns. Since they pay no corporate taxes, they are required to pay almost all their profits to investors. As a result, they often outperform the stock market.

There are three types of REITs. *Equity REITs* put their money into income-producing real estate such as shopping malls, hotels, and office buildings. Some simply provide funding to projects. Others are involved in the entire endeavor, buying, developing, and managing their properties. *Mortgage REITs* primarily invest in construction loans and mortgages in return for some ownership income. *Hybrid REITs* combine both approaches. So far, equity REITs that are involved in every aspect of their projects have exhibited the best performance of the three.

Before you rush out and invest heavily in REITs, keep in mind that, just like every other kind of investment, they're not a sure thing. Since REITs are a comparatively young investment, there are few historical benchmarks investors can use to measure performance. For this reason, and until they have more of a track record, I think they should only represent a small percentage of your total portfolio.

If you do invest, avoid start-up REITs. They have no track record at all on which to make a sound decision. Basically, you're flying blind and hoping for the best. This is *not* how one should invest one's money. You might as well take it to Las Vegas.

You should also avoid REITs that promise they'll divest themselves of all their holdings after a certain number of years and pass on huge profits to their investors. This smacks of a scam carried out in the 1980s under a different guise—the real estate limited partnership investment (RELP). These REITs charge high fees and offer no guarantees on what they'll be able to get for their holdings when they do decide to dissolve.

Don't invest in REITs that are closely tied to a particular developer. You may just be providing bailout money to someone who has gotten himself in a financial bind and is using the REIT to raise cash.

Only invest in REITs that have independent managers whose sole concern is how the REIT performs. You also need to examine the experience of those managers.

Don't invest if the REIT has only a single property or a few properties. One of the advantages of REITs is their mutual fund approach to acquisitions: The more properties a fund is invested in, the safer your investment will be.

Finally, remember that REITs face the same risks as real estate in general. Before you invest you should look carefully at the type of property the trust is involved in. How old is it? What kind of condition is it in? Pay close attention to its location. Is it in a growing area or one in decline? Is it convenient to its target demographic group? In other words, investigate the REITs holdings as you would if you were independently investing in the real estate.

RECEIVABLES

ENTREPRENEURS ARE NEVER PREPARED for the problems of collecting receivables. Having devoted all their available funds, credit, and energy to launching the company, running the operation, and landing more work, they find themselves endangered by poor cash flow because they didn't realize that the more business you do, the more operating capital you need. As a fledgling operation, they're under pressure to meet their payables immediately, but they lack the leverage and the courage to exert equal pressure to collect their receivables.

Keep the Money Moving
Obviously, the key to staying out of cash flow trouble is to receive payments from clients and customers as quickly as possible. The faster you receive payments, the less likely you will need to borrow money or raise more capital.

The frequency with which you send out invoices will have a direct bearing on how quickly your payments arrive. Ideally, you should send out an invoice as soon as you complete a job or deliver a product. That may be impractical, however. Depending on the size of your staff, you may choose to send invoices out on a regular schedule. Some businesses send them out once a week. Others send them out monthly. Whichever you choose, make sure your billing schedule provides you with adequate cash flow to meet your own obligations, including payroll, utilities, rent, and other payables.

You may choose to send invoices through the mail. I find that more and more businesses are sending them electronically as e-mail. This gets the invoice to the customer in seconds, not days, and makes the payment process that much quicker. You can also speed up payment by changing your payment terms from the standard 30 days to 15 or 20 days, providing electronic funds transfer, or offering a discount for early payment. (The traditional discount is 2 percent off the price on payments made within 10 days of receiving the invoice, which is the equivalent of giving them a 24 percent yield on their money.) I have found that many customers will agree to shorter terms without raising much of a fuss. Also, those with sufficient cash on hand will readily take up your discount offers.

Dealing with Delinquent Accounts

Regardless of your billing frequency or payment terms, there will always be a certain percentage of your customers who don't get their payments to you on time. You cannot be shy about giving them a little prod.

Many novice business owners are afraid they'll anger a client and lose his business. That's the wrong attitude. The customer incurred the debt and in doing so assumed the responsibility for paying you—on time. If he's just trying to take advantage of you, you're better off without him.

Some people have a particularly difficult time pursuing a late payment when the client is a friend. That should not be a concern, either. Business is business and friendship is friendship. An old friend—and creditor—once called me about an overdue bill. Impressed with his boldness, I asked how he so easily separated business and friendship. "What does one have to do with the other?" he asked. He was right, of course. Another friend—and creditor—took the opposite approach. She called me on the telephone and asked, "What did I do? Are you mad at me?" When I replied in the negative, she said, "Then why haven't you paid my bill?"

Both approaches work. That's because the important thing is to take action as soon as any payment becomes overdue. That establishes the fact that you are treating this as a business matter and aren't going to allow other factors to get in the way. Sometimes all it will take to inspire some action on the part of your customer is a gentle reminder over the telephone. If that fails, send another copy of the invoice along with a cover letter stating that you have already sent one invoice and that payment is late and due immediately. Most customers will get the message and respond quickly.

Some customers will try to give you a sad tale about financial difficulties in an effort to put off payment as long as possible. Don't accept this as an excuse. Instead, offer them advice. Tell them how you've periodically found yourself in difficult financial straits but managed to pay your creditors by opening a line of credit or tapping into your own assets.

If you have a customer or client who is truly having severe financial difficulty, you may have little choice but to work with him in setting up a payment schedule you can both live with. Sure, you could turn the account over to a collection agency, but that just costs you money, and it's unlikely to speed up payment. My advice is to stick with your customer for a reasonable length of time and hope he gets back on his feet. If he does, he'll be a loyal customer forever. If, even after a decent interval, he doesn't meet his obligations, turn his account over to collection, accept the loss, and write him off as a customer or client.

RECORDS AND PAPERS

I'VE NEVER MET ANYONE who saved the right amount of records and papers. When it comes to personal files, people are extremists: they seem to either throw everything out or save every scrap of paper.

Since you purchased this book I'll bet you're a saver. I'll wager you have a filing cabinet at home that's overflowing with years' worth of income tax forms, receipts, bills, canceled checks, and other records and papers. If you don't have a filing cabinet, your personal paper trail is no doubt stashed away in boxes tucked away in closets or hidden up in the attic.

Most of my clients needlessly clutter their homes and offices with such stuff. They get a sense of security from the thought that if a situation should arise that requires a bit of financial information from the past, they're ready. Need to know what they paid for an oil change on their AMC Pacer back in 1978? They'll probably be able to dig out the receipt and show me.

My advice? Establish priorities about what's important and what's not. Then start tossing things out. For example, if you don't need a record of a transaction for tax purposes, throw it out. If you do, just keep the check and throw away the receipt, or the reverse. You don't need both. The one exception is purchases of prescription medicines or business expenses. For those you'll need the receipt to prove you weren't buying cosmetics or some other personal item.

Most of the paperwork you'll receive only needs to be kept a short time. Once you've determined your checking account statement is correct, for example, there's no need to keep it. The same is true of credit card statements. Once the bill has been paid and the payment shows up on the next month's statement, you can toss the old statement. You don't need to save canceled checks and credit card receipts, either, unless you need them for tax purposes.

New insurance policies make old ones obsolete. Yet I'll bet you have several years' worth of car insurance or homeowner's insurance policies stuffed away in a file. You only need investment statements until you receive your year-end summary. Pay stubs only need to be kept until you receive your 1099 or W-2 forms.

Maintenance receipts for work done on your home and automobiles should be kept as long as you own them. When it comes time to sell a house or a car, they serve as evidence to prospective buyers that you took good care of them. For real estate, they could also help reduce the taxes that may be due on a sale. Old statements from health insurance companies detailing payments for routine doctor visits and other services can be discarded.

Once you've weeded out the most useless of your records and papers, you need to determine how long to keep the rest. Here are some guidelines.

Keep for life:

- Birth certificates

- Death certificates

- Divorce decrees

- Military papers

- Naturalization papers

- Trust agreements

- Vaccination records

- Wills

Keep for six years:

- 1099 and W-2 forms

- Accident reports

- Alimony payment records

- Charitable contribution records

- Loan records

- Medical bills

- Nondeductible IRA records

- Property tax records

- Securities transaction statements

- Tax returns

Keep for as long as item is valid, current, in force, or until it is recorded in your bank statement:

- Alimony agreements

- Certificates of deposit

- Child custody agreements

- Deposit slips

- Insurance policies

- Negotiable instruments

- Partnership agreements

- Powers of attorney

- Pre- and postnuptial agreements

Keep for as long as you own the item or home:

- Home improvement receipts

- House deeds

- Receipts for major purchases

- Stock option agreements

- Title insurance policy

- Warranties

Once you've decided what to keep, you need to decide where to keep it. I recommend dividing your papers into three categories: those you may need on short notice, those you rarely need, and those that should be kept outside your home to protect them against fire or flood.

The first category—financial records, birth and death certificates, insurance information, account statements, and the like—can be kept at home in a filing cabinet. Papers that will rarely be needed—partnership statements, marriage certificates, divorce decrees, citizenship records—should be kept at home in a fireproof box. Papers that need to be safeguarded—such as certificates of deposit, stock certificates, bearer bonds, and your household inventory—should be kept in a safe deposit box.

Finally, consider letting your lawyer keep your important legal papers such as wills, prenuptial agreements, and adoption papers. The only downside to having a lawyer hold your papers or documents is that it makes it a chore to have any other lawyer or firm do similar work for you or your executor in the future.

RENTER'S INSURANCE

THERE'S NO EXCUSE for not having renter's insurance. It costs little and the risk of being without it is enormous. If tenants lose their possessions in a fire or some other calamity, the landlord's insurance will only cover the structure and any possessions the landlord loses. Tenants' own clothing, furniture, personal effects, and any other possessions will not be covered.

Renter's insurance is quite inexpensive, so there's no reason not to be completely covered. If you rent and don't have coverage, or you have children who have moved out on their own and are renting, you should call an insurance broker immediately. Granted, the chances of something happening are slim. But what if you do find yourself the victim of a catastrophic loss?

Not Just For Property Damage

Not only does renter's insurance protect against property loss; it provides coverage against personal liability as well. This is important, since the responsibility for personal injury can be a bit confusing with rental property. For example, if someone trips coming up the front steps and breaks a leg, whose fault is it? If the rental property is a house, you'll probably be considered responsible for the entire structure and grounds and therefore considered liable for the injury.* If it's a dwelling with many apartments, however, the landlord will likely be liable, since the front steps would be considered his responsibility. Your responsibility would only include the interior of your apartment. Regardless of the court award, with renter's insurance you're protected.

Although they aren't legally required to do so, some landlords will purchase additional insurance to protect the property of their tenants. A few do it out of the goodness of their hearts. Most, however, do it because of a fear of lawsuits. Regardless, it's an easy expense for them to cover. They can just build the premiums into their rental fees. I think if more landlords were aware of how painless it is to cover their tenants' property, it would be a much more common practice than it is.

Coverage Options

Renters have several insurance options. The standard renter's policy is called an HO-4. It covers 17 or 18 different threats to your personal property, including fire, theft, vandalism, and various acts of nature. You should insure your possessions for their replacement value. If you have any collectibles such as paintings or antiques, be sure to have them appraised and photographed.

A second class of renter's insurance, HO-6, adds coverage for improvements and additions you may have made to the rental property. For example, if you purchased new kitchen cabinets or renovated the bathroom, you would be reimbursed for the loss. Keep in mind there's often a

---

*That's because you have "dominion and control."

limit of 10 percent of the face value of the policy for coverage of additions and improvements. If the work you did is worth more than that, you need to purchase additional coverage.

Whatever kind of renter's policy you buy, make sure to check the value of it liability coverage. Most policies provide $100,000 in coverage. You may decide you need more. Another $200,000 to $400,000 worth of coverage is quite affordable. I suggest you talk to a broker about buying your renter's insurance and automobile insurance from the same company. This usually results in discounted premiums and may even give you a chance to buy an inexpensive umbrella liability policy.

RÉSUMÉS

THE GREATEST RÉSUMÉ IN THE WORLD won't get you a job. All it can do is get you an interview. The rest is up to you.

Preparing a résumé is admittedly a challenging experience. It's difficult to sum up a lifetime of education, career achievements, and personal goals and successes in a couple of pages and still manage to make yourself stand out from the competition.

What can you do to make your résumé stand out? First, focus on what you shouldn't do. Forget special papers, unusual typefaces, and other gimmicks. That's just window dressing. An experienced personnel executive will laugh at your feeble attempt to get noticed. Some may even hold it against you and be less likely to grant you an interview.

The best way to get your résumé noticed is to customize it for the particular job, company, and industry you're interested in joining. You need to create subtle links between your past positions and the skills and experience the company is looking for. This means every résumé you send out will be customized and restructured to call attention to the proper information.

Let's say you know the company to which you're applying is looking for someone to streamline one of its department's expenses without resorting to layoffs. This ties in nicely with several managerial accomplishments you've had in prior positions. In one, you reduced your unit's costs 12 percent while increasing sales 10 percent. In another, you commissioned an outside consultant to visit your department and make cost-saving recommendations. His suggestions resulted in a 15 percent reduction in costs. Both these accomplishments will be given a high priority in the section of your résumé focusing on accomplishments.

You can also establish links to the company or industry in the section of your résumé that details your employment history. Describe the responsibilities you had in each position in such a manner that they seem as close a match to the position you're applying for as possible.

The reader will begin to notice these parallels early on in your résumé. If you continue to make them evident throughout the document he'll quickly recognize you as a well-qualified candidate.

Form Follows Industry or Profession

The specific form your résumé takes should follow the accepted pattern in your industry or profession. For example, someone applying for a writing job would give priority to her publication credits, job history, and education, in that order. On the other hand, someone applying for an academic position would stress her education, then give publication credits and, finally, job history. Both these résumés would be strictly paper documents, while someone looking for a broadcasting job would also include a "reel," a videotape, audiotape, or compact disc containing representative samples of her work.

If there's no industry standard in your business, the résumé structure I'd suggest would begin with a short biographical sketch of no more than four sentences, proceed to a bullet list of your top 10 achievements, move to another bullet list of your skills, jump to a reverse chronological job history, provide educational and other credentials, and finally offer some personal information.

Don't Exaggerate

While I'm all for presenting yourself in the best possible light, I'm very much against lying in a résumé. Including false information is unethical and, if you should get the job, it will come back to haunt you. Somehow or another that degree you claimed you earned from Harvard or that position you reported having held in London will suddenly be shown to be untrue and your whole world will come falling down around you.

Validate Your Job-Hopping

Some employers are put off by a résumé that shows five or six jobs in just a few years. You can allay these fears by pointing out that each new job was accompanied by increased responsibilities and a higher salary and that it brought you closer to your personal goals. You shouldn't be faulted for being both ambitious and good at what you do.

What If You Don't Have Experience?

People looking for their first job or a job in an entirely new industry are often discouraged by the fact they have no experience. In fact, they have plenty of experience. What they don't have is job experience.

If this is the case, your best bet is to emphasize the life experiences you've had that are pertinent to the position. For example, if you've just graduated from college with a major that is appropriate for the position, that is in fact a very valid experience. So are courses you may have taken, internships you participated in, and hobbies you pursued. Even an intense interest in a given area will have provided you with enough knowledge and experience to bring something positive to the position.

Profit from the Personal

Employers aren't allowed to ask for personal information. Out of fear, many will actually trash résumés that provide information such as age, marital status, or physical condition that could be the basis for any type of discrimination claim. That doesn't mean employers don't want to know—only that they can't ask. This provides you with an opportunity to keep potentially problematic information private, but to also promote information that could put you in a better light.

The best clue to an applicant's age comes from the dates included in a résumé. If you're worried about your age being an issue, you need not say when you graduated from college, only that you graduated with a particular degree from a particular school. There's also no need to list every job you've ever held if you think that might hurt your chances. Instead, list just the most recent, relevant positions, noting that a complete job chronology will be provided upon request.

Employers can't ask about your health or physical condition. But if you'd like to demonstrate that neither of these is a problem you do so subtly by noting that your hobbies include some type of demanding physical activity. An employer who reads that you're a runner won't have any doubts about your health. Someone who reads that you're captain of a local softball team will know you're a leader and a team player.

Similarly, interviewers can't ask about your marital status or whether or not you have children. Still, you can deftly demonstrate those facts by noting that you're president of your church's couples club or that you've supervised the PTA fundraiser for three years running.

Filling in the Gaps

It's not unusual for people to have gaps in their résumés. Fewer and fewer of us march lock-step through life anymore. If you have periods in your life during which you weren't working, be up front about them. Perhaps you took a year off to go trekking through Nepal or to write a book or to stay home with your young children. Most employers these days aren't as concerned by such "downtime." In fact, the more enlightened of them will recognize that such experiences make you a more well-rounded person.

If the reasons for your employment gaps are more troubling, such as a serious illness or a personal problem, don't try to explain it in your résumé. It may just lead to misunderstanding and taint you unfairly. Rather, leave the time period vacant and be prepared to discuss it during your interview.

RETIREMENT COMMUNITIES

T HERE'S NO REQUIREMENT that you retire and move to a community like Del Boca Vista in *Seinfeld.*

People's housing needs are almost always reduced when they retire. The kids are gone and they find they just don't need as much space as they used to. Some choose to sell the family home and move to either a smaller home or a condominium or apartment. This reduces their housing and maintenance costs, two important factors when living on a fixed income.

For many others the answer is a retirement community. They're often gated and thus offer a safe, comfortable environment. They usually provide activities such as golf, tennis, swimming, and boating. Most have a clubhouse with a variety of amenities such as a library, a gym, a restaurant, an art studio, and ballroom where dances and other community events are held. Life is organized and predictable. Health permitting, many people choose to spend the rest of their lives there.

Another option is a life-care community. These have many of the same amenities as retirement communities but operate differently. Rather than just buying a unit and paying a monthly maintenance fee, you purchase a membership in the community. This membership guarantees you complete care for as long as you're alive, whether in your own housing unit or, if necessary, in an affiliated assisted-living facility, nursing home, or hospital. Most life-care communities also offer communal restaurant/dining rooms that residents can use to whatever degree they choose. For example, you might decide to eat breakfast and lunch in your home but dinner in the dining room. When you die, the community, rather than your heirs, gets possession of your home.

While I certainly recognize their appeal, I personally find the idea of a retirement community stifling. Everyone is the same age and they're almost always made up of the same ethnic, religious, or racial populations. Personally, I think I would miss the stimulus of being exposed to people of different ages and backgrounds. Most of the friends my wife and I have are younger than we are.

There's also a great deal of not-so-subtle pressure to conform and participate in community events. As a chronic nonjoiner, I would find this an enormous problem. The cookie-cutter sameness that obviously provides comfort and security to some people, seems like a voluntary step toward the grave to me. I've often likened them to tribal burial grounds where, after a lifetime out in the real world, people come to die.

Another downside to retirement communities is the economic aspect. Not only should you *not* count on your property appreciating in value, you might actually find that it loses value. When a retirement community is first being built, the developer will sell the earliest units to be completed at a discount to lure buyers. As more units are completed and demand increases, prices will also increase. The last units to be completed will usually sell for the highest prices.

When units begin to go up for resale an entirely different market develops, and herein lies the problem. At first, the market will remain healthy. Prices will remain static or even go up a bit for the first few years as people who were unable to buy into the community earlier grab the first units to hit the resale market. But as the population in the community ages, demand begins to decrease.

The problem is that the first round of buyers in a retirement community are relatively close in age. After 10 or 15 years, when they begin to put up their homes for sale, they're generally trying to sell to a younger generation of retiree. People aren't interested in moving into a community in which everyone is much older. Instead, they buy into new communities with others in the same age cohort. For this reason, property values in older communities continue to decline.

Life-care communities also carry financial risk. First of all, they can be very expensive to join. Once you join you run the risk that the community won't be able to deliver on the services it promised or might even go bankrupt. If you decide you're not happy there, getting out of your contract will likely be very difficult if not impossible. You should always consult with your lawyer before you make a decision to join and proceed very carefully.

If you don't want to move to a retirement community you don't have to. If you're willing to die broke, there are sufficient financial and insurance vehicles available for you to be able to live in your current home, or at least independently in a smaller home, for your entire life.

RETIREMENT PLANNING

I MAY NOT BELIEVE in retirement, but I do believe in retirement planning. If you intend to stop working altogether at age 65 (or earlier), or if you intend to keep working for as long as you're able to (as I do), you'll need to develop a savings and investing plan. Even I, who became a partner in a new law firm at the age of 70, realize that at a certain point earned income begins to decrease. Whether by design or default, there comes a time when we will all need to rely, partly or entirely, on unearned income to maintain our lifestyle. Call that time retirement, a second career, the home stretch, a renaissance, or whatever you'd like. Just make sure you begin planning for it as soon as possible.

Many of us put off planning for "retirement" far too long. It's understandable. When you're in your twenties and thirties, working hard to build a career and raise a family, retirement seems far away. Your immediate concerns in your forties and fifties are likely to be paying off your house and putting your children through college. Then, when you hit your mid to late fifties you suddenly realize you have no retirement savings and little time to make up for the failing.

The secret is to do all you can *not* to get to that point. It's especially important for those of you in your thirties and forties because there are a number of trends that are going to make it more expensive than ever before for you to retire. One is the simple fact that everyone is living longer. The average retiree today can count on having to fund 20 or more so-called Golden Years. That means you'll need more money than previous generations. Second, the Social Security system is about to be stretched out of recognizable shape. It's highly unlikely it will provide as much as it did for your parents or their generation. Third, businesses are finding it more and more difficult to fund pension plans, so you're apt to get little or no help from your employers. And finally, there's always the quiet, relentless erosion of your money by inflation.

Start Early

All this means you need to rely a great deal on your own investments to fund a comfortable home stretch. The only way to be successful is to start early. Sure, you're going to need to invest for your children's education. But that retirement fund is equally important. If you wait until all your kids are out of the house to start putting money aside, you'll never have enough.

The important thing to remember is that investors who start early have time on their side. You may not be able to afford to save much at first, but every dollar you can set aside will have decades to appreciate in value. Starting early also means you can be a risk-taker and invest in stocks, mutual funds, and other securities that offer the potential for growth. The fact that your dotage is years away means you can afford to weather the ups and downs of the market and enjoy the long-term success that the market has traditionally provided.

Determine How Much Money You'll Need

The average retiree needs about 75 percent of his or her preretirement income to maintain the same standard of living they had while they were working. The amount you need will depend on a number of factors.

First, where do you want to live? Most retirees remain in the same house they lived in before retirement. But a considerable number make a big move, often to a warmer climate where the price of housing can be considerably lower. Determining your housing costs is critical for effective retirement planning.

You need to consider the lifestyle you hope to have. Do you plan on being a world traveler or will you be content to putter around the garden and play a little golf? Are you a big fan of dining out or will you be eating most of your meals at home? Big plans require a lot of money.

Will you continue to work for pay, full-time or part-time, or do you intend to volunteer or lead a life of leisure?

Despite Medicare, there are also medical expenses to consider. Like it or not, your older years will coincide with increasing numbers of visits to doctors, some of whom may not accept Medicare. A serious illness can have a significant effect on your financial situation. Although it's impossible to predict if and when you'll need to deal with a major health crisis, regular checkups and a healthy lifestyle can reduce your chances of becoming seriously ill.

Evaluate Your Sources of Unearned Income

Most retirees rely on three sources of income: Social Security, pension plans, and investments. As I pointed out earlier, you can't put much faith in Social Security. My advice is to not count on it at all. That way any Social Security you do get is bonus money.

If you're lucky, you work for a company with a generous pension plan that will provide a significant retirement cushion. Many companies today offer employee stock ownership plans (ESOPs), 401(k) accounts, corporate savings plans, and other retirement devices for their employees. You should start putting as much of your salary as possible into them as soon as you can. As retirement nears, you can ask your company's human resources office to calculate your estimated benefits. That will give you a ballpark idea of how much you can count on receiving each month.

The balance of your retirement income is going to have to come from your own investments. Again, starting early is the key. Time is the great equalizer when it comes to investment risk, so you can be rather swashbuckling in your younger years. Go for growth with stocks and aggressive mutual funds. As you approach your later years, you should begin to move your assets into bonds and other fixed-income securities. The services of a seasoned financial planner can be invaluable in helping you devise a long-term strategy.

Inflation: Your Biggest Enemy

No matter how much money you amass for retirement, it will be threatened by inflation. And the earlier you retire, the greater the threat. If you retire at 65, and inflation averages 4 percent, your living expenses will have increased by 80 percent by the time you reach 80. If you retire at 60, they'll more than double. Since most of your income will more than likely be fairly fixed (bond interest, pension payouts, etc.) you'll need to take this erosion of your money into account in your planning. As a hedge against inflation, you should keep some of your investment dollars in stocks and mutual funds. A nice 12 or 15 percent return can go a long way in slowing inflation's relentless assault on your money.

(See also pension plans.)

REVERSE MORTGAGES

R EVERSE MORTGAGES ARE a fabulous tool for solving one of the most worrisome problems facing older Americans: having enough money to ensure quality of life throughout
their remaining years. These mortgages will pay an older person a tax-free income to live in
their home. And yet they're not very popular. I believe that's due to misconceptions and lack of
clarity.

The concept of the reverse mortgage is beautiful in its simplicity. For many retirees, their
home is their most valuable asset. They more than likely paid for it by taking out a mortgage, a
30-year loan on which they dutifully made monthly payments until they owned the house free
and clear. If they're lucky, their home has appreciated in value well beyond their initial investment.

A reverse mortgage gets some of that money flowing back to the homeowner. It allows him
or her to tap into the value of the home to finance the golden years by borrowing against its
value. The lender agrees to provide the homeowner with a loan using the house as collateral. The
amount of the loan is based on the borrower's age, the value of the house, and the interest rate.
Because payments are based on life expectancy, the older the borrower, the more money she'll
get. (Because payments are tied to age, reverse mortgages are of most use to people 75 and over.)

The term of the loan can be a set for a defined number of years or it can be until the homeowner passes away. When the loan comes due, it must be paid off by the borrower or the borrower's estate. Although it can be paid off by other means, it almost always is covered by the
proceeds from the sale of the house when the borrower moves or dies.

Homeowners can receive the money in several ways. They can receive a lump-sum payout
from the lender or a smaller lump sum followed by monthly payments for a fixed number of
months or for life. Or they can open a line of credit to be accessed as needed. This can prove
particularly valuable in paying for home repairs and home health care if it becomes necessary.
Some homeowners, appalled at the idea of life in a nursing home, use reverse mortgages for this
very purpose.

Reverse mortgages allow homeowners to schedule the payments around their future plans.
Let's say someone will be moving to a retirement home or the home of a relative in 8 or 10
years. They can arrange to receive monthly payments until that time comes. If they desire to stay
in their home until they pass away, the payments can be adjusted to cover that period of time.
Because the payments they receive are the proceeds from a loan, not income, borrowers aren't
liable for any taxes.

One of the biggest perceived downsides is that a reverse mortgage reduces the value of the
borrower's estate. Yes, it will—but so what? I believe your goals should be to enjoy your money,
pass your assets along while you're alive, and die broke, rather than build up an estate.

If the borrower should arrange a lifetime loan and then make a mockery of the actuarial
tables and live well beyond the expected date of his or her demise, the money that's been paid

out may well be more than the value of the house. In this case, the lender takes the hit. He can't come after the borrower's heirs for the balance of the loan.

Lenders realize this, of course, and that creates another problem. Because there's a chance that the borrower will be around much longer than expected, the lender will usually agree to lend no more than 75 percent of the value of the home, and base the monthly payments on this figure. Another potential problem of reverse mortgagees is their cost. The borrower usually pays closing costs and other fees up front. Although the interest isn't paid until the loan is paid off, it can also be quite high. If the borrower should pass away soon after taking out the loan, the interest payment can be enormous.

Reverse mortgages have been around for years. But it's only been in the last half-dozen years or so that they've come to be seen as viable financial alternatives for senior citizens. Prior to that they were looked upon as an emergency strategy for impoverished seniors who had no other place to turn to for money. But with the support they've received from the federal government and the AARP, and the legions of soon-to-be-elderly baby boomers gathering on the horizon, reverse mortgages should become more popular than ever in the coming years.

Reverse mortgages can be obtained from a variety of sources, including the Federal Housing Administration (FHA) and Federal National Mortgage Association (Fannie Mae). They're also available from banks and financial services companies such as Trans America Corporation. Keep in mind, too, that children can serve as lenders and finance reverse mortgages for their parents. It's a way for them to help their parents in their dotage while ensuring that the money they pay out will be returned to them when the home is sold.

RISK VERSUS REWARD

IF YOU'RE NOT WILLING to take a chance with your money you may never lose it, but you'll certainly never make a great deal.

Risk and reward are an inherent part of any investment and are directly proportional to one another. In other words, the higher the risk, the greater the potential return. The lower the risk, the lower the potential return.

There is no absolutely risk-free place to put your money. Even government-backed investments such as Treasury bonds and insured savings accounts carry the infinitesimal risk that the federal government will fail. Plus there's the constant erosion of investment earnings by inflation.

There is one factor that mitigates risk, however—the passage of time. The longer you have until you need to begin to liquidate or cash in your investments, the more risk you can assume in your investment strategies. If you're in your thirties, you have from 30 to 40 years of prime earning years ahead of you. Your investments can weather the fluctuations that occur over time and still achieve a healthy appreciation over the long haul.

If you're in your fifties, on the other hand, you may only have 10 to 20 years of prime earning left. You'll need to make sure the money you worked so hard to save over the years is safe and will be there when your income drops. That's why investment theory suggests gradually moving assets from higher-risk investments like small-company stocks to less risky investments like bonds or stocks in Fortune 100 companies as either retirement nears or your income potential decreases.

Different investments are accompanied by different types of risk. Here are the most common.

Inflation

The one common threat to all investments is inflation, that insidious upward creep in the cost of goods and services. Keeping pace with inflation, or staying ahead of it, means your money will have the same or more purchasing power next year or in 5 years or in 10 years that it has today. If your investments don't keep pace, your purchasing power decreases.

Business Risk

Investments backed by corporations carry the risk that the corporation will do poorly. If you own stock in a company, poor performance will reduce earnings and dividends and cause the price of the stock to decline. If you hold bonds issued by the company, you run the risk that the company won't be able to pay you the interest on the bonds or repay your initial investment when the bonds mature.

Investors in municipal bonds run a similar risk. Cities and municipalities routinely issue bonds to finance all kinds of projects. If they fall on hard times—they might suffer a rapid decrease in their tax base, for example—they may have trouble meeting their financial obligations to their bondholders.*

Market Risk

If you own stock or stock mutual funds, you're vulnerable to market risk. If the stock market begins a general decline, in which stocks drop in value across the board, your investments will follow right along and you'll almost certainly see a decline in the value of your portfolio.

Marketability Risk

This is the risk that there won't be a sufficient demand for an investment when you decide to sell it. Real estate and collectibles are good examples. If you purchase a residential investment property and then need to sell it when the market is swamped with homes for sale, your chances of getting the amount you want for the property might be slim. Certain stocks, bonds, and other investments can suffer the same problem.

---

*Some municipal bonds are insured, but they will have a lesser yield.

Weighing Your Choices

Here are comparisons of some of the most common investments and the risk and potential growth associated with each one:

Investment	Risk	Growth Potential
Savings account	Limited	None to very low
Certificate of deposit	Moderate	Very low
Series EE savings bonds	Limited	None to very low
Mutual funds	None to somewhat high	None to very high
U.S. Treasury notes	Moderate	Moderate
U.S. Treasury bonds	Limited to somewhat high	Moderate
Corporate bonds	Moderate to very high	None to very high
Municipal bonds	Moderate to very high	Moderate to very high
Stocks	Moderate to very high	Moderate to very high
Precious metals	Moderate to very high	Limited to very high
Options	Very high	Very high
Futures and commodities	Very high	Very high

Interest Rate Risk

Some securities are sensitive to interest rates. Bonds are a good example. Their prices move in the opposite direction of interest rates, so when interest rates increase, bond prices fall. When interest rates fall, bond prices go up.

Liquidity Risk

Liquidity is the ability to convert an investment into cash. Generally, the greater the liquidity of an investment, the less its potential for growth. A savings account, for example, is completely liquid. You can walk into the bank, fill out a withdrawal slip, and walk out with your money. But a savings account will not earn you much money.

Your house, on the other hand, isn't at all liquid. If you decide to sell it, it may take months before you can find a buyer willing to give you the price you want and another month or two to settle and finally get a check. The good news is that if the real estate market in your town is healthy, the check will be for a lot more than your initial purchase price.

Fraud

The investment world is fertile ground for all sorts of scams and cons. Investors are anxious for advice and the opportunity to make money quickly, and there are a lot of people out there who will tell you whatever you want to hear just to get your money. If you're not careful, you'll never see it again. According to the FBI, securities fraud costs American investors $10 billion every year.

Controlling Risk

The best way to control risk is through careful asset allocation and diversification. By putting your money into investments that carry a variety of risk you balance their irregular perform-ances and increase your chances of enjoying a healthy return. Diversified portfolios rarely suffer huge losses. No matter what happens to the stock market or to interest rates, they keep investors' heads above water.

Finally, remember to protect yourself against scams. Any investment and the source of the investment must be carefully considered. If it seems too good to be true, it probably is.

SAFE DEPOSIT BOXES

Safe deposit boxes provide the ultimate in safety and security for personal papers, jewelry, and other items. Sometimes they may even be too secure . . . but more on that later.

Tucked away in bank vaults behind massive doors and steel bars and protected by full-time attendants and elaborate entry procedures, safe deposit boxes are quite formidable. So much so that, while criminals occasionally appear at tellers' windows to rob them of cash, safe deposit boxes are considered too difficult a nut to crack and so are almost always ignored.

They're also secure from internal theft. A safe deposit box requires two keys to open it. One is kept by the bank. The second is held by the customer. Without the customer's key, it's impossible for bank employees to open the box. In fact, if a customer loses both his keys (you'll usually be given two), the bank is incapable of opening the box. It must drill through the lock to get it open. By the way, should you lose your keys, the bank will charge you a fee, maybe as much as a few hundred dollars, to replace the lock on the box and provide you with new keys.

Safe deposit boxes in modest sizes rent for anywhere from $25 to $75 annually. Most banks have a few oversized boxes with higher fees. Safe deposit boxes, particularly the larger sizes, are in such demand, that there may be a waiting list for obtaining one.

If you find that to be the case, you may want to investigate businesses that offer private vaults. They'll charge more than a bank but are said to follow bank security procedures and may even offer 24-hour-a-day access. Most also allow you to rent a box under a false name, a feature that may or may not appeal to you. Many of these businesses have failed, however, so my advice would be to research carefully before renting a box from one of them.

But What If There Is a Burglary?

Safe deposit boxes are extremely secure, but they're not foolproof. They do get burglarized from time to time. Usually, however, the thieves are after a particular box or boxes and don't randomly drill through one after another in the hope of finding something really valuable. Nonetheless, if your safe deposit box should be burglarized, the bank is not responsible for your losses. (Take a look at the fine print on your contract.) Federal deposit insurance won't cover you, either. It just applies to accounts. Your homeowner policy should cover you up to its limits. But to make sure you can collect, you need to keep a careful record of what you have in your box, along with receipts and appraisals. I also suggest taking a photograph of the box and its contents and keeping the photo in a secure place at home.

Too Secure?

When you rent a safe deposit box, access to the box is limited to the person or persons named on the rental agreement. I believe there should always be two people with access. The main reason is that in some states, the safe deposit boxes of the deceased are sealed until the state can examine them to determine if any of the contents can be taxed. (Frankly, the state wants to find out if you've been stashing away millions of dollars in ill-gotten cash.) If you and your spouse or another person both have access to your safe deposit box, important papers can be removed from the box before it's sealed.

My advice is to check with the bank beforehand to find out what the rules are upon the death of a box holder. What you choose to keep in the box will depend on what you're told. If access to the box is impossible after your death, you're certainly going to want to keep your will, insurance policies, cemetery deeds, and any other important documents somewhere else. I recommend you give them to your lawyer for safekeeping.

You can skirt this issue entirely if you own a business. In this case, you can rent a business safety deposit box, which will not be sealed upon the death of the box holder. You can then use the box to store all your important papers.

Here's another issue to consider: Where should you keep your safe deposit box key? Forget the sock drawer and the cookie jar. You want to make things as easy as possible for your heirs and executors. I recommend keeping it in a place that's fairly obvious, such as a drawer in your desk. Make sure it's labeled with the bank's name and the branch where the box is located. And don't worry about what will happen if it's stolen. A crook needs more than just your key to gain access to your safe deposit box. He also has to match your signature on a card when he visits the bank. That's not going to happen.

SALARY REVIEWS

People waste far too much energy worrying about asking for a raise. It's actually a simple process that can only turn out positively for an employee.

The Four Arguments

There are only four arguments you can use to request more money from your boss.

I. The first is to keep pace with the cost of living. At the very least, all employees should be rewarded with an annual salary increase that maintains the buying power of their dollars. Otherwise, they're actually making less money each year.

2. The second argument is that you've taken on new tasks and responsibilities and the job profile has changed.

3. The third is that you're making an exceptional contribution to the company's bottom line. If you were part of a project that returned unusually large revenues to the company, you deserve to be compensated.

4. The fourth argument is based on your market value. If you're not being paid what your industry peers are being paid, you're being taken advantage of, even though it might not be the intention.

Keep these four scenarios in mind when preparing for a salary review. They will serve as the basis for your argument for more money.

For example, if you haven't had a cost-of-living increase in more than a year you're entirely justified in asking for one. It's not a raise, it's just to keep you balanced against the unrelenting surge of inflation. Explain to your employer that without a cost-of-living raise, you'll be paying a larger portion of your salary for basic goods and services than you did the previous year (any employer will be well aware of this, by the way). What has happened is your salary has actually decreased. There's no acceptable reason for him to say no to your request.

Now let's look at the second scenario. If you've been asked to take on additional responsibilities and have not seen an accompanying increase in salary, you should bring this up at your salary review. Explain how you willingly took on the new tasks you were assigned, that you've been competently carrying them out ever since, and that you feel these new responsibilities merit a raise.

If you've contributed to an extraordinary increase in revenues or otherwise helped fatten the bottom line, you're also justified in requesting more money. But again, what you're likely to get is a bonus, not a salary increase. This is because your employer may see your contribution as a one-time event. Therefore it might be rewarded with a one-time payment. If this is the case, accept the money gratefully. But if you repeat the accomplishment six or eight months later, go back in and ask for another bonus.

If your contribution will result in increased earnings year after year, however (perhaps you helped develop a new product or came up with an ongoing strategy to cut costs), then you are deserving of a salary increase. Since your contribution to the company will increase its annual revenues, your annual compensation should increase as well.

Now let's look at your market value. Show your employer that you're being paid less than what other people who do the same job in other companies are being paid. You might also hint that if your salary is not brought into line, you may have no choice but to look elsewhere for employment. A subtle way of doing that might be to ask if you're "no longer wanted." Your boss has nothing to gain by denying you the extra money. He'll know that if you leave, he'll have to increase the salary for the position, anyway. If he wants to keep you, he'll come up with the money.

Making this argument will require conducting your own compensation survey. Most industry publications track salary ranges for various positions. Check with other companies to see how your salary compares to the salaries they pay people who do your job. Examine industry

From the Other Side of the Desk

If you're an employer, you need to bring up the salary issue before your employees do. The first step is to institute cost-of-living adjustments as a matter of course. This keeps your employees at the salary level at which you hired them. It also boosts morale. Unsolicited salary increases, no matter the size, are always well received and invariably preempt the employee's own request for a larger increase.

If you can't afford a cost-of-living increase, tell your employees so and also tell them when you will be able to afford it. By being up-front about the issue, you'll have shown them that you're concerned about their welfare and are doing everything you can to take care of them.

I believe that salary increases beyond the cost of living should be directly tied to your business's bottom line. If the business isn't increasing its profits, why should you increase your labor costs? It doesn't make sense.

But if profits are increasing, I believe you should share the wealth. If an employee has made a contribution that will return increased profits year after year, reward him with a raise. All other employees should be given bonuses tied to the size of your profit. If you don't make a profit, there are no bonuses. By tying your employees' compensation directly to the bottom line, you can motivate them to work harder and give them a sense of controlling their own fortunes. I really think that's the best way to run a business.

journals for employment ads. Use the information you gather to prepare a written document that presents your argument, including the sources of your data.

A Win-Win Situation

Asking for a salary increase always turns out positively. If your request is granted, you have more money in your pocket. But if your request isn't granted you've been given the best possible indication of your value to the organization. Savvy employers always want to keep quality employees. If your request has been turned down it means:

- Your employer doesn't value your contribution

- Your employer doesn't have the money to pay higher wages

- Your employer values your contribution, but can't offer any further advancement

Whatever the reason for your rejection, it's a call to arms. You've been given irrefutable evidence that this isn't the place for you. Ask for an opportunity to revisit the issue in 90 days. Having turned you down once, your boss is unlikely to do so again. Meanwhile, revise you résumé, energize your network, and start job-hunting. Rest assured that in the long run you'll end up better off financially as well. The largest salary increases come when you switch employers.

SAVINGS ACCOUNTS

NO ONE OVER THE AGE of 10 should have money in a savings account. This is because savings accounts are the most useless investment vehicles on the market. First of all, they pay the least amount of interest and provide no other advantages. A checking account, on the other hand, will often pay as much interest and at least give you the utility of writing checks. A money market fund will pay more interest and still allow you access to your money. And a certificate of deposit will earn even more interest, although it does generally require you to keep your money invested for the full term to collect the interest.

Banks, on the other hand, love savings accounts. Since they have to pay out minimal interest, they can earn more with the money that's deposited. And they have a lot to work with. Despite the availability of so many investment vehicles with higher earnings potentials, there are an astonishing number of people in this country who, through fear or ignorance, still keep their money in a savings account.

I think the only useful function of of a savings account is to teach children about savings and interest. Banks realize this and use it as a good public relations tool. As a rule, most banks aren't interested in small savings accounts of only a few hundred dollars. The administration costs are more than the banks can earn with the money that's deposited. But they will usually agree to open a small savings account for a child under 18, provided the child is the one who actually controls the account.

The simplest approach is to open a passbook account. The bank will record every transaction in the passbook, so your child will see a record of all his deposits and interest payments. When the birthday checks arrive from Grandmom and Grandpop, or the lemonade stand has a good week, or he makes a few dollars caring for the neighbors' cat, it's off to the bank to deposit the money. It's the perfect primer to get him started on the road to learning about money and investments.

Lesson one will be understanding interest. The interest from a savings account can be compounded daily, monthly, quarterly, semiannually, or annually. Find an account that compounds interest daily to maximize its earnings and explain to your child why it's the most advantageous strategy. This will also be a good time to explain to him what the bank does with his savings to earn money for itself.

The lessons will continue as your child grows older. Once he understands interest he'll be delighted to move of his money into a CD or some other, more profitable investment. He may take a liking to investing and start doing his own research. I have a friend whose teenage son became a student of mutual funds. The broker he selected told my friend that his son knew more about mutual funds than 90 percent of his clients.

SAVINGS BONDS

I THINK SAVINGS BONDS ARE underrated, probably because most baby boomers have come to associate them with gifts they received from old relatives which were soon cashed in for less than their face value.

Granted, savings bonds are conservative tools. Of all the investment options out there, savings bonds are without question the most secure. After all, they're issued by the federal government and backed by the U.S. Treasury, so they're completely risk-free. Sure, the U.S. Treasury could go under. But if that happens, we're all going to have much bigger problems on our hands than the value of savings bonds.

Because they carry so little risk, savings bonds earn very little interest, so they're not the vehicle for those seeking rapid growth. Still, in a topsy-turvy market, or for those who find peace of mind in knowing exactly how much money they'll have at any given point in the future, savings bonds do serve a purpose.

Savings bonds are like other bonds in that the purchaser receives interest from the issuer of the bond—in this case the federal government. They differ, however, in that they can't be traded on the secondary market. They're cheap—they can be purchased for as little as $25—that's what made them very popular as holiday and birthday gifts for children. They're also a good place to invest any extra cash you might find from time to time. They can be purchased from banks or directly from the Federal Reserve.

Like zero-coupon bonds, savings bonds are purchased at a discount to their face value. Purchasers receive the full amount when the bond matures. Unlike zero-coupon bonds, however, you don't have to pay tax each year on the interest that accrues. Another plus is that when you cash in the bond, you only pay federal taxes on the interest. They're exempt from state and local taxes. Here are some other advantages:

- There are no fees for buying or selling them.

- You can hold them past maturity and they keep on generating interest. Some savings bonds will generate interest for 40 years.

- You can cash them in as soon as six months after purchase and receive some interest.

- You're not stuck with your interest rate. If you can earn a higher return elsewhere, you can cash them in and reinvest your money.

- They're not callable, so you won't have to worry about suddenly having to invest your money at a lower rate.

- You can purchase them monthly through a payroll deduction plan ($50 minimum).

- They can be redeemed at any bank.

- The U.S. Treasury issues savings bonds in series. Here is information on the two current series.

Series EE Bonds

Series EE savings bonds have been issued since 1980. They can be purchased in denominations of $50, $75, $200, $500, $1,000, $5,000, and $10,000, and you can invest up to $15,000 annually. The bonds' redemption values increase every six months, so to maximize profits it's important to cash them in just after they've passed a six-month point.

For 15 years, EE bonds carried a guaranteed minimum rate of interest. Since May 1995, however, their interest rates have been tied to the performance of Treasury securities. If a bond is held for more than five years before it's cashed in, it will receive interest at 85 percent of the average return on five-year marketable Treasury bonds. If it's held for less than five years, it will only earn the market rates of the six-month Treasury bill. There's a significant difference between the two, so if you can't afford to hold onto a savings bond for at least five years, there are better places to put your money.

If you have a child in college and cash in EE bonds to pay tuition, you may not have to pay federal taxes (this also applies to tuition for you and your spouse). This makes EEs a great investment to put in your college portfolio. To take advantage of the tax break, the following conditions must apply:

- The bonds must have been purchased after 1990.

- The bonds must be purchased in the parents' name, not in the child's name.

- Parents must be at least 24 years of age.

- The money from the bonds must be used the same year the bonds are redeemed, and all the money must be used for tuition. It cannot be used for room and board.

- Parents must meet income requirements. In 1996, the adjusted gross income for a married couple had to be $61,850 or less ($41,200 or less for a single parent) to take advantage of the tax break.

Series HH bonds

When series EE bonds mature, investors can either cash them in or convert them into another type of savings bond, the series HH bond. These bonds are issued at face value rather than at a discount and interest is paid twice a year. The Federal Reserve will either send you a check or deposit the money directly into a bank account. Because interest is paid during the life of the bond, you are responsible for federal taxes on the interest every year.

There is a distinct tax advantage to the conversion strategy. When you convert an EE bond into an HH bond, you don't have to pay taxes on the interest that the bond accrued as an EE. For example, if you cash in an EE bond that you bought for $500 and it is now worth $1,000, you will owe taxes on the $500 in interest it's earned. But if you convert the EE bond into an HH bond, you can put off reporting that $500 until you eventually cash in the HH bond. You do, however, begin to pay annual income tax on the interest the HH bond earns.

Do savings bonds have a place in the average investor's portfolio? I think so, particularly for the conservative investor with little stomach for risk. I also think they're great for kids. Just as a savings account can teach a child about savings and interest, purchasing a savings bond is a good lesson in how investing works. They're an excellent example of how time is an investor's best friend. That's a lesson that can't be learned too early.

(See also bonds.)

SCRIPTING

I'M FREQUENTLY ACCUSED by my family and friends of never being at a loss for words. They're right.

The reason I always know what to say is that I script every important conversation I have, whether it's with a client, a friend, my wife, one of my children, or the guy who fixes my car.

If there's going to be something at stake in a conversation, I'll know what I'm going to say several hours, or even several days, ahead of time. The only important conversations I don't plan for are the ones I have with my grandchildren. For those I look forward to complete spontaneity.

The more that's at stake in a conversation, the more I plan. I make lists of my goals and prepare notes about the person I'll be speaking with. I think about strategies, Then I actually make a script of the conversation. The script will take into consideration the other party's possible responses to what I have to say and then show how I might respond to each one to allow me to steer the conversation in the direction I want. If I plan correctly, I rarely come up against a situation I'm unprepared for.

I've been working with my clients for years to help them make their own scripts. Together we've prepared scripts to ask for raises, meet a new boss, fire employees, make cold sales calls on new clients, and literally dozens of other situations. They haven't all been about business, either. I once helped a wealthy client prepare a script to ask his girlfriend for a prenuptial agreement. (It worked. She didn't leave him as he feared and they're still married.) I also helped prepare a script for a client who wanted to ask his wife to lose weight. (It also worked. She didn't leave him as he feared and actually took off a few pounds.)

I'm not insisting you go to the same lengths my clients and I do, even though I think it's wise. But I do believe there are a few strategic points you should follow when entering into any important discussion.

Your first key should be to make clear what it is you want. Get the issue right on the table. That's the only way you'll have a fruitful discussion. If there's any ambiguity on your part about your goal, it will be impossible for the other party to give it to you.

The second key is to exercise control over the situation. The words you choose and your reactions to what the other party has to say can help you shape the conversation and steer it in the direction you want it to go. This doesn't mean you must dominate the conversation. You can exercise control by listening carefully to the other party and then making measured responses to what he or she has to say.

The third key is to recognize the power you have in a situation. But rather than using it right off the bat, make the other party aware that you have it and that you'll use it if necessary. Let's say you've hired a contractor to do some work on your home and have been unhappy with his work. The mere suggestion that you're considering replacing him with another contractor will give you leverage you need to get what you want.

The fourth key is to learn to handle anger constructively. Anger is the behavior of last resort. It comes from lack of control and lack of power. If the other party becomes angry, you need to deal with it without inflaming the situation further. One way is to acknowledge it: "I understand why you're angry. I would be, too." Another is to express confusion at the anger, suggesting that the person's response is inappropriate to the situation. By doing so you deflected the anger back at the other person and make him appear out of control.

The final key is to always try to have the last word, regardless of the outcome of the conversation. The ability to have the last word gives you control over the dialogue and therefore the ability to leave it on terms that are most advantageous to you. Even in defeat, having the last word can set the stage for further discussion: "I'm sorry we couldn't reach an agreement on this. What if we speak again in a couple of days?" With any luck, the next time you'll be successful.

(See also listening, negotiating.)

SECOND HOMES

OWNING MULTIPLE HOMES can be a wonderful lifestyle. Of course, I'm biased. In addition to owning an apartment in Manhattan, where my wife and I spend the work week, we own a farm in Connecticut, where we spend almost every weekend, and a beach cottage on Martha's Vineyard in Massachusetts, where we spend our summer vacation.

I know what some of you are thinking: This is a lifestyle only available to the affluent. If that's your perception, you're wrong. Second homes aren't necessarily financial drains. More often than not they represent the redirection of money, rather than an added expense. Let me explain.

Many people, when they usher their youngest child out the door or pay that final tuition bill, find themselves with more cash flow than ever before. They are in their peak earning years. The mortgage on the family home is on its way to being paid off. Suddenly all that money that for years was funneled to piano lessons and ice hockey equipment and books and tuition is gathering in little green puddles around their feet.

That could become the money for a second home. It doesn't have to be expensive. You could buy a second home that's considerably smaller than the family home, has fewer features, or needs a bit of TLC. That would make it easier to carry on your current budget. As you have more money available you can add features and fix the place up.

If you plan to eventually sell your family home and move elsewhere, a portion of retirement savings could actually be diverted to spend on what would today be a second home but will eventually become a retirement home.

If your income has taken a significant jump, rather than selling your current home and buying another, more expensive home, you could buy a second home instead.

You can also help finance a second home by using it for vacations.* If you've been budgeting several thousand dollars a years for air fare and food and lodging, redirecting that money

---

*If you're looking for a mortgage for a second home, the best sources are lenders in the area where you'll be buying, particularly if the area has a high percentage of part-time residents.

toward your second home can go a long way toward covering your expenses. Just make sure you do indeed follow your plan and stop taking vacations. Otherwise you could create cash flow problems for yourself.

A second home can even be a source of income that can be used to cover the costs of ownership. I have a number of clients who own summer homes in the Hamptons on Long Island and on the New Jersey shore. The peak rental season in these popular areas is typically Memorial Day through Labor Day. Many of my clients reserve two weeks in the summer for themselves and their families and rent their houses out by the week for the balance of the season. With rentals going anywhere from $2,000 to $4,000 a week, they can cover taxes, maintenance, utilities, and a significant portion of their mortgages, and their houses are still available for the rest of the year. I even know a few who love going to the shore for weekends in the middle of winter.

You should also consider the potential appreciation of your second home. When the economy is good, as it has been for the last decade, more and more people purchase second homes. My beach-loving clients who bought during the economic downturn of the 1980s, when homes in vacation areas were being sold for a song, have watched their investments go through the roof. The prices of homes in areas that are primarily part-time communities are admittedly much more volatile than typical residential real estate. In boom times prices soar; in economic doldrums they crash. If you time your second-home purchase wisely, it could actually turn out to be quite a good investment.

But any economic benefits are usually secondary. Most people discover, as my wife and I have, that their second home becomes more than just a retreat. They become special gathering places for their families. On any given weekend and on holidays, all my children and grandchildren visit us in Connecticut. For my wife and me, this is the best of the many benefits our little farm has brought to our lives.

SECOND-TO-DIE INSURANCE

SECOND-TO-DIE LIFE INSURANCE is one of those obscure and highly specialized insurance contracts that few people know about, yet it could be the perfect answer to a number of very vexing problems. As you might guess from the name, this is a life insurance policy on two people that doesn't pay off until both have died.

This can be a life saver in several scenarios. The first is to pay taxes due on a large estate. Let's say your father passes away, leaving your mother behind. As surviving spouse, she will likely inherit his entire estate without tax liability. But when she passes on and the estate is passed down to you and other heirs, a significant tax bill may become due. A second-to-die policy will provide a cash payment to cover the taxes and allow you to pocket the entire value of the estate.

Many tax experts recommend placing such a second-to-die policy in an irrevocable trust so that it won't be taxed as part of the estate. The premiums are paid by the trustee, presumably

Second-to-Die, but First to Divorce

Given the divorce rate these days, you should make sure that any second-to-die policy you're considering can be divided in half if your marriage should end. The policy should not require that you pass a medical exam at that point, nor should the transaction include a sales commission. There may be fees associated with the creation of the two new policies, however, and some companies may include a surrender charge.

Insurance for the Uninsurable

Second-to-die insurance could be the answer for someone who has health issues, making the purchase of necessary life insurance impossible or extremely costly. Because second-to-die insurance is priced based on the mortality of both insureds, the health conditions of one insured isn't an obstacle.

one of your heirs. If the cash to pay the premiums comes from you, it further reduces your estate. When both parties have passed away, the trust uses the payout from the policy to pay any estate taxes. The process is a bit complicated, but it does ensure the maximum amount of tax protection.

Second-to-die policies are also valuable to people who may have a child or dependent with special needs—one who may not be able to provide for himself. If one parent dies, the second will presumably be able to continue to provide for the child. When the second parent dies, the policy will provide a cash benefit that, if worth enough and carefully invested, can provide enough income to support the child the rest of his life.

One of the advantages of second-to-die insurance is the ability to accurately determine how much money you want the policy to provide. If you're concerned about protecting your estate from taxes, an accountant or tax lawyer can help you figure out how much cash your policy should generate when you and your spouse are both gone. The cost of providing for a disabled child can also be calculated and the proper policy purchased. A word of advice: Don't rely on an insurance salesman to make these calculations for you. Speak with an independent financial planner or accountant who can help you find the sources for making these estimates.

In fact, whatever the reason you're buying a second-to-die policy, I'd suggest you meet with an experience, professional insurance broker who can walk you through your options.

SEED MONEY

EVERY DAY THERE ARE thousands of people who come up with great business ideas. But only a handful ever get started. Why? Because only a handful of people in the world have the determination to overcome the most frustrating part of entrepreneurship: coming up with seed money.

Forget banks. They're not interested in sticking their necks out to back a new idea, no matter how promising it might be. They know that four out of five small businesses fail within five years. Banks can do more comfortable things with their money, thank you very much. Later on, if you're successful and have a track record, they'll want to be your best friend and will come calling on you. Until then, they don't want to know you.

So where can you get seed money? Quite frankly, anyplace you can think of. Start with yourself. The business is your idea. If you have enough confidence in it to ask others for money, you should certainly be willing to risk your own. Liquidate your investments. Max out the cash advance limits on your credit cards. Sell the second car. Have a garage sale. Take out a home equity line of credit.

Turn to Family and Friends

If that's not enough, you need to cast a critical eye on your relatives and friends. Perhaps you have an inheritance awaiting you and can ask your parents for an advance. Your brothers and sisters may be willing to make a modest investment in the business. If you have well-to-do acquaintances who are in business for themselves, ask them if they'd be interested in investing. After all, as small businesspeople themselves, they'll be more comfortable with the risky nature of start-ups. If you can convince them that your idea is a solid one, they may well be interested in getting involved. Just keep in mind that rather than just giving you a loan, they may want a piece of the business in return. At that point, you've taken on a partner, not a financier.

But let's not get ahead of ourselves. Before you start going out hat in hand to look for seed money, you need to prepare a business plan. It will determine how much money you need. This will include money to lease and furnish a location, purchase equipment and inventory, and pay for advertising and marketing. You'll also need to pay for fees and licenses.

Next, you need to calculate how much money you'll need to cover operating costs until the business reaches the break-even point. This includes your salary, so don't be conservative in your estimate. I advise clients to enter into business assuming they won't have a single customer for a year. That means they should have a year's worth of operating revenue in their account when they open their doors or business. Having such a cushion provides peace of mind. It also keeps food on the table and a roof over your head.

Making the Pitch

Once you know how much you need you can begin to approach potential investors. Keep in mind that you're forging a new relationship with them. It's not just friendship or love anymore.

It's business. If you approach the issue in a cavalier fashion, you'll likely come up short. And you'll deserve to. If you don't know enough to treat the situation with the proper degree of respect, they shouldn't loan your their money. I know I wouldn't.

This means you need to be professional and paint as thorough a picture of your proposed enterprise as possible. Explain to them how the business will work and show them projected expenses and revenues. You should be able to tell them when you expect the business to begin turning a profit. You should be able to tell them how long you'll need their money and suggest a repayment schedule. Finally, explain to them how you intend to return their money if the business should go belly-up. If there is a chance they might never see their money again, you need to make that quite plain. If you've done that, it's up to them to decide if the potential return is worth the risk.

If You Come Up Short

If you just can't come up with sufficient capital to start your business, you still have a few options. The first is to go back to the drawing board and rework your business plan. Can you reduce the scale, and therefore the start-up costs, of your business? If you can, you might be able to make it fit within a financing structure you know you can put together.

Your second option is to purchase a franchise. The proven track record of a franchise company can often loosen the purse strings of banks or other institutional lenders. Often the parent company itself will finance the business.

Your third option is to purchase an existing business. As with a franchise, lenders will find a proven business with a history of profitability an acceptable risk and will be more willing to lend you money.

Finally, you can take a huge risk and start your business undercapitalized. Just remember that undercapitalization is the number one cause of small business failure. If the day comes when you can't pay the rent, or even worse, yourself, it will be time to close the doors. On the other hand, just about every successful businessperson I've met tells war stories of flying by the seat of his pants and skirting the edge of financial disaster during the early years in business. It just may be that a taste for risk defines the true entrepreneur.

(See also business plans.)

SHOPPING

SHOPPING HAS BECOME a major leisure activity. Today, stores and malls offer entertainment as much as products or services, and they charge accordingly. Thankfully, for those, like me, who view shopping as a chore rather than fun, there are some alternatives that offer less hassle and better bargains.

Mail Order

For me, mail order is the most convenient way to shop. I can sit in the comfort of my home and, with just a few telephone calls, take care of all my shopping. It's particularly valuable at holiday time. One evening on the telephone and I've taken care of everyone.

Mail order can save you money because most mail-order businesses pass on the money they save in reduced operating costs to the customer. Some mail-order businesses have prices 20 to 30 percent below retail.

The only real downside to catalog shopping is the inability to see an item in person before you buy it. Although most high-end mail-order companies produce glossy four-color catalogs with photographs of their merchandise, the catalogs of many smaller companies have just a few line drawings or no illustrations at all. (Of course, since they save money on printing, they can often offer lower prices.) If you don't like your purchase when it arrives, or it's the wrong size, you may need to go through the hassle of sending it back for a refund or an exchange. This is why there are certain items—shoes, for instance—that I refuse to buy through mail order, since I feel the need to try them on before I buy them.

Online Shopping

Online shopping provides even greater selection for the consumer—along with a higher risk of having problems with your order. The practice has grown so quickly, and so many businesses have appeared out of nowhere, that many online retailers haven't been able to keep up with the demand. Holiday seasons, in particular, have been plagued by shortages of merchandise and delayed and lost orders.

Still, as it refines itself and as more people become conversant with this new way of buying, online shopping is sure to equal or surpass mail order in volume. But don't assume that the item you've stumbled across while surfing the Web is going to be the best deal you can find. Check other online retailers and mail-order catalogs to make sure you're getting the best buy.

Pay attention to security as well. One of the roadblocks in getting online shopping off the ground has been consumers' fears of having their credit card numbers somehow picked off during their voyages through cyberspace. Although these fears are somewhat legitimate, the industry has gone to great lengths to eliminate the problem. Most online retailers describe their security measures in great detail on their Web sites.

Outlet Centers

The outlet center has become the new Mecca for bargain-hunting consumers. Filled with name-brand stores and enormous selections, they are without a doubt enticing. But while they offer lower prices, I've found that their prices are really no different than you'd find during a regular department store sale.

Part of the problem is that much of the merchandise sold at outlets is manufactured specifically for outlets and was never intended to be sold in retail stores, so figuring out savings is difficult. Some items may be of inferior quality to retail merchandise.

One often-cited advantage of mail-order and online shopping is being able to avoid sales tax. A business is only required to charge sales tax to purchasers who live in the states where the business has physical locations. If a business has its only retail outlet in, let's say, Maine, it isn't required to collect sales tax from a mail-order or online purchaser who lives in Michigan.

Notice that I wrote that the business isn't required to *charge* sales tax. That doesn't mean the customer isn't required to *pay* the tax. That's because, according to most states' laws, residents are required to pay what's called "use tax" on purchases made outside of their home state, whether in person, over the telephone, through the mail, or online. There's actually a line on your state income tax return where you are obliged to fill in how much you owe your state.

Use tax issues seem to appear when states are having disputes. In recent memory, New York sent some of its tax personnel on "raids" into New Jersey to visit the parking lots of outlet centers just over the border. Notices were placed on the windshields of cars with New York license plates "reminding" the owners of their obligation to pay use tax. There were intimations that license plate numbers were being recorded.

Such zealous efforts are usually met with anger rather than results. Due to the incredible cost and effort that would be involved in trying to enforce use taxes, most states simply rely on consumers to voluntarily pay their share. As you may have figured out by now, most states don't count on getting much revenue from use tax.

The trick to getting the best deals in outlet centers is timing. Buying off-season merchandise is one of the best ways to save money, Sure, buying a bathing suit in February may seem a little silly, but June will arrive soon enough. Many outlet centers also have sales around holiday periods.

Of course, the real downside to outlet centers is the time and travel involved. But if you shop wisely and compare prices, you can save enough money to make the trip worthwhile.

Warehouse Clubs

These are where the real bargains are.* It's no-frills shopping at its best. Warehouse clubs sell merchandise, often in bulk, at prices barely above wholesale. Sometimes the markup is as low as 2 or 3 percent.

To be able to shop at a warehouse club, you must pay a membership fee, usually about $25.

---

*Warehouse clubs may not be for obsessives, however. I once walked out of a warehouse club with enough sardines to feed the entire island of Manhattan for a year.

At that point it's in your interest to shop at the club as much as possible. Until your savings are equal to the membership fee, you haven't saved a penny.

Warehouse clubs don't have the selection of a large grocery store, so the range of brands within any category will be limited. They also turn inventory over quite rapidly, so it's wise to stop by often to make sure you don't miss out on special deals.

SIGNAGE

How much you choose to spend on signage for your business depends on what your signs are expected to accomplish. If you have a business that relies on walk-in traffic, your storefront is your best source of advertising. You need signs that will attract customers and inform them about what they can find inside. They need to be easily seen and creative enough to attract the eye. At the same time they need to be tasteful and inoffensive.

I'm also a big fan of banners. They're relatively inexpensive to create, and they can give a business a busy and festive air as well as announce special occasions. A series of new banners over the course of a year can keep your business looking fresh and exciting. A permanent banner, perpendicular to a storefront, can attract pedestrians in the same way a traditional sign attracts drivers.

The other side of the coin is signage designed to simply inform your clients. These are more common with professionals and service businesses. If you have such a business you don't need to spend a lot of time or money on signage to attract customers. People searching for a lawyer don't walk down the street and pop into the first office whose sign appeals to them. You already have clients, either through word of mouth, previous experience, or advertising. Your signs just need to let them know they've arrived at your office or place of business.

Sometimes your signage needs will change over time. Here's a good example. I have a client who has spent his entire career in one aspect or another of the restaurant business in New York City. He has founded and then sold three very successful restaurants and is currently operating a fourth. He has been a consultant. He spent several years working for a wine importer. He also has taught at a prestigious culinary school.

Over the years this man has become renowned in New York for his expertise in food and wine, so much so that now when he opens a restaurant he has a clientele ready and waiting to patronize his business. In contrast to his early years, when he had to hustle to cultivate customers, he now has a devoted customer base that virtually ensures that every endeavor he undertakes will turn to gold.

Because he has such a devoted group of customers, he no longer needs much in the way of signage. When he opened his first restaurant, it was clearly visible to anyone walking down the street. The name of the restaurant was tastefully painted in gold leaf on the front windows. It was also on the awnings over the windows and on the canopy that extended from the front door to the edge of the street. It was hardly garish. At the same time it was impossible to miss.

Today he no longer needs that sort of attention. His current restaurant has no awnings, canopies, or painted windows. It's marked only by a small brass plaque by the door, as discreet as those used by lawyers and physicians. His customers know where he is. That small brass plaque is all they need.

SIMPLIFIED EMPLOYEE PENSIONS

WHEN MY SELF-EMPLOYED clients ask me about retirement savings options, I always direct them toward simplified employee pensions (SEPs) first.

A SEP is like a high-performance IRA (in fact, they're sometimes called SEP-IRAs) that allows you to contribute around 15 percent of your earnings rather than the $2,000 a year you're limited to in contributions to a conventional IRA. Like a Keogh, contributions reduce the amount of taxable income, which reduces your taxes, and earnings are tax-deferred. While Keoghs allow for greater contributions, SEPs are easier to manage since there's no requirement to file annual returns to the IRS on your account activities like there is with a Keogh.

Who Can Establish a SEP?

Anyone with income from self-employment, regardless of whether or not he or she has an employer, can set up an SEP. Let's say you have a 9-to-5 job teaching journalism, but you also freelance on the side writing magazine articles and books. A portion of that freelance income can be funneled into an SEP. Combined with any employer-sponsored retirement plan, the dollars could quickly add up.

Owners of small businesses can set up SEPs for themselves and their employees. In an employer-funded SEP, employees establish accounts into which their employer can direct the equivalent of as much as 15 percent of their salaries. In order for a company to offer SEPs, they must be offered to every employee and the same percentage must be contributed for all the employees in the firm. The contributions are tax-deductible for federal purposes but may or may not be tax-deductible at the state level.

Employee-funded SEPs allow employees to have money taken from their salaries and deposited into their plans. This option is only available in firms that have 25 or fewer employees, and at least half the employees must participate. Employees have various options in how the money is invested. Like any other employer-sponsored savings program, the automatic-deduction aspect of a SEP makes it an excellent choice for those who want to maximize retirement savings with minimal effort.

SEPs are easy to set up. They're available from brokerage firms, mutual fund companies, and banks. Self-employed people who miss the December 31 deadline for setting up a Keogh still have until April 15 of the following year to set up a SEP that will still be deductible for the previous year's taxes. If you get an extension to file your income taxes, you have until the deadline to set up a SEP. That could be as late as October 15.

When Can You Withdraw Funds?

SEPs are like most other retirement funds in that you can't begin to withdraw funds until age 59½ if you want to avoid penalties, and you must begin to withdraw them when you reach 70½. There's a 10 percent penalty for early withdrawal, although if you become disabled, if you die and the money in the plan is going to a beneficiary, if you have qualified medical expenses, or if you have higher-education expenses, money can be withdrawn without penalties. SEPs differ from other retirement plans in that you can't borrow from them and pay it back. The money is essentially untouchable until you begin to withdraw it.

SMALL-CLAIMS COURT

SMALL-CLAIMS COURT IS the Wal-Mart of the American legal system. It's where the average citizen can go to settle a complaint against someone else without having to spend an arm and a leg on legal representation. To invoke the name of a once-popular television program, it's truly the "people's court."

Small-claims court allows you to take on anyone, from your next-door neighbor to a multinational corporation. You can even bring action against your state government and the federal government. To be eligible for small-claims court, the claim must be for $1,000 or less, although a few states have a limit as high $5,000. Your only cost is a filing fee, which may be as little as $15 or $20.

Leveling the Playing Field

The beauty of small-claims court is that the playing field is leveled. If you have a claim against a major corporation, you can, without legal representation, bring them to court and have your argument considered by a judge. At that point it's not a David-and-Goliath story anymore. You are both equal in the eyes of the court. In fact, the corporation generally has to go to more trouble than you do, since it must often be represented by a lawyer rather than an officer or other employee.

Small-claims court is usually held at times that are convenient for most people. Most jurisdictions conduct sessions in the evening so that participants aren't forced to miss work. This is another thorn in the side of corporations. Since most lawyers charge double for working at night, the corporation stands to lose a lot more money than just the amount of your claim. This is why many will settle out of court at the mere threat of being brought to small-claims court. Sometimes they'll just fail to have a representative show up and allow the judge to issue a default judgment against them. The fact is, the bigger and more impersonal the defendant in small-claims court, the more likely you are to prevail.

Working through the Process

Your best ally in bringing a small-claims action is the clerk of the court. His or her job is to help consumers pursue their complaints. Once you've decided to sue, you should contact the clerk of the nearest small-claims court to find out in which jurisdiction your complaint will be heard. The location could be where you live, where the defendant is located, or where the problem occurred. The clerk will also guide you through the small-claims process. Many courts even have pamphlets that describe the process.*

Your first step as plaintiff is to file a statement with the court and then arrange to have the defendant notified of the action either in person or by registered or certified mail. If you're suing a business, whether it's the butcher down on the corner or General Motors, you need to include the actual name of the owner. You can get this information by contacting your local tax or licensing agency, the secretary of state's office, the state's corporation commission, or the county clerk's office and looking for a "doing business as," or DBA, form.

Prepare and Present Your Case

Once you've filed your suit you need to begin to prepare evidence to support your claim. You're doing this without a lawyer, so you need to be as thorough as possible. You need to gather all the documents that pertain to your complaint—letters, bills, receipts, contracts, warranties, photographs—and be prepared to use them to present a chronological account of the problem and clearly show why you should be awarded damages. If you have witnesses or independent experts to support your claim, ask if they must appear in person or if a signed statement is sufficient.

Although small-claims court is clearly for legal amateurs, remember that you still have the responsibility to present your case as clearly as possible. Righteous indignation alone is not enough to win a judgment in your favor. Present your arguments in a logical manner and be as concise as possible. Don't read from a prepared script. Rather, prepare notes and refer to them as needed. Answer questions directly and honestly. And don't be nervous or angry. If you've done your homework, you'll be just fine.

Here's a good way to prepare yourself for the experience. I recommend to my clients that they attend one or two small-claims sessions (they're open to the public) prior to their own hearing to familiarize themselves with the proceedings. The more comfortable you are with the surroundings and the process, the better you'll be able to state your case and the greater your chances of winning.

---

*Some courts will even have volunteer lawyers on hand to serve as mediators to try to keep cases from having to go to trial.

SOCIAL SECURITY

IT HAS BECOME FASHIONABLE to believe that the federal government isn't capable of creating and running efficient social welfare programs. Social Security, signed into law under the Roosevelt administration in 1935, disproves that argument. It has been a reliable system that has more or less accomplished what its creators had in mind. For three generations of retirees with meager savings and no pensions it has often been the difference between survival and destitution. It has also provided for widows and orphans and those whose ability to earn a living has been derailed by accidents or other disabilities.

But it's a system with one major flaw that is about to be felt in a big way, unless today's federal government is as wise as FDR's. At any point in time, the retirement money being paid to Social Security recipients is coming from the payments currently being made by those of us who are still working. This works fine as long as the working population is considerably larger than the population of Social Security recipients.

Herein lies the problem. As the baby boomers reach retirement age, the Social Security Administration (SSA) will be looking to payments being made by the gen-Xers and subsequent generations to provide Social Security benefits. But the boomers are the largest generation in our history, while the gen-Xers are a small generation. There just won't be enough money to go around. This is going to require some changes in the system. Before we look at what this might mean, let's go over how the system currently operates.

When Do Payments Start?

Social Security retirement payments begin when you turn 65. You can choose to begin to receive them as early age 62, but your monthly payment will be reduced by five-ninths of a percent times the number of months you start early. You can also choose to delay receiving benefits beyond 65. In this case your payments will be higher when you start receiving them.

The SSA has been aware of the looming demographic problems for years. In response, in 1980 it instituted new rules affecting how and when full benefits are received. Those of you born before 1938 will receive full benefits when you reach 65. If you were born between 1938 and 1942, you'll have to wait an additional two months for every year past 1937. This means that those of you born in 1942 won't be able to collect full benefits until 10 months after you turn 65.

If you were born between 1943 and 1954 you'll begin receiving full benefits at age 66. Those born between 1955 and 1959 will have to wait two months for each years beyond 1954 for full benefits. If you were born in 1960 or later, you'll have to wait until you reach 67 to receive full benefits.

How Much Will You Get?

The SSA uses complex formulas to determine benefits; too complex to describe in detail, but here's the general idea. If you've had average earnings over the course of your working life and you begin to collect benefits at age 65, you'll receive around 40 percent of your salary at the time you retired. If you had less than average earnings, you'll receive a greater percentage. Conversely, if you earned more than the average, you'll receive a lesser percentage. People who earned above the maximum income subject to Social Security tax will end up with 25 percent or less of their final salary.

Once you reach the point where you're receiving your full benefit, you'll receive the same amount each month for the rest of your life, with adjustments made for inflation.

What If You Delay Receiving Benefits?

You can put off receiving benefits until age 70 if you wish. If you do, Uncle Sam will reward you for your deferred gratification. Because the system is designed to provide you with the same amount of money once you retire, those who put off receiving benefits will get more each month. The longer you wait, the more you'll receive. It can really add up. People born before 1938 will receive an additional 3 to 4 percent for every year they wait. Those born in 1939 and 1940 get 7 percent extra and those born in 1941 and 1942 get 7.5 percent. Anyone born in 1943 or later will receive 8 percent. The adjustments for inflation you didn't receive are also included and compounded, so the final payout can be quite attractive.

How Will the Funding Crisis Affect Your Benefits?

This is the big question. As I explained earlier, the numbers just aren't there to feed the retirement needs of the baby boomers. However, I wouldn't worry about Social Security being abolished. Any politician who made such a suggestion would be committing political suicide. There is some discussion about privatizing the system and allowing individuals to manage their own funds, but the idea hasn't gone anywhere yet. There is the chance that the Social Security trust fund will be increased dramatically and left untouched. However, I think odds are that benefits will diminish. It's also possible that the qualification age will be pushed back even further.

Of course, we just may see the problem solved. The sheer size of the boomer generation will give them enormous political clout. They may demand—and receive—the same benefits their parents enjoyed. But don't count on it. They may also trade their willingness to accept lower benefits for a continued role as the dominant generation in business and government. I don't know what's going to happen, but my advice is to prepare for retirement by paying even more attention to your investments and not counting on Social Security at all. Whatever you do receive should be considered bonus money.

SOLE PROPRIETORSHIPS

OF THE THREE MOST COMMON business structures, sole proprietorship, partnership, and corporation, sole proprietorship is the simplest, easiest, and cheapest. As a result, it's also the most popular: 7 out of 10 businesses in the United States are structured as sole proprietorships.

The Advantages

The biggest advantage of a sole proprietorship is its simplicity. In many cases, all you need to do is buy a business license to get started. If you operate the business under a fictitious name, however, you'll need to register the name with the appropriate authority. You also may need to publish the name in your local paper and state that you're the person behind the business or file a certificate of doing business under a different name.

Another advantage of sole proprietorships is that you're the only one involved in making decisions. If you want to offer new products or services, change your business hours, or even close for two weeks to take a vacation, it's totally up to you. Operating alone also lets you take action quickly. If you see an opportunity, you can jump on it immediately. If you were in a partnership or a corporation, the action could only be taken after any number of meetings were held and votes were cast or your partners agreed.

Sole proprietorships also have simple forms of organization. You're alone at the top, and everyone reports to you. Neither a partnership nor a corporation will provide you with such autonomy.

Because of their simplicity, sole proprietors have the simplest accounting requirements. Ironically, they also pay the lowest taxes of any business structure. A sole proprietorship as an entity isn't taxed. The business owner pays taxes as an individual. If he or she has additional income or loss from other employment or investments, that is combined with the profit or loss from the business on one tax form.

The Disadvantages

After reading the previous section you might wonder why anyone would go into business as anything other than a sole proprietorship. The reason can be summed up in one word: liability.

As the sole proprietor of the business, you'll be responsible for every debt and obligation of the business and will have no shelter from creditors. We live in an increasingly litigious society. If you're a sole proprietor and your business is sued, your personal assets will be subject to lien to satisfy your creditors' claims against you. That means you could lose your savings, your car, and even your house.

You can protect yourself against many kinds of claims with liability insurance. But as claims against businesses have risen in recent years, so have insurance premiums. If your business has a significant liability exposure (and few today don't) and can't afford liability insurance premiums, you shouldn't go into business as a sole proprietor.

Another disadvantage to sole proprietorship is the limited access to capital. You're not a corporation, so you can't offer stock. And you don't have partners to share in business costs. You're limited to the money you can raise on your own. For most people, that's not very much.

Operating alone can also result in incredible stress. You'll be in charge of everything, and the pressure can become overwhelming.

Finally, your personal finances and those of your business will always be intertwined. The business will never really take on a life of its own.

SPEECHES

H UMILITY PLAYS NO PART in financial success. If you don't blow your own horn, no one else will. One of the best ways to trumpet your skills and abilities is to give speeches. Not only does it establish you as a leader in your industry or profession and a person with exceptional expertise; it also allows you to meet potential clients and customers. I can't overemphasize the value of these face-to-face interactions since they give you a chance to present your knowledge and philosophy to a captive audience.

The biggest fear for many people is speaking in public, so there's always a need for speakers. Be willing to speak before any group that asks you. If they think enough of you and your work to extend an invitation, you should be flattered. Besides, the more people you come in contact with, the greater your professional opportunities. From a purely mercenary standpoint, your best venues will be groups whose members have the potential to become clients or customers. Depending on the business you're in, that could include just about anybody. Industry, community, and professional groups are also valuable. They allow you expand your professional network. Your speech might also result in someone mentally filing your name away as a possible employee.

Getting Over Your Fear

For some, the thought of having to give a speech turns their knees to jelly. Even people who have no problem holding forth among their friends can find it difficult speaking in front of a group of strangers. If you find it uncomfortable, you need to overcome your fears.

My first suggestion is to enroll in a class on public speaking, through your local adult education program or at a community college. Consider joining Toastmasters International, a social organization that specializes in training its members to speak in public. Toastmasters will teach you how to organize your thoughts, relax before an audience, and pace yourself so that you can hold your audience's attention. You'll also be regularly asked to prepare and give short talks before the rest of the club. Since just about everyone else will be there for the same reason you are, it's easy to relax.

Most people's fears begin to subside with experience. I suggest you start by speaking to small groups of people. Speaking to an audience of 20 or 30 in a classroom or conference room is a lot less intimidating than speaking to an auditorium with hundreds of people. The more speeches you give the more comfortable you'll feel, and you can gradually move to larger audiences.

Preparing a Speech

Speeches need to be carefully polished. This takes a great deal of time and attention to detail. Make an outline containing all the key points you want to cover and then write the speech based on that structure. Go over your draft and streamline it as much as possible. Your audience will thank you for your efforts. They'll also be more attentive to what you have to say.

After you have your speech perfected, you need to practice it. Don't just read it back to yourself. Stand up and deliver it out loud. Decide where you'll pause and how you'll modulate your voice to emphasize key points. Practice as many times as you need to, to feel comfortable. The better prepared you are, the more confident you'll be.

Once your speech is fine-tuned, you may find you don't need to have it written out word-by-word when your deliver it. I find that reverting back to my outline allows me to be more spontaneous and hold the attention of an audience better. If you have your key points written down and you've practiced sufficiently, the rest will flow quite naturally. It will allow you to pace your speech. You won't be so inclined to bury your face in your paper and avoid eye contact with your audience.

Delivering a Speech

Go slowly. Many people have a tendency to speed up their natural cadence when they speak before a group of people. Slow it down, pause between points, and give the audience a chance to follow you. Punctuating your speech with some humor will also keep them attentive.

Your demeanor is also important. Be relaxed, smile, and make eye contact with people in the audience as much as possible. If you have a microphone that allows you to move about, take advantage of it. Be expressive, use gestures, and show some passion. Nothing will put an audience to sleep faster than a speaker who has no conviction.

When you've finished your speech and opened the floor for questions, move from behind the podium to the front of the stage or riser. This creates a more intimate feeling between you and your audience. You'll get more questions and your answers will appear more spontaneous.

Finally, on behalf of everyone who may one day hear you speak, be brief. There's no reason in the world why a speech needs to be more than 15 minutes long. If you can't get your points across in that amount of time, you need to go back and start over.

STATIONERY

YES, YOU CAN JUDGE A BOOK by its cover—it's done all the time. It may appear shallow and judgmental, but it's a quick shorthand used to make decisions when under time constraints. And today we're all under time constraints, in business and at home. We judge people by how they dress and speak. We judge stores by their signage and window displays. And we judge the writers of letters by their stationery.

I receive a great deal of correspondence. Some of it is from individuals and some is from businesses. Although I'm acquainted with a fair number of the writers, a larger number are unknown to me.

When I pick up a piece of mail, I form an immediate impression of the sender from the quality and appearance of the stationery. If it's amateurish in design, printed on cheap paper, or poorly printed, my immediate assumption is that the person or business who sent it isn't professional.

More often than not, a potential client's first contact with you is your stationery, and like it or not, image is everything. If your stationery looks unprofessional, the person can only assume that you're unprofessional as well.

Part of the problem is the ease with which we can create our own documents these days. We all have computers and color printers. There are a wide variety of word processing and design software packages to select from. Most even have templates that we can use to design our own letterhead and other business documents. In the interest of saving time and money, it's tempting to do the job ourselves.

The problem is that giving someone the tools to do a job doesn't qualify them to do the job. Take me as an example. My wife is a gourmet cook. We have a kitchen full of state-of-the-art appliances, cookware, and utensils. Does that mean I can wander in and prepare a gourmet meal? Of course not. I would never dream of it.

The same thing holds true for amateur designers. Yet I'm always amazed at the amount of material I receive that's been prepared using canned software programs and printed out on office printers. It's easy to spot. The fonts are standard Palatino or New York. They usually include poorly designed clip art that's only marginally related to the sender's service or product. Sometimes there's no obvious connection at all. And the paper is often stuff that's been preprinted with some kind of design or graphic that only distracts the eye and makes the materials seem all the more amateurish.

The sad thing is, these materials could come from people who are absolutely top-notch at what they do. Although their amateurish stationery might not harm their relationships with their existing clients, it's certainly not going to aid them in developing new business contacts.

My advice is to stick to what you know and leave the job to professionals. Your stationery should be designed by the same designer you hire to create your logo and the other pieces of your identity package. Work closely with her to help her understand the kind of image you want to convey. All your material should be designed and produced at one time and should have a consistent look. Your letterhead, envelopes, invoices, labels, business cards, fax reply sheets and other printed materials should include your logo, use a consistent typeface, and be printed on the same color paper.

Don't ignore printing, either. Everything should be produced on an offset press by a professional printer. There are some in the copying industry who maintain their products produce offset-quality documents. While they're getting close, they're not quite there yet. Besides, with the quantities you'll be producing, offset will be cheaper.

You don't have to use the most expensive paper or two-color printing. The important thing is that your stationery has a professional and consistent appearance and reflects the nature of your business. Keep in mind that every piece of paper that has your name on it has a marketing impact. You need to make sure it presents you in the best possible light.

STOCKBROKERS

WHILE THERE ARE MANY honest stockbrokers, the way they earn their money makes it easy to view them as salesmen rather than unbiased financial counselors. After all, most make money regardless of how you do when you follow their advice. If they recommend a stock and you buy it, they make a commission on the purchase. If the stock goes down the tubes and you make a frantic call to them to sell it, they make a second commission on the sale. Given this situation, it's little wonder that one of the traditional complaints against stockbrokers has been churning—the practice of keeping clients' accounts busy with excessive transactions in order to generate commissions for themselves.

Another problem has been discrimination. Studies of stockbrokers' behavior have shown that, given their druthers, most prefer to work with rich males. Women, younger investors, and investors with modest amounts of money receive much less attention. And no matter who they're dealing with, stockbrokers are not always neutral in the advice they dispense. They'll often receive higher commissions for selling mutual funds managed by their companies or stocks their companies are recommending.

All this has given the term "stockbroker" such a negative connotation that most securities firms have abandoned it in favor of "account executive," "account manager," or some other equally innocuous title. And it's really a shame, because the majority of the nations' 100,000 or so stockbrokers are highly ethical, hardworking professionals who have their clients' best interests at heart. As in many other fields, the unethical actions of a few have overshadowed the good work done by the rest of the profession.

Finding a Stockbroker

If you decide to work with a stockbroker, your first task is to find one with a good track record. The best way to do this is to ask your fellow investors. Word of mouth is usually the best way to find accomplished professionals, regardless of the field they're in.

Once you have a list of candidates, interview each to discuss your investment goals and their approaches to investing. Ask to see the performance of several clients whose investment goals are similar to your own. This will give you an idea of how well the broker's clients made out in following his advice. You should also check with your state securities administrator and the National Association of Securities Dealers (800-289-9999) to find out if the broker has had any complaints or disciplinary actions taken against him.

Beware the Day-Trading Bug

Executing your own stock transactions can lead to a behavior that has become more and more popular but has also proven to be extremely risky—day trading.

Given the availability of discount brokerages, the enormous number of financial publications on the market, and the unprecedented ability to do market research on the Web, many investors have decided to forego the advice of professionals and make investment decisions on their own. In particular, the ability to enter trades online has effectively broken the barrier between the securities industry and the average investor. If you so choose, you can now spend your days locked away in the spare bedroom, eyes glued to monitors that provide you the same up-to-date information professional traders are receiving, and your finger poised on your mouse, ready to click in buy and sell orders when you think the time is right.

Be forewarned that day trading is a very enticing but very hazardous endeavor. Unless you're willing to quit your job and totally immerse yourself in researching potential stock investments, you're almost certain to lose money. It requires knowledge, patience, infinite amounts of discipline, and more than a little luck. According to the available research, of those who have tried it, the majority have failed.

Besides, day trading flies in the face of what investing is all about. History has demonstrated time and again that to make money in the stock market all you have to do is stay with a few carefully chosen investments for the long haul. To try to zip in and out of a stock in a few hours and make a profit is to invite disaster. Just remember that old Wall Street saying: "Bears make money. Bulls make money. Pigs get slaughtered." Don't be a pig.

You'll also need to discuss commissions and other charges you may be assessed. Different types of trades will carry different commissions. There may be fees for maintaining your accounts and providing other services. Being thorough will keep you from being nickeled-and-dimed to death.

Consider a Fee-only Planner Instead

This leads to my basic complaint about stockbrokers and the reason I've usually steered clients elsewhere: they're just too expensive. My advice is to find a good financial planner—one who charges by the hour—and allow her to provide you with investment advice. First of all, her recommendations won't be biased. And second, not only will she have a good knowledge of stocks and mutual funds, she'll be able to provide you with advice on a wider range of financial choices such as annuities and reverse mortgages.

If you work with a financial adviser, you can execute your own stock transactions by setting up an account with a discount broker. This will minimize your brokerage charges and let you keep more of your gains.*

STOCKS

I BELIEVE STOCKS ARE the single best investments for almost anyone, young or old, affluent or average.† Once you peer through all the smoke and take a hard look at the statistics, I think you'll find stocks stand out from all the others.

Stocks are ownership shares that companies sell to raise capital. Over the past 75 years these tiny pieces of the American dream have outperformed every other kind of investment, averaging an 11 percent compounded return. If you've been even moderately conscious over the last few years, you're aware that we've been in the midst of the longest stock market run-up in history.

This is not to say stocks are risk-free. People can—and do—lose money in the stock market every day. But as a long-term investment, one in which you're content to ride the ups and downs of the market, stocks have proven to be the best place to put your money. This is why more than 50 million Americans have at least some part of their investment portfolios in stock.

When you purchase stock you become an owner of the company that issues the stock. Together with thousands of other stockholders, you ride the company's fortunes, for better or for worse. If you choose wisely, you may receive periodic payments called dividends, which are your share of the company's profits. If the company performs well, the price of the stock will increase, adding further to your investment profit.

Some companies are privately held, meaning their stock is owned by a few individuals and is not available to outside investors. Other companies are publicly held, meaning their stock can be owned by anyone. There are roughly 11,000 companies whose stocks are sold on the nations' securities markets. If you shop worldwide, you'll have more than 50,000 companies to choose from.

Types of Stock

Almost all stock falls within one of two categories, common and preferred. *Common stocks* are the basic ownership shares in a company. They're purchased by a wide variety of individuals and institutions and are continually traded among investors; on a busy day, 800 million or more shares will change hands.

---

*A discount broker is also a viable option for those who make their investment decisions strictly on their own and simply need someone to execute buy and sell orders.
†I believe in owning them through stock mutual funds rather than individually, however.

The Bulls and the Bears

Historically, the stock market has ebbed and flowed along with the economy and the emotions of investors. When the market is active and stock prices are rising, it's termed a "bull market." When it's slow and prices are stagnant or decreasing, it's called a "bear market."

For the last decade, the bears have been in a very long hibernation and the market has been more bullish than ever before. The Dow Jones Industrial Average topped 10,000 for the first time in 1999 and ended the year with a 22 percent gain. It was the fifth straight year the Dow had finished with a 20 percent gain or higher. In the 10 years since the Black Monday crash of October 19, 1987, the market has increased its value more than six times over.

Will the stock market continue to run with the bulls? Frankly, no one knows. History says it won't, and most experienced financial professionals concede that hard times will come eventually. But history also says the good times will continue to outweigh the bad. Despite regular setbacks over the years, the market has displayed an unrelenting overall upward movement. So for the patient investor who is content to buy in and let time work its magic, the stock market should continue to be a place to make money.

The Three Facts of Life about Stocks

No investment is entirely predictable, but decades of observation of the behavior of the stock market have revealed three basic facts about stock performance.

1. Over the short term, stock performance is very unpredictable.

2. Over the long term, stock performance is very predictable.

3. Over the long term, stocks outperform all other types of investments.

A corporation can create as many different classes of common stock as it wishes in order to meet the needs of different types of investors. For example there can be voting stock and non-voting stock, dividend-paying stock and nondividend-paying stock.

The owners of common stock often receive periodic dividends. There are no guarantees on how much a dividend will be; they fluctuate with the company's performance. If the company is doing poorly, or chooses to reinvest all its profits, dividends may not be paid at all.

A company's performance also affects its stock price. If you invest wisely, you'll enjoy watching your stock steadily appreciate at a rate that outperforms other investments. If you're unlucky, your investment will disappear as the company goes out of business. But at least your losses will stop there. Fortunately, shareholders are not responsible for a company's debts.

Preferred stocks differ from common stocks in that their dividend is guaranteed and is paid before the dividends for common stock are paid. Also, the dividend remains the same regardless of the company's performance. And although preferred stock is traded among investors, its value changes more slowly than that of common stock.

What about Risk?

Any investment carries some degree of risk, and stocks are no exception. Some stocks, such as those of the 30 companies that make up the Dow Jones Industrial Average, are considered "blue chips." They're established companies like General Motors, IBM, and Motorola. Although the fortunes of these companies can certainly ebb and flow, they have proven that they can generally be counted on to grow over time. This, in turn, means healthy dividends and a steady increase in the price of their stock. Risk is minimal.

At the other end of the spectrum are exciting young companies competing in emerging industries like biotechnology and e-commerce. Investments in these companies offer the potential for great profit. They also carry a larger degree of risk. There are many such companies out there, and the stock of many of them will outperform much of the rest of the market. Investors who choose wisely make a lot of money. Those who don't sometimes lose their shirts.

The price of some stocks is very closely tied to the overall condition of the economy. In times of economic downturn, their values fall. When the economy begins an upswing, their prices recover. Hotel stocks, for instance, usually follow this pattern. This is because when the economy is poor, people cut down on travel and vacations.

SUPPLIERS AND VENDORS

No business is an island. While entrepreneurs always think of themselves as independent, we're all dependent to some degree on our suppliers and vendors.

How dependent we are is directly related to the business or profession we're in. Take public relations writers, for example. They are their product, but they're still dependent on vendors and suppliers for equipment, stationery, office supplies, and the other minutiae of running their business. Granted, they'll survive if they temporarily run out of envelopes or staples or paper clips, though it will still cause a few problems. But now consider people who run retail businesses. They live and breathe with their suppliers and vendors. If their inventories aren't adequate to meet the demands of their customers, even if it's just for a day or two, they lose money. They may also lose customers to their competitors. Manufacturers are equally dependent on their suppliers. To operate as efficiently and profitably as possible, they need to receive parts and other items on specific days. If those parts don't arrive on time, their entire manufacturing schedule is affected. Again, this translates into lost revenues and lost customers.

This is why, regardless of your business, you need suppliers and vendors who are reliable and will be immediately responsive to your needs. It's not a relationship to be taken lightly. Entrepreneurs who are creating business plans need to spend a great deal of time getting to know different suppliers and vendors and cultivating relationships with each one. When crunch time comes—and it will, no matter what business you're in—you need to know you have reliable sources to get you the products you need as quickly as possible.

Make It a Partnership

The best supplier-customer relationships are partnerships. This is because your suppliers and vendors are as dependent on you as you are on them. Just as you can lose customers by not meeting their needs, your suppliers may lose your business if they don't deliver.

The key to functioning effectively as partners is communication. You should talk to all your suppliers and vendors on a regular basis. Keep them up to date on how your business is performing and give them as much lead time as possible if you're thinking about introducing new products or will otherwise need them to ferret out new items for you. The better their knowledge of your business, the better they can anticipate your needs.

Some suppliers and vendors will eagerly offer sales training, promotional materials and assistance, and even co-op advertising funds.* Suppliers and vendors can sometimes even be financial partners. Although this can involve them making an actual cash investment in your business, it more often takes the form of creating beneficial financial arrangements. For example, if you're a retailer, you might find suppliers who are willing to provide you with inventory on consignment. This means you don't have to pay them for the merchandise until you sell it. Or you may be granted extended payment terms, as much as 60 or 90 days. In return, you may be asked to make that particular supplier your sole source for a particular product or products or guarantee that you'll purchase a minimum amount of product each year.

Another possibility is to have a supplier or vendor drop-ship your merchandise for you. This means that you don't even need to stock the item or items your customers are purchasing. You merely pass the order on to the supplier and he ships it for you. This method of selling and shipping is quite common in the mail-order and e-commerce industries. Since these merchants don't actually deal with customers face-to-face, they have the luxury of maintaining smaller inventories.

Pay Your Bills

It goes without saying that good business relationships are only possible when you pay your bills on time. You should still negotiate to get the best terms you can—that's just smart business. But once you've agreed to payment terms, make sure you live up to them. Here's why. There will come a time when you have trouble meeting all your bills. Maybe your industry is in a slump or some other unforeseeable factor has temporarily hurt your business. Whatever the reason, your

---

*Advertising allowances.

cash flow has slowed for a period of time. When that happens, you're going to go hat in hand to your suppliers and vendors and ask for more time.

Try to let them know as soon as possible that you'll be late in paying. The more time you give them to react, the more likely they'll be able to help you. If you've been a good customer, previously paid your bills on time, and given them sufficient notice, you shouldn't have a problem. All suppliers and vendors know that businesses periodically go through some tough times. If you've fostered the proper relationship, if you've made them a partner in your endeavor, they'll be happy to give you extended terms. After all, it's in their best interest to help you succeed.

So treat your suppliers and vendors the same way you expect to be treated. Build partnerships, communicate with one another, and do your best to help one another out. It's the best way to ensure success I can think of.

SURVIVOR BENEFITS

SOCIAL SECURITY ISN'T SIMPLY a retirement program. Besides providing income for seniors, it also offers survivor benefits, whatever the age of the deceased. A spouse, dependent children or parents, and disabled children can all qualify for benefits. Under the right circumstances, even a former spouse may qualify.

For More Information

The Social Security Administration has a "Personal Earnings and Benefit Estimate Statement" to help you calculate what your survivor benefits would be. You can contact your local SSA office or call 800-772-1213 to obtain a statement.

For your family to receive survivor benefits you must have earned a sufficient number of credits while working. Prior to 1978, you would earn one credit for every three months you worked, provided you earned at least $50 during that quarter. Since then, credits have been based on how much you made during the entire year. The amount changes from year to year. In 1998, for example, workers received one credit for every $700 they earned during the year, with a maximum accumulation of four credits.

To provide benefits for your family you need to have accumulated one credit for every year from the year you turn 21 until the year before you die or the year you turn 61, whichever comes first. For example, let's say you were born in 1950 and died suddenly in 1999. You would need to have accumulated at least 27 credits (1998 minus 1971). If you reached age 61, you would need 40 credits (2011 minus 1971).

Who Is Eligible?

When you pass away your spouse qualifies for survivor benefits under a number of different circumstances. If the two of you have children under 16, your spouse will receive benefits until the youngest child turns 16. If your spouse is caring for a disabled child, the benefits will continue as long as the spouse remains the primary caregiver. If you have no young or disabled children, your spouse must reach age 60 and not have remarried to qualify for benefits (age 50 if she is disabled).

Your children qualify for benefits as long as they are under 18 (19 for full-time high school students) and unmarried. Disabled children qualify for unlimited benefits, provided they were disabled before age 22. For some reason, benefits for full-time college students were discontinued a few years ago.

Your parents qualify for benefits as long as they are at least age 62 and were dependent on you for more than half their financial support.

Your former spouse qualifies for benefits if the two of you were married for at least 10 years and he or she reaches age 60 without remarrying. If your former spouse is caring for children under age 16 or a disabled child, there is no age requirement. Nor is there a minimum length of time for the marriage.

How Much Are the Benefits?

The amount each survivor receives depends on a number of factors. At age 60, a surviving spouse or ex-spouse will receive about 72 percent of the deceased's basic Social Security benefit. That will increase to 100 percent at age 65. Spouses under age 60 who are caring for young or disabled children will receive about 75 percent. Children receive 75 percent and parents receive 75 percent each or 82.5 percent if only one is alive.

Spouses and minor children also usually receive a one-time payment of $255. Although this is usually described as a funeral benefit, there are no restrictions on how it can be spent. If three or more family members are eligible for benefits, the family will receive a predetermined maximum benefit rather than individual benefits.

To obtain survivor benefits, individuals should apply as soon as possible after the death. They'll need a copy of the death certificate and proof of their relationship with the deceased. They'll also need proof of age.

If they're over 60 and remarry while they're receiving benefits, they won't lose them. In fact, they might see them increase. This is because the new spouse's earning take precedence over the deceased spouse's earnings. If he or she had a higher income, the benefits will also be higher. A child's benefits won't be affected by a remarriage.

Finally, if you and your spouse are both receiving Social Security benefits and your spouse dies, you can elect to continue to receive your benefit or begin receiving your spouse's benefit, whichever is higher.

TAX PREPARERS

ROUGHLY HALF OF THE 120 million Americans who file tax returns with the IRS each year choose to spend money to hire a tax preparer rather than tackling the chore themselves. Much of that money is wasted.

In almost all states, tax preparers aren't required to undergo training. They don't need to be licensed or registered. All you need to do to become a tax preparer is call yourself one. It's no surprise, then, that every year irate taxpayers file for damages in the tens of millions of dollars against incompetent tax preparers.

Do You Need a Tax Preparer?

I insist that all my clients hire a CPA to prepare their taxes. But that doesn't mean everyone needs to. If your return hasn't changed dramatically from the year before, and you have a simple financial life, you might not need a tax preparer. People who can balance a checkbook, and whose income is derived primarily from wages, interest, and some investment income, shouldn't have much problem with their returns. Sure, the forms and booklets can be a bit intimidating. But if you take the time to read the instructions carefully and have your financial records in order, you can probably complete your taxes in an afternoon.

If you're planning on tackling the job yourself I recommend purchasing one of the many taxpayer guidebooks that are available. These do a great job of leading you by the hand through your return. Another option is tax-filing software, such as TurboTax, that allows you to fill out your forms on your home computer and even submit them electronically.

You can also get assistance directly from the IRS. You can download forms off the Web site or you can order a CD-ROM that contains forms. You can also get advice over the telephone or at IRS walk-in centers. While there have been reports in the past that the IRS operators don't always provide the right information, they do put their money where their mouth is. If you have an error on your return that's caused by their improper advice, you won't be hit with a penalty. You will, however, have to pay any additional tax that's owed. Make sure you keep records of your telephone conversations with any IRS employees.

If your financial life is straightforward, but you simply don't feel confident filing a return, your best bet might be to hire one of the storefront tax services. The biggest, of course, is H&R Block, which prepares more than 10 percent of U.S tax returns every year. The company's preparers attend annual courses, and you can generally have your return prepared for less than $75.

Finding a Tax Preparer

Of course, if you're like most of my clients and your finances are a bit complex, you're better off hiring an independent tax preparer. You have two choices: a certified public accountant or an enrolled agent.

CPAs are exceptionally well-trained and are quite useful if you have a complex investment portfolio, a trust, or business interests. Just make sure the CPA you choose is knowledgeable in your particular field.

Enrolled agents are certified by the IRS. Many, in fact, are former IRS employees, so they know the lay of the land quite well. Those who aren't, must pass a two-day exam that's so difficult, around 70 percent fail. Enrolled agents are required to take a certain amount of continuing education each year and are usually less expensive than CPAs.

You should interview tax preparers before you make the decision to hire one. Begin by asking about their education and professional experience. Find out what sort of continuing education programs they participate in. Ask for references from people in similar financial situations as yours. Also ask for fee information. Your previous year's return and some basic information about your financial condition should be sufficient to allow a professional to come up with an estimate. You should also check professionals out with the IRS. The agency maintains a list of preparers who have a history of problems.

When you decide who you're going to hire, don't make it a once-a-year relationship. You should touch base with your tax preparer several times over the course of the year to make sure you're adequately organized and prepared for your annual filing. The last thing you need to do is show up at her office on April 14 with a box full of papers. If that happens, chances are she'll end the relationship.

TELEMARKETERS

TELEMARKETERS ARE THE SCOURGE of the nation's evening hours. Is there any one of us who hasn't received a sales call just as we were about to sit down to dinner? If you're like me, you get several every evening. The majority of these solicitations are legitimate, if annoying. It might be a representative of your alma mater or some other nonprofit trying to squeeze a few dollars out of you. More often it's someone selling something. Frozen foods, magazine subscriptions, home improvements, securities, insurance—you name it, it's pitched over the phone.

Occasionally, however, you're going to get a call from someone trying to scam you. Armed with computerized speed dialers and detailed scripts that seem to anticipate everything we might say, they engage in high-pressure sales tactics designed to get you to commit to purchases that never materialize or turn out to be less than as advertized.

Tips for Dealing with Telemarketers

Sometimes these scams will begin with a postcard or some other solicitation in the mail. It will urge you to call a toll-free number to take advantage of some unbelievable offer. Other times you'll be cold-called over the phone. Just remember the following tips for dealing with telemarketers:

- Watch for high-pressure sales tactics. If the telemarketer seems to have an answer for everything you say, refuses to answer your questions directly, or insists that you make an immediate decision, hang up.

- Watch for "special offers." The caller will say you're one of a selected few to be made an offer or that the offer is only good for a limited amount of time.

- Never give your credit card number to someone over the telephone unless you initiated the call. Some con artists will say they need your card number as "authorization" to send you a prize or a gift.

- Some telemarketers will insist that you pay as soon as possible. They may even offer to have a representative come to your home to pick up your check.

- If they're peddling securities and insist there's "no risk," they're lying. Ask to be sent informational materials before you make any decisions. If they say they can't provide any, hang up.

- Finally, as with all solicitations, regardless of the source, if an offer sounds too good to be true, it probably isn't.

Telemarketing Rules

The FCC and the Telephone Consumer Protection Act of 1991 do have regulations in place to protect you. Here are some of the rules telemarketers are supposed to follow:

- They cannot call homes between 9 P.M. and 8 A.M.

- They must maintain lists of consumers who have requested that they not receive telephone solicitations.

- They cannot use computerized dialing systems and prerecorded messages that may interfere with public health and safety, such as calling emergency lines or hospitals.

- When using computerized dialing systems, they must identify themselves. If you hang up, they must release the line within 5 seconds.

- They cannot send unsolicited ads to fax machines.

Just Say No

My advice on telemarketers is to just hang up the second you realize who's on the other end of the phone. It's easier than ever these days now that so many of them use computerized dialers and voice-activated sales pitches. If I pick up the phone and don't get a response in a second or two, I know it's a telemarketer.

Another tip-off is the robotic voice that asks you to "please stay on the line for an important call." These things must work, otherwise telemarketers wouldn't continue the practice. Once again, my advice is to hang up.

I know some people who will toy with the person on the other end of the line. I heard of one man who was called by a well-known long-distance service and was told they were offering him "10 cents a minute." He quickly responded by thanking them for all the money and asking if they would be doing a direct deposit to his checking account or sending him a check every week. That ended that conversation.

Of course, you could use the response delivered by Jerry Seinfeld on an episode of his hit TV series a few years ago. "I'm a little bit busy right now," he told the caller. "Why don't you give me your number at home and I'll call you later tonight?"

TEMPS

IF I WAS GOING TO start my own business all over again I'd have an office full of temps. I love them. They're affordable, since there are no benefits to pay. They're efficient, so much so that I'm always amazed at their high level of competence and the quality of their work. And they're flexible. They're available nights and weekends. If you need them for a week, a month, or a year, you can count on them being there. If a project finishes early, you can end the relationship without the expense and fuss you would have with a full-time employee.

I also like temps because, unless they're around for several months, they don't get wrapped up in office politics. Their status provides just enough of a buffer that they aren't drawn into the day-to-day nonsense that goes on in most offices. They show up, do their job, and head home. It's a marvelously efficient arrangement.

Another advantage is that the temp agency serves as an in-house human resources department. If temps have a problem, they go to their agency rather than bothering me with it. If I have a problem with the temp, I go to the agency and have them take care of it. The agency eliminates the need for me to spend time on recruiting and interviewing. Spend some time selecting the right agency and that's the last interviewing you'll need to do.

Of course, I'm probably luckier than most. My business was in New York City, where there is a seemingly endless supply of talented temps and excellent temp agencies. Keep in mind that temps like the benefits of temporary work as much as do employers. They can work when they choose. They like the flexibility and variety of job assignments. For these reasons, temporary work is the perfect situation for struggling artists and writers and actors and musicians, four groups of people who are in plentiful supply in Manhattan.

The best place to find temps is at a reputable agency. Good agencies screen their temps to find those with the best talents and educations. The larger ones even test them. When you call one of these agencies you can count on getting someone who's competent, courteous, and well-dressed. If you hire your own temps, you have to waste your time conducting your own interviews and screening applicants for specific talents. I think it's easier to let the professionals do it.

If you use temps on a regular basis, you'll eventually find two or three who are particularly good fits for your office. You can match your needs to their skills. If you have a particular job that has to be done every fall, you can try to "reserve" the temp you discovered who is particularly adept at the task. At this point, the temp really becomes a vendor. You know exactly what you need and you call for the person who can provide it.

Many temps are really on the lookout for full-time employment, so you can gauge their talents on the job. If you find someone who fills the bill, you just make them an offer. Most agencies have a clause in their contracts requiring you to pay them a set amount if you do hire one of their people. But it's really no different than paying an employment agency. And in this case, you know exactly what you're getting.

Don't expect too much of temps. They're not going to be familiar enough with your business or its culture to get immediately involved in sales or marketing (although they could certainly be trained to carry out these tasks). Temps should be used for jobs that are common to any office or business: acting as receptionists, file clerks, bookkeepers, or technical professionals.

Because they're inexperienced and unfamiliar with your business, they'll need a lot more hands-on attention, at least at first. This includes regular reviews of their work. In my office I've always given temps a set period of time to develop a basic proficiency at the tasks they're expected to carry out. If I haven't gotten what I want after two days, I ask the agency to send me someone else.

One way to help them get up to speed is to provide them with written instructions. I had lists that described the duties of all the positions for which I hired temps. Newcomers were given the appropriate list the first morning they reported for work and they were walked through it step-by-step. I then checked on them at regular intervals during the day to see if they understood the work or had any questions. The system must have worked. I rarely had to ask agencies for replacements at the end of the two-day deadline.

The other issue you need to be aware of when using temps is confidentiality. A lot of your business information is easily accessed by anyone who works in your office. I recommend requiring passwords for access to sensitive computer files. I also suggest keeping confidential documents in a locked filing cabinet. Finally, any sensitive conversations you and your colleagues engage in should be carried out behind closed doors.

A Temp Instruction Sheet

Here's an example of an instruction sheet that can be given to temps when they first arrive in order to familiarize them with the customs of the workplace:

Temp Instructions

Welcome to the office of Clark Kent, certified financial planner. Here are a few things you may need to know about the office. Clark will be happy to explain anything further or answer any questions not covered.

General

Try to listen for the doorbell and answer the door quickly since Clark doesn't like to have people waiting in the hall.

Please ask all visitors, including messengers and delivery people, to step into the office instead of standing in the hall.

If you're on the telephone, someone else will get the door.

When messengers pick up deliveries, ask for a receipt.

When clients arrive, greet them at the door. Introduce yourself and ask for their name. Help them with their coats, umbrellas, etc. Direct them to the waiting area. Offer them coffee (decaffeinated or caffeinated), tea, or water. Show them where the rest room is. Tell them "Clark" (not "Mr. Kent") will be out to see them shortly. If they are a new client, give them a Client Contact Sheet attached to the clipboard on top of the cabinet nearest the door and ask them to fill it out.

Tell Clark his next appointment is here. If his door is shut, simply knock before you enter.

After the meeting give the completed Client Contact Sheet to Jimmy so he can start a new file.

The office plays classical CDs throughout the day. Please try to change them periodically (choose any you like), since they can get repetitive very quickly.

Keep track of the supply of milk and other foodstuffs in the refrigerator. If you notice we're running low, tell Lois or place an order at Gotham Bagels.

If you find we're running low of office supplies, tell Jimmy so that he can place an order.

Telephones

We answer the telephone "Clark Kent's office."

Record Clark's incoming calls on the call list. Always be sure to get telephone numbers and try to get a message too.

Clark will tell you which outgoing calls he wishes to make each day. At the end of the day go over over the call list to see who Clark didn't have time to speak with and add them to the call list for the next day. Also make note of people who haven't yet returned Clark's calls.

Messages for everyone else should go on message slips.

The answering machine will pick up if calls aren't answered promptly, so everyone pitches in to get the telephone when it rings.

Try not to keep anyone on hold for very long. If the person they're holding for doesn't pick up right away, ask the caller if they want to continue to hold or would like to leave a message.

Logs are kept for the fax machine. For incoming faxes, please note the client's name, or office, or project on the incoming fax log. For outgoing faxes, write the client's name, or office, or project on the back of the cover sheet.

First Thing in the Morning

Turn on the air conditioning and lights.

Check the answering machine and record all messages.

Turn on the photocopier and printers.

Change the date on the postage meter.

Turn on the stereo.

Turn on all the computers and open the diary/contact software.

Turn on the fish tank light and feed the fish (instructions on tank).

Update and distribute the appointment schedule.

Computers

The computers in the office are on a network so you can work from anyone's computer. To connect to someone else's hard drive, select "chooser" under the Apple menu, and then select "share." Any computer question which can't be answered internally should be addressed to Perry White at 212-555-1212.

Mailing Lists

Various mailing lists can be created from the Rolodex by highlighting the keyword. Many of these have have form letters attached.

Travel Scheduling

For domestic travel Clark uses GoUSA at 212-555-1313. For international travel Clark uses GoWorld at 212-555-1414.

TERMINATIONS

FIRING EMPLOYEES IS the most difficult part of managing. It's one thing if they're being fired because of poor performance. You feel badly, but at the same time, it's mitigated because they brought it on themselves. But when you have to let a productive employee go simply because business is down, it's an absolutely awful feeling.

Of course, if the person doing the firing is upset, you can imagine how the terminated employee feels. Being fired brings out the full range of emotions in people, from stunned silence to resigned laughter to bitter tears and anger. As a manager you must be prepared for them all.

How to Fire Someone

There are four keys to firing someone. The first is to be dispassionate and treat the termination as matter-of-factly as possible. I hate to make this analogy, but you need to think of termination as a slaughter. Do it quickly, as painlessly as possible, and leave little mess to clean up. Believe it or not, this kind of attitude is in the best interests of the employee.

The second key is to script the situation ahead of time. Know exactly what you're going to say. Once you're with the employee, say that and nothing more. Your script will hinge on your reasons for firing the person. For example, if poor performance is the issue, you'll point out that you took these actions to make the employee aware of the problem and that, despite the warnings, the employee's performance failed to improve. For that reason, you have no choice but to let him go.

This is where you must adhere to the script. The employee may attempt to bargain with you, insisting that he'll do better and asking for another chance. *Do not get into a debate.* Repeat the chain of events that led to this point and reiterate that you must let him go. It's okay to be sympathetic, but you must also let him know there's no chance that you will change your mind.

The third key is to have the fired employee leave the premises as quickly as possible. Once an employee has been given notice, his continued presence will be a drain on the morale and productivity of everyone else in the office. Have his letter of termination and severance check in hand. You should also have a closure document prepared by your lawyer for him to sign. Ask him to gather his belongings and leave as soon as he has finished. If he refuses to leave, call company security or the police.

That brings another important point to mind. If you have any reason to suspect that the employee will become abusive or violent, you must have another person with you. This serves two purposes. First, the two-on-one advantage will serve to dissuade any thoughts the employee may have of becoming violent. And second, it provides you with a witness if trouble should occur.

The fourth key to terminating an employee is the timing. It should be done as early in the week and as early in the day as possible. This gives the employee as much time as possible to regroup and begin to look for a new position. If you wait until Friday to fire someone, as used to be the common practice, you've done nothing but give them the entire weekend to stew. They'll be much better off if they can climb back onto their horse and get back in the race.

What to Do When You're Fired

If you're the one being given the pink slip, you should have just one goal in mind—getting as much out of your employer as possible.

It begins with your reaction to the news. Don't beg or bargain. Accept that the company doesn't want you. But don't agree to sign anything either. Tell your employer that you're stunned and need some time to decide on your course of action. First, you say, you need to make a few telephone calls. What your employer will hear you saying is that you're going to call your lawyer, even though you haven't uttered the "L" word. This can work to your favor. Sometimes the implied threat of a lawsuit is sufficient to sweeten the severance package.

Your ability to pull this off really depends on how much leverage you have. In other words, the more afraid your employer is of you raising a stink, the more concessions he'll be willing to make. If you're a female, a minority, gay, over 40, or nearing retirement, for example, you'll have the leverage that comes with the ability to claim discrimination. If you have documented proof that you were told by your employer that your job was not in jeopardy, that, too, will provide you with leverage. And if you've been with the company for a long period of time, or are close to retirement age, you'll have ammunition as well.

A Termination Dialog

The secret to the termination dialogue is to act and sound like a broken record. Be direct, clear, and insistent. Don't beat around the bush. Say, "I have bad news for you. Your employment here is being terminated." Explain that you have a severance check and reference letter in hand, which you'll hand over as soon as the employee signs a release. Stress that the decision is final. Note either that it was based "on your inability to rebound from two unsatisfactory performance reviews" or "on the company's bottom-line profitability and had nothing to do with your performance." Whether the employee gets angry, personal, or defensive, simply repeat your explanation, and ask for a signature on the release in exchange for the severance check and reference letter.

Threats of legal action should be taken seriously. End the meeting immediately, noting that you'll withhold the check and letter. Demands for more severance should be met with a serious effort to reach an immediate deal or the statement that there's no room for negotiation. Keep returning to your prepared statements until you've got the person out the door.

You can use your leverage to bargain for more money, continued benefits, ongoing use of the company facilities, and anything else you can think of. Talk to your lawyer and draw up a document listing what you want in your severance package. Present it at your follow-up meeting as your response to the initial severance offer.

If your leverage is sufficient, you will likely get part or all of what you ask for. But if your employer calls your bluff and you're not sure how much leverage you really have, do some hard and quick negotiating to boost your severance package as much as possible. Then take the money and run.

TIME MANAGEMENT

SAVING TIME is the single greatest business achievement. Not only does doing something quicker save money, but it also gives you more time to make more money. The better you are at managing time, the more money you'll make for your company and yourself.

It doesn't matter how you do it. Some people make to-do lists every morning and don't even think about going home until every item is crossed off. Others rely on desk diaries or personal assistants. Still others use software programs they call up on their computers when they arrive at the office. Whatever works for you is the best system for you.

Although different people use different strategies to structure their day, I believe there are a few general rules everyone should follow to maximize their work time.

Plan Ahead

The further ahead you can plan your schedule, the more efficient you'll be. For example, you may find that limiting meetings to one or two selected days every week allows you keep a better schedule. Similarly, you might set aside one or two days for nothing but uninterrupted work. You might even schedule certain tasks for the same day and time every week or every month. Granted, there will be unavoidable interruptions and emergencies, but having a predictable structure in place will allow you to be as productive as possible.

Get to Work Early

There's no better time to get work done than before the rest of the office arrives. The telephones aren't ringing. People aren't sticking their heads in your door with questions. And most of us are most alert and productive early in the morning. A few hours in the office on a Saturday or Sunday can also be amazingly productive.

Make Lists

I create a prioritized list every morning, with the most difficult tasks at the top of the list. By putting the most difficult or most unpleasant task first, I get it out of the way first thing. This also prevents me from procrastinating, which only makes the task loom that much larger. Getting it out of the way early makes the rest of the day seem a little easier. I always find that once you get started, the thing that seemed so formidable when it was hanging over your head is rarely as unpleasant as you thought it would be.

Focus on One Task at a Time

This is one of the most difficult rules to follow. It's easy to spend a few minutes on one job and then get distracted by another. At the end of the day it seems nothing has been accomplished. I try to stay completely focused on one project until I've done what I set out to do. Then the file gets put away and a new one comes out.

That brings to mind another point. An organized desktop reflects an organized mind. The materials on your desk should be related solely to what you're currently working on. All others should be filed away.

Return Telephone Calls and E-mail

Make it a practice to return every telephone call and e-mail within 24 hours. If you can't do it, have a staff member do it. If you don't, you risk angering clients and customers. This is another task you might assign to a specific time of the day. Many of the lawyers and doctors I know make it their last task of the day. If something prevents you from returning a call within 24 hours, apologize for the failure as soon as you do make the call.

Be Realistic about Deadlines

Your clients' and customers' time is just as valuable as yours. If you tell a client you'll have something ready by a certain date, make sure you can meet that deadline. If, as the date approaches, you find you can't meet a customer's deadline, call him as soon as possible and reschedule.

Or you can do what I do, offer "conditional estimates" rather than deadlines. A conditional estimate recognizes the impact of the unforeseen: "If everything goes as planned I'll have it to you by thus-and-such a date." If the unforeseen occurs, I call, describe what has happened, and offer a new conditional estimate.

Hide

Sometimes you just need to shut yourself off from the rest of the world to get your work done. I have a friend who invokes what he calls the red rule. When he absolutely has to have uninterrupted work time, he forwards his calls to his administrative assistant and hangs a piece of red paper on the outside of the door to his office. Everyone in the office understands the message: "Don't bother me unless someone is bleeding or choking!" It works for him. It just might work for you.

TIME SHARES

Time shares are one of the biggest ripoffs in the real estate industry. In fact, I shouldn't use the term "real estate." When you buy a time share you really don't own anything. All you've purchased is the right to use a vacation property for a certain number of weeks every year. If you get a telephone call from someone selling time shares, take my advice: Hang up.

Time shares work like this. A real estate developer will sell you and a number of other people shares in a vacation property that's under construction. In return, you each get to use the property for a certain number of weeks each year. The more share owners there are, the fewer weeks the property is available to each person. Many time shares are only available one week a year to shareholders.

Time shares aren't cheap. The cost of buying in can be as much as $10,000. And that's not the last check you'll write. You'll also pay a "use" fee of $400 or so for every week you use the property. The money goes to pay property taxes, maintenance, and utilities. A lot of it also goes back into the pockets of the owner of the property, who turns out to be—surprise!—the developer or a company owned by the developer. Finally, even if you don't use the property, you'll pay a brokerage fee to someone who'll be trying to rent it out in your absence.

Developers know they can't sell time shares as well over the telephone as they can in person.

That's why they arrange elaborate presentations for visitors. To lure in potential buyers, they offer gifts and prizes, such as airline tickets or free hotel stays, for attending. In reality, these are usually just certificates for minimally discounted tickets or lodging.

Once they have you in their office, the salespeople will put on an elaborate sales presentation that will include a video, a tour of an elaborately furnished unit, and emotional testimonials by other share owners who just love the time they get to spend at their vacation home. The pressure to buy is relentless, and financing is usually available right there in the office to anyone who can breathe and whose eyes are clear. The salespeople know that if they don't get your signature while you're there, they will likely never get it.

It's no wonder the sales pitch is so hard. Let's look at how lucrative time shares can be for developers. Say a developer is building condominiums at a beach-front resort and is selling them for $350,000 each. He's also selling time shares in some units—50 shares per condo at $8,000 each. The shareholders each get to use the condo one week a year, for which they pay an additional $400. The developer will leave two weeks open to do maintenance on the property.

You can do the math. The developer has raised $400,000 from each condo he managed to fill with shareholders. That's $50,000 more per unit than he would have received by selling them. In addition, at $400 for each week of use, each unit provides a revenue stream of $20,000, a large portion of which will be profit.

The shareholders, in the meantime, have each shelled out $8,000 and are committed to another $400 a year regardless of whether they use the unit or not. If they don't pay, the developers will eventually turn their debt over to a collection agency or even sue. The fewer shareholders there are, the more weeks each shareholder is responsible for.

There are other risks as well. If the developer becomes insolvent, the property may be sold and you'll lose your access to it. You'll also have no control over how the property and the grounds are maintained, even though you'll be helping to pay for the maintenance. If you're unhappy with the condition of the property, there's not going to be much you can do about it. Granted, you might be able to rally other shareholders to your cause. Of course, that assumes you know who they are. Chances are you won't.

Shareholders can usually rent their weeks out if they don't want to use them. They can also sell their shares—if they can find a buyer. A few do. But time shares are notoriously difficult to resell. Once you buy one, chances are you'll be stuck with it forever.

Or at least until you die. And that brings up one last point. If you inherit a time share, my advice is that you disavow the inheritance. All you're inheriting is a guaranteed bill every year and a host of potential headaches.

TOYS

No other consumer group can generate greater product demand than children. And no other group can react to this demand as irrationally as parents. That's why toys have become a significant budget line for any family with children.

When a toy takes off—like the Furbys of a few years ago or, more recently, Pokémon—the resulting behavior becomes absolutely bizarre. Lines form outside toy stores hours before they open. Pushing and shoving breaks out. Prices soar on the resale market. Parents will go to any length and pay any price to come home with that one toy their child covets more than anything else.

They might be better off saving their money. Toy manufacturers have admitted that no one really knows what makes one toy take off and another one flop. One thing they do know, however—it's not for lack of marketing. Toy manufacturers spend more than half a billion dollars on advertising every year. But increasingly, their advertising is being criticized for hawking overly expensive toys that fail to deliver what they promise.

There's also the safety issue. More than 100,000 children are injured by toys ever year. A few die. Parents must pay special attention to toy safety and advertising to protect both their children and their wallets.

Safety: Your Primary Concern

There are several lines of defense against unsafe toys. The U.S. Consumer Product Safety Commission is responsible for keeping unsafe toys off the market. The toy industry also funds two organizations to provide oversight and standards. Ultimately, though, you are the final line of defense. Here are some of the hazards to watch out for when shopping for toys:

Toys with small parts: Choking is the biggest risk to children under 3. Any toy with small parts that may come off is a threat. So are balloons and small balls.

Cords and ropes: Any cord more than 12 inches long is considered unsafe. They can become entangled around a child's throat and cause strangulation. They're particularly dangerous in confined areas like cribs.

Toys that use electricity: If they're not assembled or maintained correctly, toys that require a power source can cause burns or shocks.

Noisy toys: Toys that make loud noises can injure a child's hearing.

Chemicals: Some toys contain chemicals that can be hazardous. Chemistry sets are an obvious culprit. More benign examples include models with glues and paints.

Riding toys: All riding toys—bicycles, skateboards, roller blades—present a risk of falling or running into something. To minimize the risk, look for riding toys that are constructed of sturdy materials and, if appropriate, have strong brakes. This is not an area to try to save money. Quality aside, the way a riding toy is used is the real factor in its safety. No child should be allowed to use one without wearing a helmet and other protective gear such as elbow and knee pads and wrist guards. Children should also be taught safe practices to minimize their chance of injury.

Play sets: Play sets should be well constructed with no exposed nuts or bolts that can grab fabric or cause cuts. Watch out for sharp edges. Keep in mind, too, that they all present the risk of falling, no matter how safely they're designed. For that reason, all play sets should have a surface of sand or wood mulch beneath them to soften the inevitable landings.

Dealing with Toy Advertising

Advertising aimed at children is relentless. Just sit in front of the television some Saturday morning and watch for a while. First of all, there's more time devoted to advertising than there is in the evening. There are product tie-ins galore. Sometimes it's hard to tell when the shows end and the ads begin.

One of the most annoying practices in toy advertising is using the names and likenesses of celebrities or movies and television shows to promote a toy. While this practice grabs the imagination of the child, it puts a real dent in the parent's wallet. Toys with tie-ins can cost twice as much as comparable toys.

One way to fight back against tie-ins is to stall. Many are fads that will quickly fade away in favor of the next hot thing. Chances are your child will lose interest quickly. You should also try watching television with your kids to give them the proper perspective on a lot of the ads they're seeing. Instilling a little skepticism early in life isn't necessarily a bad thing.

You might also consider a toy allowance. Give each of your children a small budget and let them make their own purchases. If, after being swayed by a glitzy ad, they find they don't get much bang for their buck, they'll be more careful next time.

Of course the ultimate way to minimize the effects of advertising and avoid being constantly hounded for new toys is to restrict your children's television viewing. Give it a try. There will be some grumbling at first, but perhaps they'll learn how to amuse themselves by other means—including playing with the toys they already own.

Finally, when you do buy toys, make sure you're doing it for your child, not for yourself.

TRAVEL INSURANCE

Anyone who has seen *Titanic* knows that sometimes trips don't go as planned. Airline flights or cruises can be delayed or even abruptly canceled due to the default of a tour operator or some other problem beyond your control. When that happens, getting your money back could be difficult. A personal emergency might require that you cancel your travel plans at the last minute, which can also cause you to lose your money.

While overseas, your own illness or that of a traveling companion could require immediate medical attention. Many health insurers, HMOs, and even Medicare offer little or no protection in the event of an overseas emergency. A family problem might require that you cut your trip short and make emergency arrangements to return home. The change in travel plans and the cancellation of the balance of your trip are sure to be expensive.

This is why travel insurance is a good idea. It can protect you against almost any kind of disaster that might befall you while on vacation or on a business trip. Because the coverage is for such a short term—the duration of your trip—the premiums are very affordable. It really makes no sense to not protect yourself. Here are the most common kinds of coverages. Some can be purchased individually. Many insurers bundle some of them as part of a travel pack.

Trip cancellation: If you cancel your trip, this coverage will reimburse you for the nonrefundable portion of your arrangements. If you have to change your travel plans, it will cover the cost of making the adjustments necessary to meet your new itinerary. It also will reimburse your for nonrefundable land or sea arrangements.

Travel delay: If your trip is delayed for 12 hours or more, this plan will provide you with a stipend (usually around $50 a day for a maximum of five days) for each covered member of your party until travel becomes possible.

Travel interruption: If your trip is interrupted, this will reimburse you for the costs of catching up to your original itinerary or travel group.

Accident and sickness medical expense: If you should become ill or injured while traveling, this will cover your emergency medical expenses. Dental expenses can also be covered. Some policies will also cover the cost of sending your minor children home while you're being treated, including an escort, if necessary.

Emergency medical evacuation and assistance: If you fall ill or become injured while traveling, this will pay for your transportation to the nearest medical facility. If, after treatment, it's determined that you should return home, that cost will also be covered. Considering that the cost for such emergency transportation could reach $25,000, this coverage makes a great deal of sense.

Principal sum: If you suffer accidental death, dismemberment, or loss of sight within a certain number of days after an accident, this coverage will pay you the amount you've selected in your policy.

Homeward carriage: This coverage, also known as "repatriation of remains," pays to have your body returned home if you should pass away while on a trip. It can save your family a great deal of trouble and expense.

Travel baggage: This will pay for lost luggage or the emergency purchase of essential items if your luggage is delayed en route to your destination.

What Does Travel Insurance Cost?

For the peace of mind it provides, and because there are no deductibles, travel insurance is really quite reasonable. For example, a 30-day policy that provides $100,000 for accidental death, $3,000 for emergency medical expense, and $10,000 for homeward carriage can be purchased for around $50. Travel baggage premiums, however, are a bit higher, which should not be a surprise considering the amount of luggage that disappears every year. A policy for $1,000 worth of coverage for the same 30-day trip would be around $70. Trip cancellation coverage is usually sold in increments of $100. You can usually purchase up to $10,000 worth for about $5 per $100.

Read the Fine Print

The purchase of travel insurance is usually a wise move. Just make sure to read the fine print so you understand the various exclusions from the policy. For example, most accidental death and dismemberment policies don't cover suicide, diseases, infections, or death while participating in high-risk activities such as skydiving or mountain climbing (Mount Everest climbers, take note).

Similarly, most medical policies don't cover preexisting conditions, treatment not approved by a physician, or injuries suffered during high-risk activities. Laptop computers aren't covered by travel baggage policies (although you can arrange coverage through your homeowner's policy). And if war breaks out, you're basically on your own.

My advice is to investigate the various packages that are available from different insurers, select coverages that best match the duration and nature of your trip, and then relax. Sure, it costs a little extra money. Just consider it part of the cost of your vacation.

UNEMPLOYMENT COMPENSATION

Losing a job is traumatic. And while the emotional and psychological impact may be profound, they pale beside the most immediate crisis: your loss of income. Once again, you can offer thanks to FDR.

Unemployment compensation is a federal program created by the Social Security Act of 1935 and implemented through the Federal Unemployment Tax Act. It provides workers who have lost their jobs through no fault of their own with an income to avoid financial distress until they can find another job. Each state administers its own program. The rules regarding eligibility, the amount of money that's received, and other factors are determined by a combination of federal and state law.

The program is funded by a combination of federal and state taxes paid by employers. The revenues generated are deposited in an Unemployment Trust Fund in which each state maintains an account.

Who Is Eligible for Unemployment Compensation?

You should apply for unemployment compensation as soon as possible after you lose your job. Each state has its own requirements for eligibility. Most include the following:

- You must meet your state's minimum requirements for wages earned or time worked during the year prior to the claim.

- You must have become unemployed through no fault of your own. If you quit, you can't collect. If you're fired because of misconduct or because of a strike, you can't collect.

- You must be able to work during each of the days for which you're claiming benefits.

- You must be available for work immediately. You must also have transportation and not be required to stay home to care for children or other dependents.

- You must actively look for work. The state doesn't feel responsible to pay you if you're spending all day out on the golf course.

Maintaining Eligibility

To remain eligible you must report to a local unemployment office as requested to file claim forms and document your applications for employment. If you're not asked to report, you can file your forms by mail. If you're offered a suitable job, you must take it. If you don't, you'll lose your eligibility.

The issue of what's "suitable" and what's not is a bit murky but generally relies on common sense. If you lost your job as chief financial officer of a large manufacturing business, the unemployment office isn't going to expect you to immediately start pumping gas or flipping burgers at McDonald's. But if a financial management position should become available at another company, you may be required to take it, even if you don't want to. Just remember that it only has to be temporary. You can continue your search until the right job comes along.

Special Unemployment Assistance

There are several situations in which special unemployment compensation may be available. Workers in areas that have been declared federal disaster areas qualify for disaster unemployment assistance. If your job was affected by foreign trade you can receive a trade readjustment allowance. There are also special programs for nonprofits and governmental agencies, including the armed services. Some states also provide special assistance for workers who are disabled. The Railroad Unemployment Insurance Act provides compensation for railroad workers who lose their jobs.

How Much Will You Get?

Unemployment compensation generally provides about 50 percent of what you made while you were working, up to a ceiling that's set by each state. Most states pay benefits for up to 26 weeks.

Granted, that's not likely to pay all your bills. You will probably need to tap into your savings or liquidate some investments to tide you over until you find a new job. You're also going to need to tighten up the family budget. Forget about restaurants and vacations and new clothes. Until things are back on track you'll need to concentrate on feeding your family and keeping a roof over their heads.

Some states with unusually high unemployment rates have extended benefits. This allows them to give workers an extra 13 weeks—or even 20 weeks if things are bad enough—to find a new job. These emergency funds are built into an "extended unemployment account" within the Unemployment Trust Fund. Availability of the funds in this account is triggered when a state's unemployment rate reaches a certain level.

If you quit or are terminated for cause you are not eligible for unemployment compensation. That determination is made during the application process. The former employer is contacted and informed of the application for unemployment compensation.

There's no reason why you shouldn't try to negotiate with your former employer. Ask if he'll agree with your categorizing yourself as being fired without cause so you can collect unemployment compensation. You have nothing to lose. The worst he can do is say no—he's already fired you. Who knows, he may feel guilty enough to help you out.

Recipients of extended benefits are required to intensify their search for employment. There are also stricter rules on what constitutes "suitable" employment. This means that while you still might not be expected to start flipping burgers under the Golden Arches, you may be expected to accept the manager's job if it's offered to you.

U.S. TREASURY BILLS, NOTES, AND BONDS

FOR RISK-FREE INVESTING, nothing matches U.S. Treasury securities. They are sold in three forms—bills, notes, and bonds. Like U.S. savings bonds, another virtually risk-free investment, they usually offer lower yields than other comparable securities in return for their safety. Still, they present investors with the added advantage that they're only liable for federal taxes and are exempt from state and local taxes. Unlike savings bonds, U.S. Treasury securities can be bought and sold on the secondary market.

Buying Treasury Securities

Treasury securities can be purchased from a bank, a brokerage house, or in the open market. You can also buy them at a Treasury auction by establishing a Treasury Direct account with the Federal Reserve Bank. When you make your first purchase, an account is set up for you and all your subsequent purchases are kept in that account. You can keep up to $100,000 worth of securities in your account without charge. If you have more than that amount, there is a nominal annual charge.

An advantage of using a Treasury Direct account to purchase and store Treasury securities is that the federal government, not a brokerage firm, is the custodian of your securities, so they're safe. There are no transaction fees. When a security matures, you can either have the money wired at no charge directly to an personal account of your choosing or have it reinvested in new issues.

A downside of using Treasury Direct is that you can only purchase Treasury securities at auction. Later, if you want to sell them before maturity, you have to transfer them to a brokerage firm or a bank. This causes delays in getting your money. You also can't borrow against securities held in a Treasury Direct account. Again, they first have to be transferred to a brokerage firm or bank.

Treasury Bills

Treasury bills (T-bills) are a popular place for affluent investors to ride out storms in the stock market. I say "affluent" because the minimum investment in a T-bill is $10,000 with additional purchase increments of $5,000. Because they have maturity terms of 13 weeks, 26 weeks, or 52 weeks, they're great short-term parking spots for your money.

T-bills are issued at auction every Monday so investors can buy new issues at any time. T-bills with 52-week terms are usually offered quarterly. Like zero-coupon bonds, you pay a discounted rate and then receive the face value of a T-bill at maturity. Federal taxes are due in the year they mature.

Because of their fairly hefty minimum investment requirement, T-bills are seldom purchased by small investors. They're more commonly purchased by the managers of big pension funds, money market funds, corporations, and governments as a safe short-term investment while they consider more long-term plans for their money.

Treasury Notes

Treasury Notes have a minimum purchase requirement of $5,000, so they're a more viable investment for the average investor. Rather than being offered at a discount, they're sold at par value and the interest is distributed periodically until maturity. Treasury notes also have longer terms to maturity than T-bills, from 2 to 10 years. They are usually offered at the Treasury auction quarterly and can also be purchased in the over-the-counter market.

Treasury Bonds

Treasury bonds have even longer terms to maturity—from 10 to 30 years. They're also sold at par value and pay interest until maturity. The minimum investment is $1,000, with $1,000 increments. Because it's backed by the federal government, the 30-year Treasury bond is usually considered the benchmark against which all other bonds are measured.

One way to generate immediate income from a Treasury bond is to sell off all its interest coupons to other investors. For example, if you purchase a 10-year $10,000 bond paying 6 percent, and the interest is to be distributed every 6 months, you'll have 20 coupons to sell. At 6 percent, the bond will pay $600 a year, so each coupon would be worth $300 when it's redeemed. Of course, any buyer will want to purchase them at a discount so they can get a larger yield.

The price you receive from investors for each coupon will depend on its payment date. The further off the date, the less the coupon is worth. To investors, each coupon is like a mini zero-coupon bond: they pay you a discounted rate and then collect the coupon's full value when it becomes redeemable.

Once you've sold the coupons, you'll be left with a $10,000 zero-coupon bond that will come due in 10 years. Since you have already received income for the coupons, you can reinvest it and, hopefully, earn more than the 6 percent the coupons would have returned. As with other types of zero-coupon bonds, you'll be liable for the annual federal tax on the income you would have received but you'll be exempt from state and local taxes.

Patience Is the Key

Like any investment that has a specified maturity date, Treasury securities should be purchased with money you know you're not going to need for a certain amount of time. It's not that they can't be sold early—they can—but you run the risk that they may actually be worth less than their face value at the time you sell them.

So buy them, sock them away in a safe place, and enjoy the fruits of your patience when they mature. That's how they're designed to be used and that's how you should treat them.

_____

(See also bonds.)

VACATION HOME RENTALS

THE BIGGEST PROBLEM WITH vacation rentals is that an astounding number of renters don't see what they rented until July or August when they pull up to the front door. The only information they've received may have come from a classified ad, the owner of the property, or a real estate agent. Upon arrival, they often find that what they were told and what they see before them aren't exactly the same thing.

The term "ocean view" can be translated a number of different ways, after all. To the renter, it means an expansive vista of sand and surf. The reality may be a tiny glimmer of blue that's barely visible between the edges of two houses down the block, which you can see from the window above the toilet. If you don't like it, there's not a whole lot you can do about it. You just grin and bear it and chalk it up to experience.

There are only two ways to ensure your vacation paradise doesn't turn out to be a dump. You can either visit it yourself, which may or may not be practical, or enlist someone else to check it out. If you have a friend within a reasonable drive of the house in question you may be able to get him to give you an appraisal. Barring that, you need a local real estate agent who you're confident is not given to hyperbole.

Regardless of who visits the property, there will be certain basic things that need to be checked. The first, obviously, is cleanliness. The water, air conditioning, heating system, electrical system, septic system, and appliances should all be in working order. The place should be adequately furnished and the furnishings should be in good repair. The kitchen should be fully equipped. Find out the number, size, and distribution of the beds and bedrooms so that you can plan ahead.

Have the outside inspected as well. If it's advertised as a 60-second walk to the beach, make sure it is. If you're interested in boating or golfing or some other activity, make sure there are facilities close by. Check to see how close it is to shops and restaurants, too. You're going to be on vacation, remember.

Read the lease carefully and be prepared to negotiate changes. The lease should clearly spell out who is responsible for utilities, garbage pickup, and other services, such as cleaning and lawn care. It should specify whether linens are provided. There should also be a local person named who can be contacted to make repairs in case something breaks. Your only obligation should be to leave the house in the same condition in which you found it.

Most vacation rentals require a deposit—usually half the total rent—with the balance payable on the day you arrive. That's fine. Just visit the property first to make sure everything is still in good condition. Rental properties have one renter after another moving through them. A lot can happen between your first inspection and the day you arrive for your vacation. If there are problems, withhold payment until they're corrected. Try to ensure that someone other than the landlord holds the deposit, perhaps the real estate broker or even the landlord's lawyer.

Here's another tip. The best way to find your dream rental is to look around while you're on vacation. If you visit the same location year after year, take an afternoon to drive around. You may find a house you'd like to rent the following season.

———————————

(See also second homes.)

VIATICALS

ONE OF THE BEAUTIES of the financial services industries is that whenever a need evolves, a product is is created to fill that need. There are times, however, when those products can seem a bit troubling. For me, that's the case with viaticals.

God forbid you've been diagnosed with a terminal illness and given a year or so to live. You'd like to take advantage of the time you have left to travel and do some of the other things you'd always hoped to accomplish. The problem is, you're concerned you might not be able to afford it and still cover the enormous medical and other costs you know you'll soon face. The solution is a viatical.

How Viaticals Work

You can sell your life insurance policy to a viatical company and receive the cash you'll need to have one last fling. The amount you receive will depend on the value of the policy and your doctor's opinion on how long you have to live. The less time you have left, the more money you'll receive. Many companies prefer to deal with patients who have a year or less to live, although some will buy policies from patients who have as much as five years left. Depending on the predicted date of your demise, you can receive anywhere from 60 to 90 percent of the face value of the policy. When you die, the viatical company receives the full amount from your insurance company.*

Viaticals (the name comes from the Latin word *viaticum*, a payment Roman officials would receive before leaving on a journey) are a bit like reverse mortgages. Both provide you with an income for your remaining years. The difference is that your life insurance policy, not your house, is the asset providing you with money. Viaticals began to take off in the late 1980s as a strategy for terminally ill AIDS patients to generate cash. Because the proceeds are tax-free, thanks to a 1996 act of Congress, they're now more popular than ever. Although cancer and AIDS patients still make up a large portion of sellers, increasing numbers of reasonably healthy seniors are putting their policies up for bid under the theory that you may as well enjoy your money while you can. As more and more baby boomers reach retirement age, this may eventually become the most popular type of viatical transaction.

There's a bit of a gamble on both sides of a viatical. If you should sell your policy for a steep discount because you've been given several years to live but then check out in a few months, you'll have received much less than you should have. Granted, this won't affect you, but it will affect your estate and leave less to your heirs.

The other side of the coin is when you suddenly take a turn for the better and live much longer than predicted. In this case the viatical company stands to lose money. If you live long enough, it may even have to start to pay premiums to keep your policy active.

Before you rush out and sell your insurance policy, you should take several things into consideration. First, make sure you understand how this large infusion of cash could affect other aspects of your financial life. For example, the income you receive may disqualify you from Medicaid and other government programs for low-income citizens. You also need to shop around. There's no set formula for how much a policy is worth. Different companies will make you different offers. Take the time to find the best price you can. And make sure you read the fine print and don't pay an outrageous brokerage fee. Finally, you can choose to sell just a portion of the policy and keep the rest for your heirs. You can also keep just the accidental death portion of your policy.

Viaticals As Investments

Not surprisingly, viaticals have attracted the interest of investors. Unfortunately, many have fallen victim to scams arranged by shady brokers. Many promise inflated returns and fail to adequately explain the considerable investment risk to their clients. Look at it this way. If you pay $85,000 for a $100,000 policy and the seller dies in a year, you'll receive 18 percent on your investment. But if the person hangs on for three years, your return will be less than 7 percent. If he lives longer, your return is reduced even further.

Some brokers have been selling fraudulently obtained policies that turn out to be worthless.

---

*There are some insurance companies today that are offering viatical options on their life insurance policies.

Others will "guarantee" a rate of return, which is flat-out impossible. Viaticals also are quite illiquid, so investors will have a difficult time trading them in if they should have a financial emergency.

The problems have been numerous enough that, as of this writing, regulators were considering restricting or even temporarily halting the practice. Hopefully this won't occur. Viaticals are a proven strategy for the terminally ill to enhance the final months of their lives. The insurance industry has recognized this fact by beginning to offer accelerated death benefits that provide the terminally ill with some part of the proceeds from their policies before they die.

For more information on selling or buying viaticals and to keep up with the latest on industry regulations, you should contact the Viatical and Life Settlement Association of America in Washington, D.C. (800-842-9811) or the National Viatical Association in Waco, Texas (800-741-9465).

WEB SITES

Whether the world wide web becomes the primary marketplace for business or just the twenty-first-century equivalent of the Yellow Pages is anyone's guess. But whatever happens, no business, large or small will be unaffected. Online sales are increasing by quantum leaps. More and more people are logging on every year. And the technology continues to move in a direction that will make it cheaper and more accessible. It won't be long before access to the Web will be available to almost everyone from almost everywhere.

What does that mean for you and your business? It's already clear that any business that doesn't have a Web site is missing the boat. Some use their sites for advertising and marketing. A keyword search for a subject like "arbitration," for example, will return links to dozens of firms that provide mediation and arbitration services. It's already even more comprehensive than the Yellow Pages.

Many other businesses are using their sites to sell goods and services. Although business-to-business sales continue to make up the majority of online transactions, retail sales are quickly catching up.

A few days of Internet wanderings will demonstrate the importance of having a well-designed Web site. It will also show that an awful lot of businesses out there should do some digital demolition and rebuild their sites from the ground up. For these businesses I have one piece of advice: Don't try to do it yourself. That was most likely your problem the first time around. Hire an experienced Web designer and work with her to create a site that has the following characteristics:

Ease of Use. Poorly designed Web sites make it difficult to get from point A to point B. A well-designed site should be as easy to navigate as a real-world store. Customers should be able to peruse your merchandise, make selections, and pay for them with as little fuss as possible. If they can't, they'll leave and never come back.

Logical Organization: The best Web site designs are almost intuitive. They begin with a home page that presents an overview of the entire site. Pages are linked together in a rational manner. And above all, a visitor never gets "trapped" within a site. Every page in the site has a link back to the home page.

Straightforward Content: Content is the most important part of any site. Keep it to the point and change the content from time to time to keep your site fresh. Visitors quickly lose interest in static sites. If they think there's nothing new to see, they stop dropping by.

Simple Graphics: The more graphics you have, the longer it will take for your site to download. Keep in mind that a lot of your visitors may be operating with relatively slow modems. If they get impatient waiting for your site to download, they'll back out and go elsewhere.

Page Size: The standard Web page is 640 pixels wide and 480 pixels high. This allows users with 12-to 14-inch monitors to see the entire page. If you use anything larger, you'll be forcing them to scroll up and down and from side to side to see your entire page. Most won't bother. They'll just leave.

Brief Copy: The printed word is sill the key to effective communication on the Web. There's nothing more intimidating to a visitor than huge blocks of copy that run across the entire page. Keep your messages short and to the point and spread them around the page in small blocks. Also, use black-on-white for your copy. Any other color combinations will be difficult to read. Use a serif font and make sure your font sizes are large enough to read easily. Also, make sure your copy is grammatically correct and there are no misspellings. Information on the Web should be delivered with the same care as information in printed publications. To do anything less makes you appear careless and unprofessional.

E-mail Link: One last thing: Since you're not standing behind the counter of your online enterprise, you need to provide a means of communication for your customers. You should have an e-mail address they can use for questions and comments. You can set up a listserv they can join to receive up-to-the-minute information about new products or services. And don't forget that old-fashioned but nonetheless effective communication tool—the telephone. Sometimes it works better than anything else.

WEDDINGS

WEDDINGS ARE SUPPOSED TO BE celebrations, not sideshows. The day belongs to the bride and groom, not the parents. This isn't an opportunity for you to show off your new house or dazzle your friends and colleagues with an ostentatious display of wealth. And it should certainly never be used as a business function. When the event itself starts to become more important than the two people it's designed to honor, I guarantee that warfare will quickly follow, and in every conceivable permutation: bride versus mother, mother versus father, father versus future son-in law, and future son-in-law versus caterer. About the only person who might not get involved is the clergyman, and with the prevalence of interfaith marriages today there's not even a guarantee of that.

By their very nature, weddings are ripe for chaos. First there's the cost. Thousands upon thousands of dollars may be involved, and not all the parties to the event are going to be in agreement over what is and is not necessary. Then there's all the emotion. Add to that the years of dreaming, the months of planning, and the last-minute decision making and you can see why nerves can easily become frayed.

It's not just the couple and their family members who create turmoil. There's also the seemingly endless lineup of vendors. They'll gleefully help you spend every last penny you have and are quite adroit at talking you into flourishes you don't need. (I knew one client who finally drew the line at a small flock of doves being released at the critical moment in his daughter's wedding ceremony.) They'll also prey on your emotions and guilt, constantly pointing out that this is a "once-in-a-lifetime" event and that your owe it to the happy couple (actually, the bride) to make it as memorable a day as possible.

My experience as the father of three daughters and one son has taught me a few things you can do to ensure that your wedding and those of your children are joyful and celebratory events. Here are some of the most important.

Make Decisions as a Family

Everyone involved, from both families, should meet to discuss what kind of wedding will be held, where it will be held, how many guests will be invited, who will be responsible for various costs, and other important decisions. Don't stand on ceremony or let delays and subtle hints take the place of honest discussion. Later confusion can only lead to sore feelings. Sure, you may not be able to achieve a consensus. But if all the parties involved get a chance to air their ideas, there will be less chance for bruised egos.

Organize Around Your Guests

If a wedding is to be a true celebration, both families will want to have their closest friends and family members in attendance. Create the guest list first, then decide what kind of a party you can throw for that number of people. If you want and can afford a sumptuous sit-down dinner with wines and champagne, by all means go for it. If you can only afford a cocktail party, that's fine, too. The important thing is that the people everyone cares about are there to share the special day.

Be a Wise Consumer

Be prepared for the hard sell when dealing with vendors. Caterers will try to talk you into more expensive food and fancier place settings than you really need. They may also suggest top-shelf liquor and overly expensive champagnes when less expensive brands would do just fine. Every other vendor, from the photographer to the florist to the baker, will do the same. Stay within your budget and don't be talked into things that you don't want or need.

Be Extra Careful Selecting a Band

Music can make or break any occasion. You should hear any band you're considering hiring at least once before you make a decision. And make sure they play music that's appropriate for your guests. The best wedding bands are equally adept at light jazz, pop, and other musical styles. Insist that the band you hear is the band that will actually play at your party.

Hire a Wedding Planner

If you can afford it, a wedding planner can be worth her weight in gold. You can tell her what you want and how much you have to spend, and then sit back and let her go to work. Just makes sure she charges a flat fee and not a percentage of the total cost of the wedding. Ask for the names of her three most recent clients, call each, and ask about the planner's services.

Have the Wedding at a Hotel

Many good hotels have their own wedding planners on staff, as well as banquet departments that can handle any size affair you choose. You can choose from "small and simple" to "sky's the limit." They'll be able to provide everything except the dress using their in-house or regular vendors.

Try Bribery

One more thing: You can avoid all the hassle by offering the bride and groom a check for what you would have spent on the whole thing and urging them to elope. I just hope you're luckier than I was. I tried it three times. It didn't work once.

WILLS

Do you have a will? If you don't, put down this book immediately and get on the telephone with a lawyer. I'm not joking. It's that important.

A will is a legal document that spells out how you wish to have your assets handled after your death. If you don't have one, you run the risk of creating problems for your heirs. When you die intestate (i.e. without a will), the court takes over your estate and appoints an administrator to dispose of your assets. If there are relatives who qualify, the court will likely appoint one of them as administrator. If there are no relatives, or they are all minors, the court will appoint an outside administration, perhaps using the appointment as political patronage. The administrator follows state law in deciding how to divvy up your property and his decisions will be final.

In most states, that means only your immediate relatives will be included. The percentage of your estate each member of your immediate family receives will be determined by law and not necessarily according to your wishes. Your favorite nephew, your lifelong friend from home, and your best buddy from your golf club won't get a thing. If you have a partner but the two of you aren't married, he or she will be excluded. Your stepchildren, and possibly even your grandchildren, may be excluded.

It can be a disaster. Your spouse, to whom you intended to leave the bulk of your estate, may end up having to share it with your grown children and thus have insufficient funds to live on. If you own a business, it may need to be sold or worse, liquidated, because the estate is not permitted to operate it. It's almost certain that disputes will break out among those you leave behind and everyone will be angry at you.

That's bad enough. It's even worse if you have minor children, because the court will also take control of their fate. It won't matter that you may have discussed with family and friends your wishes about who will raise your children if you should die. The court will decide whose home they'll move into. And although it will likely be that of a relative, there's no guarantee it will be the one you've chosen.

Start Early

You should have a will drawn up as soon as you begin to acquire assets or have a child, whichever comes first. That way guardianship and asset transfer problems can be avoided. It's a simple process—so simple, in fact, I just don't understand why so many people fail to carry out this most basic of life responsibilities. Shockingly, two out of three Americans die without wills.

You can even do it yourself, although I strongly advise against it. The best way to make a will is to consult with a lawyer who will help you craft a document with no ambiguities. The whole thing can take less than an hour. After all, the art of making wills is centuries old. There's plenty of precedent to fall back on. If you do it yourself, either with a boilerplate form you buy from a stationers or with a software program, you may leave the probate judge scratching his head in confusion and jeopardize your true wishes.

Make only one original of your will and consider having your lawyer keep it for you.* If it's

---

*As I note in the entry on "Records and Papers," having your own lawyer hold onto your will could make it a chore for your executor to use any other lawyer to handle the estate.

in a safe deposit box or stashed away somewhere in your home, it could confuse and delay the probate process. You can have copies of the will made for yourself and anyone else you choose to have one.

Once you have a will, you need to regularly review it to make sure it reflects your current assets and wishes. Over time, most of us will enjoy a growth in income, acquire new assets, and experience changes among our friends and family members. This will affect how you choose to have your assets distributed. A thorough annual review of your will should keep it up to date. Make sure all your assets are listed and that the disposal of each one is clearly spelled out. If you want Cousin Bobbie to get the dinette set, the will needs to state exactly that. You should also have your will checked when you move to a new state to make sure it adheres to that state's probate practices.

If you need to make changes in your will, you can execute a formal codicil that is signed, dated, and witnessed according to your state's practices. You can also have your existing will invalidated and a new one written. There are two ways to accomplish this. You can literally destroy your old will, in front of witnesses, or have your new will clearly state that it revokes all wills and codicils that precede it.

WINES AND LIQUORS

T HERE'S NO DENYING THAT augmenting a perfect meal with a carefully selected merlot or sauvignon blanc can add immeasurably to any dining experience. There's also no denying it can set you back a small fortune.

I'm not a drinker, but I have a number of friends who fancy themselves experts of the grape and who maintain impressive wine collections. Sitting down with a few ounces of an exceptional liquor can also be a pleasure. I know people who are serious students of single-malt scotches and rare vodkas and spend a great deal of time and effort searching for the elusive perfect spirit. Still, these are expensive pleasures.

I've been told that being knowledgeable about wines and liquors can also be a benefit professionally. If you're entertaining clients, either at home or at a restaurant, the ability to offer an interesting selection of liquors and wines may make you appear more sophisticated and worldly. If there are serious enthusiasts within the group, you'll be able to hold your own in discussions about different liquors and wines.

There are indeed proven medical benefits to moderate consumption of wines and liquors. Red wine, for example, has been linked to a reduced risk of heart attack. People who consume one or two drinks a day may be less likely to suffer a stroke than teetotalers.

My only complaint about wines and liquors—other than over consumption, of course—is the expense. With an excellent bottle of wine selling for $20 or more and a top-quality liquor for more than $50, it's not a hobby for everyone. The trick is to find the best quality you can afford.

Buying Wine

Enjoying wine begins with discovering what kinds of wine you enjoy. The best approach is to determine your price range and then sample various wines within it. Try a selection of reds—cabernet sauvignon, merlot, and pinot noir are traditional favorites—and whites such as chardonnay, sauvignon blanc, and chablis. Try both imported and domestic. France and Italy, of course, are well-known for their wines. But Spain, Portugal, Germany, and Chile also produce fine selections. California is the biggest wine producer in the United States. New York, Oregon, and a few other states also have growing wine industries.

When you find wines you like, write down the labels and keep them on file. Researching properly will require a good wine store, and the bigger the better because you'll get the best selection. You'll also get the best prices. Even more important, you'll have access to knowledgeable experts who can make recommendations and help you learn more about various wines. For example, if your budget has you in the $8 to $10 a bottle range, the store's wine experts can work with you to help you find labels you really like.

Once you've determined which wines that you like, there's only one way to buy—a case at a time. Most wine stores will give you a 12 to 15 percent discount on a case of twelve 750-ml bottles or six 1.5-liter bottles, or "magnums." If you wish, most will let you mix a case rather than buying a dozen bottles of the same label.

Buying Liquors

After suffering a decline in popularity in the 1980s and early 1990s, liquors began to make a comeback as the twentieth century drew to a close. Well-to-do baby boomers and precocious gen-Xers discovered the pleasures of single-malt scotches and smooth small-barrel bourbons. Expensive imported vodkas enjoyed a rebirth, as did some tequilas and rums.

Of course, not all of us can afford to sample our way through the products of the storied small distilleries of Scotland, Tennessee, and Kentucky. Part of the problem is that expensive liquors are "tiered," with products moving from distillery to distributor to wholesaler to retailer. There's a markup every step of the way. The most popular brands also benefit from enormous marketing and advertising efforts, which adds further to the cost.

The best approach to finding affordable liquors is to sample a wide variety of products and then find cheaper brands that duplicate the taste. Once again, a knowledgeable expert and a large selection are the key to getting the best buys. If you happen to fall in love with a $60 single-malt scotch, for example, the dealer can help you find a $15 blended scotch that comes close.

You can also save money with coupons. Liquors (and wines) frequently have rebate forms either right on the bottle or attached to the store shelf. These can save you up to 20 percent. The only problem is that, unlike a grocery store, where the discount is taken off your bill, the rebate form has to be mailed in. The distiller, of course, counts on the fact that many of us will never get around to doing it once we get home. They're often right.

WITHHOLDING

Y OU'LL GET FAR MORE bang for your buck working on your tax withholding than you will struggling with your tax returns.

The majority of your tax liability will be covered through withholding or estimated tax payments—money that's taken out of your paycheck or prepaid to your state treasury and to Uncle Sam. As a general rule, to avoid possible penalties, you need to have had withheld or prepaid at least 90 percent of the taxes that will be due for the current year or 100 percent of the taxes you paid the previous year.

High earners must now follow slightly different rules. If your adjusted gross income for the previous year is more than $150,000, you'll need to pay more than 100 percent of the previous year's tax: for 2000 and 2001, you must pay 105 percent of the previous year's liability; for 2002 and later, the figure will rise to 112 percent.

Withholding payments only need to be correct by the end of the year. That means if you're behind, you can make adjustments toward the end of the year to increase your withholding. Estimated quarterly payments, on the other hand, must be for the tax due on the income received that quarter. You can't play catch-up at the end of the year without incurring a penalty.

Fine-Tuning Your Withholding

The amount of money that's withheld from your paycheck is determined by the information you include on your W-4 form. The key pieces of information will be your marital status and the number of exemptions you claim. For example, if you have three children, less money will be withheld from your paycheck than from someone who is childless. This is because you receive exemptions for those three children that will lower your tax liability. If you have no children, you won't receive those exemptions. Your tax liability will be higher so the amount withheld from your paycheck will be higher.

Many people simply trust that the formulas used to calculate their withholding will be accurate. My advice is to check it yourself several times during the course of the year and make adjustments if necessary. Everyone's financial situation, and tax status, is unique. There's no guarantee the formula used by your employer's business office will come up with the proper withholding. Work with your accountant to figure out as accurately as possible what your liability will be for the year and then make sure your withholding is sufficient.

Some people prefer to have more withheld than they're going to owe in order to guarantee a refund. They see it a sort of forced savings plan. The only problem is that the money you receive as your refund will not have earned any interest during its time in Uncle Sam's coffers. You'd be better off fine-tuning your withholding to reflect your exact liability and investing the extra money you would have had withheld. If you don't have the self-control to put the money aside, have your employer direct the money to your retirement plan or a company-sponsored investment plan.

If you want to find out if your current withholding is adequate to meet your tax liability, contact the IRS and order publication 919, "Is My Withholding Correct?" It contains a worksheet that will allow you to plug in your withholding to date and then calculate how much you will need to have withheld by the end of the year. If your current withholding is insufficient to meet that figure, you can have it adjusted upward.

Fine-Tuning Your Estimated Payments

Most self-employed individuals automatically make estimated tax payments equal to their prior year's tax liability in order to avoid penalties. That's fine if your income is consistent or ever-increasing. But if your income rises and falls from year to year you might find yourself paying taxes based on a high-earning year during a year when your income is down.

The solution is to make some solid estimates of your income for the coming year, sit down with your tax adviser, and work out an estimated payment plan based on those projections. Then, calculate your approximate tax rates—say 33 percent for federal tax and 7 percent of state tax. During the year, keep track of how your actual income compares to your tax-time projections. If you begin to earn more than you projected, increase your subsequent estimated payments by adding the relevant percentage.

For instance, let's say you've projected earnings of $100,000 and you pay about 33 percent to the federal government and 7 percent to your state. During the year you earn that $100,000 and then start to pass it. For every dollar over $100,000 you earn, you should add 33 cents to your next federal estimated payment and 7 cents to your next state payment. This will keep you from having to face a large tax bill. While you may indeed incur a small penalty, it will be far less damaging than if you had to make payments based on an income far in excess of what you actually earned.

WORD OF MOUTH

T HE MOST POWERFUL FORMS of marketing are unbiased recommendations. Recommendations from "experts" in the media, are very difficult to obtain, and constantly pursued by businesspeople. Recommendations from average people are quite simple to get, yet are rarely the focus of entrepreneurs' marketing efforts. That's ironic because the latter are much more effective.

The simplest way to make sure you get word-of-mouth advertising is to ask for it, often. When clients or customers tell you they're happy with your work, thank them and then tell them that you'd really appreciate it if they passed their opinion on to their friends and business colleagues. If you're an employee, add that a brief message to your superiors would help too.

Don't feel embarrassed by doing this. Your clients and customers will realize that your business depends on such referrals. If they're happy with your work or your products, they'll be more than happy to tell other people about you. Consider it your bonus for exceptional performance.

There's also an odd psychology involved. If people feel you have exceptional skills, they'll actually get a kick out of telling other people about you. I hesitate to use the comparison, but it's similar to when people discover a wonderful new restaurant. Those in the know earliest gain a certain amount of currency within their social and business circles. By passing on your name, it makes them appear more competent and savvy. This gives them added stature in the eyes of their friends and business associates.

There are additional benefits. If a client recommends you to someone and he is pleased with your work, he owes your client a favor. That little chit can sit quietly for a long time until it's needed.

You might also consider offering clients discounts or bonuses for referrals.* Make it part of your standard service agreement. If a client recommends you to someone and that person hires you, you'll give the person who recommended you a rebate or a discount the next time she needs your services. That kind of incentive can keep your name on the tip of a lot of tongues. In fact, it becomes another reason for them to recommend you.

It's important to realize that you can't rely solely on word of mouth—not at first, anyway. While you're working to build your word-of-mouth marketing, you need to augment it with other forms of promotion and advertising. The bottom line is that the more people who see your name, hear your name, and think of your name when your profession becomes the topic of conversation, the better off you'll be.

One last thing: Word of mouth is great when you can get it. Just remember that to get it you have to earn it. If you want people to recommend you, you'd better perform. If you don't, I guarantee you'll still get plenty of word of mouth—only it will be the wrong kind.

WORKING CAPITAL

NO FLEDGLING SMALL BUSINESS has sufficient working capital. You've turned over every rock you can think of just to raise enough money to get your business off the ground. Once you're up and running, there's usually not a lot left over.

That's not an ideal situation. The less working capital you have, the more vulnerable you are. The slightest interruption in your cash flow can make it difficult to pay your bills, your rent, your employees, and yourself. It's no surprise that being undercapitalized is the number one cause of small business failure. But, most of the successful businesspeople I know teetered on the brink of financial disaster more than once during their early years and managed to survive. They learned a lot of valuable lessons in the process.

*In general, professionals such as doctors, lawyers, and CPAs don't offer such discounts.

Plan for Cash Flow Problems

My advice is to accept the fact that you'll have working-capital crises and be prepared for them. That means having strategies in place to come up with cash when you need it. The first step is to visit a bank to talk about credit. Chances are, it will be the same institution that refused to give you a business loan when you were scrounging for seed money. But now that you have some cash behind you, and some inventory, the bank may be more likely to see you as a worthwhile risk.

You can do one of several things. You can ask for a line of credit. This will allow you to infuse your accounts with cash as soon as you recognize there's going to be a cash flow problem. You can obtain a credit card with the highest limit you can get. If you can't use your business to obtain the line of credit or credit card, take one out as an individual. You can also obtain a secured loan from a bank, using either business or personal assets as collateral. Finally, you can go to a noninstitutional investor and obtain a loan based on your accounts receivable.

Once you've obtained a line of credit, use it periodically just to keep the account active and establish a pattern of responsible use. Take out a small advance and then pay it back immediately when the statement arrives. Do this every six months or so. Be aware that, for bookkeeping purposes, most banks will require you to pay off the line of credit at the end of the year and not use it for another 30 days.

Understand and Stimulate Your Cash Flow

The next step in adequately preparing for a crisis is to understand your cash flow. If you're billing your receivables correctly, you know when to expect payments. Likewise, if you stay on top of your payables, you know exactly when you need to write a lot of checks. Experienced, successful businesspeople have an almost visceral sense of the movement of their money. The better you understand your cash flow, the easier it will be to spot problems. And the earlier you can spot a problem, the better you can prepare for it.

There are a couple of ways you can stimulate your cash flow. One is to make your terms of payment 15 days instead of the more standard 30 days. Another is to offer a small discount—perhaps 2 or 3 percent—if the bill is paid before a certain number of days. Finally, be prepared to tap into your personal funds if money gets tight. After all, it's your business. If you don't have enough confidence in it to lend yourself money, that might be a good indication that it's time to close up shop.

Of course, the easiest way to avoid a crisis is to have adequate working capital on hand from the day you open for business. One seasoned entrepreneur I know tells his protégés they should assume they're not going to generate a penny of revenue for a year. If they're prepared for that, then they have enough working capital. Chances are, you won't be that fortunate. But if you pay attention to your cash flow and have some emergency plans in place, you should be just fine.

(See also cash flow, receivables.)

YARD SALES

ONE MAN'S TRASH is another man's treasure. That's why yard sales (some people call them garage sales) are so popular. On any given Saturday morning, you can find legions of suburban and rural bargain hunters traveling from one yard sale to another. The merchandise includes everything imaginable, from useful goods, such as clothing and housewares, to collectibles and just plain junk.

Whatever is offered, though, you can be sure you're getting a bargain. Most merchandise at yard sales is priced anywhere from 10 percent to 30 percent of its original cost. Do a bit of dickering and you can get the price down even further. And although everyone dreams of finding that rare item that turns out to be worth a fortune, it's unlikely to happen. Most people today have a pretty good idea of what their possessions are worth.

Still, there's always an exception. As this book was being written, the national news picked up on a story of a man who bought a painting at a flea market for $20. A few weeks later he sold it at auction in New York City for more than $1 million dollars.

Advice for Buyers

Getting the best deals at yard sales requires some planning. Here's how to do it right:

1. *Start early.* The competition for the best stuff is fierce. Most of the action will take place during the first few hours. By the afternoon, most of the bargains will be gone.

2. *Dress down.* Leave the Mercedes at home and wear old clothes. If sellers see you decked out in your Sunday best, they'll assume you can pay top dollar.

3. *Plug it in.* Make sure things work. If you're considering appliances, electronic equipment, power tools, or anything else that runs on electricity or some other power source, ask the seller to demonstrate that it works. There's no point in saving $50 on an item and then spending $60 to get it repaired.

4. *Negotiate the price.* You should never pay the asking price at a yard sale. Remember the seller has no use for the item you're thinking of buying. If it doesn't sell, he'll either store it away back in the attic, throw it away, or donate it to the Salvation Army or some other charity. He'd much rather have a few dollars for it. He's prepared to bargain and will have set his price higher than what he actually expects to get. Also, the later in the day your arrive at the sale, the more likely a seller will be to accept your offer.

5. *Show the money.* It's the oldest trick in the book but it still works. If you want to offer $40 for a $50 item, flashing a couple of twenties might persuade the owner to see things your way.

Advice for Sellers

If you're planning on having a yard sale, here are a few tips to make it successful:

1. *Recruit the neighbors.* Neighborhood yard sales with 10 or more families participating offer buyers a greater selection. They always draw a big crowd.

2. *Advertise.* Put ads in your local paper and signs at the entrance to your neighborhood. Give plenty of advance notice. Many yard sale enthusiasts plan their schedules several weeks in advance.

3. *Start early.* If the sale starts at 8 in the morning be ready by 7. Savvy yard sale shoppers always arrive before the advertised starting time.

4. *Be prepared to bargain.* You've already read my advice to buyers. Few are going to offer you your asking price on an item.

5. *Watch out for thieves.* Unfortunately, yard sales do sometimes attract folks who are less than honest. Keep an eye on your property, particularly when things are busiest.

6. *Make it a family affair.* Get your spouse and the kids involved. They can be helpful in dealing with buyers and moving merchandise. And the extra eyes can also protect you against the thieves I just mentioned.

7. *Consider hiring pros.* There are yard sale professionals who, in exchange for either a flat fee or a percentage of sales, will come into your home and run the entire sale, from pricing

objects to advertising and negotiating sales. These pros have their own clientele and tend to attract more serious buyers. If you're moving or dissolving an estate, hiring them often makes sense.

Have Fun

Whether you're a buyer or a seller, yard sales can be a lot of fun. They bring together neighbors who normally don't see each other. They provide an opportunity to interact with a wide variety of people. And everyone ends the day with either a bunch of bargain purchases or a tidy bundle of cash.

ZERO-COUPON BONDS

ZERO-COUPON BONDS ARE the perfect investment tools for psychics. Actually, they're not just for oracles; they're for anyone who knows ahead of time that they will need a specific amount at a specific date.

Most bonds carry two types of payments: they pay interest periodically until they mature, and then when they finally do mature, they pay their face value. For instance, a $10,000, 10-year bond paying 10 percent interest will generate annual interest payments of $1,000 each year. Then, when it finally matures, it will pay the bondholder its face value, $10,000.

A zero-coupon bond is one that pays only upon maturity. The derivation of the name comes from the historic physical appearance of bonds. Printed bonds used to have a main section, to be redeemed at maturity, and individual interest coupons, to be redeemed each time interest came due up until maturity. (Today, bonds are no longer printed with interest coupons; interest is directly credited to registered owners.) Zero-coupon bonds, however, are bonds created without periodic interest payments; they have, symbolically, had all their interest coupons removed.*

Because a zero-coupon bond pays no interest to the bondholder, it is sold at a deep discount from its stated value. For instance, that $10,000 bond with all the interest coupons stripped off might be sold for only $5,000.

---

*Brokerage firms also offer instruments in which the right to interest payments is packaged and sold to one group of investors, and the bond itself is sold to another investor group. As this security is sold at a discount, it is the equivalent of an initially structured zero coupon.

Most of my clients who buy zero-coupon bonds use them to finance their child's college education. After having concentrated on amassing savings during their child's younger years, these investors eventually shift over to zero-coupon bonds as a way to guarantee they'll have the funds available to pay tuition. By carefully timing their purchases they can insure that a bond will mature just prior to the arrival of an annual or semiannual bill.

There are a couple of downsides to zero-coupon bonds. First, because they pay no interest, selling them prior to maturity can be problematic. There is a secondary market, but it is quite volatile and there's no guarantee you'll get back what you paid. Second, you are responsible for paying taxes on the imputed interest the bond is generating, even though you're not receiving it. That's one reason why these bonds are often held in retirement accounts or in accounts bearing a child's Social Security number. You can avoid this tax problem with municipal zero-coupon bonds as well.

Despite these drawbacks, zero-coupon bonds remain one of the best investment options for college financing.

A NOTE OF GRATITUDE

Can one man be another's mentor, partner, and sometimes son? As well as his friend and occasional brother? The answer, I have been lucky enough to discover, is yes, if that man is Mark Levine, my coauthor for the past fifteen years.

Although we are separated by a great gulf of age, geography, and background, Mark and I have developed a closeness over the years I could never have expected when we set out together on this writing adventure. That adventure has given me the opportunity to live two lives in a single lifetime, one of them with a creative and collaborative joy nothing in my past had prepared me for.

So to Mark Levine, on the occasion of our fifteenth book together, I offer my gratitude, admiration, and love.

—Stephen M. Pollan